DONNIE O'QUINN

PHOTOSHOP 6

SHOP MANUAL

New Riders

201 West 103rd Street, Indianapolis, Indiana 46290

Photoshop 6 Shop Manual

International Standard Book Number: 0-7357-1130-5

Library of Congress Catalog Card Number: 20-01087700

Printed in the United States of America

First Printing: August 2001

05 04 03 02 01   7 6 5 4 3 2 1

Interpretation of the printing code: The rightmost double-digit number is the year of the book's printing; the rightmost single-digit number is the number of the book's printing. For example, the code *01-1* indicates that the first printing of the book occurred in 2001.

Trademarks

Warning and Disclaimer

David Dwyer
Publisher

Karen Whitehouse
Executive Editor

Donnie O'Quinn
Series Editor

Matt LeClair
Technical Editor

Sarah Kearns
Managing Editor

Karen Whitehouse
Project Editor

Donnie O'Quinn
Cover & Interior Designer

Cheryl Lenser
Indexer

Kathy Malmloff
Product Marketing Manager

Contents at a Glance

Table of Contents

11   The Layer Menu   351

12   The Select Menu   415

13   The Filter Menu   435

14   The View Menu   555

18   The Swatches Palette   593

19   The Styles Palette   599

20   The History Palette   605

23 The Channels Palette

24 The Paths Palette

A   Automation Techniques   697

B   Selection Techniques   713

C   Cropping & Resizing Techniques   739

J   Custom Ink Techniques   893

K   Retouching & Pattern Techniques   911

L   Path Editing Techniques   923

Preface

More than any previous version, Photoshop 6 is the most intensive and established applications in the graphics arts industry.

On one hand, it's one of the few universally indispensable tools. Professional users in all facets of the graphics industry—print, the Web, multimedia, and video—turn to Photoshop again and again to refine the images that define our world.

On the other hand, the program as a whole is impossible to master. Photoshop's sprawling interface caters to an incredible variety of needs. In a deadline-driven world, it's hard enough to fully explore the tools that apply to one line of work; when trying to expand your skill set, the challenge to understand Photoshop's inner workings can be downright daunting.

That's where this book comes in. Even after you've learned the basics, it's difficult to remember the function of every tool, every palette, and every item of every dialog box of every command. And the newest features: Do they replace old tools? How are they used in conjunction with an existing workflow? Are they really as effective as the marketing reports would have you believe?

This book contains no tutorials. It doesn't hold your hand or strive to entertain you with witty asides. Like you, I use Photoshop for a living. When the clock is ticking, I know you don't want to flip through page after page of unnecessary text for the information you need. I've presented the facts—and only the facts—so you can get in, get out, and get back to work.

The Interface

The main text of this book covers the entire interface of Photoshop 6. Each tool and command receives the following treatment:

Specific Function

A summary of the purpose and function of each item. This section even places seemingly insignificant items into an easy to understand, production-oriented context.

Mistakes to Avoid

A list of complex but avoidable misuses of the software. Since many aspects of Photoshop are so non-intuitive, this section explains the common mistakes—and offers realistic solutions.

Issues to Consider

A list of advice, warnings, guidance, and shortcuts. Photoshop never works in a vacuum, and this section fleshes out an item's relationship with other commands, issues, and techniques.

The Dialog Box

Definitions and recommended settings for each option in every dialog box. Because the real power of Photoshop rests in its on-screen controls, users must understand the cause-and-effect relationship of every setting.

Techniques Appendices

The back of this book contains 12 appendices that list over 170 step-by-step techniques, ranging from simple selections, to advanced layer and channel editing, to complex color adjustments. This list further illustrates the most demanding and production-enhancing uses of Photoshop. With a few print-specific exceptions, they represent a core set of skills that you can apply to images for any medium.

Topic Numbering

Every topic in this book is numbered for fast and easy reference. In the main text, the topics also reflect the layout of Photoshop's interface. For example, if a particular issue involves the Curves command, a cross reference would appear as follows:

(For more information, see *10.22, Image: Adjust:* **Curves**.)

This indicates that in Photoshop, the Curves command is found in the Image menu, under the Adjust submenu. In the book, the Curves command is the 22nd topic listed in Chapter 10; to find it, flip to the Table of Contents to locate the page number, or refer to the footers at the bottom of each page.

Considerable effort was made to include as many cross-references as possible. Each topic contains a "Related Topics" section, which lists the tools, commands, and techniques most commonly encountered when using a specific part of Photoshop.

Macintosh and Windows Commands

Keyboard shortcuts are included for Macintosh and Windows users. Mac keys appear in parentheses, Windows keys appear in brackets. For example:

- (Command) [Control]-click an item in the Channels palette to convert it to a selection.

- Choose (Option-Command) [Alt-Control]-N to create a new image layer.

Visit *www.newriders.com*

On the publisher's Web site, you'll find information about their other books, the authors they partner with, book updates and file downloads, promotions, discussion boards for online interaction with other users and technology experts, and a calendar of trade shows and other professional events. We hope to see you around.

Call or Fax New Riders

You can reach the publisher toll-free at (800) 571-5840 +0 (ask for New Riders). If outside the U.S., call 1-317-581-3500 and ask for New Riders. If you prefer, you can fax them at 1-317-581-4663, Attention: New Riders.

Contact the Author

Contact Donnie O'Quinn at *donnie@maine.rr.com*.

Acknowledgements

Many thanks to the people who helped make this book possible: Karen Whitehouse, Cheryl Lenser, and the rest of the New Riders staff; David Rogelberg and the crew at StudioB; Matt LeClair, for preparing the dialog box screenshots; John Foxx Images, for the continued use of their excellent stock image library; Troy Mott, for his assistance in developing earlier versions of the content; Steve Kurth, Chris Fournier, and Greg Heald of iSET Educational Services; iSET's students, for their continued input and questions. Special thanks to Gina Lewis, Tim Plumer, Don O'Quinn, Lois O'Quinn, and Sharon O'Quinn, for keeping the homefront secure.

Selection Tools

Selection Tools Overview

The most important editing technique you can master doesn't alter even a single pixel value. When you work in Photoshop, there's always a choice: Apply an edit to the entire image, or target a specific part of the image. In the vast majority of cases, the only way to apply a focused adjustment is to create a selection.

Selecting in Photoshop is different than in a page layout or illustration program. Those applications are object-oriented, meaning that every element exists as a standalone shape you can individually click, edit, layer, and position. When you select something, the edges are highlighted with a series of dots, and subsequent commands only affect that particular item.

That sense of separation doesn't exist in a pixel-based image. For example, Photoshop doesn't know the difference between a palm tree and the blue sky behind it, a car and the road beneath it, or a face and the hair that surrounds it. You can't select something by clicking what you only perceive to be a separate object. (Of course, this assumes that an image doesn't already consist of layers, a process heavily based on selections.) The only "objects" Photoshop recognizes are the individual pixels that comprise the image. To make a selection, you create an outline that surrounds the targeted element. A *selection* is simply a boundary, a sort of mask that enables you to edit one part of an image while protecting the rest.

Common Reasons to Select

On its own, a selection does nothing. It must be used in conjunction with other commands to produce a visible result. The most common uses of a selection include the following:

- **Editing specific image areas.** Make a selection to edit the color or tone of a specific part of your image. For example, you can safely raise or lower the value of one color without compromising the remaining pixels. You can also protect sensitive areas from erroneous mouse clicks when painting or retouching.

- **Layering individual image elements.** Active selections enable you to create new layers based on the contents of an open image. After making a selection, this is most often done by copying and pasting, choosing one of the Layer: **New** options, or dragging a selected element into another open image. (For more information, see *11.1, Layers Overview.*)

- **Creating masks.** When you save a selection, its shape and edge information are stored in the image as an additional 8-bit channel. You can use these "alpha channels" for additional spot color plates in a page layout, the transparent pixels of a web graphic, advanced image composition, and a wide variety of special effects. (For more information, see *23.1, Channels Palette Overview.*)

- **Cropping.** You can use any rectangular selection as a basis for reducing the overall canvas size. Also, the Crop tool is found among Photoshop's selection tools (for more information, see *10.42, Image: **Crop** and *1.11, Crop Tool*).

Editing Selections

When you are creating a selection, your first attempt does not need to be perfect. Each selection tool can be used to further alter the shape of an active selection outline:

- **Add to a selection.** Hold down the Shift key and use a selection tool to add to the existing outline. As you do, the cursor displays a small plus sign. Or, without holding down any keys, click the Add to Selection button in the Options bar and draw the desired outline. (For more information, see *1.2, Rectangular Marquee Tool.*)

- **Subtract from a selection.** Hold down the (Option) [Alt] key and use a selection tool to remove pixels from the existing outline. As you do, the cursor displays a small minus sign. Or, without holding down any keys, click the Subtract From Selection button in the Options bar and draw the desired outline. (For more information, see *1.2, Rectangular Marquee Tool.*)

- **Intersect two selections.** Hold down the (Option-Shift) [Alt-Shift] keys and use a selection tool to deselect all but the overlapping portions of the two outlines. As you do, the cursor displays a small X. Or, without holding down any keys, click the Intersect With Selection button in the Options bar and draw the desired outline.

- **Transforming a selection.** It's possible to scale, rotate, skew, flip, and distort a selection without affecting its contents. (For more information, see *12.14, Select: Transform Selection.*)

Mistakes to Avoid

Making the right selection, but choosing the wrong layer. You can choose any item in the Layers palette while a selection is active. When you apply a command, it affects the current layer within the boundary of the selection.

Forgetting that the selection edges are hidden. After choosing View: **Hide Edges,** you still must choose Select: **None** when finished with the selection. Otherwise, future edits will be confined to the selected area.

1.2
_____

Rectangular Marquee Tool   Type "M"

Use this tool to draw square-edged selections. When you click and drag to create a selection, a preview outline extends outward from your starting point. When you release the mouse button, the preview converts to an active selection. From there, continue editing the selection or apply a command to the selected pixels.

Issues to Consider

Toggling between Marquee tools. By default, when you type the letter M, you only activate the Marquee tool that is currently visible in the Toolbar. To toggle between the Rectangular and Elliptical Marquee tools, press Shift-M. (To toggle between them without holding down the Shift key, choose Edit: Preferences: **General** and uncheck the "Use Shift Key for Tool Switch" option.)

Positioning a marquee as you drag. If you need to reposition the entire preview marquee, hold down the spacebar and continue dragging. You don't have to release any keys you may be holding down. Release the space bar to continue shaping the selection.

You can only select to the edge of the image window. Any pixels that exist beyond that point cannot be included in any selection. These hidden pixels can be edited only after clicking on the appropriate layer in the Layers palette, without making a selection.

Rectangular Marquee Tool Options

When the Rectangular Marquee tool is active, the Options bar contains the following settings. (Set the desired values *before* drawing a selection—the options have no affect on an existing outline.)

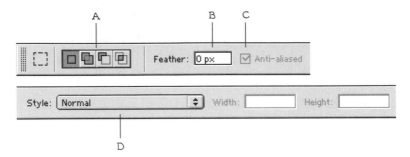

A. **Operations**

These buttons enable you to use the Marquee tool to refine the shape of an existing selection. Their function is exactly the same as the keyboard shortcuts listed under "Editing Selections," earlier in this chapter (see *1.1, Selection Tools Overview*). Here, you achieve the desired effect by clicking the appropriate button before using the Marquee tool.

(Be aware that when you click a button, it remains activated until you manually choose another—even when you quit and relaunch the program. This can easily become confusing if you're not paying attention.) From left to right, the buttons are as follows:

New Selection

Click this button to draw a new selection outline. Any existing selections are deactivated as soon as you begin.

Add to Selection

Click this button to increase the area of an existing outline. As long as this button remains activated, you can continue adding shapes to the selection. Currently selected areas are unaffected by this option.

Subtract from Selection

Click this button to decrease the area of an existing outline. As long as this button remains activated, you can continue removing shapes from the selection. Non-selected areas are unaffected by this option.

If you ultimately encircle the entire existing selection with this option enabled, you trigger an alert that states, "Warning: No pixels were selected." When you click OK to proceed, all selections are deactivated.

If no selection exists when you first drag a marquee using this option, you're able to create a normal selection outline.

Intersect with Selection

> Click this button to deselect all but the overlapping portions of the two selection outlines.

B. **Feather** (0–250 pixels)

This value applies a feathered edge to the next selection. (For more information, see *12.6, Select: **Feather**.*)

C. **Anti-aliased**

Check this box to anti-alias the edge of the next selection, or apply a one-pixel transition into the surrounding image information. Unless you have a reason for turning it off, leave this box checked. (For more information, see *B.1, Determining Selection Edge Transition.*)

D. **Style**

The options under the Style pop-up menu control the process of drag-selecting with the Rectangular or Elliptical Marquee tools.

Normal

> The most common option, this allows you to manually shape the selection by watching the preview outline while you click and drag.

Constrained Aspect Ratio (Width and Height: 0.001–999.999)

> This option fixes the ratio between a selection's width and height, regardless of how big or small you draw the outline. The ratio is based on the values in the Width and Height fields. These values are based on proportional units instead of actual measurements. For example, if you enter 2 under Width and 1 under Height, the width of your selection is always twice the height. This option is only available for the Rectangular and Elliptical Marquee tools.
>
> The aspect ratio of a typical monitor is 1.3 to 1, the same as your television set. Duplicate this ratio by entering 1.3 under Width and 1 under Height. Other noteworthy aspect ratios include most modern movies (1.8 to 1) and wide-angle Panavision (2.4 to 1).

Fixed Size

> This option enables you to set a specifically-sized marquee. You don't click-drag to draw a selection—instead, a marquee automatically appears, reflecting the values entered in the Width and Height fields. As long as you hold down the mouse button, you can change the position of the outline; as soon as you release the button, you've placed the selection.
>
> The very first time you choose this option, the units in the Width and Height fields are based on pixels. As soon as you enter a value, the fields revert to the current ruler units. In other words, if the rulers are currently set to display inches, Photoshop assumes that any number entered in the Width and Height fields are intended to be inches. (For more information, see *14.36, View: **Show Rulers**.*)

To override the current ruler units, enter the appropriate abbreviation after each value: px = pixels, in = inches, cm = centimeters, pt = points, and picas = picas.

You're also able to create a fixed-size marquee based on a percentage of the current width and height. For example, to place a marquee measuring one-half of the image's width and height, enter "50%" in the fields.

By default, fixed-size marquees appear to the lower-right of the cursor. To center the marquee to the cursor, hold down the (Option) [Alt] key as you click.

Related Topics

1.3

Elliptical Marquee Tool   *Type "M"*

This tool enables you to create elliptical or round selections. Beyond that, the techniques, issues, and Options bar settings are exactly the same as the Rectangular Marquee tool. (For full descriptions, see *1.2, Rectangular Marquee Tool.*)

1.4

Single Row Marquee Tool   *Type "M"*

Use this tool to select a single row of pixels that extends all the way across the image. When you click and drag, a horizontal line appears, which can only be positioned up or down.

Issues to Consider

Image resolution determines the selection thickness. The Single Row and Single Column tools create selections that are only one pixel thick. The actual thickness depends on the current resolution. This makes them best suited for editing low-resolution images such as screen-captures or web graphics. Their effects may not be visible in a 300 ppi print image.

1.5

Single Column Marquee Tool   *Type "M"*

Use this tool to select a single column of pixels that extends from the top to the bottom of the image. When you click and drag, a vertical line appears, which can only be positioned left or right.

1.6

Move Tool   *Type "V"*

Use this tool to reposition the contents of a selection, layer, or channel. Common uses of the Move tool include the following:

Moving the contents of a selection. Here, the effect of the Move tool depends on the following:

- When repositioning a selected element, make sure that you click-drag from within the outline. Otherwise, you move the entire layer along with the selection.
- If the background layer is active when you move a selection, the left-behind pixels are filled with the current background color. If an image layer is active, moving the selection reveals transparent areas. If you're editing a particular channel, moving a selection leaves behind the Grayscale equivalent of the current background color.
- If you try dragging a selection while one of the selection tools is still active in the Toolbar, you only succeed in moving the selection outline. If this happens, immediately choose Edit: **Undo**, click the Move tool, and try again.
- Make sure you've activated the correct layer before dragging a selection. If the Move tool appears to be affecting the wrong information, or if you receive an alert that states, "Could not move the selection because the selected area is empty," choose Edit: **Undo**, and double-check the Layers palette.
- As long as you drag a selection with the Move tool, its contents remain part of the same image layer. When you deactivate the selection, that information is "fused" into place, obscuring any pixels that

may have existed beneath it. To gain more editing flexibility, consider choosing Layer: New: **Layer Via Cut** after creating the initial selection. This places the selected pixels into a new layer, which you can move around at will until you merge or flatten the image.

Moving an entire layer. Here, the effect of the Move tool depends on the following possibilities:

- To move the contents of the active layer no matter where you click-drag onscreen, make sure the Auto Select Layer box is not checked in the Options bar.

- When the Auto Select Layer box is checked, you must click-drag directly on the target image element. If you click a transparent area (or any element that resides on a different layer), you automatically activate a different item in the Layers palette.

- To move the contents of more than one image layer, they must be linked in the Layers palette. (For more information, see *22.16, Linking Layers.*)

Moving an entire channel. When you drag the contents of an entire channel with the Move tool, you reveal an area along at least one of the image edges. Unlike image layers, channels cannot fill this area with transparency—it has to be filled with a particular gray level. The exact value depends on the type of channel:

- When you drag an alpha channel (with no active selection), Photoshop automatically fills the exposed edge areas with black or white, whichever preserves the current mask effect. For example, if a saved selection is represented by white pixels, the masked areas are colored black. When you drag this channel with the Move tool, the exposed edges are filled with black, producing the appearance of having the capability to reposition the selection info.

  Unlike dragging an active selection, this effect has nothing to do with the current background color—instead, it depends on whatever Color Indicates option was in effect when you created the channel. (For more information, see *23.10, New Channel.*)

- When you reposition a single color channel (with no active selection), the value applied to the exposed area depends on the color mode. In a Bitmap image, dragging the Bitmap channel reveals white pixels. In a Grayscale image, you cannot drag the entire contents of the Gray channel (although you can choose Select: **All** and drag the selection with the Move tool, which exposes the current background color). In an RGB or CMYK image, dragging a color channel reveals white. In a Lab Color image, dragging the Lightness channel reveals white; dragging the a or b channels reveals 50% gray.

- As long as you're focusing on a single channel, you can move the contents beyond the edge of the image with no consequences. As soon as you activate another channel, however, any hidden information is clipped. If you try to drag it back onto the screen, you'll find it replaced with the base values described above.

– When an image contains multiple layers, you are not able to reposition the contents of a color channel. When you try, you receive an alert that states, "Could not use the move tool because the target does not include all the composite channels." If necessary, choose Image: **Flatten Image** before continuing.

Nudging in one-pixel increments. To nudge a selected area one pixel at a time, make sure the Move tool is active and press the arrow keys on your keyboard. To nudge while you're still using a selection tool, hold down the (Command) [Control] key while pressing the arrow keys—otherwise, you only nudge the selection outline. If no selection exists, the arrow keys nudge the entire contents of an image layer.

Nudging in 10-pixel increments. To nudge an item 10 pixels at a time, hold down the Shift key while pressing the arrow keys. If you're currently using another tool, hold down (Command-Shift) [Control-Shift] while nudging.

Cloning a selection. To copy a selected area with the Move tool, hold down the (Option) [Alt] key and drag. Be aware that the copy is not placed into a new image layer—when you deactivate the selection, the pixels may obscure other information in the layer. To achieve a greater degree of editing flexibility, consider choosing Layer: New: **Layer Via Copy** after creating the selection. This way, the copy is placed into a new layer that you can position and edit at will.

Cloning a layer. To copy the contents of an entire layer with the Move tool, make sure there are no active selections, then (Option) [Alt]-drag. When you do, the copied layer appears as a new item in the Layers palette.

Cloning and nudging simultaneously. To copy a layer or selection as you nudge, hold down the (Option) [Alt] key and press an arrow key. Most often, this is done when you want to continue nudging the new copy. If this is the case, make sure you release the (Option) [Alt] key after the first copy—otherwise, you create a fresh copy every time you hit the arrow key. (You can use this shortcut in conjunction with the nudge technique described earlier in this section.)

Dragging-and-dropping into another image. The Move tool enables you to drag a background layer, image layer, channel, or selection directly from one image into another. You can even drag-and-drop an image element into another application (although the results ultimately depend on the program in question).

Positioning and removing ruler guides. Although you can place new ruler guides while using any item in the Toolbar, you can only reposition or delete a guide using the Move tool. (For more information, see *14.36, View: **Show/Hide Rulers**.)

Mistakes to Avoid

Moving the selection outline instead of the selection contents. If you click and drag a selection while a selection tool is still chosen, you only reposition the outline. In earlier versions of Photoshop, this would affect the selected pixels. Now, the outline moves independently. To move the selected pixels, you must use the Move tool.

Issues to Consider

Constraining motion. When dragging anything with the Move tool, hold down the Shift key to constrain the motion to 45° angles.

Accessing the Move tool while using another tool. Although you can pause at any time during your editing and choose the Move tool from the Toolbar, it isn't necessary. To temporarily access the Move tool while using another tool, hold down the (Command) [Control] key. This way, you can quickly refine the position of an element distraction. Release the key to revert to the currently active tool. This shortcut works with every tool except the Pen tool (where it accesses the Direct Selection tool), any shape tool (it accesses the Path Component Selection tool), the Slice tool (it accesses the Slice Select tool), or the Hand tool (it accesses the Zoom tool.)

Using the Info palette. When repositioning an element, refer to the upper-right panel of the Info palette for precise measurements.

Move Tool Options

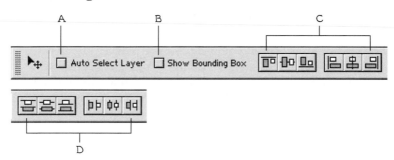

A. **Auto Select Layer**

When this box is checked, clicking an image element with the Move tool automatically activates its item in the Layers palette. This allows you to click and drag more intuitively. When this box is unchecked, you can only affect the currently active layer, regardless of where you click. However, you can still choose layers on-the-fly by (Control) [Right]-clicking an image element and choosing the appropriate item from the context-sensitive menu that appears. Or, you can hold down the (Command) [Control] key, which temporarily enables you to select a layer by clicking onscreen.

B. Show Bounding Box

When this box is checked, the contents of the active layer are surrounded by an editable box, similar to the transform box used by the Edit: Transform commands. This box serves two purposes. First, it delineates the contents of a particular layer, enabling you to target it more efficiently. Second, by using a series of modifier keys, you can apply transformation commands to a layer. (For more information, see *9.13, Edit: Free Transform.*)

C. Align Options

These buttons enable you to align the contents of two or more layers, as long as their items are linked in the Layers palette. (For more information, see *11.85, Layer: Align Linked.*)

D. Distribute Options

These buttons enable you to apply equal spacing values to the contents of three or more layers, as long as their items are linked in the Layers palette. (For more information, see *11.92, Layer: Distribute Linked.*)

1.7

Lasso Tool *Type "L"*

The Lasso tool enables you to create a selection outline by hand. As you click and drag, you draw a thin line. Make a selection by drawing a free-form outline around the desired portion of the image. When you release the mouse button, the ends of the line automatically connect, completing the selection. From there, continue editing the selection or apply a command to the selected pixels.

Issues to Consider

Remember to "close the loop." For best results, always end on the same point from which you started. Otherwise, the straight line that connects the start and end of the outline may cut off part of the image you want to select.

Toggling between Lasso tools. By default, when you type the letter L, you only activate the Lasso tool that is currently visible in the Toolbar. To toggle between the Lasso, Polygon Lasso, and Magnetic Lasso tools, press Shift-L. (To toggle between them without holding down the Shift key, choose Edit: Preferences: **General** and uncheck the "Use Shift Key for Tool Switch" option.)

Free-form selection tools can be limited. The Lasso tools offer a little more freedom than the Marquee tools, enabling you to draw a more flexible outline. When accuracy is important, this isn't always a perfect solution—success depends on your hand-eye coordination, how comfortable you are using a mouse to draw (if you don't have a tablet), and your patience. Even with the most practiced hand, the Lasso tools are mostly appropriate for quick and simple selections. For the most accuracy—as well as the ability to access the same selection over and over again—you're much better off using the Pen tool to create a vector-based outline.

Lasso Tool Options

A. Operations

These buttons enable you to use the Lasso tool to modify an existing selection. (For full descriptions, see *1.2, Rectangular Marquee Tool.*)

B. Feather (0–250 pixels)

This value applies a feathered edge to the next selection. (For more information, see *12.6, Select: Feather.*)

C. Anti-aliased

Check this box to anti-alias the edge of the next selection, or apply a one-pixel transition into the surrounding image information. Unless you have a reason for turning it off, leave this box checked. (For more information, see *B.1, Determining Selection Edge Transition.*)

Related Topics

1.8

Polygon Lasso Tool *Type "L"*

Use this tool to create a selection by clicking a series of straight lines.

Rather than drag to draw a selection, you click a series of points. Each mouse-click adds a straight segment to the outline. To complete the outline and convert it to a selection, you must end on the same point you first clicked. Before you click to complete a selection, the cursor displays a small circle, which indicates a closed outline. If desired, you could double-click anywhere on the image to complete the selection, but this method gives you less control over the position of the final segment.

Mistakes to Avoid

Don't use a series of polygons to simulate a curved selection edge. If you're uncomfortable with the Lasso tool, it's tempting to try to create detailed selections by clicking a multitude of tiny straight lines with the Polygon Lasso tool. Unfortunately, it's easy to spot these edges. If you need to draw curved selections but cannot effectively use the Lasso tool, consider drawing a path with the Pen tool and converting it to a selection.

Issues to Consider

Escaping a polygon selection in-progress. If you have not completed a selection with the Polygon Lasso tool, you cannot select any other tools or access any palettes. Instead, the current straight segment follows your cursor around the image, waiting for you to click the next point. Press the Escape key to remove the existing outline.

"Cheating" with a polygon selection. Many users, uncomfortable with drawing a free-form selection, use the Polygon Lasso tool to create *all* of their selections out of tiny straight lines. There's nothing inherently wrong with this approach. However, if you create a curved outline using straight lines, they may be visible after you continue editing the image. For example, if you select an apple this way and lift it into a new layer, it may wind up looking more like a stop sign than a natural piece of fruit. If you must do it this way, use tiny straight lines—or better yet, use the Pen tool. There, even if you click straight lines, you can continue to edit the outline before converting it to a selection, and you can easily re-access it in the future.

Toggling between Lasso tools. By default, when you type the letter L, you only activate the Lasso tool that's currently visible in the Toolbar. To toggle between the Lasso, Polygon Lasso, and Magnetic Lasso tools, press Shift-L. (To toggle between them without holding down the Shift key, choose Edit: Preferences: **General** and uncheck the "Use Shift Key for Tool Switch" option.)

Polygon Lasso Tool Options

A.   **Operations**

These buttons enable you to use the Lasso tool to modify an existing selection. (For full descriptions, see *1.2, Rectangular Marquee Tool.*)

B.   **Feather** (0–250 pixels)

This value applies a feathered edge to the next selection. (For more information, see *12.6, Select: Feather.*)

C.   **Anti-aliased**

Check this box to anti-alias the edge of the next selection, or apply a one-pixel transition into the surrounding image information. Unless you have a reason for turning it off, leave this box checked. (For more information, see *B.1, Determining Selection Edge Transition.*)

Related Topics

1.7   *Lasso Tool*
B.7   *Including Edge Pixels in a Polygon Tool Selection*
B.8   *Including Free-Form Outlines in a Straight-Edge Selection*

1.9

Magnetic Lasso Tool   *Type "L"*

This tool allows you to draw a selection that adheres to a contrasting color or shape. In theory, this allows you to avoid drawing a complex selection by hand. In reality, like most automatic selection tools, the results are uneven at best. Even casual users are better off learning to use the Pen tool to create these types of selection outlines.

Unlike the standard Lasso tool, you do not create a selection outline by click-dragging. After setting the desired values in the Options bar, creating a selection involves the following:

1.   Click once onscreen to insert the start of the selection outline. Do not hold down the mouse button.

2.   Direct the cursor around the object you wish to select. As you do so, Photoshop automatically places an outline around the object. If unhappy with its location, back up the cursor and draw again. Additionally, anchor points appear along the more prominent edges of the selected shape. To remove a point on-the-fly, press Delete. To remove a series of

points, press Delete multiple times. To add your own points (which better directs the placement of the outline), click as you move the cursor.

3. Activate the selection by clicking once on the first point you placed. Or, double-click to close the outline with a straight line.

Mistakes to Avoid

Attempting to select finely detailed or low-contrast images. Because of the difficulty in pinpointing the precise values, this tool is a poor choice for making delicate selections. It works best in high-contrast situations, such as isolating an object photographed in front of a white backdrop. For more accurate selections, you're better off using the Pen tool, or using alpha channel techniques to create a complex mask. (For more information, see *3.4, Pen Tool* and *12.16, Select: **Save Selection**.*)

Using this tool to select a single element contained in an image layer. You can select the entire contents of a layer by (Command) [Control]-clicking the appropriate item in the Layers palette.

Issues to Consider

You must still trace the contour of the target element. Unlike the Lasso tool found in such ancient paint programs as MacPaint and SuperPaint, an outline made with this tool never instantaneously "snaps" to a specific shape—even if it's a black box on a white background. You still have to move the cursor along the contour of the shape you wish to select.

Adding straight segments to an outline. To add a straight segment to the selection outline, hold down the (Option) [Alt] key while clicking a point, similar to the standard Lasso tool. A straight line extends from the cursor, waiting for you to place the next point. Release the (Option) [Alt] key to revert to normal behavior.

Toggling between Lasso tools. By default, when you type the letter L, you only activate the Lasso tool that is currently visible in the Toolbar. To toggle between the Lasso, Polygon Lasso, and Magnetic Lasso tools, press Shift-L. (To toggle between them without holding down the Shift key, choose Edit: Preferences: **General** and uncheck the "Use Shift Key for Tool Switch" option.)

Magnetic Lasso Tool Options

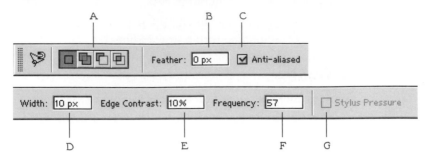

A. Operations

These buttons enable you to use the Lasso tool to modify an existing selection. (For full descriptions, see *1.2, Rectangular Marquee Tool.*)

B. Feather (0–250 pixels)

This value applies a feathered edge to the next selection. (For more information, see *12.6, Select: **Feather.***)

C. Anti-aliased

Check this box to anti-alias the edge of the next selection, or apply a one-pixel transition into the surrounding image information. Unless you have a reason for turning it off, leave this box checked. (For more information, see *B.1, Determining Selection Edge Transition.*)

D. Lasso Width (1–40)

This value determines how closely you must move the cursor to the edge of the object you wish to select. For example, if the value is 10, you can drag the cursor within 10 pixels of the target shape, and the outline will still shrink to fit. If the cursor is more than 10 pixels away, you may include unwanted pixels in your outline.

For the best results, raise this value for higher-contrast target shapes, and lower it for lower-contrast shapes. If the Other Cursors option in the Edit: Preferences: **Display & Cursors** dialog box is set to Precise, the cursor will display as a circle, sized at the current value.

You can change this setting as you drag. Press the open-bracket key to lower the value in increments of 1. Press the close-bracket key to raise the value in increments of 1.

E. Frequency (0–100)

This value determines how often anchor points are placed as you move the cursor. Typically, Photoshop loosely matches your movements. A point will occasionally appear if you keep the cursor in one spot for more than a couple of seconds.

Raise the value to place points more frequently. Lower the value for fewer points. For the best results, use a higher value when selecting rough-edged images, and use a lower value when selecting smooth-edged images.

F. **Edge Contrast** (0–100%)

This value determines how much contrast must exist between the object you wish to select and the surrounding pixels. Higher values mean that there must be more contrast; lower values will accommodate less contrast. For the best results, raise the value when selecting high-contrast images, and lower it when less contrast exists.

G. **Stylus Pressure**

This option is only available when using a drawing tablet. When this box is checked, the Lasso Width value will automatically lower when you apply more pressure, and automatically raise when you apply less. When unchecked, the Lasso Width behaves the same as described earlier in this chapter.

1.10

Magic Wand Tool   *Type "W"*

This tool enables you to create a selection by clicking on the image. A specific range of colored pixels is included in the outline, controlled by the Tolerance setting in the Options bar.

Starting from where you click, the Magic Wand tool selects adjacent pixels that fall within the established tolerance. For example, if an image contains two separate red circles on a black background, clicking on a circle only includes that one shape in the selection. To select the other, you must do one of the following: Hold down the Shift key and click the second circle with the Magic Wand tool, or choose Select: **Similar** to add all similar image colors to the current selection. (Or, you can uncheck the Contiguous box in the Options bar before clicking the first color.)

The Magic Wand tool can be quite useful, as long as you work within its limitations. For example, it is an excellent tool for selecting non-anti-aliased colors, such as line art images converted to Grayscale mode or rasterized Illustrator artwork. On the other hand, if you want to target all the greens in a scanned fabric pattern, you're usually better off using the Select: **Color Range** command.

Mistakes to Avoid

Attempting to isolate an image element with the Magic Wand tool. At many photo shoots, products are shot in front of a single-colored, high-contrast backdrop. This is done to assist the efforts of the production specialists tasked with creating the necessary silhouettes or clipping paths. Some users assume that the Magic Wand tool enables them to select all the pixels that surround the product, after which they can fill the selection with white (to create a silhouette) or convert it to a work path (to create a clipping path). Unfortunately, the tool's unpredictability—and its inability to recognize anti-aliased information—make it almost impossible to produce an accurate selection. If the element in question has hard, clearly defined edges, trace it with the Pen tool. This way, if you need a silhouette, you can convert the path to a selection; if you need a clipping path, you can use the same path. (For more information, see Appendix I, *Silhouetting Techniques.*)

Attempting to select objects in continuous-tone images. Because of the method it uses to recognize pixels, the Magic Wand tool is a poor-to-fair choice for making selections in continuous-tone images.

Attempting to make selections in a bitmap image. Although the solid colors seem perfect for the Magic Wand tool, this is the only selection tool that doesn't work when an image is in Bitmap mode. Convert the image to Grayscale to use the tool. If necessary, convert the image back to Bitmap when editing is complete.

Selecting the transparent pixels of an image layer. This results in an inaccurate selection because the edge pixels of the layer's contents can be mistakenly included in the selection. For the best results, (Command) [Control]-click the appropriate item in the Layers palette, then choose Select: **Inverse**.

Issues to Consider

Try examining the individual color channels before using the Magic Wand tool. If the element you want to select appears solidly colored and highly contrasting on a particular color channel, the tool may work more efficiently. Make the selection in the color channel, then switch back to the composite channel to continue editing. If you cannot make a clean selection, you'll have to resort to other selection tools.

Magic Wand selections vary according to color mode. The Magic Wand tool generates different results in RGB, CMYK, and Lab Color images, even if you click on the same color with the same Tolerance value. This is due to the different information in the color channels.

Increasing the Tolerance of an existing selection. There are three ways to increase the Tolerance of an active selection:

- **Shift-click to add pixels.** This method is inaccurate. You increase the number of selected pixels, but the exact range is determined by the value of the second pixel you click.

- **Increase the Tolerance and try again.** This method is also inaccurate. Unless you click on precisely the same pixel, the selected range will differ from the first selection.

- **Choose Select: Grow.** This method automatically increases the Tolerance of the existing selection, using the value currently entered in the Tolerance field. If desired, enter a new value before choosing the command.

Magic Wand Tool Options

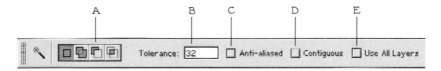

A. Operations

These buttons enable you to use the Lasso tool to modify an existing selection. (For full descriptions, see *1.2, Rectangular Marquee Tool*.)

B. Tolerance (0–255)

This value determines the range of pixels included in your selection. A value of 0 includes only the exact color of the targeted pixel in the selection. Higher numbers gradually increase the range.

Contrary to popular belief, the Magic Wand tool does not base a selection on color values. It measures the brightness values of the targeted pixel. The value you enter in the Tolerance field actually corresponds to the 256 possible tones in an 8-bit color channel. If the image is in RGB, CMYK, or Lab Color mode, it reads the values of each color channel.

Photoshop defines the range by adding and subtracting the Tolerance from the brightness value of the initial pixel. Assuming the Tolerance is set to its default of 32, clicking a pixel with a brightness value of 100 expands the range to include adjacent pixels between 68 and 132 in the selection. If you select an RGB pixel with values of R: 160, G: 50, and B: 35, the range includes all adjacent pixels with values between R: 128 and R: 192, G: 18 and G: 82, and B: 3 and B: 67.

The range cannot extend beyond values of 0 or 255. For example, if you click on a pixel valued at 10 and the Tolerance is set to 32, Photoshop selects all adjacent pixels between 0 and 42. Because of this, you select the greatest range when you click on a pixel in the midtones. Clicking lighter or darker pixels results in smaller selections.

C. **Anti-aliased**

Check this box to anti-alias the edge of the next selection, or apply a one-pixel transition into the surrounding image information. Unless you have a reason for turning it off, leave this box checked. (For more information, see *B.1, Determining Selection Edge Transition.*)

D. **Contiguous**

By default, this box is checked. This way, the Magic Wand tool only reads pixels adjacent to the initial click-point before making a selection. When this box is unchecked, the tool includes pixels throughout the entire image, whether they are contiguous or not.

E. **Use All Layers**

Check this button to allow Photoshop to use all visible pixels when defining the range of a selection. Otherwise, Photoshop uses only the pixels of the active layer. Even if you use the Magic Wand tool with the Sample Merged box checked, the selection only affects the currently active layer.

Related Topics

1.11

Crop Tool   *Type "C"*

When cropping an image, you mimic the conventional technique of cropping a photograph. There, you'd mark the photo to specify the rectangular portion you wish to use. In Photoshop, you accomplish the same thing by drawing a *crop marquee*, then discarding the pixels that fall outside its boundaries.

Create a crop marquee by dragging with the Crop tool. You can easily refine the size and orientation of this box, so don't worry if it isn't perfect the first time. Use the following techniques:

• **Move.** Place the cursor inside the marquee and drag to reposition it. Don't drag directly on the target that appears in the center of the marquee, because doing so will only reposition the target.

• **Resize.** Drag any of the points on the corners and sides of the marquee to resize it. Hold down the Shift key while dragging to scale the marquee proportionately.

- **Rotate.** Drag anywhere outside the marquee to rotate it. Hold down the Shift key while dragging to rotate in 15-degree increments. When you apply a rotated marquee, the cropped image rights itself, becoming rectangular. Use this approach to straighten crooked scans. By default, the marquee rotates around its center; to establish a new pivot point (for example, if you want to rotate around one of the corners), drag the target that appears in the center of the marquee to the desired spot.

- **Cancel.** Press the Escape key at any time to remove the crop marquee from the image.

- **Crop.** To apply the Crop command, do one of the following: double-click inside the marquee, click the checkmark button in the Options bar, or press the (Return) [Enter] key.

Issues to Consider

The Crop tool is similar to using the Image: Canvas Size command. There, you crop an image by entering new values for image width and height. Many users turn to that command when the image information they want to retain is in a fixed location, such as the upper-right or lower-left corner. Instead of dragging a marquee, they simply plug in the new values, specify the position of the uncropped pixels, and let Photoshop do the rest. The Canvas Size command is also the only option available when you want include an automated Crop command in an action, droplet, or batch process to use the Crop tool, you'd have to include a stop in the action, manually apply the crop, then continue. (For more information, see *C.14, Decreasing the Canvas Size.*)

Crop Tool Options (Before Drawing Marquee)

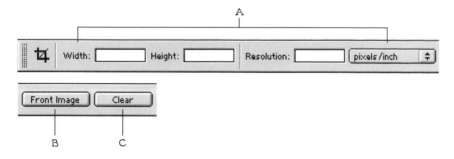

A. Fixed Target Size Options

If desired, you can use these fields to set a specific final width, height, and/or resolution of the cropped image. They essentially combine the Crop tool with the effects of the Image: **Image Size** dialog box—useful when you need to crop a series of irregularly-sized images to the same dimensions. (For more information, see *C.5, Cropping to a Specific Width and Height.*) The following options are available:

Width and Height (1.000–30,000.000 pixels)

Enter the desired width and height of the cropped image in these fields. Choose your preferred unit of measurement from the pop-up menus. Now, as you draw the crop marquee, the ratio between the width and height is constrained. When you crop, the image is resized to match your settings.

Resolution (1.000–30,000.000)

Enter the desired resolution of the cropped image in this field. When you crop, the image resolution is increased or decreased, depending on your setting.

B. **Front Image**

Use this button to automatically enter the dimensions of a pre-existing image in the Width, Height, and Resolution fields. This way, the target image acts a template, enabling you to crop and resize future images to the same dimensions. To use this option, open the image in Photoshop, bring it to the front of any other images, and click the button.

C. **Clear**

Click this button to clear all the fields in the Options bar.

Crop Tool Options (After Drawing Marquee)

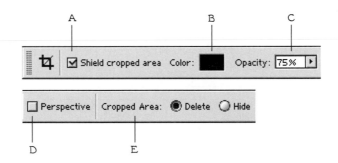

A. **Shield Cropped Area**

When this box is checked, Photoshop applies a semi-transparent overlay to the area that will be discarded when you apply the crop marquee. This shaded area simply makes it easier to tell which information you're trimming away. Uncheck the box to turn off this option—when you do, the crop marquee appears identically to earlier versions.

B. **Color**

This swatch enables you to change the overlay color that appears when the Shield Cropped Area option is enabled. The color has no bearing on the actual image—for example, in a Grayscale image, you can set this value to any RGB color. Change the current value only when it is too similar to the image colors.

C. **Opacity** (0–100%)

This field sets the transparency level of the colored overlay. For most uses, the default of 75% is sufficient. Change it only when the current value obscures any hard-to-see detail, and resetting the overlay color doesn't produce the desired effect.

D. **Perspective**

Although this option is called "Perspective," it is actually intended to *eliminate* the appearance of perspective. For example, imagine that you've taken a photograph of a painting, only to discover that the camera was just a touch off-center. When you try to crop the image, the four edges aren't aligned. After checking this box, you can manipulate the corners of the crop marquee to make it flush with the off-kilter edges. When you apply the crop, you pull the image back to the desired dimensions. The effect is similar to the Image: Transform: **Perspective** command, but with some limitations. (For more information, see *C.4, Correcting Perspective While Cropping.*)

If the neighboring Cropped Area option is set to Hide, the Perspective box is not available.

E. **Cropped Area**

The following options determine how Photoshop handles the data cropped from an image. Note that when an image only consists of a single background layer, these items are not available; to access them, an image must have at least one image layer.

Delete

When you choose this option, the cropped information is entirely removed from the image. This method was the only one used by earlier versions of the program.

Hide

When you choose this option, the cropped information isn't trimmed away. Instead, it remains part of the file, and simply extends beyond the new image boundaries. This way, you can continue to access the cropped portion of the image. You reveal the hidden data by repositioning one of the layers with the Move tool. (Any hidden information is also revealed if you use the Image: **Canvas Size** command to expand the image boundaries.)

Related Topics

1.12

Slice Tool   Type "K"

Although you can't tell by looking at them, many large web graphics are comprised of smaller segments. For example, a complex set of site navigation controls may appear to be a single image, but different parts of it are linked to different locations. This is possible only by splitting the image into separate files, assigning the necessary HTML code to each one, then knitting them back together—a process known as *slicing*. The Slice tool enables you to manually divide a large web graphic (or even an entire page mock-up) into the smaller components that are later assembled in an HTML editor.

In Photoshop 5.5, you had to open a file in ImageReady (or another web graphics program) to add slices. In version 6, you can add simple, rectangular slices and a basic level of HTML code—although you still have to use a different program to create animations, rollovers, and other web-specific effects.

When you click and drag with the Slice tool, two types of slice appear. The one you've drawn is a *user slice*, which you can resize and recolor. The user slice is automatically surrounded by a series of *filler slices*—Photoshop adds as many of them as needed to cover the remaining image space. The filler slices automatically adjust to accommodate any new user slices. When you choose File: **Save for Web** to create the final version, the image is physically split into a series of files based on the size and shape of the original slices. (Photoshop also adds an HTML page that enables you to properly display the image in a browser.)

The Slice tool only creates new slices. To select, resize, re-orient, and otherwise edit any existing slices, use the Slice Select tool. (For more information, see *1.13, Slice Select Tool*.)

Issues to Consider

Slices let you apply different compression settings to the same image. An increasingly popular aspect of the Slice tool is that it enables you to apply different levels of optimization to a single web graphic. For example, text typically looks better when saved as a GIF, while a scanned photo looks better as a JPEG. If your graphic combines text and continuous-tone detail, you can create a slice that encompasses the text, and slices for the rest of the image. Later, the File: **Save for Web** dialog box enables you to select one or more of these slices, entering different compression settings for each part. Another approach is to apply heavy compression to parts of the image without significant detail, and use maximum quality only where it really matters, to create the smallest possible file size.

Don't confuse slices with an image map. Slices can only be rectangular— they're intended to provide a simple, quick way to divide a single image into multiple links. If you want the linked areas to be based on irregular shapes, you must create an *image map*, which you cannot do in Photoshop. In ImageReady 3.0, which ships with Photoshop 6, you're able to convert the contents of a layer into a linked item, regardless of its shape.

Creating a template before slicing. Many users prefer to draw a slice at the exact size they require, rather than eyeball and hope for the best. For the surest results, use the ruler guides to specify the desired locations. You can place the guides with mathematical precision, then trace them with the Slice tool.

Creating a layer-based slice. You're not restricted to using the Slice tool to mark areas in a flattened image. If desired, you automatically place a slice around the contents of an image layer. Click the desired item in the Layers palette, then choose Layer: **New Layer Based Slice**. Although the new slice matches the width and height of the image element, it does not conform to its shape—it's still rectangular.

Viewing and clearing slices. To hide any existing slices from view, choose View: **Show Extras** (or uncheck the Slices item in the View: **Show** submenu). To remove a single slice, click it with the Slice Select tool and press the (Delete) [Backspace] key. To remove multiple slices, Shift-click them with the Slice Select tool before deleting. To remove all slices at once, choose View: **Clear Slices**.

Slice Tool Options

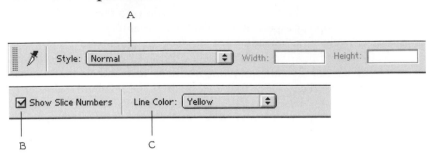

A. Style

The options under the Style pop-up menu control the process of dragging with the Slice tool. *Normal* enables you to drag a slice that you can shape and size at will. *Constrained Aspect Ratio* maintains a specific relationship between the width and height. *Fixed Size* enables you to place a slice with predetermined measurements.

In terms of pure function, these options are identical to the Style pop-up menu in the Marquee Tool Options bar. (For full descriptions, see *1.2, Rectangular Marquee Tool.*)

B. Show Slice Numbers

When this box is checked, the numbers assigned to each slice are displayed on screen. Photoshop uses the numbers to differentiate between files when you save the final sliced image. When unchecked, the slices appear only as dotted lines (although you can't see them, they remain numbered). Uncheck this option when the slice information obscures your view of the image.

C. Line Color

This pop-up menu controls the onscreen color of unselected slices. It defaults to Light Blue; when the image colors make it difficult to see the slices, choose a new item.

Related Topics

1.13

Slice Select Tool

Use the Slice Select tool to activate and edit any existing slices. Use the following guidelines:

- **Selecting slices.** To select a single slice, click it with the Slice Select tool. To select multiple items, hold down the Shift key while selecting. Note that you can only select and edit user slices. Before applying any of the following edits to a filler slice, you must select it and click the Promote to User Slice button in the Options bar.

- **Resizing slices.** To change a slice's size and shape, select it and click-drag the handles that appear around its perimeter. To set specific dimensions, double-click the item to access the Slice Options dialog box, then enter the desired values in the Width and Height fields.

- **Repositioning a slice.** To move a user slice, click and drag within its shape. The filler slices automatically shift to accommodate the new position.

- **Duplicating a slice.** To clone a slice, hold down the (Option) [Alt] key while moving it.

- **Removing a slice.** To remove a slice, select it and press the (Delete) [Backspace] key.

- **Changing the stacking order of a slice.** To re-order any overlapping slices, use the Arrange Slice buttons in the Options bar.

- **Applying web-specific information.** To add the desired HTML attributes to your slices, you must access the Slice Options dialog box by either double-clicking a slice, or selecting it and clicking the Slice options button in the Options bar.

Issues to Consider

Slices are editable in the File: Save for Web dialog box. Before saving the final version of a sliced image, you can use the Slice Select tool that appears in the Save for Web work area to perform any of the tasks listed above.

Slice Select Tool Options

A. Arrange Slice Options

These buttons enable you to change the stacking order of your slices. By default, this isn't necessary. Filler slices are never an issue—they automatically shift to accommodate the position of a user slice. However, when two user slices overlap, you may want to address their arrangement. For example, a new slice may split an existing slice into several items; even though the individual pieces retain the same Slice Options settings as the original, you now have to contend with multiple slices. By sending the new item backward in the stacking order, you're able to retain the shape of the original slice. (Note that you can always switch to ImageReady to apply more powerful slice-oriented commands, including linking, combining, and special effects.) From left to right, the Arrange Slice buttons are as follows:

Bring to Front

> This button places the currently selected slice at the top of the stacking order. Any underlying slices are hidden.

Bring Forward

> This button places the currently selected slice forward one level in the stacking order.

Send Backward

> This button places the currently selected slice backward one level in the stacking order.

Send to Back

> This button places the currently selected at the very bottom of the stacking order. Any underlying slices are revealed, which subdivide the current slice into multiple items.

B. Promote to User Slice

Click this button to convert a selected filler slice to a user slice. This way, you can edit the size and shape of the item.

C. Slice Options

Click this button (or double-click a slice) to access the Slice Options dialog box. There, you enter the information necessary for the image to behave as desired in a web browser.

Slice Options Dialog Box

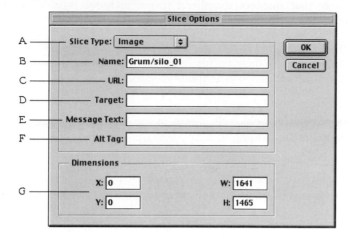

A. Slice Type

A slice displays image information or text in a web browser, depending on the option set in this pop-up menu:

No Image

> When you set this option, the slice will not display the image data it initially contained—it displays text instead. A field titled "HTML" is available in the dialog box where you enter the desired text and format it using standard HTML tags. Note that you cannot preview the appearance of this effect in Photoshop—you must save the sliced image and open it in a web browser.

Image

> When you set this option, the slice displays any image data that it encircled in Photoshop, and retains any linking or text data you enter in the dialog box. (The options specific to this setting are listed below.)

B. Name

By default, the name of each slice (which subsequently becomes the name of each component file) is based on the filename of the current image, followed by the slice number. To change this setting, enter the desired data in this field.

C. URL

To convert the slice into a clickable button, enter the address of the target page in this field. (If the page will be stored in the same folder as the sliced image, you can simply enter the filename. Otherwise, enter the *entire* URL.)

D. **Target**

If the page that displays the sliced image includes frames, enter the appropriate frame tag in this field.

E. **Message Text**

When a user moves their cursor over the slice in a browser, any text entered in this field displays at the bottom of the window.

F. **Alt Tag**

Text entered in this field is displayed in the location of a slice while its image contents are loading in a web browser window.

G. **Dimensions**

These options are available whether Image or No Image is set in the Slice Type pop-up menu. They enable you to refine a slice's size and position.

X & Y

Here, X represents the position of the slice's left edge. Y represents the position of the top edge. Entering new values only moves the slice—it doesn't affect the size.

W & H

Here, W represents the slice width, as measured from the left edge—when you enter a new value, only the right edge moves. H represents the slice height, as measured from the top edge; when you enter a new value, only the bottom edge moves.

The Paint Tools

Paint Tools Overview

The Paint tools provide three functions:

- **Painting.** The Airbrush, Paintbrush, Pencil, Eraser, Pattern Stamp, Gradient, and Paint Bucket tools apply new color information to an image.

- **Retouching.** The Eraser, Clone, and Smudge tools primarily use existing pixel values as the basis for editing.

- **Tone editing.** The Focus and Toning tools affect the sharpness and saturation of the existing image information.

These tools are placed in the same category because, for the most part, they use a brush shape to apply or affect image colors, similar to traditional paintbrushes. Pressure-sensitive drawing tablets enable you to further emulate traditional brush techniques. The appropriate Options bar item is available only when a tablet is properly connected to your workstation.

Issues to Consider

Create a new layer before applying a Paint tool. Be careful when using any Paint tool that adds color to an image, such as the Paintbrush, Pencil, and Clone Stamp tools. Many users simply jump in and apply brushstrokes directly onto existing image information, which seriously restricts their ability to edit, arrange, or otherwise refine their work. When you create a new image layer before painting, your brushstrokes remain separate from the underlying information, enabling you to continue editing them without damaging the image. (For more information, see *11.8, Layer: New: **Layer**.*)

2.2

The Brush Picker

The Brushes palette found in earlier versions of Photoshop has been replaced by the *brush picker*, a pop-up item in the Options bar that contains the brush shapes used by Photoshop's Paint tools. Although the ultimate behavior of each brush depends on the specific tool, their essential characteristics are defined and stored here. The brush picker is used for the following:

- **Selecting brushes.** Choose a new brush shape by clicking one of the small icons in the picker.

- **Loading a series of pre-defined brushes.** Similar to the Swatches palette, you can save brush sets for future use, rather than clutter the palette with too many options. Also, Photoshop supplies a series of predefined sets, as do many third-party developers.

The active brush is highlighted by a thick black border. To select a new brush, click on any other icon in the brush picker. A brush is always active whenever a Paint tool is selected, even if that tool has never before been used. Paint tools also retain their last-used brush. For example, if you choose a small brush for the Airbrush tool then a large brush for the Smudge tool, the Airbrush tool remembers the small brush until a new one is selected.

Issues to Consider

Revealing the brush picker. There are two ways to access the contents of the brush picker:

- **From the Options bar.** In the Options bar, click the thin vertical strip on the immediate right of the brush icon. When you do, the brush picker appears directly underneath. (Make sure you don't click the actual icon by accident—when you do, the Edit Brush pop-up item will appear.)

- **On-the-fly.** If you're currently using a Paint tool, press the Return or Enter key. The brush picker appears to the lower right of the cursor, whatever its current position. This enables you to access a brush without the disruption of returning to the Options bar.

Although the menu is automatically hidden when you start painting, try to avoid this method—it results in too many unwanted brushstrokes. Hide the brush picker by pressing the Return or Enter key, or by simply double-clicking the desired item.

Resizing the brush picker. Change the size of the brush picker by dragging from the lower right corner. The new dimensions will remain, regardless of how you access the menu, until you quit and relaunch the program.

Using virtual brushes. If you want a brush size that's not currently available in the menu, you don't necessarily have to create a new item. Instead, click the Brush icon in the Options bar. The Edit Brush controls appear, enabling you to change the settings of the current brush. If you simply continue editing, you're using a *virtual brush*, or a temporary brush that will disappear as soon as you choose another item. If you believe you'll need to use the same brush in the future, click the pop-up's New Brush button to add it to the menu. (For more information, see *2.3, Brush Picker Submenu*.)

To cancel the Edit Brush pop-up without applying any changes, press the Escape key.

Brush selection shortcuts. If desired, use the following keyboard shortcuts in the brush picker:

- **Scroll through all items in the brush picker.** Use the arrow keys.
- **Choose the item that appears before the current brush.** Press the comma key.
- **Choose the item that appears after the current brush.** Press the period key.
- **Select the first brush in the palette.** Press Shift-comma.
- **Select the last brush in the palette.** Press Shift-period.
- **Increase the current brush width in 10-pixel increments.** Press the open bracket key ([).
- **Decrease the current brush width in 10-pixel increments.** Press the close bracket key (]).

Previewing the size of the current brush. Photoshop defaults to Standard paint cursors under Edit: Preferences: **Display & Cursors**, which does not show the size of a selected brush onscreen. By setting the preference to Brush Size (or to Precise and pressing the Caps Lock key), the cursor changes to an outline that matches the brush size. While this does allow for more accurate use of the brush, only parts of the brush with an opacity of 50% or more are outlined—in other words, the outlines of very soft brushes appear smaller than the area they affect.

2.3

Brush Picker Submenu

The commands of the brush picker submenu enable you to create, modify, and delete brush shapes. You can also save and load predefined groups of brushes.

New Brush

Use this command to create a standard elliptical brush shape. The results are different from using the Edit: **Define Brush** command (which converts image information into a custom brush) and changing the settings of a brush on-the-fly (which creates a temporary brush)—here, you establish the settings of a brush that remains in the brush picker until you manually delete it.

The New Brush command is not available if a non-standard brush is currently highlighted in the brush picker. If you find the command dimmed, try clicking a standard brush first—when the New Brush dialog box appears, it initially displays the settings of the currently selected brush. When you change the settings and click OK, a new item is added to the brush picker.

Issues to Consider

Understanding standard brushes. These brushes imitate the behavior of actual paint brushes. If you use a drawing tablet, these brushes can emulate natural, non-digital media. Their shape is always elliptical. Unless an image is in Bitmap mode (or the Pencil tool is being used), they are always anti-aliased, and can even be softened to create a diffuse, feathered effect. All of Photoshop's default brushes are standard.

Low Spacing values may impact brushstroke speed. When Spacing is set very low (under 20%), there may be a delay between the time it takes to apply the brush stroke and the time it takes for the effect to appear onscreen. The lower the spacing, the more times Photoshop has to draw the brush shape in a given space. Increasing the value increases the speed of the stroke. The trick is finding a balance between smoothness and speed, instead of using one universal low Spacing value.

Manually setting the angle of a new brush. Set Angle and Roundness manually using the Brush Outline in the lower left of the dialog box. Click-drag the two points to reset the Roundness. Click-drag anywhere else to reset the Angle. The preview in the lower right displays the changes on-the-fly.

The New Brush Dialog Box

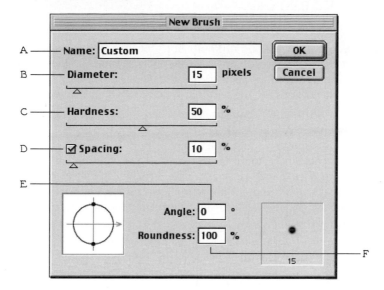

A. Name

If desired, name a new brush in this field. Be specific—the icons used to display a brush are difficult to interpret visually, and can only appear accurately up to a relatively small size.

To rename an existing brush, double-click its icon in the brush picker. The Edit Brush controls appear.

B. Diameter (1 to 999 pixels)

The Diameter measures the widest part of the brush, regardless of its shape. Since the value is measured in pixels, the same brush has different relative sizes in low- and high-resolution images. Set the Diameter by dragging the slider to the proper width. If desired, enter a value in the Diameter field.

Brushes under 74 pixels in diameter appear in the lower-right preview window at their actual size. Larger brushes appear as large as possible, but are reduced in scale in order to preview the entire brush.

C. Hardness (0% to 100%)

Lowering the Hardness value softens the outer edge of a brush. A Hardness value of 100% results in a totally opaque brush, except for a thin anti-aliased edge. By entering a lower value, the center point of the brush fades to transparency. The lower the value, the softer the edge.

This effect is an attempt to emulate specific real-world brush types. Harder brush edges are like stiff-bristled paint brushes, which produce crisp and even strokes. Softer brush edges mimic soft-bristled paint brushes, which apply heavier densities of paint at the center of a brushstroke.

As the Hardness value lowers, the effective size of the brush increases beyond its defined value.

D. **Spacing** (0% to 100%)

When you paint with one of Photoshop's brushes, you're actually applying a repeating series of brush marks. When those shapes are spaced close enough together, they create the appearance of a solid line. If they're spaced far enough apart, the individual shapes become visible.

Spacing controls the distance between brush marks. This value is based on a percentage of the Diameter, or the width of the brush. Values under 100% produce overlapping brush marks, and values over 100% produce evenly spaced but separate brush marks. If the Spacing option is turned off, spacing then depends on how fast or slow the stroke is made. Slow strokes make solid lines, while faster movements begin to separate the brush marks. Spacing should only be turned off when such an artistic effect is desired.

For most purposes, a spacing value of 25% produces brush strokes that appear solid. Large brushes, usually with Diameters higher than 75 pixels, usually need a lower Spacing percentage. If bumps appear along the brush stroke, reduce this value.

E. **Angle** (0° to 360°)

The Angle determines the slant of an elliptical brush. This is similar to the angle of a flat paintbrush or calligrapher's pen. Round brushes are unaffected by this value.

Set the brush angle by entering a value in the Angle field, or use the Angle and Roundness box in the lower-righthand corner of the New Brushes dialog box. Click anywhere on the circle to change the angle to that degree.

F. **Roundness** (0% to 100%)

This value determines the overall shape of a standard brush. A Roundness of 100% produces a perfectly circular brush, while lower values result in thinner shapes. All elliptical brushes are a combination of Roundness and Angle settings.

Set the brush roundness by entering a value in the Roundness field, or use the Angle and Roundness box in the lower-righthand corner of the New Brushes dialog box. Click and drag on either black dot, found at the edge of the circle, to set the roundness.

Reset Brushes

This command restores Photoshop's default set of brushes. When you select Reset Brushes from the submenu, an alert appears, offering two options: Click OK to delete the entire set of current brushes before restoring the defaults, or click Append to add the defaults to the existing set of brushes.

Issues to Consider

Resetting may delete any unsaved brushes. If you have added custom shapes to the Brushes menu or have any standard brushes with special settings, save the contents of the menu before restoring the default brushes. The Reset Brushes command cannot be reversed with Edit: **Undo**.

Load Brushes

This command enables you to access groups of pre-defined brush shapes. The set you choose is added to the existing set of brushes.

Issues to Consider

Adding saved brushes to the loadable brush picker list. To add a saved group of brushes to the list that appears at the bottom of the brush picker submenu, place the file in the following folder: Adobe Photoshop 6/Presets/Brushes. The next time you launch the program, the brush set will appear in the submenu, enabling you to load it whenever you want.

Save Brushes

Use this command to save all current brushes and their settings into a separate file. Name each file descriptively and save them into Photoshop's Brushes folder (found in the Presets folder). To load saved brushes, use the Load Brushes or Replace Brushes commands.

Replace Brushes

This command is similar to Load Brushes, except that it deletes all existing brushes and replaces them with the selected set. If necessary, save the current set of brushes before choosing this command.

Delete Brushes

Permanently remove a brush by selecting the brush in the brush picker and choosing Delete Brush from the Brushes picker flyout menu. Or, bypass this step by holding down the (Command) [Control] key and clicking the unwanted brush.

Viewing Options

The following options determine how the icons that represent the individual brushes appear in the brush picker. You still choose a brush by clicking it, regardless of the current setting.

- **Text Only.** When you choose this option, only the names of the brushes are visible, listed in alphabetical (or numerical) order. Only use this option when you've given your brushes clear, specific names.

- **Small Thumbnail.** This option is Photoshop's default. Here, each brush appears in a 24-pixel box, with its diameter printed directly underneath. (Any brush up to 24 pixels wide appears at actual size.)

- **Large Thumbnail.** Here, each brush appears in a 64-pixel wide box, with its diameter printed directly underneath.

- **Small List.** Here, the brushes appear in a scrolling alphabetical list. The brush shapes appear to the left of each item in a 12-pixel wide box.

- **Large List.** Here, the brushes again appear in a scrolling alphabetical list. The brush shapes appear to the left of each item in a 24-pixel wide box.

2.4
___

Brush Dynamics

The Brush Dynamics controls, found on the far right of the Options bar, enable you to use a drawing tablet to apply more realistic attributes to your brushstrokes. As you apply pressure to the stylus of a tablet, you dynamically change the function of the current brush. The following options control the results:

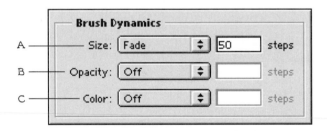

A. **Size** (1 to 9999)

Different levels of pressure affect the thickness of the brushstroke. Full pressure applies the current brush at its full width; less pressure results in a thinner stroke.

B. **Opacity** (1 to 9999)

Full pressure applies the foreground color at full opacity, assuming the opacity slider in the Options bar is set to 100%. Less pressure results in increasingly transparent brushstrokes.

C. **Color** (1 to 9999)

Full pressure applies the current foreground color; very slight pressure applies the current background color. As you apply levels of pressure in between, the result is a blend between the two colors, creating a sort of flexible gradient.

Issues to Consider

Using the Fade option. The Airbrush, Paintbrush, Eraser, and Pencil tools enable you to apply tapered brushstrokes. You must enter a number of steps for this effect to work.

The Steps value refers to the Spacing setting of the current brush. A brushstroke is actually a repeating series of brush shapes—when you taper a brushstroke, the distance of the fade is based on a specific number of these shapes. Therefore, brushes with higher Spacing values take longer to fade. A brushstroke can fade to one of two values:

– **Transparent.** Choose this option to fade the current foreground color into completely transparent pixels.

– **Background.** Choose this option to fade the current foreground color into the current background color.

2.5

Brush Modes

The Options bar for every Paint tool contains a pop-up menu of different brush modes. These options affect how the color of a brush stroke combines with the colors of the existing image pixels.

When you apply any Paint tool, the basic effect is the same: The color of every pixel involved is recalculated, or changed to a new value. Therefore, painting involves three values:

• **Base Color.** The base color is the value of a pixel before you apply a brushstroke.

• **Blend Color.** The blend color is the value applied by a Paint tool. It can be a single value (such as the foreground color when using the Paintbrush tool), or a series of colors (such as the image information used by the Clone tool).

• **Result Color.** The result color is the value produced by combining the blend color and with the blend modes used in the Layers palette. Although the options in both lists are pretty much the same, the techniques required to apply them are different. Blend modes affect the contents of an entire layer; using the Paint tools, you can apply different brush modes to parts of a single layer.

Normal

This mode applies the full value of the current blend color. If a tool does not apply color—such as the Blur or Sharpen tools—it simply edits the existing colors based on the remaining settings in their Options bar.

Threshold

Images in Bitmap or Indexed Color mode contain this option instead of Normal. Since both modes contain a limited number of colors, painting in this mode applies the available value closest to the current blend color.

Dissolve

This option affects soft-edged or semi-opaque brushes. Any application of a blend color less than 100% opaque is converted to randomly scattered, 100% opaque pixels. The result is a rough-textured brushstroke with no anti-aliasing. The quantity of scattered pixels is determined by the transparency value of the brush. If its opacity slider is set to 60%, then 60% of the pixels within the painted area are changed to the foreground color. Forty percent of the pixels retain the original base color.

Behind

This mode is available only when an image layer is active. Here, only pixels less than 100% opaque are affected by the blend color. Fully transparent pixels are painted with 100% of the foreground color. Semi-transparent pixels are colored at opacity levels equal to the inverse of their transparency levels. For example, a 40% transparent pixel is colored with 60% of the blend color.

Clear

Only the Paint Bucket tool can use Clear, and only when an image layer is selected. Instead of applying color, this option changes pixel transparency. A fully opaque blend color results in completely transparent pixels. A semi-opaque blend color sets the transparency of the base pixels to the inverse value of the Options bar's opacity slider. For example, an opacity setting of 80% results in 20% opaque pixels. (This option also appears in the Edit: **Fill** and **Stroke** dialog boxes.)

Multiply

This mode multiplies the brightness values of the base and blend colors to create a darker tone.

When the blend color is white, the base color is not affected. When the base color is white, the blend color is unaffected. When either color is black, the result color is black as well. When the blend color is a shade of gray, Multiply darkens the base color without changing its hue. This makes it an effective choice for applying shadows to a color image.

Screen

This mode produces the opposite effect of Multiply, resulting in lighter colors.

When the blend color is black, the base color is not affected. When the blend color is white, the result color is always white. Shades of gray lighten pixels without changing their hue, making it an effective choice for applying highlights to a color image.

Overlay

The effect of this mode is the same as either Multiply or Screen, depending on the values of the base color. The hues of the base color shift toward the blend color, and the general contrast is increased. When either the blend color or the base color is neutral gray, this mode has no effect.

Soft Light

The effect of this mode is similar to Overlay, only less intense.

Hard Light

The effect of this mode is similar to Overlay, only more intense.

Color Dodge

This mode lightens the base color, shifting its hue toward the values of the blend color. Lighter blend colors cause more intense changes, while darker colors produce a more subtle effect. The result of Color Dodge is similar to using the Dodge tool, with an added element of color bias. When the blend color is black, this mode has no effect.

Color Burn

This mode darkens the base color, shifting its hue toward the values of the blend color. Darker blend colors cause more intense changes, while lighter colors cause a more subtle effect. The result of Color Burn is similar to using the Burn tool, only the resulting hues are shifted toward the blend color. When the blend color is white, this mode has no effect.

Darken

This mode compares the brightness values of each color channel. The resulting color is formed by the darkest channel values of the blend and base colors. (For example, if you apply R: 160, G: 70, B: 220 to a base of R: 80, G: 120, B: 155, the result is R: 80, G: 70, B: 155.)

Lighten
(Option-Shift) [Alt-Shift]-L

This mode compares the brightness values of each color channel. The resulting color is formed by the lightest channel values of the blend and base colors. (For example, if you apply R: 160, G: 70, B: 220 to a base of R: 80, G: 120, B: 155, the result is R: 160, G: 120, B: 220.)

Difference
(Option-Shift) [Alt-Shift]-E

This mode compares the brightness values of each color channel. The resulting color is formed by subtracting the smaller values from the larger values. (For example, if you apply R: 160, G: 70, B: 220 to a base of R: 80, G: 120, B: 155, the result is R: 80, G: 50, B: 65.)

When the blend color is white, the base color inverts. When the blend color is black, this mode has no effect.

Exclusion
(Option-Shift) [Alt-Shift]-X

The effect of this mode is similar to Difference, but the resulting colors are more likely to contain neutral grays.

When the blend color is white, the base color inverts. When the blend color is black, this mode has no effect. When the blend color is middle gray, it replaces the base color completely.

Hue
(Option-Shift) [Alt-Shift]-U

This mode replaces the hue value of the base color with the value of the blend color. The saturation and lightness levels of the base color are not affected. (For more information, see *10.1, Image: **Mode** Overview*.)

Saturation
(Option-Shift) [Alt-Shift]-T

This mode replaces the saturation value of the base color with the value of the blend color. The hue and lightness levels of the base color are not affected. (For more information, see *10.1, Image: **Mode** Overview*.)

Color
(Option-Shift) [Alt-Shift]-C

This mode replaces the hue and saturation values of the base color with the values of the blend color. The lightness level of the base color is not affected. This mode makes it easy to hand-tint an image (after converting a Grayscale file to RGB or CMYK Color, or by applying Image: Adjust: **Desaturate** to a color image.)

Luminosity
(Option-Shift) [Alt-Shift]-Y

This mode replaces the lightness value of the base color with the value of the blend color. The hue and saturation levels of the base color are not affected. (For more information, see *10.1, Image: **Mode** Overview*.)

2.6

Set Opacity

An Opacity slider appears in the Options bar for every Paint tool that applies color. This option enables you to apply semi-transparent brushstrokes. (For more information, see *11.6, Opacity.*)

Before using this feature, however, ask yourself what you're trying to achieve. Unlike changing the opacity of an image layer, you can't automatically reset the opacity of a brushstroke after you've applied it. Think of it this way: To apply overlapping, semi-transparent brushstrokes to a single layer, use the Paint tool's Opacity slider. To give your brushstrokes a uniform opacity value, create a new layer before painting, then set the value in the Layers palette. (For more information, see *22.1, Set the Opacity.*)

2.7

Airbrush Tool
Type "J"

This tool applies a continuous feed of color, similar to an actual airbrush. While painting, holding the cursor in one position results in a wider application of color. Use the Airbrush tool to create soft, gradual brushstrokes.

Airbrush Tool Options

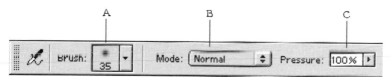

A. **Brush**

Click the vertical bar to access the brush picker; click the Brush icon to edit the current brush settings. (For more information, see *2.2, The Brush Picker.*)

B. **Mode**

These options determine how colors applied with the Airbrush tool will interact with the existing image colors. (For more information, see *2.5, Brush Modes.*)

C. **Pressure** (1% to 100%)

This value controls how quickly color is applied to the image, simulating the flow of paint from an airbrush. It defaults to 50%, which applies a diffuse, semi-translucent line. For the most delicate work, use a very low pressure—for example, 10 to 20%—and overlap your brushstrokes to gradually build the desired color values.

2.8

Paintbrush Tool   Type "B"

This tool applies a brushstroke of uniform width. Its brushes have either soft or anti-aliased edges.

Paintbrush Tool Options

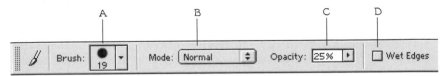

A. **Brush**

Click the vertical bar to access the brush picker; click the Brush icon to edit the current brush settings. (For more information, see *2.2, The Brush Picker.*)

B. **Mode**

These options determine how colors applied with the Paintbrush tool will interact with the existing image colors. (For more information, see *2.5, Brush Modes.*)

C. **Opacity** (0 to 100%)

This slider controls the opacity of a brushstroke. The value is applied in addition to the opacity of the current layer. (For more information, see *2.6, Set Opacity.*)

D. **Wet Edges**

When this box is checked, the resulting brushstrokes resemble a water-color. The color in the center of the brush is washed out and semi-transparent, while the edges appear slightly darker.

This effect appears to be a blend mode, but it's not. Rather, Photoshop manipulates the opacity of the brush: The center of the brush is set to roughly half of the current opacity setting. The edges are set to roughly three-quarters of the current opacity.

2.9

Pencil Tool *Type "B"*

This tool applies a brushstroke of uniform width. Like an actual pencil, its brushes have hard edges. Closely related to the very first digital paint tools, the Pencil tool cannot use soft or anti-aliased brushes.

Pencil Tool Options

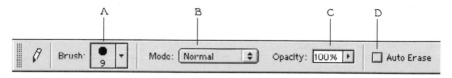

A. Brush

Click the vertical bar to access the brush picker; click the Brush icon to edit the current brush settings. (For more information, see *2.2, The Brush Picker.*)

B. Mode

These options determine how colors applied with the Pencil tool will interact with the existing image colors. (For more information, see *2.5, Brush Modes.*)

C. Opacity (0 to 100%)

This slider controls the opacity of a brushstroke. The value is applied in addition to the opacity of the current layer. (For more information, see *2.6, Set Opacity.*)

D. Auto Erase

This option allows you to apply the background color over areas colored with the current foreground color.

Although it's available in all color modes, the effect of Auto Erase is most apparent on a Bitmap image. Assuming the colors are set to default black and white, painting on white pixels applies black, similar to drawing on paper. If you start painting by clicking on a black pixel, the Pencil tool applies white, similar to erasing black from a white page.

Related Topics

2.10

Clone Stamp Tool *Type "S"*

Formerly known as the Rubber Stamp tool, this item enables you to copy and paste brush-sized segments of pre-existing image colors.

As a production tool, the Rubber Stamp is most often used to retouch an image. For example, scratches or dust on a 35mm slide may become visible when the image is scanned. To retouch the flaw, the Clone tool requires that you do two things:

- **Sample.** Typically, you'll copy pixels from an area with similar color, tone, and texture to the pixels surrounding the flaw. When you sample, you specify the exact pixels you want to clone. Do this by holding down the (Option) [Alt] key and clicking the appropriate area. This results in no visible changes.

- **Clone.** To apply the sampled pixels, move the cursor over the flaw and click. This act copies pixels from the defined sample area and pastes them wherever you clicked. By using the surrounding pixels, you keep visible artifacting to a minimum.

Overall, the Clone tool is not well-suited for cloning a specific image element, such as a tree or rock. To create multiple copies of an existing element, you're much better off using one of Selection tools to isolate the desired pixels, and copying it to a new layer. From there, it's much easier to duplicate and reposition the item. However, if your intent is to *remove* the rock or tree, the Clone tool is the most effective option.

The exact behavior of the sample and clone commands depends on the settings of the Options bar.

Issues to Consider

Create a new layer before using the Clone Stamp tool. Doing so makes it much easier to approach particularly complex retouching tasks—if you don't like the results, discard the layer and start over; if you like them, merge the layers. (For more information, see *2.1, Paint Tools Overview*.)

The Clone Stamp tool can read information from a separate image. Open the image and (Option) [Alt]-click to define a sample area. Open another image and click to clone the sampled information.

Sample by clicking, not by dragging the brush. When you retouch an image with the Aligned box checked, avoid cloning by dragging the cursor. This often results in visible artifacting and the inclusion of unwanted details. For the best results, start with a small, soft-edged brush and clone one click at a time.

Clone Stamp Tool Options

A. **Brush**

Click the vertical bar to access the brush picker; click the Brush icon to edit the current brush settings. (For more information, see *2.2, The Brush Picker.*)

B. **Mode**

These options determine how colors applied with the Clone Stamp tool will interact with the existing image colors. (For more information, see *2.5, Brush Modes.*)

C. **Opacity**

This slider controls the opacity of a brushstroke. The value is applied in addition to the opacity of the current layer. (For more information, see *2.6, Set Opacity.*)

D. **Aligned**

When checked, this option samples and clones visible pixels, as described above. Its title refers to the relationship between the sample area and the clone area—here, their relative positions remain constant. For example, assume your sample area is two inches to the right of the clone area. If you continue clicking various spots throughout the image, you continue sampling information from a point two inches to the right of every click.

When unchecked, the sample area remains constant, regardless of where and how many times you click to define a clone area.

E. **Use All Layers**

When this box is checked, the Clone Stamp tool samples pixels from all visible layers. To prevent a layer's contents from being included, hide the layer before cloning. When unchecked, the Rubber Stamp only samples from and edits the currently active layer.

Checking this option allows you to clone into a new, empty layer. Neither option allows you to clone fully transparent pixels.

Related Topics

2.11

Pattern Stamp Tool *Type "S"*

Although this item is referred to as a Stamp tool, it doesn't involve any sampling or cloning. Instead, it applies the information contained within any
pattern created via the Edit: **Define Pattern** command.

Issues to Consider

There are better ways to apply a pattern. When you use the Pattern Stamp
tool, you're pretty much stuck with what you get: You can't scale or rotate
the pattern, or change it on-the-fly, or easily change the area on which
it appears. However, you can gain considerable editing flexibility if you
bypass this tool in favor of creating a new Pattern Fill layer. This way,
you can use the mask thumbnail that automatically appears in the Layers
palette to reveal or hide the desired information. Additionally, you can
always double-click the pattern thumbnail to change or scale the current
pattern. (For more information, see *11.41, Layer: New Fill Layer: **Pattern**.*)

Pattern Stamp Options

A. **Brush**

Click the vertical bar to access the brush picker; click the Brush icon
to edit the current brush settings. (For more information, see *2.2, The
Brush Picker.*)

B. **Mode**

These options determine how colors applied with the Pattern Stamp tool
will interact with the existing image colors. (For more information, see
2.5, Brush Modes.)

C. **Opacity**

This slider controls the opacity of a brushstroke. The value is applied in
addition to the opacity of the current layer. (For more information, see
2.6, Set Opacity.)

D. **Pattern Menu**

This pop-up menu enables you to target the pattern that the tool refers
to. (For more information, see *9.29, Edit: **Define Pattern**.*)

E. **Aligned**

When this box is checked, the pattern is always aligned as you paint, regardless of the number of times you click or drag. The illusion is that the pattern has already been applied to the image, and the Clone tool is simply revealing it.

When unchecked, the pattern is re-aligned every time you click with the Pattern Stamp tool. Rather than align to an invisible grid, the center of the pattern aligns to the center of every brushstroke.

Related Topics

2.12

History Brush Tool

Type "Y"

This brush refers to the contents of the History palette, enabling you to apply information from previous incarnations of the image. Target the tool's source pixels by clicking the paint-enable icon beside the desired snapshot or history level in the History palette. (For more information, see Chapter 20, *The History Palette*)

Mistakes to Avoid

Painting with the incorrect History Palette item selected. Since the History palette contains up to 100 histories and allows for multiple snapshots, you must make sure the appropriate one is active before painting. Make sure you double-check the palette and click the paint-enable icon beside the desired snapshot.

Attempting to use this tool after modifying the image dimensions. If you've changed the image's width, height, resolution, or color mode since the last snapshot was defined, the History Brush is disabled. For the best results, apply the desired dimension, resolution, and mode changes before using this tool. If this is impossible, then you'll be restricted to using only History palette items that occurred after such edits.

Issues to Consider

The History Brush tool is not the only way to selectively revert an image. This tool is essentially the same as (Option) [Alt]-painting with the Eraser tool (or erasing with the Erase to History box checked in the Options bar). Unlike the Eraser tool, you can choose from the list of Brush Modes while painting with the History Brush.

History Brush Options

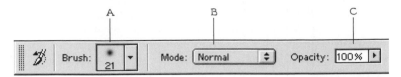

A. **Brush**

Click the vertical bar to access the brush picker; click the Brush icon to edit the current brush settings. (For more information, see *2.2, The Brush Picker.*)

B. **Mode**

These options determine how colors applied with the History Brush tool will interact with the existing image colors. (For more information, see *2.5, Brush Modes.*)

C. **Opacity**

This slider controls the opacity of a brushstroke. The value is applied in addition to the opacity of the current layer. (For more information, see *2.6, Set Opacity.*)

Related Topics

2.13

Art History Brush Tool   *Type "Y"*

Like the History Brush tool, the Art History Brush refers to the contents of the History palette. However, instead of applying an accurate representation of a history state, it uses a series of unpredictable brush effects to distort and redistribute the information. The history state you target almost doesn't matter—the only information that survives the effect of the tool are the colors contained in the state.

This tool is an expansion of the "Impressionist" feature that was part of the Clone Stamp tool options in earlier versions of the program. There, you had no control at all over the appearance of the brushstrokes. The Art History Brush does indeed give you more options to influence the results, but you should still think twice before using it. You only have vague control over the effect of the brushstrokes, and their appearance is immediately identifiable to almost anyone who has ever used Photoshop.

Art History Brush Options

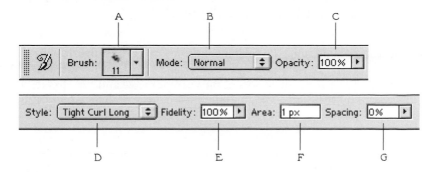

A. Brush

Click the vertical bar to access the brush picker; click the Brush icon to edit the current brush settings. The size of the current brush will influence the overall effect of the tool—the degree will depend on the item set in the Style pop-up menu. (For more information, see *2.2, The Brush Picker.*)

B. Mode

These options determine how colors applied with the Art History Brush tool will interact with the existing image colors. (For more information, see *2.5, Brush Modes.*)

C. Opacity

This slider controls the opacity of a brushstroke. The value is applied in addition to the opacity of the current layer. (For more information, see *2.6, Set Opacity.*)

D. Style

This pop-up menu contains a list of custom brush options. Their overall size and shape are based on the item currently set in the brush picker, but each item here determines the extent and pattern of the tool's random color placement. The options are reasonably self-explanatory. For example, items marked "Long" use longer patterns to apply color; items marked "Tight" place the brushstrokes closer together.

E. Fidelity (0 to 100%)

This option determines how accurately the tool will adhere to the colors that exist in the targeted history state. When set to 100%, the tool only applies values found in the targeted state. As you reduce the setting, the tool expands the range of possible colors. If you use an older or slower computer, lower settings may extend the redraw time of the tool.

F. **Area** (0 to 500 pixels)

This setting determines how close together the individual custom brush-strokes will appear. Lower values pack the strokes into a smaller space; higher values stretch them out over a wider area.

G. **Spacing** (0 to 100%)

This value determines the tolerance of the Art History Brush. When the value is set to 0%, you can apply new colors anywhere on the image. As you raise the setting, the colors of the current image and the targeted history state must be increasingly different before any change takes effect.

2.14

Eraser Tool *Type "E"*

Although the Eraser tool appears to delete pixels, it actually does no such thing. Instead, it changes existing color values to one of two values:

* **Background color.** When the Eraser tool is used on the background layer, it applies the current background color. This effect is the same as making a selection and pressing the Delete key.

* **Transparent.** When this tool is used on any other image layer, it applies no color at all. Rather, it converts colored pixels to fully transparent ones. This effect most closely resembles "erasing" pixels.

To increase your editing options, Photoshop enables the Eraser tool to mimic the brush behavior of multiple Paint tools.

Issues to Consider

Lower the opacity setting to paint semi-transparency onto an image layer. By lowering the opacity setting for the Paintbrush or Pencil option, you can use the Eraser tool to add transparency to specific parts of an image layer. For example, applying a 40% erasure to a 100% opaque layer results in 60% opaque pixels.

Erasing while preserving transparency. If a layer's Lock Transparent Pixels box is checked, the Eraser tool applies the background color.

Erase to Saved shortcut. Hold down the (Option) [Alt] key while using any brush type or mode to access the Erase to Saved option.

Eraser Tool Options

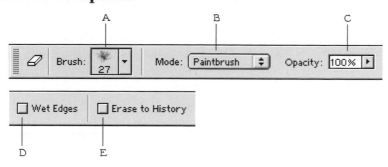

A. **Brush**

Click the vertical bar to access the brush picker; click the Brush icon to edit the current brush settings. (For more information, see *2.2, The Brush Picker.*)

B. **Mode**

Brush modes are not available when using the Eraser tool. Instead, the options in this pop-up enable the Eraser tool to mimic the characteristics of the Airbrush, Paintbrush, or Pencil tool. The fourth option is Block, the same non anti-aliased square brush shape used by earlier versions of the program.

When you choose a Paint tool from the pop-up menu, the Options bar displays the appropriate slider and Stylus Pressure controls.

C. **Fade**

Check this box to erase with a tapered brushstroke. (For more information, see *2.4, Brush Dynamics.*)

D. **Wet Edges**

This option is available only when Paintbrush is chosen from the Brush Type pop-up. Here, the brushstroke resembles a watercolor, similar to using Wet Edges with the Paintbrush tool. The effects are reversed, however, to create the appearance of erasing.

This effect appears to be a blend mode, but it's not. Rather, Photoshop manipulates the opacity of the brush: The center of the brush is set to roughly half of the current opacity setting. Its edges are set to roughly one-quarter of the current opacity.

E. **Erase to History**

When this box is checked, the Eraser tool applies the pixels found in the currently targeted History palette item. When unchecked, you can still use this function by holding down the (Option) [Alt] key while using the tool. When this box is checked, you can still access the standard Eraser tool by holding down the (Option) [Alt] key. (For more information, see *20.1, History Palette Overview.*)

2.15

Background Eraser Tool

Type "E"

The Background Eraser tool enables you to erase what you *perceive* to be the background of an image. For example, imagine a dog standing in front of a blue wall. Before you can place the dog over a different background, you must separate it from the surrounding pixels. You can use the Background Eraser tool to erase only the blue pixels, leaving the dog as an isolated image element.

This tool is not the best option for creating a complex silhouette. It's more appropriate for rough-and-ready extractions, when speed is more important than quality. For the best results, follow these guidelines:

- **Use on images with a high-contrast background.** The more the background colors differ from the foreground element, the easier it is to remove them with the Background Eraser tool. If the color values are too close together, the tool cannot discern between the element and the surrounding pixels.

- **Only paint the colors you want to remove.** When clicking and dragging with the Background Eraser tool, focus on the small crosshair in the middle of the brush shape. Whenever you click, the crosshair must remain over the background color. Let the outer edge of the brush shape move over the target element—as long as you start on a background color, the object is safe. If you happen to click the item you're trying to extract, you'll erase part of it.

- **If possible, downsample the image after erasing the image.** As effective as this tool seems to be, it doesn't produce perfectly clean edges. Often, the process of downsampling the image after extracting will compensate for the lack of detail. For this reason, the most successful Background Eraser extractions start as a 300 ppi image, and end as a 72 ppi web graphic. (For more information, see *C.8, Downsampling an Image.*)

- **Be prepared to deal with an image layer.** If you use this tool on a background layer, it automatically converts to an image layer. This is the only way that the tool can leave behind transparent pixels.

Issues to Consider

Applying more effective extraction techniques. Photoshop offers a number of silhouetting techniques far more successful than what you can produce with the Background Eraser tool. When the quality of an extracted element really matters—and it usually does—ignore this tool and spend a little more time on the necessary steps. (For more information, see *10.55, Image: Extract, I.5, Creating a Complex Silhouette: Hair,* and *I.7, Creating a Complex Silhouette: Tree.*)

Resizing brushes on-the-fly. Decrease or increase the size of the current brush by pressing the open bracket ([) and close bracket (]) keys, respectively. If the brush diameter is 100 pixels wide or less, it changes in 10-pixel increments. If the diameter is between 101 and 199 pixels wide, it changes in 25-pixel increments. When the diameter is 200 pixels wide or more, it changes in 50-pixel increments.

Toggling between hard and soft brushes. To switch to a hard-edged brush, press Shift-open bracket ([). To switch to a soft-edged brush, press Shift-close bracket (]).

Be prepared to clean up your extraction. Like most automatic extraction methods, the Background Eraser tool tends to leave behind stray pixels or a semi-transparent halo. Unfortunately, you may not detect this noise until you flatten the image. At the very least, you'll need to perform a basic clean-up of the silo edges. (For more information, see *1.4, Cleaning an Extracted Silhouette.*)

Background Eraser Options

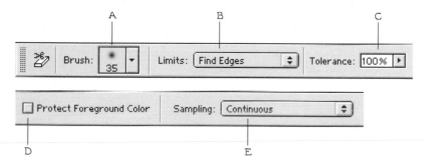

A. Brush

Click the vertical bar to access the brush picker; click the Brush icon to edit the current brush settings. (For more information, see *2.2, The Brush Picker.*)

B. Limits

The crosshair in the center of the Background Eraser tool's cursor is continually sampling color information. Based on the current sample, the items in this pop-up menu determine how the colors within the brush shape are erased.

Contiguous

Here, the tool erases similarly-colored pixels as long as they are contiguous to the crosshair.

Discontiguous

Here, the tool erases all similarly-colored pixels falling within the brush shape, whether or not they are contiguous.

Find Edges

This option attempts to exaggerate the edges of the element you're extracting, presumably to add a degree of sharpening. However, its effect is difficult to predict, and even harder to control. Avoid it.

C. **Tolerance** (1 to 100%)

This option determines the Background Eraser's color sensitivity. Higher values enable you to erase a wider range of colors. Lower values restrict the range, enabling you to work with finer details more successfully.

D. **Protect Foreground Color**

When this box is checked, the tool will not affect any pixels colored with the current foreground color.

E. **Sampling**

The options in this pop-up control how the Background Eraser addresses the current background color.

Continuous

The default setting, this option continually samples the color beneath the center crosshair, basing its editing decisions on the current value.

Once

When this item is set, the tool only recognizes the first color sampled when you click with the tool. This way, as you drag the cursor, only the original color is recognized and erased. To specify a new color, release the mouse button and click again.

Background Swatch

When this item is set, the Background Eraser only recognizes the value of the current background color—no sampling occurs. This option is useful if you need to re-extract an image that has already been silhouetted and flattened—as long as the background color is set to white, you can quickly trace the edge of the element.

2.16

Magic Eraser Tool *Type "E"*

The Magic Eraser tool enables you to erase ranges of similarly-colored pixels. It's closely related to the Magic Wand tool—the only difference is that the Magic Wand selects a color range, and the Magic Eraser converts a color range to transparent pixels.

Issues to Consider

Eliminating the white pixels in a line art image. In earlier versions of Photoshop, it was time-consuming at best to convert the white areas in a 1-bit image to transparency. After converting the image to Grayscale mode, it typically involved converting the background layer to an image layer, making a Magic Wand selection, choosing Select: **Similar**, and pressing the Delete key. Now, as long as the image no longer exists in Bitmap mode, the Magic Eraser tool can convert every white pixel with a single click.

Erasing a layer with locked transparency. The Magic Eraser always produces transparent pixels, with one exception: If the Lock Transparency box is checked for the target layer, clicking with this tool fills the pixels with the current background color. The effect is similar to using the Paint Bucket tool. (For more information, see *22.3, Lock Options.*)

Magic Eraser Options

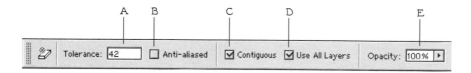

A. Tolerance (0 to 255)

This setting determines the sensitivity of the tool. When set to 0, it only recognizes the precise color value of the click-point. As you increase the setting, you increase the range of affected colors. A setting of 255 includes every color in the layer.

B. Anti-aliased

When checked, this option attempts to add a one-pixel thick transition between the transparent and colored areas. Whether or not you use it depends on the image type in question: Full-continuous tone images usually benefit from anti-aliasing; however, if the image consists of solid, hard-edged shapes (such as line art), anti-aliasing only gets in the way.

C. Contiguous

When this box is checked, the Magic Eraser tool only affects pixels adjacent to the initial click-point. When unchecked, it includes pixels throughout the entire image, whether they are contiguous or not.

D. Use All Layers

When this box is checked, the tool refers to all colors visible in the image when making its decisions, even if they appear on different layers. However, only the currently active layer is affected.

E. Opacity (0 to 100%)

This setting reduces the intensity of the tool, leaving behind semi-transparent pixels instead of transparent.

Related Topics

H.8   *Adding Multiple Colors to B&W Artwork*
H.9   *Colorizing Line Art: Using Flat vs. Process Black*
H.10   *Colorizing Line Art: Using an Anti-Aliased Template*

2.17

Gradient Tool   *Type "G"*

Use this tool to create a *gradation,* or a progression of colors that blend gradually from one to the next. (The term *gradient* is actually a bit misleading, implying a mathematical rate of inclination.)

For example, to create a linear gradient, drag a line with the Gradient tool. The start of the line represents the first color of the gradient; the end represents the last color. If a gradient consists of more than two colors, the remaining values are evenly spaced between ends of the line. Photoshop automatically inserts a series of tones between each defined color to create smooth transitions.

The Gradient tool is commonly used for the following:

- **Filling a selection.** When a selection is active, only its contents are filled. If more than one area is selected, they are affected by the same progression.

- **Filling an entire layer.** When no selections are present, the entire active layer is filled, replacing any existing information. Note that you can produce this effect more efficiently by creating a gradient fill layer. (See *Issues to Consider,* below.)

- **Filling the contents of a layer.** By choosing a layer and checking the Lock Transparency box in the Layers palette, the gradient is only applied to the non-transparent pixels. This enables you to add a custom fill to information, such as type.

- **Filling a layer mask or alpha channel.** Apply a gradient to a mask channel or an image in Quick Mask mode to create a diminishing selection.

Issues to Consider

Avoid creating a gradient that is too long, resulting in shade-stepping. Any blend between two colors has a limited number of possible tones. For example, if you create a blend between black and white, up to 254 shades of gray can be generated between them. As you lengthen the gradient, you widen the individual tones. When a gradient is extended too far, the tones become visible. The exact point at which banding occurs depends on two things:

- **The tonal difference between two colors.** For example, a black-to-white gradient can extend to approximately eight inches before banding occurs. A blend between two medium grays contains fewer tones, and can extend only a fraction of the distance.

– **The linescreen value of a printed image.** As you increase the linescreen of a printed image, you reduce the number of tones an output device can reproduce. If the linescreen exceeds a printer's recommended limit, banding will occur—and gradients are the first elements visibly affected.

When filling an entire layer with a gradient, create a gradient fill layer. The gradient tools are most effective when you need to address a specific image area, such as an active selection. However, when filling an entire layer with a gradient, they're no longer the most effective choice. If you create a gradient fill layer, you'll retain the ability to scale, rotate, invert, and otherwise edit a gradient fill. (For more information, see *11.40, Layer: New Fill Layer: **Gradient**.*)

Resizing the Gradient Editor. Resize the Gradient Editor dialog box by dragging the tab in the lower right corner. This will give you a better view of a large list of presets and gradient preview.

Gradient Tool Options

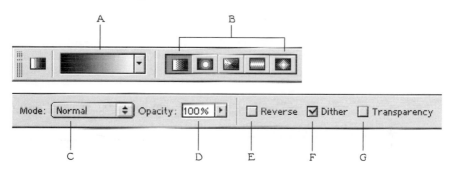

A. Edit Gradient

Click directly on the Gradient icon to access the Gradient Editor dialog box. From there, you can edit the contents of an existing gradient, or define a new one altogether. (For more information, see **The Gradient Editor Dialog Box (Solid)** and **The Gradient Editor Dialog Box (Noise)**, later this section.)

B. Gradient Picker

Click directly on this thin vertical bar to access the gradient picker. The pop-up palette that appears—similar in form and function to the brush picker—enables you to choose from a series of existing gradient fill options. To close the picker, press the Return or Enter key, or double-click the desired item.

The gradient picker submenu, found in the upper right of the pop-up item, contains the following items:

New Gradient

Choose this command to add a new item to the picker. It only creates a duplicate of the last-used gradient—to customize the values, close the picker and click the Edit Gradient icon to access the Gradient Editor dialog box.

Reset Gradients

Choose this command to replace the current contents of the gradient picker with Photoshop's factory default items.

Load/Save Gradients

If you frequently define a large number of gradients, you can save the entire list into a separate, easy-to-organize file. Choose the Load option to access a saved list.

Replace Gradients

Choose this command to replace the current contents of the picker with gradients that have been saved in an external file.

Rename Gradient

Choose this command to change the name of an existing gradient.

Delete Gradient

Choose this command to permanently remove the currently selected gradient from the picker. Bypass this command by (Option) [Alt]-clicking any unwanted item.

Loadable Gradients

By default, a number of factory-supplied gradient sets appear at the bottom of the picker submenu. When you load one, you have the option to add them to the current picker (by clicking Append) or replacing the entire contents of the picker (by clicking OK). To add your own saved set to the list, place the file in the following folder: Adobe Photoshop 6/Presets/Gradients. It will appear the next time you launch the application.

C. Gradient Types

Choose the desired gradient shape from this row of buttons:

Linear Gradient

The default option, it produces a gradient that extends straight from the click-point to the release-point.

Radial Gradient

Click this option to create a concentric gradient, starting at the click-point and extending to the point where you release the mouse button. The final color of the gradient is applied beyond the release-point.

Angle Gradient

> Click this option to create a circular gradient that rotates around the initial click-point. To eliminate any harsh transition between colors, define a gradient that starts and ends on the same color.

Reflected Gradient

> Click this option to create a linear gradient that mirrors itself on either side of the click-point.

Diamond Gradient

> This tool is similar to the Radial Gradient tool, except the overall effect is diamond-shaped.

D. **Mode**

When adding a gradient to an existing layer, these settings determine how its colors combine with any underlying pixels. (For more information, see *2.5, Brush Modes.*)

E. **Opacity** (0 to 100%)

When applying a gradient to an existing layer, this slider enables you to create a semi-transparent gradient.

F. **Reverse**

When this option is checked, the gradient starts with the color at the left of the Edit Gradient preview. When checked, the gradient starts with the color at the right of the preview.

G. **Dither**

Check this box to slightly randomize the distribution of colored pixels. This helps prevent *banding*, or the visible shade-stepping that occurs when too few tones are extended over too great a distance. Unless you have a specific reason to turn it off, leave this box checked for the best results.

H. **Transparency**

When you apply a gradient that contains transparent or semi-opaque pixels, check this box to maintain those values. Otherwise, the gradient appears as 100% opaque.

The Gradient Editor Dialog Box (Solid)

When you set Solid in the Gradient Type pop-up menu, the following options appear in the Gradient Editor dialog box.

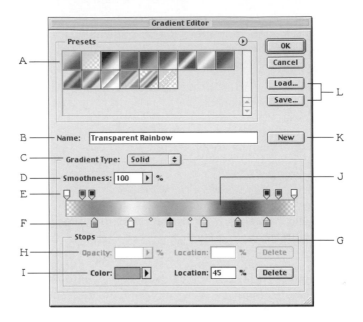

A. Presets

This field displays all gradients currently available in the picker. To edit one, click it once and use the remaining controls. To add a new gradient swatch, click an empty area within the presets field. Double-click an existing swatch to access the Gradient Name dialog box.

B. Name

This field enables you to either enter a name for a new gradient, or rename an existing gradient.

C. Gradient Type

This pop-up enables you to choose between Photoshop's two gradient variations:

Solid

Here, you manually specify the position, opacity, and value of each color in a gradient. It's "solid" because the transitions between each color are smooth and unbroken.

Noise

Noise gradients are composed of thin, randomly-colored striations. You cannot manually edit the values (there are far too many colors involved to be handled by stops)—instead, you can change the color intensities by manipulating a group of color sliders. (For more information, see *The Gradient Editor Dialog Box (Noise)*, later this section.)

D. **Smoothness** (0 to 100%)

When you place a color stop, the value it represents appears at a certain width. The Smoothness slider controls the width applied to every color stop. At 100% (the default), the target colors are widely dispersed, resulting in a more diffused appearance. As you reduce the setting, the width is reduced, resulting in a more focused appearance. Reduce this value at your own risk—beyond a certain point, the gradient looks forced and unnatural.

E. **Opacity Stop**

It is possible to add levels of transparency to a gradient, just like adding different colors. This way, you can see through portions of the gradient to the underlying information. Opacity stops are arranged along the top of the gradient preview.

When you create a new gradient, Photoshop adds two opacity stops by default, at the beginning and end (both are set to 100% opaque). To add a new stop, click above the gradient preview. To add semi-transparency, click the desired stop and set a value in the Opacity field at the bottom of the dialog box. Any changes are immediately reflected in the gradient preview.

To remove a stop, drag it away from the preview, or click it once and press the Delete button at the bottom of the dialog box. To duplicate a stop, (Option) [Alt]-drag it.

Note that when a gradient contains transparency levels, the Transparency box must be checked in the Options bar—otherwise, the values are ignored.

F. **Color Stop**

These triangular markers enable you to define the values and location of a gradient's key colors.

Photoshop defaults to two color stops: one each at the beginning and end of the gradient. To add a new stop, click below the Gradient toolbar. To remove a stop, drag it away from the Toolbar.

Add a color to a gradient by changing the value represented by a color stop. After clicking once on the stop to select it, click the color swatch at the bottom of the dialog box. The color picker appears, enabling you to define a new value.

G. **Midpoint**

A diamond-shaped marker appears between every two stops. These represent the midpoint, or the point where both colors (or opacity values) are equally blended. Extend the impact of one stop by moving the midpoint marker closer to the other.

H. **Opacity Stop Controls**

Use these options to fine-tune the currently selected opacity stop:

Opacity (0 to 100%)

This option controls the current opacity value. At 100%, the stop is completely opaque. Reduce the setting to increase the level of transparency.

Location (0 to 100%)

This field displays the current position of a selected opacity stop or midpoint. When a stop is selected, the percentages indicate positions across the gradient preview—the left edge is 0%, the right edge is 100%. When a marker is selected, the percentages indicate its position between the two stops.

Delete

Click this button to remove the currently selected stop. (You cannot delete the stops on the far left or right of a gradient.)

I. **Color Stop Controls**

Use these options to fine-tune the currently selected color stop:

Color (0 to 100%)

This option enables you to attach a new color value to a color stop. After selecting a stop, click this swatch to access the color picker. Set the desired color and click OK to apply the change.

Location and Delete

These options function exactly the same way as their opacity stop counterparts. (For more information, see *"Opacity Stop Controls,"* earlier this section.)

J. **Gradient Preview**

This bar displays the current settings as a linear gradient—the left side represents the starting color, the right represents the end. It acts as a guide as you edit the gradient's color and transparency values.

K. **New**

This button creates the basis for a new gradient. After naming the new item, it defaults to a two-color gradient, based on the current foreground and background colors.

L. **Load and Save**

If you frequently define a large number of gradients, you can save the entire list into a separate, easy-to-organize file. Choose the Load option to access a saved list.

The Gradient Editor Dialog Box (Noise)

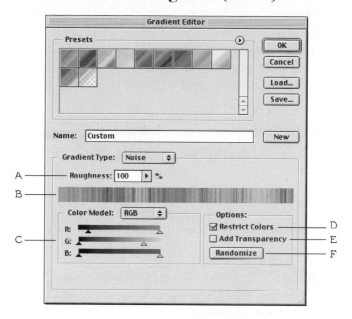

When you set Noise in the Gradient Type pop-up menu, the following options appear in the Gradient Editor dialog box. (Any value not listed here is covered under *The Gradient Editor Dialog Box (Solid)*, earlier this section.)

A. **Roughness** (0 to 100%)

This option determines the intensity of the gradient's colored striations. At 0, the gradient is reduced to two colors. As you raise the value, the thin bands become more pronounced. At 100% (the default), they stand out in high contrast.

B. **Gradient Preview**

This bar displays the current settings as a linear gradient—the left side represents the starting color, the right represents the end. It acts as a guide as you edit the gradient's overall color and transparency values. (Note that you cannot add opacity or color stops to a noise gradient.)

C. **Color Sliders**

This option enables you to specify the range of colors available to a noise gradient. Choose one of three color models—RGB, HSB, or Lab—and move the underlying sliders. Only that values that fall between the positions of each pair of sliders are included in the gradient.

Be aware that this option is incredibly imprecise. The colors of the sliders themselves don't change to reflect the current range, and there are no numerical readouts to aid your decisions. They only way to predict the impact of an edit is to examine the gradient preview, a small and uncalibrated strip of pixels. Consider these controls—if not the entire noise gradient feature—an interesting but unpredictable special effect.

D. Restrict Colors

When this box is checked, Photoshop will prevent any aberrant, oversaturated colors from appearing in the gradient. When unchecked, the gradient may include much more vivid, unnatural color values.

E. Add Transparency

When this box is checked, Photoshop randomly inserts bands of transparency throughout the gradient, as if you'd added several dozen opacity stops. (Note that the Roughness value has no effect on these transparent areas.)

F. Randomize

Click this button to randomly rearrange any color and transparency values in the gradient. If desired, continue clicking until you're satisfied with the results.

2.18

Paint Bucket Tool *Type "K"*

Although its title suggests otherwise, the Paint Bucket tool is not a Paint tool—it's a modified Fill command. This tool enables you to apply color by clicking on an image. A specific range of pixels are affected, controlled by the Tolerance setting in the Paint Bucket tool Options bar.

Starting from where you click, the Paint Bucket tool only affects adjacent pixels that fall within the established Tolerance. For this reason, this tool has limited uses. If you're editing an image that contains strongly defined solid colors, this tool works fairly well. Because of the method it uses to recognize pixels, however, it's a poor choice for coloring continuous tone images.

Issues to Consider

Much more effective fill options exist. Using the Paint Bucket tool, it's almost impossible to get accurate results on anti-aliased shapes—the edge colors are difficult to include in the Tolerance range without affecting additional pixels. Typically, in the time it would take to pinpoint the exact range, you could create a selection outline and use Edit: **Fill**, a far more capable command. Better still, use a solid fill layer, which enables you to change the settings at any time. (For more information, see *9.11, Edit: **Fill*** and *11.39, Layer: New Fill Layer: **Solid Color**.*)

Paint Bucket Options

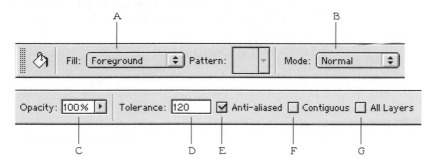

A. Fill

Choose the type of fill you want to apply from this pop-up:

Foreground

> This option uses the current foreground color.

Pattern

> This option uses the currently defined pattern. (For more information, see *9.29, Edit:* **Define Pattern.**)

B. Mode

When applying color, these settings determine how they combine with the existing pixels. (For more information, see *2.5, Brush Modes.*)

C. Opacity (0 to 100%)

When adding color, this slider enables you to apply semi-transparent fill.

D. Tolerance (0 to 255)

This value determines the range of pixels affected by the fill. A value of 0 changes only the exact color of the targeted pixel in the selection. Higher numbers gradually increase the range.

Contrary to popular belief, the Paint Bucket tool does not base a selection on color values. It measures the brightness values of the targeted pixel. The value you enter in the Tolerance field actually corresponds to the 256 possible tones in an 8-bit color channel. If the image is in RGB, CMYK, or Lab Color mode, it reads the values of each color channel.

Photoshop defines the fill range by adding and subtracting the Tolerance from the brightness value of the targeted pixel. Assuming the Tolerance is set to its default of 32, clicking a pixel with a brightness value of 100 expands the range to paint all adjacent pixels between 68 and 132. For example, if you select an RGB pixel with values of R: 160, G: 50, and B: 35, the range includes all adjacent pixels with values between R: 128 and 192, G: 18 and 82, and B: 3 and 67. This process makes the effect of the Paint Bucket tool difficult to predict.

E. **Anti-aliased**

Check this box to add a thin, soft edge transition to the fill. When filling solid-colored areas that do not already have anti-aliased edges, turn this option off.

F. **Contiguous**

When this box is checked, the Paint Bucket tool only applies color along a series of contiguous pixels. For example, if you click a white pixel, the fill color only extends to the edges of that particular white area. When this box is unchecked, the fill is applied to every occurrence of the targeted color. In other words, clicking the same white spot replaces every white pixel in the image with the fill color.

G. **All Layers**

This option enables the Paint Bucket tool to recognize colors outside the currently active layer. When you click to add color, the Tolerance value considers all visible colors, regardless of their layer. The actual fill, however, is applied only to the current layer.

2.19
_____

Sharpen & Blur Tools *Type "R"*

The Focus tools enable you to manually emphasize or de-emphasize the level of detail in an image:

- **Sharpen tool.** Painting with this tool sharpens the image, boosting the amount of contrast between neighboring colored areas. It achieves this effect by increasing the saturation values of the edge pixels.

- **Blur tool.** Painting with this tool blurs the image, reducing the amount of contrast between colored areas. It achieves this effect by averaging the color values of the edge pixels of neighboring colors.

The basic effect is similar to the Blur and Sharpen filters, only the Focus tools enable you to "paint" the intended effect. This method lacks the numerical precision of Filter: Blur: **Gaussian Blur** or Filter: Sharpen: **Unsharp Mask**, but it does enable you to specifically target part of an image.

Issues to Consider

You cannot use one tool to reverse the effect of the other. If you are unhappy with the effect of a brushstroke, choose Edit: **Undo** and try it again.

Sharpen & Blur Tool Options

The following options are available for the Sharpen and Blur tools:

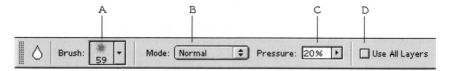

A. Brush

Click the vertical bar to access the brush picker; click the brush icon to edit the current brush settings. (For more information, see *2.2, The Brush Picker.*)

B. Mode

Because this tool doesn't apply new color values, it ignores most of the brush modes. The remaining items affect the redistribution of the existing colors. (For more information, see *2.5, Brush Modes.*)

C. Pressure (1 to 100%)

This slider controls the intensity of the Sharpen and Blur tools. Lower values produce very slight effects; higher values exaggerate the results.

D. Use All Layers

Ordinarily, the Focus tools only affect pixels in the active image layer. By checking this box, you include any visible color values, regardless of the layer in which they exist. As you apply a tool, the new colors appear in the currently active layer.

2.20

Smudge Tool *Type "U"*

This tool smears existing color values as you apply a brushstroke, similar to
running your finger through wet paint. Many people use this tool to create
distorted effects—however, the Liquify command is usually what they're trying to emulate. (For more information, see *10.56, Image: **Liquify**.*)

Smudge Tool Options

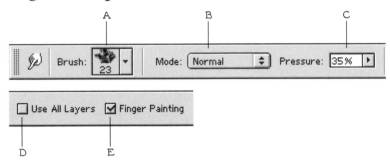

A. **Brush**

Click the vertical bar to access the brush picker; click the Brush icon
to edit the current brush settings. (For more information, see *2.2, The
Brush Picker.*)

B. **Mode**

Because it doesn't apply new color values, this tool ignores most of the
brush modes. The remaining items affect the redistribution of the existing colors. (For more information, see *2.5, Brush Modes.*)

C. **Pressure** (1 to 100%)

This controls the intensity of the smudge, similar to the pressure of your
finger as you smear wet paint. Lower values result in very slight smudging, while higher values exaggerate the effect. When the value is 100%,
the Smudge tool lifts the portion of the image you initially clicked, and
repeats the edge pixels of the brush as you drag.

D. **Use All Layers**

Ordinarily, the Smudge tool only affects pixels in the active image layer.
By checking this box, you include any visible color values, regardless of
the layer in which they exist. As you smudge, the new colors appear in
the currently active layer.

E. **Finger Painting**

When this box is checked, the Smudge tool initially applies the current foreground color, similar to dipping your finger in pigment before smearing wet paint. The length of this effect is determined by the Pressure setting. Lower values result in short applications of the foreground color, while higher values extend the distance. When the value is 100%, the Smudge tool applies only the foreground color, just like the Paintbrush tool.

Hold down the (Option) [Alt] key as you paint with the Smudge tool to temporarily access the Finger Painting option.

2.21
___

Dodge, Burn & Sponge Tools   *Type "O"*

The Dodge, Burn, and Sponge tools enable you to manually affect the tone and saturation of the existing image colors. Each tool mimics a conventional photographic technique:

- **Dodge tool.** As you paint with this tool, you lighten the tones of the image colors. In photography, this effect is achieved by diffusing the light used to expose a negative.

- **Burn tool.** As you paint with this tool, you darken the tones of the image colors. In photography, this effect is achieved by focusing the light used to expose a negative.

- **Sponge tool.** As you paint with this tool, you only affect the saturation value of the colors. On a Grayscale image, however, this tool affects overall contrast. The Desaturate mode lowers the contrast, bringing all tones closer to middle gray. The Saturate mode increases the contrast, or brings all tones closer to black or white.

Dodge, Burn & Sponge Tool Options

The following options are available for all three Toning tools:

A. **Brush**

Click the vertical bar to access the brush picker; click the Brush icon to edit the current brush settings. (For more information, see *2.2, The Brush Picker.*)

B. **Modes**

These tools cannot apply color or redistribute pixels, so the standard brush modes do not apply. When using the Dodge or Burn tool, this pop-up menu displays the following options:

Shadows

Here, the tool primarily targets the darkest image tones, although the remaining tones are affected as well.

Midtones

Here, all tones except the very lightest and darkest are targeted.

Highlights

Here, the tool primarily targets the lightest image tones, although the remaining tones are affected as well.

When using the Sponge tool, choose one of the following:

Desaturate

This option reduces the saturation value of the painted colors, bringing them closer to neutral gray. (For more information, see *10.1, Image: Mode Overview.*)

Saturate

This option increases the saturation value of the painted colors, or increases their intensity. (For more information, see *10.1, Image: Mode Overview.*)

C. **Exposure/Pressure** (1 to 100%)

The Exposure value mimics the intensity of light a photographer uses to expose a negative. The pressure value controls the intensity of the Sponge tool. For both, lower values result in slight edits, while increasing the value exaggerates the effect.

The Vector Tools

3.1

Path Component Selection Tool   *Type "A"*

Sometimes referred to as the *black arrow*, this tool enables you to reposition and edit an entire path. (To edit the individual points and segments that comprise a path, you must use the Direct Selection tool.) Common uses include the following:

- **Selecting a path.** Click anywhere within the path outline to select it. Or, drag a marquee that touches part of the path.

- **Selecting multiple paths.** Hold down the Shift key and click a series of existing paths. Or, drag a marquee with the tool—any paths included in the box are selected when you release the mouse button.

- **Deselecting all paths.** Click on the image, away from the path. The paths remains visible, but no points are selected.

- **Deselecting one path at a time.** When multiple paths are selected, deselect one at a time by (Option) [Alt]-clicking it. The path remains visible, but no points are selected.

- **Duplicating a path.** (Option) [Alt]-drag a path to create a clone.

- **Transforming a path.** There are two ways to scale, rotate, and otherwise transform a selected path: Choose one of the Edit: **Transform Path** commands; or, turn on the Show Bounding Box feature in the Options bar.

Issues to Consider

Accessing the black arrow tool. To access the black arrow while using another path or shape tool, hold down the (Command) [Control] key. (The black arrow must be visible in the Toolbar—otherwise, this shortcut accesses the white arrow tool.)

Path Component Selection Options

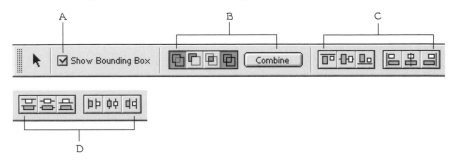

A. Show Bounding Box

When this box is checked, selected paths or shapes are framed by a *bounding box*, an editable marquee virtually identical to the one used by Edit: **Free Transform Path**—in fact, as soon as you edit the bounding box, the Options bar displays the standard Transform settings. When this option is turned off, clicking a path or shape simply highlights the anchor points.

B. Shape Blending Options

When two or more overlapping shapes share the same item in the Paths palette, these buttons enable you to change their appearance.

Add to Shape Area (+)

When this button is active, the path fill remains solid, even in the overlapping areas.

Subtract from Shape Area (–)

Click this button to remove the shape of the selected path from a neighboring path. Any shape tagged with this option is essentially hidden—you can't even convert the subpath to a selection.

Intersect Shape Areas

Click this button to hide all but the overlapping shape areas.

Exclude Overlapping Shape Areas

Click this button to punch out the overlapping shape areas.

Combine

Click this button to permanently apply the current blending option.

C. **Alignment Options**

These options enable you to align two or more selected paths. The effect is similar to using the Layer: **Align Linked** options.

D. **Distribute Options**

These options enable you to manipulate the spacing between three or more selected paths. The effect is similar to using the Layer: **Distribute Linked** options.

Related Topics

9.15   Edit: *Free Transform Path*
11.85 Layer: *Align Linked*
11.92 Layer: *Distribute Linked*

3.2

Direct Selection Tool

Type "A"

This tool—often referred to as the *white arrow* tool—enables you to move and manipulate the different components of a path. Common uses include the following:

- **Selecting a point.** Click on a single point to independently select it. This displays the curve handles, if any have been extended. If desired, you can reposition the point by dragging it.

- **Selecting multiple points.** Hold down the Shift key and click a series of existing points. Or, drag a marquee with the tool—any points included in the box are selected when you release the mouse button. If desired, reposition multiple points by dragging them.

- **Selecting a path.** Hold down the (Option) [Alt] key and click the path. Or, drag a marquee around the entire path. If desired, reposition the entire path by dragging it.

- **Deselecting a path.** Click on the image, away from the path. The path remains visible, but no points are selected.

- **Repositioning a segment.** When you drag a straight segment, it moves along with the two points on either end. When you drag a curved segment, you either increase or decrease the curve—the points do not move.

- **Dragging a curve handle.** To change the shape of a curved segment, select a point to reveal its curve handles. Drag the handles to reshape the segment.

- **Duplicating a path.** Hold down the (Option) [Alt] key while dragging a path.

Issues to Consider

Accessing the white arrow tool. To access the white arrow while using another path or shape tool, hold down the (Command) [Control] key. The white arrow must be visible in the Toolbar—otherwise, this shortcut accesses the black arrow tool.

Accessing the black arrow tool. Hold down the (Command) [Control] key while using the white arrow tool to access the black arrow.

3.3

Type Tool
Type "T"

Use this tool to add editable type to an image. Unlike earlier versions of Photoshop (which require that you enter and edit text in a separate dialog box), you can enter, format, and refine type directly on screen.

The quickest way to add text is to click once on the image with the Type tool. A flashing cursor appears, indicating that you're able to start typing. To set the character attributes, use the settings in the Options bar (while using the Type tool) or the Character palette (while using any other tool). To set paragraph attributes, use the Paragraph palette.

Photoshop handles type differently than other graphics applications. Page layout and illustration programs have object-oriented type tools—once you add text to a document, they enable you to edit at will, similar to a word processing program. When working in Photoshop, on the other hand, type exists in five forms:

- **Live type.** When you initially add type to an image, it appears in a type layer, identified in the Layers palette by a capital "T". The contents of a type layer exist as editable text—to edit it, choose the Type tool and click on screen to insert the cursor. As long as type exists in this form, you can only apply a few image-editing commands to it, such as color, opacity, blend modes, transformations, and layer styles. If you embed the type in the image, the font files are required for correct output.

- **Path type.** Here, the contents of a type layer are converted to standard paths, as if drawn with the Pen tool. This way, you're able to use the outlines as a clipping path, or copy and paste them into an Illustrator file for further editing. (For more information, see *11.46, Layer: Type: **Create Work Path**.*)

- **Shape type.** Here, the contents of a type layer are converted to vector-based shapes. The effect is similar to converting type to outlines in Illustrator or FreeHand: You can no longer edit the information as text, but you're able to use the path-editing tools adjust the character shapes. If you embed the vector data in the image, the font files are no longer required for proper output. (For more information, see *11.47, Layer: Type: **Convert to Shape**.*)

- **Rendered type.** To treat type as pixel-based image information, you must render the type layer, or fully convert it to editable pixels. Do this by selecting the type layer in the Layers palette and choosing Layer: Type: **Render Layer**. Once type is rendered, you cannot convert back to an editable-text format. Make sure the text is accurate before rendering. (For more information, see *11.57, Layer: Rasterize: Type.*)

- **Mask type.** When you use the Type tool's Create Mask option, the character shapes appear as an active selection. This way, you're able to adjust the selected area directly, create a layer mask, or save the selection for future editing. (For more information, see *Create Mask or Selection*, below.)

Issues to Consider

Using point text and paragraph text. When you place point text, you simply click the image to add the flashing cursor. It has no boundaries—you have to add line breaks manually—and the alignment commands are based on the position of the original click-point. (To change existing point text to paragraph text, choose Layer: Type: **Convert to Paragraph Text**.) When you place paragraph text, you drag a box with the Type tool, defining a frame that contains the characters. This way, you're able to manipulate the box to redirect the text flow. (To change existing paragraph text to point text, choose Layer: Type: **Convert to Point Text**.)

Using keystrokes to highlight text. You're not restricted to click-dragging to highlight the If desired, use the following keystrokes when manually selecting type in the text box:

- **Highlight a single character to the right.** Press Shift-right arrow.
- **Highlight a single character to the left.** Press Shift-left arrow.
- **Jump cursor right one word.** Press (Command) [Control]-right arrow.
- **Jump cursor left one word.** Press (Command) [Control]-left arrow.
- **Select a single word.** Double-click the word.
- **Select a specific range of characters.** Insert cursor at start of desired range, then Shift-click and end of range.
- **Highlight the word to the right.** Press (Command-Shift) [Control-Shift]-right arrow.
- **Highlight the word to the left.** Press (Command-Shift) [Control-Shift]-left arrow.
- **Select line above.** Press Shift-up arrow.
- **Select line below.** Press Shift-down arrow.
- **Select entire contents of field.** Press (Command) [Control]-A while editing text, or double-click the layer's thumbnail in the Layers palette.

Using the Type tool without installing Adobe Type Manager. When using PostScript Type 1 fonts, ATM uses the output information stored in a font to render its shapes smoothly on screen. Without it, Photoshop cannot utilize the vector data stored in the printer font files.

Type Options

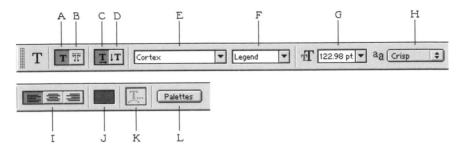

A. **Create Text Layer**

Choose this button to add a new text layer when you click the image with the Type tool.

B. **Create Mask or Selection**

When you choose this button, the Type tool does not produce a vector-based type layer. Instead, it creates a selection that matches the exact shape of the formatted characters.

When you first click the image, the entire window is covered with a semi-transparent overlay. As you add characters, their shapes appear in the mask. When finished, press the Enter key (or click the checkmark button in the Options bar) to convert the overlay to a selection. If necessary, use Photoshop's selection tools to continue editing the outlines. (For more information, see *1.1, Selection Tools Overview.*)

C. **Horizontally Orient Text**

When you choose this button, the contents of the new type layer flow horizontally, from left to right. If desired, you can convert horizontal text to vertical by choosing Layer: Type: **Vertical**.

D. **Vertically Orient Text**

When you choose this button, the contents of the new type layer flow vertically, from top to bottom. The orientation of the individual letters depends on the status of the Rotate Character command, in the Character palette submenu. When disabled, the text flows sideways, like horizontal type rotated 90° clockwise. When enabled, the characters are stacked. (For more information, see *25.15, Rotate Character.*)

E. Set Font Family

All font families currently available to your operating system appear in this pop-up. Unless you're using TrueType fonts, you must use Adobe Type Manager for the best results. Otherwise, type will appear jagged and formless on screen. (For more information, see *25.2, Set Font.*)

F. Set Font Style

When a font contains multiple variations, the different styles are listed in this pop-up. Choose the desired style after setting the font family. (For more information, see *25.3, Set Font Style.*)

G. Set Font Size

Enter the desired size of the type in this field. (For more information, see *25.4, Set Font Size.*)

H. Anti-aliasing Method

This pop-up menu enables you to set different levels of *anti-aliasing*, or the built-in edge transition applied to the character shapes. Ordinarily, there are only two options: off and on (you may have noticed that your selection tools only offer a single Anti-aliasing checkbox). However, because shape integrity is so important to type—especially at small sizes or low resolutions—Photoshop now enables you to tweak the value.

None

This option applies no anti-aliasing. It is often the best choice for small, low-resolution type samples, which tend to be obliterated by anti-aliasing.

Crisp

This option applies the least amount of anti-aliasing, maintaining high-contrast edge detail. If this option doesn't provide enough edge-smoothing, choose the Smooth option.

Strong

This option attempts to compensate for the slight loss of character thickness normally produced by anti-aliasing. It is sometimes the best choice for small, low-resolution serif typefaces. If this option makes the text too heavy, choose the Smooth option.

Smooth

This option applies a balanced level of edge smoothing. If the edges are too blurred, choose the Crisp setting; if the characters lose too much weight, choose Strong.

I. Alignment Options

These options determine the horizontal alignment of the type. When applied to point text, these options align to the original click-point. When applied to paragraph text, they align to the margins of the bounding text box. (For more information, see *26.2, Alignment Options.*)

J. **Set Color**

This option determines the color of the type. It defaults to the current foreground color, but by clicking the swatch and accessing the color picker, you can apply a new value. (For more information, see *25.11, Set Text Color.*)

K. **Warp Text**

Click this button to access the Warp Text dialog box. (For more information, see *11.53, Layer: Type: **Warp Text**.*)

L. **Palettes**

Click this button to reveal the Character and Paragraph palettes.

Related Topics

1.1   Selection Tools Overview
*11.45 Layer: **Type***
25.1   Character Palette Overview
26.1   Paragraph Palette Overview

3.4

Pen Tool

Type "P"

Use the Pen tool to manually create an object-oriented path. These are based on *Bézier curves*, the same technology utilized by programs like Adobe Illustrator and Macromedia FreeHand. Paths offer an impressive array of editing capabilities. However, the techniques required to create and modify a path are completely different than any other facet of Photoshop.

Issues to Consider

Storing a path. Any path you create automatically appears in the Paths palette, which contains all the commands you need to make the path interact with your image. Once a path appears there, however, the terminology changes: There, a path is any specific grouping of object-oriented shapes. One specific shape, whether open or closed, is called a subpath.

Editing a path. The Pen tool is only used to create the initial path. Unless you create a path perfectly the first time—which rarely happens—you must use the black and white arrow tools to modify its shape.

Transforming a path. To transform the shape of a path using techniques similar to Illustrator or FreeHand, select the entire shape and choose one of the Edit: **Transform Path** commands. Or, turn on the Path Component Selection tool's Show Bounding Box option, which enables you transform a path on-the-fly. To apply a transformation to a single point or partially-selected shape, use Edit: **Transform Points**.

Components of a Path

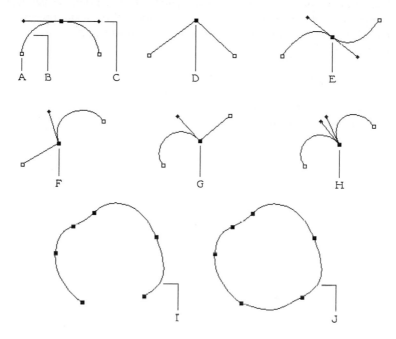

A. Point
Click with the Pen tool to place a single point. Paths are created one point at a time—they're the hot-spots, acting like the dots in a connect-the-dots puzzle.

B. Segment
As you click, a line connects the new point with the previous point. These segments ultimately form the shape of a path.

C. Curve Handles
Each point contains two curve handles. When you simply click to place a point, both handles are hidden. If you drag the cursor before you release the mouse button, you extend the handles. Manipulate them with the Arrow tool to curve the segments connected to the point. It's not necessary to reveal the handles, but without them, you can only create straight lines.

Each curve handle affects a segment on one side of a point. Therefore, a segment can be controlled by two curve handles—one on each end.

D. Corner Point
This point displays no handles, resulting in straight segments. Place a corner point by simply clicking with the Pen tool.

E. **Smooth Point**

This point displays two locked and symmetrical handles, allowing two segments to meet in a smooth, continuous curve. Place a smooth point by click-dragging with the Pen tool to place a smooth point.

F. **Single-Curve Point** (straight segment into curved)

This point displays one handle, resulting in a straight segment meeting a curved segment. After clicking to place a corner point (which forms the straight segment), click and drag from the same point to reveal one handle. This adds curve to the following segment, which appears when you place the next point.

G. **Single-Curve Point** (curved segment into straight)

This point displays one handle, resulting in a curved segment meeting a straight segment. After placing a smooth point (which forms the curved segment), hold down the (Option) [Alt] key and click the same point to hide the forward handle. This results in no curve being added to the following segment, which appears when you place the next point.

H. **Double-Curve Point**

This point displays two unlocked handles, allowing you to separately adjust the two segments on either side of the point. To create a double-curve point with the Pen tool, start by placing a smooth point. Hold down the (Option) [Alt] key and drag from the same point to redirect the forward handle. This adds an independent curve to the following segment, which appears when you place the next point.

I. **Open Path**

A path with a distinct beginning and end is considered *open*. A path consisting of two points and a connecting segment is the simplest example. Using the Stroke Path command in the Paths palette, this type of path is commonly used as the basis for creating curved lines in an image.

K. **Closed Path**

A path with no distinct beginning and end is considered *closed.* As you create a path, close it by targeting your last mouse-click on the very first point of the path. A circular path—a shape with no beginning or end—is the simplest example. Depending on the command chosen from the Paths palette, this type of path is commonly the basis for filled shapes, clipping paths, and new selections.

Pen Tool Options

A. **Create New Shape Layer**

Click this button to start drawing a layer-based shape with the Pen tool. This option is only available before you begin—once you start placing points, the buttons are replaced with the Shape Blending options (described under *3.1, Path Component Selection Tool*). As long as you remain in the Pen tool, the Options bar displays settings for layer styles, blend modes, and opacity.

When you need to draw an accurate shape—for example, if you're tracing a particularly complex element—it's usually more convenient to draw the item as a standard path, then convert it to a shape when finished. This way, you're able to view the underlying pixels as you edit. (For more information, see *L.8, Converting a Path into a Shape.*)

B. **Create New Path**

Click this button to start drawing a standard path. This option is only available before you begin—once you start placing points, the buttons are replaced with the Shape Blending options (described under *3.1, Path Component Selection Tool*).

If you've begun drawing a shape instead of a path (the path will contain fill content of some sort), you don't have to start over. Either convert it to a standard path and continue editing, or wait until you're finished before converting. (For more information, see *L.9, Converting a Shape into a Path.*)

C. **Auto Add/Delete**

When this box is checked, you're able to use the Pen tool to add or delete anchor points. When you position the cursor over a segment, the Add Anchor Point tool is temporarily accessed, and you can click to add a single point. When you position the cursor over a point, the Delete Anchor Point tool is temporarily accessed, and you can click to remove the point. When unchecked, you must manually choose the necessary tools to add or delete points, or apply their shortcuts while editing with the white arrow tool.

D. **Rubber Band**

When this box is checked, the Pen tool previews the shape and curve of the segment that will appear when you place the next point. When unchecked, you cannot see the segment until you actually place the next point.

Related Topics

3.5

Freeform Pen Tool   Type "P"

This tool enables you to create a path by simply drawing the desired shape. An outline appears on screen as you drag the cursor, allowing you to monitor your progress. As soon as you release the mouse button, Photoshop assigns the points and curve handles necessary to duplicate the outline as a path.

Issues to Consider

Adding polygonal segments. To add a straight segment to the path, hold down the (Option) [Alt] key while clicking a point, similar to using the Polygon Lasso tool. A straight line extends from the cursor, waiting for you to place the next point. Release the (Option) [Alt] key to revert back to normal behavior. Note, however, that if you release the mouse button before releasing the (Option) [Alt] key, the path will automatically close with a straight segment.

Creating open and closed freeform paths. This tool can be used to create both open and closed paths:

- Create a closed path by placing the cursor directly on top of the first inserted point and releasing the mouse button.

- Create an open path by releasing the mouse button when the cursor is not touching the first inserted point.

- If you accidentally create an open path when you wanted a closed path (usually, by releasing the mouse button too early), you cannot use the Freehand Pen tool to close the path. Instead, with the standard Pen tool, click one endpoint of the open path, then the other.

Creating finely-detailed paths or tracing low-contrast images with the Magnetic Pen tool. Because of the difficulty in pinpointing the precise values, this tool is a poor choice for drawing delicate paths. It works best in high-contrast situations, such as isolating an object photographed in front of a white backdrop. For more accurate selections, you're better off using the Pen tool, or using alpha channel techniques to create a complex mask. (See *12.16. Select: **Save Selection** for more info.)

The Magnetic Pen tool only creates closed paths. To use an automatic path tool to create an open path, you can do one of two things:

- Use the Pen tool or Freehand Pen tool to draw the desired shape.
- Draw a closed path with the Magnetic Pen tool. Since the path is closed, you must locate the segment that connects the two points you wish to separate. Use the Add Point tool to place a new anchor point between these two points. Select only the new point and press Delete, opening the path.

Freeform Pen Tool Options

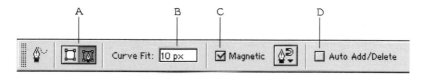

A. **Shape/Path**

These buttons determine whether the Freeform Pen tool creates a filled shape or standard path. (They're described in full under *3.x, The Pen Tool.*)

B **Curve Fit** (0.5 10 pixels)

This option determines the overall smoothness of the path. The value actually represents the amount of detail, measured in pixels, that the tool will ignore as it applies curve to each segment. For example, if the value is 5, the tool will ignore any detail measuring less than 5 pixels in size. The lower the value, the more intricate the path; the higher the value, the smoother (and less accurate) the path. The field defaults to 2—most users prefer a value between 2 and 5.

C. **Magnetic**

Check this box to draw a path that snaps to the edge of a contrasting color or shape. In theory, this enables you to avoid manually drawing a path with the standard Pen tool. In reality, like most automatic path creation tools, the results are uneven at best. Unlike the Pen tool, you do not create a path by click-placing points and adjusting handles. After setting the desired values in the Options bar, creating a path with this tool involves the following:

- Click once on screen to insert the first point of the path.
- Direct the cursor around the object you wish to select. As you do so, Photoshop automatically places a series of points and segments around the object. If unhappy with the outline, back the cursor up

and draw again. Additionally, anchor points appear along the more prominent edges of the selected shape. To remove a point on the fly, press Delete. To remove a backward series of points, press Delete multiple times. To add your own points (which better directs the placement of the outline), click as you move the cursor.

– Complete the path by clicking once on the first point you placed. Or, double-click to automatically close the outline.

Once you've finished drawing the path, adjust it with the remaining path editing tools. To cancel a path before its completion, press the Esc key, or double-click to complete the path and immediately press Delete.

When this feature is enabled, you're able to access the Magnetic Pen Options pop-up palette, which contains the following items:

Pen Width

This value determines how closely you must move the cursor to the edge of the object you wish to trace with a path. For example, if the value is 10, you can drag the cursor within 10 pixels of the target shape, and the outline will still shrink to fit. If the cursor is more than 10 pixels away, you may include unwanted image pixels in the path.

For the best results, raise this value for higher-contrast target shapes, and lower it for lower-contrast shapes. If the Other Cursors option in the File: Preferences: **Display & Cursors** dialog box is set to Precise, the cursor will display as a circle, sized at the current value.

You can change this setting as you drag. Press the open-bracket key to lower the value in increments of 1. Press the close-bracket key to raise the value in increments of 1.

Edge Contrast

This value determines how much contrast must exist between the object you wish to trace and the surrounding pixels. Higher values mean that there must be more contrast; lower values will accommodate less contrast. For the best results, raise the value when tracing high-contrast images, and lower it when less contrast exists.

Frequency

This value determines how often anchor points are placed as you move the cursor. Typically, Photoshop loosely matches your movements. A point will occasionally appear if you keep the cursor in one spot for more than a couple of seconds.

Raise the value to place points more frequently. Lower the value for fewer points. For the best results, use a higher value when selecting rough-edged images, and use a lower value when selecting smooth-edged images.

Stylus: Pressure

This option is only available when you're using a drawing tablet. When checked, the Pen Width value will automatically lower when you apply more pressure, and automatically raise when you apply less. When unchecked, the Pen Width behaves the same as described above.

D. **Auto Add/Delete**

When this box is checked, you're able to use the Freeform Pen tool to add or delete anchor points. When you position the cursor over a segment, the Add Anchor Point tool is temporarily accessed, and you can click to add a single point. When you position the cursor over a point, the Delete Anchor Point tool is temporarily accessed, and you can click to remove the point. When unchecked, you must manually choose the necessary tools to add or delete points, or apply their shortcuts while editing with the white arrow tool.

Related Topics

3.6

Add Anchor Point Tool   *Type "P"*

Use this tool to add a new point to a path. It cannot place new points to continue a path, like the Pen tool—rather, you click on a path segment to insert a point where none existed before. Long segments have limited flexibility; adding points enables you to edit the shape of a path more accurately. If you add a point to a curved segment, Photoshop automatically extends the curve handles to maintain the segment's shape.

Issues to Consider

Accessing the Add Anchor Point tool. To access the Add Point tool while using the white arrow tool, hold down the (Option-Command) [Alt-Control] key. Click on a segment to add a point.

3.7
Delete Anchor Point Tool
Type "P"

Use this tool to delete an existing point. If you delete a point by selecting it with the Arrow tool and pressing the Delete key, you also remove the two segments on either side. By clicking a point with this tool, you remove it while leaving the segment intact. However, when you delete a point, you also remove the effect of its curve handles. Therefore, the path doesn't retain its shape.

Issues to Consider

Accessing the Delete Anchor Point tool. To access the Delete Point tool while using the white arrow tool, hold down the (Option-Command) [Alt-Control] key. Click a point to delete it.

3.8
Convert Point Tool
Type "P"

After creating a path, use this tool to convert a point from one type to another. Common uses include the following:

- **Converting a corner point to a smooth point.** Drag from a corner point to reveal two locked curve handles.

- **Converting a smooth point to corner point.** Click on a smooth point to hide the handles.

- **Converting a smooth point to double-curve point.** Drag one of the curve handles of a smooth point. It moves independently of the other handle.

- **Converting a double-curve point to smooth point.** Drag one of the curve handles of a double-curve point. The other handle snaps into a symmetrical position.

Issues to Consider

Accessing the Convert Point tool. To access the Convert Point tool while using the white arrow tool, hold down the (Option-Command) [Alt-Control] key.

3.9

Shape Tools

These tools enable you to add shapes to an image by dragging a predefined outline. Although they're referred to as "shape tools," you can use them to draw vector shapes, standard paths, or editable pixels.

Common Shape Tool Options

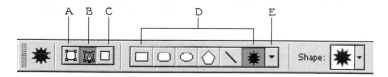

The following items appear in the Options bar when any Shape tool is active.

A. **Create New Shape Layer**

Click this button to add a vector-based shape layer. When you choose this setting, the Options bar displays settings for layer style, blend mode, and opacity.

As soon as you start drawing, the Create buttons are replaced by the Shape Blending options (described in full under *3.1, Path Component Selection Tool*).

B. **Create New Work Path**

Click this button to add a standard path.

C. **Create Filled Region**

Click this button to add a pixel-based fill. Here, new shapes are based on the current foreground color. The effect is the same as drawing a selection and filling it with a solid color. For the most flexible results, create a new, blank item in the Layers palette before using this option. This way, you can edit the shape separately from the rest of the image.

D. **Shape Options**

These buttons display the same Shape tool options found in the Toolbar. To select a different tool, click its button at any time.

E. **Geometry Options**

Click this vertical strip to display a list of options specific to the currently active Shape tool (items described in detail in the following sections.)

3.10
_____

Rectangle Tool

Use this tool to draw perfectly aligned rectangles or squares.

Rectangle Shape Options

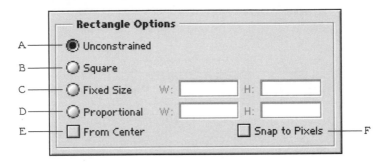

A. Unconstrained

Choose this option to drag rectangles of any width or height.

B. Square

Choose this option to constrain the effect of the tool, drawing perfect squares only. If desired, ignore this option and hold down the Shift key while dragging to produce the same effect.

C. Fixed Size

Choose this option to place rectangles of a specific width and height. Enter the desired values in the Width and Height fields.

D. Proportional

Choose this option to constrain a rectangle to a specific aspect ratio. Enter the desired ratio (or dimensions that reflect the desired ratio) in the Width and Height fields.

E. From Center

Check this box to radiate a rectangle from the initial click-point. If desired, ignore this box and hold down the (Option) [Alt] key *after* you start dragging to produce the same effect.

F. Snap to Pixels

Check this box to snap the edges of a rectangle to the grid formed by the image pixels.

3.11

Rounded Rectangle Tool   *Type "U"*

Use this tool to draw a rectangle with rounded corners. This effect is produced by a *corner radius*, or the distance from a rectangle's corner to the starting point of the rounded edge. As the radius increases, the curve begins farther away from the corner, thus producing a more "rounded" effect. As long as this tool is active, you can enter a Radius value between 0 and 1000 pixels in the Options bar.

The Rounded Rectangle options are identical to those listed under *3.10, Rectangle Tool.*

3.12

Ellipse Tool   *Type "U"*

Use this tool to draw elliptical and circular shapes.

Ellipse Shape Options

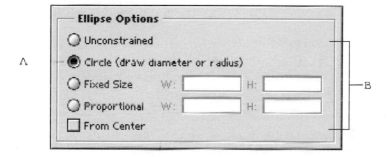

A. **Circle (draw diameter or radius)**

Choose this option to constrain the effect of the tool, drawing perfect circles only. To "draw diameter," drag without holding down any keys; the circle's diameter is based on the distance between the click-point and the final position of the cursor. To "draw radius," (Option) [Alt]-drag the shape; the circle's radius is based on the distance between the click-point and the final position of the cursor.

B. **Remaining Options**

The remaining Ellipse Shape options are identical to those listed under *3.10, Rectangle Tool.*

3.13

Polygon Tool

Type "U"

Use this tool to draw a shape with a specific number of sides. As long as this tool is active, you're able to enter the desired number of sides in the Options bar. (Enter a value between 3 and 100.)

Polygon Shape Options

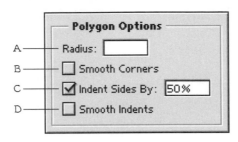

A. **Radius** (1 to 15000 pixels)

Choose this option to create polygons of a specific size. This value measures the distance from the center of a shape to its outermost edge.

B. **Smooth Corners**

Choose this option to round the edges of a polygon. The effect is arbitrary—you cannot control the degree of the effect, as you can with the Rounded Rectangle tool.

C. **Indent Sides By** (1 to 99%)

Choose this option to draw a starburst. Photoshop produces this effect by placing points in the center of each polygon segment, and moving them toward the center of the shape. The requested percentage refers to the polygon's radius, and determines how far to move these additional points. For example, if you enter 50%, the tool moves them halfway toward the centerpoint. Higher values produce more extreme starbursts; lower values produce more subtle rounding.

D. **Smooth Indents**

Check this box to round off the additional points used to produce the starburst effect. The effect is similar to revealing their curve handles.

3.14

Line Tool

Use this tool to add lines to an image. Establish the desired line thickness in the Width field (enter a value between 1 and 1000 pts). The Line Options enable you to add arrowheads.

Line Options

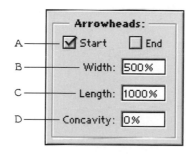

A. Start & End

Check the Start box to add an arrowhead at the beginning of a line, or at the point you initially click with the Line tool. Click the End box to add an arrowhead at the end of a line, or at the point you release the mouse button. Check both boxes to add arrowheads to both ends of a line.

B. Width & Length

Enter percentages between 10% and 5000%. These values are based on the current line width. For example, the default arrowhead is 500% wide, 1000% long. On a 4-pixel line, the arrowhead is 20 pixels wide and 40 pixels long. On a 10-pixel line, the arrowhead is 50 by 100 pixels.

C. Concavity

This value defines the shape of the arrowhead, and is also based on the current line width. Enter a value between -50% and 50%. Positive values result in a familiar, convex arrowhead. Negative values result in a diamond-shaped, concave arrowhead.

3.15

Custom Shape Tool   Type "U"

Use this tool to place a preset shape, originally specified using the Edit: **Define Custom Shape** command. This tool is little more than a simple clip-art library—although you're able to place these shapes as rendered pixels, they all start as vector-based objects. Before dragging with the tool, choose the desired shape from the available pop-up menu.

Custom Shape Options

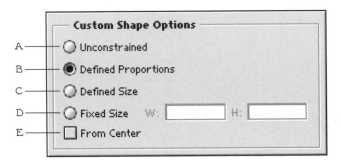

A. **Unconstrained**

Choose this option to drag custom shapes to any width or height.

B. **Defined Proportions**

Choose this option to constrain the effect of the tool to the proportions of the originally-defined shape.

C. **Defined Size**

Choose this option to constrain the effect of the tool to the size of the originally-defined shape.

D. **Fixed Size**

Choose this option to place rectangles of a specific width and height. Enter the desired values in the Width and Height fields.

E. **From Center**

Check this box to radiate a rectangle from the initial click-point. If desired, ignore this box and hold down the (Option) [Alt] key *after* you start dragging to produce the same effect.

Special Tools

Notes Tool

Type "N"

This tool enables you to add written comments to an image. The text isn't added directly to the image—instead, it exists in a small window that you (or another user) can reveal and hide at will. The basic idea of Photoshop's annotation tools is that you can exchange comments with clients, superiors, and colleagues during the editing stages of an image. In practice, this method of communication is not expected to supplant email, phone calls, or physical print-outs anytime soon. Nevertheless, a number of users have embraced this feature as a down-and-dirty way to pass along image-specific information.

To create a new annotation, click–drag a marquee with the Notes tool. A pop-up window appears, enabling you to manually type a message or copy/paste text from another source. When you close the window, the note is represented on screen by a small note-paper icon. Double-click the icon to open the note.

At any time (and with any tool), you can reposition the note-paper icon across the screen. Remove a note by clicking it once and pressing (Delete) [Backspace].

Issues to Consider

This tool has limited editing capabilities. You cannot create intricately for-matted notes with this tool. In fact, you can only set the typeface and overall size. Beyond that, your ability to format is dependent on how well you can hit the Return and spacebar keys. Additionally, you can only store text in the pop-up window—you cannot add editing marks, circles, arrows, or any other notations you may already use in a production environment.

Saving annotations along with an image. Only three file formats are able to retain any messages you've added with the Notes tool. The native Photoshop (PSD) and TIFF formats enable other users to read the notes when the image is open in Photoshop. The Photoshop PDF format enables another user to access the notes in Adobe Acrobat 4.0 (or Acrobat Reader), as well. Regardless of the format you choose, you must make sure that the Annotations box is checked in the Save As dialog box.

Dragging notes beyond the image edges. It's possible to drag a note-paper icon or message window beyond the edge of the image window. It may look like the note has disappeared, but it hasn't. If you expand the size of the window (by dragging the lower-left corner, or by zooming out with the Resize Windows to Fit option disabled), you'll find the icon in the gray area that surrounds the image. Many users place their notes to the side of the image in this way to avoid obscuring the image with any icons or windows.

Gathering notes from other images. To import the textual and audio notes contained in another image, choose File: Import: **Annotations**. In the nav-igational window that appears, locate the target image and click Load. Any notes are copied and placed into the currently open image. To import the notes from multiple images, Shift-click the desired files in the naviga-tional window before clicking Load.

Notes Tool Options

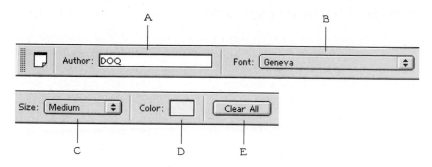

A. Author

The information entered in this field appears in the title bar of the message window. Often, a person enters his or her name, so people know who authored the message. To further establish identity, many users set their own color value, as well (see *Color*, below). When you enter a new name, it's applied to every subsequent item created with the Note tool.

B. Font

This menu displays all of the typefaces currently available to your operating system. The one you choose is applied to the entire message—you cannot highlight certain passages and format them separately.

C. Size

This pop-up menu offers a series of size options in lieu of standard point sizes. Similar to an email program like Outlook Express, you can only choose from Smallest, Smaller, Medium, Larger, and Largest. The actual size of the characters ultimately depends on your monitor and screen resolution, so simply choose an option that you find most comfortable. Like the Font pop-up menu described above, the option you set here affects the entire note.

D. Color

This swatch enables you to change the color of the note-paper icon and the title bar of the message window. When you click it, the color picker appears, enabling you to set the desired value. For the best results, choose a color that contrasts with the current image, as well as any notes created by other users. If you routinely exchange notes with other users, consider picking one color and sticking with it (for easier identification).

E. Clear All

Click this button to delete every annotation in the image, whether they were created with the Note tool or Audio Annotation tool.

4.2

Audio Annotation Tool

Type "N"

The Audio Annotations enables you to add a recorded voice message to an image. (It assumes that you have a microphone, sound card, and speakers.) When you click an image with this tool, you're given a small set of controls to record, stop, and play back a message. Afterward, the note is represented on screen by a small speaker icon.

No production-oriented facility in their right mind would use this feature. Voice messages offer nothing that can't be accomplished with a simple phone call, they almost always take longer to listen to than to read the equivalent text, and they tend to annoy the listener after more than a two or three plays. And most importantly, even short messages will quickly bloat the file size of an image. Most users perceive this tool as more of a consumer-level feature, suitable for recording the cooing of a newborn baby to accompany a photo sent to a relative.

The overall function of this tool (and the items that appear in the Options bar) are largely identical to the Notes tool. (For more information, see *4.1, Notes Tool.*)

4.3

Eyedropper Tool

Type "I"

This tool provides a simple method of defining a new color value. Although many dialog boxes contain eyedropper tools—Image: Adjust: **Curves** and Select: **Color Range** come to mind—they do not redefine the foreground or background colors. Rather, their use is restricted to the purpose of the specific dialog boxes.

Common uses for the Eyedropper tool include the following:

Defining a new foreground color. Select the Eyedropper tool and click on any color in an open image. If you hold down the mouse button, you can see the different colors cycling through the foreground color swatches.

Defining a new background color. Hold down the (Option) [Alt] key and click on any color in an open image.

Paint tool shortcut. While using any Paint tool, set a new foreground color by holding down the (Option) [Alt] key and clicking the desired color.

Issues to Consider

The Sample Size setting affects the eyedroppers used by the dialog boxes. For the most accurate results, especially when sampling in color-specific commands, set the Sample Size pop-up menu to 3 by 3 Average.

At times, the Eyedropper tool may appear to be working backwards. If the background color swatch is selected in the Color palette, this tool defines the background color, and you must (Option) [Alt] click to define a new foreground color.

Toggling between measurement tools. When you type the letter I, you only select the currently visible Eyedropper tool. Toggle between this tool, the Color Sampler tool, and the Measure tool by pressing Shift-I. (To toggle without holding down the Shift key, choose Edit: Preferences: **General** and uncheck the "Use Shift Key for Tool Switch" option.)

Eyedropper Tool Options

A

A. **Sample Size**

This option determines how the Eyedropper tool reads the values of a sampled color:

Point Sample

Here, the tool reads the value of the single targeted pixel.

3 by 3 Average

Here, the tool reads the average color value of a nine-pixel square surrounding the targeted pixel.

5 by 5 Average

Here, the tool reads the average color value of a nine-pixel square surrounding the targeted pixel.

4.4

Color Sampler Tool   *Type "I"*

Use this tool to add up to four *color samplers* to an image, or targets used for evaluating the color value of a specific location. When you add a sampler, the Info palette expands to display the values of the pixels located directly beneath it. This makes it possible to continually monitor the effects of your adjustments on critical or sensitive portions of the image. Unlike the standard Eyedropper tool, it does not change the current foreground or background color.

Add samplers by clicking the image. (Option) [Alt]-click an existing sampler to delete it. Reposition a sampler by dragging it with this tool, or by Shift-dragging with the Eyedropper tool.

The Options bar for this tool lists two items: the Sample Size pop-up menu (described in full under *4.3, Eyedropper Tool),* and a button labeled Clear (click this button to remove any existing samplers).

Issues to Consider

Reading the Info palette. When you have placed all four color samplers, the first panel in the Info Palette still displays the color values beneath the cursor, allowing you to read additional information.

Toggling between measurement tools. When you type the letter I, you only select the currently visible Eyedropper tool. Toggle between this tool, the Eyedropper tool, and the Measure tool by pressing Shift-I. (To toggle without holding down the Shift key, choose Edit: Preferences: **General** and uncheck the "Use Shift Key for Tool Switch" option.)

Color Sampler Tool Options

A   B

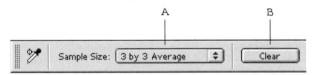

A. **Sample Size**

The settings in this pop-up menu are described in full under *4.3, Eyedropper Tool.*

B. **Clear**

Click this button to remove all color samplers from the image.

4.5

Measure Tool *Type "I"*

Use this tool to measure distance and angle values in an image. Add a measurement line by click-dragging with the tool. The angle and length of the line appear in the second panel of the Info palette, as well as the Options bar.

Reposition the line by click-dragging a segment. Re-orient a segment by click-dragging an endpoint. Hide the current measurement line by selecting another tool. Whenever you select the tool again, the most recent line appears. Create a new line by clicking away from the current line and dragging.

Issues to Consider

Adding another measurable segment. You can only draw one line at a time. However, you can split a single line into two segments by using the *protractor* feature. After drawing a single line, (Option) [Alt]-drag from either end. The line divides into two segments, and the Info palette changes to accommodate the new values: D1 lists the length of the first segment, D2 lists the length of the second, and A lists the angle that exists between the two.

Establishing angles before rotating. This tool is often used to set the desired angle before rotating an element. When you position a single segment with the Measure tool then immediately choose Edit: Transform: **Rotate**, the current selection or image layer snaps to the same angle. (If you've used the protractor feature, this field will display the angle inherent between the two measurement lines.)

Toggling between measurement tools. When you type the letter I, you only select the currently visible Eyedropper tool. Toggle between this tool, the Eyedropper tool, and the Color Sampler tool by pressing Shift-I. (To toggle without holding down the Shift key, choose Edit: Preferences: **General** and uncheck the "Use Shift Key for Tool Switch" option.)

Measure Tool Options

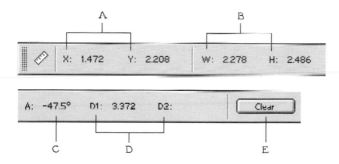

A. X & Y

These values display the location of the first point of the measurement line. X indicates its position across the horizontal ruler; Y indicates its position down the vertical ruler. The values are based on the current ruler settings, as established in the Edit: Preferences: **Units & Rulers** dialog box.

B. W & H

These values display the location of the cursor as you drag the second point of the line. W indicates how far to the left or right the second point is, compared to the first. H indicates how far above or below the second point is, compared to the first.

C. **A**

This value displays the current angle of the measurement line. When only a single line exists, the angle is relative to a horizontal plane. When you use the protractor feature, the angle is relative to the two line segments.

D. **D1 & D2**

These values display the current length of the line segments. D1 represents the first line segment; when you use the protractor feature, D2 represents the second segment.

E. **Clear**

Click this button to remove the measurement line. This is only required when you want to create a new measurement—if you're finished with the current line, it is hidden from view when you choose another tool.

4.6

Hand Tool *Type "H"*

Use the Hand tool, to scroll within the image window by click-dragging. It's only effective when the image is larger than the window displaying it. Use this tool instead of the scroll bars on the right and bottom sides of the window.

Access the Hand tool at any time by holding down the spacebar. Regardless of the currently selected tool, you can scroll the image by clicking and dragging. Release the spacebar to switch back to your original tool. You'll find one or two occasions when this shortcut doesn't work; for example, while you're entering text using the Type tool, or while you're drawing a selection with a marquee tool.

Issues to Consider

The Hand tool is much more flexible than using the scroll bars. Not only can you drag the image in any direction at will, but you can scroll when the image is in Full Screen View, which hides the scroll bars. (For more information, see *14.3, Image Window: **Scroll Bars**.*)

4.7

Zoom Tool *Type "Z"*

Use the Zoom tools to increase or decrease the magnification percentage of the image window. The current percentage is displayed in the lower left corner of the window, as well as in the title bar, just after the file name. (For more information, see *14.1, Image Window: **Magnification Box**.*)

This tool defaults to the Zoom In tool, which increases the magnification. Here, the cursor appears as a magnifying glass with a plus sign. There are two ways to zoom in:

- **Click on the image.** When you do, the point you click upon snaps to the center of the image window. Starting from 100%, the automatic magnifications are 200%, 300%, 400%, 500%, 600%, 700%, 800%, 1200%, and 1600% (the maximum).

- **Drag a zoom box.** When you do, the contents of the box fill the window, regardless of the exact percentage. This allows you to precisely target part of an image for close-up editing.

Hold down the (Option) [Alt] key to access the Zoom Out tool. The cursor changes to display a minus sign. Starting from 100%, the automatic percentages are 66.7%, 50%, 33.3%, 25%, 16.7%, 12.5%, 8.33%, 6.25%, and 5%. The smallest possible percentage ultimately depends on the width, height, and resolution of the open image. You cannot drag a zoom box to decrease the magnification.

Issues to Consider

Temporarily accessing the Zoom tools. You can quickly switch to one of the Zoom tools while using any other tool. Hold (Command) [Control]-spacebar to access the Zoom In tool; hold (Option-Command) [Alt-Control]-spacebar to access the Zoom Out tool.

The Zoom tools mimic the View: Zoom In and Zoom Out commands. You can also set the magnification on-the fly by adjusting the controls of the Navigator palette.

Zoom Tool Options Palette

A. **Resize Windows to Fit**

When this box is checked, the image window resizes to match the new magnification. When unchecked, the window dimensions do not change when you zoom in or out.

B. **Ignore Palettes**

When this box is checked (along with Resize Windows to Fit), the image window will expand behind any palettes currently positioned along the edge of the screen. When checked, the image window only expands to the edge of the palettes.

C. **Actual Pixels**

Click this button to increase the magnification percentage until the size of the image pixels match the size of your monitor's screen pixels. (For more information, see *14.23, View: **Actual Pixels**.*)

D. **Fit On Screen**

Click this button to set the magnification so that the image occupies as much screen area as possible without the need to scroll. (For more information, see *14.22, View: **Fit On Screen**.*)

E. **Print Size**

Click this button to set the magnification so that the image appears on screen as closely as possible to the printed size of the image. (For more information, see *14.24, View: **Print Size**.*)

Color Controls

5.1

Color Controls Overview

Sooner or later, every Photoshop user must define colors. Nearly every command and tool in the program exists to either manipulate existing colors or apply new values.

The magnitude of your color decisions depends on the type of work you're producing. If you scan line art for output, your colors are limited to black and white. If you scan and adjust halftones, you work with tints of black between 0% and 100%. If you create onscreen images, you can choose from millions of possible colors—but if you generate graphics for the Web, you may be limited to the 256 colors of an indexed palette. If you create full-color print images, you work with CMYK percentages—and the slightest variation may result in unexpected color shifts.

When you digitally acquire an image, the resulting colors depend on the quality of the scanner and the experience of the operator. Scanning has nothing to do with *defining* color, which takes place only after you open an image in Photoshop. Regardless of an image's destination, Photoshop's color controls enable you to define colors properly before you apply them.

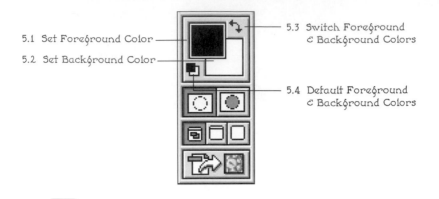

5.1 Set Foreground Color

5.2 Set Background Color

5.3 Switch Foreground
& Background Colors

5.4 Default Foreground
& Background Colors

5.2

Set Foreground Color

The foreground color is Photoshop's active color, similar to the paint an artist selects from her palette. When you apply a command that *adds* new color information, Photoshop uses the values defined in this swatch.

Photoshop always retains the last-applied foreground color. To define a new value, you must use one of the following methods:

• Click the swatch to access the color picker. (For more information, see *5.7, The Adobe Color Picker*, later this chapter)

• Use the Eyedropper tool to sample a color from any open image.

• Manipulate the sliders of the Color palette after selecting the foreground color swatch. (For more information, see Chapter 17, *The Color Palette*.)

• Click a predefined item in the Swatches palette. (For more information, see *18.1, Swatches Palette Overview*.)

5.3

Set Background Color

The background color is Photoshop's passive color. It's similar to the color that remains when a painter scrapes the canvas with a palette knife: when you apply a command that *removes* existing color information, the values defined in this swatch are left behind. Additionally, some commands work by creating a relationship between this color and the foreground value.

Photoshop always retains the last-applied background color. To define a new value, you must use one of the following methods:

• Click the swatch to access the color picker. (For more information, see *5.6, The Adobe Color Picker*).

- Hold down the (Option) [Alt] key and use the Eyedropper tool to sample a color from any open image.

- Manipulate the sliders of the Color palette after selecting the background color swatch.

- Hold down the (Option) [Alt] key and click an item in the Swatches palette.

Most often, users define a new background color for the following purposes:

- Using the Eraser tool on the background layer.

- Pressing the Delete key when a selection is active in the background layer.

- Using the Auto Erase feature of the Pencil tool.

- Applying Edit: **Fill** or **Stroke** (although it is not required that you use the background color).

- Filling a selection or any image layer by holding down the (Command) [Control] key and pressing Delete.

- Defining the ending color of a gradient that specifically blends between the foreground to the background colors.

Issues to Consider

When filtering, the background color is strictly a secondary value. Although many filters use the background color in conjunction with the foreground color–Filter: Sketch: **Chalk & Charcoal** and **Photocopy** are two examples–no filters use only the background color value.

The background color is most likely to appear on the background layer. Using the Eraser tool or deleting a selection on an image layer results in transparent pixels instead of the background color.

Reset to the default value. Click the Default Colors button to set the background color to white (see *5.5, Default Foreground and Background Colors*, later in this chapter).

5.4

Switch Foreground & Background Colors
Type "X"

Click this icon to swap the foreground and background color swatches. Click it again to swap them back.

5.5

Default Foreground and Background Colors

Type "D"

Clicking the Default Colors icon appears to set the foreground color to black and the background color to white. More specifically, it sets the lightest and darkest possible color values. The default colors for each color mode are as follows:

- **Bitmap.** The foreground color is 100% black. The background color is 0% black.

- **Grayscale.** The foreground color is 100% black. The background color is 0% black.

- RGB. The foreground color is R: 0, G: 0, B: 0. The background color is R: 255, G: 255, B: 255. If you intend to convert an RGB image to CMYK, however, be aware that the black values are not absolute. The converted values are ultimately determined by the current settings in the Edit: **Color Settings** dialog box.

- CMYK. The background color is C: 0, M: 0, Y: 0, K: 0.

  The default black of a CMYK image, however, depends on the Black Ink Limit and Total Ink Limit, both of which are established in the Edit: **Color Settings** dialog box.

  The Black Ink Limit is the maximum allowable percentage of black. When this value is set to 100%, the black component of the default foreground color is also 100%. If it's lowered to 90%, the default black component is 90%.

  The Total Ink Limit is the ceiling placed on the combined percentages of cyan, magenta, yellow, and black. To determine the CMY values of the default black, Photoshop subtracts the Black Ink Limit from the Total Ink Limit. The remaining CMY percentages add up to the remaining value, but in order to remain a neutral gray, the cyan percentage must be slightly higher than magenta and yellow.

  For example, if the Total Ink Limit is 300% and the Black Ink Limit is 100%, the combined CMY percentages total 200: The default black is C: 75, M: 63, Y: 62, K: 100. If the Total Ink Limit is 280% and the Black Ink Limit is 90, the combined CMY percentages total 190: The default black is C: 72, M: 60, Y: 58, K: 90.

- **Lab Color.** The foreground color is L: 0, a: 0, b: 0. The background color is L: 100, a: 0, b: 0.

Mistakes to Avoid

Using different values for black in the same general area. This can cause visible artifacting. For example, if you apply a manually defined 100% black brushstroke to an area of enriched black, the lack of CMY inks make the brushstroke appear washed out after printing. Unless you have specific reasons to do otherwise, keep your black percentages consistent.

Issues to Consider

The default black for RGB and Lab Color images are always the same. The black that results when you convert the image to CMYK, however, is based on the settings in the Edit: **Color Settings** dialog box.

Default blacks in a CMYK image are always *enriched*, or comprised of all four process inks. This helps create a deeper black with better paper coverage. It also reduces the need for trapping four-color artwork containing black outlines. (See *10.xx, Image: Trap Overview* for more information.)

Related Topics

9.37   *Edit: Color Settings*
10.1   *Image: Mode Overview*
10.54 *Image: Trap Overview*

5.6

The Color Picker

The color picker is Photoshop's primary tool for defining color values. Although it's strongly associated with defining the foreground or background color, the color picker is used for a variety of other purposes:

- **Defining endpoint target values.** Double-click one of the eyedroppers in the Image: Adjust: **Levels** or **Curves** dialog boxes.

- **Editing an indexed color.** Double-click one of the colors in the Image: Mode: **Color Table** dialog box.

- **Defining a duotone color.** Click one of the swatches in the Image: Mode: **Duotone** dialog box.

- **Editing the color of onscreen tools.** This includes the transparency pattern, gamut warning, ruler guides, grid, and Quick Mask overlay. The color picker appears when you click the appropriate swatch.

- **Defining a background color for an image burned to a color slide.** Click the Background button in the File: **Page Setup** dialog box.

- **Defining multiple gradient colors.** Click the color swatch in the Gradient Editor.

Mistakes to Avoid

Attempting to use the Apple or Windows color picker. Both additional pickers lack the flexibility and power of the default color picker. Neither allows you to define output values, CMYK percentages, Lab colors, or colors from custom libraries. Also, you are not warned if you choose a color falling out of CMYK's reproducible gamut. They are adequate for only the most rudimentary color selections, and therefore are not recommended. (See *5.9, Additional Color Pickers* for more information.)

Issues to Consider

The same color picker is used in different locations. When you access the color picker in a dialog box, though, it usually does not affect the current foreground and background color.

Apply specific CMYK values *after* you convert the image to CMYK Color mode. Otherwise, the values will likely change during the conversion from RGB. If necessary, refer to process color swatchbooks like Trumatch or Pantone Process to select precise color values.

The bit-depths of the color slider and field refer to the number of colors displayed by each option. Being 8-bit, the slider contains 256 (or 2^8) colors. Being 16-bit, the field displays 65,536 (or 2^{16}) variations of each color or tone selected in the slider. Multiply the two numbers to produce 16,777,216 (or 2^{24})—the precise number of colors your monitor is capable of displaying.

5.7

The Adobe Color Picker

This is Photoshop's default color picker, and by far the most powerful. It contains the following options:

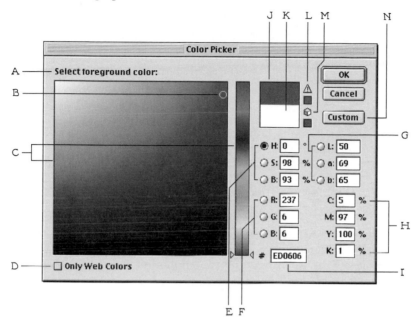

A. Task

The intended use of the new color appears in the upper-left corner of the dialog box.

B. Color Indicator

This circular marker pinpoints the location of the current color in the color field. It moves when you click elsewhere in the field, click on the Gamut Alert swatch, click on the Previous Color swatch, or enter values in the Numerical Fields.

C. Color Field and Slider

The large color field and the vertical slider work together to provide access to more than 16 million colors.

Their contents depend on the radio buttons located directly to the right of the slider. Each option fills the slider with a particular 8-bit range and the field with an opposing 16-bit range. By manipulating the slider arrows and clicking somewhere in the field, you can properly target your desired color.

D. **Only Web Colors**

Check this box to restrict the number of available colors in the color field and slider to the 216 "browser-safe" values. Immediately, you'll notice that the color field is reduced to a few patches of solid color, instead of the smooth color-to-color blends normally found there. To choose a particular color, click anywhere in the desired patch. Or, if desired, enter the necessary hexadecimal code in the "#" field. (For more information, see *10.x, Photoshop Color Models.*)

Note that whenever you check this box, the value currently defined in the color picker is pushed to the closest browser-safe option; the change can be considerable. Off-checking the box does not switch the value back.

E. HSB **Buttons**

Choosing any of these buttons sets the color field and slider to the HSB color model. Their effect is as follows:

H (Hue)

This button is always the default option whenever you first open the color picker. It fills the slider with the visible spectrum of colors, similar to the contents of the RGB/CMY color wheel. Move the arrows to select a particular hue, such as blue, yellow, or orange. The color field then displays all possible variations of the chosen hue: colors from left to right differ in saturation, or color intensity; colors from top to bottom differ in brightness, or tone.

S (Saturation)

This option fills the slider with the full range of possible saturation levels. The chosen hue appears fully saturated at the top of the slider, and progresses to fully desaturated, or gray, at the bottom.

In the color field, colors from left to right differ in hue. Colors from top to bottom differ in brightness.

B (Brightness)

This option fills the slider with the full range of possible brightness levels. The chosen hue appears at the top of the slider, and progresses to black at the bottom.

In the color field, colors from left to right differ in hue. Colors from top to bottom differ in saturation.

F. RGB **Buttons**

Choosing any of these buttons sets the color field and slider to the RGB color model. Their effect is as follows:

R (Red)

This option fills the slider with the full range of red, as it affects the currently selected color. The top of the slider displays the current color with the red level boosted to maximum (255). The bottom of the slider displays the current color with the red level reduced to the minimum (0).

In the color field, colors on the right contain maximum blue levels; colors on the left contain minimum blue levels. Colors on the top contain maximum green levels; colors on the bottom contain minimum green levels.

G *(Green)*

This option fills the slider with the full range of green, as it affects the currently selected color. The top of the slider displays the current color with the green level boosted to maximum (255). The bottom of the slider displays the current color with the green level reduced to the minimum (0).

In the color field, colors on the right contain maximum blue levels; colors on the left contain minimum blue levels. Colors on the top contain maximum red levels; colors on the bottom contain minimum red levels.

B *(Blue)*

This option fills the slider with the full range of blue, as it affects the currently selected color. The top of the slider displays the current color with the blue level boosted to maximum (255). The bottom of the slider displays the current color with the blue level reduced to the minimum (0).

In the color field, colors on the right contain maximum red levels; colors on the left contain minimum red levels. Colors on the top contain maximum green levels; colors on the bottom contain minimum green levels.

G. Lab Buttons

Choosing any of these buttons sets the color field and slider to the Lab color model. Their effect is as follows:

L *(Lightness)*

This option fills the slider with the full range of lightness values, as they affect the currently selected color. The top of the slider displays the current color with the Lightness value boosted to maximum (100). The bottom of the slider displays the current color with the Lightness value reduced to 0 (which always results in black).

In the color field, all the hues of the RGB/CMY color wheel are displayed. The hues remain as you reposition the slider, changing lightness values as specified. (For more information, see *10.2, The RGB/CMY Model.*)

a *(Green to Magenta)*

This option fills the slider with the range of values between magenta and green, as they affect the currently selected color. The top of the slider displays the current color with the a value boosted to maximum (127), which indicates that the value is positioned all the way to the magenta end of the Lab spectrum. The bottom of the slider displays the current color with the a value reduced to −128, which indicates that the value is positioned all the way to the green end of the spectrum.

The color field reflects the influence of the remaining Lab values. Colors to the left contain maximum blue values, and colors to the right contain maximum yellow—a direct reflection of Lab's b component. Colors to the top of the field have a Lightness value of 100, and colors to the bottom have a value of 0—a direct reflection of Lab's Lightness component. (For more information, see *10.4, The Lab Model.*)

b (Blue to Yellow)

This option fills the slider with the range of values between yellow and blue, as they affect the currently selected color. The top of the slider displays the current color with the b value boosted to maximum (127), which indicates that the value is positioned all the way to the yellow end of the Lab spectrum. The bottom of the slider displays the current color with the b value reduced to −128, which indicates that the value is positioned all the way to the blue end of the spectrum.

The color field reflects the influence of the remaining Lab values. Colors to the left contain maximum green values, and colors to the right contain maximum magenta—a direct reflection of Lab's a component. Colors to the top of the field have a Lightness value of 100, and colors to the bottom have a value of 0—a direct reflection of Lab's Lightness component. (For more information, see *10.4, The Lab Model.*)

H. **Numerical Fields**

The numerical fields allow you to enter specific color values. Use these instead of the color slider and color field when you know the exact color you need to define. If desired, use the tab key to jump from one field to the next. (See *10.1, Image: Mode Overview* for more information.)

I. **#**

When you first open the color picker, this field displays the hexadecimal code of the last-defined (or currently sampled) color. As you use the picker's controls to set a new color, the # field changes to display its hex value. If desired, you can enter a value directly into the field. (For more information, see *16.2, Panel One: Primary Color Info.*)

J. **Current Color**

This swatch constantly changes to display the currently selected color. When you click OK, the color that appears here is the one defined.

K. **Previous Color**

This swatch displays the color that existed before you accessed the color picker. For example, if you clicked the foreground color swatch to access the color picker, it displays the previously defined foreground color.

L. **Warning: Out of Gamut for Printing**

The Gamut Alert triangle appears when you select a color that falls out of the reproducible range of process inks. The small swatch below the triangle represents the closest CMYK equivalent of the out-of-gamut color. Click on the triangle or the swatch to automatically select that value.

While this feature seems helpful, it has limited uses. Its results depend on the current color mode of an image:

- CMYK. The only advantage is the appearance of the foreground or background color swatch. Even if you apply an out-of-gamut color to the image, it applies the same values that appeared in the Gamut Alert swatch. However, if you add that color to the Swatches palette for later use, you add the out-of-gamut color. Clicking the Gamut Alert swatch while defining the color enables you to apply the same values to the image as well as the Swatches palette.

- RGB and Lab Color. It's easy to believe that the values of the Gamut Alert swatch are the same as if you applied the out-of-gamut color, then converted the image to CMYK. That's not necessarily the case. When Photoshop determines the nearest CMYK equivalent, it refers to the Edit: **Color Settings** dialog box to compensate for the expected dot gain. If you click on the Gamut Alert swatch, apply the color, then convert the image to CMYK, Photoshop compensates for dot gain again. The color doesn't change by much—only by one or two percentage points—but it's enough to cause a visible shift, especially when printing to an ink jet, thermal wax, or color laser printer.

M. **Warning: Not a Web Safe Color**

This cube-shaped gamut warning appears in the color picker whenever you specify a value that is not one of the 216 browser-safe web values. Because the huge majority of colors fall outside this particular range, the warning is almost always visible. If necessary, you can click the small swatch that appears underneath the cube to set the current color to the closest browser-safe option.

N. **Custom**

Click this button to access the Custom Colors dialog box. (For more information, see *5.8, The Custom Color Picker*.)

5.8

The Custom Color Picker

Photoshop enables you to select colors from a series of predefined color libraries. Each library has a corresponding printed swatchbook, which you can purchase from a graphic supply company or directly from the manufacturer. There are two types of color library:

- **Process colors.** Most predefined samples consist of CMYK percentages. The swatchbooks themselves are organized in different ways for different purposes, but the individual colors are all intended for four-color printing. When you choose a color from one of these libraries, you automatically enter the preset values in the CMYK fields of the standard color picker.

- **Spot colors.** You can also define spot colors, or solid inks. The PANTONE library is the de facto standard for spot colors.

Most often, spot colors are defined in the following circumstances:

- **Selecting a color from a printed sample.** The swatchbooks allow you to do something that you cannot do with any of Photoshop's onscreen tools: define a color based on an actual printed sample. This is as close as you can get to predicting how a color will appear after printing—otherwise, you have to rely largely on memory, guesswork, and your knowledge of color theory when defining a specific color.

- **Creating spot-color duotones.** When you create a monotone, duotone, tritone, or quadtone that contains at least one spot color, you'll choose it from the custom color picker. (See *10.8, Image: Mode:* **Duotone** for more information.)

- **Adding a spot color channel.** When you add a spot channel to an image, you specify a particular color from a spot library. Most often, you choose it from the custom color picker.

- **Calibrating a non-standard ink system.** Occasionally, a process ink is replaced by a spot ink. To ensure proper separation, you must use a PANTONE ink's Lab values, accessible only by defining the color in the custom color picker.

Mistakes to Avoid

Assuming that *choosing* a spot color from the Custom color picker is the same as *defining* one. Unless you create a duotone or add a spot color channel, Photoshop does not let you define and separate spot colors. If you try, Photoshop automatically converts the color to its closest CMYK equivalent—which contradicts the most common reasons to use spot colors in the first place.

Issues to Consider

When you define a custom process color, your image must already be in CMYK mode. If you apply a custom color to an RGB or Lab Color image, its values are altered when you convert to CMYK. This is due to the settings in the Edit: **Color Settings** dialog box.

Most spot colors do not convert accurately. Although each Pantone spot color has a CMYK equivalent, only about 15–20% of the library can be accurately reproduced with process inks.

Each supported library has a corresponding printed swatchbook. Unless you refer to one while choosing a color, your decisions are no more accurate than if you were using the standard color picker.

The Custom Color Dialog Box

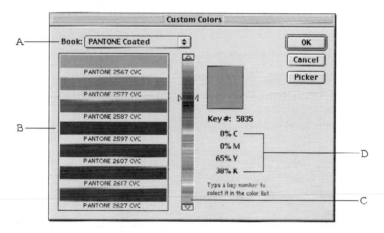

A. **Book**

Select your desired color library from this pop-up menu. Photoshop supports the following:

ANPA Color

Short for *American Newspaper Publisher's Association,* this library contains the colors that reproduce most successfully on newsprint. This organization has recently changed its name to the Newspaper Association of America (NAA).

DIC Color Guide

Short for *Dainippon Ink and Chemicals, Inc.,* this process color library is rarely used outside Japan.

FOCOLTONE

From the United Kingdom, this library contains 763 CMYK combinations selected for their ability to form a *process bridge,* or share enough color components to reduce the need for trapping.

HKS

> The HKS library is a German spot-color system. Unlike the PANTONE spot inks, however, each HKS color has a direct CMYK equivalent. There are four HKS catalogs, each one intended for a grade of paper stock: HKS E (for continuous stationary), HKS K (for coated, glossy paper), HKS N (for uncoated paper), and HKS Z (for newsprint). You'll notice that each library offers more or less colors, depending on what the target paper stock is capable of reproducing accurately.

PANTONE Coated

> This contains the PANTONE Color Formula Guide 1000. Select this option if the color will be printed to coated stock. Although inks from the Coated library have the same CMYK values as their Uncoated counterparts, they use a different naming convention, which can cause problems when you import the image into a different application. Also, these colors display slightly darker on screen in an attempt to simulate their actual printed appearance.

PANTONE Process

> This library contains more than 3,000 CMYK combinations.

PANTONE ProSim

> Short for *Process Simulation*, this library shows the printed effect of converting Pantone's spot-color library to CMYK. This way, you can determine how closely a spot color's CMYK equivalent matches the actual ink.

PANTONE Uncoated

> This contains the PANTONE Color Formula Guide 1000. Select this option if the color will be printed to uncoated stock. Although inks from the Uncoated library have the same CMYK values as their Coated counterparts, they use a different naming convention, which can cause problems when you import the image into a different application. Also, these colors display slightly lighter on screen in an attempt to simulate their actual printed appearance.

TOYO Color Finder

> This is another Japanese color standard, rarely used outside that country.

TRUMATCH

> This is a highly organized library of more than 2,000 CMYK colors. Here, the range of printable color is divided into 50 different hues, each with 40 tints. This allows a designer to choose a lighter or darker version of a color with a minimal shift in color cast.

B. **Color List**

This scrolling list displays all the colors of the selected library. Type the title of your desired color to automatically scroll to its location.

C. **Color Slider**

The slider displays the hues of the currently loaded library. Reposition the slider arrows to move to another location in the library.

D. **Key Number and Color Information**

When you select a custom color, its title appears as the key number in the lower right of the dialog box. Below that, the CMYK values for the selected color appear.

5.9

Additional Color Pickers

Photoshop lets you use two additional color pickers, one each for the Macintosh and Windows versions. To switch from the default Photoshop picker, you must open the Edit: Preferences: **General** dialog box and select the second option from the color picker pop-up menu.

The Apple Color Picker

This is the standard color picker of the Macintosh operating system. Here, you can define colors based on several different models, including CMYK, HSB, RGB, and a set of generic crayons. Most users justifiably avoid this option. The controls are extremely limited, you cannot define Lab colors, and you are not warned if you choose a color falling out of CMYK's reproducible gamut.

The Windows Color Picker

This is the standard color picker of the Windows operating system. Here, you can choose from a series of basic colors, or you can define up to 16 custom colors based on the HSB or RGB color models.

Quick Mask Tools

6.1
Quick Mask Tools Overview

Use the Quick Mask tools to create selections using Photoshop's paint tools.

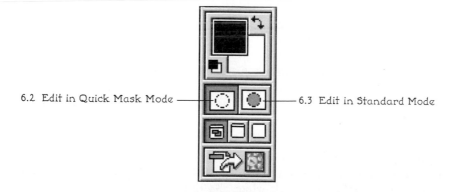

6.2 Edit in Quick Mask Mode ——— 6.3 Edit in Standard Mode

There are two ways to create a Quick Mask selection:

- **Create a new selection.** Do this by switching to Quick Mask mode, painting with the desired tool, and clicking the Edit in Standard Mode tool.

- **Enhance an existing selection.** Here, you draw a selection using one of the standard Selection tools, switch to Quick Mask mode, and use the paint tools to add the desired changes.

In Quick Mask mode, a selection appears as a semi-transparent overlay. As long as you remain in this mode, the overlay is the only information affected by your brushstrokes and adjustments. The altered overlay is converted into a new selection outline as soon as you exit Quick Mask mode.

This process is similar to editing an alpha channel, made by drawing a selection and choosing Select: **Save Selection**—both use an additional 8-bit channel to contain an editable selection, and both channels are visible in the Channels palette. When you edit a mask channel, you can use paint tools, adjustment commands, and filters to alter the appearance of the selection before making it active again. You can edit a Quick Mask this way as well; the only difference is that a Quick Mask uses a temporary channel, while alpha channels remain in the image until you discard them.

The capabilities of this method fall squarely between manual selections and mask channels. On one hand, you can create more complex selections than the selection tools allow. For example, you can add soft edges of varying widths and define partial selections, neither of which you can do with the Marquee or Lasso tools. On the other hand, these selections are one-shot deals. They can't be loaded again unless you save them as a mask channel.

Quick Mask is a down-and-dirty technique, and the quality of its selections often shows it. When the most precise selections are required, take the extra time to create a mask channel. If desired, you can edit a saved selection just like a Quick Mask.

6.2

Edit in Quick Mask Mode Tool *type "Q"*

Click this button to switch into Quick Mask mode. When you do, a temporary mask channel, titled "Quick Mask," appears in the Channels palette. As long as you remain in Quick Mask mode, your edits affect only the contents of this channel. Because its view button is checked in the Channels palette, its contents appear on screen as a semi-transparent overlay.

If a selection is active when you switch to Quick Mask mode, it changes to form the basis of the overlay. If you switch to Quick Mask mode without an active selection, no overlay appears at first. Either way, you can begin painting with any brush-based tool, using the existing image information as a guide.

Creating a Quick Mask is different than editing the regular image. Because you're really editing a Grayscale channel while in Quick Mask mode, the only colors you can define are black, white, and tones of gray:

Black

Painting with black applies the overlay color. Black is really being applied to the Quick Mask channel. Depending on the Color Indicates option set in the Quick Mask Options dialog box, areas painted with black are either fully selected or fully ignored when you click the Edit in Standard Mode tool.

White

Painting with white removes the overlay color. White is really being applied to the Quick Mask channel. When you paint over a black area there, that part of the Quick Mask overlay is removed.

Gray

Gray areas in a Quick Mask result in partially-selected areas. In other words, the area is masked with a semi-opaque selection. The actual amount depends on the current Color Indicates setting in the Quick Mask Options dialog box. For example, if you apply 25% black while creating a Quick Mask, the Selected Areas option produces a 25% selection. On the other hand, the Masked Areas option produces a 75% selection. (For more information, see *1.1, Selection Tools Overview.*)

Issues to Consider

As long as you're in Quick Mask mode, all colors defined with the Color Picker appear as gray tones. Most users paint in black or white; press the D key to automatically set the foreground color to black and the background color to white. To define precise gray values, use the Color palette with the Grayscale Slider chosen from the palette submenu. This way, you can target specific percentages when creating partial selections.

Toggling back and forth between the Masked Areas and Selected Areas settings. Do this by holding down the (Option) [Alt] key and clicking the Edit in Quick Mask Mode tool. The tool's icon displays the current option. If you toggle while in Quick Mask mode, the overlay reverses to reflect the change.

Painting a Quick Mask with the foreground and background colors. Press the X key to swap the current foreground and background swatches in the Toolbar, which in turn enables you to increase or lessen the area included in the Quick Mask.

The Quick Mask Options Dialog Box

Double-click either Quick Mask button to access this dialog box.

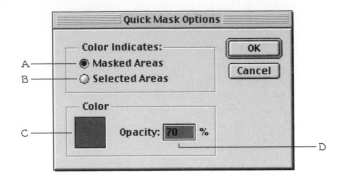

A. Masked Areas

Photoshop defaults to this option. Here, all pixels not colored by the overlay are included in an active selection when you click the Edit in Standard Mode tool. As you paint the overlay, you cover the areas you don't want included in the selection. This method may be more intuitive if you have created opaque masks during conventional stripping or platemaking.

B. Selected Areas

With this option, all pixels colored by the overlay are included in an active selection. As you paint the overlay, you cover the areas that you want included in the selection.

C. Color

This box controls the color of the overlay. Photoshop defaults to red, emulating the opaque rubilith tape used to make conventional masks. If the overlay is too close to the colors in the image, click on this swatch and define a new color in the Color Picker. The color itself is only an onscreen reference; changing colors has no impact on the final selections.

D. Opacity

This value controls the opacity of the overlay. It's set to 50% by default, and there is little need to change this setting. If the opacity is too high, the image is obscured; too low, and the overlay is difficult to see.

Related Topics

6.3

Edit in Standard Mode Tool   *type "Q"*

Click this button to switch from Quick Mask back to normal editing mode. All areas masked by the overlay form the basis for the new selection. If no masked areas exist in the Quick Mask mode, no selection appears.

Issues to Consider

Toggling between selections and Quick Masks. After a selection is made active, you can turn it into a mask channel by choosing Select: Save Selection. Or, you can switch back to Quick Mask mode and continue refining the selection.

View Controls

View Controls Overview

The View Controls at the bottom of the Toolbar affect the display of the image window. These buttons have no effect on the image itself.

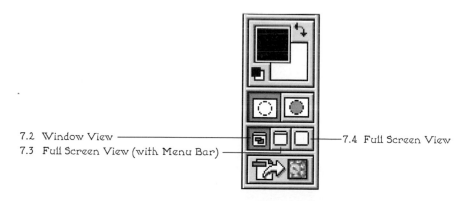

7.2 Window View

7.3 Full Screen View (with Menu Bar)

7.4 Full Screen View

Issues to Consider

Using View Controls shortcuts. The following shortcuts apply to all three view modes:

- **Change views.** Scroll through all three options by repeatedly pressing the F key.
- **Hide all palettes.** Press the Tab key to hide all open palettes, including the Toolbar. Press the Tab key again to reveal the palettes.
- **Hide all palettes except the Toolbar.** Hold down the Shift key and press the Tab key. Press Shift-Tab again to reveal the palettes, or press Tab to hide the Toolbar.

7.2

Window View

This is the default view for every image opened in Photoshop. It displays the image window, allowing access to the scroll bars, title bar, magnification box, and image data box.

Issues to Consider

This is the only view that allows you to see any underlying information. This includes other open images, open applications, and the desktop.

Different images can be set to different views. If the active image is in Window view, it sits in front of images in Full Screen view.

Related Topics

7.3

Full Screen View (with Menu Bar)

This view hides the edges of the image window. The image rests on a solid gray background, which conceals all underlying information. This increases the total area that can be occupied by the image, which is especially useful when editing large graphics.

Issues to Consider

The menu bar and all of its commands remain visible. This view is often the choice of artists who want to maximize their workable space, but want constant access to all tools and commands.

Photoshop uses a simple trick to display an image this way. It enlarges the bounds of the image window until the edges, including the scroll bars and title bar, are positioned just beyond your monitor's display area. If you ever connect a second monitor to your workstation, you'll be able to detect the window edges. (The same process is used when you display the image in Full Screen view.)

7.4

Full Screen View

This view hides the menu bar and replaces the gray background with solid black. This increases the total area that can be occupied by an image to include the entire screen.

Issues to Consider

Even though the menu bar is hidden, you can still access a command by selecting its keyboard shortcut. To apply a menu command without a shortcut, you must switch to another view. You can also select a particular tool by typing its one-letter shortcut.

This is primarily a display mode, especially with all the palettes hidden. The black background provides a high-contrast viewing area with no potentially influencing color bias. Also, if you're working on images that are exactly the same size as your monitor (for example, if you're creating CD-ROM graphics on a 640-by-480 screen), only this option allows you to see the image at 100%.

The File Menu

File: New

(Command) [Control]-O

Use this command to create a new image window. New images are commonly used for the following tasks:

- Creating a new canvas for original artwork generated in Photoshop.

- Creating a temporary workspace for image information the user wishes to separately edit, then re-incorporate into the original image.

- Creating a new, separate file for a selection copied from a larger image.

Mistakes to Avoid

Failing to accommodate bleeds and trimming. If a new image will bleed off the page in your layout, you must extend its width and/or height to accommodate the trimming. For most purposes, an extra .125 to .25 inches added to each bleeding edge will suffice.

Entering a resolution too low for the image's intended use. Every image has its own resolution requirements, and the new image should reflect its intended use. Pay close attention when the new image contents will be blended with a second image—the resolution of the new image should match its destination. For example, if you plan to add information to a 300 ppi image, the resolution of the new image should be 300 ppi as well.

Issues to Consider

Creating a new image via copying and pasting. If you copied a selected area before choosing File: **New**, then the values of the New dialog box reflect the dimensions, resolution, and color mode of that image information. If the intention is to create a new image out of a copied selection, choose Edit: **Paste** after creating the new window. To ignore the contents of the Clipboard, choose (Option-Command) [Alt-Control]-N, or hold down the (Option) [Alt] key while choosing File: **New**. This way, the last values entered in the dialog box are retained. (Remember that if you paste information into a new image, it appears in a separate image layer. Although it may not look like it, you'll need to choose Image: **Flatten Image** before saving the file.)

When blending, start with Transparent Pixels. By default, Photoshop will create an image filled with white pixels. However, if you intend to blend any new info with another image, the surrounding white pixels may render that task impossible. Play it safe and create the image using transparent pixels, which makes it much easier to add anti-aliased or soft information to another image.

Entering the dimensions of an open image. To automatically plug in the values of an open image, choose the file's title from the Windows menu while the New dialog box is open.

Determining the default unit of measurement. The default unit of measurement can be changed in two places—under Edit: Preferences: **Units & Rulers** or the pop-up menu in the lower-left of the Info palette.

The New Dialog Box

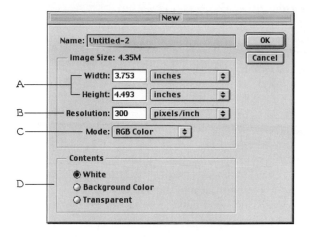

A. **Width and Height** (1 to 30000, regardless of unit)

Before entering the image dimensions, select the preferred units of measurement from the Width and Height pop-up menus. Choices under both include pixels, inches, centimeters, points, and picas. The Width menu has an extra option called Columns. Here, you set the width of an image to a number of columns in your page layout (images with a width of two or more columns include a preset value for gutters). Establish these widths in the Edit: Preferences: **Units & Rulers** dialog box.

B. **Resolution** (1.000 to 10000.000)

The Resolution value must match the target resolution requirements. Graphics for web or on screen presentation rarely exceed 72 dpi, while print-destined images can range from 150 to 300 ppi (for Grayscale and color) to 1200 ppi (for black-and-white artwork).

C. **Mode**

The image mode determines the color type of an image: Bitmap displays only black and white; Grayscale displays 256 shades of gray; RGB, CMYK, and Lab all display in full color. Since color information can be lost or poorly translated when converting to another mode, the proper mode should always be selected when creating a new image. (For more information, see *10.1, Image: Mode Overview.*)

D. **Contents**

These options determine what the new image will contain: white pixels, the current background color, or transparency.

Related Topics

9.8   Edit: **Paste**
9.51   File: Preferences: **Units & Rulers**
11.5   Transparency
E.1   Setting Resolution for Scanned Line Art
F.4   Setting Resolution for Scanned Halftones

8.2

File: *Open* *(Command)/[Control]-O*

Most frequently, this command is used to open pixel-based images, such as stock and PhotoCD files, scans made using proprietary software (like Scitex or Optronics), or any pre-existing Photoshop image. You can also use it to open vector-based artwork from programs such as Adobe Illustrator, Macromedia FreeHand, or Adobe Dimensions.

Issues to Consider

Images may not open directly into Photoshop. For the most part, accessing an image with the File: **Open** command is the same as double-clicking a file on your hard drive. However, if a file was not originally saved from Photoshop, it may not open directly into the program. For example, if it was scanned using a stand-alone program, double-clicking it will likely relaunch the scanning application; if the file is a downloaded web graphic, double-clicking it may launch a system-level viewing utility; if the file was created in a graphics program from a different platform, you may receive an "Application Not Found" message. Avoid these problems by opening the images from within Photoshop.

Drag-and-drop to open images. Make an Alias (Mac) or Shortcut (Windows) of Photoshop's application icon and place it on your computer's desktop. This way, files created in outside programs can be dragged onto it, simultaneously launching Photoshop and opening the images.

This approach is also useful when you've installed multiple versions of Photoshop on the same system. When you double-click an image on the hard drive, it automatically launches the latest version (unless the earlier version is already open). If you have aliases on your desktop, you can drag the image icons onto the desired version.

Opening vector-based graphics. When you open a graphic that was created in an object-oriented program (such as Illustrator or Freehand), you must convert the shapes to editable pixels. Before the image opens, you're prompted to enter the desired width, height, color mode, and resolution. (For more information, see *D.2*, **Opening a Vector-Based File**.)

Opening multiple files. You can open more than one image by Shift-clicking the desired files in the Open dialog box.

The Open Dialog Box

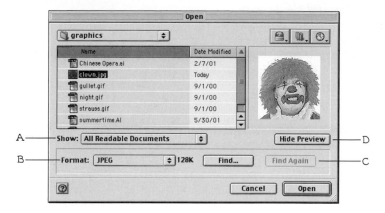

A. Show

This pop-up menu enables you to narrow the range of images listed in the window to a specific file format. For example, if you set it to Photoshop, only images saved in Photoshop's native file format are visible; if you set it to TIFF, only images saved as TIFFs (from any program) are visible. If you set it to All Documents, the window lists every file on the drive, whether Photoshop can open it or not. If you set it to All Readable Documents, the window only displays the images that Photoshop recognizes.

B. Format

When you choose a non-Photoshop image in the window, this pop-up menu automatically anticipates the file format, enabling Photoshop to open it successfully. If it can't recognize the file type, it sets the Raw option, which rarely succeeds. If you happen to know the file's actual format, set it in this pop-up before opening. If you don't know the format, you can try choosing some logical options, but you should probably track down the file's creator for more information.

C. Find/Find Again

This option enables you to search for an image based on all or part of its file name. The search is very basic—only one file at a time is displayed in the Open window. Selecting Find Again lets you flip through the matching files until you find the one you need.

D. Show/Hide Preview

When you click the Show Preview button, the dialog box makes room to display in image thumbnail—assuming one is built into the file. This only works when the preview is saved into the image file (by checking the Thumbnails options in the Edit: Preferences: **Saving Files** dialog box). If you attempt to preview a PICT image, it may be possible to generate a thumbnail by clicking the Create button.

Related Topics

8.3

File: *Open Recent*

This submenu displays a list of the most recently opened images. This way, you can access a file by choosing its name from the submenu, as opposed to using the Open command.

The only files that do not appear here are new images that are closed without saving, and image duplicates created using the As Copy option in the Save As dialog box.

By default, Photoshop lists the last four images. To change this setting, enter the desired value in the Recent File List Contains field, in the Edit: Preferences: **Saving Files** dialog box.

Related Topics

8.4

File: *Close* (Command) [Control]-W

Choose this command to close the active image window. If any changes have been made since the last time you saved, a prompt appears, asking whether to Save, Don't Save, or Cancel.

8.5

File: *Close All* (Command-Shift) [Control-Shift]-W

Choose this command to close all open images. No matter which one is active, Photoshop closes the images in the reverse order in which they were opened. If any changes have been made since the last time you saved, a prompt appears, asking whether to Save, Don't Save, or Cancel.

8.6

File: Save

(Command) [Control]-S

This command enables you to write the information contained in an image to a file on your hard drive. Saving actually involves two processes:

- **Preserving the current image state.** It allows you to save your work as you go along, lowering the possibility of time-consuming frustration if your system crashes.

- **Placing the file.** You can use the Save dialog box to place saved images in the right place on your hard drives or removable storage media.

Save images soon and frequently. When scanning images directly into Photoshop, save them before making any corrections, eliminating any need to rescan. When working on original images, save them just after creating the new image window. If translating graphics from a different program, save them just after opening them in Photoshop, overwriting the originals if they are no longer needed.

When you initially save an image, take the opportunity to place the file in its proper location. Once an image has been saved, selecting File: **Save** updates the current file without bringing up the Save As dialog box.

Mistakes to Avoid

Choosing the Save keyboard shortcut by accident. The shortcut for Select: Deselect—(Command) [Control]-D—is dangerously close to the shortcut for File: Save. Many users have accidentally saved a file when attempting to remove a selection outline. This would prevent you from reverting to the last saved version to reverse a series of commands.

Saving an image in the wrong file format. Every image destination has its own file format requirements. (For more information, see *8.8 Supported File Formats.*)

Saving an image in the wrong color mode. Every image use has its own color mode requirements. (For more information, see *10.1, Image: Mode Overview.*)

Using lazy or disorganized file names. Doing so makes it hard to locate the appropriate image down the road. Many designers fall into the habit of creating multiple versions of an image, adding the numbers "2", "3", or "4" after each variation. Then they tag the word "final" at the end of their preferred file. If they make a series of last-minute edits, they wind up with file names containing "final FINAL," "REAL final," or "USE THIS ONE," which easily leads to the wrong graphic getting imported and used. File names should be as clear and simple as possible. Often, this means using a numerical job-tracking system for scans, but some users name them after the focus or purpose of the image itself.

Failing to include the proper extension in the file name. After typing in a file name, add a dot and the abbreviation for the file format you have selected—for example, *USflag.eps, HenryAaron.gif,* and *rhubarbpie.tif.* This enables you to immediately see what types of images you have, which is beneficial if you need to troubleshoot problematic graphics. Also, Photoshop sometimes relies on the existence of this code when attempting to open an image from a different platform. You can tell Photoshop to automatically add a three-letter extension to every file by going to Edit: Preferences: **Saving Files** and choosing an option under Append File Extension.

Issues to Consider

You can't undo a Save command. However, if you choose the command by accident, you can revert to the desired state in the History palette and re-save.

Macintosh is the only platform that recognizes four-letter image codes. Windows, UNIX, and other platforms require the same three-letter codes that Photoshop applies automatically. For Mac users, this only becomes an issue when images are being prepared for distribution across platforms.

Avoid adding file extensions manually. Although you can easily type in an extension on your own, try not to, unless you're absolutely sure. There are dozens of Photoshop-specific file extensions, and literally hundreds of different possibilities. If you add the incorrect extension to a file on a Mac, you may not be able to read it on a PC. For example, one designer created an Illustrator graphic on a Mac, added ".aif" after the filename (assuming it meant "Adobe Illustrator File"), and sent the file to a Windows-based company. Since that extension actually stands for "Audio Interchange Format", the PC recognized it as a sound file. It couldn't be opened, even when they tried from within Illustrator. As soon as they changed the extension, it worked perfectly. Also, some users mistakenly add four-letter extensions, such as ".tiff" or ".jpeg", which work fine on a Mac, but make no sense to a PC. If you need to add an extension to an image and you're not sure what it is, re-open it in Photoshop, and choose File: **Save As** to save a copy with the correct extension.

Don't delete the extension when naming the file. Photoshop automatically adds the file extension, but it doesn't prevent you from accidentally removing it. When you first access the Save As dialog box, only the file name (and not the extension itself) is highlighted, which enables you to quickly enter a new name. However, if you highlight part of the current name to modify it, it's easy to include the extension as well, and replace it with whatever text you add.

While working on an image, leave it in the native Photoshop format. It's the only one that retains multiple layers. It also opens and saves more quickly than other formats, and that can make a big difference when editing 100 MB-plus images. Save the image to the proper format when editing is complete.

Removing unwanted file formats from the list. If you get tired of looking at obscure file formats that you never use in your Formats pop-up menu, delete the items from the following folder: Adobe Photoshop 6/Plug-ins/File Formats.

Related Topics

8.7   File: *Save As*
8.8   Supported File Formats
9.48   Edit: Preferences: *Saving Files*
10.1   Image: *Mode* Overview

8.7

File: *Save As* (Command-Shift) [Control-Shift]-S

This command enables you to save an additional copy of an image. It's similar to the first time you save. From the same dialog box, you name the file, choose a file format, and place the new image somewhere on the hard drive. There's an important difference, however. This time, the original file is left untouched, and a new image containing all the most recent edits is written.

File: **Save As** uses the same dialog box that appears when you choose File: **Save** for the first time. Photoshop automatically inserts the current file name in the Document Name field.

Mistakes to Avoid

Creating unnecessary copies of an image. Avoid this for two reasons. First, it leads to confusion about which image to finally use. Second, Photoshop images can be very large (a single 9- by 12-inch CMYK scan can exceed 40 MB). Multiple copies can devour hard drive space, wasting the scratch disk space Photoshop uses to facilitate its commands.

Accidentally overwriting the original image. If you intend to create a separate file, you must change the name. Leaving the name unchanged and saving it to the same location as the original image overwrites the original with the new copy, just as if you'd chosen File: **Save**.

Saving a new copy to the wrong place. If you assume that Photoshop automatically places the new copy in the right place, it may wind up in the Photoshop application folder, on the Desktop, a previous job folder, or any other location on your hard drive.

Issues to Consider

Duplicate the image to create a temporary copy. You can also create a copy of the current image by choosing Image: **Duplicate**. This way, both the original image and its copy remain open at the same time. Although the Duplicate Image dialog box allows you to enter a new file name, be aware that the image that initially appears is unsaved. Use this command when you need to compare and contrast two editing approaches, or when you want to test a series of commands before applying them permanently.

The Save As Dialog Box

A. Name

Enter the desired file name in this field. When you first open the dialog box, the name is highlighted, enabling you to start typing immediately. If you've set Photoshop to add a file extension to the name, only the characters of the name are highlighted—you can start typing without replacing the extension.

If you accidentally delete the extension, don't enter it manually unless you're sure of the letters. Otherwise, choose a different file format, the choose the desired format again. The extension resets. (If you do enter the extension by hand, don't forget the period between it and the file name.)

B. Format

Set the desired file format in this pop-up menu. (For more information, see *8.8 Supported File Formats.*)

C. As a Copy

This box enables you to save a copy of an image. When checked, the saved file doesn't opened—it's placed on the hard drive, separate from the current image. By default, the word "copy" is added to the end of the current file name. When unchecked, you only save or update the open image. (Note that this box may be turned on automatically, depending on the remaining settings in the Save As dialog box.)

D. Alpha Channels

This option is only available when an image contains one or more alpha channels. When checked, you can save them into the following file formats: Photoshop, PDF, PICT, PICT Resource, TIFF, and DCS 2.0. To save the file without the channels, uncheck the box, which creates a copy of the image. (For more information, see *23.1, Channels Palette Overview*.)

E. Layers

This option is only available when an image contains multiple layers. When checked, you can save them in the following file formats: Photoshop, PDF, and TIFF (with the Advanced TIFF option enabled). When unchecked, you're able to save a flattened copy of the image.

F. Annotations

This option is only available when the image contains a note or audio annotation. When checked, the annotations are included in the file; when unchecked, they're stripped out.

G. Spot Colors

This option is only available when an image contains one or more spot channels. When checked, you're able to save the image as a Photoshop, PDF, TIFF or DCS 2.0 file (however, remember that DCS 2.0 is the only file format that can successfully output spot channels). When unchecked, the saved file discards the spot channels, without merging them.

H. Use Proof Setup

This option enables you to embed the profile currently established in the View: **Proof Setup** submenu. When you save the image, its colors are converted to the space defined by the profile. This approach can be useful when saving a document for the sole purpose of sending it to a specific output device. (You can also convert an image's color space using Image: Mode: **Convert to Profile**.)

This option is only available for the following file formats: PDF, Photoshop EPS, DCS 1.0, and DCS 2.0.

I. Embed Color Profile

Check this box to embed the current RGB working space into an image. This option is available for the following file formats: Photoshop, PDF, JPEG, TIFF, Photoshop EPD, DCS 1.0, DCS 2.0, and PICT.

Related Topics

8.8
_____

Supported File Formats

Unless an image is saved in the right file format, it can't be used. The one you ultimately choose depends on the medium you're working in and the type of image you've generated. Although Photoshop supports many different formats, in each of the major graphics categories—print, multimedia, and the Web—you will typically use only two:

- Print graphics exist as either TIFF or EPS.

- Web graphics exist as either GIF or JPEG (although PNG is slowly being used more frequently).

- Multimedia graphics exist as either PICT (Mac) or BMP (Windows).

The following section lists all the file formats that appear in the Save As dialog box.

Photoshop

This option is Photoshop 6's native format; images saved this way are recognized only by Photoshop 5 or 6. It's the only format that saves every feature the program offers, such as multiple layers. Because you can save and re-open images much more quickly, use this format until editing is complete. Then flatten your layers, double-check your color mode, and save it into its appropriate file format. Unless you flatten the image, this is the only option available under the File Format pop-up.

Photoshop 2.0

This file format can be recognized by early versions of Photoshop, but cannot contain separate layers. Its safe to assume that nearly all Photoshop users have upgraded to version 3.0 or higher, so you can ignore it.

BMP

Short for Windows *Bitmap*, this format is compatible with Microsoft Paint, the bitmap editing program included with Windows 95. Use this format only for the following:

- When handing images over to someone who will continue editing using Paint or another Windows-based program.

- If the images will be used in onscreen presentations using Windows-based software.

CompuServe GIF

Because GIFs take up very little disk space—which means shorter download times—they've become the standard for onscreen web graphics. One of the reasons for their smaller size is their reduced color palette (always fewer than 256 colors), which you achieve by converting an image to Image: Mode: **Indexed Color**. The other is its compression scheme. Like TIFF files, GIFs use LZW compression, which results in no loss of image information. GIFs come in two forms:

- **GIF87a,** the default setting when you select CompuServe GIF from the File: **Save** dialog box.

- **GIF89a,** which supports transparent pixels. (For more information, see *8.9, File: Save for Web.*)

Issues to Consider

GIFs are most appropriate for solid colors. Because GIFs have such a limited color palette, they are best suited for images with areas of solid color, such as boxes, buttons, cartoon characters, corporate logos, and the like. For more continuous-tone images, use JPEG.

Only an image with 256 colors or less can be saved as a GIF. So unless it exists in Bitmap, Grayscale, or Indexed Color mode, the CompuServe GIF file format is not available in the File: **Save As** dialog box. Similarly, if you export an image to the GIF format using File: **Save for Web,** the range of colors is automatically reduced.

Related Topics
8.9   File: *Save for Web*
10.9 Image: Mode: ***Indexed Color***

Photoshop EPS

Along with TIFF, this is the only format intended for print-related images. Note how it's called "Photoshop EPS," instead of simply "EPS". This was done to eliminate confusion with graphics from vector-based illustration programs like Illustrator or FreeHand. That artwork is comprised of PostScript-defined shapes, can be infinitely scaled, and has no specific resolution until it's either output or imported into Photoshop. Images edited in Photoshop, even if they originated as vectors, are always subject to pixel-based scaling and resolution requirements.

The only time you need to save an image as an EPS file is when PostScript-based commands or behaviors are being built into it. The most common examples include clipping paths, duotones, custom screen angles, and transfer curves.

Mistakes to Avoid

Attempting to re-color or trap EPS images in a page layout program. Images in this file format cannot be edited in another program, unlike TIFF files.

Issues to Consider

If an EPS image is going to be used on a UNIX or Windows-based platform, set the encoding to ASCII. If this is the case, do not select a TIFF preview—these are binary, and will prevent the image from being recognized by the platform.

Saving a bitmap image as an EPS. When you save an image in Bitmap mode as an EPS, an option for Transparent Whites appears in the EPS Options dialog box. When checked, the white pixels remain transparent when imported into a layout document, behaving the same as TIFF line art. When unchecked, the pixels remain white, knocking out any underlying page information.

The EPS Options Dialog Box

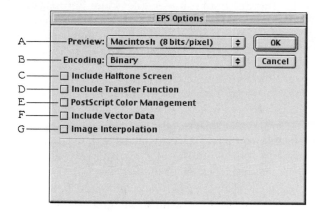

A. **Preview**

An EPS image is actually made up of two parts: The high-resolution information that's downloaded to an output device, and a low-resolution preview. When you import an EPS image into a layout document, you actually import the preview. This is why EPS images import so much more quickly than equally-sized TIFFs, which force a preview to be generated on-the-fly by the software importing them. Mac users should select "Macintosh (8 bits/pixel)," which adds a 256-color PICT preview. Windows users should select "TIFF (8 bits/pixel)," which adds a 256-color TIFF preview. Selecting either a lower bit-depth or "None" results in a preview that's difficult at best to see on screen, while saving only nominal disk-space in return.

B. **Encoding**

This option involves how the code representing the image file is written to the disk. All major graphics software supports Binary (the default selection), which results in smaller file sizes, quicker imports, and faster downloading times than ASCII. Anyone still using a PostScript Level 1 output device may have better luck using ASCII encoding, but those printers have become scarce indeed. The JPEG compression selections should be avoided at all costs. True, they result in much smaller file sizes, but it always comes at the expense of image quality. Its easy to get away with that on the Web, but hardly ever in print.

C. **Include Halftone Screen**

By clicking the Screen button in the File: **Page Setup** dialog box you can enter custom screen angles and halftone dot shapes. Unless you check this button, you can't override the Printer's Default settings. Any image using Photoshop's predefined set of Duotone Curves must include the halftone screens.

D. **Include Transfer Function**

By clicking the Transfer button under File: **Page Setup**, you can create tone curves that lighten, darken, or add contrast to images on output. Unless you check this button, the output device does not know to apply the curve.

E. **PostScript Color Management**

When this box is checked, a printer is able to convert the image to the device's color space. This way, you're able to convert the space without permanently altering the image data (unlike using the Image: Mode: **Convert to Profile** command). However, do not use this option if you intend to import the image into a color-managed layout—it may conflict with the document's management system.

When working with CMYK images, this option is only possible on a PostScript Level 3 output device. Achieve the same results on a PostScript Level 2 printer by converting the image to Lab Color mode before saving.

F. **Include Vector Data**

Check this box to embed live vector-based information (such as type or filled shapes) into a file. This way, you're able to output the vectors with the same crisp edges as an Illustrator or FreeHand file, even when combined with overlapping pixel-based detail. If the file contains vectors and you uncheck this box, the image is flattened when you save it.

Be aware that if you've used this option, the image is rasterized when you open it again. If you need to preserve the vector data, make sure you save a copy of the image in Photoshop's native format.

G. **Image Interpolation**

This option acknowledges the fact that images are often scaled in a page layout document. Ordinarily, when you increase the size of the image, you simply increase the size of the pixels. When this box is checked, the scaled image is upsampled during output, just as if you used the Image: **Image Size** command in Photoshop. This feature only works when images are sent to a PostScript Level 3 printer.

Related Topics

Filmstrip

Adobe Premier, the industry-standard QuickTime movie editing suite, cannot edit individual movie frames—its commands only control fades, edits, merges, sound synching, and so forth. Filmstrip files consist of a vertical series of movie frames, each one editable using any of Photoshop's tools or commands (except Image: **Image Size** and **Canvas Size**, which renders the file unreadable by Premier). Editing a sequence of frames is known as *rotoscoping.*

JPEG

JPEG (short for Joint Photographic Experts Group, the developers of the format) offers powerful compression for Photoshop images by averaging the color values of groups of adjacent pixels. Because it always comes at the expense of image quality, it should never be used on images destined for print reproduction—artifacting and pixelization invariably occurs. If images are going to be used over the Web, JPEG is perfect. Here, the smaller a file is, the better—even if quality takes a hit. For example, a 3 by 3-inch, 72 ppi RGB image takes up 136K of disk space. Downloading at 1 or 2K per second, the average modem could take over two minutes to retrieve this image. Using JPEG compression, you can reduce the file size to under 20K, allowing it to download in seconds. (For more information, see *8.9, File: Save for Web.*)

Issues to Consider

JPEG images work best for tone-sensitive images like photographs and flesh tones. Images containing solid colors become blocky and pixelized—for these, consider using the GIF file format.

JPEGs are recompressed every time they're saved. Every time you save and close a JPEG image, you eliminate a little more detail. (This doesn't occur when you save the image while the file remains open.) Retain as much quality as possible by saving as little as possible. Preferably, you should save the image as a Photoshop native file, then covert to JPEG when editing is complete.

The JPEG Options Dialog Box

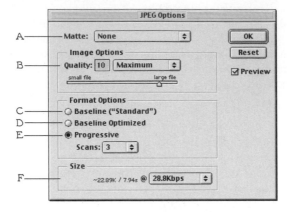

A. Matte

This option enables you build the appearance of transparency into a JPEG image. It only appears when the image contains an element surrounded by transparent pixels. When you choose a color from the pop-up menu, it replaces the image's transparent areas. (Choose the Custom item to define your own value.) When you save the file, the image is flattened.

B. Quality Slider

How small you make a file depends on the amount of image quality you want to retain. This slider allows you to set a Quality value from 0 (lowest quality, smallest size) to 10 (highest quality, largest size). Many users decide upon one preferred value for all of their images—we've found that a value of 4 or 5 avoids most of the visible artifacting while producing a satisfactory file size.

C. Baseline

JPEGs saved under this option appear in your browser one line at a time, from top to bottom.

D. Baseline Optimized

This option uses a different encoding from that used for standard Baseline, which slightly reduces the file size. Baseline JPEGs are used by fewer web designers these days because of the additional time it takes for a viewer to see the entire image.

E. Progressive

These images appear in a series of passes, giving the viewer a rough-and-ready idea of a graphic before it's fully refreshed. Determine the number of passes by selecting a number from the Scans pop-up menu. Higher numbers begin refreshing sooner, but take longer to complete. For consistency, set all graphics used in a website to the same value.

F. Size

This pop-up enables you to choose between different modem speeds, so you can gauge the anticipated download time of the current settings.

PCX

Images in this format are similar to BMP files, but the PCX extension indicates the image is compatible with *PC Paintbrush,* an ancient DOS-based paint program still in widespread use. Older versions of this file format had only one color channel, used for indexed color, Grayscale, or line art images. Current versions support 16 million colors.

Photoshop PDF

Adobe's Portable Document Format allows you to create images or page layouts viewable by anyone using Adobe Acrobat, regardless of their platform. Usually, these files originate as QuarkXPress or PageMaker documents, then are exported to PDF files and distributed over the Internet or CD-ROM. This format is suitable for giving a client a proof for approval when they don't have a copy of Photoshop.

The PDF Options Dialog Box

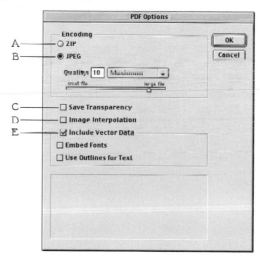

A. ZIP

Choose this item to use ZIP compression, a lossless method more suitable for images that contain areas of solid color.

B. JPEG

Choose this item to use JPEG compression, a lossy method more suitable for continuous tone images. (For more information, see *"JPEG,"* above.)

C. **Save Transparency**

If the image contains transparent areas, check this box to preserve them when you open the file in another application. (If you open the image in Photoshop or ImageReady, transparent areas are retained whether or not you check this box.)

D. **Image Interpolation**

When this box is checked, the image will be resampled when scaled up or down by another application. (For more information, see *"Photoshop EPS,"* above.)

E. **Include Vector Data**

Check this box to embed any existing vector-based shapes into the file. If the image contains a text layer, the following options are available:

Embed Fonts

Check this box to embed the necessary font information into the file. This way, the end-user does not have to load the fonts into his system to display the image properly. Note that this option results in a larger image.

Use Outlines for Text

Check this box to convert all text to vector-based shapes. The font information is not embedded, enabling you to load the image in an application that does not read embedded fonts.

PICT File

Used on the Macintosh platform, the PICT file format is used primarily for onscreen multimedia images. Occasionally, PICTs are used in print because they're more likely to be compatible with lower-end graphics features found in word-processing programs, but they should never be used in a document intended for high-res output or color separation. Common uses for this format include images for interactive applications, CD-ROM images, still images for video, and slide show presentations

Mistakes to Avoid

Attempting to separate a color PICT file. Although you can set the resolution of a PICT to 300 ppi and above, color PICTs can only exist in RGB or Indexed Color mode, neither of which will output successfully. Use TIFF or EPS for any print-related image.

Issues to Consider

PICTs should only exist at 72 ppi. Anything more only slows down the software used to import the image.

The PICT File Options Dialog Box

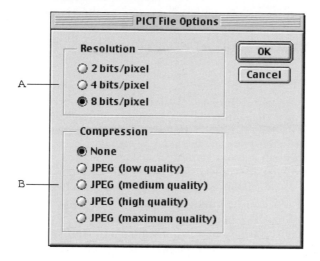

A. Resolution

Select either 16 or 32 bits/pixel, which determines how much color information can be contained in the file. Choosing 16 bits/pixel gives a slightly smaller file with fewer colors. It imports and displays more quickly in your multimedia applications, but banding and posterizing may occur in your blends and continuous tones. 32-bit PICTs not only retain photographic tones, they allow you to save an additional color channel into the file (many video editing suites, for example, require an alpha channel for masking purposes).

B. Compression

If QuickTime is installed on your system, you can save a 32 bit PICT using JPEG compression. Bear in mind that this is QuickTime's proprietary version of JPEG, not Photoshop's. The quality of compression is a little worse, and opening and re-saving these PICTs leads to an image being compressed multiple times, trashing additional image data. If you wish to create a JPEG file, use the JPEG format—otherwise, leave the option alone.

PICT Resource

This format is used by onscreen images accessed by the Macintosh operating system. The most common appearances of PICT Resource files are application splash screens, images saved in the Scrapbook, and system startup screens.

Issues to Consider

Importing PICT Resource images. To import PICT Resources from sources containing more than one, like applications or the Scrapbook file, see File: Import: PICT **Resource**.

Creating a Macintosh startup screen. The startup screen is the image that appears on screen as your system boots. To create your own screen, follow these steps: Create a 72 ppi image that matches your monitor's dimensions (you can determine this value by choosing the Monitors & Sound control panel). Choose File: **Save** to access the Save As dialog box. Name the image "startupscreen," direct the file to your system folder, and click OK. In the PICT Resource Options dialog box, enter "SCRN" in the Name field and click OK. The next time you restart your workstation, the image will display as your system extensions load.

Pixar

If you've watched Disney's computer-animated *Toy Story*, you've seen the type of work created by Pixar. Although they create versions of their 3-D rendering software for the more common graphics platforms, the ultra high-end work you see in the movies is generated on their own proprietary workstations. Even so, Photoshop can open individual frames rendered by Pixar software. RGB and Grayscale images saved in this format can be incorporated into a Pixar rendering.

PNG

Portable Network Graphics (or "ping") files are a rising alternative to CompuServe GIFs for designers of web graphics. So far, they have only limited support from the major browser manufacturers. Stronger support is expected soon, since PNG compatibility can be built into a software package without its developers paying royalties—unlike GIFs. (For more information, see *8.9, File: Save for Web.*)

Issues to Consider

Anticipating PNG's image quality. As far as image size and quality go, PNG falls somewhere between JPEG (which are smaller due to compression) and GIF (which have a smaller color palette). This makes them a better choice for images that are smaller in width and height but contain important details and tones, like highly stylized buttons or online advertisements.

PNG files can contain semi-transparency. PNG files can contain an additional masking channel that allows the image to be part opaque, part transparent. By manipulating the gray levels of the mask, you create semi-transparent pixels in your web graphics.

The PNG Options Dialog Box

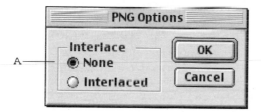

A. Interlace

Although the choices are between None and Interlaced, it's actually a choice between On and Off. Select Interlaced if you want the graphic to refresh on screen in a series of passes.

Raw

A relatively rare file format, raw images exist only as strings of code. There are no colors, no channels, no pixels, nothing you've learned to recognize as an image component. Typically, information like this is downloaded from mainframe computers—a platform not known for its high-end imaging capabilities—or older proprietary systems with image types Photoshop doesn't recognize.

The Raw Options Dialog Box (When Saving)

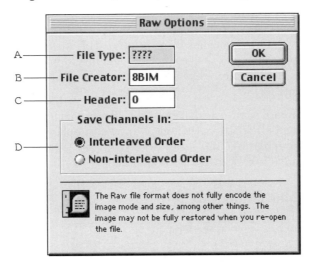

A. File Type

Presumably, you enter the four-letter image code—PICT or TIFF, for example—in this box. Only Macs pay any attention to it, though, so ignore it if the file is headed for another platform.

B. File Creator

This value is used to specify which application created the image. It defaults to "8BIM", Photoshop's four-digit code. Leaving or changing the code has little if any impact on the file.

C. Header

The header is the data written at the start of the code that the computer uses to identify the image type and contents. This box is asking for the byte-size of the header. Setting a value higher than 0 (the default) means you would have to use third-party code editing software to actually create the header.

D. Save Channels In

Interleaving has to do with how the color data is stored in the file. Remember, every single pixel in the image is defined by a length of code. Since each pixel in an RGB file, for example, has three different values (red, green, and blue), there are two different ways the file can communicate them to a computer. Choosing Non-Interleaved means that all the red pixels are listed first, then all the green, then all the blue. Choosing Interleaved means that all three RGB values for the first pixel are listed, then all three for the second pixel, and so on. Interleaved graphics should open more quickly, but the platform receiving them must be able to recognize the command.

The Raw Options Dialog Box (When Opening)

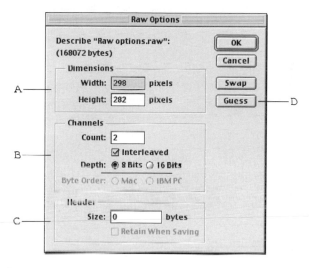

A. Dimensions

If the width and height of the image has been provided, enter them here. The Swap button on the right of the dialog box switches these values back and forth.

B. Channels

The Count value alerts Photoshop to the number of channels an image is supposed to contain—Grayscale images have one, RGB images have three, CMYK images have four. To know if you should check Interleaving (described above), you must determine whether the image information was originally saved in that form. Depth refers to the number of bits contained in each color channel. The vast majority of graphics contain 8 bits per channel, but graphics from more obscure platforms may contain 16. If this option is chosen, you must select Mac or PC to determine the Byte Order.

C. **Header**

Here, enter the byte-size of the file's header (described above), so Photoshop will not attempt to open that portion of the data as an image.

D. **Guess**

If you lack any of the specs listed above, click the Guess button in the upper left of the Raw Options dialog box. Photoshop takes a half-hearted stab at discerning the necessary information, but it's rarely successful. A better bet is to contact the creators of the file, or at least someone who can read the image on its original platform.

Scitex CT

Many service bureaus and printers use high-end Scitex scanners and work-stations, which provide powerful image acquisition, editing and correcting capabilities. Most often, a Photoshop user sees this file format in the form of a raw scan, ready for adjusting on a color correcting station. The only time to save an image in this format is if it's going to be opened on a Scitex system— and even then, double-check with the system's operator. Scitex systems can read other formats, and operators may prefer to import the image using their own color tables.

Targa

Images saved in this format can be imported and combined with digital video sequences driven by video boards from TrueVision, Media 100, and Radius. These images often contain a chroma-key color (to be masked out and replaced by video, like the big maps behind a TV weatherman), or an additional alpha channel.

TIFF

Along with EPS, TIFF (short for Tagged Image File Format) is the primary file format used for outputting an image to paper or film. Unlike Photoshop EPS files, which communicate complex PostScript commands as well as pixels to an output device, TIFFs only handle pixel-based information.

Photoshop 6 has updated its approach to the TIFF format, and offers an expanded set of options. To ignore these options, choose Edit: Preferences: **Saving Files** and uncheck the Enable Advanced TIFF Save box. This way, the same TIFF Options dialog box found in Photoshop 5 appears, enabling you to set the Byte Order and Compression.

Issues to Consider

TIFFs are widely accepted. TIFFs are the most widely used print-oriented format, fully compatible with Macs and PCs alike.

TIFFs can be recolored. Although line art and grayscale TIFFs import as black-and-white images into your page layout programs, you can apply a different color to them in your page layouts. EPS files cannot be recolored.

TIFFs can be trapped. Some trapping commands, such as those found in QuarkXPress or Adobe TrapWise, can affect the contents of an imported TIFF. EPS files are closed to these commands, and must be trapped using the original software.

TIFFs use LZW Compression. Unlike JPEG, LZW reduces file size without destroying image data. It does this by abbreviating lengths of repetitive pixel values. If 200 consecutive pixels share the same color, an uncompressed file lists all 200 of those values. LZW lists the value of the first pixel, then inserts a character essentially stating, "the next 199 pixels are the same color as this one." With this in mind, LZW works better on images containing fewer colors. Line art, only consisting of two colors, compresses to as low as 10% of the original file size. Grayscale images have more tonal variation, but are limited to 256 possible shades. With less potential for repetitive values, files will typically reduce to 40–50% of original size. Full color images hardly reduce at all, since the chances of repetitive values are remote.

TIFFs support multiple layers. When saving a TIFF, you can check the Layers option in the Save As dialog box, enabling you to save multiple layers in the file. Some users mistakenly assume that this is a great way to include transparent areas in an image. If they create a complex silhouette, they think, they can place it in a layout, and the underlying page elements will peek through the fine details. However, when you use this option, Photoshop builds a flattened version of the image into the file, and this is what your layout program imports and outputs. When you re-open the image in Photoshop, the flattened version is ignored, enabling you to edit the layers.

The TIFF Options Dialog Box (Expanded)

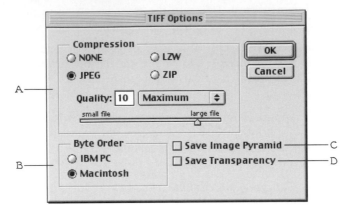

A. Compression

Set the desired compression method from the following options:

None

> When you choose this item, no compression is applied to the new TIFF, resulting in the largest file size (but the highest level of compatibility).

LZW

> Choose this item to reduce the file size using LZW compression, the method recognized by the vast majority of graphics applications.

JPEG

> Choose this option to use JPEG compression. Be aware that while this method produces a smaller file than LZW—especially when applied to color images—it does so at the expense of image detail. (For more information, see *"JPEG,"* above.)

ZIP

> Choose this option to use ZIP compression, the same method used by PDF files. It produces roughly the same size and level of quality as LZW, but is compatible with far fewer applications. (For more information, see *"Photoshop PDF,"* above.)

B. Byte Order

These enable you to specify the image's target platform, to accommodate the slightly different system requirements. (Note that on either platform, Photoshop can read both variants.)

C. Save Image Pyramid

Choose this option to create a *tiled* image, where the file consists of an internal stack of images, all of different resolutions. It's referred to as a "pyramid," because the high resolution version acts as the foundation, and the image variations decrease in resolution all the way to the top. This way, if another application needs to perform a simple command, it bases the effect on the data near the top of the pyramid; when it needs to apply an intensive, detail-oriented command, it references a variation toward the bottom. The idea is that commands are executed more efficiently. In reality, very few graphics applications recognize tiled images, so you should ignore this option unless you're sure you can put it to work.

D. **Save Transparency**

If the image contains transparent areas, check this box to preserve them when you open the file in another application. (If you open the image in Photoshop or ImageReady, transparent areas are retained whether or not you check this box.)

Photoshop DCS 1.0

When saving a CMYK image, you can create a Desktop Color Separation file. Originally introduced by Quark, this process splits the image into five separate files: the low-res preview, plus the individual channels containing the cyan, magenta, yellow, and black information. Typically, this process is used by service bureaus or print shops who perform high-end scanning services for their clients. Rather than transport potentially enormous files back to their page layouts, clients take the previews, which are only about 10% of the original file size. These files are imported, scaled, and rotated as FPO (For Position Only) graphics, then the layout files are taken back to the service bureau for processing. The imported previews are re-linked to the high-res files just prior to output. If a designer has scanning done in-house, this feature is probably not required. In fact, ignore this option unless you have a good reason for using it. Without the high-res parts, the preview cannot be edited in Photoshop, and if any one of the five image files are accidentally deleted, the graphic is worthless.

Issues to Consider

The separate files representing the channels must be kept together. If you lose the preview file of the five DCS components, you cannot import or output the remaining four color channels. However, you can reopen these files in Photoshop, merge them into a single CMYK image (using the Merge Channels command of the Channels Palette submenu), and resave the file as desired. This technique will not work if any of the non-preview files are lost.

The DCS 1.0 Format Dialog Box

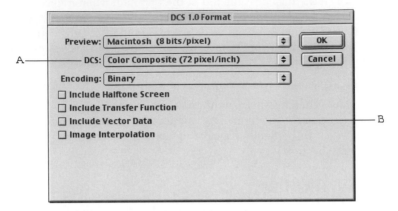

A. DCS

The items in this pop-up determine the type of preview file included with the color components.

No PostScript Preview

When selected, this option results in no additional PostScript preview. A smaller fifth file is produced that can be imported into a layout document, but it's only suitable when outputting the image directly to film. If you intend to proof the image on a laser printer or color device, select another option.

Grayscale Composite (72 pixel/inch)

This option results in a 72 ppi preview, suitable for laser output.

Color Composite (72 pixel/inch)

This option results in a 72 ppi full color preview. It's considerably larger than the other two options, but allows for better proofing before final output.

B. Remaining Items

The remaining options are identical to the items found in the EPS Options dialog box. (For more information, see *"Photoshop EPS,"* above.)

Related Topics

8.8   *Supported File Formats (EPS and DCS 2.0)*

Photoshop DCS 2.0

This file format differs from DCS 1.0 in three ways:

- It supports files in Bitmap and Grayscale mode, as well as CMYK. Additionally, it will support Duotone images, if the file is converted to Multichannel mode before saving.

- It's the only file format that supports spot channels produced using the New Spot Channel command in the Channels Palette.

- You have the option of saving the image as a single-file DCS, or as many component files as the image requires.

If your image does not meet any of the above criteria, you don't require this file format.

The DCS 2.0 Format Dialog Box

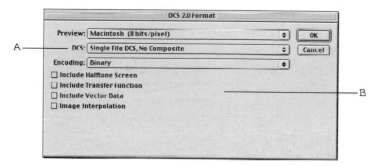

A. DCS

The items in this pop-up determine the type of preview file included with the color components.

Single File DCS, No Composite
> This option results in a single file, with no PostScript composite included.

Multiple File DCS, No Composite
> This option results in a series of component files, with no PostScript component included.

Single File with Grayscale Composite (72 pixel/inch)
> This option results in a single file, with a 72 ppi Grayscale composite included.

Multiple File with Grayscale Composite (72 pixel/inch)
> This option results in a series of component files, with a 72 ppi Grayscale composite included.

Single File with Color Composite (72 pixel/inch)
> This option results in a single file, with a 72 ppi full color composite included.

Multiple File with Color Composite (72 pixel/inch)
> This option results in a series of component files, with a 72 ppi full color composite included.

B. **Remaining Options**

The remaining options are identical to the items found in the EPS Options dialog box. (For more information, see *"Photoshop EPS,"* above.)

Related Topics

8.8   *Supported File Formats (Photoshop EPS and DCS 1.0)*

8.9

File: Save for Web

When creating an image for the Web, this command enables you to preview the effect of multiple compression settings and file format options. This way, you can determine the appropriate combination of image quality and file size. For the best results, choose this command when an image is in RGB mode.

Issues to Consider

This command exports a copy of the current image. Although this item is listed as a Save command, it actually exports a copy of the image, based on the established settings. The original image remains open, and is not affected by the command. Using this command, you can continue editing and exporting multiple versions of the same image at different settings, without over-compressing the original detail.

Editing slices. The Save for Web command enables you to save an image based on multiple slices (as produced by the Slice tool). When you export the image, it splits into a series of smaller files; The HTML code required to reassemble the image in a web browser is saved with the components. (For more information, see *"Slice Select Tool,"* below.)

Don't be intimidated by the glut of features. The Save for Web command is practically a stand-alone application, and brims with unlabeled buttons, arcane language, hidden settings, and buried dialog boxes. Its interface is awkward at best; for the user who simply wants to generate smaller web graphics, it can be a nightmare. However, the Save for Web command is more efficient than saving an image directly into the desired file format. Once you determine the settings that work best for your particular images, you'll quickly realize that you can ignore most of the features in the dialog box.

The Save for Web Dialog Box

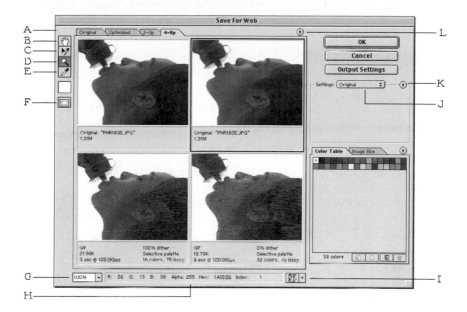

A. View Tabs

These tabs control the preview images that display in the Save for Web dialog box:

Original

Choose this option to display only the original image, with no applied compression.

Optimized

This option displays a single compressed version of the image, based on the current settings of the dialog box.

2-up

This option displays the original image, plus an optimized version (based on the current settings in the dialog box). As you manipulate the settings, the optimized version changes to reflect the new values. This way, you can compare the compressed image to the original.

4-up

This option displays the original image, plus three compressed versions. One is based on the current settings, and the other two are automatically given settings that further reduce the quality and file size. This way, you can pinpoint the settings that give you the best balance between size and quality, and still compare them to the original.

Click a preview to specify the settings you want to apply when you click OK.

B. **Hand Tool**

Use this tool to scroll the images within the preview frames. When you drag one preview, any others move as well. This way, you can continue to compare the same image areas.

C. **Slice Select Tool**

When the current image contains multiple slices, this tool enables you to select one or more of them by clicking or Shift-clicking. You can't change the size or position of the slices, but you're able to apply different compression settings to each one. Remember that a sliced image ultimately exists as a series of different files; therefore, each one can receive different settings, and can even exist in a different file format. For example, you can draw a slice around an important image area, then apply settings to it that retain the most detail. You can set the remaining slices to a much lower compression setting, producing an image that takes much less time to display on screen. (For more information, see *1.13 Slice Select Tool*.)

Double-click a slice to access the Slice options dialog box. For the most part, it's the same as the one accessed by the standard Slice Select tool. However, when you access it from the Save for Web dialog box, two additional options are available:

– **Linked.** This icon indicates that the selected slice is linked to another in the image. When present, the optimization settings you apply in the Save for Web dialog box are automatically applied to any linked item. (You can't manually link slices in Photoshop—you have to switch to ImageReady to do that. However, filler slices are automatically linked. To unlink the current slice, double-click the icon.)

– **Background.** If the image currently contains transparent pixels, you can set this option to replace them with a particular color value. To retain the transparency value, leave this item set to None.

D. **Zoom Tool**

Use this tool to enlarge or reduce the images in the preview frames. When you click one preview with the Zoom tool, the others respond in kind. This enables you to continue comparing the same image areas.

E. **Eyedropper Tool**

Use this tool to sample color values from the image preview. The targeted value appears in the color swatch, located directly beneath the Eyedropper tool.

F. **Toggle Slices Visibility**

When an image contains multiple slices, click this button to display or hide them in the preview frames.

G. Zoom Level

This option enables you to choose a predefined zoom percentage from the available pop-up. To zoom to a particular percentage, manually enter the desired value in the field.

H. Color Readouts

The Info palette does not function when the Save for Web dialog box is open. However, these items display the current RGB and hexadecimal values of the preview color currently underneath the cursor.

I. Preview In

This option enables you to preview the current image in the web browser of your choice. When you click this button, your operating system launches the designated browser and opens the image in a new window.

To set a different browser, choose an item in the Select Browser menu, to the button's immediate right. To add a new browser to the list, choose Other from the menu, then direct Photoshop to the desired program.

J. Settings

This pop-up menu displays a list of 12 predefined settings for creating GIF, JPEG, or PNG images. You're not committed to using these settings; however, many people use them as a starting point by choosing an option then fine-tuning the values. It's also possible to add your own settings to list (for more information, see *"Optimize Menu,"* below.)

K. Optimize Menu

This flyout menu contains the following items.

Save Settings

Choose this command to save the current settings into a separate file, stored in Photoshop's Optimized Settings folder. The settings are then available as an item in the Settings pop-up menu.

Delete Settings

Choose this command to delete the item currently established in the Settings pop-up menu.

Optimize to File Size

Choose this command to access the Optimize to File Size dialog box, which enables you to compress a web graphic to a specific file size. From there, you can fine-tune the level of quality by tweaking the remaining settings.

In the dialog box, you can tell the command to use the current Save for Web settings, or you can let it choose GIF or JPEG on-the-fly, based on which option produces the best results. Also, if the image contains multiple slices, you can tell the command to apply the size limitation to the currently selected slice, to each image slice, or to the total size of all slices combined.

Repopulate Views

Choose this command to draw new image previews, based on the settings of the currently selected frame. When the dialog box is set to 4-up, the new previews consist of the following: The original, the preview that was selected when you chose the Repopulate Views command, and two previews that result in smaller file sizes.

L. **Preview Menu**

The items in this flyout menu enable you to affect the display of the preview images.

Browser Dither

Choose this option to simulate how a web graphic will display on an 8-bit color monitor, the type most widely in use around the world. This way, you can anticipate the amount of dithering that will result from the reduced number of colors.

Color Spaces

These options enable you to evaluate the appearance of an image under the influence of a different color space. Choose Uncompensated Color to view the image as it would display in a browser on your particular monitor. Choose Standard Windows Color to simulate the appearance of a typical PC monitor. Choose Standard Macintosh Color to simulate the appearance of a typical Macintosh monitor. Choose Use Document Color Profile to display the preview in the current RGB working space. (For more information, see *14.5, View: Proof Setup.*)

Download Times

These options determine the download time listed at the bottom of each preview.

GIF Optimization Controls

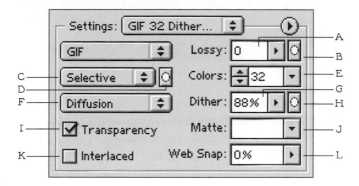

The following settings are available when you choose GIF in the Settings pop-up menu. (Many of the options also appear in the Image: Mode: **Indexed Color** dialog box.)

A. **Lossy**

This slider determines how much detail is retained in a GIF image. Low values retain more detail, resulting in higher file sizes; higher values reduce the level of detail, resulting in a lower file size.

B. **Use a Channel to Modify Lossy Setting**

This option enables you to protect part of a GIF from excessive compression. To use this feature, you must select the area and create an alpha channel before opening the Save for Web dialog box. (For more information, see *25.5 Save Selection as Channel.*)

Click this button to access the Modify Lossiness Setting dialog box. In the Channel pop-up, set the desired alpha channel. By manipulating the Min and Max sliders, you're able to independently control the amount of compression applied to the masked and unmasked areas.

The starting position of the sliders is based on the current Lossy setting. For example, if the Lossy slider is set to 30, the Min and Max sliders default to 30 and 100, respectively. This means that the area protected by the alpha channel receives the least amount of compression (30), and the unprotected area receives the most (100). If you move the Max slider down to 60, you limit the amount of compression applied to the unmasked areas. If you move the Min slider, you change the current Lossy setting, which in turn increases or decreases the amount of compression applied to the masked area.

For the most intuitive results, set the desired Lossy setting, then manipulate the Max slider to produce the desired balance.

C. **Color Reduction Algorithm**

The options in this pop-up menu determine the method used to create a GIF image's color table. Choose from the following categories:

Dynamic Options

The Perceptual, Selective, and Adaptive options use an algorithm to create a table based on the relationship between the image colors and the value entered in the Colors field. The table's values are regenerated any time you edit or re-optimize the image.

Fixed Options

The Web, Mac OS, Windows, Black & White, and Grayscale options are *fixed*, or use a predefined palette of colors. The set of available colors is always constant, but the actual table depends on the colors available in each particular image.

The Custom Option

This option refers to a custom-designed or pre-existing color table. For example, if you modify a color table or optimize an existing GIF, the table is considered Custom.

For full descriptions of the color reduction options, see *"Palette,"* under *10.9, Image: Mode: **Indexed Color**.*)

D. **Use a Channel to Influence Color Reduction**

This option is essentially the same as *"Use a Channel to Modify Lossy Setting,"* described above. Here, the dialog box determines that any colors masked by an alpha channel are reproduced more accurately during the conversion process. (Unlike the other command, this option does not offer sliders for Minimum or Maximum values.)

E. **Colors**

The Color setting establishes the maximum number of colors available to a new color table. This option is the same as the Colors option in the Indexed Color dialog box. (For more information, see *"Colors,"* under *10.9, Image: Mode: **Indexed Color**.*)

F. **Dithering Algorithm**

The dithering method determines how the indexed colors are distributed throughout the image. This option is the same as the Dither pop-up menu in the Indexed Color dialog box. (For more information, see *"Dither,"* under *10.9, Image: Mode: **Indexed Color**.*)

G. **Dither Amount**

Available only when you set Diffusion in the Dither pop-up, this field determines the degree of smoothness between color transitions. Higher values result in smoother transitions, but larger file size; lower values result in harsher transitions, but smaller file size.

H. Use a Channel to Modify Dither Setting

This option is essentially the same as *"Use a Channel to Modify Lossy Setting,"* described above. Here, the dialog box determines that any colors masked by an alpha channel are reproduced more accurately by the dithering process.

I. Transparency

This box enables you retain a transparent area in the converted image. In order to work, an element must already exist on an image layer, already surrounded by transparent pixels, when you choose the Save for Web command. When you check this box the transparent area is built into the exported GIF.

J. Matte

This option enables you to build the appearance of semi-transparency into a GIF. (For a full description, see *"Matte,"* under *10.9, Image: Mode: Indexed Color.*)

K. Interlaced

Check this box to produce an interlaced GIF, or one that gradually refreshes on screen in multiple passes. When unchecked, the GIF loads all at once.

L. Web Snap

This option enables you to gradually convert each image color to its closest equivalent in the browser-safe palette. At low values, only the colors that differ slightly from their closest equivalent are affected; at higher values, more colors are converted.

In the dialog box's color table, any color converted to its closest browser-safe equivalent is tagged with a small white diamond.

JPEG Optimization Controls

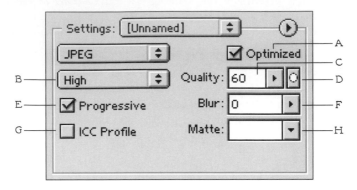

The following settings are available when you choose JPEG in the Settings pop-up menu. Many of the options also appear in the JPEG Options dialog box. (For more information, see *8.8, Supported File Formats.*)

A. **Optimized**

Presumably, this option "optimizes" the compression method applied to a JPEG image. However, it has little if any impact on the overall file size, and it produces an image that may be incompatible with other image-editing programs.

B. **Compression Quality**

The items in this pop-up menu enter preset values in the Quality field. They serve no other purpose than to be a shortcut to a particular point on the Quality slider.

C. **Quality**

How small you make a file depends on the amount of image quality you want to retain. This slider allows you to set a Quality value from 0 (lowest quality, smallest size) to 100 (highest quality, largest size). Many users decide upon one preferred value for all of their images—a value of 40 or 50 avoids most of the visible artifacting while producing a satisfactory file size.

D. **Use a Channel to Modify Quality**

This option is essentially the same as *"Use a Channel to Modify Lossy Setting,"* described under *GIF Optimization Controls*, earlier this section. Here, the dialog box determines that the area masked by an alpha channel is reproduced with less compression, resulting in higher detail.

E. **Progressive**

Progressive images appear in a series of passes, giving the viewer a rough-and-ready idea of how a graphic appears before it's fully refreshed. When this box is unchecked, the image is saved as a baseline JPEG, which appear in your browser one line at a time, from top to bottom.

F. **Blur**

This option hinges on the fact that JPEG compression reduces the size of soft transitions more successfully than hard color breaks. In theory, it stands to reason that blurring the image would enable you to reduce the file size without raising the compression setting. In practice, however, raising the blur setting above zero produces little more than a blurry image. Ignore this option and lower the Quality slider, if necessary.

G. ICC **Profile**

When this box is checked, the image's color profile is included in the JPEG file. However, the average browser cannot recognize embedded profiles. Leave this option unchecked and save the addition 3–4K in file size.

H. **Matte**

This option enables you build the *appearance* of transparency into a JPEG image. It only appears when the image contains an element surrounded by transparent pixels. When you choose a color from the pop-up menu, it replaces the image's transparent areas. (Choose the Custom item to define your own value.) When you save the file, the image is flattened.

PNG-8 Optimization Controls

The options that appear when PNG-8 is set in the Settings pop-up menu are also available when optimizing a GIF. (For full descriptions of their purpose, see *GIF Optimization Controls*, earlier this section.)

PNG-8 files can contain up to 256 separate colors. Like GIF, it is appropriate for areas of solid color, and sharp details such as line art or type. A PNG-8 file uses a more advanced compression scheme than GIF, and therefore tends to be 10–30% smaller than a GIF of comparable dimensions. However, browser support for this format is limited.

PNG-24 Optimization Controls

The options that appear when PNG-24 is set in the Settings pop-up menu are also available when optimizing a GIF. (For full descriptions of their purpose, see *GIF Optimization Controls*, earlier this section.)

PNG-24 files support 24-bit color. Like JPEG, they are appropriate for preserving the fine details of a continuous-tone image. Like GIF and PNG-8, it is able to preserve crisp detail, such as line art, logos, or type. PNG-24 also supports *multilevel transparency*, which preserves up to 256 levels of transparency to smoothly blend the edges of an image with the background color. A PNG-24 file uses the same lossless compression method as PNG-8, and therefore tends to be larger than a JPEG of comparable dimensions. Browser support for this format is limited.

Color Table Controls

Only GIF and PNG images contain a color table, which lists every color currently available to the image. For all intents and purposes, this feature is identical to the indexed color palette located in Photoshop's Color Table dialog box. (For more information, see *10.16 Image: Mode: Color Table.*)

The commands in the color table's submenu enable you to sort, select, and otherwise interact with the different values.

Image Size Controls

The Image Size options are essentially a scaled-down version of the Image: **Image Size** command. They perform the same function, but without the increased flexibility. Most users complete their resizing before choosing File: Save for Web. (For more information, see *10.40, Image: Image Size.*)

8.10

File: Revert

This command tells Photoshop to reload the most recently saved version of a file, clearing any edits made since then. Successful reverting requires that you save an image at the stage you want to be able to get back to, such as after color correcting or after creating a series of layers. At the very least, save an image whenever making a change you know you want to keep.

In earlier versions of Photoshop, the success of this command was highly contingent on when and how you saved the last version of the file. Now, File: **Revert** appears as a state in the History palette, enabling you to undo the reversion, or refer to it with the History Brush or Fill command. (For more information, see *20.1, History Palette Overview.*)

8.11

File: Place

This command enables you to import the contents of an EPS graphic. Common scenarios for placing images include the following:

*   **Importing and rasterizing vector-based EPS files.** This command bypasses the Rasterize EPS dialog box and uses the dimensions of the active image.

*   **Importing Photoshop EPS images.** This command will not recognize a Photoshop image in any other file format.

After choosing a graphic in the Place dialog box, a low-res preview appears in a bounding marquee. Scale the graphic by dragging the corner points of the box, rotate it by dragging the cursor outside the box, and position it by dragging the box or using the arrow keys. Double-clicking on the box or pressing the Return key tells Photoshop to permanently apply the artwork. It appears in a new image layer.

Mistakes to Avoid

Failing to account for different color modes. For example, if you place a CMYK file into an RGB image, the CMYK percentages are converted to RGB brightness values. If you later convert the image to CMYK, the resulting colors will differ from the original values.

Over-transforming a placed pixel-based image. Excessive scaling and rotation, particularly when combining graphics of different resolutions, quickly degrades the quality of the added image.

Issues to Consider

Canceling the command. When the bounding box is present, you can cancel the Place command by pressing the Escape key. Immediately after you apply the command, you must choose Edit: **Undo** to reverse the effect.

Related Topics

D.2   *Opening a Vector-Based File*
D.3   *Importing Vector-Based Artwork*
D.4   *Retaining Layers in a Rasterized Illustrator File*

8.12

File: *Import*

The File: **Import** options enable you to access graphics from external sources, such as scanners and digital cameras. You can also acquire images from software formats that Photoshop doesn't immediately recognize, like system resources that contain multiple graphics. The import commands are based on different plug-ins, only a few of which are present when Photoshop is installed. Whenever a third-party input device like a scanner or camera is connected to a workstation, you must install the plug-in that ships with it into the following folder: Adobe Photoshop 6/Plug-ins/Import-Export. Choosing the plug-in from the submenu launches the software interface that allows you to capture or transfer images into an editable form.

8.13

File: Import: *Anti-Aliased* PICT

Use this command only if you use a less-powerful vector-based drawing program, like the ones found in integrated software packages like Microsoft Works, AppleWorks, or certain word processors. Although native files from these programs are not recognizable by Photoshop, their graphics can be saved as PICT files. Simply opening these graphics via File: **Open** gives you a 72-ppi image with the same width and height as the original graphic. By importing it, Photoshop attempts to anti-alias the edges of the shapes, gently blending them into their surrounding pixels.

Issues to Consider

Changing the dimensions of an imported PICT. The PICT opens at 72 ppi, but you can change the size of the resulting image by increasing or decreasing the width and height. Checking Constrain Proportions locks the ratio between the two values. To create a file of higher resolution than 72 ppi, increase the width and height to double or triple the actual size, then increase the resolution under Image: **Image Size** while leaving the Resample Image box unchecked.

At best, this command is reasonably adequate. You get a much higher quality image when placing or opening vector-based artwork existing in true EPS form. If you find yourself importing these types of PICTs often, consider investing in a more powerful software package, like Adobe Illustrator or Macromedia FreeHand.

Related Topics

8.14

File: Import: PDF *Image*

This command enables you to extract one or more images from an existing PDF file. This way, when you only need a particular image, you're not restricted to rasterizing an entire PDF page, then cropping away the unwanted information. (For more information, see *D.6, Opening a PDF File.*)

A navigational window appears when you choose this command, allowing you to target a specific PDF file. Doing so accesses the PDF Image Import dialog box, where you can scroll through the available images until you find the item you need. Click OK to open the image in Photoshop. If desired, click the Import All Images button to open all of the images in the PDF file.

Issues to Consider

The quality of an imported image depends on the original PDF compression settings. Most images in a PDF file are compressed when the file is created. The amount of compression—and therefore the level of quality—is determined by the settings in the program that produces the file. For example, if your copy of Acrobat Distiller is set to produce small PDF files suitable for online distribution, the images are probably reduced to 72 ppi. In a PDF file properly distilled for on-press reproduction, the images may not be reduced in size at all. When you open any PDF image, you can only open the compressed version, whether or not the settings were appropriate for its intended use.

8.15

File: Import: PICT Resource

Using this import command, you can tap into a file (usually an application) containing multiple PICT images. A scrolling dialog box appears, allowing you to browse through the different graphics, select one you want, and import it into an active Photoshop window.

Common uses for this command include the following:

- **Acquiring application-specific graphics.** Images like cursors, splash screens, and icons are often difficult or time-consuming to grab using a screen-capture program. Select File: Import: **PICT Resource**, find the application you desire, and click open. After scrolling through the selections in the PICT Resource dialog box, click Open to access the desired image in Photoshop.

- **Browsing through images saved to the Scrapbook.** Many screen-capture programs like Capture or Snapz save images to the Scrapbook file, and many frequently-used Photoshop images are placed there as well. After taking your screen shots, you can scroll through the PICT Resource dialog box to open images one at a time.

Issues to Consider

Not all applications will contain the images you desire. Some, like Macromedia Director, have over 200. Others, like Adobe PageMaker, have only two.

Adobe Photoshop is the only application that cannot be tapped into with this command. This is to prevent application and system crashes—telling any program to open itself invariably leads to trouble.

8.16

File: Import: TWAIN Acquire

TWAIN is a multi-platform scanner interface. It dates back to 1990, before scanners came bundled with their own interface in the form of a Photoshop plug-in. Back then, a scanner's interface shipped as a kind of stand-alone application (or source module) you'd have to launch, use, and close before being able to edit the scans in Photoshop. The biggest problem was the lack of standardized controls. They looked and acted differently for each scanner, there was seldom a preview window for pre-scanning, and the process itself was non-intuitive. By linking a program like Photoshop to a connected scanner's source module, TWAIN offers users a predictable and more user-friendly interface.

Issues to Consider

The meaning of "TWAIN." TWAIN was developed by Hewlett-Packard and initially promoted by such companies as Aldus, Caere, Logitech, and Kodak. According to legend, TWAIN stands for *Technology Without An Impressive Name*, or *Toolkit Without An Interesting Name*. More realistically, Logitech claimed it was named after the relationship it developed between input devices and applications, and how they were finally able to meet *"in the 'twain."*

8.17

File: Import: TWAIN Select

Use this command to select an active TWAIN device to access from within Photoshop. Only one device can be active at a time, so this command must be chosen whenever you need to focus Photoshop's attention onto a different one. (For more information, see *8.16, File: Import: TWAIN Acquire.*)

8.18

File: Import: Annotations

Choose this command to import any written or audio annotations from a PDF file (it does not recognize other Photoshop images). The Load dialog box opens, enabling you to pinpoint the desired file on your hard drive. Any annotations that it contains are copied into the open image, and placed in the same relative position. You're able to continue editing the annotations using Photoshop tools, if desired.

Related Topics

4.1	*Notes Tool*
4.2	*Audio Annotation Tool*

8.19

File: *Export*

Export information from Photoshop when you need to access a specific image feature in a different application. Any export command is based on different Plug-ins, only a few of which are present when Photoshop is installed. Whenever certain third-party products are installed in a workstation, you must install the plug-in that ships with it into the Plug-ins' Import/Export folder. Choosing the plug-in from the submenu enables Photoshop to create the appropriate files.

8.20

File: Export: *Paths to Illustrator*

Use this command to export items from the Paths palette into an Adobe Illustrator file. From there, you can open the files in Illustrator or FreeHand and continue editing. Later, if desired, the stroked and filled shapes can be rasterized using File: **Open** or imported into a Photoshop image using File: **Place**.

When you choose this command, a navigation window appears, requesting that you place the new file somewhere on your hard drive. In the Write pop-up menu, choose the item you want written into the file: You can choose a single path, all paths, or just the document bounds (which exports object-oriented crop marks matching the width and height of the image).

Mistakes to Avoid

Deleting the crop marks that are automatically placed in the Illustrator file. The crops reflect the dimensions of the original Photoshop image, and this is what maintains the path's original position. If you don't change the crops or move the path, you can place the new graphic back in its original position.

Issues to Consider

Paths exported from Photoshop have no stroke or fill color. When opened in Illustrator or FreeHand, they're not visible unless the Preview mode is turned off. In Illustrator, choose (Command)[Control]-E to switch to Artwork mode. In FreeHand, choose (Command)[Control]-K to switch to Keyline mode. After color has been applied, turn Preview back on to continue editing the shapes in color.

If you use Illustrator, you can copy Photoshop paths and paste them directly into an Illustrator document. If you use FreeHand, you cannot paste Photoshop paths, but you can open the Illustrator file containing the exported path.

Related Topics

3.4   *Pen Tool*
8.11   *File:* ***Place***
9.8   *Edit:* ***Paste***
24.1   *Paths Palette Overview*

8.21

File: *Manage Workflow*

The Manage Workflow commands make possible a collaborative online imaging environment, in which multiple users are able to download, edit, and upload the same images without the risk of accidentally overwriting or losing the files. This workflow is based on Web Distributed Authoring and Versioning (WebDAV) server technology, now supported by Photoshop 6 and ImageReady 3.

When files (or *assets*) are managed by a WebDAV server, the user experience is as follows:

- Multiple users can download copies of the same asset.

- One user at a time can *check out* an asset, or lock the original file on the server while editing a copy of it in a remote location.

- After making changes to an asset, the user can then upload the changes to the server. This way, other users are able to download the new information, but not make changes to it.

- When finished with an asset, the user *checks it in*, or makes the new version available for downloading and editing.

You must be able to connect to an existing WebDAV server before using this feature. (For additional information, visit *www.webdav.org.*)

8.22

File: *Manage Workflow:* ***Check In***

This command is only available after you've checked out an asset from a WebDAV server, and the file is open in Photoshop or ImageReady. Choose it upload to your changes to the server and release your lock on the file.

8.23

File: Manage Workflow: Undo Check Out

This command enables you to check in an asset without updating changes to the server. The original file is untouched, as if it were never checked out. Use this option when you don't want to save any changes you've made.

8.24

File: Manage Workflow: Upload to Server

Choose this command to update an asset's original file on the server, without releasing your lock on the managed file. Other users can download the file, but they cannot make changes to it until it is checked out.

8.25

File: Manage Workflow: Add to Workflow

Use this command to add a file to a WebDAV server, thereby making it a managed asset. (To add an existing asset to the server under a different name, use the Add to Workflow As option.)

When you choose this command, the Add to Workflow dialog box appears, requesting the URL for the precise location of the server. (You must include the filename in the URL; be sure to include the proper file extension if the asset will be downloaded to a Windows workstation.) To check out the file, activate the Keep This File Checked Out for Editing option.

8.26

File: Manage Workflow: Open from Workflow

You must download a copy of a managed file to your workstation before you're able to view and edit it. This command enables you to place a copy of an asset onto your hard drive. You only need to choose this command once per file; after a copy exists, you can download any changes manually or automatically, depending on the settings in the Workflow Options dialog box.

To download a copy of a managed asset, choose the Open Workflow command. In the Open from Workflow dialog box, enter the full URL of the file (including the filename) and click OK

Issues to Consider

Downloading changes only. To download any changes to an asset from its managed file on the server, open the local file and choose File: Manage Workflow: **Download from Server**.

Setting download options. To access the download option preferences, choose Edit: Preferences: **Workflow Options**. Set one of the following items in the Download from Server pop-up menu:

– **Always.** When you set this item, Photoshop automatically downloads any changes to the asset when you open the local file.

– **Ask.** Here, when you open the local file, a dialog box will appear if any changes have been made to the original asset.

– **Never.** Here, no dialog box appears when changes have been made to the original asset. You must update the local file manually, by choosing File: Manage Workflow: **Open from Workflow**.

8.27

File: *Automate*

The commands in this submenu are applied to multiple images simultaneously, saving you the time and tedium of performing the same task over and over again. While third-party developers may provide their own automated commands, Photoshop ships with the following.

8.28

File: Automate: *Batch*

When you batch process, you automatically edit multiple images, instead of just one. Here, it refers to having Photoshop apply the same Action to a series of images. The images do not have to be opened—they only need to be stored in the same folder.

Batch processing is a valuable time-saver whenever you have a series of images that need to share the same characteristics. Common uses include the following:

• **Color and tonal adjustments.** For example, you can apply a group of Adjustment Layers to a series of color images. Each image may need some fine tuning, but the tedious task of defining the Adjustment Layers would be automated.

• **Importing and editing images from a remote device.** This includes scanners, digital cameras, and any other device that supports Photoshop's technology.

Mistakes to Avoid

Failing to prepare the images of a batch process. (For more information, see *A.24, Preparing to Batch Process*.)

Failing to properly flatten batch images. If you are batch processing a series of images containing multiple layers, be sure to include a Layer: **Flatten Image** in the Action. Otherwise, the Action is only applied to the layer selected when the image was last open.

Issues to Consider

Running an action that requires an open image. The Action you wish to perform may require a specific image to be open—for example, if the Action loads a selection based on a channel in another image. To avoid conflicts, open that image first, then run the Batch command with the Override Action "Open" Commands box checked.

Increasing batch efficiency. Two common methods of increasing the efficiency of a batch process are as follows:

– In the Edit: Preferences: **Image Cache** dialog box, lower the Cache Levels setting to 1. This reduces the number of low-res on screen previews Photoshop holds in memory as each image is opened, processed, and closed.

– In the History Palette's History Options dialog box, turn off the Automatically Create First Snapshot option. This prevents Photoshop from taking a new snapshot when each image is opened.

The Batch command can be included while recording an action. This enables you to apply multiple actions in the same batch. To do this, record a new action, in which you choose the Batch command for each action you wish to apply.

Adding multiple folders to the batch folder. To include multiple folders in a batch process, add aliases (or shortcuts) of each additional folder inside the targeted batch folder.

The Batch Dialog Box

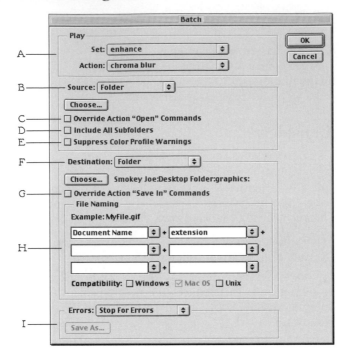

A. Play

These options determine the action applied to a series of images. In the Set pop-up, choose the Actions Palette set that contains the script you wish to run. (If you have created no additional sets, "Default Actions" automatically appears.) In the Actions pop-up, choose the desired script.

B. Source

From this pop-up, select the location of the images to be included in the batch:

Folder

If your images have been placed in a Source folder as described above, choose this option from the Source pop-up menu. When the source is a folder, the Choose button appears. Click this button to target the folder containing your images. In the navigation window that appears, find the right folder, select it, and click the Select Folder button. The name of the folder is listed next to the Choose button.

Import

To import a series of images from a digital camera or similar source, choose this option from the Source pop-up. The From pop-up appears, listing the same options as the File: **Import** submenu.

C. Override Action "Open" Commands

If the Action you wish to apply contains the File: **Open** command, check this box. Since batch processing repeats the same Action every time, leaving this option unchecked tells Photoshop to open the same image over and over. An alert appears claiming that "This document is already open," interrupting the batch process.

D. Include All Subfolders

When this box is checked, the batch command will recognize the contents of any other folders (or their aliases) placed inside the Source folder. When unchecked, those images are ignored.

E. Suppress Color Profile Warnings

This option enables you to ignore any profile conflict alerts that would otherwise appear when the batch images are opened. This is only an issue if your color management policies are set to Ask When Opening. (For more information, see *9.43 Color Settings: **Color Management Policies**.*)

F. Destination

From this pop-up, select the destination of the processed images.

None

This option leaves the images open without saving any changes. Select None if you want to continue editing the images before saving them.

Save and Close

This option saves the images back into the Source folder, overwriting the originals. This option is not available when importing a series of images.

Folder

This option allows you to target a Destination Folder. When you select Folder from the pop-up, the Choose button appears. Click this button to target the folder receiving the processed images. In the navigation window that appears, find the right folder, select it, and click the Select Folder button. The name of the folder is listed next to the Choose button.

G. Override Action "Save In" Commands

If the Action you wish to apply contains File: **Save** or File: **Save As** command, check this box. This tells the Batch command to save the images into the Destination folder, instead of the location defined in the Action.

Checking this box does not override the File Format setting in the Save command, allowing you to specify format changes while batch processing.

H. **File Naming**

This option is only available when the Destination submenu is set to Folder. These fields enable you to specify that all file names produced by the Batch sequence contain certain information, such as dates, sequential numbers, and so forth. To add more than type of information, determine the order in which you want the to appear, and enter the data in the appropriate fields.

I. **Compatibility**

Here, check the box that dovetails with the destination platform of the processed files. The current platform is always activated by default.

J. **Errors**

This pop-up determines how Photoshop handles any processing errors that may occur while running the batch.

Stop for Errors

Here, the process is suspended until you manually confirm the error.

Log Errors to File

Here, the batch runs through completion, and any errors are logged in a separate file. When errors occur, you are notified at the end of the process.

Related Topics

8.29

File: Automate: *Create Droplet*

This command enables you to save the settings of the Batch dialog box into a separate file (called a *droplet*) onto your hard drive. When you drag-and-drop an image onto the droplet icon, Photoshop automatically launches and executes the batch instructions. This offers two benefits: You can apply the same batch settings more than once without choosing File: Automate: **Batch** each time; and, you're able to distribute a droplet to other Photoshop users, enabling them to apply the same settings.

The Create Droplet dialog box is virtually the same as the Batch dialog box. The only difference is the Save Droplet In button, which enables you to specify the destination of the droplet file. (For more information, see *8.28 File: Automate: **Batch**.*)

Issues to Consider

Anticipating the folders referenced by a batch. If the batch that drives a droplet references other folders (for example, if it saves the current image to a particular location), that information may not carry over to another workstation. Therefore, if the droplet is handed over to another user, there are two ways to address this issue: Duplicate the original hierarchy on the new workstation, or leave the save command open-ended in the batch, enabling the user to specify the location of each item.

Droplets require Photoshop to be present. All a batch does is direct the implementation of a program's commands; the program itself must be open and available. Therefore, if you distribute a droplet to other users, they must have a working copy of Photoshop on their workstations.

Related Topics

8.28   File: Automate: **Batch**
21.1   Actions Palette Overview

8.30
File: Automate: *Conditional Mode Change*

This command converts an image from one color mode to another. It is largely intended for use in batch processing. If an action requires an image to be in a specific mode, include this command somewhere at the start of the action. By allowing you to select from a variety of original modes, you can run images of differing color modes through the same batch process, without receiving any mode-specific error messages.

If desired, you can use this command to change the mode of a single open image. However, this offers no advantage over manually choosing a new mode from the Image: **Mode** submenu.

The Conditional Mode Change Dialog Box

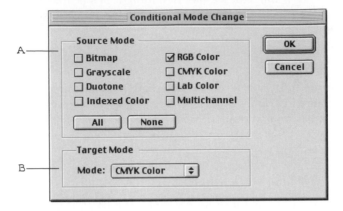

A. Source Mode

Here, specify the color modes that will be recognized by the command. For example, if you intend to convert a series of RGB and CMYK images to Grayscale, check RGB and CMYK here. Any other mode will be ignored by the command. In the same example, if you fail to check RGB, any RGB images in the batch process will not convert to Grayscale.

Click the All button to check every box. Click the None button to uncheck every box. (Although you can uncheck every box, at least one source mode must be selected for the command to have any effect.)

B. Target Mode

In this pop-up, choose the mode to which you want to convert the images.

Related Topics

10.1   Image: **Mode** *Overview*

8.31
_____

File: Automate: ***Contact Sheet II***

Use this command to output an entire folder of images as a series of small thumbnails, grouped together on a single sheet. While not a particularly powerful tool, it does allow you to quickly output large quantities of images in a catalog-style format.

The "contact sheet" is actually a large Photoshop file, created when you exit the command. Each image in the source folder is opened, and its contents are copied, pasted into the contact sheet, scaled, and put into position.

All images in the target folder must be closed before running this command.

The Contact Sheet II Dialog Box

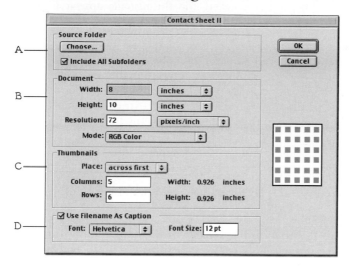

A. **Source Folder**

Click the Choose button to target the folder that contains the images you wish to include on the contact sheet. Check the Include All Subfolders box to force the command to recognize the contents of any folders (or their aliases) contained within.

B. **Document**

The following options establish the dimensions of the contact sheet file:

Width and Height

Similar to using File: **New**, these values determine the width and height of the contact sheet image. More often than not, the image will be on the larger side (6 x 9 inches and above), to accommodate the specified number of thumbnails.

Resolution

Here, specify the resolution of the contact sheet.

Mode

From this pop-up, choose the desired color mode of the contact sheet.

C. **Thumbnails**

The following options determine the placement and orientation of the images.

Place Across First

When this item is checked, the thumbnails appear in alphabetical order from left to right, top to bottom.

Place Down First
> When this item is checked, the thumbnails appear in alphabetical order from top to bottom, left to right.

Columns and Rows (1 to 100)
> Enter the desired number of columns and rows in these fields. Multiply the two values to determine the maximum number of thumbnails the contact sheet can contain. Since Photoshop will not create additional contact sheets for extra thumbnails, you should either make sure these values at least total the number of images in the target folder, or be prepared to divide the images between multiple folders, and run the command more than once.

Width and Height
> These fields display the ultimate width and height of the thumbnails.

D. **Use Filename as Caption**
> Check this box to include the name of each file underneath each printed image. Use the available controls to set the desired typeface and point size of the captions.

8.32

File: Automate: *Fit Image*

This command is essentially the same as using Image: **Image Size**, but with a small twist. Here, you determine a maximum width and height not for the image, but that the image can fit into. For example, assume the width is 640 pixels and the height is 480. Different images will be resized as follows:

- A landscape image (width larger than height) wider than 640 pixels is proportionately scaled down until the width is 640.

- A portrait image (width smaller than height) taller than 480 pixels is scaled down until the height is 480.

- A landscape image less than 640 pixels is scaled up until the width is 640.

- A portrait image shorter than 480 pixels is scaled up until the height is 480.

Issues to Consider

An image resized with this command retains the original resolution. The image is resampled, and the file size increases or decreases, depending on its new dimensions.

The Fit Image Dialog Box

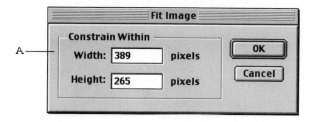

A. **Constrain Within**
Enter the image's maximum width or height in these fields.

Related Topics

*10.40   Image: **Image Size***
C.7   Resampling an Image
C.10   Resizing Without Interpolation

8.33

File: Automate: *Multi-Page PDF to PSD*

Use this command to open all or part of a PDF file as a series of Photoshop images. The width and height of the images are based on the original dimensions of the PDF.

Issues to Consider

Once a PDF page is converted, it exists solely as an image. Text will no longer output with PostScript clarity, all images (regardless of their original color space) will appear in the same mode, and every page element will exist at the same resolution.

This command only converts the PDF files—it does not open the images upon completion. You must open them manually after the command has finished converting all the targeted pages.

The Convert Multi-Page PDF to PSD Dialog Box

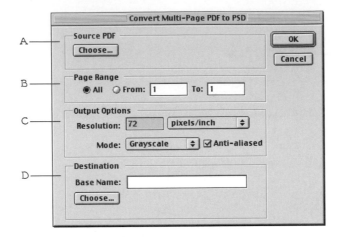

A. **Source PDF**

Click the Choose button to locate the desired PDF file.

B. **Page Range**

To convert every page in the file, click All. To convert a specific range, enter the first page of the range in the From field, and the last page of the range in the To field. To convert non-continuous ranges from the same PDF, you must run this command more than once.

C. **Output Options**

These options determine the remaining dimensions of the converted images:

Resolution

Enter the desired pixel frequency of the converted images in this field.

Mode

Choose the desired color mode from this pop-up.

Anti-aliased

Check this box to anti-alias all colored shape edges.

D. **Destination**

These options affect the location and name of the new images:

Choose

Click this button to target the folder that will contain the new images.

Base Name

By default, the original name of the PDF file appears here. When pages are converted, each new image is titled the base name, followed by the page number. If desired, change the base name before converting.

8.34

File: Automate: Picture Package

This command enables you to place multiple copies of a single image on a page, similar to a sheet of photos provided by a studio.

The Picture Package Dialog Box

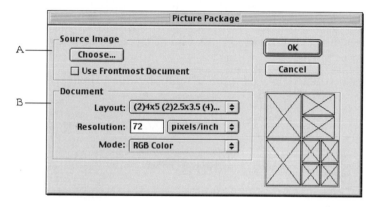

A. **Source Image**

To package an image that is not currently open, click the Choose button and direct Photoshop to the desired file. To package the currently open image, ignore the button and check the Use Frontmost Document box.

B. **Document**

The options in this section determine the form of the packaged file:

Layout

Choose the desired arrangement from this pop-up menu. When you choose an option, a preview of the layout appears on the right of the dialog box.

Resolution

Enter the resolution of the new image in this field. Bear in mind that the image may letter- or tabloid-sized; higher resolutions may result in exceptionally large file sizes.

Mode

Set the desired color mode of the new image in this pop-up menu.

8.35

File: Automate: *Web Photo Gallery*

Use this command to collect a group of images into a *web photo gallery*. A typical gallery consists of a home page that displays the images as a series of thumbnails, which visitors can click to view larger versions. Each page contains links for easy navigation.

This command places the following HTML and JPEG files into in the folder you specify as the destination:

- A gallery home page named "index.htm." Open this file in your web browser to preview the gallery.

- JPEG gallery images, placed inside a subfolder titled "Images."

- HTML pages, placed inside a subfolder titled "Pages."

- JPEG thumbnail images, placed inside a subfolder titled "Thumbnails."

The Web Photo Gallery Dialog Box

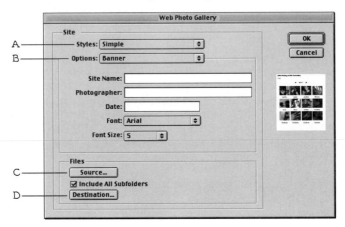

A. Styles

Choose a predefined layout for the web gallery from this pop-up menu. A preview of the current style appears to the right of the dialog box.

B. Options: Banner

The following items are available when you set Banner in the Options pop-up menu:

Site Name

Enter the name of the gallery in this field.

Photographer

Enter the name of the person or organization responsible for the images in this field.

Date

> Enter the date that will appear on each gallery page in this field. By default, Photoshop enters the current date.

Font and Font Size

> Use these options to determine the appearance of the banner type.

Options: Gallery Images *(Settings not shown)*

The following items are available when you set Gallery Images in the Options pop-up menu:

Border Size

> In this field, enter the desired width of the border that will be applied to the gallery images.

Resize Images

> To change the dimensions of the source images, check this box and set the desired width (in pixels).

JPEG Quality

> Use this slider to set the desired level of JPEG compression. (For more information, see *8.8, Supported File Formats.*)

Options: Gallery Thumbnails *(Settings not shown)*

The following items are available when you set Gallery Thumbnails in the Options pop-up menu:

Captions

> These options determines the text that appears underneath each thumbnail. When no boxes are checked, no text appears. When Use Filename is checked, the image's filename appears underneath its thumbnail. When Use File Info Caption is checked, the photo gallery displays the information listed in the image's File: **File Info** (Caption) field.

Font and Font Size

> Use these options to format the thumbnail text.

Size

> This option determines the size of each thumbnail. To establish a new value, either choose a predefined setting from the pop-up menu, or enter your own value (in pixels) in the field.

Columns and Rows

> Use these fields to determine the number and orientation of the images that will appear on the gallery's home page.

Border Size

> This option determines the thickness of the border applied to each thumbnail.

Options: Custom Colors *(Settings not shown)*
The following items are available when you set Custom Colors in the
Options pop-up menu:

Background
>Click this swatch to specify the background color of the gallery.

Banner
>Click this swatch to specify the color of the banner.

Text
>Click this swatch to specify the color of the gallery text.

Link Items
>Click these swatches to specify the color of the gallery's link infor-
>mation.

C. **Source**
>Click this button to direct Photoshop to the web gallery images. In the
>navigation window that appears, select the folder that contains the
>images and click OK.

D. **Destination**
>Click this button to direct Photoshop to the folder that will contain the
>images and HTML files.

8.36
___

File: File Info

This feature enables you to annotate your images with creator information,
category tags, tags, copyright details, even captions and website addresses. It's
never required to use this feature, but many professionals, like photographers
and digital illustrators, routinely create original graphics. These are often sent
to newspapers, ad agencies, stock image distributors, and other large production facilities. If that's the case, then this feature builds necessary
information right into the image, avoiding the need to send handwritten documents or READ ME files.

A common use for this feature would be annotating a file for cataloging software. Many file retrieval applications are used to search for key textual
information built into a file.

Mistakes to Avoid

Adding information not used by the end-receiver. Not all locations receiv-
>ing digital images make it an official practice to refer to this built-in
>information. Be sure to inquire ahead of time, at least until this feature
>becomes more widely used—if it ever does. It's rather ironic; you use this

feature to cut down on extra documentation, but you still have to supply extra documentation to let people know the feature has been used.

Issues to Consider

If you have a series of images that share File Info, you can save each section into a small text file. Choosing Load and opening that file relieves you from having to type the information again. Or, choose Append, find an image that contains the same information, and import it into the section.

The File: Info Panels

Caption

You can insert up to 2,000 characters in the Caption field. If you output an image from Photoshop, this information prints beneath the image if you check the Caption box under File: **Page Setup**. If the image must be handled or treated in a specific way, enter a description under Special Instructions.

Keywords

Here, enter any number of words associated with the image, so search software can seek and find it at the user's command.

Categories

Many publishing organizations use codes to describe different categories of information. If you know a specific code, enter it here, along with any supplemental categories that may apply. If instructed to enter how time-sensitive an image is, choose an option from the Urgency pop-up menu.

Credits

Enter the name of the image creator, his/her title, any acknowledgment to another person or company, and the person or company that owns the image.

Origin

Here, describe the image's history, including file name, creation date, and the location of production.

Copyright & URL

Add the desired copyright notice, and determine if that information displays in browser or catalog software. You can also list a website address that applies to the image, such as one containing additional work by the same artist. Anyone clicking on the Go to URL button will automatically connect to the listed address.

8.37

File: Print Options

The Print Options dialog box enables you to establish a series of printer-level options, such as page position and scale. You cannot save the settings, nor are they built into an image; you have to choose this command every time before you print.

The Print Options Dialog Box

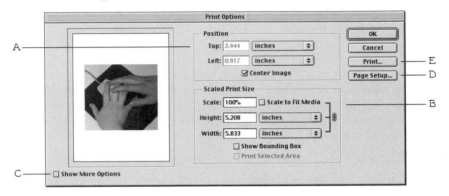

A. **Position**

The Position options determine the placement of the image on the printed page:

Top and Left

These values refer to the page position of the upper-left corner of the image. When both values are set to 0, the image is placed flush in the upper left of the page. Increase the Top value to move the image down; increase the Left value to move the image to the right.

Center image

Check this box to place the image in the center of the page. The Top and Left fields automatically reflect the coordinates.

B. **Scaled Print Size**

These options enable you to change the size of the printed image:

Scale

To scale the printed image at a particular percentage, enter the desired value in this field. When you do, the Width and Height fields automatically reflect the new size.

Scale to Fit Media

Check this box to scale the printed image to the largest dimensions possible, based on the dimensions of the target paper size.

Width and Height

To scale the printed image to a particular width or height, enter the desired value in the appropriate field. When you do, the Scale field automatically reflects the new percentage.

Show Bounding Box

Check this box to add a bounding box to the image in the preview window. This way, you can scale the image manually by dragging one of the box's corner points.

Print Selected Area

This option is only available when the image contains an active selection. When checked, it only prints the selected pixels.

C. **Show More Options**

When you check this box, the Print Options dialog box expands to display an increased number of options. When you set Output in the top left pop-up menu, the settings of the File: **Page Setup** dialog box appear. When you set the pop-up menu to Color Management, the options of the File: **Print** dialog box appear.

D. **Print**

Click this button to access the File: **Print** dialog box. To print without accessing the dialog box, (Option) [Alt]-click the button.

E. **Page Setup**

Click this button to access the File: **Page Setup** dialog box.

8.38

File: Page Setup   *(Command-Shift) [Control-Shift]-P*

In one sense, the Page Setup dialog box is where you fine-tune the output behavior of a file before downloading the information to a printer. More realistically, it is used to build certain customized output commands into a file before it's saved, imported into a page layout program, and output. For reasons discussed under File: **Print**, you'll rarely output images from Photoshop, even though the application has a range of printing commands.

The top half of the Page Setup dialog box contains the same information found in most other applications: paper size, orientation, selected printer, and so forth. The ones that ultimately appear depend on your type of output device and the print driver installed in your operating system.

The remaining options are specific to Photoshop (you may need to access the Adobe Photoshop 6 options from a pop-up menu). Most of these functions only apply to images output directly from the program. The Screens and Transfer buttons, however, contain commands you can build into an image, ready to be applied when printed from another application. Therefore, these are the most commonly used features in the Page Setup dialog box.

The Page Setup Dialog Box

The check boxes only apply to images being output from Photoshop; they're seldom used in print publishing. (Note that the Screen and Transfer buttons are covered separately. For more information, see *8.39, File: Page Setup: Screen* and *8.40, File: Page Setup: Transfer.*)

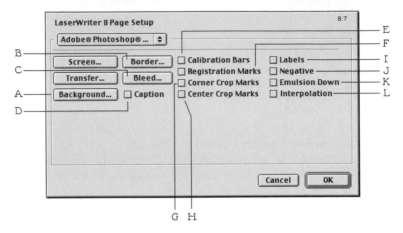

A. **Background**

This button brings up the Color Picker. Here, define a value to be used as a background color when an image is shot to slides using a film recorder. It does not affect the original image—the color is only applied during printing.

B. **Border**

Also intended for film recorders, this command adds a black border to the image at a width you specify.

C. **Bleed**

This command only applies to images being separated directly from Photoshop. It allows image areas to be printed beyond standard page sizes, which are then trimmed, giving the appearance of an image printed all the way to edge of a page. Most offset printing requires at least an eighth of an inch of bleed (9 points), but other press types require a little more. If an image is being printed from a page layout program, don't worry about this command. Create bleeds simply by placing an imported image over a page's boundary.

D. **Caption**

This option prints the caption entered under File: File Info: **Caption** under the image. It's not intended for any design purposes, and the position, typeface, and type size cannot be altered.

E. Calibration Bars

This option adds a strip of 10 gray squares, ranging from 10% black to 100% black in 10% increments. These bars are output alongside any separated image or page layout file, and they are used to test the accuracy of an imagesetter's halftone dot values.

F. Registration Marks

These marks are crosshairs that print in the exact same position on each film separation. Strippers—the prepress professionals responsible for imposing plate separations into useable flats—use these marks to properly align page films. In this case, however, the only time they'd be of any use is if you printed some raw film separations from Photoshop for a color proof (a process where we still prefer to use QuarkXPress or Adobe PageMaker). This option also places two star targets. These are used to measure image resolution while a press plate is burned, and to indicate the integrity of the plate during printing.

G. Corner Crop Marks

Crops mark the page boundaries of a printed image. They tell the person trimming the pages where to cut. This option places crops in each corner of the image.

H. Center Crop Marks

This option places crosshairs marking the center of each side of an image.

I. Labels

Checking this box prints the title of an image above it, in the same typeface as the Captions option.

J. Negative

Check this box to invert the printed image. As with most traditional separations, white pixels are represented by black areas, and black pixels are represented by white (or, if printing to film, clear) areas. If printing the image as a composite to a color printer, this option will invert the color values.

K. Emulsion Down

Emulsion refers to the silver halide emulsion that coats one side of lithographic film. This is the material that is exposed to a finely-focused beam of light. This box determines which direction the image will face upon output: right-reading up or right-reading down. Leaving the box unchecked results in film printing with the emulsion up.

L. Interpolation

This option will anti-alias a low-res graphic by resampling the image to twice the original size and resizing back to 100%. It only works on PostScript Level 2 or 3 printers—and it doesn't even work that well.

Related Topics

8.39

File: Page Setup: Screen

Halftoning is the method used to reproduce the smooth, continuous tones of your images on press. In it, a grid of different sized dots is used to create an illusion. For an easy example, examine a Grayscale image printed on your laser printer: Dark areas are reproduced using large dots; light areas are reproduced using small dots. The varying dot sizes combined with the white spaces between them create what the eye perceives to be tone.

Reproducing full-color images takes this concept one step further. Since it has only four different inks (cyan, magenta, yellow, and black) to reproduce millions of onscreen colors, the printing process overlays four different grids of halftone dots. Process inks are transparent, so whenever dots of different colors are printed on top of each other, they blend to form new colors. Using this method, you can reproduce thousands of different colors—not enough to reproduce all the colors you see on screen, but enough to adequately reproduce most high-quality photographic images.

For print-oriented work, then, the entire purpose of Photoshop is to prepare these tone-rich images for translation into halftone dots. You'll use other tools for adjusting the image's color content. The Screens dialog box is used to adjust the structure and behavior of the halftone dots themselves, independent of the colors they represent.

Before making any changes, understand that in most cases you don't have to touch this dialog box. Photoshop defaults to a setting called Use Printer's Default Screens. If you leave the Screens dialog box untouched, the screen values are based on two different sources: the output device (which contains its own screening information), and the page layout program (which allows to set the linescreen value for the entire document).

Common uses for this command include the following:

- **Setting angles and linescreen for a duotone.** There are two ways to create a duotone, and both require changing the screen angles. You can define your own duotone curves or use the pre-defined curves that Adobe supplies with Photoshop. Either way, consult with the person running the job on press. Many print shops prefer a specific set of duotone angles for their presses. (For more information, see *10.8, Image: Mode:* **Duotone**.)

- **Triggering stochastic screens.** Imagesetters that support stochastic (or randomized) screens need to be told when to discard standard screening for an image. Usually, an obscure linescreen value, like 102 or 108, is used to trigger the new screens. In this case, you don't need to change the screen angles—they will be ignored.

- **Embedding images of a different linescreen.** When a page layout file contains images reproducing at a different frequency than the rest of the document, those values must be entered in the Screens dialog box.

Mistakes to Avoid

Failing to make consistent changes to every color plate. If you make only one change under Screens, you must make sure that the rest of the information is correct. For example, if you enter custom screen angles but do not set the linescreen to the desired value, the image prints with the correct angles at the incorrect frequency (and the default is about 47 lines per inch, meaning the dots will be about twice as large as those found in the average newspaper).

Entering inappropriate screen angles. If the angles for a multicolor image are incorrect, a moiré pattern will result on-press. If there is any question about which angles to use, consult with your printer.

Issues to Consider

When setting custom screen data, always save as an EPS file. Whenever you make any alterations to the Screens dialog box, you have to make sure that your page layout program can understand the changes. The only way to do this is to save the image as an EPS file, and check the Include Halftone Screen box in the EPS Options dialog box.

Changing the default screen settings. To change the default settings, first make the desired changes. Then (Option)[Alt]-click the Save button. Before you click, you'll notice that its title changes to Default. (Option)[Alt]-click the Load button to restore the original factory-installed defaults.

The Screens Dialog Box

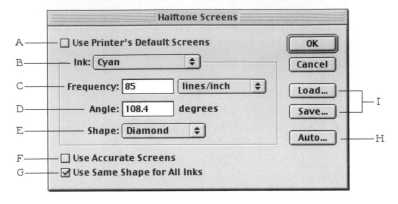

A. Use Printer's Default Screens

When this box is checked, the image is printed using the target output device's built-in screening method. Uncheck this box to access the remaining controls.

B. Ink

Set values one color at a time. If you're changing a Grayscale image, the only option is black. If it's a duotone, choose the first or second color ink. Full-color images let you edit cyan, magenta, yellow, and black separately.

C. Frequency

Enter a linescreen value. Unless you're creating some sort of visible effect, these values remain constant for all color plates. Be careful—setting a value for one color does not automatically set the rest.

D. Angle

Every color must output at a different screen angle. The only time to deviate from the default setting is when you have it on good authority— meaning the person who will be running the job on press—what the preferred screen angles should be. Identical screen angles result in muddy, low-quality reproduction, and incorrect angles result in moiré, a blotchy pattern formed by conflicting halftone grids.

E. Shape

The universal default dot shape is elliptical. The majority of printed materials use these dots because they are predictable, time-tested, and effective. In rare cases, some people use square or diamond-shaped dots, believing the crisper shapes capture more of an image's fine details. Also, many designers use custom screens to create a special effect, such as reproducing an image with line-shaped dots at a low screen value.

F. Use Accurate Screens

This option allows you to use the new screen angle technology available on PostScript Level 2 printers when making color separations. This only applies when outputting images directly from Photoshop.

G. Use Same Shape for All Inks

Checking this button ensures that once a dot shape is changed on one ink, it automatically changes the remaining ink. It does not affect any other values.

H. Auto/Auto Screens

This is a shortcut to use only when you want to change the screen frequency on all color plates at once. In the dialog box, enter the resolution of your output device and your intended linescreen value. Clicking OK applies the screen frequency to all colors.

I. Load and Save

When applying the same changes to multiple images, save the changes made to the first image, and then load them into the remaining ones to automatically apply the same values.

Related Topics

8.40

File: Page Setup: Transfer

The Transfer button refers to *transfer functions*. This feature enables you to create tone curves similar to the ones encountered using the Image: Adjust: **Curves** command. Unlike those curves, a transfer function does not change the color values of an image's pixels—rather, the change is applied by the RIP when the image is output. Common uses include the following:

- **Applying a tonal adjustment without affecting the original image.** Since the curve is applied during output, you can make adjustments without changing the original tones and colors. Often, a curve is created to compensate for dot gain.

- **Using the same corrected image in a variety of reproduction methods.** In the print industry, it usually means inserting a correcting curve that compensates for different presses and paper stocks. For example, an image printed on coated stock at 150 lpi using a finely-tuned digital press will not reproduce identically to the same image printed on a 70-year-old Heidelberg on uncoated paper. If you're aware of the capabilities of the different presses—which requires making contact with the print shop—you can attempt to compensate for the areas that will darken or lighten.

Mistakes to Avoid

Attempting to apply finely detailed adjustments. The Transfer Curve is less precise than the Image: Adjust: **Curves** command, and it is difficult at best to preview the changes. For the most important adjustments (and any color correcting), use the standard Curves dialog box. If necessary, create a duplicate of the original image.

Loading a Transfer curve into the Curves command to preview its effect. In a perfect world, you could save the curves from the Transfer Functions dialog box, load them into the Image: Adjust: **Curves** dialog box, and temporarily apply them to test the results of the transferred curve. This only works on composite curves, which affect all channels equally. Unfortunately, the Curves dialog box often misinterprets curves intended for specific color channels as being meant for the entire image, which doesn't help at all.

Issues to Consider

Transfer curves require research and guidance. It's important to realize that building transfer functions into full-color images requires direct contact with the service bureau outputting the files and the printer reproducing the images. All decisions must be based on profiles of the printing presses in question, and the predicted behavior of different combinations of linescreen, paper stock, and ink densities.

The Transfer Functions Dialog Box

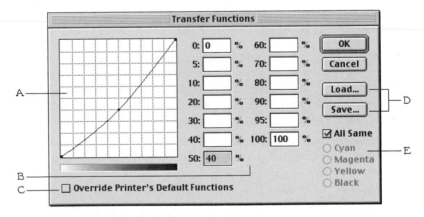

A. The Curve

This panel is a graph that plots pixel values against final output values. Ordinarily, an area of pixels colored 30% black outputs as a 30% screen. The curve, which starts as a diagonal line, changes the relationship between onscreen color and the output value without editing the actual image.

For example, if you want to lighten the midtones of a Grayscale image to compensate for dot gain while leaving the original image untouched, you might consider editing the transfer curve.

B. **Percentages**

Use these boxes to enter your desired changes numerically instead of manually. To duplicate the above example, enter "40" in the field labeled "50". Leave the other fields blank if they are not being specifically changed—entering a number anchors the curve to that value, and the ability to smoothly add changes may be compromised.

C. **Override Printer's Default Functions**

This button forces the image to ignore any transfer functions already built into an output device. When you're making your own transfer curve, it seems like the right thing to do, but bring it to the attention of your service bureau nonetheless. Clicking this button may also override all of their imagesetter's calibration data, leaving the ultimate quality of the image up to fate and chance.

D. **Load and Save**

To apply the same transfer curve to multiple images, save the values of the first and load them into the subsequent files.

E. **Color Buttons**

An option only when editing full-color images, it allows you to create separate curves for each channel. To edit all channels at once, leave the All Colors button checked.

Related Topics

8.41   File: *Print*
10.22   *Image: Adjust:* **Curves**
F.14   *Manually Compensating for Dot Gain*

8.41

File: *Print*   *(Command) [Control]-P*

This command enables you to output a single image to a printer or your hard disk. Most often, this is done to output a calibrated proof to a color device.

Although Photoshop has quite an array of printing options, you'll rarely print final, separated color from the program. Photoshop is rarely used in a vacuum—it's usually part of a larger suite of software, regardless of your industry. For publishers, this includes a page layout program (like Quark or PageMaker), an illustration program (like Illustrator or FreeHand), and other sundry utilities and system extensions.

The settings that appear in the Print dialog box depend on the printer driver currently recognized by your operating system. Outputting to different devices typically results in different printer options.

Mistakes to Avoid

Attempting to mimic a page layout or illustration program. In terms of output, Photoshop has some serious limitations:

- You cannot manually adjust the position of a printed graphic.
- It becomes more difficult to incorporate graphics and text from other programs.
- Unless you establish a series of vector-based shapes, you cannot reproduce crisp, PostScript-defined lines, like artwork created in Illustrator or type set in Quark.

Issues to Consider

Designers occasionally output separations from Photoshop to check the color of an image in progress. If you do this, the screen frequency must be set appropriately in the File: Page Setup: **Screen** dialog box; otherwise, the values default to roughly 47 lpi, far too low to get an accurate representation of the final printed image. Also, the dot shape must be set to the same one you'll ultimately use—different halftone dot shapes can slightly alter your perception of an image's color. For the most predictable results, print test separations from the same program using the same values you'll use to output the final project. This way, you duplicate the final output environment.

The Print Dialog Box

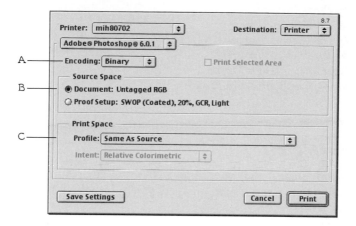

A. Encoding

The options in this pop-up menu determine the form taken by the image information on its way to an output device. It defaults to Binary, the most widely accepted option.

JPEG-encoded files typically consume the least amount of space, but the compression method hinders image quality. Also, many output devices (especially older models) cannot process this types of data. ASCII images are universally accepted, but they can be twice the size of a Binary-encoded image.

B. Source Space

This option determines the conversion settings applied to a non-CMYK image. When set to Document, the image retains the currently embedded profile; no conversion takes place. When set to Proof Setup, the image is converted to the current CMYK working space. (For more information, see *9.40, Color Settings: CMYK Working Space.*)

C. Print Space

This option enables you to convert the image to the output device's color space. This way, you're able to convert the space without permanently altering the image data (unlike using the Image: Mode: **Convert to Profile** command).

When printing an image in CMYK mode, the Proof Setup option only works when printing to a PostScript Level 3 device. When printing to a Level 2 device, convert the image to Lab Color mode before printing.

Related Topics

8.42

File: Quit/Exit   *(Command) [Control]-Q*

This command forces the operating system to discontinue running Photoshop. If any open images are unsaved, you're prompted to Save, Don't Save, or Cancel.

The Edit Menu

9.1

Edit: Undo/Redo
(Command) [Control]-Z

Undo works the same as in any other program: Selecting it reverses, or "undoes," the last applied command. Unlike other graphics programs, Photoshop has only one Undo level, so only the very last command can be reversed. Choosing Undo again reapplies the command. Toggling back and forth between Undo and Redo is the only way to see the before-and-after effects of a command on an entire image.

Issues to Consider

Attempting to undo a command after choosing Select: Deselect. After applying a command or filter to a selection, many users click on screen to make the selection disappear. If you try to undo the command, you can't— the selection path just reappears. Clicking to make a selection disappear is the same as choosing Select: **Deselect**, an impossible command. To temporarily hide a selection from view, turn off the View: Show: **Selection Edges** option.

Partially undoing the entire effect of a command. Use Edit: **Fade** to partially undo the effect of a command. There, you can move a slider to blend an applied command from zero (total Undo) to 100% (no Undo) with the previous image.

Undoing specific areas of an image. To restrict the Undo effect to specific parts of an image, target the previous state in the History palette and paint the areas you want to "undo" with the History Brush tool.

Simulating multiple undo levels. The History palette allows you to mimic the multiple-undo capability found in other applications: Press (Option) [Alt]-Z to activate previous editing states; press (Option-Command) [Alt-Control]-Z to move forward.

Not all commands can be undone. Edit: **Undo** applies to all paint, selection, and palette-based commands. Commands that can't be reversed include the following:

- Commands that create or manipulate information on the hard drive, such as File: **Open**, **Close**, **Save**, **Import**, and **Export**.
- Splitting and merging channels from the Channels palette submenu.
- Deleting the contents of RAM using the Edit: **Purge** commands.

Related Topics

9.2

Edit: Step Forward   (Command-Shift) [Control-Shift]-Z

Choose this command to activate the next state down in the History palette. If the last state is currently highlighted, this command is not available. Most often, this command is chosen after choosing Step Backward. (Note that this command is the same as the Step Forward item in the History palette submenu.)

9.3

Edit: Step Backward   (Option-Command) [Alt-Control]-Z

Choose this command to activate the next state up in the History palette. Repeatedly stepping back to previous states creates the effect of multiple undo levels. (Note that this command is the same as the Step Backward item in the History palette submenu.)

9.4

Edit: *Fade*
(Command-Shift) [Control-Shift] F

Use this command to incrementally reduce the effect of a filter or Image: **Adjust** command. This item must be chosen immediately after applying an effect. If desired, fade the filter using an available blend mode, which affects how the filtered image combines with the unfiltered version.

Issues to Consider

A more efficient way to fade. You can reproduce the effect of the Fade command in a way that gives you much more control over the final results. When applying a filter, duplicate the target layer (if already using multiple layers, choose Layer: **Group with Previous** to group the two items together). Apply the desired filter to the top layer. Fade the effect by reducing the top layer's opacity; set a blend mode to affect the faded values. This way, you're able to change the fade level whenever you want, or even remove the entire effect later. When applying an Image: **Adjust** command, use an adjustment layer and follow the same steps described above.

Related Topics

10.19   Image: *Adjust Overview*
11.78   Layer: *Group with Previous/Group Linked*
11.42   Layer: New: *Adjustment Layer*

9.5

Edit: *Cut*
(Command) [Control]-X

This command deletes selected image information from view while copying it to the Clipboard. Later, you can reapply the information using Edit: **Paste**. This command is only available when an open image contains an active selection, or when text in a field is highlighted.

Issues to Consider

Cutting vs. copying a selected area. Copying leaves the selected information intact; cutting removes it from the image entirely. In some cases—for example, when lifting a selected area into a new layer—choosing Cut may produce a fringe around the extracted element. When this occurs, choose Undo and use Edit: **Copy**.

Edit: Cut only works on the current layer. To copy information on multiple layers to the Clipboard, use Edit: **Copy Merged**.

Cutting and pasting a selection is the same as choosing Layer: New: Layer Via Cut, but with one big difference—cutting and pasting places the new image in the dead center of a new layer; Layer Via Cut maintains the selection's original position.

Related Topics

9.6   Edit: **Copy**
9.7   Edit: **Copy Merged**
9.8   Edit: **Paste**
11.14   Layer: New: **Layer Via Cut**

9.6
_____

Edit: Copy   *(Command) [Control]-C*

Edit: **Copy** saves a selected area to the Clipboard, a section of "short-term" memory that applications use as an invisible holding area. You can apply that information to the same image or a new image using Edit: **Paste**. Although this command is called *copy*, that term only applies to the act of copying to the Clipboard. To create a copy of a selected image area on screen, you must select a paste command after copying to the Clipboard. Unlike Edit: **Cut**, copied information is not removed from the image.

Mistakes to Avoid

Leaving large amounts of information in the Clipboard. If you copy an image larger than the amount of RAM available to Photoshop, then the application is forced to use virtual memory, considerably slowing the computer. This can happen when copying large portions of print-specific graphics, which easily grow to dozens of megabytes in size. Unless your machine has RAM to spare, select Edit: Purge: **Clipboard** after copying and pasting large images.

Issues to Consider

Edit: Copy only works on the current layer. To copy information on multiple layers to the Clipboard, use Edit: **Copy Merged**.

Information copied to the Clipboard is dynamic, meaning active RAM is required to store it. After pasting the contents of the Clipboard, the information remains in memory until one of two things happens:

– Another selected area is copied, replacing the previous one.

– The contents of the Clipboard are purged (or deleted) using Edit: Purge: **Clipboard**.

Copying into another image. Copy a selection from one open image to another by holding down the (Command) [Control] key and dragging. The selection will be placed into a new layer. Watch out, though—if you don't hold down the key, you only drag the selection path to the second image, not the selected pixels.

9.7

Edit: *Copy Merged*   *(Command-Shift) [Control-Shift]-X*

Where Edit: **Copy** only copies the information in the current layer, this command copies all the visible information in an active selection, regardless of the number of layers involved. The individual layers are not maintained; when you paste the information into a new layer or new image, everything is reduced to one "merged" layer.

Note that this command only works on layers that contain editable pixels. Information such as shapes, paths, layer masks, alpha channels, or the contents of an adjustment layer are not recognized by this command.

9.8

Edit: *Paste*   *(Command) [Control]-V*

Pasting places the contents of the Clipboard into the active image.

Mistakes to Avoid

Failing to account for different color modes. When you paste pixels from a different mode, they assume the mode of the image into which it is being pasted. For example, RGB colors convert to process percentages if pasted into a CMYK file, or convert to a limited palette when pasted into an Indexed Color file.

Failing to account for different resolutions. When copying and pasting from images of different resolutions, the results can be surprising. For example, if you paste an inch-wide selection from a 72-ppi image into a 300-ppi image, it pastes as 0.24 inches wide. On the other hand, if you paste a 300-ppi selection into a 72-ppi image, it appears so large that it might not fit in the image window. This is because Photoshop maintains the exact number of pixels in the selection rather than attempting to create new pixels.

Issues to Consider

Using layers to mimic the effect of pasting. To automatically place the contents of a selection into a new layer without using Copy or Paste, choose Layer: New: **Layer Via Copy** or **Layer Via Cut**. The information in each new layer retains its original position.

Photoshop will not paste into an existing layer. To achieve this effect, select the existing layer in the Layers palette before choosing Edit: **Paste**. Immediately after the new layer appears, choose Layer: **Merge Down**. The new layer combines with the one underneath.

Text copied from another program retains no formatting when pasted into Photoshop. If you want to paste formatted type, create it in Adobe Illustrator. To retain the ability to continue editing the type, you must export the Illustrator file as a Photoshop image that preserves the type. (For more information, see *D.4, Retaining Layers in a Rasterized Illustrator File.*)

Pasting pixels in the same image. The most common occurrence of pasting involves selected pixels. When you paste a selection, it automatically appears in a new layer:

- If you choose Select: **None** before pasting, then the new layer is slightly offset from its original position.
- If you leave the selection active while choosing Edit: **Paste**, the new layer retains its original position.

Pasting into a channel. The only time a pasted selection is not placed into a new layer is when you paste into an individual channel:

- If you paste into an existing color channel (like the Red channel in an RGB image), you replace the brightness values that Photoshop uses to display color. The result appears as a color change in the composite channel.
- If you paste into a selection channel, you affect the information that Photoshop reads when a saved selection is made active.

Pasting from another pixel-based application. Photoshop accepts information copied from any other pixel-based editing program. Successfully handling this information depends on two things:

- The color depth present in the other program. If it only works in 8-bit color or uses a limited color palette, pasting into a 24-bit Photoshop image does not automatically increase the range of colors. You can add them as you edit the image further, but if certain colors are dithered in another program, they paste that way in Photoshop.
- Whether the image will be pasted back into the first program. If the original program cannot handle the color depth of a Photoshop image, much of the color information may be lost or inaccurately displayed.

Pasting text. You can paste any text-based information into the text fields in Photoshop's dialog boxes. You can also paste text copied from another program, such as QuarkXPress or Microsoft Word. The only time you would do this is when you want to paste into one of Photoshop's larger text fields, such as the Caption field under File: File Info: **Caption** or while using the Type tool.

Related Topics

9.5   Edit: **Cut**
9.6   Edit: **Copy**
11.13 Layer: New: **Layer Via Copy**
11.14 Layer: New: **Layer Via Cut**
D.4   Retaining Layers in a Rasterized Illustrator File.

9.9
___

Edit: *Paste Into*   (Command-Shift) [Control-Shift]-V

This command enables you to paste the contents of the Clipboard into an active selection. This is really an alternative method of creating a layer mask. Here, the selection acts like a mask, letting only a portion of the information you paste show through. Two things happen when this command is applied: The pasted selection is placed into a new layer, and the selection is automatically converted to a layer mask. (For more information, see *11.65, Layer: **Add Layer Mask**.*)

Issues to Consider

Inverting the new mask. By holding down the (Option) [Alt] key while applying this command, you invert the mask, creating the impression of pasting behind the active selection.

Repositioning the pasted information. Depending on how you manipulate the Layers palette, you can move the pasted information in two different ways: If you activate the link between the image and layer mask thumbnails, you can reposition the image as well as the mask. If you deactivate the link, you can reposition the image without moving the mask.

9.10
___

Edit: *Clear*

Choosing Edit: **Clear** is the same as pressing the Delete (or Backspace) key.

Issues to Consider

Clearing when layer transparency is unlocked. Clearing a selection on an image layer with unlocked transparency fills the selection with transparent pixels.

Clearing when layer transparency is locked. Clearing a selection on the background layer or on a layer with locked transparency fills the selection with the background color.

9.11

Edit: Fill

This command fills a selection or layer with colored pixels. The fill information can be based on the foreground or background color, a pattern, a History palette item, or the last saved version of the file. All these options can be applied at different opacities and blend modes. Common uses include the following:

- **Filling an active selection.** The most common use of the Fill command, it enables you to accurately determine which portion of an image is filled, and which is left untouched.

- **Filling a layer without a selection.** Applying the Fill command with no active selection fills the entire layer.

- **Filling a layer with locked transparency.** If you have a portion of an image residing in a separate layer, you can fill its exact shape without creating a selection.

Mistakes to Avoid

Using the Black option to fill an area in a CMYK image. Filling with Black in a CMYK image creates a total ink density of 400—far too high for any printing process. If you need to fill part of an image with black, select the default black (which gives you lower percentages of C, M, and Y) and fill with the foreground color.

Issues to Consider

Applying a semi-opaque fill. For the most part, the Opacity option is a holdover from earlier versions of Photoshop. The problem is, after you apply a semi-opaque fill, you can't increase the opacity later. You have more control if you fill at 100% Opacity, then use the slider in the Layers palette to reset the value. Or better yet, create a solid color fill layer, then manipulate its opacity.

Using a blend mode fill to colorize an image. One of the more popular uses of this command is to colorize part or all of an image. Photoshop 6's solid color fill layers enable you to apply the same techniques much more efficiently (see *Appendix H, Colorizing Techniques*); however, if you must use this command, you're better off filling an empty layer with the target color, then setting the blend mode in the Layers palette. This way, you can preview the colors before making them permanent.

Use the black, gray, and white options with caution. Normally, you don't fill with Black, 50% Gray, or White for a visible color effect. These are neutral colors, used in conjunction with the blend modes applied in the Layers palette. For example, if you fill a layer with 50% Gray and apply the Soft Light blend mode, the neutral color is hidden from view. However, if you edit that layer with filters and adjustments, the new tonal variations affect the underlying layers (For more information, see *11.8, Layer: New: New Layer.*)

Keyboard shortcuts. Use the following Fill shortcuts:

- **Access the Fill dialog box.** Press Shift-Delete.
- **Fill with background color.** Press (Command) [Control]-Delete.
- **Fill with background color, preserving transparency.** Press (Command-Shift) [Control-Shift]-Delete.
- **Fill with foreground color.** Press (Option) [Alt]-Delete.
- **Fill with foreground color, preserving transparency.** Press (Option-Shift) [Alt-Shift]-Delete.
- **Fill a selection with transparent pixels.** Make a selection on an image layer and press Delete. (If the selection is on the background layer, pressing Delete fills with the background color.)

The Fill Dialog Box

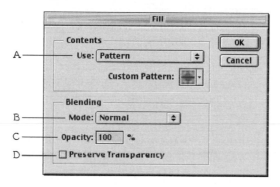

A. **Use**

The options in this pop-up menu determine the information used to fill a selection or layer:

Foreground Color
This option fills with the current foreground color.

Background Color
This option fills with the current background color.

Pattern
This option fills with a repeating tile created using Edit: **Define Pattern**. Choose the desired tile from the available pop-up menu.

Saved
This option fills with the last saved version of a file.

History

> This option fills with the contents of the targeted snapshot or state in the History palette. If the image's resolution, color mode, or width and height have changed since the snapshot was created, this option is not available.

Black

> This option fills with the darkest possible color. In a grayscale image, the value is K: 100. In an RGB image, it fills with R: 0, G: 0, and B: 0. In a CMYK image, choosing Black fills with 100% of each component color. This option is intended for use as a neutral color for certain blend modes. (For more information, see *22.2 Set the Blending Mode.*)

50% Gray

> This option fills with a neutral value of exactly half of the darkest possible color. In a grayscale image, that value is K: 50. In an RGB image, it's R: 128, G: 128, B: 128. In a CMYK image, it fills with 50% of each component color. This option is intended for use as a neutral color for certain blend modes

White

> This option fills with the lightest possible color. This option is intended for use as a neutral color for certain blend modes

B. **Opacity**

By lowering this value, you decrease the opacity of the specified fill content, letting the underlying information show through.

C. **Mode**

Selecting a mode from this pop-up forces the fill contents to blend differently with the underlying layers. (For more information, see *22.2 Set the Blending Mode.*)

D. **Preserve Transparency**

This box is the same as the one in the Layers palette. Checking it before you fill prevents any transparent pixels from being affected by the command. If you leave it unchecked, the entire layer or selection fills completely and uniformly.

Related Topics

9.12

Edit: Stroke

When you *stroke* part of an image, you apply a colored border of a specified width. Edit: **Stroke** applies that border two different ways: Around the edge of an active selection, or around the outer edge of an image layer (with no selection required).

Issues to Consider

You can't stroke type, vector shapes, or layer masks. Here, you can only stroke editable pixels. To add a much more flexible stroke option (including one you can apply to almost any image element), choose Layer: Layer Style: **Stroke**. As long as it exists as a layer style, you're able to change the color, weight, and blend mode of the stroke whenever you like. You're also able to stroke with gradients, patterns, and other customized fill types, which you cannot do with this command.

Creating a editable, standalone stroke. It's possible to create a vector-based stroke that you can edit with the Pen tools, similar to working in a program like Illustrator or FreeHand. (For a full explanation, see *24.6 Stroke With Foreground Color Path*.)

Applying a stroke with Preserve Transparency checked. If the box is checked in the Stroke dialog box or the Layers palette, the Center and Outside options do not apply properly.

Stroking the background layer. When editing the background layer, Edit: **Stroke** is not available unless you have an active selection. To use this command to stroke the entire background layer, choose Select: **All**, then choose the Inside option in the Stroke dialog box. (To produce the equivalent of adding an Outside stroke around the background layer, don't use this command. Instead, set the desired stroke color as the background color, then use the Image: **Canvas Size** command to increase the width and height by twice the desired stroke width.)

Centering a stroke with an odd-numbered width. When you apply an odd-numbered pixel width, Photoshop cannot precisely center the stroke over the selection path. The extra pixel is always placed inside the selection. For example, a centered stroke width of five pixels places two pixels outside the selection, three pixels inside. This is only noticeable in low-resolution images.

The Stroke Dialog Box

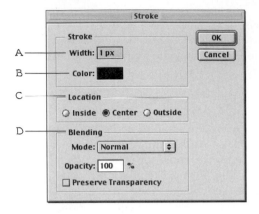

A. **Width** (1 to 250 pixels)

Apply a stroke thickness in the Width field. In other programs, you enter stroke values in point sizes. In Photoshop, you must enter a number of pixels. Therefore, a five-pixel stroke appears much thicker in a 72-ppi web graphic than in a 300-ppi print graphic. Often, the only way to determine the right thickness of a stroke is to apply a series of different values, choosing Edit: **Undo** after each one, until the correct value is found.

B. **Color**

When you first open the Stroke dialog box, this swatch defaults to the current foreground color. To set a different value, click the swatch to access the color picker.

C. **Location**

These options determine the placement of the stroke, in relation to the edge of the target item.

Inside

This option applies a stroke inside the selection path or layer.

Center

This option applies a stroke that straddles the selection outline or layer.

Outside

This option applies a stroke outside the selection path or layer.

D. **Blending**

The Opacity, Mode, and Preserve Transparency options function the same as the Edit: **Fill** dialog box, described previously in this chapter.

Related Topics

9.13

Edit: *Free Transform* *(Command) [Control]-T*

The Free Transform command enables you to apply any of the transformation commands through a series of keystrokes. Using them successfully requires an understanding of the following basic issues:

- **The bounding box.** As with other dynamic transformations, Free Transform uses a transform box to preview the changes. Holding the (Command) [Control], (Option) [Alt], or Shift key is necessary to apply certain changes.

- **The pivot point.** When you first choose this command, a crosshair appears in the geometric center of the box. This crosshair acts as a focal point for the transformations. At any time during editing, you can click-drag the crosshair to reposition it.

- **Applying a change.** After manipulating a transformation box, apply the changes by pressing Return or double-clicking inside the box.

- **Canceling.** To cancel a transformation in progress, press the Escape key.

- **Cloning while transforming.** To transform a copy of the active layer, hold down the (Option) [Alt] key while choosing Edit: **Free Transform**. As soon as you manipulate the transformation box, a new layer (containing the contents of the box) appears in the Layers palette.

- **Entering numerical values.** When using this (or any other) transformation command, the current settings are visible in the Options bar. If desired, you can enter a new value to apply a numerical change.

Mistakes to Avoid

Over-manipulating the transformation box. It is possible to move the handles of the transformation box to such a degree that the mathematics of re-interpolating the image become impossible for Photoshop to calculate. When this happens, the lines of the bounding box change from solid to dotted, indicating that you are asking Photoshop to do the impossible. To correct this, move the handles until the dotted lines become solid again or cancel the transformation and begin again.

Applying multiple transformations individually. Every time you transform an image, you force Photoshop to recalculate the data for every pixel. While Photoshop does an excellent job at this, some information will be lost. Typically, this means a loss of detail, resulting in a slightly blurred image. This increases with every transformation. Apply all your transformations at once to minimize this loss of detail information.

Issues to Consider

When a transformation box is visible on screen, the remaining image-editing commands are shut down. In fact, the only commands available are File: **Close**, File: **Quit**, the Edit: **Transform** options, and the View Menu. If you click on a visible palette, an alert sounds. If you select another tool from the Toolbar, a dialog box appears, asking you to choose Apply, Don't Apply, or Cancel.

This command is not available if any of the Pen tools are currently selected. If a path is visible and a Pen tool is active, one of the path transform options is available. If no path is visible and a Pen tool is active, Edit: **Transform Path** appears in the menu, but is unavailable. To access the standard Transform command, select any other tool.

Transforming a background layer. Background layers cannot be transformed, but selected parts of the background layer can. To transform the entire image, convert it to an image layer (by double-clicking its item in the Layers palette).

Changing transformation options on-the-fly. To switch from one command to another while the transformation box is active, use the context-sensitive menus. Control-click (Mac) or right-click (Windows) inside the transformation box to bring up a complete list of available transformations.

Move

Click inside the transform box and drag to reposition its contents.

Scale

Drag any handle to change the height and width of the selection. Use the following keystrokes:

- **Scale proportionately.** Shift-drag a corner handle.
- **Scale from the centerpoint.** (Option) [Alt]-drag a corner handle.
- **Scale proportionately from the centerpoint.** (Option-Shift) [Alt-Shift]-drag a corner handle.

Flip

To flip the image, drag a handle past a handle on the opposite side of the transform box.

- **Flip horizontally.** Drag a handle on the left-hand side of the transform box past a handle on the right-hand side.

- **Flip vertically.** Drag a handle from the top of the box past one on the bottom.

- **Flip proportionally.** Hold down the Shift key while dragging a corner handle to keep things in proportion.

- **Flip proportionally from the center.** Hold the Option and Shift keys down while dragging a corner handle to flip proportionally from the center.

Rotate

Move the pointer outside of the transform box and drag clockwise or counter-clockwise to change its angle. Hold down the Shift key while dragging to constrain the rotation to 15° increments.

Distort

Hold down the (Command) [Control] key and drag a corner handle in any direction to distort the box. Use the following keystrokes:

- **Distort symmetrically from the center of the transform box.** (Option Command) [Alt-Control]-drag any handle.

- **Constrain the motion of a corner handle to the current shape of the box.** (Command-Shift) [Control-Shift]-drag a corner handle.

Skew

Hold down the (Command) [Control] key and drag any non-corner handle to skew the image. Use the following keystrokes:

- **Constrain the motion of a corner handle to the current shape of the box.** (Command-Shift) [Control-Shift]-drag a corner handle.

- **Skew opposite sides of the box simultaneously.** (Option-Command-Shift) [Alt-Control-Shift]-drag a non-corner handle.

Perspective

Hold down the (Option-Command-Shift) [Alt-Control-Shift] keys and drag a corner handle to apply perspective.

9.14

Edit: Free Transform Point

This command is available when you draw a path using one of the Pen tools and select one or more individual points. As you apply transformations, the point positions, handle configurations, and segment shapes change as needed to display the new shape.

The key commands and shortcuts required here are the same as Edit: **Free Transform**, described above.

Issues to Consider

This command is not always available. Transform Point is not available if no points are selected or if all points are selected. In both cases, Edit: **Free Transform Path** appears here.

Entering numerical values. When using this (or any other) transformation command, the current settings are visible in the Options bar. If desired, you can enter a new value to apply a numerical change.

9.15

Edit: Free Transform Path

This command is available whenever a path is active in the Paths palette. As you apply transformations, the entire path shape changes as needed. This allows you to edit paths with the same flexibility found in such vector-based programs as Illustrator and FreeHand.

The key commands and shortcuts required here are the same as Edit: **Free Transform**, described above.

Issues to Consider

You don't have to select a path to access this command. For best results, simply click the desired item in the Paths palette before editing.

This command is not always available. When a path is visible (and no points are selected), you can only access this command when one of the Pen tools is active. If any other tool is selected, the standard Free Transform options appear instead.

Entering numerical values. When using this (or any other) transformation command, the current settings are visible in the Options bar. If desired, you can enter a new value to apply a numerical change.

9.16

Edit: Transform

All layer transformation commands except for Free Transform are located under the Edit: **Transform** menu. The actions, shortcuts, and techniques required to edit points and paths are the same as those used to edit pixel-based information.

Issues to Consider

Transform vectors or pixels with the same commands. These commands can also be used to transform vector-based points and paths:

- If a path is visible on screen and some or all of its points are selected, the command appears as Edit: **Transform Points**. It does not matter which tool is currently active.
- If a path is visible on screen and no points are selected, the command appears as Edit: **Transform Path**. Here, this option is only available when one of the Pen tools is currently selected. If any other tool is active, the standard Edit: **Transform** command appears.

Transforming selection outlines. The Edit: **Transform** commands enable you to alter the contents of a selection. To edit only the shape of the outline—leaving the selected pixels untouched—use Select: **Transform Selection**.

Related Topics

9.13   *Edit: Free Transform*
9.14   *Edit: Free Transform Points*
9.15   *Edit: Free Transform Path*
12.14 *Select: Transform Selection*

9.17

Edit: Transform: Again   *(Shift-Command) [Shift-Control]-T*

This command re-applies the most recent transformation to the currently targeted item. It doesn't matter whether the last transformation was generated using Edit: **Free Transform** or one of the Edit: **Transform** items.

Issues to Consider

Cloning while transforming. If you hold down the (Option) [Alt] key while choosing this command, the result appears in a new layer, leaving the original layer untouched.

Transforming multiple layers. Some users choose this command to apply the same transformation values to different layers. Avoid these unnecessary steps by linking the desired layers in the Layers palette and applying a single transformation.

Applying the same values to layer-based information as well as points and paths. For example, you can rotate the contents of a layer, then select a path, make sure one of the Pen tools is active, and choose Edit: Transform Path: **Again** to apply the same value.

9.18

Edit: Transform: *Scale*

This command enables you to change the height and width of a targeted item. Use the following keystrokes:

- **Increase or decrease the height.** Drag the top or bottom center handles.

- **Increase or decrease the width.** Drag the left or right center handles.

- **Change height and width simultaneously.** Drag the corner handles.

- **Change the height and width proportionally.** Hold down the Shift key while dragging the corner handles.

- **Scale proportionately from the center of the box.** (Option-Shift) [Alt-Shift]-drag a handle.

- **Flip the image while scaling.** Drag any handle past the anchor point.

9.19

Edit: Transform: *Rotate*

This command enables you you to change the angle of a targeted item. This item is the only dynamic transform command that does not use the handles to make changes. Instead, click and drag anywhere outside the transformation box. Hold down the Shift key while dragging to rotate in 15° increments. Double-click inside the image to apply the rotation.

Issues to Consider

Don't use the Rotate tool for straightening crooked scans. It increases the canvas size and still requires the extra step of cropping the image. Instead, use the Crop tool to simultaneously rotate and crop the image.

9.20
Edit: Transform: *Skew*

This command constrains the movement of the handles to the same direction of the lines of the transformation box. You can only drag the handles in one direction at a time. Use the following keystrokes:

- (Option) [Alt]-dragging a corner handle is the same as dragging a center handle.

- (Option) [Alt]-dragging a center handle skews the image while anchoring the two adjacent center handles.

9.21
Edit: Transform: *Distort*

This command enables you to move any handle in any direction. As with any dynamic transformation, moving a center handle moves the entire side of the transformation box. Use the following keystrokes:

- Hold the Shift key to constrain the distortion, similar to Skew.

- Hold the (Option) [Alt] key while dragging to make the opposite handle mirror the new position.

9.22
Edit: Transform: *Perspective*

This command constrains the movement of the handles to the direction of the lines of the transformation box. When you drag one corner handle, the opposite handle moves an equal distance in the opposite direction.

9.23
Edit: Transform: *Rotate 180°*

This command turns the targeted element upside-down.

9.24
Edit: Transform: *Rotate 90° CW*

This command turns the targeted element onto its right-hand side.

9.25
Edit: Transform: **Rotate 90° CCW**

This command turns the targeted element onto its left-hand side.

9.26
Edit: Transform: **Flip Horizontal**

This command turns over the targeted element from left to right, like flipping a transparent colored overlay.

Issues to Consider

Horizontally flipping an entire image. Use Image: Rotate Canvas: **Flip Horizontal** to perform this correction on an image consisting solely of a background layer, or when all image layers need to be rotated.

Related Topics

*10.45 Image: **Rotate Canvas***

9.27
Edit: Transform: **Flip Vertical**

This command turns the image over from top to bottom, like flipping a transparent colored overlay. At the same time, it rotates the image 180°.

Issues to Consider

Vertically flipping an entire image. Use Image: Rotate Canvas: **Flip Vertical** to perform this correction on an image consisting solely of a background layer, or when all image layers need to be rotated.

Related Topics

*10.45 Image: **Rotate Canvas***

9.28

Edit: Define Brush

Use this command to convert the contents of a rectangular selection into a custom brush shape. Color information is not included in the brush—this information is used to *apply* new color, not to reproduce it. Instead, the relative brightness values of the selected area determines the brush's opacity. 100% black equals 100% opacity, 75% black equals 25% opacity, 50% black equals 50% opacity, and 25% black equals 75% opacity. If the initial selection contains any white information, it translates to fully transparent pixels.

Issues to Consider

Creating irregularly-edged brushes. Don't be put off by the fact that you can only use a rectangular marquee to create a new brush. To create a brush with irregular edges, take the time to place the desired information on a white background, then encircle the entire shape with a selection. Any part of the brush based on white pixels will not apply color.

Custom brushes are based on active selections between 1 and 999 pixels wide. If the brush is larger than 27 x 27 pixels, only the upper left of the brush is displayed in the palette. If the width or height of the active selection exceeds 999 pixels, a dialog box appears, informing you that the selection is too large to be used as a brush.

Custom brushes are useful to traditional artists who find the elliptical standard brushes too constraining. Many users scan in a series of different real-world brush marks (sponges, cotton balls, even cut potatoes are good examples), adjust them appropriately, and use the individual shapes to create custom brushes.

9.29

Edit: Define Pattern

Use this command to turn a rectangular selection into a pattern, or a repeating series of tiles. Defining a pattern is simple: Once you've designed and staged the tile you wish to use as a pattern, use the Rectangular Marquee tool to target the desired area. Choose Edit: **Define Pattern**. After naming the pattern, you can access it from a number of locations, including pattern fill layers, layer styles, and the Pattern Stamp tool.

Issues to Consider

Save any patterns you want to keep for future use. If you plan to use a new pattern more than once, do one of two things. At the very least, quit and relaunch Photoshop. Otherwise, if the program should happen to crash, any unsaved patterns are lost. However, this may not protect you if you ever need to re-install Photoshop. To keep a permanent record of a pattern, use the Present Manager to save them into a separate file.

Before you create a pattern, you must have some sense of how it's going to be used. As evidenced by the number of available techniques, one simple pattern does not satisfy all purposes. Some must be seamless, some require transparent pixels, some work best with overlapping information. The most successful patterns are the result of planning and focused editing.

Related Topics

2.11   *Pattern Stamp Tool*
9.11   *Edit:* **Fill**
9.36   *Edit:* **Preset Manager**
10.6   *Image: Mode:* **Bitmap**
11.41 *Layer: New Fill Layer:* **Pattern**
K.3   *Defining a Pattern with Non-Adjacent Edges*
K.4   *Defining a Staggered Pattern with Non-Adjacent Edges*
K.5   *Defining a Non-Continuous Pattern*
K.6   *Creating a Seamless Pattern*
K.7   *Creating a Seamless Image Pattern*
K.8   *Defining a Pattern that Includes Transparent Pixels*

9.30
___

Edit: Define Custom Shape

Choose this command to load a vector-based item as a custom shape. This way, you're able to use the Custom Shape tool to place copies by clicking and dragging.

This command is only available when a shape or path is visible onscreen. They don't have to be selected—only active in the Layers or Paths palette. If a palette item contains more than one shape, they're all included in the custom shape.

Related Topics

3.15   *Custom Shape Tool*
9.36   *Edit:* **Preset Manager**

9.31

Edit: Purge

Whenever you copy any information to RAM, it takes up space. If too much active RAM is occupied, Photoshop uses virtual memory, or megabytes from the hard drive, to compensate. This seriously hinders the performance of your workstation—so make it a point to purge the contents of RAM when you no longer need that information, or if you start to experience slowdowns during heavy editing.

9.32

Edit: Purge: Undo

Photoshop always retains a copy of an image as it existed before the last command. Whenever you choose Edit: **Undo**, Photoshop merely replaces the visible image with this invisible Undo image. Selecting Edit: Purge: **Undo** removes this image from RAM, but it will be replaced as soon as the next command is applied.

9.33

Edit: Purge: Clipboard

Purging the Clipboard deletes any information placed there by the Edit: **Cut** or Edit: **Copy** commands

9.34

Edit: Purge: Histories

This option deletes every item that currently appears in the History palette. If you find yourself choosing this command often, consider lowering the number of Maximum History States in the History Options dialog box (choose History Options from the History palette submenu).

9.35

Edit: Purge: All

This option purges all information currently occupying RAM (the four items listed above).

9.36

Edit: Preset Manager   *(Command-Shift)[Control-Shift]-K*

The Preset Manager gives you one-stop access to every predefined setting currently stored in Photoshop's internal database. It exists only for your convenience—it offers nothing that you can't accomplish in various locations throughout the program.

For example, even though you only define a pattern in one place (Edit: **Define Pattern**), you can access the pattern controls in the Pattern Stamp Options bar, as well as the Bitmap, Layer Style, and Pattern Fill dialog boxes. In each one, you're able to choose a new pattern, save a series of them into a separate file, load a pre-saved set, and so forth. The main advantage to using the Preset Manager is that you can jump directly to the desired presets without searching for a particular tool or working halfway through an unwanted command. Any additions or deletions are automatically reflected throughout the application.

The Preset Manager Dialog Box

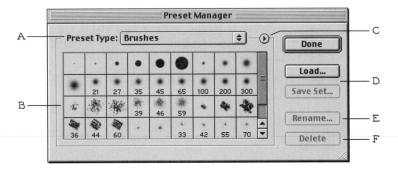

A. **Preset Type**

Select the group of presets you want to edit from this pop-up menu. Choose from the following:

– **Brushes.** For more information, see *2.2, The Brush Picker.*

– **Swatches.** For more information, see *18.1, Swatches Palette Overview.*

– **Gradients.** For more information, see *2.17, Gradient Tool.*

– **Styles.** For more information, see *19.1, Styles Palette Overview.*

– **Patterns.** For more information, see *9.29, Edit: **Define Pattern.***

– **Contours.** For more information, see *11.18, Layer: **Layer Style.***

– **Custom Shapes.** For more information, see *3.15, Custom Shape Tool.*

B. Thumbnails

When you set an item in the Preset Type pop-up menu, all of the currently available samples appear in this window. Click a thumbnail to select it. Shift-click to select more than one. (Option) [Alt]-click a thumbnail to remove it. Double-click a thumbnail to rename it.

C. Submenu

Each group of presets has its own set of organizational commands, found under this submenu.

D. Load/Save

To load a pre-saved set of presets, click the Load button. To save the current range into a separate file, click Save. (These options are also available under the submenu.)

E. Rename

Click this button to rename the selected thumbnail. (This command is available in the submenu; you can also double-click an item to rename it.)

F. Delete

Click this button to delete the selected thumbnail. (This command is available in the submenu; you can also press the Delete key to remove an item.)

9.37
___

Edit: *Color Settings*   *(Command-Shift) [Control-Shift]-K*

The Color Settings options serve two purposes: They control the colors that appear on your monitor, and they control the conversion of RGB colors to CMYK output values.

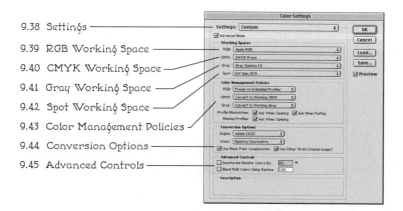

9.38 Settings

9.39 RGB Working Space

9.40 CMYK Working Space

9.41 Gray Working Space

9.42 Spot Working Space

9.43 Color Management Policies

9.44 Conversion Options

9.45 Advanced Controls

Before adjusting the settings found in the following dialog boxes, however, it is important to understand Photoshop's new approach to handling color images. Photoshop is compatible with ICC profiles, or hardware descriptions used by Apple's ColorSync management utility to track consistent values from initial image acquisition to final output. These profiles allow for *device independent* color, which means that the values contained in an image can be altered to accommodate the unique ranges of the different devices used during the typical color editing process.

This enhanced function is not intended for every Photoshop user. Ultimately, profiles are better suited for professionals establishing a larger-scale color managed workflow. For example, they're proving to be an invaluable tool for newspapers, magazines, and other high-volume, closed-loop environments. If you don't have the resources to invest in such a project—or if it simply does not fit with your current methodology—you can easily bypass the use of profiles, enter some basic settings, and continue processing color images the way you did in Photoshop 4 or 5.

Even though most devices utilize a common color space (RGB), each device interprets the same source values differently. For example, the Green phosphors in your scanner do not match the Green phosphors of your monitor, resulting in inconsistent values. When devices are profiled, their unique ranges are defined in comparison to a standardized reference space. ICC-aware applications can then calculate the values required to match colors from device to device, program to program. This method is not necessarily a solution—it doesn't result in perfect color from beginning to end. Rather, when used properly, it gets you as close as possible, working within the limitations posed by your different tools.

It's important to note that profiles are not specific to Photoshop. Rather, they are separate files that reside in your operating system. They require a conversion engine, such as ColorSync, which applies the profile to an image as a sort of filter. You'll encounter three types of profiles:

- **Input (or Source).** These describe the color space of a device used to acquire color images, such as scanners or digital cameras. (For more information, see *10.17, Image: Mode: **Assign Profile*** and *10.18, Image: Mode: **Convert to Profile**.*)

- **Display.** These describe the onscreen color space of a particular monitor. In Photoshop, they're used to define an RGB working space.

- **Output (or Destination).** These describe the available color space of a device used to reproduce an image, such as a color composite proofer, a film-based laminate proof, offset press, or digital press. These profiles can also be used to soft-proof, or display the final colors on your monitor before printing. (Profiles are not used for black-and-white laser printers.) In Photoshop, they're used to define a CMYK working space.

Additionally, a profile that describes the color space used while editing the image in Photoshop can be embedded into an image. A file that contains an embedded profile is referred to as *tagged.*

Issues to Consider

Complete the following tasks before implementing a color-managed workflow:

- **Determine your working color spaces.** Here, determine the most appropriate RGB space for your monitor and the setup for your CMYK conversions. When editing in RGB, it is recommended that you choose a space other than the working space of your own monitor, such as sRGB or Adobe RGB (for more information, see *9.39, Color Settings: RGB Working Space*). Since the values of these spaces are already known and tabulated, the same image can be successfully viewed and edited on different monitors within the same color-managed workflow.

- **Determine the color space to apply to your legacy files.** Photoshop enables you to convert untagged images (for example, Photoshop 4 images, which use the device-dependent RGB space of your monitor) to your working color space, or you can tell it to apply a specific profile. These settings are established in the Color Management Policies controls.

- **Determine whether or not you will embed profiles in your images.** When working as part of a color managed system, you will almost always want to do this. The only time you would not embed a profile is when specific color values are more important than the way they are visually perceived. (To save an image without an embedded profile, choose File: **Save a Copy** and uncheck the Embed Color Profile box.) Examples include the following:

  - If you are producing work, such as an application interface, that relies on colors from the system palette.
  - If you are producing web graphics using colors from the browser-safe palette.
  - If you are producing a test image for calibration, where specific numerical values must be reproduced in order characterize a device.

- **Determine a methodology for handling images tagged with a color space different than your own.** When Photoshop attempts to open an image with a conflicting profile, the Profile Mismatch dialog box will appear. Here, you can apply a new profile, if desired.

9.38

Color Settings: *Settings*

When you first open the Color Settings command, this pop-up menu offers a list of factory-installed setups. Choosing one resets the values as necessary throughout the dialog box. The proper context for some of these options is obvious—for example, Color Management Off and Emulate Photoshop 4 are geared for environments that avoid the use of profiles altogether. The remaining settings sound useful, but it can be difficult to predict if they dovetail with your specific requirements.

For the best results, establish your own settings and save them as a separate CSF file. Photoshop automatically places the file in the Application Support/Adobe/Color/Settings folder on your system. The filename subsequently appears in the Settings pop-up. (As you save, you're also able to enter comments that will appear in the Description field.)

9.39

Color Settings: RGB *Working Space*

An image's color mode is different from the *working spaces* you set in Photoshop. Color mode determines all potential colors an image can contain; the working space takes into account how those colors will appear when output or displayed on a specific device. For example, if you output the same image to an IRIS inkjet, Epson inkjet, or Canon color laser printer, the results are all slightly different—and none match the values you see onscreen. Setting the appropriate working spaces will enable you to view, soft-proof, and convert images in a consistent color environment.

The RGB working space determines how colors display on your monitor. To get the most out of this working space, Photoshop must be made aware of certain information, including the type of monitor you're using, the device used to acquire an image, the intended proofing methods, and the image's final destination. Photoshop 6 uses ICC profiles (based on the standards of the International Color Consortium), which attempt to maintain consistent color throughout your workflow by identifying the origin of an image, and communicating its color values consistently between different monitors and output devices. Its not simple—in fact, most off-the-shelf monitors cannot be easily calibrated, which means they cannot take full advantage of ICC profiles.

The RGB pop-up menu lists the following items when the Advanced box is unchecked:

- **Monitor RGB.** This option results in Photoshop simply using the current color space of the monitor, with no further adjustments. If desired, profile your monitor using the Adobe Gamma utility to modify the display.

- **Adobe RGB (1998).** The recommended choice for print work, this option displays a much wider color range than sRGB, Apple RGB, or ColorMatch

RGB. Adobe intends this color space to be a viable option for prepress professionals requiring the largest gamut possible. Interestingly, its gamut includes many values that cannot even display, let alone print. When this occurs, some colors are clipped, which means that two or more similar color values are averaged together into one. However, this phenomenon is rarely noticeable in print, and in fact it allows for a little more flexibility when adjusting color.

- **Apple RGB.** Based on the range of an Apple 13-inch Trinitron monitor, this option is the color space used by earlier versions of Photoshop (and most other design applications).

- **ColorMatch RGB.** This option represents the range of a Radius PressView monitor.

- **sRGB.** Short for standard RGB, this option represents the color space of HDTV, and is promoted primarily by Hewlett-Packard and Microsoft. If you're not part of a workflow using this space, there is little need for this option. Some users convert web graphics to sRGB, because this space displays the same characteristics of most PC monitors. However, its range is smaller than the color space used by earlier versions of Photoshop—and when you consider that many CMYK values fall outside the sRGB gamut, you can see that it's a poor choice for print professionals.

When the Advanced button is checked in the Color Settings dialog box, the RGB pop-up is expanded. It displays all color profiles currently available to your system, and you're also able to save and load RGB profiles that haven't been installed into your operating system. To create a custom RGB working space, choose Custom from the top of the pop-up (For more information, see *The Custom RGB Dialog Box*, below.)

Mistakes to Avoid

Using sRGB in a print environment. While this standard is well-suited for previewing smaller-gamut images such as web graphics, it's a poor choice for the print professional. If sRGB remains as the default, you run the risk of reducing the color range of print-destined images—especially when opening images originally processed in Photoshop 4. Unfortunately, once you accidentally reduce an image's color range by converting its profile, you cannot regain the lost information. However, you can set a new default to avoid this problem in the first place, such as Adobe RGB. To maintain the settings used by earlier versions of Photoshop (and many other design applications), set the RGB pop-up to Apple RGB.

Assuming that these settings result in a "calibrated" monitor. Choosing an RGB working space is sometimes referred to as *monitor calibration*, but that's only true in a sense. True calibration requires that additional tools, such as a calibration cup or accelerator card, be used every day to ensure that your monitor displays those colors as consistently as possible.

Issues to Consider

Space prohibits a full discussion of the intricacies of profiling. However, the Adobe Gamma utility—included for free—offers a basic method of profiling the displayable range of your monitor.

The Custom RGB Dialog Box

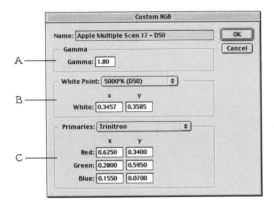

A. **Gamma** (0.75 to 3.00)

Essentially an overall correction to a monitor's contrast, the gamma value depends on the work you do as much as the monitor you use. The standard for print-oriented work is 1.8. Workstations connected to an NTSC-compatible video screen work in a slightly darker color space, which usually requires a higher gamma of 2.2.

B. **White Point** (each field: 0.0000 to 1.0000)

Here, choose the temperature of the light in which your work is viewed. Doing so determines the red, green, and blue intensities required to display pure white on your monitor.

Light is measured by the Kelvin scale. Zero degrees Kelvin is absolute zero, the point at which all molecular motion ceases. The temperature of light ranges from 1900°K for weak candlelight to 7500°K for bright daylight. Rather than attempt to determine the ultimate viewing conditions for all printed pieces, print publishers typically use a single lighting standard. In the U.S., it's 5000°K.

The X and Y fields are coordinates in the CIE XYZ color space, enabling you to enter the values determined by a calibration device.

C. **Primaries** (each field: 0.0000 to 1.0000)

This option determines how Photoshop handles the primary colors generated by the electron guns inside your monitor. Since the method used to produce red, green, and blue differ from medium to medium, you can duplicate the desired effect by choosing the appropriate item.

If your monitor type is not listed, you're able to manually enter the necessary red, green, and blue chromaticity coordinates in the X and Y fields.

9.40
___

Color Settings: CMYK Working Space

The CMYK working space determines the output values created when an image is converted from RGB to CMYK. This item will also work in conjunction with the current RGB space to display the colors as accurately as possible on screen.

Most often, the CMYK space is based on the separation settings established in the Custom CMYK dialog box. However, you can also load a profile for a particular color output device, enabling you to soft-proof an image before printing. (For more information, see *14.5, View: **Proof Setup**.*)

Using predefined device profiles. Profiles of several color printers are included in the Ink Colors pop-up menu, but they should only be accessed when an image will output solely to one of those devices.

The Black Generation setting impacts the use of CMYK information throughout Photoshop. For example, the default black of an image in CMYK mode is directly based on the current setting. (For more information, see *5.5, Default Foreground and Background Colors.*)

You must apply a UCR or GCR value when converting an RGB image to CMYK. By doing so, you determine that equal values of cyan, magenta, and yellow—which form gray—are replaced with black ink. This cuts down ink density, material costs, and drying time.

The Custom CMYK Dialog Box

The controls of this dialog box enable you to establish your own CMYK conversion settings. (For more information, see *G.2, Common CMYK Conversion Setups.*)

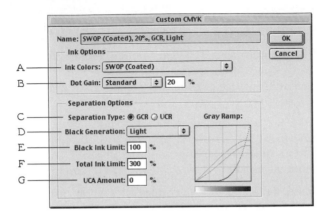

A. Ink Colors

Selecting an ink set allows Photoshop to refer to an internal model of how those particular printed inks appear. Photoshop's default is the North American standard—SWOP (Specifications for Web Offset Printing)—but it's not universal. For example, Japan uses the Toyo set and Europe uses Eurostandard. If there is any question about the type of ink used to reproduce an image on-press, consult your printer. Each standard has a setting for coated paper, uncoated paper, and newsprint. Selecting one over the other alters the Dot Gain value.

B. Dot Gain (-10 to 40%)

Dot gain is the tendency of printed halftone dots to expand slightly as the ink is absorbed into the paper. If ignored, dot gain darkens any halftone reproduced on-press. The amount of the darkening depends on the absorbency of the paper—coated paper absorbs the least, uncoated paper a little more, and newsprint the most.

Selecting an ink standard automatically enters a value for dot gain. When a full-color image is converted to CMYK from RGB, you don't see this change—but when the separations are output, they are lightened slightly to compensate for the gain on-press. The amount depends on the ink standard and paper type. This value can be changed independently of the Ink Colors pop-up, so consult your printer to determine the expected amount of dot gain.

C. **Separation Type**

This command controls the generation of black information. Two methods are available:

UCR

UCR stands for Under Color Removal, because color is literally being removed from under a gray area. UCR dictates that cyan, magenta, and yellow are replaced with black only in neutral areas—so when CMY combine to make gray, it's replaced with a black screen. For example, a color consisting of C: 20, M: 20, and Y: 20 is replaced with K: 20. This typically removes unneeded ink in the shadows, but leaves the remaining image full of CMY ink. This makes images affected by UCR more difficult to control on-press.

GCR

GCR stands for Gray Component Replacement, which takes UCR one step further. It replaces all of the gray it can, swapping any areas consisting of gray combinations with black information. For example, a color consisting of C: 50, M: 30, and Y: 20 could become C: 30, M: 10, and K: 20. This is more powerful, but can be destructive to the image. If you replace every single gray with black ink, the human eye begins to notice the difference in the lightest tones. To counter this effect, use the remaining controls.

D. **Black Generation**

This setting determines the black highlight, or where substitution will begin. For example, choosing Light from the pop-up sets the starting point at 40%, meaning all tones under 40% are left unchanged. The values for each option are as follows:

- **None.** No black is generated, resulting in a CMY image.
- **Light.** Black generation starts at 40%.
- **Medium.** Black generation starts at 20%.
- **Heavy.** Black generation starts at 10%.
- **Maximum.** Black is substituted for all colors.

Choosing Custom from the pop-up allows you to set a custom black generation curve. Edited similarly to the curves used to correct color, use it to manually determine the extent that black replaces the remaining CMY components. Typically, these are created for difficult-to-print, high-key images like white, snowy mountain tops or low-key images, like dark cityscapes. High-key images, with little information, tend to lack color. Low-key images tend to be too rich in black. Use the Image: **Histogram** dialog box to evaluate image key.

E. **Black Ink Limit** (0 to100%)

This value states the darkest percentage of black that Photoshop allows to exist. Where Black Generation was used to define the black highlight, this value determines the black shadow. Typically, the only time to reduce this value is when you're reducing the total ink limit. Otherwise, leave it at 100%. Any necessary changes can be made during color correction.

F. **Total Ink Limit** (200 to 400%)

This value sets the maximum amount of ink laid down on-press. This decision is based on the type of press being used as well as the material receiving the ink. Too much ink, and it shows through the material. Too little, and the colors are not as rich as they could be. If the amount is set to below Photoshop's default—we actually recommend that anyone unsure of their press requirements set this value to 280%—it is wise to reduce the Black Ink Limit to 90%.

G. UCA **Amount** (0 to 100%)

Short for Under Color Addition, it compensates for the rather severe effects of GCR. UCA replaces some of the black removed from neutral shadow areas. Even at the highest value, it only affects tones darker than 50%, so you still receive the benefit of reduced ink coverage. Typically, only 10-20% of UCA is required.

9.41

Color Settings: *Gray Working Space*

The Gray working space determines how a Grayscale image displays on your monitor. There are two options. First, you can choose a *gamma* setting, which enables you to base the display quality on a typical Mac (1.8) or PC (2.2) monitor. Or, choose a *dot gain* setting, which darkens the onscreen image, enabling you to anticipate the effect of dot gain during on-press reproduction. (To set your own dot gain profile, choose Custom from the top of the pop-up.) Note that these values only lighten or darken the *appearance* of an image—the actual output values are not affected.

If you work in a closed-loop print environment (such as a newspaper's prepress department), choose or establish the necessary dot gain value. If working on images that will display on screen, choose the gamma setting for the predominant viewing platform. If working in both print and web, consider setting this pop-up to Gray Gamma 2.2. This way, you're able to anticipate the viewing conditions of a PC monitor (important for web graphics), and the darkening is roughly equivalent to a 25% dot gain setting.

9.42

Color Settings: *Spot Working Space*

This working space determines the appearance of any spot color channels. For the best results, choose or establish the anticipated dot gain. If unsure, choose 20%.

9.43

Color Settings: *Color Management Policies*

ICC profiles can cause as many problems as they try to resolve. One of the most common issues are images that already contain an embedded profile. Here, you must determine whether the profile will be retained, replaced, or discarded outright. Also, when you open Photoshop 4 images (which couldn't use profiles) or images that were intentionally created without profiles, you must determine whether or not to convert them to your current working space.

This is important, because profiles were never intended to be swapped around with wanton abandon. If you mistakenly convert an image tagged with one profile to another, you can literally change its color content, which in turn produces unexpected on-press color shifts. Fortunately, the Color Management Policies act as a series of roadblocks that alert you whenever a potential conflict arises. From there, you can make any necessary changes. (Recommended settings appear after each item, in italics.)

The Color Management Policies Controls

A. **RGB** (*Convert to Working RGB*)

These options determine how Photoshop will process an RGB image with a mismatched or missing profile.

Off

When this option is set, Photoshop doesn't recognize any embedded profiles, nor does it convert to the working space. The color appearance is not affected. Color management is essentially off for the image, and all adjustments and conversions must be performed manually.

Preserve Embedded Profiles

Here, Photoshop recognizes and retains a profile embedded in an image.

Convert to Working RGB

Here, Photoshop converts the image to the current RGB working space. Most of the time, this option is the best choice—

it enables you to convert an image into a color space optimized for your viewing conditions. (Give yourself a choice by checking the Ask When Opening box under "Profile Mismatches," below.)

B. CMYK *(Preserve Embedded Profiles)*

These options determine how Photoshop will process an CMYK image with a mismatched or missing profile.

Off

When this option is set, Photoshop doesn't recognize any embedded profiles, nor does it convert to the working space. The color appearance is not affected.

Preserve Embedded Profiles

Here, Photoshop recognizes and retains a profile embedded in an image. Because CMYK working space is based on a target output method, don't be quick to discard or replace any embedded CMYK profiles—choosing the incorrect one could result in a flawed conversion, ruining the image.

For the best results, lean toward keeping any embedded CMYK profiles, until you have a specific reason to set another one. (Give yourself a choice by checking the Ask When Opening box under "Profile Mismatches," below.)

Convert to Working CMYK

Here, Photoshop converts the image to the current CMYK working space. If you've already opened the image without converting, you can perform the conversion independently. (For more information, see *10.18, Image: Mode:* **Convert to Profile**.)

C. **Gray** *(Off)*

Users have discovered that there is little if any benefit to tagging a Grayscale image with a profile. Even converting to the working gray may result in a clipped tonal range, which makes itself quickly known when an image is comprised of only 256 shades of gray. Therefore, Off is the only logical setting for this pop-up.

D. **Profile Mismatches** *(Ask When Opening)*

These options determine how Photoshop responds when you open an image that conflicts with the established working space.

Ask When Opening

When this option is checked, Photoshop displays a Profile Mismatch dialog box, enabling you to accept, change, or refuse the current color management policy. When unchecked, the current policy is automatically followed.

Ask When Pasting

This option is an issue if you routinely copy information from one image and paste it into another. When this option is checked,

Photoshop displays a Profile Mismatch dialog box, enabling you to accept, change, or refuse the current color management policy. When unchecked, the current policy is automatically followed.

E. **Missing Profiles**

These options determine how Photoshop handles an image that doesn't include an embedded profile. For most purposes, the following settings are sufficient:

9.44

Color Settings: **Conversion Options**

The following options determine the properties in effect when you convert an RGB image to CMYK.

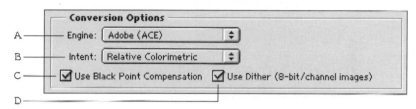

A. **Engine**

In this pop-up, choose the desired color management module. It defaults to *Adobe (ACE),* Photoshop's internal CMM (formerly known as "Built-In"), the best choice when working primarily in this application. Depending on your workflow, you may require choosing a different CMM, such as Kodak's Digital Science Color Management System or Apple's ColorSync.

B. **Intent** *(Perceptual)*

Set the desired *rendering intent* in this pop-up, or the method used to convert color spaces.

Perceptual (Images)

Here, the relative color values of the original image are maintained as they are converted to the target color space. While the overall color may change, the visual relationship between them is preserved.

Saturation (Graphics)

Here, the relative saturation values of the original image are maintained as they are converted to the target color space. Any values outside the intended gamut retain their original saturation values, but are moved just inside the gamut.

Relative Colorimetric

Here, color values falling outside the target gamut have the same lightness value, but are positioned just inside the gamut.

Absolute Colorimetric

This option ignores white point matching during conversion. This typically results in the poorest translation, and should be avoided.

C. **Use Black Point Compensation**

This option determines how the darkest image information will be handled during conversion. In almost every instance, you'll want to leave it checked. This way, the darkest neutral color of the original color space is mapped to the darkest neutral color of the new color space. Otherwise, the darkest neutral color is simply mapped to black, which may push the overall colors out of balance.

D. **Use Dither (8-bit/channel images)** *(On)*

When this option is checked, Photoshop will blend and combine certain values during a conversion, in an attempt to prevent subtle tonal and color transitions from degrading or banding.

9.45

Color Settings: Advanced Controls

The following options are only available when the Advanced box is checked at the top of the Color Settings dialog box.

A. **Desaturate Monitor Colors By** (0 to 100%)

This option enables you to compensate for a minor shortcoming in the Adobe RGB color space. It recognizes such a wide range of vivid colors, that the brightest values tend to flatten out on screen, making it more difficult to evaluate the level of detail. As long as this box is checked, the onscreen colors are slightly desaturated, the lightest details easier to see. This option does not affect the final conversion—however, as long as it remains on, the colors display far less accurately.

B. **Blend RGB Colors Using Gamma** (1.00 to 2.20)

Here, "blending" refers to the way that red, green, and blue light is combined to generate onscreen color values. When this option is unchecked (the default setting), Photoshop bases this phenomenon on the gamma of the current RGB working space. If the current profile produces artifacting around edge details, checking this box will attempt to apply a more "colorimetrically appropriate" gamma. (For more information, see *9.39 Color Settings:* **Working Spaces**.)

9.46

File: Preferences

Every major graphics application has a vast and complex interface. Because there are so many variables and so many different uses for the program, there are certain elements that can be altered to better suit your working environment. These are called *preferences,* or default settings, and can be changed on-the-fly whenever Photoshop is open.

These preferences are stored in the Adobe Photoshop Preferences file, located in the Preferences folder in the System Folder. To reset all the Preferences at once, delete the file and let Photoshop create a new one the next time the program is launched. Also, if the program begins acting inconsistently—certain values keep resetting, or colors keep changing—deleting the preferences file will often solve the problem.

There are eight Preferences panels (where we specifically prefer a setting, we've included it after the title of the preference):

9.47

File: Preferences: General   *(Command) [Control]-K*

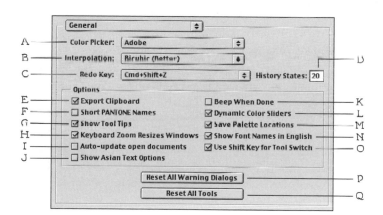

A. **Color Picker** (Mac only): *Photoshop*

Choose between Photoshop's built-in picker or the one developed by Apple. The Apple picker is found in many other programs, but only defines RGB and HSB (Hue, Saturation, Brightness) colors. Photoshop's picker also defines Lab and CMYK colors, displays a gamut warning, and allows you to select custom colors supported by different swatch book systems. (For more information, see *5.7 The Adobe Color Picker.*)

B. **Interpolation:** *Bicubic*

When Photoshop re-sizes an image or the information in a transform box, it must figure out how to rearrange the pixels. It does this by comparing pixel values to get an educated guess about what to do. This is called *interpolation.* The highest-quality option is *Bicubic,* the factory default, because it looks at the highest number pixels before making its decision. *Nearest Neighbor* offers the lowest quality, not attempting to interpolate the pixels at all. *Bilinear* falls in the middle. (For more information, see *10.40 Image: **Image Size.**)*

C. **Redo Key**

This option enables you to set the keystroke for Edit: **Redo**, which reverses the Undo command.

(Cmd-Shift) [Ctrl-Shift]-Z

When you set this item, you're able to press (Command) [Control]-Z—the Undo shortcut—over and over again to step backward through an image's editing history.

(Cmd) [Cntrl]-Z (Toggles Undo/Redo)

When you set this item, pressing the Undo shortcut repeatedly toggles between Undo and Redo.

(Cmd) [Cntrl]-Y

This option enables you to mimic a Redo shortcut commonly used by other graphics programs.

D. **Maximum History States** (1 to 100)

This value determines the largest number of states the palette can contain. If the number of your edits exceeds this amount, the earliest states will be replaced with new ones. However, this number can be changed on-the-fly.

When you increase the maximum number of states, Photoshop will require more RAM to hold them in memory. If an alert appears stating that Photoshop is running low on memory, choose Edit: Purge: **Histories**, or clear the current states by choosing Clear History from the palette submenu. If this occurs frequently, consider lowering the maximum number of states.

When this value is set to 1, the History palette is essentially rendered useless (except for the ability to contain multiple snapshots). It contains the same number of undo levels as earlier versions of Photoshop.

E. **Export Clipboard:** *Off*

This option tells your computer to hold copied information in memory when you quit the program—although it is unlikely you will paste it into another program. (For more information, see *9.6, Edit: **Copy.**)*

F. **Short Pantone Names:** *Off*

When Pantone names are selected as part of a duotone (the only way to define a spot color in Photoshop), the short version of the name—PMS 506 CV rather than Pantone 506 CV is a good example—is used. The short names are used by almost all print-related graphics software.

G. **Show Tool Tips:** *On*

This option displays a tiny, single-letter keyboard shortcut when the cursor is placed over a tool or palette.

H. **Keyboard Zoom Resizes Windows:** *On*

When this box is enabled, the shortcuts for zooming will resize an image window automatically. When unchecked, the window remains unchanged by the Zoom command.

I. **Auto-Update Open Documents**

This option is intended for images being shared over a network. When enabled, the changes saved by one user automatically update the version being referenced by another user. When disabled, a user has to close and reopen the image to view any changes saved by another user.

To undo another user's changes while editing the same image over a network, press (Option-Command) [Alt-Control]-Z.

J. **Show Asian Text Options**

This option determines whether or not Photoshop's Asian text options are available in the Character and Paragraph palettes.

K. **Beep When Done:** *Off*

This option tells Photoshop to sound an alert whenever a command is finished processing.

L. **Dynamic Color Sliders:** *On*

This option displays an active preview of colors formed using the sliders in the Colors palette.

M. **Save Palette Locations:** *On*

This option forces Photoshop to remember where you place the floating palettes on screen.

N. **Show Font Names in English**

When using a Chinese, Japanese, or Korean version of Photoshop, this option enables the font names in the Options bar and Character palette to display in English.

O. **Use Shift Key for Tool Switch**

Every tool in the Toolbar can be accessed by pressing a single key. When this option is checked, you must hold down the Shift key to cycle through the different options represented by a single letter. When unchecked, pressing only the letter cycles through the tools.

P. **Reset All Warning Dialogs**

Photoshop displays a series of warning dialog boxes that you're able to turn off by checking a "Don't Show Again" box. Click this button to uncheck all of those boxes, enabling the warnings to display again.

Q. **Reset All Tools**

Click this button to restore the options for every tool to the original default settings.

9.48

File: Preferences: *Saving Files*

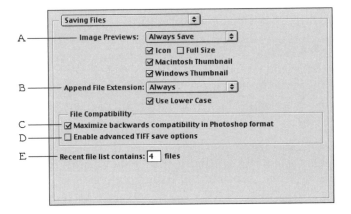

A. **Image Previews**

Previews are small renderings of an image created by Photoshop when saving a file. Checking Icon creates a 32 x 32 pixel image used as the image's icon, presumably for visual identification. Checking Macintosh or Windows Thumbnail creates the small preview referred to the Open dialog. Checking Full Size builds in an actual-size 72 ppi preview for quicker importing into another program—the image can be imported more quickly into another program, but it also slightly increases the file size.

B. **Append File Extension:** *On*

This option tells Photoshop whether or not to automatically add the three-letter code for an image's file format at the end of the title. Although it uses the Window-style method of file extensions, it's always preferable to include the extension, whether you do it automatically or manually (For more information, see *8.6, File: Save*).

C. **Maximize Backward Compatibility in Photoshop Format:** *Off*

This option includes a flattened version of the image in the file, presumably to ensure better compatibility with image editing programs that do not support layers. Since this option drastically increases file size (sometimes by as much as 200%), it should be turned off altogether. If you need backward compatibility, just save a flattened copy of the file when you need it.

D. **Enable Advanced TIFF Save Options:** *On*

When this option is enabled, the dialog box that appears when you save a TIFF image offers an expanded range of settings. When disabled, it displays the same TIFF Options dialog box that appeared in earlier Photoshop versions.

E. **Recent List Contains**

This field determines how many previously opened files Photoshop will "remember" in the File: **Open Recent** submenu.

9.49

File: Preferences: Display & Cursors

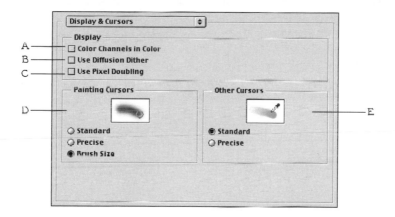

A. **Color Channels in Color:** *Off*

This option colorizes the separate channels in a color image with the same colors they are supposed to represent. The colors are only visible when you view an individual channel by clicking it in the Channels palette. This can reduce the possibility of editing the wrong channel, but the colored versions display with less contrast and clarity than their Black counterparts.

B. **Use Diffusion Dither:** *On*

For users of 8-bit (256 color) monitors, this option tells Photoshop to use a more randomized pixel diffusion method as it attempts to mimic a monitor with more colors.

C. Use Pixel Doubling

When this box is checked, Photoshop cuts the onscreen resolution of an image element in half as you drag it with the Move tool. This way, the image refreshes more quickly, enabling you to reposition it in real-time. The speed increase is most noticeable on high-res images and less-powerful workstations.

D. Painting Cursors: *Precise*

When using any Paint tool, Standard tells Photoshop to display the descriptive but wholly inaccurate tool-shaped cursor. Selecting Precise replaces the cursor with a crosshair, which is more accurate, to a certain point. When using a brush tool such as the Airbrush or Paintbrush tool, selecting Brush Size uses a round cursor the exact size of the selected brush. We prefer the Precise option because the Brush Size feature can be activated by depressing the Caps Lock key, giving us easy access to both options on-the-fly.

E. Other Cursors: *Standard*

This option applies to any tools that don't use brushes. Similar to the Painting Cursors above, we choose Standard because we can easily access the Precise tools by depressing the Caps Lock key.

9.50

File: Preferences: Transparency & Gamut

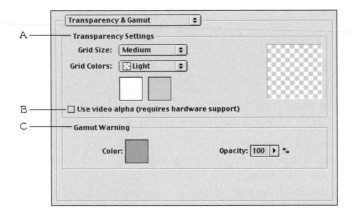

A. Transparency Settings

In order to illustrate the transparent pixels Photoshop uses when you start working with multiple layers, Adobe devised a checkerboard pattern that only appears where there are no color values whatsoever (not even white). Here, select the size of the grid and the color of the tiny squares. Change the colors by using the pop-up, the two color pickers below, or by clicking and (Option)[Alt]-clicking anywhere on an open image. To be honest, we prefer the default settings, but changing this information hurts nothing.

B. **Use Video Alpha**

This option is for anyone using a video board supporting chroma-key functions. Checking this box allows a television signal to display in any transparent area.

C. **Gamut Warning**

Clicking on this box opens the color picker, where you choose the color that the View: **Gamut Warning** command uses to highlight colors that are out of the reproducible CMYK gamut. Lowering the opacity value turns the highlight color semi-transparent. (For more information, see *14.19 View:* **Gamut Warning**.)

9.51

File: Preferences: *Units & Rulers*

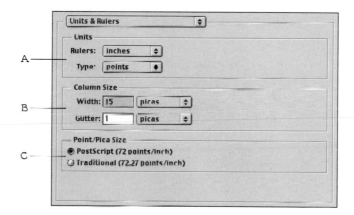

A. **Rulers**

Select the preferred units from the pop-up. Web and multimedia designers tend to use Pixels, while most print publishers use Picas or Points (For more information, see *14.36 View:* **Show Rulers**.)

B. **Column Size**

This option is referred to in the File: **New** dialog box when Columns is chosen as a Width value. It's asking for the width of a column used in a page layout, as well as the gutter, or the space in between columns. Now, when you enter a number of columns as an image width, the proper size, gutters included, is created.

C. **Point/Pica Size**

The conventional measurement of a point is a tiny bit bigger than the digital measurement. PostScript—and by extension, all graphics applications—have shortened that value to 72 points per inch. This doesn't usually cause a problem. However, some environments that employ conventional and digital technology must keep their base measurements consistent.

9.52

File: Preferences: *Guides & Grid*

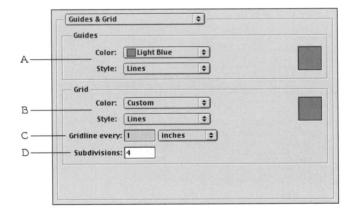

A. **Guides**

Use the pop-up menu, the color picker, or click anywhere in an open image to choose a color for the horizontal and vertical ruler guides. From the Style pop-up, choose whether the guides will be solid or dotted lines.

B. **Grid**

Use the pop-up menu, the color picker, or (Option) [Alt]-click anywhere in an open image to choose a color for the grid. From the Style pop-up, choose whether the grid will be solid or dotted lines.

C. **Gridline Every**

This value determines the distance between the gridlines displayed over an image.

D. **Subdivisions**

This value determines how many thinner lines are placed between the gridlines. For example, if you have gridlines every inch with a subdivision of four, the result is a criss-cross pattern of quarter-inch increments that Photoshop uses to align selections and layers.

9.53

File: Preferences: *Plug-ins & Scratch Disk*

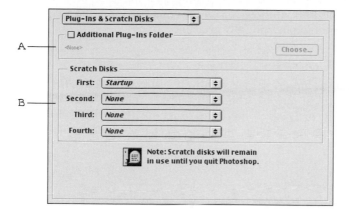

A. Plug-ins Folder

The Choose button enables you to select a different folder from which Photoshop reads the information. The only time to change that folder is when you use other applications that support plug-ins, like Painter or After Effects. If so, you may consider creating one central Plug-ins folder that each program is told to read. This way, each program has access not only its own plug-ins, but to all the others as well.

After clicking the Choose button, you must highlight the desired folder and click the Select button at the bottom of the navigation window. Pressing Return or Enter will not automatically choose the folder.

Some power users may have hundreds, if not thousands, of plug-ins. Loading this many modules when launching the software can take a prohibitively long time, especially on older model computers. If so, consider dividing your plug-ins into multiple folders, rather than one primary folder. This way, if you hold down the (Option-Command) [Alt-Control] keys while launching Photoshop, you can select your desired Plug-ins folder on the fly.

B. Scratch Disks

When Photoshop runs low on available RAM, it temporarily uses available space on the hard drive, a process known as *virtual memory* (For more information, see *14.2, Image Window: Image Data*). If you only have one hard drive, Photoshop automatically uses that as a scratch-disk, searching out the largest free chunk of drive space and using it to help process the commands you apply. If you have multiple drives, Photoshop defaults to the startup drive, but allows you to use up to four additional drives as scratch disk space. For example, if the drive set in the First pop-up runs out of room, Photoshop will switch to the second drive, and so on.

Photoshop only uses the largest contiguous (not containing any fragmented files) space for its scratch files. To keep this space constant, consider creating a 100 MB partition on one of your hard drives. This partition will appear in the First pop-up, just like a separate hard drive. As long as no files are ever copied into this partition, the space will always remain contiguous and fully available.

Issues to Consider

Don't be tempted to use removable storage media for scratch disk space. Almost anyone who has tried can tell you from experience that using a Zip or Jaz as a scratch disk is inconvenient, unreliable, and potentially dangerous. Regular hard drives are the only safe choice.

9.54
***

File: Preferences: *Image Cache*

Image caching is a scheme that speeds the on screen redraw of high-res images. When it's enabled, Photoshop uses lower resolution versions of an image to update the image on-screen when performing operations like transformations, compositing, and color adjustments.

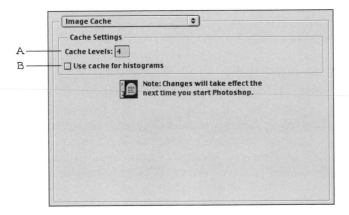

A. **Cache Levels**

Setting a Cache Levels value determines the number of different sized low-res previews that Photoshop holds in memory. The default is 4, which means previews for four zoom percentages from 100% down are maintained in RAM. The image redraws faster when editing at these zoom percentages, but it comes at a cost: Photoshop requires more RAM. Therefore, users with large amounts of RAM (48 MB and above) can safely increase the Cache Levels to 8, the maximum. Workstations with less RAM should reduce the value.

B. **Use Cache for Histograms**

Checking this button tells Photoshop to use the information of one of its cache levels to generate the histograms found in the Image: Adjust: **Levels** and Image: **Histogram** dialog boxes. The information won't be totally accurate, but histograms are rarely used for anything more than a general overview of an image's tonal range. Because leaving this option on uses a bit more RAM, turn it off if the Cache Level is set below 4.

Related Topics

The Image Menu

Image: Mode Overview

In a Photoshop image, color is defined by two things:

- **Its color model,** which is a mathematically-defined color gamut used by Photoshop to generate a color image.

- **Its color mode,** which, on the other hand, provides a file structure that enables that range of color to be displayed, edited, and—if necessary—printed.

Photoshop Color Models

Color models are only used to generate full-color images. In an attempt to compensate for our very subjective perception of color, two- or three-dimensional models are used to mathematically represent a color's position in a particular space. This method ensures that color information is accurately communicated between your computers, software, and peripheral devices.

In Photoshop, images with 256 colors or less—including Bitmap, Grayscale, Duotone, and Indexed Color images—are not represented by any particular model.

Establishing Color Mode

An image never automatically appears in the appropriate color mode. After understanding the differences between Photoshop's supported color models, you must first determine the appropriate mode, then create it. Consider the following factors when determining an image's mode:

- **The ultimate use of the image.** Just as an image must be saved in the right file format, it must also exist in the right mode. RGB files, for example, cannot separate on an imagesetter; CMYK images cannot display on the Web.

- **The number of available colors.** One-color images require a mode that displays only one color. On the other hand, when working with full-color images, you usually edit in a mode with a wide range of colors (like RGB) before converting to a smaller gamut (like CMYK).

- **The editing tools available to that mode.** Not all commands are available to all modes. This largely depends on the number of colors in an image. If you're editing an RGB image, which can contain 16.7 million colors, you have access to all filters and color adjustment tools. If you're editing a Bitmap image, which contains only one color, you can't use any of those commands.

Color Depth

A color mode is actually a file structure. Different types of color image can be displayed only if a file contains the appropriate components. This boils down to two things: an image's pixel depth and the number of color channels.

Pixel depth describes the color potential of a single pixel. In any Photoshop image, each pixel can be only one color. As far as your computer is concerned, color is defined by binary data, or strings of 1's and 0's. Each character is called a *bit*. The more bits used to describe a pixel, the more possible colors that pixel can be:

1-bit Color

The most common example of 1-bit color is black-and-white line art. Its pixels are one of only two colors: black or white. Here, black pixels are described with a "1", white pixels are described with a "0". There are fewer than 256 colors, so only one color channel is required.

Since so little information is required to display these colors, 1-bit images have the smallest relative file size.

8-bit Color

The perfect example of 8-bit color is a Grayscale image. Here, each pixel is described with eight bits of information. There are 256 possible combinations of 1's and 0's in a string of eight characters, so there are 256 possible levels of gray. This is the maximum amount of information that can be contained in a single color channel—to display full color, an image requires additional channels.

Eight-bit images contain eight times the amount of information as a 1-bit image. Therefore, a similarly configured image is eight times as large.

24-bit Color

An RGB image is made of three internal Grayscale channels, each one representing a different color. Now each pixel is described by three 8-bit values—or 24 total bits.

Containing three times the amount of information as a single-channel, 8-bit image, 24-bit images are three times as large.

Pixel depth should not be confused with the bit depth of a scanner. An RGB image may be limited to 8 bits of information per color channel, but many scanners acquire up to 16 bits per channel. This extra information is not written directly into the file, but it almost always results in a higher-quality scan.

Color Gamut

Every color model embodies a unique range of colors, known as the *gamut.* Of the models described in this section, Lab color has the largest gamut, encompassing all the colors of RGB space, and then some. In turn, RGB contains more colors than CMYK, the smallest gamut.

Gamut becomes an issue when you convert an image from one color space to another, particularly when you convert from Lab or RGB to CMYK. When this happens (and one way or another, it has to, if you want to reproduce an image on press), Photoshop must re-describe the colors of one range with combinations of CMYK values, based on the information established in the CMYK Setup dialog box. If a color falls outside the CMYK range and cannot be described, it's pushed back to the closest borderline color.

Unfortunately, this causes two problems. First, many shades and subtle differences in tone are lost. Extreme colors, such as bright blues and vivid greens, will flatten and darken considerably. Two slightly different RGB colors can even be changed to the same CMYK value. Second, you only get one chance to move between color spaces. Converting to CMYK irreversibly clips any out-of-gamut colors—you cannot regain them by switching back to the previous model.

This phenomenon poses one of the greatest challenges of color correcting. Not only must you balance the colors of an image to match the original material, you must do so in a space that contains far fewer colors than your eyes can see, a camera can recognize, and your scanner can capture. Like working with halftones, it's an illusion, a process of highly managed loss.

10.2

The RGB/CMY Model

The RGB model is used to reproduce the spectrum of visible light, and represents anything that transmits, filters, or senses light waves (like your monitor, scanner, or eyes). It's commonly described as the *additive primary* model. The absence of all light is black; to create different colors, you must add levels of the primary colors (red, green, and blue).

You can't discuss RGB color without mentioning its opposite, the CMY model. This model represents *reflected* light, or the colors you see in printed inks, photographic dyes, and colored toner. CMY is described as the *subtractive primary* model. Here, full values of the primary colors (pure cyan, magenta, and yellow) *produce* black; to produce different colors, you must reduce the levels of the primaries. **A**

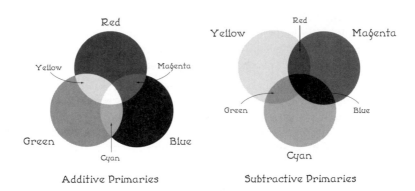

Additive Primaries   Subtractive Primaries

A *When you combine full intensities of the additive primaries (the basis of transmitted light), the result is white. When you combine full intensities of the subtractive primaries (the basis of reflected light), the result is black. Note how combining two primaries of one model produces a primary of the other (see color insert).*

Because RGB and CMY are the inverse of each other, they share a special relationship. When you display this information as a single color wheel, the colors alternate between RGB and CMY. If you combine two RGB colors, you produce a CMY value; if you combine two CMY colors, you produce an RGB value. For example, in the CMY model, red is described as the combination of magenta and yellow. In the RGB model, magenta is described as the combination of red and blue.

Examine the RGB/CMY color wheel. When two colors of one model are combined to create a color of the other, there's one left over. This is known as the new color's *complement*. For example, magenta and yellow combine to produce red; therefore, the complement of red is cyan. As you can see in the color wheel, cyan appears as the direct opposite of red. **B**

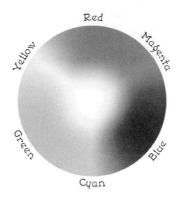

B *The RGB/CMY color wheel alternates between the additive and subtractive primaries. To determine a color's complement, look for the value directly across the wheel (see color insert).*

The following table lists the component and complementary colors of the RGB/CMY primaries.

Color	Components	Complement
Red	Yellow + Magenta	Cyan
Green	Cyan + Yellow	Magenta
Blue	Magenta + Cyan	Yellow
Cyan	Blue + Green	Red
Magenta	Red + Blue	Green
Yellow	Green + Red	Blue

Issues to Consider

RGB, the most commonly used color space, has one strength and one weakness. On one hand, this model is extremely useful for high-res image editing. It displays a wide range of values, and images in RGB mode can take advantage of nearly all of Photoshop's commands and filters. On the other hand, RGB is device dependent, meaning that regardless of a color's numerical definition, the way it appears depends entirely on the hardware used to display it. Environmental factors such as monitor age and the amount of ambient light make displaying color consistently on multiple devices almost impossible.

Components and complements are an important part of a color adjusting workflow. For example, assume you're scanning an item that you perceive to be too yellow. You want to reduce the amount of yellow at the time of the scan, but your scanning software doesn't contain any controls for yellow—only red, green, and blue. You have two ways to address this problem. First, according to the color wheel, yellow is a combination of red and green. Reducing these colors during scanning produces the same effect as reducing yellow. Second, the complement of yellow is blue. Increasing blue is the same as reducing yellow. Given these choices, the former is usually more effective. It's easier to compensate by pulling color out, as opposed to pushing it in. Complementary colors are important to an image's tone and sharpness; if you create too steep an imbalance during scanning, you may not be able to correct it afterwards.

10.3

The CMYK Model

You are prevented from printing RGB color by the very laws of physics. One way or another, when you have an RGB image destined for print, you must convert its additive color values to CMY, a purely subtractive state.

The CMYK color model represents the four colors used to reproduce full-color images: cyan, magenta, yellow, and black. In theory, CMY inks are sufficient to reproduce the full range of colors—in fact, color photography is *trichromatic*, meaning cyan, magenta, and yellow dyes are pure enough to produce a full range of color. However, this is impossible in print. CMY inks always contain slight impurities, and different types of paper stock absorb different levels of light, further affecting your perception of color. As a result, combining 100% levels of CMY inks produces more of a muddy brown color than black. To compensate, black ink is added to balance the range of colors.

Because CMYK represents a much smaller range of color than RGB, it is impossible to reproduce all the colors that appear on your monitor. When you convert an RGB image to CMYK in order to reproduce the colors in print, many of the values will change.

Issues to Consider

Understanding the "K" in CMYK. You may have wondered why black is represented by a "K" instead of a "B". Many people assume that this was done to avoid confusion with the blue of RGB color. Not so. When printers started using black ink as a full-color component about 80 years ago, it was referred to as the key color. Black was the first color laid down, providing the basis for registering the remaining inks.

10.4

The Lab Model

The Lab model was developed in 1976 (and continues to be refined) by the *Commission Internationale d'Eclairage*, a scientific organization that's main concern is measuring color. This model is unique in that it's device independent. The RGB and CMYK models describe colors by component values (how they're *supposed* to appear), but cannot accommodate the variability of your hardware and environment (which determines how they *ultimately* appear). The Lab model is constructed according to how color actually exists, and how it is perceived in different environments.

The basic idea is this. While your eye is most sensitive to red, green, and blue, you cannot detect different colors until three additional neural responses register in your brain: a magenta-green relationship, a yellow-blue relationship, and a lightness (or black-white) relationship. Magenta contains no green; yellow contains no blue; white contains no black. The Lab model correctly assumes that any conceivable color can be described by quantifying its position between these complements. When a Lab specification is told to account for certain lighting conditions, it can further refine a color value, based on how the human eye would respond to it.

"Lab" is actually an acronym for the three components of the color space. The "L" represents Lightness, or how bright a color is; "a" represents a color's position between magenta and green; and "b" represents the position between yellow and blue.

You probably don't realize it, but Lab is one of the most commonly used models in the print industry. Whenever you convert an image from one color mode to another, Photoshop internally converts to Lab first. As you set your printing and separation preferences (as described later in this chapter), Photoshop uses Lab space to determine the correlating RGB and CMYK values, then builds an index called a *look-up table* (LUT). During conversions, Photoshop uses this table to produce the necessary colors.

Lab is a superlative model for communicating color information among machines. Most device-independent color management systems and many scanners use Lab in their reckoning of color. Kodak's YCC color space (which it developed for its PhotoCD system) is also based on Lab space. Entire books have been written about it by esteemed color scientists, and a small cadre of hard-core, high-end specialists swear that Lab is the only way to go.

Does this mean you should consider performing your color adjustments in Lab Color mode? Absolutely not. Being abstract and highly mathematical, it does a horrible job describing color to ordinary human beings. (Try telling your printer that you need to boost an image's "a" component sometime, and see what response you get.) It's difficult to comprehend, let alone master. Your time is better spent focusing on the relationship between RGB and CMYK color; pursue Lab only if the demands of your workplace specifically require it.

10.5

The HSB Model

This model defines color using three criteria that people recognize intuitively: hue, saturation, and brightness. **A**

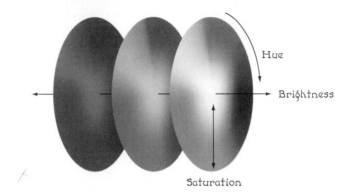

Hue

Brightness

Saturation

A *The HSB color space is cylindrically shaped. Hue refers to a color's position around the RGB/CMY color wheel. Saturation determines the intensity of a color, or its position between the center of the wheel to the outer edge. Brightness determines how light or dark a color appears, or its position between the front and back of the cylinder (see color insert).*

Hue refers to a particular color, such as purple, orange, or red. When HSB space is represented as a three-dimensional cylinder, the visible spectrum of colors encircle its circumference, with each color assigned an angle. Red is positioned at 0°, and the remaining colors are arranged the same as the RGB/CMY color wheel: Yellow is at 60°, green at 120°, cyan at 180°, blue at 240°, and magenta at 300°.

Saturation refers to a color's intensity. For example, a soft pastel orange has a low saturation value; the blaze orange of a traffic cone is highly saturated. In the HSB cylinder, colors in the center have a saturation value of 0, which produces a gray tone. As a color moves closer to the outer edge, the saturation increases.

Brightness refers to a color's tone, or how light or dark it appears. Lower brightness values darken a color, creating what you perceive to be a deeper tone. In the cylindrical model, brightness moves from front to back. At one end, brightness is at full value; at the other, all colors are reduced to black.

HSB is referential, as opposed to the RGB and CMYK spaces. Those color models are actually instructions that tell a monitor or printer how to construct a color. However, you can use hue, saturation, and brightness as the basis for creating adjustments in every color mode. They're available in Photoshop's color picker and the Image: Adjust: **Hue/Saturation** and **Replace Color** commands.

10.6

Image: Mode: *Bitmap*

Images in Bitmap mode are 1-bit color, so pixels are either black or white. Most often, Bitmap images are used for the following types of artwork:

- Creating line art for print.

- Generating specialized, one-color effects.

- Creating small-sized, one-color web graphics.

Issues to Consider

You can only convert Grayscale images to Bitmap mode. To convert a color image to Bitmap, convert to Grayscale first, then to Bitmap.

The Bitmap Dialog Box

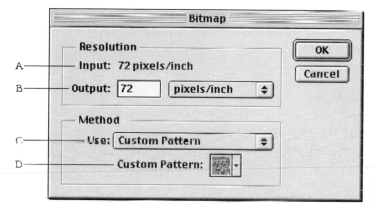

A. **Input**

This value states the current image resolution in pixels per inch. You cannot change it.

B. **Output**

This option enables you to change the image resolution when converting to Bitmap mode. Its uses are limited, but quite effective. For example, when creating a 1-bit halftone, you can convert a 300 ppi Grayscale image to a 2400 ppi screen. Or, when creating a dithered-tone image, you can raise or lower the resolution to fine-tune the effect.

Bear in mind that this option does not affect the appearance of an image already converted to black-and-white tones (for example, by using the Image: Adjust: **Threshold** command, or by converting a low-res line art file to Grayscale and back again).

C. Use

The options in this pop-up menu determine the method used to convert an image to black-and-white pixels.

50% Threshold

This conversion method changes all image tones into pure black or white. It makes no attempts to shade or simulate tone, producing the same effect as a 1-bit line art scan. It does this by applying a *threshold*, or a dividing line, at 50% black. All tones above 50% become black, all tones below become white. This method is appropriate for artwork containing bold, solid areas or ultra-fine details.

If you're looking for this type of effect but don't want to change the color mode, use Image: Adjust: **Threshold**. It enables you to reposition the 50% threshold, changing the number of tones that become black or white—and, the image retains its original mode.

Pattern Dither

By *dithering* pixels, Photoshop scatters them in an attempt to simulate the tones of a Grayscale image. The Pattern method uses a predefined geometric pattern that produces awkward, blotchy results, similar to the patterns used in the earliest paint programs. Those of you wishing to simulate tone in a 1-bit image should use Diffusion Dither.

Diffusion Dither

Instead of using a pattern, this method randomizes the individual pixels to simulate tone. This method is ineffective at resolutions above 300 ppi. (For more information, see *E.9, Creating a 1-bit Random-Screened Image.*)

Halftone Screen

This method reduces the tones of gray to a series of halftone dots. After choosing this option, set one of the following items in the Halftone Screen dialog box. The *Frequency* value determines the size of the simulated halftone dots. The *Angle* value determines the angle of the screen frequency, or the rotation of the halftone grid. Select a halftone dot shape from the *Shape* pop-up menu: Round, Diamond, Ellipse, Line, Square, or Cross.

At higher resolutions (1200 ppi and up), this option is able to simulate the appearance of a screened Grayscale image. At lower Frequency values (45 lpi and below), you can create a variety of specialized screening effects. (For more information, see *E.8, Creating a 1-bit Halftone.*)

Another alternative is the Filter: Pixelate: **Color Halftone** command—when applied to a Grayscale image, it changes the tones to smooth, anti-aliased dots without converting the color mode. The only available shape is Round, however—any other shape must be created with the Bitmap dialog box.

D. **Custom Pattern**

This option uses a pattern already defined using Edit: **Define Pattern** to create a customized screen. The same idea of the 50% Threshold applies here; the information is reduced to black and white, but the repeating pattern only appears in areas darker than 50% black.

Related Topics

8.39   *File: Page Setup:* **Screens**
9.29   *Edit:* **Define Pattern**
10.7   *Image: Mode:* **Grayscale**
10.33 *Image: Adjust:* **Threshold**
Appendix E, Line Art Editing Techniques

10.7

Image: Mode: Grayscale

Grayscale images are also known as 8-bit files, meaning each pixel is one of 256 possible tones of gray. Once you start working with this many tones, there are two ways to interpret the information: as brightness values or output values. The method you use typically depends on whether an image is going to be used onscreen or printed.

Pixels in a Grayscale image are given a value between 0 (no brightness, or black) and 255 (full brightness, or white). The higher the value, the lighter gray the pixel will be. When your monitor displays a Grayscale pixel, it's actually displaying equal values of red, green, and blue, which gives the appearance of different gray levels. Most Grayscale images, however, are intended for output and printing. To assist you, the tones are presented as output values, or halftone dot sizes from 0% (white, or no ink) to 100% (black, or full ink coverage).

Common uses for images in Grayscale mode include the following:

- Generating halftones for print.

- Converting a color image to be used as a printed halftone.

- Creating the appearance of a black-and-white photograph for a web or on-screen graphic.

- Converting a 1-bit image to a mode you can edit with a wider range of tools.

- Converting a color image, en route to Bitmap mode.

Mistakes to Avoid

Producing a quadtone by converting a Grayscale image to CMYK. The most successful way to make this type of image is to convert to Image: Mode: **Duotone**. Otherwise, the CMYK image is larger and much less flexible than its Duotone counterpart. There are only two reasons to bypass the Duotone mode:

- If you prefer to have access to individual color curves in the Image: Adjust: **Curves** dialog box when editing a quadtone.

- If you're going to be changing some part of the image to a more vivid color, which isn't possible in a duotone.

Issues to Consider

Every other Photoshop mode can be converted directly to Grayscale. Conversely, a Grayscale image can be converted to any other mode.

Simulating Grayscale in a color image. To reduce a color image to the appearance of a Grayscale image without changing modes, choose Image: Adjust: **Desaturate**. By applying this command to a selected area, you can reduce smaller portions of an image to gray tones.

Converting to Grayscale may result in unexpected tonal shifts. When you convert a color image to Grayscale, Photoshop attempts to maintain the relative brightness of the colored pixels. Since different colors can share the same brightness level, some colors may convert into the same tone of gray. Because of this, you can't always expect a satisfactory Grayscale version of a color image. Usually, you'll need to adjust the image using Image: Adjust: **Levels** or Image: Adjust: **Curves**.

Converting to Grayscale using RGB or CMYK channels. Before converting to Grayscale, a common technique is to examine the individual color channels. Occasionally, one channel looks better than the Grayscale image that results from converting the entire file. If you choose a channel and select Image: Mode: **Grayscale**, the brightness values of that one channel are used, while the others are discarded.

Converting to Grayscale via Lab Color mode. If you're not satisfied with the results of converting a color image directly to Grayscale, try converting to Lab Color mode first. In the Channels palette, click the Lightness channels. Choose Image: Mode: **Grayscale** to discard the hidden channels. The images produced using this approach are typically lighter in the midtones, and require less fine-tuning.

The Grayscale Dialog Box

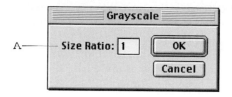

A. **Size Ratio**

Photoshop defaults to a size ratio of 1. This means the new Grayscale image is exactly the same size as the original Bitmap. Any number higher than this produces a smaller image: A ratio of 2 reduces to 50%, a ratio of 3 reduces to 33%, 4 reduces to 25%, and so forth. You cannot enter a value less than 1 to generate a larger image.

Related Topics

10.10   Image: Mode: RGB Color
10.11   Image: Mode: CMYK Color
10.20   Image: Adjust: Levels
10.22   Image: Adjust: Curves
10.26   Image: Adjust: Desaturate
Appendix F, Halftone Adjusting Techniques

10.8

Image: Mode: Duotone

Duotones, tritones, and quadtones enable you to expand the tonal range of a printed halftone. The average printing press is capable of reproducing 40–60 different tones of a single color ink—far less than the 256-level range that Photoshop supports. In a duotone, multiple inks are used to reproduce a halftone. This broadens the number of reproducible tones, adding depth and range to the printed image.

Duotones can be made of process or spot inks, but they must begin as a Grayscale image. Unlike a color image (or an image that contains a spot color channel), only one channel exists in the file; the duotone retains the brightness values of the original Grayscale image. This color mode simply tells an output device to print the image differently, much like embedding a transfer curve (for more information on transfer functions, see *8.40, File: Page Setup: Transfer.*) Before you create a duotone, the image must be adjusted, sharpened, and optimized for the target press conditions as needed.

Mistakes to Avoid

Using an incorrect PANTONE ink name. When you specify a PANTONE ink, it is imperative that you keep its name consistent with the colors defined in your layout program and any other project files. Unlike process colors, which are always based on CMYK combinations, images tagged with a custom ink are separated to an individual plate. If you use different names to reference the same color, you'll likely wind up with extra color plates during output. In other words, if your layout already contains "PANTONE 2705 CVC," don't be tempted to create a duotone based on "Purple" or "PMS 2705." If you use any variation on the name, your layout program may not understand that they're supposed to be the same color, and page elements intended for the same plate will separate to different plates.

Different programs tend to use their own PANTONE abbreviations, but Photoshop images have historically caused the most problems. For example, if you specify PANTONE 2705 in an Illustrator or FreeHand file, your layout program will recognize the color, whether it's named "PANTONE 2705 CVC," Pantone 2705 CVU," or "PMS 2705". However, if the spot color name of a duotone is even one letter different from the version defined in the layout file, your program will see both occurrences of PANTONE 2705 as different colors. The moral is this: Simply choosing an ink name is not enough; you must double-check the convention used by the importing program to make sure the names are identical.

Saving a duotone incorrectly. Regardless of the type of duotone you create, two things must happen before you can import and output the image:

- If you used a duotone preset, these angles are automatically set. If you set your own curves, you must set your own screen angles in the File: Page Setup: **Screens** dialog box. Otherwise, they all output at the same angle, ruining the image. If unsure of which angles to use, consult your printer.

- Make sure the Include Halftone Screens box is checked in the EPS Options dialog box. Otherwise, the colors separate at the same angle.

Issues to Consider

In presets, the ink order targets different parts of the tonal range. Define the darkest color in your duotone as Ink 1—it reproduces most of the shadow detail. Ink 2 colorizes the image, providing most of the highlight information. When additional inks are added, Ink 3 warms the image by affecting the midtones, and Ink 4 primarily focuses on the three-quarter tones.

The maximum number of inks in a duotone is four. Even though many designers create projects consisting of five, six, or more colors, the Duotone Options dialog box cannot combine more than four inks.

The Duotone Options Dialog Box

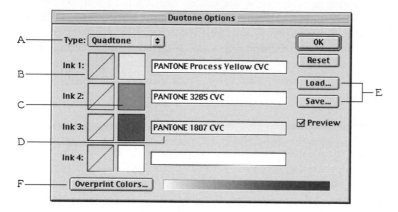

A. Type

By choosing an option from this pop-up, you determine how many inks are used to reproduce the image:

Monotone

> Monotones use only one ink, typically a Pantone color, to reproduce a halftone.
>
> Usually, there's no need to create a monotone in Photoshop. If you save a Grayscale image as a TIFF and import it into a page layout program, you can recolor it with any color defined in the program.
>
> The only reason to make a monotone is if you want to recolor a halftone, but you have to save it as an EPS. This happens for one of two reasons: if you import the image into a program that doesn't support TIFF images; or, if the image already contains a PostScript command, such as a transfer function or clipping path.

Duotone

> Although Photoshop refers to all images in this mode as duotones, that term really describes images reproduced with two inks. The majority of duotones use black as one of the two colors.

Tritone

> Tritones use three different inks to reproduce a halftone.

Quadtone

> Quadtones use four inks. The majority of them use combinations of cyan, magenta, yellow, and black to reproduce a halftone, although combinations of spot inks are possible.

B. Curve

The distribution of each ink is controlled by a gamma curve, which works the same as File: Page Setup: **Transfer** or Image: Adjust: **Curves**. Since two or more colors are going to be combined, they must be combined intelligently. If you don't adjust the curves, equal amounts of both inks are printed in all areas of the image, causing it to shift and darken significantly. Manually adjusting duotone inks is a complex science—they are difficult at best to proof, and standard color correcting techniques do not apply. To assist you, Adobe provides a series of preset curves for a great variety of duotones. They can be manipulated to suit most of your needs, and we recommend using them instead of attempting to set your own curves.

C. **Swatch**

Clicking this box accesses the custom color picker. For a duotone containing spot colors, choose the appropriate PMS ink from this list. To select a process color—for example, if you're making a black and cyan duotone as part of a four-color job—click on the Picker button to switch to the standard color picker.

D. **Color Name**

Once you select a color and click OK, its name will appear in this field. If you've chosen a spot color, make sure the name matches the name in your page layout program. Using the incorrect spot color name results in an additional color plate during output.

If you choose a process tint as a color, no name appears in the field. You must enter a name manually in order to apply the curves to the image.

E. **Load and Save**

Using these buttons, you can save the information in the Duotones Options dialog box to load and apply to another image. Most often, these buttons are used to load the preset duotone curves that ship with Photoshop.

F. **Overprint Colors**

Duotones create tonal depth by overlapping different inks. In an attempt to display this effect on screen, this option lets you change the colors that result when your inks combine. Clicking on any swatch accesses the color picker, enabling you to define a new color. This only affects the onscreen appearance of the active duotone, and Photoshop's first guess is usually about as accurate as it gets. Unless your monitor is rigidly calibrated, changing these values accomplishes little.

Related Topics

8.39   File: Page Setup: **Screens**
10.22 Image: Adjust: **Curves**
Appendix J, Custom Ink Techniques

10.9

Image: Mode: *Indexed Color*

When you convert an image to Indexed Color, you reduce the number of colors it can display to 256 or less. By doing so, you reduce the amount of information contained in the file, which results in a smaller file size. For this reason, all web graphics saved as CompuServe GIFs have indexed color palettes. Also, multimedia designers often use Indexed Color graphics because of their faster display times. Print professionals, however, have no use for this color mode.

When you convert to Indexed Color, Photoshop creates a color *look-up table* (LUT), or a small index that describes the image's few remaining colors. Only the colors present there appear in the image. Although the color table can contain 256 colors, you'll usually specify a lower number to further reduce the file size. Photoshop attempts to recreate the original range of colors as closely as possible, based on the final number of colors you choose.

Mistakes to Avoid

Creating double-dithered graphics. Although the Diffusion dither option may look best on your monitor, it may not be the best choice for your web graphics. The vast majority of people using the Internet use 8-bit monitors, which use their own dithering scheme to display colors on screen. An image dithered twice—once by the Indexed Color dialog box, and once by the viewer's monitor—suffers in quality. Choosing None as a dithering option at least results in the most predictable quality.

Converting to Indexed Color before editing is complete. Make sure your editing is completed before you convert an image to Indexed Color. The lost colors cannot be regained by converting back to RGB, and most editing functions—including filters, Image: **Adjust** commands, anti-aliasing, and feathering—are not available in this mode.

Issues to Consider

Converting to Indexed Color versus File: Save for Web. This command is not the only way to create an Indexed Color graphic. The same options are available in the File: **Save for Web** command, which also enables you to preview a series of compression settings before exporting the file.

The only color mode you can convert to an indexed palette is RGB. If you wish to index the colors of a Lab or CMYK image, convert first to RGB, then to Indexed Color.

Editing a Color Table. After you convert an image to Indexed Color, you can further edit its color palette under Image: Mode: **Color Table**. There, you can increase or decrease the number of colors, as well as change the color values.

For most GIF images, the visual difference between 256 colors and 128 is negligible. You can usually cut the number of available colors down to 128 without noticing any additional image degradation—and save considerable file size in the process.

Converting a Grayscale image. Since Grayscale images contain 256 tones or less, the Indexed Color dialog box does not appear when you convert to that mode. Instead, it automatically applies the Exact palette. To access the dialog box, switch the Grayscale image back to RGB before converting to Indexed Color.

The Indexed Color Dialog Box

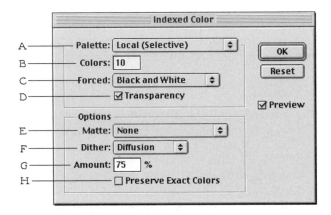

A. Palette

Select a palette type from this pop-up menu:

Exact

> This palette is automatically chosen when the original image contains 256 colors or less, such as a screen shot, logo, or highly posterized image. It also appears if the original image was Grayscale. It means that Photoshop uses precisely the same colors that appear in the image to construct the color table. If the original image contains more than 256 colors, this option is not available.

System (Macintosh) and System (Windows)

> This option uses the default color palette of your operating system. Macintosh and Windows may use many of the same colors, but they are arranged differently. Therefore, use this palette if you're sure the image only will be viewed on the same platform as yours. Most often, the System palette is applied to graphics that enhance the operating system itself. For example, someone creating specialized icons or Finder-level graphics for the Macintosh should select the System (Macintosh) option.

Web

> This palette represents the 216 color recognized by most major web browsers. When a browser displays a color not included in this palette, it must dither the color on screen, or combine colored pixels in an attempt to simulate the color. This results in visible artifacting, which most web designers prefer to avoid. Many designers load these colors into the Swatches palette, so they can refer to them directly when designing web graphics.

Uniform

> This palette contains an evenly-stepped sampling of colors from the RGB spectrum. Initially, it's the same as the web palette (216 colors), but it has a touch more flexibility—you can reduce the number of colors to as low as eight.

Adaptive (Local and Master)

> This palette generates a color table based on the colors that appear most frequently in the original image. Less-used colors are discarded, and their original values are changed to the indexed colors they most closely match. Use this option when you want to maintain the most accurate colors possible.

> The Local setting is appropriate when working on a single image, and you want the Adaptive option to focus only on the colors at hand. The Master option enables you to broaden that focus to a series of open images, enabling you to apply the same table to each one.

> You may need to redirect the color decisions made by the Adaptive method, especially if part of your image is tone-sensitive and you're using a particularly low number of colors. Select the important part of the image before converting to Indexed Color. Photoshop bases the new color table on the values within the selection.

Perceptual (Local and Master)

> This option is similar to Adaptive (described above)—however, instead of including the most frequently-occurring colors, it attempts to use only the values that produce more even transitions between colored areas. Use this option when smooth transitions are more important than color integrity.

> As with Adaptive, choose the Local option when working on a single image, and the Master option when you want a series of open images to use the same color palette.

Selective (Local and Master)

> This option is similar to Adaptive (described above)—however, it restricts the palette to a certain range of key values, including the 216 browser-safe colors.

> As with Adaptive, choose the Local option when working on a single image, and the Master option when you want a series of open images to use the same color palette.

Custom

> This option automatically opens the Image: Mode: **Color Table** dialog box, where you can import a previously saved color palette.

Previous

> Selecting this option automatically applies the last-used color palette. This is useful if you are applying the same values to a series of images, whether it's a 3-bit Adaptive palette or an extensively edited custom table. This option is only available when at least one image has been converted to Indexed Color since the last time Photoshop was launched.

B. **Colors**

> This field enables you to enter the specific number of colors that will appear in the palette. This option is only available when you set Uniform or one of the Local Master options in the Indexed Color Palette pop-up menu. The rule is simple: lower numbers of colors produce smaller file sizes. The trick is finding a balance between file size and image quality. The field defaults to 256, but that number is almost always too high. Most users start with 64, then move up or down, depending on the image requirements.

C. **Forced**

> When setting an Adaptive palette—especially with a low number of colors—it's easy to lose the image's most important values. The Forced option enables you to lock certain colors, ensuring that they appear in the converted image.

None

> The default setting, this option doesn't lock any values.

Black and White

> This option locks only black and white.

Primaries

> This option locks black and white, plus the primary colors: red (R:255, G:0, B:0), green (R:0, G:255, B:0), blue (R:0, G:0, B:255), cyan (R:0, G:255, B:255), magenta (R:255, G:0, B:255), and yellow (R:255, G:255, B:0).

Web

> This option locks any of the 216 browser-safe values that exist in the image.

Custom

> This option enables you to lock specific values before converting the image. When you choose it from the Forced pop-up menu, the Forced Colors dialog box appears; 256 swatches are available, but only black and white are set by default. Add a new color to the table by clicking a blank swatch. The color picker appears, where you can

either enter the target values, or move the cursor over the image to click the desired color. To remove a color from the table—thereby unlocking it—(Command) [Control]-click it.

If desired, save the color table you've created by clicking the Save button. To make it available in the Preset Manager, place the file in the following folder: Adobe Photoshop 6/Presets/Optimized Colors. To add the colors of a pre-saved table, click the Load button.

D. Transparency

This box enables you retain a transparent area in the converted image. In order to work, an element must already exist on an image layer, already surrounded by transparent pixels, when you choose the Indexed Color command. When you check this box, the transparent area is built into the GIF. (For more information, see *I.1, Creating a Simple Silhouette.*)

This approach replaces the separate GIF89a Export command of earlier Photoshop versions. Bear in mind that a transparent GIF can only consist of hard edges—you cannot use soft or feathered transitions. (For more information, see *"Matte,"* below.)

E. Matte

This option works in conjunction with the Transparency feature in two ways. Both methods require that you know the background color of the web page that will display the graphic.

First, when the Transparency box is checked, it encircles any soft-edges in the image with the value established in the Matte pop-up menu. This way, when a browser loads the graphic, the edges appear to fade into the background. It doesn't fill the entire image with the matte color—it only fills to the outer perimeter of the edge detail, adding transparency beyond that point. This way, you retain a little flexibility when placing the graphic.

When the Transparency box is unchecked, it fills all transparent and semi-transparent areas in the current with the established Matte color. This way, you retain the *appearance* of a transparent GIF, without actually building transparency into the file.

F. Dither

The dither method determines how the indexed colors are distributed throughout the image:

None

With no dithering selected, Photoshop simply changes each image pixel to its closest equivalent in the color table. In images with more continuous tones, this usually results in harsher color transitions and visible banding. This option does result in smaller GIFs, since LZW compression works best with contiguous color areas.

Pattern

This method is only available when System (Macintosh) is the selected palette. It uses a predefined pattern to redistribute the colors, attempting to compensate for the lost tones. It does a poor job, and should not be used.

Diffusion

This method randomizes the colored pixels, creating the illusion of additional colors.

Noise

This method is similar to Diffusion, but it randomizes pixels more evenly throughout the image.

G. **Amount**

Available only when you set Diffusion in the Dither pop-up menu, this field enables you to determine the degree of smoothness between color transitions. Higher values result in smoother transitions, but larger file size; lower values result in harsher transitions, but smaller file size.

H. **Preserve Exact Colors**

Available only when you set Diffusion in the Dither pop-up menu, this option removes any dithering that would otherwise occur in solid-colored areas.

Related Topics

10.10

Image: Mode: RGB Color

RGB is the most commonly used color mode. All scanners acquire images in RGB, even if some scanning software automatically converts them to CMYK.

An RGB file consists of three Grayscale color channels: one red, one green, and one blue. Like a standard Grayscale image, each channel uses 8 bits of data per pixel to display color, which translates into 256 brightness levels per channel. Therefore, each image pixel is defined by three brightness values from 0–255, one for each color. When all three values are 0, the color is black. When all three are 255, the color is white. When all three are equal numbers between 0 and 255, the color is some shade of gray.

Images in RGB Color mode are most commonly encountered in the following situations:

Editing a scan before converting to CMYK. Since RGB contains a much wider range than CMYK, the first round of editing is usually performed in RGB mode. This ensures that as much information as possible is present in the image. It's then converted to CMYK, a mode containing much less color information, for proofing and printing.

Editing a graphic before converting to Indexed Color. All web and multi-media graphics are viewed on RGB monitors, even if they don't necessarily remain in RGB mode. By editing them in RGB, you have more control over how they ultimately display.

Mistakes to Avoid

Converting from RGB and back. Once an RGB image is converted to another mode, it may not be wise to convert back for further editing. You cannot regain any lost color information by converting back to RGB.

Issues to Consider

RGB values are never displayed as output values, because the mode does not exist in a printable form. However, Photoshop already knows how it will convert an image to CMYK at any given moment. Show both RGB and the relative CMYK values by selecting Palette Options from the Info palette submenu. There, set First Color Readout to RGB, and Second Color Readout to CMYK.

Related Topics

10.11

Image: Mode: CMYK *Color*

Images in CMYK Color mode contain the information necessary to produce four-color process separations. Each image is comprised of four Grayscale channels, one each for the cyan, magenta, yellow, and black information. When you separate a CMYK image, the color channels output as four individual halftones. For that reason, all CMYK colors are read as output values, or percentages from 0 to 100. Often, color images are edited in RGB or Lab Color mode, then converted to CMYK just prior to printing. Because CMYK images are only destined for print, they are almost always saved as either TIFF or Photoshop EPS files.

Images in CMYK Color mode are most commonly encountered in the following situations:

Preparing a full color image for print. CMYK is the standard mode used to produce color separations on a laser printer, imagesetter, or digital press.

Make additional adjustments to a CMYK image. Some high-end scanning software automatically convert RGB scans to CMYK. If your service bureau provides color proofs with their scans, then those images are converted to CMYK. Also, if you rasterize a CMYK-colored, vector-based graphic, you'll continue editing in this mode. Never switch to another mode to make additional edits.

Mistakes to Avoid

Failing to correct the color of high-res scans. Accurately adjusting and reproducing color is one of the most complex tasks in the print publishing industry. Although an image may look acceptable on screen, proper color correcting requires a calibrated monitor, an understanding of the Image: Adjust: **Curves** dialog box, and the ability to read the output percentages in the Info palette.

Failing to adjust the Color Settings. The Edit: **Color Settings** controls determine how Photoshop converts an RGB image to CMYK values. These settings must be tailored to match the anticipated press conditions.

Defining out-of-gamut colors. There are three ways to identify RGB and Lab colors that fall out of CMYK's gamut. The first two, the Info palette and the color selection window in the Color Picker, display an exclamation point when an out-of-gamut color is targeted. The third is the View: **Gamut Warning** command, which temporarily masks out-of-gamut colors.

Related Topics

10.12

Image: Mode: *Lab Color*

Understanding the information in the individual channels of a Lab image can be difficult, since people are generally accustomed to dealing with color as the product of a device, not as an independent entity.

The L channel represents Lightness, or how bright a color is. Values in the Lightness channel range from 0, which is black, to 100, which is the full intensity of the color. The a and b channels represent the location of the color on the standard color wheel. The a channel represents the colors between green and magenta, which are directly opposite each other on the color wheel; 0 is the exact center of the color wheel. Values between 1 and 100 are towards the center of the magenta spectrum of the color wheel, and values between -1 and -100 are toward the green center of the spectrum. Similarly, the b channel represents the colors between blue and yellow.

Lab Color images are most often used in workflows that are specifically geared for getting the most out this color space, such as outputting to IRIS printers (or similar devices), or correcting images on certain color management systems.

Issues to Consider

PostScript Level 2 (and up) output devices can print Lab Color images directly to CMYK separations. However, most users prefer editing in CMYK. If an image already exists in CMYK mode, you gain nothing by converting it to Lab Color before outputting.

When you examine the individual a and b channels, they make no intuitive sense. The shades of gray do not represent brightness or output values, but locations on the color wheel. Darker values in the b channel indicate more blue and less yellow. Lighter values in the a channel represent more magenta, less green.

Related Topics

10.13

Image: Mode: *Multichannel*

An image in Multichannel mode simply contains multiple channels. Unlike the other color modes, no relationship exists between them, regardless of how many there are. This mode has no composite view. There are two ways to convert an image to Multichannel:

Select Image: Mode: Multichannel while a color image is open. This removes the relationship among the color channels, allowing them to simply exist within the structure of a single image. If an RGB or Lab Color image is converted, then the Multichannel image contains three channels. If a CMYK image is converted, it has four.

Delete one of the channels in a color image. This forcibly destroys the relationship among the color channels, since removing one of them alters the basic structure of the mode. Rather than attempt to deal with this type of effect on screen, Photoshop converts the image (and the remaining channels) to Multichannel.

Only images that initially contain more than one channel can be converted to Multichannel mode.

Related Topics

10.14

Image: Mode: *8 Bits/Channel*

This command is used to convert 16 bit-per-channel images—such as those generated by certain scanners and digital cameras—back to the standard 8 bits. Sixteen-bit graphics can only be acquired with special plug-ins that ship with those input devices. These files contain twice as much color information as an average file, so the user has more flexibility when making adjustments. Convert to this setting when you have completed the editing of the file.

A checkmark appears next to this command to indicate an image's status as 8 Bits/Channel.

Issues to Consider

Nothing is gained by converting an 8 Bits/Channel image to 16 Bits/Channel. It does not give you any additional color data, nor any more flexibility in editing.

10.15

Image: Mode: *16 Bits/Channel*

Although you're able to convert any Grayscale or RGB image to 16 Bits/Channel, you have no need to do so. This command exists to indicate whether a digitally acquired image contains that much image data. If it does, it must be converted to 8 Bits/Channel before the final image is saved and used.

Because these images contain twice as much color data as 8-bit images, the relative file sizes are twice as large.

10.16

Image: Mode: *Color Table*

Once you've converted an image to Indexed Color, there are two ways to edit the existing values:

- Convert back to RGB to access the 24-bit spectrum. Unfortunately, converting back and forth between the two modes can result in additional image degradation.

- Edit the image's color table using the Image: Mode: **Color Table** dialog box.

This command is only available when an image is in Indexed Color mode. Once you open the dialog box, there are two ways to edit the color palette: Select a pre-defined palette, or edit colors individually.

Issues to Consider

Most often, indexed graphics are saved using the Adaptive palette option. To make any changes to these custom palettes, you must selectively edit individual color values in the Color Table dialog box.

The Color Table Dialog Box

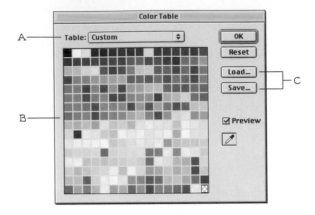

A. Table

If desired, select a custom palette from this pop-up menu:

Custom

> This appears whenever any other palette except System (Macintosh) or System (Windows) was selected in the Indexed Color dialog box. The colors specific to your settings appear in the swatches below.

Black Body

> This palette is supposedly based on the colors emitted by a super-heated slab of black iron—they exist as a gradient from black, to red, to yellow, to white. While this table can be applied to interesting effect on an indexed Grayscale image, the results of this table are unpredictable, and the values do not necessarily translate over the Internet. It's rarely used for anything useful.

Grayscale

> This option only appears if you've converted a Grayscale image to Indexed Color. Otherwise, selecting it remaps the colors of the image to the 256-level gray scale. You have little control over which colors are converted to which grays, so it's a poor technique to convert a colored Indexed image to gray levels. Do this more effectively by converting an image to Grayscale mode before converting to Indexed Color.

Macintosh System

> This option appears if you selected System (Macintosh) in the Indexed Color dialog box.

Spectrum

> The colors of this option appear as gradient between the primary hues of the spectrum. Again, the results of applying this table are unpredictable at best.

Windows System

> This option appears if you selected System (Windows) in the Indexed Color dialog box.

B. **The Color Palette**

This grid contains all the colors of the indexed file. To edit a specific value, click once on the color.

C. **Load and Save**

These buttons allow you save and reload a customized color palette.

Related Topics

10.9   *Image: Mode:* ***Indexed Color***

***

10.17

Image: Mode: Assign Profile

This command tags an image with a new color profile, enabling you to preview its final appearance more accurately before converting between color modes. No pixel values are altered when you re-assign a profile—the only thing that changes is the way they are displayed on screen.

Use this command only as part of a color managed workflow. Even then, assigning a new profile is only suitable for certain situations. For example, if an image is acquired with a device that is not ICC-aware, you can open the image in Photoshop and apply the appropriate profile. Or, if you receive an image that you know contains an incorrect profile, you can easily assign the proper one. You're also able to assign a profile to an image that has none, or remove a profile altogether.

Issues to Consider

Determining an image's profile status. If you routinely use the Assign Profile command, get used to referring to an image's title bar. If no profile is currently assigned to an image, a pound symbol (#) appears after the color mode in the title bar. If the profile assigned to an image is different from your current Working RGB space, an asterisk (*) appears. If the profile assigned to an image is the same as your Working RGB space, no symbol appears.

Assign Profile Dialog Box

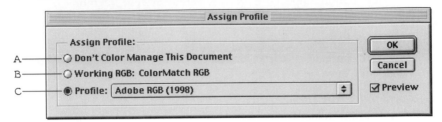

A. **Don't Color Manage This Document**

If the current image doesn't have a profile assigned to it, the Assign Profile dialog box defaults to this option. If an image does contain a profile, setting this option removes it.

B. **Working RGB**

This option represents the profile currently set as your Working RGB space in the Edit: **Color Settings** dialog box. If an image is set to a different profile (or has no profile), set this option to assign your working space to it.

C. **Profile**

This pop-up menu displays the list of ICC profiles currently available to Photoshop. If a profile other than your current Working RGB space is assigned to an image, this option is set by default. To assign a different profile, select it from the pop-up menu.

Related Topics

9.37   Edit: **Color Settings**
10.17 Image: Mode: **Convert to Profile**

10.18

Image: Mode: Convert to Profile

Use this command to convert an image's profile and color space. When you do, the color values of the image are changed, but the way they display on screen remains reasonably constant. Like Image: Mode: **Assign Profile**, this command should only be used as part of a color managed workflow. (It essentially performs the same function as Photoshop 5's Image: Mode: **Profile to Profile** command, with some increased flexibility.) Most notably, it enables you to embed a profile other than your current Working RGB space into an image.

Issues to Consider

This command may convert an image's color mode. If you apply a profile based on a different space, Photoshop may convert color modes in order to create the proper values. For example, if you're editing an RGB image and apply the US Sheetfed Coated profile (a CMYK space), the image is converted to CMYK Color mode. Unlike simply converting an image to CMYK Color, this command enables you to convert modes and assign a working space at the same time.

Convert to Profile Dialog Box

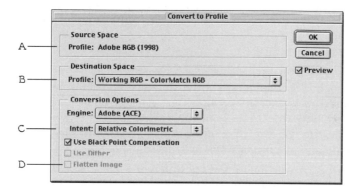

A. Source Space

This item displays the Working RGB space currently assigned to an image.

B. Destination Space

This pop-up menu displays the list of ICC profiles currently available to Photoshop. Set the color space you want to convert to here.

C. Conversion Options

The Engine, Intent, Black Point Compensation, and Dither options enable you to fine-tune the settings currently established in your Edit: **Color Settings** dialog box. (For full descriptions, see *9.37, Edit: Color Settings.*)

D. Flatten Image

This option is only available when the current image contains multiple layers. When checked, the image is flattened during the conversion process, making it easier to include the Flatten Image command in an action or batch process. (For more information, see *11.105, Layer: Flatten Image.*)

Related Topics

Image: *Adjust Overview*

The Image: **Adjust** commands enable you to *remap* pixel values, or change a targeted color from one value to another. These commands are used for two purposes:

- **To adjust the tones and colors of scanned images.** Due to limitations of scanning technology, every halftone or color image requires some degree of correction. Traditionally, this was true only of print-oriented images. Today, now that multimedia and the web have matured, the Image: **Adjust** tools are more widely used than ever.

- **To generate special effects.** Rather than use these commands to make small corrections, you can use them to radically alter an image's color content.

Adjusting color is arguably the most complex and demanding Photoshop-driven process in the graphic arts. Even though Photoshop measures color with scientific models and precise numerical values, individual perception of color is highly subjective. To make matters worse, the act of correction itself quickly reduces the amount of color information in an image—so you have only a small degree of latitude when making adjustments.

Color correction actually involves many different tools and commands, most of which are found in the Image: **Adjust** submenu. As you become more familiar with the process, it pays to develop a consistent workflow strategy. Adjusting color without a plan is like cutting hair with an electric clipper and no comb. Fixing one section usually throws another out of whack. Fixing that one impairs another. Soon, you have nothing left but an irreparably bad haircut. (For more information, see *F.1, Establishing a Halftone Editing Strategy* and *G.1, Color Scanning and Adjusting Checklist.*)

Common Image: Adjust Options

Most Image: **Adjust** dialog boxes share the following options.

Previewing Adjustments

You can preview the effects of most Image: **Adjust** commands before they are applied. The only exceptions are Auto Levels, Desaturate, Invert and Equalize—these only produce one effect, so they don't need to be previewed. There are two ways to preview:

- **Leave the Preview button unchecked.** Here, Photoshop uses the computer's own graphics card to generate previews using the card's *video color lookup table* (VLUT). The effect is applied to the entire screen, not just the image. Since the preview is hardware-based, it's much faster—but it's a less accurate representation of the final adjustment. Temporarily turn off the hardware preview by clicking the title bar of the open dialog box.

- **Check the Preview button.** Here, Photoshop itself generates the preview. Only the part of the image being adjusted is affected by the preview. It takes longer to generate than the hardware-based preview, but it provides an exact representation of the final adjustment.

Accessing Previously Used Settings

Any Image: **Adjust** command with an editable dialog box recalls its last-entered values when you hold down the (Option) [Alt] key while selecting the command. If there is a keyboard shortcut, such as (Command) [Control]-L for Image: Adjust: **Levels**, then hold down the (Option) [Alt] key in addition to the standard shortcut.

Numerical Field Shortcuts

Many Image: **Adjust** dialog boxes use sliders to edit color content or tonal values. Every slider has a field that displays the associated numerical values. To bypass the slider, insert the cursor in the field (press the Tab key to scroll through them). (Option) [Alt]-click the up and down arrows to increase or decrease the values in increments of one. Shift-click to increase or decrease in increments of 10.

Cancel/Reset

Clicking Cancel closes the dialog box, leaving the image unchanged. However, holding down the (Option) [Alt] key changes the Cancel button into the Reset button. Clicking the reset button restores the original settings without closing the dialog box.

Save and Load

If an Image: **Adjust** command has multiple settings, they can be saved into a separate file and reloaded later. This is useful when the same settings must be applied to multiple images, or to multiple layers of the same image.

Depending on the situation, using the Actions palette may be more efficient than saving and loading settings. If you're batch processing, or applying the same commands to a number of images in quick succession, then record an action. If you intend to use the settings again at some unspecified time in the future, then save them.

Access Color Samplers

You can access the Color Sampler tool while an Image: **Adjust** dialog box is open by holding down the Shift key and moving the cursor over the image area. When you click, you place new color samplers instead of simply reading color values with the Eyedropper tool. (For more information, see *4.4, Color Sampler Tool* and *16.8, Show/Hide Color Samplers.*)

10.20

Image: Adjust: Levels *(Command) [Control]–L*

This command enables you to remap the brightness values of an image by manipulating controls that represent its shadows, midtones, and highlights. By repositioning the Levels sliders and referring to a graph that displays the image data, you compress, expand, or clip the existing tonal range. This command is commonly used for the following tasks:

- Evaluating the tonal range of a scan.

- Targeting and applying endpoints for print.

- Simple image enhancing.

Mistakes to Avoid

Attempting delicate or complex image adjustments. Image: Adjust: **Curves** offers much more powerful and accurate tools.

Over-adjusting the tonal range. Whenever a tonal range is expanded, no new values are created—the existing tones are simply spaced farther apart to cover a broader range. When a range is expanded by too much, visible shade-stepping occurs.

Setting endpoints using the Output Values sliders. Doing so is similar to setting endpoints for print, but with two problems. First, the tones are displayed as brightness values, instead of print-specific output percentages. Second, your adjustments are applied even-handedly—you have little control over which pixels are affected. For the best results, use the Eyedropper tools.

Issues to Consider

"Levels" actually refers to brightness levels. This command only controls pixel brightness, or values that range from 0 to 255—unlike the Curves dialog box, which has the option of displaying output percentages. Accuracy ultimately depends on your understanding of this system.

The Levels Dialog Box

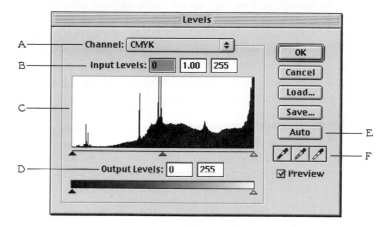

A. Channel

This pop-up menu enables you to edit either an individual channel of a color image, or a composite representing all channels at once. When you select a different channel, the histogram displays its specific content.

B. Input Levels

The left and right fields respond in two ways. They allow the user to enter values for the shadow and highlight areas, or they display the changes made when you adjust the black-and-white sliders. For example, if the shadow value is raised from 0 to 45, all pixels with brightness values of 45 and below become black. Similarly, lowering the highlight value from 255 to 210 turns every pixel with a value of 210 or more to white.

The middle field controls *gamma*, in this case the brightness value of neutral gray. This value always starts at 1.00, even if it was changed in a previous edit. Gamma values can range from 0.1 to 9.99—any changes up or down darken or lighten the tones of an image without changing the white or black points.

Readjusting the midpoint expands one part of the tonal range while compressing the other. For example, raising the gamma from 1.00 to 2.00 remaps the brightness value of 64 to 128. The values between 0 and 64 are expanded to range from 0 to 128, while the values between 64 and 255 are compressed to range from 128 to 255.

C. The Histogram

This graph plots the tonal range of an image or a channel, similar to Image: **Histogram**. It contains up to 256 vertical lines, each one representing a brightness level from black to white. If a particular value colors a larger number of pixels, the line appears taller; if it colors a smaller number of pixels, the line is shorter. Areas where no lines exist are tones not present in the image.

D. **Output Levels**

The Output Values restrict the darkest and lightest possible tones. For example, setting the shadow value to 40 remaps all pixels so the darkest value is 40 (85%), rather than black. Likewise, setting the highlight value to 230 (10%) remaps the pixels so the lightest value is 230. (For more information, see *F.9, Using Levels to Set Endpoints.*)

This is a more obvious form of tonal compression—as the endpoints are pushed closer together, the number of possible tones decreases, causing the image to lose contrast.

E. **Auto**

Click this button to reposition the tonal endpoints of an image. It's the same command as Image: Adjust: **Auto Levels**. The values it follows are set using the Eyedropper tools.

F. **Eyedroppers**

Use the black-and-white Eyedropper tools to manually set the endpoints of a halftone image.

The gray Eyedropper tool is only available in color images, and is used to establish neutral gray. In theory, you would include a swatch of neutral gray (one of the PANTONE Cool Grays, for example) with a scan—when you click that swatch with the gray eyedropper, it removes any color bias, bringing it (and the remaining image grays) into neutral spec. In practice, it provides only a cursory adjustment with unpredictable results.

Related Topics

10.21

Image: Adjust: Auto Levels

(Command-Shift) [Control-Shift]-L

This command is the same as clicking the Auto button in the Image: Adjust: **Levels** and **Curves** dialog box. It remaps the highlight and shadow value, based on the values set by double-clicking the black-and-white Eyedropper tools. Keep the clip value low—from 0.5% to 1.5%—for the best results.

Even though this command is automatic, you still have some control over the pixels it targets. In either the Levels or Curves dialog box, hold down the (Option) [Alt] key. The Auto button changes to Options, which enables you to access the Auto Range Options dialog box.

The Auto Range Options Dialog Box

A. **Black Clip**

This option lets you ignore a certain percentage of the darkest pixels before applying the changes. This way, a few extreme pixel values don't throw off the effects of the command. Enter a value between 0.5% and 9.99%. The higher the percentage, the more severe the effect.

B. **White Clip**

This option functions the same as Black Clip, but it pertains to the adjustment of the highlight dot.

10.22

Image Adjust: Curves   *(Command) [Control]-M*

This command is Photoshop's most powerful tool for remapping pixel values. Unlike Image: Adjust: **Levels**, you can change the value of one pixel to virtually any other. Common uses for this command include the following:

- Adjusting an image for contrast.
- Adjusting a halftones for dot gain
- Identifying and adjusting a color cast
- Adjusting neutral values in a color image
- Applying half-cast removals, and other delicate adjustments

Mistakes to Avoid

Applying curves that are too steep. When color correcting, even changes of 2-3% are noticeable.

Applying too many curves. Each change reduces the number of tones, and the image eventually becomes washed out or posterized.

Issues to Consider

If unsure of a particular color or tone value, move the cursor over the image. It changes to an Eyedropper. When you click on the image, a small *feedback circle* appears, indicating the click-point's value on the curve. When editing a color channel (red, for example), the circle indicates the red component of whatever color you've clicked. However, in a CMYK image, you cannot display a feedback circle when the composite channel is selected—this technique only works when editing an individual color channel.

Dynamically place a curve point. To add a point to the curve based on the image information, (Command) [Control]-click the image. If the composite channel is selected in the dialog box, no change is visible—but if you switch to any of the color channels, a point appears at the appropriate value. If a color channel is selected when you (Command) [Control]-click, a point is only inserted for that color. To add a point to all color channels regardless of the selected color, (Command-Shift) [Control-Shift]-click the image.

You can add up to 14 points to a single curve. This number includes the endpoints. Remove a point by dragging it off the graph.

The Curves Dialog Box

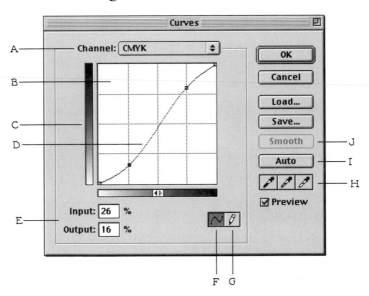

A. **Channel**

The Channel pop-up enables you to edit individual channels in a color image, or edit a composite representing all channels at once. When a single color is selected, you edit the Grayscale values of that color's channel. When the composite is selected, you edit all channels simultaneously.

B. **Tone Graph**

The tonal graph is the heart of the Curves command. It plots the tonal content in two ways: The horizontal axis represents *input levels*, or the values that existed before you opened the dialog box; the vertical axis represents *output levels*, or the values that will exist after you apply a curve. When you adjust the curve, you move points from one area to another, changing their position on the graph. The extent of change determines the new values.

By default, the graph is divided into a four-by-four grid, which makes it easier to target the primary image tones: highlights, quarter tones, mid-tones, three-quarter tones, and shadows. If desired, (Option) [Alt]-click the graph to convert it to a 10-by-10 grid.

C. **Values Gradient**

The bar at the bottom and to the left of the graph are gray ramps, representing all the possible tones from black to white. By looking at this, you know which end of your curve represents shadows and which represents highlights.

The bottom gradient also determines whether the dialog box measures in brightness values or output percentages. Photoshop defaults to bright-ness values, which many users prefer for reading RGB color. Most print professionals, however, prefer reading color in terms of halftone dot sizes. Click once on the gradient to change the measurement values.

D. **The Curve**

Make your adjustments by manipulating the diagonal line bisecting the graph. This line represents all the possible tones from lightest to darkest, even though your image may contain a shorter range. This command is called "Curves" because although this line is straight, it bends into a curved shape as you make corrections. This curve helps distribute your changes more smoothly throughout the rest of the image, avoiding more jarring results like posterizing and unexpected color shifts.

Make adjustments by placing and repositioning points along the curve. Click on the curve to insert a point. Drag this point above or below its original position to lighten or darken the tones of the image. Refer to the Input/Output values in the lower right of the dialog box to track your changes.

Curve points have two different uses. They adjust tone and color, as will happen when you drag a point from one point to another, thereby remap-ping the values. Also, you can use them to anchor the curve, enabling you to target one part of the tonal range. For example, if you only want to edit the highlights, click to add points at 25%, 50%, and 75%. Now, you can edit the lightest values without affecting the remaining tones.

E. **Input/Output**

As you apply changes to the curve, the before-and-after values appear in these fields. The Input field displays the color values that existed before you opened the Curves dialog box. The Output field displays the remapped values that will exist after you apply the curve.

When you initially open the dialog box, the fields change to display the current position of the cursor. As soon as you place a point, however, the fields become editable. If desired, you can select a point by clicking it and enter a new position numerically. Shift-click the graph to close the fields and display the current values again.

F. **The Point Tool**

This option is Photoshop's default, and enables you to click-drag points, as described above.

G. **The Pencil Tool**

Here, you can manually draw curves on the graph. Usually, this option is casually dismissed as just another special effect. While it's true that you can create off-the-wall color adjustments, you can also switch to the pencil tool to make discreet edits that may be more difficult with the point tool.

H. **Eyedropper Tools**

The Eyedroppers are used to define and apply endpoint values. (For more information, see *10.20, Image: Adjust: **Levels**.*)

I. **Auto**

The Auto button applies the same command as Image: Adjust: Auto **Levels**. (For a full description, see *10.20, Image: Adjust: **Levels**.*)

J. **Smooth**

Use the Smooth button to convert a manually-drawn curve to one based on points. Clicking the button again slightly flattens the adjustments made to the curve. Continued clicking ultimately straightens the curve completely.

Related Topics

10.23

Image: Adjust: **Color Balance** *(Command) [Control]-B*

This command enables you to adjust colors by changing their position in the RGB/CMY color wheel. Similar to the color controls of your scanner's software, you make adjustments in one of three ways:

- **Add a color by moving its slider toward it.** For example, add yellow by moving the bottom slider toward Yellow.

- **Subtract a color by moving its slider away from it,** or toward its complement. For example, subtract yellow by adding blue.

- **Add or subtract a color by adjusting its two components.** Referring to the RGB/CMY color wheel, you can subtract yellow by adding red and green.

Issues to Consider

Although easy to use, this tool has limited function. Its edits are not based on exact color values, and you cannot target specific tones to correct. If anything, this tool is best suited for adjusting onscreen images. Print images require the precision of Image: Adjust: **Levels** or **Curves**.

The Color Balance Dialog Box

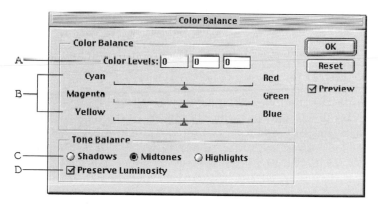

A. Color Levels

From left to right, these fields display the values of the top, middle, and bottom color sliders. If desired, enter the values manually.

B. **Color Sliders**

Each slider in the dialog box pairs a color with its complement on the color wheel. The values of the sliders default to 0, but range from -100 to 100. Unless you're creating a special color effect, keep your adjustments small. Any changes more than 3–5 units above or below 0 are likely to create another color cast.

C. **Tone Balance Buttons**

Here, you target the part of the tonal range you wish to adjust: Shadows, Midtones, or Highlights. Each option actually affects the entire range of the image—but by choosing one of these options, you determine which portion receives the brunt of the changes. The Shadows option primarily affects tones above 75%. Midtones primarily affect tones between 25% and 75%. Highlights primarily affect tones below 25%.

D. **Preserve Luminosity**

Check this button to preserve the luminosity, or the overall lightness values, of the image. If you edit with this button unchecked, the tonal balance is affected along with the color content.

Related Topics

10.24

Image: Adjust: Brightness/Contrast

This command may be the most intuitive adjustment tool, but it's also the least useful. It suffers from two major drawbacks: Its effects are applied to all channels simultaneously, and it provides no precision beyond oversimplified curve adjustments. Users are advised to use Image: Adjust: **Levels** or **Curves** instead, even for the most basic edits.

The Brightness/Contrast Dialog Box

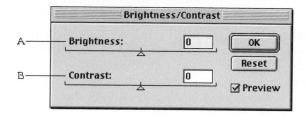

A. Brightness

Moving this slider to the right lightens the overall image. It has the same effect as opening the Curves dialog box and moving the shadow straight toward the highlight value. Moving the slider to the left darkens the overall image, creating the same effect as dragging the highlight point straight toward the shadow value.

B. Contrast

Moving this slider to the right exaggerates the difference between the lighter and darker image tones. It has the same effect as opening the Curves dialog box and moving the highlight and shadow endpoints horizontally toward 50%–light information becomes white while dark information becomes black. Moving this slider to the left reduces contrast, producing the same effect as dragging the endpoints vertically toward 50%. All tones eventually turn gray.

10.25

*Image: Adjust: **Hue/Saturation*** *(Command) [Control]-U*

This command enables you to edit colors based on the HSB color model. Rather than use specific color values, you change the position of one or more colors in the HSB spectrum. (For more information, see *10.1, Image: **Mode Overview*.) Common uses for this command include the following:

- Adjusting color using HSB-based controls.

- Colorizing a black-and-white image (after converting it to a color mode).

Issues to Consider

Editing color versus tone. Most Hue/Saturation corrections are made to edit specific colors, not tones. Tonal edits are far more accurately performed using Image: Adjust: **Levels** or **Curves**.

Using HSB controls to edit a Lab Color image. When editing an image in Lab Color mode, you only have four color options: yellow, green, blue, and magenta. These correspond to the color ranges represented by the a and b channels.

When you select the Colorize option, Photoshop automatically applies the highest saturation level. The Saturation slider is altered to read only from 0 to 100, meaning you can only reduce the saturation.

Colorizing an entire image at once. If your intent is to apply only one color to the entire image, using a solid color fill layer with a blend mode is a more flexible option. There, you can specifically define the color you want with the color picker, rather than depend on more abstract HSB values. (For more information, see *H.7, Colorizing an Image: Retaining Deep Tones.*)

The Hue/Saturation Dialog Box

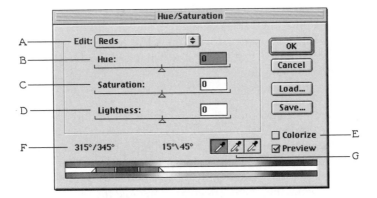

A. **Edit**

This pop-up determines the color range affected by this command. Photoshop defaults to the Master setting, which results in all color values being adjusted in equal amounts. To target a more specific color, select one of the additional color items: Reds, Yellows, Greens, Cyans, Blues, and Magentas—or, as you may have noticed, the six primary colors of the RGB/CMY color wheel.

When editing one of these colors, the Hue slider only has a range from -60° to +60°, or the distance between the selected color's two components on the color wheel. For example, if you select Reds and adjust the Hue slider, you change red values to anything between magenta and yellow—the degree of change is apparent in the small swatch next to the color's button. You can also use the Saturate slider to affect only the colors containing red.

Selecting individual colors is more flexible than editing with Master selected. You can apply different values for each color, allowing for relatively specific edits.

B. **Hue Slider**

Hue pertains to a color's location on the RGB/CMY color wheel. The values you see when moving this slider are actually degrees; moving the slider all the way to the left or right places the color halfway around the color wheel, or 180° from its original position. For example, if you adjust red by moving the slider 60° to the right, the color becomes yellow. Sixty degrees to the left, it becomes magenta. Adjusting this slider, then, is like moving any color in a perfect circle around the color wheel.

C. Saturation Slider

Moving this slider affects the intensity of a color, or its distance from the center of the color wheel. Lowering the saturation value moves the color closer to the center of the wheel, or reduces it closer to gray. Raising the saturation moves a color closer to the edge of the wheel, a color's brightest point.

D. Lightness Slider

This slider affects brightness levels, similar to the Brightness slider in Image: Adjust: **Brightness/Contrast**. Here, adjustments move colors closer to one end or the other of the cylindrical HSB model. Moving the slider to the left gradually darkens the overall image tones, eventually turning them black. Moving it to the right gradually lightens the tones, eventually turning them white.

E. Colorize

Checking this option does two things. First, it partially *desaturates* the images, or removes the individual colors, by lowering the Saturation value to 25. Then, it applies one hue to the entire image.

The effect here is different from creating a monotone (using Image: Mode: **Duotone**) or recoloring a halftone in another program. The deepest tones remain black, but all lighter brightness values are tinted with one color. When you move the Hue slider, that one color cycles through the different stages of the color wheel.

This option is commonly used to colorize different portions of a Grayscale image, an effect similar to antique, hand-tinted photographs. The image must be converted to a color mode in order to access the command, and the best results are achieved in RGB. From there, use the selection tools to isolate portions of the image. Each time, you will need to open this dialog box, choose Colorize, and apply your desired color.

F. Color Range Controls

When you select a specific range of colors from the Edit pop-up menu, the following controls appear along the color bars at the bottom of the dialog box, enabling you to broaden or reduce the targeted values.

Affected Range

The dark gray bar in the center of the controls represents the color range affected by the command. View the width of the bar against the color ramps to visually gauge the colors in question.

Range Boundaries

The small blocks on either side of the dark gray bar determine the length of the affected range. Broaden the range by dragging the bars apart—the new positions of the range appear as degrees in the above values.

Fuzziness Range

The lighter gray bars on either side of the affected range represent the fuzziness, or the transition between the affected and unaffected colors. Wider ranges result in smoother transitions; shorter ranges result in more abrupt transitions.

Fuzziness Sliders

Reposition the triangular sliders to lengthen or shorten the fuzziness range. The new values appear as degrees above the color ramps. The starting and ending points of these sliders ultimately determine the entire range of colors affected by this command.

G. **Eyedroppers**

Use the standard Eyedropper to determine a color range by clicking in the image—the color ramps change to display the new range. To add colors to the currently defined range, click with the Add Eyedropper tool (or Shift-click with the standard Eyedropper). To remove colors from the current range, click with the Remove Eyedropper tool (or (Option) [Alt]-click with the standard Eyedropper).

Related Topics

10.26

Image: Adjust: *Desaturate* (Command-Shift) [Control-Shift]-U

This command reduces the saturation of all colors to 0, creating the effect of a Grayscale image without changing modes. The result is the same as selecting Image: Adjust: **Hue/Saturation** and moving the Saturation slider all the way to the left.

Issues to Consider

Converting JPEG images to Grayscale mode sometimes results in small, black artifacts. This is especially common with certain CD-ROM stock images. This is a flaw in the conversion scheme resulting from the compression used on the images. Avoid this problem by applying Image: Adjust: **Desaturate** before converting them to Grayscale.

10.27

Image: Adjust: *Replace Color*

With this command, you target a range of colors and change their values using Hue, Saturation, and Lightness controls. Colors are targeted by clicking on the image or a thumbnail with a series of Eyedropper tools, avoiding the need for potentially complex selections.

A common use of this command is for editing information such as continuous tones, blends, and gradients. It is also reasonably effective on areas of subtly varying color, such as fleshtones.

Issues to Consider

This command is of limited use. This command is strikingly similar to making a selection using Select: **Color Range** and editing color using Image: Adjust: **Hue/Saturation**. On one hand, it saves time because only one command is used instead of two. On the other, it offers only a pared-down version of the Hue/Saturation tools. The only advantage to using Replace Color is the lack of active selections.

The Replace Color Dialog Box

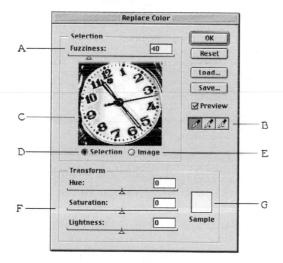

A. Fuzziness

This slider determines the range of targeted colors. Lower values include fewer colors in the selection; higher values include more. A fuzziness value of 0 means only the exact color you click on can be changed.

B. Eyedroppers

Use the three Eyedropper tools to define the editable colors. The plain eyedropper simply selects a particular color. Clicking elsewhere selects a different value. To add values to the selection, use the plus-Eyedropper or hold down the Shift key while selecting with the standard Eyedropper. To subtract values from the selection, use the minus-Eyedropper or (Option) [Alt]-click with the standard Eyedropper.

Drag with one of the Eyedroppers to add or subtract a wider range of tones.

C. **Image Map**

Use this thumbnail to facilitate your color selection. If there is an active selection, only that information appears in the image map. If no selection exists, then the entire image appears.

D. **Selection**

This mask displays the currently selected colors. The portions of the image editable with the Transform options appear white, and the unselected areas remain black.

E. **Image**

This displays a full-color version of the image.

F. **Transform Options**

These include the same three Hue, Saturation, and Lightness sliders found in the Image: Adjust: **Hue/Saturation** dialog box. The Sample swatch displays any color encountered by the Eyedropper tools.

Related Topics

10.28

Image: Adjust: Selective Color

This command attempts to simplify the color correcting process by adjusting CMYK values with sliders, similar to the Image: Adjust: **Color Balance** dialog box. Rather than target specific process percentages, you correct more intuitively by focusing on Reds, Blues, Yellows, and so forth. The idea is that you make adjustments the same way you would evaluate a color proof.

Although this command is based on a good idea, it falls short of being an effective color editing tool. It relies too much on onscreen appearances and guesswork to be considered accurate, and you have no reliable method of measuring your color changes.

Issues to Consider

Although available in RGB mode, this command is most effective on a CMYK image. RGB images must still be converted to CMYK, and those values ultimately depend on the settings in the Edit: **Color Settings** controls.

The Selective Color Dialog Box

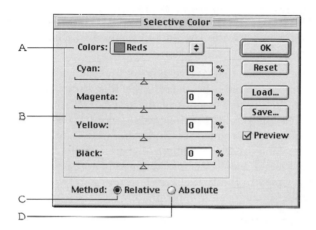

A. Colors

Select a general tonal range from this pop-up menu. For example, if you notice a yellow cast in the red tones, select Reds and edit the Yellow slider. Also included are options for Whites (for editing the diffuse highlight), Neutrals (for the gray tones), and Blacks (for shadows).

B. CMYK Sliders

One slider exists for each process component. By manipulating them, you either add or subtract ink from a chosen range. Although the numerical fields measure in percentages, they do not refer to output percentages. Their meaning depends on the option selected under Method.

C. Relative Method

This method evaluates the range you've chosen to adjust and attempts to apply your changes proportionately. In theory, if you wanted to make the Reds 5% more magenta, Photoshop would determine the actual red values and then add 5% magenta. There are two problems with this method, however. First, you have no control over what Photoshop determines to be "red"—you have to take the program's word for it. Second, this command may use multiple components to make the change, especially with larger percentages. You're not only unaware of which pixels are being edited, you have no idea what's being done to them until you click OK and check the Info palette.

D. **Absolute Method**

This method is no less confusing. Changes are based on a percentage of the actual values. For example, if you lessen an area containing 75% magenta by 25% magenta, the result is 56% (25% of 75 is 18.75. Subtract that from 75% to get 56%).

10.29

Image: Adjust: ***Channel Mixer***

Use this command to replace the contents of a specified channel with combined values of any channels in the image.

A simple example: assume that you're editing an RGB image, and Red is selected as the output channel. By default, the Red slider is positioned at 100%, representing the current values of the channel. The Green and Blue values appear as 0%, indicating that their values currently have no affect on the Red information. If you reduce the Red value to 0% and move the Blue slider to 100%, the contents of the Red channel are completely replaced with the values of the Blue channel. The actual Blue channel is not touched—its values are simply copied to the Red channel, resulting in two identical channels. The overall image colors shift appropriately.

In the same example, assume you reduced the Red value to 0% and set the Blue slider to 50%. Here, the contents of the Red channel are replaced with the contents of the Blue channel at half-intensity (as if the channel had been affected by a 50% ghost). If you then increase the value of the Green slider, you start adding the contents of the Green channel as well, darkening the overall effect. Again, once the dialog box is closed, the Green and Blue channels are not affected—only the Red channel (the output channel) is adjusted.

Most of the time, the most effective new channel values are a result of mixing smaller values of the remaining channels with a decreased value of the original.

Common uses of this command include the following:

- **Creating a Grayscale image using more delicate methods than simply converting to Grayscale or desaturating.** Checking the Monochrome box before adjusting the sliders enables you to work solely with gray values as you combine channel information. Convert the image to Grayscale after applying the command.

- **Quickly swapping channel information.** This command enables you to exchange channels without using the Split or Merge Channels commands of the Channels palette.

- **Creating lightly-tinted images.** Do this by checking the Monochrome box, making an overall adjustment, then unchecking the box. When you make a small adjustment to a source channel slider, you begin adding a hue to the image. If desired, check the box again to reduce the values to all gray, then uncheck again to add a new color tint.

- **Off-the-wall color adjustments.** Since it is difficult to predict the ultimate effect of this command, broad changes can create a wide range of interesting effects that you cannot accomplish using the remaining Image: **Adjust** commands.

Issues to Consider

To access this command, the composite channel must be active in the Channels palette. If a single color channel is active, the command is not available.

Editing multiple channels. You can alter the contents of more than one channel at a time by choosing another item from the Output Channel pop-up.

Maintaining consistent tonal values. To produce brightness levels in the new values that are similar to the original channel, make sure the combined percentages of the sliders total 100.

This command only utilizes color channels. You cannot access any alpha channel, layer mask, or QuickMask information.

The Channel Mixer Dialog Box

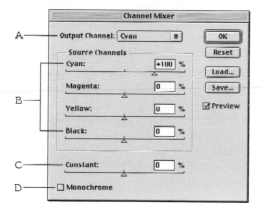

A. **Output Channel**

Choose the channel you wish to affect from this pop-up menu.

B. **Source Channels** (-200–200%)

These sliders determine the amount of information added to or subtracted from the current output channel. Positive values add source channel information to the output channel. When you set a negative value, the source channel information is inverted before being added to the output channel.

C. **Constant**

This slider essentially controls the overall lightness or darkness of the command's effect. When you apply a positive value, the effect is similar to placing a semi-opaque white layer over the output channel's information. When you apply a negative value, the effect is similar to placing semi-opaque black layer over the output channel's information.

D. **Monochrome**

When this box is checked, every channel is treated as the output channel (in fact, Black appears in the Edit pop-up menu, as if you were editing a Grayscale image). This enables you to combine channel values to create a desired Grayscale version of the current image. Remember that you must still convert the image by choosing Image: Mode: **Grayscale** after applying this command.

10.30

Image: Adjust: Gradient Map

This command remaps the entire color range of an image, layer, or selection, basing the changes on the values contained in a gradient. Essentially, the mapping works like this: First, the command invisibly desaturates the available colors, reducing them to pure tonal data. Then it replaces each tone with one of the values of the selected gradient. The effect can be subtle or outrageous, depending on the gradient's complexity.

Although it's nearly impossible to predict the overall results of a gradient map (this command is strictly a special effect, more like a filter than an adjustment tool), it's easy to determine how the gradient will impact different parts of the tonal range. Take a look at the Gradient Map dialog box. When you set a gradient, it appears as a linear preview, running left to right. Now imagine a black-to-white gradient, exactly the same size, sitting below it—this gradient represents the image's tonal range. If you were to draw a line from the black-to-white gradient up to the colored gradient, you'd find the color that would replace the tone when you applied this command.

Gradient Map Dialog Box

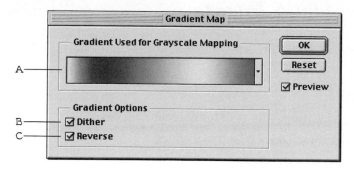

A. Gradient Used for Grayscale Map

This preview thumbnail displays the currently selected gradient. To select a different one, click the thin vertical bar to the right of the preview. A pop-up menu appears, displaying the available options. To edit the current gradient, click directly on the preview. The Gradient Editor appears, enabling you to adjust the current settings. (For more information, see *2.17, Gradient Tool.*)

B. Dither

Check this box to slightly randomize the distribution of colored pixels. This helps prevent *banding,* or the visible shade-stepping that occurs when too few tones are extended over too great a distance. Unless you have a specific reason to turn it off, leave this box checked for the best results.

C. Reverse

Check this box to reverse the direction of the gradient, which in turn reverses how the colors impact the image.

Related Topics

2.17   *Gradient Tool*
10.7   *Image: Mode:* **Grayscale**
10.26   *Image: Adjust:* **Desaturate**

10.31

Image: Adjust: *Invert*   *(Command) [Control]-I*

This command changes each image pixel to its opposite value, creating an effect similar to a film negative. Photoshop determines the new values by changing a pixel's brightness to 255 minus the original value. For example, a dark pixel with a value of 40 is changed to a much lighter value of 215 (255–40=215).

This command is commonly used for the following tasks:

- Reversing color values as a special effect.

- Generating true colors from a scanned negative.

- Reversing image components such as selection masks and layer masks, thereby reversing their effect.

When inverting color images, the values of each color channel are reversed. Because of this, the inverted result depends on an image's color mode. CMYK images in particular tend to darken considerably after inverting, because the black channel typically contains much less information than the other three. When the entire image is inverted, the black channel then contains more information than the others, darkening the overall image.

Mistakes to Avoid

Double-inverting a feathered selection. Although you can safely reapply the command to an entire image without suffering any degradation, inverting a selection twice leaves artifacts around feathered or anti-aliased selections. If you change your mind about inverting a selection, choose Edit: **Undo** rather than invert again.

Issues to Consider

Inverting a CMYK image. When inverting all or part of a CMYK image, invert only the cyan, magenta, and yellow channels. This way, the image is not compromised by a sudden influx of black information.

10.32

Image: Adjust: Equalize

This command redistributes an image's tonal range by maximizing the values of the lightest and darkest pixels. It does two things when applied. First, it locates the lightest and darkest pixels in the image. Second, it remaps those pixels so the lightest becomes white and the darkest becomes black. The remaining tonal range is expanded to accommodate the new endpoints.

Mistakes to Avoid

Attempting to color correct with this command. While it is somewhat similar to the Image: Adjust: **Auto Levels** command, Equalize only looks at a couple of factors, and provides no ability to adjust its effect.

Issues to Consider

Equalizing may produce unexpected results. Since this command is applied to the individual color channels, the colors black and white do not necessarily appear in the image. In a CMYK image, for example, the cyan or magenta of a pixel may maximize to white, but the remaining components may still contain gray values.

The Equalize Dialog Box

This dialog box only appears when an active selection exists.

A. **Selected Area Only**

This option applies the command only to the selected area.

B. **Entire Image Based on Area**

This option applies the command to the entire image, based on the color values found within the selection.

Related Topics

10.33

Image: Adjust: *Threshold*

This command reduces an image to two colors: solid black and solid white. It has the effect of converting an image to 1-bit color—similar to scanned line art—without converting to a different image mode. A *threshold* is the dividing line between the tones that become black or white. This command enables you to easily reset the threshold to any value.

Mistakes to Avoid

Failing to convert line art to Bitmap mode. If you apply this command to a Grayscale image to create detailed line art, you must convert it to a 1-bit color file to have it output properly.

Issues to Consider

When you apply this command to a color image, you may see a range of colorful splotches in the preview. This is just a side effect of the Video LUT Animation preference, and it displays Photoshop's attempt to apply the same threshold level to each color channel. Avoid the colors by turning the Preview option on. Or, duplicate the colors you see by manually applying the command the each channel.

The Threshold Dialog Box

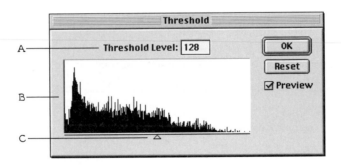

A. Threshold Level

This field indicates the current threshold value. It can range from 1 to 255—a level of 1 turns all pixels white, and a level of 255 turns all pixels black. When you first select the command, the level defaults to 128, or the midpoint between black and white. In the future, the dialog box will retain the last applied value. If desired, you can manually enter a threshold value.

B. **Histogram**

Similar to Image: Adjust: **Levels** and Image: **Histogram**, this graph represents the entire range of image tones. It acts as a loose guide while determining the location of the threshold.

C. **Threshold Slider**

Move this slider to reposition the threshold. Moving it to the left results in a lighter image, to the right results in a darker image. The threshold is reflected in the Threshold Level field, above the histogram.

Related Topics

10.6   Image: Mode: *Bitmap*
10.20 Image: Adjust: *Levels*
10.52 Image: *Histogram*
F.6   Targeting Endpoints for Press
E.7   Optimizing Finely Detailed Line Art
G.11   Identifying Endpoints in a Color Image

10.34

Image: Adjust: *Posterize*

The Posterize command reduces the number of tonal levels in an image. Unlike Image: Adjust: **Threshold**, which reduces only to black and white, Posterize averages the 256 tone levels of each color channel into the number of levels you specify

Mistakes to Avoid

Using this command to reduce the number of colors for a web graphic. For this technique, use Image: Mode: **Indexed Color**.

Applying a Levels value of 2 to a Grayscale image, in an attempt to create line art. For this effect, use Image: Adjust: **Threshold**, then convert to Bitmap mode

Issues to Consider

Use this command to simplify an image before auto-tracing it. Although this command is primarily used to create a silkscreen-style special effect, it can be used to simplify an image before converting it to vector-based artwork. This gives you more control over specific image areas—especially if you're using an automatic tracing program like Adobe Streamline.

The Posterize Dialog Box

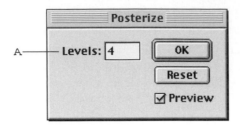

A. Levels

To posterize an image, enter a value from 2 to 255. Lower values result in obvious banding, or identifiable patches of color. Higher levels result in less apparent changes. The image previews dynamically as you enter different values in the dialog box, giving the best indication of the final effect. The lowest value you can enter is 2, since a value of 1 would render the image either all white or all black. A value of 255 leaves the image unchanged.

Related Topics

10.9   *Image: Mode:* **Indexed Color**
10.33 *Image: Adjust:* **Threshold**
J.5   *Adding a Gray Ramp to Evaluate Duotone Edits*

10.35

Image: Adjust: Variations

This command combines the tools found in the Brightness/Contrast, Hue/Saturation, and Color Balance commands. These items are controlled by an expansive interface that displays a series of small previews. Each preview represents a possible color correction, and you click on the desired effect to change the image.

The advantage to using Variations is that you can edit the colors of an image while watching the direct result of your actions. This is an intuitive and dynamic method of adjusting color. The disadvantage is that you have no direct control over the actual color values. Since the dialog box takes up nearly the entire screen, your decisions are based on very small, low-res thumbnails—hardly an accurate indication of subtle color changes. For this reason, this command is best used for adjusting onscreen images.

Issues to Consider

Since the image thumbnails are so small, previewing smaller selections is difficult at best. Also, you are unable to see any changes in relation to the rest of the image. Therefore, this command is best used on the entire image.

Adjusting tone in a color image. The tone controls that appear when editing a color image are similar to the Saturation slider in the Image: Adjust: **Hue/Saturation** dialog box, but the end result may be slightly different. This command adjusts saturation without changing any brightness values, so the colors may appear deeper and more intense than those edited with Hue/Saturation.

Undo and redo the results to gauge the impact of the command. After clicking OK to apply an adjustment, make it a practice to double-check the new values by choosing Edit: **Undo** and **Redo** while examining different portions of the image with the Info palette. There is no other way to evaluate the degree of change.

The Variations Dialog Box (Grayscale)

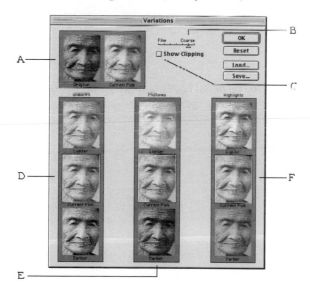

A. Status Thumbnails

The thumbnail marked Original represents the image that existed before you opened the dialog box. Click on this image at any time to restore the original values. The thumbnail marked Current Pick represents the current status of the image, with all the new changes. Clicking on this image does nothing.

B. **Intensity Slider**

This slider controls the amount of change that occurs each time you click one of the tone-correction thumbnails. A Fine setting results in very small changes, or an approximate 1% increase or decrease per click. A Coarse setting results in very large changes, or an approximate 35% increase or decrease per click. It defaults to the midpoint.

C. **Show Clipping**

If this box is checked, any color that is pushed beyond black or white is colored with a gray mask in the Preview thumbnails. This is done to alert you that the command is generating patches of solid black or white. Once you click OK, the mask is not applied to the image.

D. **Shadows**

This column adjusts shadows, or the values between 75% and 100%. Lighten the shadow tones by clicking the Lighten thumbnail. Darken the shadows by clicking the Darken thumbnail. The degree of change is determined by the Intensity slider as well as the number of times you click.

E. **Midtones**

This column adjusts the midtones, or the values between 25% and 75%. Again, lighten or darken this range by clicking on the appropriate thumbnail. Changes to the midtones have the most visible effect on the image.

F. **Highlights**

This column adjusts the highlights, or the values from 0% to 25%. Be aware that over-lightening the highlights quickly results in large areas of burnout, or 0% black.

The Variations Dialog Box (Color)

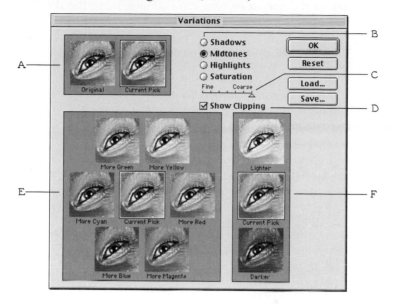

A. **Status Thumbnails**

Similar to the Grayscale option described above, these represent the Original image and current status. Click on Original at any time to restore the original image values.

B. **Tone Selections**

Choosing the Shadows, Midtones, or Highlights button focuses the command on that portion of the tonal range. You can select and edit more than one area while the dialog box is open.

There is also a button for Saturation. When this is selected, there are only three thumbnails available: Less Saturated, which lessens the overall color intensity; More Saturated, which increases the overall color intensity; and Current Pick, which displays the current status.

C. **Intensity Slider**

This slider works the same as in the Variations dialog box for Grayscale images, described above.

D. **Show Clipping**

Turning on this option acts as a gamut warning. If you begin making extreme adjustments, you'll notice bizarre, unexpected colors appearing in the thumbnails. These inverted values represent values that have extended beyond the available gamut, indicating that certain colors will not display accurately when you click OK. If you apply the adjustment, the colors simply appear flatter than you may expect.

Many users find the gamut warning a nuisance, and leave the option turned off. At the very least, you can continue using the thumbnails to make basic color decisions.

E. Hue Thumbnails

These buttons are similar to the color sliders in the Image: Adjust: **Color Balance** dialog box. Arranged in the same order as the RGB/CMY color wheel, you edit color content by clicking the appropriate hue. Add color by clicking the color you want to add. Subtract a particular color by clicking on its complement, or the opposite button. For example, to add yellow to an image, click More Yellow. To subtract yellow, click More Blue.

When you click a color button, the Current Pick thumbnail reflects the new edit. The remaining thumbnails are altered to show the new possible changes.

F. Brightness Thumbnails

Use these buttons to lighten or darken the tonal content of the image, while leaving the hue and saturation untouched.

Related Topics

10.22   *Image: Adjust:* **Curves**
10.23   *Image: Adjust:* **Color Balance**
10.24   *Image: Adjust:* **Brightness/Contrast**
10.25   *Image: Adjust:* **Hue/Saturation**
G.3   *Adjusting RGB vs. CMYK Color*

10.36

Image: **Duplicate**

This command creates an unsaved copy of the open image.

Issues to Consider

This command is most useful when you want to test a series of commands on an image. Simply duplicate the image and edit the copy. This provides the unique opportunity to compare the altered image with its original. If you want to keep the changes, then save the copy, close the original, and continue editing. If you don't want to keep the changes, close the copy without saving.

Bypassing the dialog box. Bypass the Duplicate Image dialog box by holding down the (Option) [Alt] key while selecting the command. This shortcut leaves all multiple layers unmerged.

The Duplicate Image Dialog Box

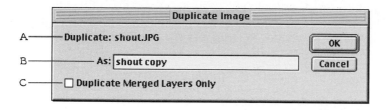

A. Duplicate

This non-editable field displays the name of the image being duplicated.

B. As

This editable field enables you to name the duplicate image. It defaults to the name of the original file with the word "copy" tagged on the end. You don't need to rename the new image, but it keeps things organized when making multiple duplicates. Naming a new image is not the same as saving it—if you want to keep a duplicate, you must select File: **Save** to write it to your hard drive.

C. Merged Layers Only

This option is available only when duplicating an image with multiple layers. Checking the box flattens all the layers in the new image. Leaving the box unchecked creates an identical duplicate.

10.37

Calculations Overview

Image: **Apply Image** and Image: **Calculations** are largely holdovers from early versions of Photoshop. Before this program had advanced channel-editing tools and multiple layers, these commands were the only way to composite images from different files. If you wanted to create a montage back then, you had to forcibly merge the pixel values of one image (the source) with the active image (the target). Today, with very few exceptions, every technique they're capable of can be performed using other, more intuitive tools.

While these commands are certainly powerful, they contain three significant limitations:

- They possess the most non-intuitive interface found in Photoshop. Often, it's impossible to predict the results of your settings.

- They only work on images sharing the exact width, height, and resolution.

- Once an effect is applied, it cannot be further adjusted or "tweaked." The result typically has all the flexibility of a flattened image.

If you're new to image compositing, there's little to be gained by mastering these commands. Your time is much better spent working with the Layers palette and Channels palette. If you're more comfortable with the ideas involved there, you may be intrigued by the ability of both commands to produce complex combinations of masking channels.

10.38

Image: Apply Image

This command combines the contents of layers or channels to create composite images. It reads information from either one or two equal-sized images.

Issues to Consider

It can be difficult to preview the image if a color channel is selected as the target. Ordinarily, when you select a channel from the Channels palette, the remaining colors are hidden—unless you click the View eyeball next to the composite channel *after* you select your desired color channel. Now, when you open the Apply Image dialog box, you can preview the overall effect of targeting one color channel.

The Apply Image Dialog Box

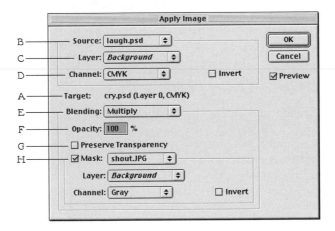

A. **Target**

Located in the center of the dialog box, this lists the image and layer affected by the command. To target an image layer, select it from the Layers palette before choosing the command. To affect one particular channel, select it from the Channels palette. Once the dialog box is opened, this information cannot be altered—so make sure the appropriate layer or channel appears in parentheses. All other options determine how this information is changed.

B. **Source**

This pop-up menu lists all available open images. It defaults to the target image, or the image that was active when you opened the dialog box. Select the image from which you want to pull information.

C. **Layer**

This pop-up menu lists all the available layers in the selected source image. If no multiple layers exist, then Background Layer is the only choice. To blend the target image with a specific layer, select the layer from this list. Choose Merged from the list to treat all visible layers as one.

D. **Channel**

From the source image, you can access either one specific channel or the overall composite. This allows for a variety of effects, depending on the channels selected in the target image (RGB mode is used for the following examples):

Target Image: RGB; Channel Pop-Up: RGB
The red, green, and blue channels of both images are combined.

Target: RGB; Channel: Red, Green, or Blue
The one color channel is applied equally to the red, green, and blue channels of the target image.

Target: Red, Green, or Blue; Channel: RGB
A composite Grayscale version of the source image is combined in that one channel.

Target: Red, Green, or Blue; Channel: Red, Green, or Blue
The contents of those two channels are combined.

Depending on the contents of the source image, four additional options may appear in the Channels pop-up menu:

Masking Channels
If the source image contains any saved selections, their numbers appear in the pop-up menu.

Selection
If the source image contains an active selection, choosing this item results in a mask channel based on the selection.

Transparency
If the source image contains transparent pixels, this item results in a mask channel based on the transparent areas.

Layer Mask
If the source image has a layer mask attached to it, this item results in a mask channel based on the layer mask.

E. Blending

This pop-up controls the method used to combine the source image with the target image. Twelve of the standard blend modes are available, including Add and Subtract, which are only available here and under Image: **Calculations**. The effects of these blend modes are simple: Add essentially lightens the result, while Subtract darkens.

F. Opacity

The opacity value affects the source image as it combines with the target image. It's functionally identical to the Opacity slider in the Layers palette.

G. Preserve Transparency

If the target image contains any transparent pixels—for example, an object on its own layer, like a placed EPS graphic—checking this box tells the Apply Image command to ignore the transparent pixels. Compositing only occurs on the colored pixels, similar to a layer mask.

H. Mask

By checking this box, you can use part of the source image as a mask when you combine it with the target image. It can be an active selection, layer mask, or even a regular color channel. For example, if the source image contains an active circular selection, you can use it to mask the rest of the image. Only information inside the selection appears in the target image.

The dialog box expands, displaying another Source, Layer, and Channel menu. Source and Layer work together—use them to choose the image and particular layer you want to use as a mask. From Channel, select your desired color channel. Like the first Channel pop-up menu, selections, transparency, and layer masks will appear on this list when available.

Check the Invert button to reverse the effect of the mask.

Related Topics

10.39

Image: *Calculations*

This command is nearly the same as Image: **Apply Image**. The primary difference is that Apply Image is used to combine two source *images* into a target image—Image: **Calculations** is used to combine two source *channels* into a target channel. This command is often used for the following tasks:

- Creating a replacement for an existing color channel.

- Creating a new selection channel.

- Creating a new Grayscale image.

However, the layers, blend modes, and filters offered by Photoshop 6 are much more convenient and flexible tools to accomplish any of these jobs. It is difficult to recommend this command for anything in particular.

The Calculations Dialog Box

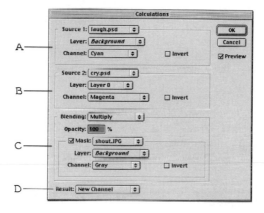

A. Source 1

Here, define your first image. Choose the file name from the Source popup. Choose your desired layer from the Layer pop-up. Finally, choose the channel you want to blend from the Channel pop-up. Click Invert to reverse the channel's values.

B. Source 2

Here, define your second image. Like with Source 1, choose the appropriate file name, layer, and channel from the pop-up menus. Click Invert to reverse the channel's values.

C. Blending

To further affect the compositing of the two channels, select a blend mode from the Blending pop-up. Both the blend modes and the opacity value affect Source 1, as if it was in a layer above Source 2.

If desired, choose a third channel to act as a mask between the two sources. Such a mask affects the Source 2 channel. Click Invert to reverse the effect of the mask.

D. **Result**

These pop-up menus determine the location of the new channel. To create a new Grayscale image, choose New from the Result pop-up. To replace a color channel in an existing image, select the image from the Result pop-up and choose the appropriate color from the Channel pop-up. To create a new masking channel in an existing image, select the image from the Result pop-up, and choose New from the Channel pop-up.

10.40

Image: *Image Size*

Resizing an image in Photoshop is different than scaling an image in a page layout program. There, you can only change the width and the height, with no control over the number of image pixels. With Image: **Image Size**, you can dictate exact values for all three image dimensions: Width, Height, and Resolution.

This command is commonly used for the following:

- **Resizing an image.** Here, you change the width and height, but not the number of image pixels. Similar to a page layout program, the resolution increases if you make the image smaller, and decreases if the image is made larger. Because the number of pixels remains constant, the file size stays the same. This technique is useful for converting a large low-res image into a small print-oriented image.

- **Resampling an image.** This is the most common use of Image: **Image Size**. Here, you force Photoshop to change the number of image pixels, either by downsampling, or decreasing the resolution, or by upsampling, or increasing the resolution. This can be done while leaving the width and height untouched, or by setting them to disproportionate values.

Mistakes to Avoid

Upsampling by too much. Photoshop downsamples with virtually no image degradation, since it only removes unnecessary pixels. Upsampling, however, makes Photoshop add pixels where none existed. The program is not very good at guessing, and the result appears pixelated. If you must upsample a scan, you're better off rescanning. To upsample placed artwork, import it again at a higher resolution. If you created the image in Photoshop, you must upsample at your own risk.

Issues to Consider

Once an image is imported into a page layout, it should not be scaled by more than 20%. If you need to make the image smaller, downsample it to a smaller size using Image: **Image Size**. If you need to enlarge it, the best option is to have the image rescanned at the proper dimensions.

Entering the dimensions of another image. To automatically apply the dimensions from another open image, open the Image Size dialog box and choose the name of the other image from the application's Window menu.

The Image Size Dialog Box

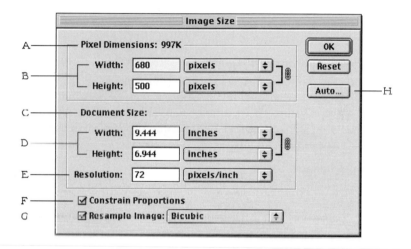

A. Pixel Dimensions

This displays the current file size. As you change the values in the dialog box, this number changes to reflect the new size, while putting the original size in parentheses.

B. Pixel Width and Height

These values display the current width and height in terms of pixels. Use these fields to resize images to a specific pixel value, such as monitor widths for multimedia presentations. If desired, select Percent (rather than Pixels) from the pop-up to reduce or increase the image size by percentages. If the Resample box is unchecked, these values cannot be edited.

C. Document Size

These values represent the printable image size, or the image dimensions as they apply to importing, printing, and output.

D. Print Width and Height

By default, these two values are constrained—if you change one, the other changes to maintain the original proportions. Choose a unit of measurement from the pop-ups: percent, inches, centimeters, points, or picas. Just like the File: **New** dialog box, the Width pop-up has an option for Columns, which enables you to set a new image width based on the values defined in File: Preferences: **Units & Rulers**.

E. Resolution

This field represents the current image resolution. Entering a different value sets a new resolution, but the method used to apply it depends on the remaining settings. If the Resample Image box is checked (or if Constrain Proportions is unchecked), changing the resolution either downsamples or upsamples the image. If Resample Image is unchecked, the resolution is constrained to the Width and Height values.

F. Constrain Proportions

Checking this button connects certain values in order to maintain the original image proportions. If Resample Image is checked, Width and Height are constrained. If Resample Image is unchecked, Width, Height, and Resolution are constrained. Unchecking this box enables you to edit all three values independently.

G. Resample Image

When you resample an image, Photoshop must use one of three interpolation methods to calculate the new pixels:

Bicubic

This method takes the longest, but it results in the highest quality distribution of pixels.

Bilinear

This takes less time, but it does a poor job.

Nearest Neighbor

This option uses no interpolation at all. It simply adds or discards pixels without averaging any new values.

H. Auto

Theoretically, this option optimizes image resolution for print. Clicking the Auto button brings up the Auto Resolution dialog box, where you enter the target linescreen. Based on this value and your selected Quality setting, Photoshop enters a new resolution in the Image Size dialog box. For example, if you target linescreen is 150 lpi, clicking Draft sets a value of 150 pixels per inch (lpi x 1). Good sets a value of 225 ppi (lpi x 1.5). Best sets a value of 300 ppi (lpi x 2).

In practice, this option is of little use. If your image was scanned at the appropriate resolution, it does not need to be changed. If the original resolution is too low for print, then Photoshop would have to upsample the image, hindering its quality.

Related Topics

10.41

Image: *Canvas Size*

This command changes an image's width and height. Unlike Image: **Image Size**, it does this without affecting the resolution. This command is commonly used for the following:

- **Cropping an image.** Lowering the width and height clips existing pixels, resulting in a smaller image window. When you crop an image this way, an alert appears, warning you that pixels are going to be clipped from the current image; click Proceed to apply the new measurements.

- **Expanding the canvas.** Increasing the width and height adds pixels around the existing image, resulting in a larger image window.

Issues to Consider

If an image only contains a background layer, then the new pixels appear as the current background color. To add transparent pixels instead, duplicate, and delete the background layer in the Layers palette. Then apply Image: **Canvas Size**.

Revealing information positioned beyond the edge of the image window. Occasionally, filter or transformation-based edits places image information off the canvas. To avoid clipping part of your image, undo the command and use Image: **Canvas Size** to temporarily enlarge the image window. If necessary, use Image: **Image Size** or Edit: Transform: **Scale** to reduce the image back to its original dimensions.

The Canvas Size Dialog Box

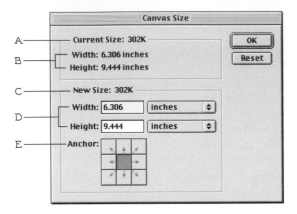

A. **Current Size**

This displays the current file size.

B. **Width and Height**

These display the current width and height in terms of pixels.

C. **New Size**

This displays the higher or lower image size that will result from the new dimensions.

D. **Width and Height**

Enter new values in these fields to change the width and height of the current image window. Units of measurement include percentages, inches, centimeters, points, and picas. Like the File: **New** dialog box, the Width pop-up has an option for Columns, which enables you to set a new image width based on the values defined in File: Preferences: **Units & Rulers**.

E. **Anchor**

With this grid, you determine the placement of the current image in the new window.

If cropping the image, the anchor grid enables you to preserve a specific portion of the image. For example, if you reduce the height by one inch and click the top center square, the inch is cropped from the bottom of the image. If you click the center square, a half-inch is removed from the top and bottom.

If expanding the canvas, this grid determines the position of the original image in the larger window. For example, if you add two inches to the width and height and click the center square, one inch is added all the way around the image. If you click the upper left square, two inches are added to the right, and two inches are added to the bottom.

Related Topics

10.42

Image: *Crop*

This command crops an image based on an active selection. When you crop, Photoshop discards all the image information outside the selection area, resetting the width and height while maintaining the resolution.

Issues to Consider

Trimming away information that exists beyond the edge of the image window. By choosing Select: **All** and applying Image: **Crop**, you discard any layer information that extends beyond the image boundaries. This will prevent such image data from bloating the file size of your images. (To expand the image boundaries out to the edges of the hidden areas, use Image: **Reveal All**.)

Related Topics

10.43

Image: *Trim*

Use this command to automatically crop an image, eliminating a specific range of solid edge color. For example, a series of web graphics may contain a black border that needs to be removed. The Crop tool is inefficient, because you have to draw a marquee by hand; the Canvas Size command isn't perfect, because the width of the borders may vary by a pixel or two. The Trim command enables you to pinpoint the desired value, and then discard only those edge pixels.

Issues to Consider

Use this command to resize a silhouette or vignette. When you create a silhouette, you usually have to crop some of the leftover space from the image. This can be difficult, especially when working with very light or soft-edge detail. If you crop too closely by hand, the final image suffers from noticeable clipping. Using the Trim command, you can automatically discard surrounding white or transparent edge pixels, leaving even the lightest values untouched. (For more information, see *I.1, Creating a Simple Silhouette* and *I.2, Creating a Vignette.*)

Trim Dialog Box

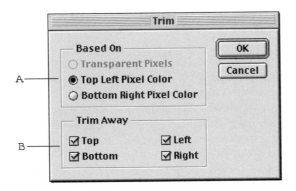

A. **Based On**

The following options determine the pixel value that will be discarded by the Trim command:

Transparent Pixels
> Click this option to crop away any transparent edge pixels. The most common example would be a silhouetted element, sitting in its own image layer.

Top Left Pixel Color
> Click this option to crop away any edge pixels based on the same value as the top left corner of the image.

Bottom Right Pixel Color
> Click this option to crop away any edge pixels based on the same value as the bottom right corner of the image.

B. **Trim Away**

The following options enable you to focus the Trim command on different edges of the image. Once you've specified a color, you're not committed to cropping every edge—instead, check as many boxes as you need.

Top
> Check this box to crop the Based On color from the top edge of the image.

Bottom
> Check this box to crop the Based On color from the bottom edge of the image.

Left
> Check this box to crop the Based On color from the left edge of the image.

Right
> Check this box to crop the Based On color from the right edge of the image.

Related Topics

10.44

Image: *Reveal All*

This command is only available when information in an image layer extends beyond the boundary of the image window. When you choose this command, the image canvas is increased to the very edge of the hidden information, fully revealing it. If multiple image layers contain hidden data, the canvas is increased to accommodate the outermost edges.

10.45

Image: *Rotate Canvas*

Unlike the Edit: **Transform** options, which can rotate selected areas, these commands rotate the entire canvas.

10.46

Image: *Rotate Canvas: 180°*

This option rotates the entire image 180°, or half of a circle's circumference.

10.47

Image: *Rotate Canvas: 90° CW*

This option rotates the entire image 90° to the right.

10.48

Image: Rotate Canvas: 90° CCW

This option rotates the entire image 90° to the left.

10.49

Image: Rotate Canvas: *Arbitrary*

This option rotates the entire image by an amount you define, either to the left or right. Since Photoshop only displays images in upright-rectangular windows, the canvas size is increased to accommodate the tilted corners.

Issues to Consider

If your image only contains one layer, applying an arbitrary rotation fills the new canvas area with the background color. Avoid this by duplicating and deleting the background layer before rotating the image. The new pixels now appear as transparent areas.

10.50

Image: Rotate Canvas: *Flip Horizontal*

This option flips the image on a vertical axis, providing a horizontal mirror-image.

10.51

Image: Rotate Canvas: *Flip Vertical*

This option flips the image on a horizontal axis, providing a vertical mirror-image.

10.52

Image: *Histogram*

This histogram is Photoshop's most thorough and accurate graph of an image's tonal values. It does not perform any specific commands—it's used only to evaluate existing information.

Although this dialog box gives very detailed information about an image, most of it is simply academic. Indeed, knowing the exact number of pixels in an image of is little help when making tonal corrections. The Histogram is commonly used for the following tasks:

- **Checking the distribution of image tones captured by a scanner.** If any gaps exist, or if certain tones such as shadows or highlights were not acquired, rescan the image before applying any corrections.

- **Determining image key.** Certain images have a naturally higher concentration of light or dark colors. For example, a scan of a snow-covered field is considered high-key, because it consists primarily of quarter- and highlight-tones. A scan of a cityscape at night is low-key, consisting mainly of three-quarter and shadow-tones. This information helps you create a better color correcting strategy.

- **Checking the status of an image during correction.** As you apply Image: **Adjust** commands, you consistently remove levels of information from the image. If the number of tones is reduced by too much, the image appears grainy and posterized. Checking the histogram channel lets you know how much information remains in each channel.

Note that if the image contains an active selection, only those values are represented in the histogram.

The Histogram Dialog Box

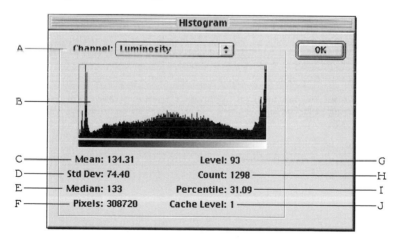

A. Channel

Choose the channel you wish to review from this pop-up. To see a composite of all color channels, select Luminosity. If the active image is in Grayscale mode, the pop-up is replaced by a single option: Black.

B. The Histogram

From left to right, this graph displays the darkest to lightest pixel values. The vertical lines each represent one of 256 possible tones. The higher the line, more of that particular tone will exist in the image.

The histogram for the Luminosity channel is particularly useful. This displays the overall range of the image, enabling you to determine the distribution of light and dark tones.

This graph differs from the histogram found in Image: Adjust: **Levels**. There, the composite histogram overlays the values of all color channels. For example, a value of 255 means at least one of the channels contains all-white information—regardless of the values of the remaining channels. The Image: **Histogram** composite averages the values of all channels before graphing them. Now, a value of 255 only occurs when every color channel is maxed.

C. Mean

This value displays the average brightness level for all image pixels. It's based on two things: the range from endpoint to endpoint and the tonal emphasis. For example, a high-key image may share the same tonal range as a low-key image, but since it has an abundance of lighter tones, the mean value is higher.

D. Std Dev

Short for Standard Deviation, this value represents the difference in brightness of the average pixel from the Mean.

E. Median

This value represents the value in the exact center of the existing tonal range. For example, if a Grayscale image contains brightness values from 10 to 240, the Median is 125. With color images, a different value typically applies to each channel.

F. Pixels

This value displays the total number of image pixels.

G. Level

To target the brightness value of an individual point on the histogram, position the cursor over it and click. The value appears under this option. If you click-drag to highlight a range of values, the darkest and lightest points appear here, separated by an ellipsis.

H. Count

When you click on the histogram to see a brightness value under Levels, this value displays the number of image pixels containing that value.

I. Percentile

This value displays the percentage of existing image pixels that possess a value darker than the selected value.

J. Cache Level

The option reflects the current setting of the Image Cache, as established in the Edit: Preferences: **Image Cache** dialog box. If the value is 1, it indicates that the histogram is based on every pixel value in the image. If the value is higher than 1, it indicates that the histogram is based on one of the magnification levels, as directed by the "Use Cache for Histograms" option in the Image Cache dialog box. If necessary, you can bypass that preference by holding down the Shift key while choose Image: **Histograms**.

Related Topics

9.54   Edit: Preferences: **Image Cache**
10.20 Image: Adjust: **Levels**

10.53

Image: *Trap Overview*

Trapping is a time-honored conventional prepress technique, and applies only to images containing more than one ink color. To compensate for any misregistration that may occur on-press, the color of one object is slightly expanded into its adjacent color. By creating this thin overlap, you prevent tiny gaps from appearing between colored objects in your printed piece.

Although trapping is an important part of any print job, the question is whether or not you need to use this particular command. The vast majority of CMYK images are one of two types:

- Continuous tone images, like scanned photographs, containing a wide and varied range of cyan, magenta, yellow, and black inks.

- Artwork or logos with colors that share multiple CMYK components.

Ninety-five percent of the time, these images do not need to be trapped. This is due to a *process bridge*, which essentially states that two adjacent colors sharing at least 20% of one component do not need to be trapped. Should misregistration occur, that color prevents any gaps from showing.

Most often, the only time you need to use Image: **Trap** is when an image consists of colors that do not share a process component. For example, a pure cyan shape abutting a pure black shape needs to be manually trapped, since they share no components.

Trapping Imported Vector-Based Artwork

Whether or not imported graphics need to be trapped depends on the content of the image and the techniques that were used in creating it. First and foremost, an illustration created using process colors must be imported as a CMYK image. Importing it as RGB and then converting to CMYK alters all the color values. Beyond that, most trapping needs can be taken care of before the image is imported:

- If the shapes in the image share a process bridge, they do not need to be trapped.

- If you added trap to a vector-based illustration before importing it into Photoshop, those color commands translate into the new image.

- If the image contains black outlines—like a cartoon character or a box with a frame—set them to Overprint before importing the image.

10.54

Image: *Trap*

This command enables you to apply a trapping value to any CMYK image. (It's not available when editing an image in any other color mode.) Once applied, Image: **Trap** seeks out all abutting colors and traces them with a thin, colored line. Since trapping consists of one color expanding into another, this command uses the following guidelines:

- All colors expand into black.

- Lighter colors expand into darker colors.

- Yellow expands into cyan, magenta, and black.

- Pure cyan and pure magenta expand into each other equally.

Mistakes to Avoid

Applying this command to a continuous-tone image. Doing so may visibly distort the tones in the cyan, magenta, and yellow channels.

Issues to Consider

If you apply your own traps, always contact your printer for advice on appropriate trap widths. Different press types and printing methods all have unique requirements.

The Trap Dialog Box

A. Width

Here, determine the width of the overlapping line. Choose points, pixels, or millimeters as a unit of measurement. Other programs with trapping functions use points, so this may be the most intuitive unit.

10.55
___

Image: *Extract*   *(Option-Command) [Alt-Control]-X*

The Extract command enables you to lift a detailed image element from the pixels that surround it. It bases its decisions on two things:

- **A user-defined transition edge.** In every extraction, you must paint the transition between the edge of the target element and the background. The exact approach will depend on the image type.

- **Contrast between the target element and the background.** As with all automatic targeting commands, this one works best on high-contrast images. For example, it's much easier to extract an image of a dog when it's photographed against a clear blue sky, as opposed to the branches of a tree.

It's easy to expect too much from this command. It doesn't work miracles—in fact, it's rather sloppy and time-consuming, and most of its extractions need to be cleaned up. However, as long as the element stands out in high contrast against the background, the edge detail is too fine to capture using standard selection techniques, and other methods have failed, the Image: **Extract** controls will often do the trick. (For more information, see *1.5, Creating a Complex Silhouette: Hair.*)

Issues to Consider

Using Image: Extract to create a selection. Even though this command is used to isolate an image element, it's also a surprisingly effective selection tool. To mask an element (as opposed to lifting it from the background), duplicate the target layer, then apply the extraction. Convert the new layer into a selection, then save the selection. Delete the extracted layer. (For more information, see *B.21, Creating a Complex Mask.*)

Using Image: Extract versus the Background Eraser tool. This command essentially produces the same results as the Background Eraser tool, only with more options and a clunkier interface. When the element you need to extract is reasonably straightforward, try the Background Eraser first. (For more information, see *2.15, Background Eraser Tool.*)

The Extract command offers reasonably powerful silhouetting controls, but its uses are limited. It's most suitable for finely-detailed edges, such as hair, fur, or even flame. However, it stumbles when you try to create a hard-edged silhouette, such as a product shot. The amount of cleanup that would be involved is time better spent using a selection-based technique.

Undoing your edits in the Extract dialog box. You can choose (Command) [Control]-Z to undo your most recent edit in the Extract dialog box, but you're restricted to a single undo level—you cannot step backward or forward.

Extract Dialog Box

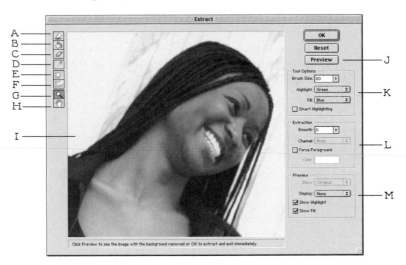

A. **Edge Highlighter Tool**   *Type "B"*

Use this tool to establish the edge of the targeted element. When creating a standard silhouette, paint all the way around the perimeter (if the element extends beyond the image boundaries, follow them off the edge). Make sure you straddle the line between background pixels and edge data—you're not creating the silhouette at this point, you're simply telling Photoshop where to focus. Use thin brush sizes for hard edges, larger brush sizes for soft details. Make sure no gaps appear in the painted outline.

When using the Force Foreground option to base an extraction on a targeted color (such as a flame against a black background), you're not defining an outline. Here, cover the entire element with the Edge Highlighter tool.

B. **Fill Tool**   *Type "G"*

Use this tool to establish the overall shape of the extracted element. After targeting the edges with the Edge Highlighter tool, click inside the outline with the Fill tool. Only the inside should fill. If the fill color appears beyond the outline, double-check the edges and close any gaps with the Edge Highlighter tool.

C. **Eraser Tool**   *Type "E"*

Use this tool to erase the outline applied by the Edge Highlighter tool. If desired, access this tool while painting by holding down the (Option) [Alt] key.

D. **Eyedropper Tool**   *Type "I"*

This tool is only available when the Force Foreground box is checked. Use it to sample the dominant color of the element you want to preserve in the extraction.

E. **Cleanup Tool**   *Type "C"*

This tool is only available when after you click the Preview button. At this point, the preview extraction is like a layer mask: parts of it are visible, parts are hidden. Use this tool to hide or reveal parts of the original image, similar to painting a layer mask with the Paintbrush tool. Paint a transparent part the preview to reveal part of the background. Hold down the (Option) [Alt] key while you paint to hide part of the foreground. Use this approach to compensate for any dropped-edge pixels or fringe colors before applying the command.

Change the pressure of the brush on-the-fly by pressing a key from 1 to 9. The zero key produces the highest pressure. Higher values produce harder, more direct edits.

F. **Edge Touchup Tool**   *Type "T"*

Like the Cleanup tool, this item is only available after you've created a preview. Rather than hide or reveal parts of the image, the Edge Touchup tool increases the level of edge contrast when you apply brushstrokes along the edges of the preview. The function is similar to the Background Eraser tool, but with more limited options. This tool is most appropriate for touching up the harder edges of the extraction; its impact on finer detail tends to be heavy-handed and obvious.

Change the pressure of the brush on-the-fly by pressing a key from 1 to 9. The zero key produces the highest pressure. Higher values produce harder, more direct edits.

G. **Zoom Tool**   *Type "Z"*

Use this tool to zoom in or out of the preview window. Click to zoom in; (Option) [Alt]-click to zoom out. To zoom in while using another tool, hold down the (Command) [Control] key and the spacebar and click. To zoom out, hold down the (Option-Command) [Alt-Control] keys and the spacebar and click

H. **Hand Tool**   *Type "H"*

Use this tool to scroll throughout the preview window. To scroll while using another tool, hold down the spacebar and drag.

I. **Preview Window**

This window displays the current status of the target extraction. If you've already created a preview, toggle between the extraction and the original image by pressing the X key.

J. **Preview Button**

Click this button to evaluate the success of your extraction settings. It actually generates a mask that is referenced only by the Extract dialog box. Sometimes you can edit this mask directly (for example, with the Cleanup or Edge Touchup tools); other times, you must click the Preview button again to generate a new mask (for example, when you change the Smooth setting).

When creating a standard silhouette, you cannot access this button until you've filled the outline with the Fill tool.

K. **Tool Options**

These options enable you to fine-tune the effect of the Edge Highlighter and Fill tools:

Brush Size (1 to 999)

Adjust this slider to increase or decrease the size of the current brush. Lower values produce smaller brushes; higher values produce larger brushes (which may also take longer to apply). The established brush size is referenced by every tool.

Highlight

This pop-up enables you to change the color laid down by the Edge Highlighter tool. Change it only if the current color doesn't stand out in high contrast against the image. To define a color other than red, green, or blue, choose Custom from the pop-up menu to access the color picker.

Fill

This pop-up enables you to change the color applied by the Fill tool. Change it only if the current color doesn't stand out in high contrast against the image. To define a color other than red, green, or blue, choose Custom from the pop-up menu to access the color picker.

Smart Highlighting

This option enables you to apply more intelligent brushstrokes with the Edge Highlighter tool. When checked, the tool's brush cursor contains crosshairs, enabling you to center the brush directly on the targeted element's edges. As you paint, the brushstroke automatically increases or decreases, based on what it perceives to be important detail. For the best results, be prepared to uncheck this box and perform a quick couple of touch-ups with the Edge Highlighter tool before extracting.

L. **Extraction**

These options enable you to fine-tune the current extraction settings:

Smooth (0 to 100)

This option enables you to reduce the level of sharp or jagged artifacts in the extraction's edges. As you raise the setting, you risk reducing the amount of detail. In many cased, however, the difference between low values and high values is subtle.

Channel

This option is only available when the current image contains at least one alpha channel. It enables you to load a channel into the preview window, as if you've drawn it with the Edge Highlighter tool. If you continue to edit the channel in the Extract dialog box, the pop-up automatically switches to Custom.

The way you prepare the channel will impact your ability to use it for an extraction. Black ranges appear as painted areas when you load a channel; white areas remain clear. You may need to invert a channel in the Channels palette before choosing Image: **Extract**.

Force Foreground

This option enables you to extract softer, more variably-toned image elements. A good example is flame against a high-contrast background. You can't trace the outline of the shapes, like you would with a standard selection—too much of the background color shows through. Instead, you can base the extraction on a source color value. This way, the background colors throughout the element are replaced with semi-transparent values, enabling you to blend the results more easily.

This approach has two requirements. First, you must completely paint over the targeted element with the Edge Highlighter tool—don't try to trace it. Second, you must use the Eyedropper tool to target the source color. You'll most likely need to preview several times, changing colors to Smooth settings.

Color

This swatch displays the color value currently targeted for the Force Foreground option. There are two ways to establish a new value: Use the Eyedropper tool, or click the swatch to access the color picker.

M. Preview Options

These items enable you to adjust the preview settings of the extraction:

Show

> Once you've clicked the Preview button, you can switch back and forth between the original image and the preview by choosing an item in this pop-up menu. You can achieve the same results by pressing the "X" key.

Display

> The items in this pop-up menu enable you to apply the extraction preview against different background colors. This way, you can assess the quality of the extraction before making the changes permanent. To display Photoshop's transparency checkerboard, select None. To set a colored mask, choose the desired value. To display the entire effect as an 8-bit mask, choose Mask. Toggle between the current setting and None by pressing the "D" key.

Show Highlight

> Check this box to display whatever you've painted with the Edge Highlighter tool. Most users only reveal the outline when they need to adjust it—otherwise, uncheck the box to hide it from view.

Show Fill

> Check this box to display whatever you've colored with the Fill tool. Most users only reveal the fill when they need to adjust it somehow—otherwise, uncheck the box to hide it from view.

Related Topics

10.56

Image: Liquify   *(Shift-Command) [Shift-Control]-X*

The Liquify command enables you to apply distortion effects through a series of brushstrokes. (The results are similar to those produced by the Smudge tool or the Distort filters, but with far more flexible options.) As you drag the cursor over an image, the pixels are pushed and pulled on-the-fly, producing effects similar to third-party warp-envelope utilities like Kai's Power Goo. There are two basic approaches:

- **Paint an effect.** When you apply a brushstroke, you're actually applying an algorithm that displaces the underlying pixels in a particular direction. Therefore, the larger the brush size, the greater the effect.

- **Pinpoint an effect.** The distort commands will affect the image whether you drag the cursor or not. Therefore, if you simply click the mouse button, most of the tools will affect the underlying pixels. This enables you to precisely target effects such as Twirl or Pucker.

Similar to working with a mask or a selection, you're able protect (or *freeze*) parts of an image before affecting it, which gives considerable control over the placement of the distortions. However, users must understand that if this tool is used without restraint, it produces obvious, mawkish effects that virtually scream, "I was made with the Liquify command."

Issues to Consider

This command often works well with the History Brush tool. For example, one of the most common uses of this command is to manipulate an image of a person's face. Because the distortions are so pronounced, it tends to destroy the subtle detail that lends realism to the image, such as whiskers and fleshtones. After distorting a face, use the History Brush tool to restore the image areas you didn't want to affect, painting carefully around the edited areas that you want to retain.

Liquify Dialog Box

A. **Warp Tool**   *Type "W"*

Use this tool to push pixels across the image, as if you dragged your finger through wet paint. Under Tool Options, increase the Pressure setting to make the effect more pronounced. (Clicking without dragging has no effect.)

B. **Twirl Clockwise** *Type "R"*

Use this tool to spin the pixels underneath the cursor to the right. Under Tool Options, decrease the Pressure setting to make the effect twirl more slowly, giving you more control. (Click without dragging to focus the effect.)

C. **Twirl Counterclockwise** *Type "L"*

This tool is the same as Twirl Clockwise, except that it spins the underlying pixels in the opposite direction.

D. **Pucker Tool** *Type "P"*

Use this tool to draw the underlying pixels directly toward the center of the cursor. Under Tool Options, decrease the Pressure setting to make the effect pucker more slowly, giving you more control. (Click without dragging to focus the effect.)

E. **Bloat Tool** *Type "B"*

Use this tool to push the underlying pixels toward the outer edges of the cursor. Under Tool Options, decrease the Pressure setting to make the effect bloat more slowly, giving you more control. (Click without dragging to focus the effect.)

F. **Shift Tool** *Type "S"*

Use this tool to displace the underlying pixels perpendicularly. When you drag to the left, the pixels move down. When you drag down, the pixels move to the right. When you drag to the right, the pixels move up. When you drag up, the pixels move to the left. To displace in the opposite directions, hold down the (Option) [Alt] key as you drag.

Drag in small circles to mimic the effect of the Pucker or Bloat tools, depending on which way you move the cursor.

G. **Reflection Tool** *Type "M"*

This tool doesn't really *reflect* information. Instead, it clones pixels from one area underneath the cursor and applies them to an area on the other side. The sides in question depend on the direction you're currently dragging the cursor (see "Shift Tool," above).

H. **Reconstruct Tool** *Type "H"*

Use this tool to slowly restore the image to its original condition. The exact results depend on the current option set in the Mode pop-up menu, under the Reconstruction options.

I. **Freeze Tool** *Type "F"*

Use this tool to paint over any image areas you want to protect. It doesn't matter if you've already applied a distortion to the area—as soon as you freeze it, you cannot adjust it with a Distortion tool.

Unfortunately, your editing options are restricted. You don't have access to any Paint tool options—instead, you can only control the Brush Size and Pressure settings. If the Pressure value is under 100, you only apply a partial mask to the image. The lower the pressure, the more your future edits will distort the underlying pixels.

To produce the most accurate protected area, create an alpha channel before choosing Image: **Liquify**. You can load the channel in the Freeze Area options, enabling you to create much more accurate masks. (For more information, see *B.18, Saving a Selection.*)

J. **Thaw Tool** *Type "T"*

Use this tool to liberate any frozen image areas. From an editing standpoint, this tool is functionally identical to the Freeze tool. (If you want to thaw the entire image, don't bother with this tool—click the Thaw All button.)

K. **Preview Window**

This window displays the current status of the image. You cannot zoom in or out.

L. **Tool Options**

These options enable you to fine-tune the distortion tools' brush settings.

Brush Size (1 to 150)

Adjust this slider to increase or decrease the size of the current brush. Lower values produce smaller brushes; higher values produce larger brushes (which may take longer to apply). The established brush size is referenced by every tool.

Brush Pressure (1 to 100)

Adjust this slider to increase or decrease the intensity of the distortion effect. Lower values result in slower, more gradual distortions; higher values produce quicker, more extreme results.

Stylus Pressure

If you use a drawing tablet, check this box to apply pressure dynamically, increasing or decreasing the distortion intensity on-the-fly.

M. **Reconstruction Options**

These options enable you to fine-tune the command's reversion settings.

Mode

The items in this pop-up determine the reversion method used by the Reconstruct tool. Each mode represents a different way of restoring the command's *warp mesh*, or the grid that you manipulate to produce distortion effects. (See "Show Mesh," later this section.)

Revert enables you to restore the the original image directly, with a minimum of back-end distortion.

Rigid ensures that the warp mesh gridlines between frozen and unfrozen areas remain at right angles. (Presumably, this retains a more natural transition between the two areas, but in practice, the results are awkward and hard to control.)

Stiff lessens the intensity of a distortion effect as you move away from a frozen area.

Smooth and *Loose* don't really revert the image at all. Instead, they continue distorting the warp mesh. The main difference between them is that Loose results in smoother transitions between frozen and unfrozen areas.

Displace enables you to apply a fully restored version of the image— however, the position of the new image is offset from the original. The exact position depends on the pixel you initially click with the Reconstruct tool. For example, if you click a distorted pixel that was originally the subject's nose, the restored nose appears at the click-point, and the rest of the image falls into place around it.

Amplitwist uses the same concept as Displace, but the restored image retains the angle and scaling of the click-point, as well as its position.

Affine uses the same concept as Displace and Amplitwist, but every attribute of the distorted pixels are retained when painting in the restored version.

Reconstruct

When you click this button, the image restores itself, almost as if it were replaying your edits in reverse. (It's not available when Displace, Amplitwist, or Affine appears in the Mode pop-up.)

Revert

Click this button to restore the original version of the image.

N. Freeze Area Options

These options enable you to fine-tune the frozen areas on the warp mesh.

Channel

This pop-up menu is only available when an alpha channel is available in the image. If so, you can base a frozen (or unfrozen) area on the contents of a predefined mask. This way, you can use much more accurate selection techniques to create a frozen area.

Invert

Click this button to invert any frozen areas.

Thaw All

Click this button to remove the mask from any frozen areas.

O. View Options

These options enable you to fine-tune the view settings of the Liquify dialog box.

Show Frozen Areas

Check this box to display any frozen areas. Uncheck it to hide the areas, enabling to to edit with a clean line of sight.

Show Image

Uncheck this box to hide the preview image from view. You can only hide the image when Show Mesh is checked.

Show Mesh

Check this box to display the gridlines of the warp mesh, the basis of the Liquify command. The manipulations that you apply to this grid are directly translated to image distortions.

Mesh Size

The items in this pop-up affect the cell-size of the warp mesh. This is for visual purposes only—different sizes have no impact on the quality of the distortions.

Mesh Color

The items in this pop-up enable you to change the color of the warp mesh. Change it only if you need a more contrasting value.

Freeze Color

The items in this pop-up enable you to establish the mask color applied by the Freeze tool. For the best results, use a value that contrasts with the image colors.

Related Topics

The Layer Menu

Layers Overview

Layers enable you to work with image elements as if they were on a series of transparent overlays.

Without layers (which debuted in version 3.0), you could only edit one flat canvas of pixels. To make a focused adjustment, you had to draw a selection outline to isolate the targeted area. When creating image composites or montages, you were mostly limited to complex channel techniques and the Image: **Calculations** commands.

With layers, the effect is similar to working in a page layout or illustration program. There, you treat each element as an independent entity. By selecting one item, you can make changes without affecting the others. You can easily rearrange an item, placing it above or below the others at will.

There are three types of layer (background, image, and content), and a variety of methods to mask and organize them in the layers palette.

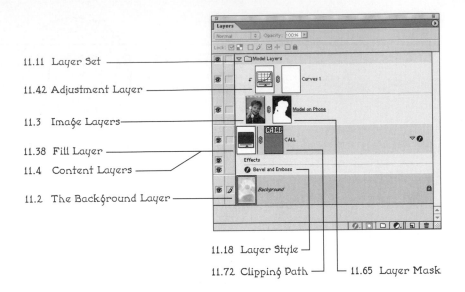

11.11 Layer Set

11.42 Adjustment Layer

11.3 Image Layers

11.38 Fill Layer

11.4 Content Layers

11.2 The Background Layer

11.18 Layer Style

11.72 Clipping Path

11.65 Layer Mask

11.2

The Background Layer

The background layer is Photoshop's default layer. It's fully opaque, similar to the single canvas used by early versions of Photoshop, or any other pixel-based editing software that does not support multiple layers. Background layers automatically appear in the following images:

- **Scans.** When you use a scanning Plug-in to acquire an image while Photoshop is open, the sampled data appears on a background layer.

- **Images saved in any file format other than native Photoshop.** Only native Photoshop images can contain multiple layers. Images saved as a GIF, EPS, or any other file format can only contain a single layer.

- **New images with non-transparent contents.** When creating a new image with the File: **New** dialog box, setting the Contents to White or Background Color results in a background layer.

- **Flattened images.** Applying Layer: **Flatten Image** converts all multiple image layers to a single background layer.

Mistakes to Avoid

Confining all of your edits to the background layer. A background layer is not required to continue editing. As soon as you require additional layers, the restrictions of the background layer can prove cumbersome:

- A background layer cannot possess transparent pixels or an opacity value of less than 100%.

- A background layer cannot be repositioned in the Layers palette.
- If a portion of the background layer is selected and deleted, the selected area is filled with the current background color.
- Increasing the image dimensions using Image: **Canvas Size** fills the new pixels in the background layer with the current background color.

Avoid these problems by creating a new image layer before applying a command or technique that adds new information to an image (retouching and painting are good examples). When making tonal or color corrections, consider using an adjustment layer.

Issues to Consider

An image can only contain one background layer. It is always titled "Background" in the Layers palette.

Adding a background layer. If an image doesn't already contain a background layer, you can add a new one by choosing Layer: **New: Background Layer**. While an image layer cannot be converted to a background layer, you can simulate this effect by adding a new background layer, positioning the desired image layer just above it, and choosing Layer: **Merge Down**.

Converting the background layer. Avoid the limitations of the background layer by converting it to an image layer:

- **Double-click the background layer in the Layers palette.** After entering a new name in the Make Layer dialog box and clicking OK, it appears as an image layer. The Layer: **Layer From Background** command produces the same results.
- **Duplicate the background layer.** Either choose the background layer and select Duplicate Layer from the Layers palette submenu, or drag the background layer item onto the New Layer control button. The copy appears as an image layer, allowing you to hide or delete the original background layer.

Related Topics

11.3

Image Layers

Image layers are created in addition to the background layer, enabling you to isolate an image element smaller than the entire window. Each layer appears as a separate item in the Layers palette, giving you independent control over their position and front-to-back arrangement. Since these layers support transparent pixels, you can see the image data contained in underlying layers.

When you choose Layer: New: **Layer**, the result is an empty, fully transparent layer. This enables you to paint, fill, or otherwise add new color to an image without affecting any existing pixels. More often, however, new layers are based on existing image information

Once an image contains multiple layers, you can only apply changes to the layer currently chosen in the Layers palette. There are three exceptions to this rule:

- Changing the color mode of an image.

- Applying an Edit: **Transform** command to a linked layer.

- Changing the width, height, or resolution of an image using Image: **Image Size** or **Canvas Size**.

Issues to Consider

Most file formats do not support multiple layers. As long as an image is open in Photoshop, it can contain multiple layers—even if the image was originally saved in a file format that doesn't support them. However, once an image contains anything but a background layer, it can only be saved in the native Photoshop file format. To save an image containing multiple layers into a different file format, you have two options:

- **Flatten the image.** This combines all visible layers into a single background layer, enabling you to save the image into any available file format.

- **Save a flattened copy.** Do this by checking the As a Copy box in the File: **Save As** dialog box. This enables you to save a separate, flattened copy of the open image into any available file format.

Related Topics

11.4

Content Layers

Content layers don't contain pixel-based data. Instead, they contain the settings of an Image: **Adjust** or Edit: **Fill** command. At first, the effects appear as if applied directly from the source, but there are two key differences:

- **They affect all underlying layers.** Instead of adjusting a single layer, content layers act as a sort of lens, affecting the appearance of any underlying image information.

- **The settings remain editable.** Each content layer contains a small thumbnail in the Layers palette that represents the original dialog box. By double-clicking this icon, you're able to make further adjustments.

As with image layers, you're able to restrict the area affected by a content layer:

- **Edit the layer mask.** In the Layers palette, every content layer automatically contains an empty layer mask. By clicking the mask thumbnail and applying brushstrokes, you're able to hide or reveal parts of the content layer. If a selection is active when you create a content layer, the new item is automatically masked. (For more information, see *11.66, Layer: Add Layer Mask: Reveal All.*)

- **Add a layer clipping path.** After creating a content layer, you're able to force an existing path to clip it, or draw a new clipping item with one of the Vector tools. If a path is active in the Paths palette when you create a content layer, the new item is automatically masked. (For more information, see *11.72, Layer: Add Layer Clipping Path.*)

- **Create a clipping group.** To restrict the effect to the pixels of an image layer, use the Layer: **Group With Previous** command. (For more information, see *22.17, Grouping Layers.*)

Issues to Consider

Masking tips for subtle content layers. Since you do not apply visible color to the image, it may be difficult to apply precise brushstrokes. Use the following shortcuts to facilitate this process:

- Hold down the (Option) [Alt] key and click the adjustment layer thumbnail to display the contents of the mask. (Option) [Alt]-click again to return to the normal editing mode.

- Hold down the (Option-Shift) [Alt-Shift] keys and click the adjustment layer thumbnail to view the mask as a semi-transparent overlay, similar to the one used by the Quick Mask tools. (Option-Shift) [Alt-Shift]-click again to hide the overlay.

Related Topics

11.5

Transparency

When a single element is added to an image layer, it is surrounded with transparent pixels. These pixels contain no color information, and enable you to "see through" the unused portions of a layer to the underlying information. This is sometimes referred to as a *transparency mask*.

Photoshop displays a checkerboard pattern to indicate transparency values. This pattern does not print or appear in any other application—it is only used to differentiate transparent areas from any other colors. The pattern is visible when the background layer has been removed or hidden from view, or when no color information appears on a specific portion of all visible layers.

Issues to Consider

Coloring transparent pixels. Most Photoshop commands only affect *existing* color information—the Image: **Adjust** commands are good examples. Transparent pixels can only be affected by actions that add *new* data.

Transparent pixels consume no space. Since transparent pixels contain no image data, they do not contribute to the overall file size. Only colored pixels increase the file size.

Related Topics

11.6

Opacity

When a layer is 100% opaque, its contents completely conceal any underlying information. When you reduce the opacity of a layer, you create the appearance of fading the image, allowing the underlying colors to show through. At 75% opacity, 75% of the visible information is contained in the visible layer, and 25% comes from the layers beneath. When the opacity is set to 50%, the active layer and the underlying layers appear at equal intensities. When you lower the opacity of an adjustment or fill layer, you decrease the impact of its adjustment values.

Most often, layer opacity is set with the opacity slider in the Layers palette. It does not permanently alter the pixel values until you apply either **Layer: Merge** or **Flatten Image**.

Related Topics

2.6   *Set Opacity*
11.100 *Layer: Merge*
11.105 *Layer: Flatten Image*
22.1   *Set the Opacity*

11.7

Layer: New

Each command in this submenu adds a new item to the Layers palette.

11.8

Layer: New: Layer

This command adds a new image layer to the Layers palette, placing it above the currently active item. Common uses include the following:

- **Creating a new, blank image layer.** Most often, this is done when applying an edit that adds new color values, such as retouching or painting.

- **Filling a new layer with a neutral color.** This is done to create a carrier layer for a blend mode effect, such as a lens flare or lighting effect. (See *Issues to Consider*, below.)

Issues to Consider

Understanding neutral color effects. Many filters, such as Filter: Render: **Lens Flare** or **Lighting Effects**, cannot be applied to the transparent pixels of an empty image layer. By choosing a blend mode and checking Neutral Color for Blend Mode, you can affect this new layer without permanently altering any underlying color values. This technique offers three distinct advantages:

- You can continue editing the underlying information, independent of the filter's effect.

- You can adjust the intensity of the effect by manipulating the layer's opacity slider, or by choosing different blend modes that share the same neutral color.

- You can reposition the effect, since it resides on a separate layer.

The New Layer Dialog Box

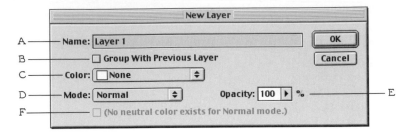

A. Name

Photoshop automatically enters a name in this field, loosely based on the number of layers that already exist. If desired, enter a new layer title of up to 32 characters.

B. Group with Previous Layer

Check this box to create a clipping group between the new layer and the item directly beneath it in the Layers palette. If the underlying layer is already part of a group, this option adds the new layer to the existing group.

C. Color

The values in this pop-up menu affect the appearance of a layer in the Layers palette. They have no effect on the actual contents of a layer.

D. Mode

This pop-up menu enables you to apply any of the 17 available blend modes to the new layer.

This setting isn't permanent—you can always choose a new blend mode at any time during editing. Most often, a specific blend mode is chosen from this dialog box to take advantage of the Neutral Color for Blend Mode option, described below.

If the current image does not contain a background layer, an additional listing appears at the bottom of the pop-up menu: *Background.* Choose this item to add a new background layer. You cannot enter a new title in the Name field when Background is chosen.

E. Opacity

The value in this field sets the opacity slider of the new layer. This value isn't permanent—you can reset the slider at any time during editing.

F. Neutral Color for Blend Mode

When certain blend modes are set in the Mode pop-up menu, checking this box fills the new layer with their *neutral color,* or the tone that results in no visible effect on the underlying information.

The available neutral color depends on the blend mode set in the Mode pop-up menu:

- **Black.** The neutral color for Screen, Color Dodge, Lighten, Difference, and Exclusion.
- **White.** The neutral color for Multiply, Color Burn, and Darken.
- **50% Gray.** The neutral color for Overlay, Soft Light and Hard Light.

Related Topics

11.9

Layer: New: *Layer From Background*

Choose this command to convert an image's background layer into an image layer. This way, you're able to incorporate transparency into the layer by erasing, masking, or repositioning the pixels.

If an image contains multiple layers, you don't have to activate the background layer before applying this command. If an image does not contain a background layer, this command appears as "Background from Layer."

Related Topics

11.10

Layer: New: *Background From Layer*

Choose this command to convert the active image layer into a new background layer. If an image already contains a background layer, this command appears as "Layer from Background."

To make a solid white background layer, create a new blank layer just before choosing this command. (To base the background layer on a different color, first set the desired value in the Toolbar's background color swatch.)

Related Topics

11.11

Layer: New: *Layer Set*

Layer sets enable you to organize the contents of the Layers palette by placing items into a series of folders. Sets are only necessary when an image contains a large number of layers, or a complex sequence of effects. For example, if you've expanded a layer style into its component layers, you can place all of them into a folder. This way, when the set is closed, you can continue to treat the effect as a single element; when the set is open, you're able to edit the individual items. Use the following techniques:

- **Expanding and closing a set.** To reveal the layers inside a set, turn down the small arrow to the left of the folder icon. Turn up the arrow to hide the contents.

- **Renaming a set.** Double-click a layer set in the Layers palette to access the Layer Set Properties dialog box.

- **Repositioning a set.** Click-drag a set in the Layers palette to change its position up or down in the stacking order.

- **Adding and removing layers.** Add a layer to a set by dragging its palette item directly into the folder. To remove a layer, expand the set to reveal the contents, then drag the desired item to a new position.

- **Duplicating sets.** Make a copy of a set by dragging its palette item directly onto the Create New Layer button.

- **Linking within sets.** You're able to link layers in different sets, link layers to sets, and link multiple sets by activating the target item and clicking the desired status boxes.

- **Transforming sets.** To apply a transformation to an entire set, activate the set in the Layers palette before choosing the desired Edit: **Transform** command. To transform a single item within a set, expand the set and activate the desired item.

- **Converting a set to a selection outline.** (Command) [Control]-click a layer set's icon to create a selection based on the outer edge of the overlapping layers inside.

Issues to Consider

Preserving multiple blend modes in a layer set. When the contents of a layer set are affected by different blend modes, a new option appears in the Blend Mode pop-up menu: Pass Through. This option is set automatically to ensures that the blend mode settings remain intact. If you apply a new blend mode to a layer set, every layer inside is set to the same mode.

Placing complex layer sequences into a set. If you need to preserve the relationships between a series of layers, don't place them into a set by dragging one-by-one—doing so may cancel important group settings. Instead, link the items you want to place, then choose Layer: New: **Layer Set From Linked**.

The New Layer Set Dialog Box

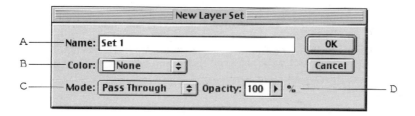

A. Name

If desired, enter the name of the new layer set in this field. Otherwise, the items are automatically named "Set 1," "Set 2," and so forth.

B. Color

This pop-up menu enables you to apply a color to the item that appears in the Layers palette. This is for organizational purposes only—it has no effect on the actual contents of the set.

C. Mode

To apply a single blend mode to the contents of a set, select one from this pop-up menu. By default, this item is set to Pass Through, which retains the original layer settings.

D. Opacity

If desired, lower the opacity of the entire set. This value is applied in addition to the Opacity settings applied to the individual layers.

Related Topics

11.12

Layer: New: **Layer Set From Linked**

Choose this command to place all items currently linked in the Layers palette into a new layer set. This way, you're able to organize the layers without dragging them manually.

11.13

Layer: New: **Layer Via Copy** *(Command) [Control]-J*

Choose this command to place the contents of an active selection into a new image layer, similar to making a selection and choosing Edit: **Copy** and **Paste**. The base layer is untouched, and the contents of the new layer maintain their original position.

Issues to Consider

Accessing the New Layer dialog box. Hold down the (Option) [Alt] key while choosing this command to access the New Layer dialog box. It's the same item that appears when you choose Layer: New: **Layer**, but without the Fill with Neutral Color option.

Related Topics

9.6   Edit: **Copy**
9.8   Edit: **Paste**
11.8   Layer: New: **Layer**

11.14

Layer: New: **Layer Via Cut** *(Command-Shift) [Control-Shift]-J*

Choose this command to place the contents of an active selection into a new image layer, similar to making a selection and choosing Edit: **Cut** and **Paste**. The contents of the new layer maintain their original position, but the base layer is affected: If the information came from an image layer, the selection area is filled with transparent pixels; if the information came from a background layer, the selection area is filled with the current background color.

Issues to Consider

Accessing the New Layer dialog box. Hold down the (Option) [Alt] key while choosing this command to access the New Layer dialog box. It's the same item that appears when you choose Layer: New: **Layer**, but without the Fill with Neutral Color option.

Related Topics

9.6   *Edit:* **Copy**
9.8   *Edit:* **Paste**
11.8   *Layer: New:* **Layer**

11.15

Layer: Duplicate Layer

Choose this command to create a copy of the currently active layer. Common uses include the following:

- Duplicating a layer to the same image.

- Duplicating a layer to another open image.

- Creating an entirely new, unsaved image from a layer.

Issues to Consider

The duplicate layer's position. Regardless of the image to which a layer is duplicated, the new item is listed above the active layer in the Layers palette.

Changing color modes may alter color content of layer. If the color mode of the destination image is different than the source image, the color values of the duplicate layer convert to match the destination image.

When copying a layer from one image to another, it's not necessary to access the Duplicate Layer dialog box. Drag the appropriate item from the Layers palette in the source image onto the image window of the destination image. When a black border appears around the image window, release the mouse button. The item appears in the Layers palette of the second image.

The Duplicate Layer Dialog Box

A. **Duplicate**
This non-editable field displays the name of the original layer.

B. **As**
This field contains the name of the new layer. When duplicating the layer into the same image, Photoshop automatically enters the original layer name with "copy" added at the end. When sending the new layer to another image, the automatic name is loosely based on the number of existing layers. If desired, enter a new title of up to 32 characters.

C. **Destination**
The options in this pop-up menu determine the location of the new layer:

Document

This pop-up menu lists all open images, and defaults to the image containing the original layer. To duplicate the layer to another image, select its name from the pop-up. To convert the duplicate into a new image, select New from the pop-up.

Name

When New is selected in the Document pop-up, this field enables you to name the new image. Entering a name here does not automatically save the image—you must still choose File: **Save**.

Related Topics
8.6   File: **Save**
22.10 Create New Layer

11.16
___

Layer: Delete Layer

This command permanently removes the active layer from a multilayer image. When an image contains only one layer, this command is not available. Unlike clicking the Delete Layer button in the Layers palette, this command does not offer an alert before deleting.

11.17

Layer: *Layer Properties*

Choose this command to rename a layer and change its color in the Layers palette. You can also access the Layer properties dialog box by (Option) [Alt]-clicking the desired palette item.

11.18

Layer: *Layer Style*

Layer styles enable you to apply and edit several popular techniques typically associated with Photoshop, such as diffuse glow, soft shadows, and custom emboss effects. In earlier versions of the program, executing these techniques required reasonable skill and patience, and the results were often difficult to edit. By applying a layer style, you can edit and re-adjust the effect in real-time, save the settings for future use, even copy and paste the settings to different layers.

When a layer style is applied, a small *"f"* appears on the target item the Layers palette. To view the list of styles currently applied, turn down the small arrow next to the character. To access the Layer Styles dialog box, double-click the name of the desired style.

Issues to Consider

Use the Layer Style commands with restraint. Layer styles can quickly spin out of control. The main dialog box enables you to apply up to 12 effects at once, manipulating dozens of controls in seconds flat. One or two clicks in the wrong direction, and your work becomes exactly what every professional should strive to avoid: a highly-stylized mishmash, recognizable by most people as a computer-edited image. Like the Image: **Adjust** commands, the most successful layer styles are usually the ones that quietly supplement an image, not the ones that strive to be an image all by themselves.

In the Layer Styles dialog box, checking a box is not the same as viewing the settings of a style. To apply a style, click the name of the desired item; the box is automatically checked. To remove a style, uncheck the unwanted box. Be aware that if you simply check a box, you don't automatically activate the settings—you must still click the style name for that. If you don't, you could edit the incorrect settings.

Toggling between the layer style options. While the Layer Style dialog box is open, you can toggle through the different options:
- **Drop Shadow.** Press (Command) [Control]-1
- **Inner Shadow.** Press (Command) [Control]-2
- **Outer Glow.** Press (Command) [Control]-3

- **Inner Glow.** Press (Command) [Control]-4
- **Bevel & Emboss.** Press (Command) [Control]-5
- **Satin.** Press (Command) [Control]-6
- **Color Overlay.** Press (Command) [Control]-7
- **Gradient Overlay.** Press (Command) [Control]-8
- **Pattern Overlay.** Press (Command) [Control]-9
- **Stroke.** Press (Command) [Control]-Zero

Bumping the field values. When one of the fields in the Layer Style dialog box is highlighted, press the up or down arrow key to increase or decrease the value in increments of 1. Hold down the Shift key to increase or decrease in increments of 10.

Preserving the settings of a layer style. Save a particular range of settings by adding them to the Styles palette. There are three ways to do this:

- Click the New Style button in the Layers Style dialog box.
- Click a blank spot in the Styles palette.
- Drag and drop the target layer from the Layers palette onto the Styles palette.

Once you add a combination of settings to the Styles palette, you can apply them to a layer with a single mouse-click. (For more information, see *19.6, New Style.*)

Viewing and hiding the effects of a layer style. To hide the influence of a style, make sure the list of styles is visible in the Layers palette. To hide all styles, click the view box to the left of the item named "Effects," just below the target layer. To hide a single style, click the view box next to the desired item. Click the view box again to reveal any hidden styles. (For more information, see *22.4, View/Hide Layer.*)

Converting a style to editable layers. For the most part, layer styles do nothing more than automatically perform what you can accomplish using normal layer editing techniques. In fact, you can convert the effects of one of these commands to their component image layers and clipping groups by selecting the appropriate item in the Layers palette and choosing Layer: Layer Style: **Create Layers**.

11.19

Layer: Layer Style: Blending Options

Choose this command to open the Blending Options panel in the Layer Style dialog box. These settings offer more advanced methods to blend the contents of an image layer with the underlying values.

The Layers palette enables you to set the blend mode and opacity for the entire contents of a layer. However, layer styles are applied *in addition* to the contents of an image. By manipulating Blending Options, you're able to affect the original information separately from the layer style.

The Blending Options Controls

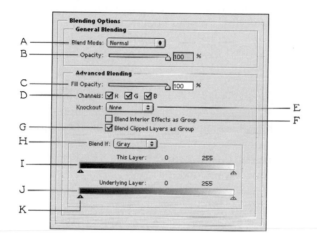

A. Mode

Setting a new blend mode here is the same as choosing an option from the Blend pop-up menu in the Layers palette.

B. Opacity

Setting a new opacity value here is the same as manipulating the opacity slider of an existing layer.

C. Fill Opacity

This slider affects the area covered by the layer's original contents. For example, if a layer originally contained an extracted silhouette of a monkey wrench, this slider only affects the pixels that comprise the wrench. Any applied layer styles that affect part of the fill boundary are also controlled by this option. (For example, the results of Inner Glow, Inner Shadow, Satin, and the Overlay styles are adjustable here; the influence of Drop Shadow and Outer Glow are not.)

Use the underlying Blend checkboxes to determine whether the contents fade separately from any layer styles that overlap the same area, or whether the original contents and overlapping styles fade together. This effect is applied separately from the Opacity slider at the top of the dialog box.

D. Channels

These checkboxes enable you to turn off the influence of one or more color channels. For example, assume you're editing an RGB image. If you uncheck the R box, the contents of the current layer appear as if there is no information in the Red channel. The Red data of any underlying information is untouched. (To achieve this effect manually, you'd have to copy/paste the layer into a new image, delete the data in the Red channel, then copy/paste it back to the original image.)

The available options depend on whether an image is in RGB, CMYK, or Lab Color mode. You can achieve a wider variety of color variations by temporarily converting modes before unchecking a channel (this approach is not recommended for color-sensitive, print-oriented images). Unchecking all the boxes renders the layer invisible.

E. Knockout

When the contents of a layer *knock out*, it acts as a sort of window, letting the contents of an underlying layer show through. The lower the Fill Opacity, the more information shows through. The required relationship between layers is a tricky one, and the results are so specific that most users don't consider them worth the effort. The Knockout pop-up menu contains the following options:

None

When this item is set, no knockout occurs—the layer contents are unaffected.

Shallow

In order for this option to work, the target layer must be part of a layer set or clipping group. When the layer is part of a set, this item reveals the next layer down. When part of a group, this item reveals the group's base layer.

Deep

When the target layer is part of a set, this item reveals the background layer. (If there is no background layer, transparent pixels are revealed.) When part of a clipping group, this item produces the same effect as Shallow.

F. Blend Interior Effects as Group

This option only addresses any layer style information that overlaps the original layer contents. When checked, the original contents and the layer style are both affected by the Fill Opacity slider. When unchecked, only the original fill is affected.

G. **Blend Clipped Layers as Group**

This option can only be applied to the base layer in a clipping group. When checked, the remaining group layers are affected by the blend mode applied to the base layer. (This is in appearance only—the remaining layers are not actually set to a different blend mode.) When unchecked, the blend mode applied to the base layer does not affect the remaining layers.

H. **Blend If**

This pop-up menu enables you to isolate the Blend command to a specific color channel.

When editing an RGB or CMYK image, choose Gray from the pop-up to include all color channels in the blend. This designation is inconsistent with the rest of Photoshop's controls, which refer to this composite channel as "RGB" or "CMYK". No composite is available when editing a Lab Color image. When editing layers in a Grayscale image, Black is the only available option.

I. **This Layer**

This bar represents the brightness values of the active layer. When the two sliders are positioned at 0 and 255, all colors in the layer are visible. By repositioning a slider, you hide a range of visible brightness values. For example, moving the right slider from 255 to 200 forces all values between 201 and 255 to become transparent.

J. **Underlying Layer**

This bar represents the brightness values of the underlying image information. The effect is the opposite of the This Layer bar: By repositioning a slider, a range of underlying colors becomes visible through the active layer, regardless of the active layer's brightness values. For example, moving the left slider from 0 to 30 forces the active layer to reveal all underlying values between 0 and 29.

K. **Smooth Transition Sliders**

If the layers contain continuous tones, moving the blend sliders can result in harsh transitions between the visible and hidden color values. By holding down the (Option) [Alt] key and dragging one side of a slider, it splits in two. This adds a range of increasing semi-opacity between the hidden and visible colors, creating a smoother transition.

For example, moving the left slider of the bar to 20 and (Option) [Alt]-dragging its right half to 40 creates a smooth transition. When applied to the This Layer bar, values between 0 and 19 are transparent, values between 20 and 39 gradually increase in opacity, and values above 40 are fully opaque. When applied to the Underlying bar, values between 0 and 19 are fully opaque, values between 20 and 39 gradually increase in transparency, and values above 40 are not visible.

Once you have separated the two sections of a slider, you can reposition them without holding down the (Option) [Alt] key.

L. **Preview**

Check this box to see the effect of your adjustments on screen while the Blending Options dialog box is still open.

11.20

Layer: Layer Style: *Drop Shadow*

Use this command to apply a soft-edged shadow beneath the contents of the currently selected image layer.

The Drop Shadow Controls

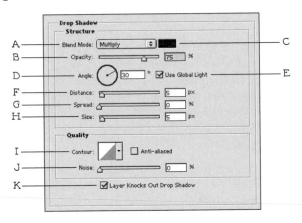

A. **Mode**

Choose the desired blend mode from this pop-up menu. It determines how the shadow color combines with the pixels in underlying layers. This option defaults to Multiply, which enables a shadow to overprint underlying colors. (For more information, see *22.2, Set the Blending Mode.*)

B. **Opacity** (0 to 100%)

This value determines the opacity of the shadow only—it has no effect on the original layer information. (For more information, see *22.1, Set the Opacity.*)

C. **Color Swatch**

Click this swatch to access the color picker, where you define the color of the drop shadow.

D. **Angle** (-180° to 180°)

This value determines the angle at which the shadow falls away from the object.

E. **Use Global Light**

When this box is checked, this effect uses the value entered in the Global Angle dialog box. (For more information, see *11.34, Layer: Layer Style: **Global Light**.*)

F. **Distance** (0 to 30000)

This value determines how far away from the original layer information the shadow is placed. Ultimately, the placement of the shadow is a combination of the distance and the angle. If desired, you can move the cursor onto the image and click-drag to manually position the shadow. The Distance and Angle values reflect the change.

G. **Spread** (0 to 100%)

This value determines the softness of the shadow's edge, similar to applying Filter: Blur: **Gaussian Blur**. Low values result in a harder edge; higher values result in a soft, feathered edge. The amount of blur applied varies according to the resolution of the image.

H. **Size** (0 to 250)

This option enables you to expand the shadow's edge beyond its original perimeter. It may increase the level of edge softness (depending on the current Spread setting), but remember that this is a simple scale command—it only increases the size of the edge, as if using the Image: **Image Size** command.

You can't use this option to make a drop shadow smaller than the original layer element. To produce this effect, choose Layer: Layer Style: **Create Layer** to split the style into separate layers, then choose Edit: Transform: **Scale** to reduce the size of the shadow.

I. **Contour**

A shadow fades from a base color (black, for example) to full transparency. In most cases, the fade is smooth and straight, similar to a linear gradient. This option enables you to apply a curve that redirects the fade values. Changes can be simple, such as a gradual curve that fattens the edge (similar to the Choke setting in Photoshop 5), or extreme, such as sharp spikes that add halos or neon-style effects.

To edit an existing contour, click the small thumbnail. The Contour Editor dialog box appears, enabling you to plot a curve on a graph. The top of the graph represents fully opaque values; the bottom represents fully transparent values. The left side of the graph represents the outer boundary of the shadow; the right side represents the inner boundary. Place and position points on the curve to redirect the transition of the shadow edge. (For the best results, apply a drop shadow and zoom in to preview the effect of your edits.)

Check the Anti-aliased box to add a thin, one-pixel blend to the edge transitions in the shadow. The effect is more noticeable in harsh or sharp contours—soft shadows don't really benefit from anti-aliasing.

J. **Noise**

This option adds an adjustable level of randomized pixels to the shadow. The effect is similar to applying the Dissolve blend mode, except you're able to increase or decrease the amount of dithering that occurs.

K. **Layer Knocks Out Drop Shadow**

When this box is checked, no shadow information is placed behind the layer contents. If you reduce the Fill Opacity (in the Blending Options controls), only the visible shadow edge remains. When unchecked, reducing the Fill Opacity reveals shadow information beneath the layer.

Some users uncheck this option to produce the effect of a semi-translucent element casting a shadow. However, such items don't cast single-colored shadows. For example, hold a slide or color film negative over a sheet of white paper; the "shadow" is actually a diffuse version of the same colors. Produce this effect by duplicating and blurring a color layer.

11.21

Layer: Layer Style: Inner Shadow

This command applies a reverse shadow to the layered element. Instead of the element casting a shadow on the underlying image information, it appears as if the surrounding information casts a shadow on the element.

The Inner Shadow controls are identical to the items in the Drop Shadow panel. (For more information, see *11.20, Layer: Layer Style: Drop Shadow.*)

11.22
___

Layer: Layer Style: *Outer Glow*

This command applies a diffuse glow around the outer boundary of the layered element.

The Outer Glow Controls

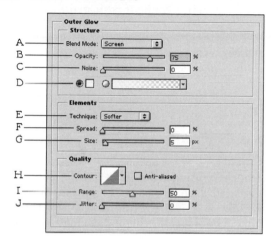

A. Blend Mode

Choose the desired blend mode from this pop-up menu. It determines how the glow color combines with the pixels in underlying layers. This option defaults to Screen, which tends to produce more natural highlights. (For more information, see *22.2, Set the Blending Mode.*)

B. Opacity

This value determines the opacity of the glow only—it has no effect on the original layered element. It defaults to 75%.

C. Noise

This option adds an adjustable level of randomized pixels to the shadow. The effect is similar to applying the Dissolve blend mode, except you can increase or decrease the amount of dithering that occurs.

D. Fill Type

These options enable you to set the color values used in the glow effect:

Color

Click this button to base the glow on a solid color. To change the color, click the small swatch to access the color picker. By default, the color is based on a blend to transparency, similar to a drop shadow.

Gradient

> Click this button to base the glow on a gradient. To access the gradient editor, click the thumbnail. To select from a list of predefined gradients, click the small vertical bar to the right of the thumbnail. (For more information, see *2.17, Gradient Tool*.)

> To anticipate the effect of a gradient, examine the thumbnail. The left side represents the outer edge of the glow; the right side represents the inner edge. The entire gradient is shaped by the contour setting.

E. Technique

This option is actually a calculation method that affects the current contour setting. For the most part, it determines how a glow effect bends around sharp corners.

Softer

> When you choose this item, the corners of the effect are rounded, as they would appear if the element were actually glowing.

Precise

> When you choose this item, the glow follows the shape of the element more accurately, enabling it to handle sharp corners and steep angles. The effect is not as natural, but is sometimes more useful when affecting a more angular-shaped element, such as type.

F. Spread (0 to 100%)

This value determines the softness of the glow's edge, similar to applying Filter: Blur: **Gaussian Blur**. Low values result in a harder edge; higher values result in a soft, feathered edge. The same value may produce different results, depending on the size and resolution of the image.

G. Size

This option enables you to expand the edge of the glow effect beyond its original perimeter. It may increase the level of edge softness (depending on the current Spread setting), but remember that this is a simple scale command—it only increases the size of the edge, as if using the Image: **Image Size** command.

H. Contour

A typical glow fades from a base color to full transparency. In most cases, the fade is smooth and straight, similar to a linear gradient. This option enables you to apply a curve that redirects the fade values. (For more information, see *11.20, Layer: Layer Style: **Drop Shadow**.*)

I. Range (0 to 100%)

This slider enables you to reset the midpoint of the current contour curve. It defaults to 50%, indicating the midpoint's original position. By decreasing the value, you push the midpoint closer to the outer edge (the result is a fatter interior, and a thinner soft edge). By increasing the value, you push the midpoint closer to the inner edge (the result is a wider, softer edge).

J. Jitter

This option enables you to randomize the pixels in a glow effect. It only works when you've set a gradient fill type based on two or more colors. No new colors are added by this item.

11.23

Layer: Layer Style: Inner Glow

This command applies a glow that appears around the inner contour of the layered element.

Inner Glow Controls

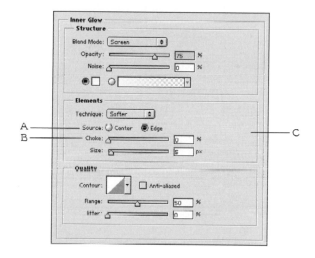

A. Source

This option enables you to specify the starting point of the glow effect.

Center

Here, the glow emanates from the center of the layer contents, expanding outward.

Edge

Here, the glow emanates from the outer edge of the layer contents, expanding inward.

B. Choke

This value determines the softness of the glow effect, similar to applying Filter: Blur: **Gaussian Blur**. Low values result in a harder edge; higher values result in a soft, feathered edge. The same value may produce different results, depending on the size and resolution of the image.

C. Remaining Options

The remaining controls are identical to the items in the Outer Glow panel. (For more information, see *11.22, Layer: Layer Style:* **Outer Glow**.)

11.24

Layer: Layer Style: *Bevel & Emboss*

This command enables you to apply a series of three-dimensional edge effects to the contents of a layer.

The Bevel & Emboss Controls

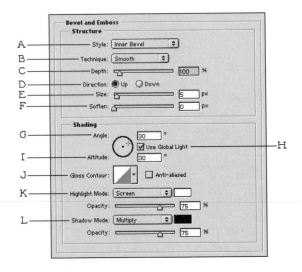

A. Style

The items in this pop-up menu determine the overall style of the layer effect.

Outer Bevel

This option applies a semi-translucent beveled edge around the outer contour of the layered element.

Inner Bevel

This option applies a solid beveled edge along the inner contour of the layered element.

Emboss

This option is the same as applying the Outer Bevel and Inner Bevel options simultaneously.

Pillow Emboss

This option is the same as Emboss, except the inner bevel is reversed, making it appear as if the edges of the layered element are slightly sunk into the surrounding image information.

Stroke Emboss

This option only produces an effect when a Stroke layer style is currently applied. Here, the stroke acts as a colored, beveled edge that surrounds the layer contents.

B. Technique

The items in this pop-up menu determine the level of sharpness apparent in the cut edges of a beveled element:

Smooth

This option adds soft transitions between shaded areas, producing the effect of smooth, rounded edges.

Chisel Hard

This option adds hard transitions between shaded areas, producing the effect of hard-cut edges.

Chisel Soft

This option also produces hard-cut edges, but as if they were based on smaller, more finely-detailed strokes.

C. Depth (1 to 1000%)

This slider increases the steepness of the beveled edges, or the apparent angle of their cut. This is accomplished by raising or lowering the amount of contrast between the highlight and shadow areas.

D. Direction

This option enables you to flip the direction of the light source. In theory, this makes the difference between a raised bevel and lowered bevel; in practice, it looks the same either way, with a different lighting angle. When you choose Up, the highlight area appears to face the light source; when you choose Down, the highlight area appears to face away.

E. Size (0 to 250 px)

This value determines the perceived height of the beveled object.

F. Soften (0 to 16 px)

This value determines the edge softness of the beveled edges, similar to applying Filter: Blur: **Gaussian Blur**. Low values result in a harder edge; higher values result in a soft, feathered edge. The amount of blur actually applied varies according to the resolution of the image.

G. Angle (-180° to 180°)

This value determines the angle of the light source that appears to strike the beveled object.

H. Use Global Light

When this box is checked, the effect uses the value entered in the Global Light dialog box. (For more information, see *11.34, Layer: Effect: Global Light.*)

I. Altitude (0 to 90°)

Where the Angle field indicates the position of a light source in relation to the layer, this option determines its height. Decrease the value to produce the effect of a low-altitude light source; use a higher value to raise the apparent altitude of the light source.

J. Gloss Contour

This option uses the Contour curves to establish the reflectivity of the beveled edges. (For more information, see *11.20, Layer: Layer Style: Drop Shadow.*)

K. Highlight Mode

The values in this section of the controls affect the blend mode, opacity, and color of the effect's highlight information, or the portion that appears angled toward a light source.

L. Shadow Mode

The values in this section of the controls affect the blend mode, opacity, and color of the effect's highlight information, or the portion that appears angled away from a light source.

The Contour Options

When you choose this option, you're able to use the Contour curves to adjust the fades between the highlight/shadow colors and transparency, similar to adjusting the same items in the Shadow or Glow styles.

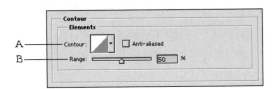

A. Contour

Click this thumbnail to edit the current Contour curve. To apply a preset curve, click the vertical bar to the right of the thumbnail. (For more information, see *11.20, Layer: Layer Style: Drop Shadow.*)

B. Range (0 to 100%)

This slider enables you to reset the midpoint of the current contour curve, or the halfway-points between the solid and transparent areas. (For more information, see *11.20, Layer: Layer Style: Drop Shadow.*)

The Texture Options

When you choose this option, you're able to use a pattern as an embossed overlay. These settings only have an effect when one of the Emboss options is set in the style's main controls. Use the Shading options in the Bevel and Emboss controls to further refine the pattern's appearance.

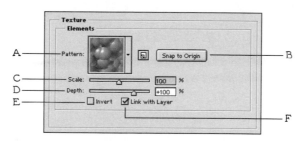

A. Pattern

Click this thumbnail to choose a pattern from the list of presets. You must define a swatch as a pattern before it is available in the pattern picker. (For more information, see *9.29, Edit: **Define Pattern**.*)

After choosing a swatch, you can click-drag onscreen to position the repeating pattern as desired.

B. Snap to Origin

If you've repositioned the pattern on screen, click this button to restore it to its original location.

C. Scale (1 to 1000%)

Use this slider to affect the size of the pattern tile. It defaults to actual size: 100%. Lower values reduce the size of the pattern, and higher values enlarge it. Be careful—if you scale a pattern too high, the components will appear washed out and pixelated.

D. Depth (-1000 to 1000%)

This slider increases or decreases the steepness of the embossed edges. This is accomplished by raising or lowering the amount of contrast between the highlight and shadow areas. Positive values accentuate the current highlights and shadows; negative values reverse the highlights and shadows, making the pattern appear to be embossed in the opposite direction.

E. Invert

Check this box to invert the values of the embossed layer, making the emboss direction appear to reverse. The results are identical to setting the additive inverse of the current Depth value. For example, if the Depth slider is set to 100%, checking Invert is the same as setting the value to –100%.

F. **Link to Layer**

When this button is checked, the embossed pattern is attached to the target layer; when repositioning the layer, the pattern moves with it. When unchecked, the pattern does not move when the layer is repositioned.

11.25

Layer: Layer Style: *Satin*

This command enables you to use the Contour curves to apply and manipulate a series of single-colored waveforms. In certain situations, the complex, overlapping strings vaguely recall the play of light on a swatch of satiny fabric. Beyond that, the results are impossible to predict.

Satin Controls

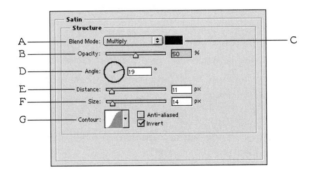

A. **Blend Mode**

Choose the desired blend mode from this pop-up menu to determine how the waveforms combine with the colors of the target layer. This option defaults to Multiply, which darkens the overall values. (For more information, see *22.2, Set the Blending Mode.*)

B. **Opacity** (0 to 100%)

This value sets the opacity of the waveforms—it has no effect on the original layered element. It defaults to 50%. (For more information, see *22.1, Set the Opacity.*)

C. **Color**

Click this swatch to specify the color applied to the waveforms. You can only set one color per style.

D. **Angle** (-180° to 180°)

This option enables you to set the orientation of the entire style. The effect is similar to rotating the contents of a layer. If desired, drag the image window to set an angle manually (doing so adjusts the Distance, as well).

E. **Distance** (1 to 250 px)

This value determines the onscreen placement of the Contour curves. Lower values place the effect on the edges of the layer, leaving a solid-colored field in the center. Higher values expand the curves, creating a series of overlapping waveforms. If desired, drag the image window to set the Distance manually (doing so adjusts the angle, as well).

F. **Size** (0 to 250 px)

This option enables you to adjust the thickness of the waveform by increasing the level of softness applied to the shapes. At low values, the waveforms are thin and hard-edged; at higher values, they soften and fade.

G. **Contour**

The Contour curves form the basis of the Satin layer style, overlapping and rotating a series of blends from the target color to transparency. (For more information, see *11.20, Layer: Layer Style: **Drop Shadow**.*)

11.26

Layer: Layer Style: Color Overlay

This command enables you to apply a range of solid color to a layer. For the most part, the effect is the same as adding a new layer by choosing Layer: New Fill Layer: **Solid Color**, then grouping it to the desired layer. Adding the information this way makes it easier to incorporate the colors into another layer style. When using a colored overlay for other effects (such as the recoloring techniques covered in Appendix H), use a solid color fill layer, instead. (For a description of the settings, see *11.39, Layer: New Fill Layer: **Solid Color**.*)

11.27

Layer: Layer Style: Gradient Overlay

This command enables you to apply a colored blend to a layer. For the most part, the effect is the same as adding a new layer by choosing Layer: New Fill Layer: **Gradient**, then grouping it to the desired layer. Adding the information this way makes it easier to incorporate the colors into another layer style. (For a description of the settings, see *11.40, Layer: New Fill Layer: **Gradient**.*)

11.28

Layer: Layer Style: *Pattern Overlay*

This command enables you to apply a pattern to a layer. For the most part, the effect is the same as adding a new layer by choosing Layer: New Fill Layer: **Pattern**, then grouping it to the desired layer. Adding the information this way makes it easier to incorporate the colors into another layer style. (For a description of the settings, see *11.41, Layer: New Fill Layer:* **Pattern**.)

11.29

Layer: Layer Style: *Stroke*

This command enables you to add a stroke that borders all exposed edges of a layer. The results are similar to those produced by the Edit: **Stroke** command, but this option is far more flexible. Because it is separate from the actual layer, you can change its color, width, and orientation at any time, as well as remove it altogether without compromising the image.

Issues to Consider

Outputting a vector-based stroke. One of the problems with pixel-based strokes is that their edge-crispness is limited by the image's resolution and target linescreen. However, it's possible to output a stroke with the same PostScript-based crispness as the objects created in Illustrator or FreeHand. To do this, you must apply the Stroke layer style to a vector-based shape. When finished, leave the image unflattened and save it as a Photoshop EPS file. As long as your workflow supports embedded vectors, the stroke will output cleanly, regardless of the image's resolution.

Note that the only way to apply a PostScript stroke to an image layer is to mask the contents with a layer clipping mask. This way, when you apply the stroke to the layer, it is applied to the path, enabling you to embed the information as vector data.

Stroke Controls

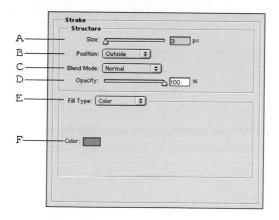

A. **Size** (1 to 250 px)

Use this slider to set the width of the stroke, as measured in pixels.

B. **Position**

The items in this pop-up menu determine the placement of the stroke, in relation to the boundary of the image contents:

Outside

This item places a stroke along the outer edge of the boundary.

Inside

This item places a stroke along the inner edge of the boundary.

Center

This item places a stroke that straddles the edge of the boundary.

C. **Blend Mode**

Choose the desired blend mode from this pop-up menu to determine how the stroke combines with the colors of the target layer. This option defaults to Normal, which results in a solid color. (For more information, see *22.2, Set the Blending Mode.*)

D. **Opacity** (0 to 100%)

This value sets the opacity of the stroke—it has no effect on the original layered element. It defaults to 100%. (For more information, see *22.1, Set the Opacity.*)

E. **Fill Type**

The items in this pop-up menu enable you to change the type of information that appears in the stroke:

Color

Choose this option to fill the stroke with a solid color. When you do, a color swatch appears in the dialog box, enabling you to specify the desired value.

Gradient

Choose this option to fill the stroke with a colored blend. When you do, the Gradient options appear in the dialog box. (For more information, see *11.40, Layer: New Fill Layer: **Gradient**.*)

Pattern

Choose this option to fill the stroke with a predefined pattern. When you do, the Pattern options appear in the dialog box. (For more information, see *11.41, Layer: New Fill Layer: **Pattern**.*)

11.30
*Layer: Layer Style: **Copy Layer Style***

As a way of saving time, you can copy and paste the style settings from one layer to any other. Choose this command to tell Photoshop to remember the style settings of the active layer.

Issues to Consider

Copy Effects does not involve the Clipboard. If you've copied any other information before choosing this command, it remains intact.

11.31
*Layer: Layer Style: **Paste Layer Style***

After copying the style settings of a layer by choosing Layer: Effects: **Copy Layer Style**, select another item in the Layers palette and choose this command. The same effect is applied to the new layer.

Issues to Consider

Pasting a style into multiple layers. To apply the same effect to multiple layers, link them in the Layers palette before using this command.

11.32
*Layer: Layer Style: **Paste Layer Style to Linked***

This command enables you to paste the values of a layer effect to more than one image layer at a time. When you choose this paste command, the copied layer effect values are applied equally to any image layers linked to the active layer.

11.33

Layer: Layer Style: Clear Layer Style

Choose this command to remove any style settings from the active layer. Linked layers are not affected—to clear layer effects from more than one layer, you must select them one at a time and choose this command.

11.34

Layer: Layer Style: Global Light

When you choose this command, you can enter a single Angle value in the Global Light dialog box. By clicking the Global Light option in any of the Layer Style dialog boxes, you can ensure that all effects contain the same value.

You're also able to set an Altitude value, which determines the relative height of the light. Decrease the value to produce the effect of a low-altitude light source; use a higher value to raise the apparent altitude of the light source.

11.35

Layer: Layer Style: Create Layer

Choose this command to convert any applied layer styles into their component layers and clipping groups. From there, you can continue editing using standard layering techniques. Once converted, however, you cannot revert back to the automated state of a layer style.

11.36

Layer: Layer Style: Hide All Effects

To conceal the values of the current layer effects, choose Layer: Layer Style: **Hide All Effects**—only the original layer information displays. To reveal the styles again, choose Layer: Layer Style: **Show All Effects**.

11.37

Layer: Layer Style: Scale Effects

Use this command to scale the style settings applied to a layer all at once. This way, you don't have to re-open the Layer Style dialog box and manipulate the individual sliders and fields; the values are calculated and entered automatically.

11.38

Layer: *New Fill Layer*

The commands in this submenu add a content layer that contains a temporary, editable fill.

Issues to Consider

Changing the contents of a fill layer. In the Layers palette, the fill type is represented by a small thumbnail on the left side of the palette item. The main benefit of a fill layer is that you can double-click the thumbnail at any time to specify a new value. This is quite valuable when using fill layers in a high-volume recoloring or pattern workflow.

You can't apply adjustment commands, filters, or brushstrokes to a fill layer. You can only change the fill type. To apply these effects, you must convert the layer to editable pixels by choosing one of the commands in the Layer: **Rasterize** submenu. (For more information, see *11.56, Layer:* **Rasterize***.*)

Fill layers form the basis for Photoshop's vector-based shapes. If a standard path is active when you create a new fill layer, it automatically converts to a layer clipping path, forming the outline of a filled shape.

11.39

Layer: *New Fill Layer: Solid Color*

This command produces a fill layer based on a solid color value. When you first choose it, the New Layer dialog box appears, where you can set blend mode, opacity, and group options. (If desired, you can handle these settings later in the Layers palette.) When you click OK, the Color Picker appears, enabling you to enter the desired values.

Related Topics

11.40

Layer: New Fill Layer: Gradient

This command produces a fill layer based on a gradient blend. When you first choose it, the New Layer dialog box appears, where you can set blend mode, opacity, and group options. (If desired, you can handle these settings later in the Layers palette.) When you click OK, the Gradient Fill dialog box appears, enabling you set the desired values.

Gradient Fill Dialog Box

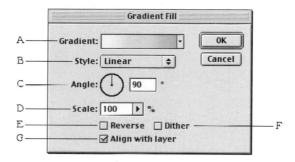

A. Gradient

Click directly on the Gradient icon to access the Gradient Editor dialog box. From there, you can edit the contents of an existing item, or define a new one altogether. To choose an existing gradient, click directly on the thin vertical bar to access the gradient picker.

Note that after you specify a gradient, you can fine-tune its position by dragging on screen while the Gradient Fill dialog box is open.

B. Style

Choose the desired gradient shape from this pop-up menu. (For more information, see *2.17, Gradient Tool.*)

C. Angle (-180° to 180°)

Set the angle of the gradient in this field, or drag the small pointer in the Angle wheel to the desired position.

D. Scale (10 to 150%)

Use this slider to increase or decrease the size of the fill. The results depend on the style of gradient.

E. Reverse

Check this box to flip the direction of the gradient.

F. Dither

Check this box to slightly randomize the distribution of colored pixels. This helps prevent banding, or the visible shade-stepping that occurs when too few tones are extended over too great a distance. Unless you have a specific reason to turn it off, leave this box checked for the best results.

G. **Align with Layer**

When this box is checked, the gradient endpoints are based on the bounds of the layer. When unchecked, they're based on the bounds of the entire image. The only time there is any difference between the two is when the gradient fill is affected by a clipping path or layer mask.

Related Topics

11.41

Layer: New Fill Layer: Pattern

This command produces a fill layer based on a pattern. When you first choose it, the New Layer dialog box appears, where you can set blend mode, opacity, and group options. (If desired, you can handle these settings later in the Layers palette.) When you click OK, the Pattern Fill dialog box appears, enabling you set the desired values.

Pattern Fill Dialog Box

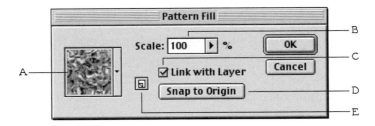

A. **Pattern**

Click this thumbnail to access the pattern picker, which enables you to select from a list of predefined pattern swatches. Only patterns created using Edit: **Define Pattern** are available to this command.

Note that after you choose a pattern, you can fine-tune its position by dragging on screen while the Pattern Fill dialog box is open.

B. **Scale** (1 to 1000%)

Use this slider to increase or decrease the size of the pattern.

When the pattern first appears (at 100%), Photoshop attempts to maintain the proportions of the original swatch. For example, assume the original tile was 1.5 x 1.5 inches, at 150 ppi. Even if you use this command to apply it to a 300 ppi image, the pattern is still based on a 1.5 x 1.5-inch tile. Bear in mind that if a tile is scaled up too much, it will begin to appear jagged or pixelated, just as if you oversampled an image using the Image: **Image Size** command.

C. **Link with Layer**

When this button is checked, the embossed pattern is attached to the target layer; when repositioning the layer, the pattern moves with it. When unchecked, the pattern does not move when the layer is repositioned.

D. **Snap to Origin**

If you've dragged on screen to move the pattern, you can reset it to its original position by clicking this button.

E. **Add to Presets**

Click this button to add the current pattern to the list of default presets. This approach is especially useful when you define a pattern and immediately create a pattern fill layer—it's a way of ensuring that you'll be able to access the pattern again.

Related Topics

11.42

Layer: New Adjustment Layer

An adjustment layer doesn't contain any image information—it contains the values of an adjustment command, such as Levels or Curves. The layer acts like a lens, affecting the values of any layer that sits beneath it in the Layers palette.

When you choose a command from this submenu, the New Layer dialog box appears, where you can set the standard blend mode, opacity, and group options. (If desired, you can handle these settings later in the Layers palette.) When you click OK, the adjustment command's dialog box appears, enabling you set the desired values.

The main benefit of using adjustment layers is that any color or tonal adjustments aren't set in stone, as they are when you simply apply the commands to an image. As long as the adjustment layer exists, you can tweak the values, even remove them entirely. The effect isn't final until you flatten the image, or merge the adjustment layer with any underlying image layers.

Issues to Consider

Limiting an adjustment to a single layer. To restrict the adjustment values to a single image layer, group the two together. There are two ways to do this. To group them as you create the adjustment layer, check the "Group With Previous Layer" box to group the new layer with the item currently selected in the Layers palette. If you've already created the adjustment layer, move it over the target layer and choose Layer: **Group With Previous**.

Editing the adjustment settings. To change the values of an adjustment layer, double-click its item in the Layers palette. The adjustment command's dialog box opens again, enabling you to tweak the settings as needed.

Related Topics

11.43

Layer: *Change Layer Content*

This command enables you to change the fill type of a content layer to any other type. For example, if you've determined that you want to base an adjustment layer on Curves instead of Levels, or apply a gradient fill instead of a solid color, you don't have to delete the layer and start over. Activate the item you want to change in the Layers palette, then choose the desired option from this submenu. The pertinent dialog box appears, enabling you to establish the new settings. Be aware, however, that the settings of the original layer are removed, and they don't carry over into the new layer type.

Related Topics

11.4   Content Layers
11.38 Layer: New Fill Layer
11.42 Layer: New Adjustment Layer

11.44

Layer: *Layer Content Options*

Choose this command to access the settings of the current fill layer. The effect is the same as double-clicking the fill thumbnail on the layer's item in the Layers palette.

11.45

Layer: *Type*

The commands in this submenu only affect the contents of a live text layer. These items are not available while the Type tool is in use—you must choose another tool and make sure the target item is active in the Layers palette.

11.46

Layer: *Type: Create Work Path*

This command creates a new path from the contents of a text layer. The original text layer is not affected, and remains in the Layers palette. A new item appears in the Paths palette, which you can edit using any of the path tools or commands. For the best results, save the path as soon as you create it (by double-clicking its palette item).

It's important to note that this command produces a *path*, not a shape. It doesn't retain masking, fill types, colors, blend modes, or any other color information. Instead, the paths are based on the same vector-based data used to output fonts at high resolutions, and match the outlines of the characters precisely. Common uses of this command include the following:

- **Using type as the basis for a layer clipping path.** This technique enables you to mask one or more layers with the type outlines, retaining the ability to edit the points and curves of the outlines. (Note that you can produce the same effect by creating a clipping group based on a live text layer, then converting the type into a shape.)

- **Using type as the basis for a print-oriented clipping path.** Creating a clipping path enables you to preserve the mask effect as you import the image into a page layout document.

- **Editing type characters before converting them into a shape layer.** Many users prefer to edit character shapes with the Pen tools, customizing the original appearance of a typeface. If the intended fill type of the shapes is too distracting, convert the type to a path first, perform your edits, then convert them to a filled shape.

- **Converting type to a reloadable selection.** When type outlines are saved as a path, you're able to load them as a selection as often as necessary, without the extra file size produced by an alpha channel.

- **Bringing type outlines into Illustrator for further editing.** Although you cannot import filled shapes into Illustrator, you can copy and paste converted paths, then continue adding color and effects. This way, you can access type effects not readily available in Illustrator, like the Text Warp options.

Related Topics

11.47

Layer: Type: Convert to Shape

This command converts the contents of a text layer into filled, vector-based shapes. In the Layers palette, the original layer is replaced by a shape layer, where the character outlines are embedded in the clipping path thumbnail.

The new layer is always based on a solid color fill. If no other color is applied to the type, the new solid color fill defaults to black. If the original text layer forms the base of a clipping group, the converted group remains intact.

If you've applied layer styles to a text layer, the converted shapes are tagged with the same styles.

For the most part, you can't see any difference between live type and converted shapes. However, converted type offers the following advantages:

- **You can edit the shapes with the Pen tools.** Although you can transform and warp live type, you can't edit the character shapes until they're converted.

- **You can embed "safe" vectors in the file.** When you embed live type in a Photoshop EPS file, you don't require the font files for successful output. However, if you give the native Photoshop version of the image to another user, they require the font files even to nudge the type by a pixel or two. When type is converted to a vector shape, fonts are no longer necessary to display and print the characters.

- **Path-based masks are easier to handle than layer masks.** The crisp edges of a layer clipping path tend to be easier to view and edit than a comparable layer mask—and if you embed the shapes into a Photoshop EPS file, they print without the need for anti-aliasing. As soon as you want to soften the edges of the type, however, use a layer mask.

Related Topics

11.48

Layer: Type: *Horizontal*

Choose this command to make vertical text flow horizontally, from left to right.

11.49

Layer: Type: *Vertical*

Choose this command to make horizontal text flow vertically, from left to right. The orientation of the individual letters depends on the status of the Rotate Character command, in the Character palette submenu. When disabled, the text flows sideways, like horizontal type rotated 90° clockwise. When enabled, the characters are stacked. (For more information, see *25.15, Rotate Character.*)

11.50

Layer: Type: Anti-Alias

This pop-up menu enables you to set different levels of *anti-aliasing*, or the built-in edge transition applied to the character shapes. (These options are described in full under *3.3, Type Tool.*)

11.51

Layer: Type: Convert to Paragraph Text

When the current text layer contains *point text* (that is, you originally clicked the image with the Type tool to insert the flashing cursor), this command converts it to paragraph text. The text is surrounded by a bounding box, which you can utilize in formatting efforts.

11.52

Layer: Type: Convert to Point Text

When the current text layer contains *paragraph text* (that is, you originally dragged a bounding box with the Type tool), this command converts it to point text. The box is removed, and the characters are no longer be restricted by enforced margins.

11.53

Layer: Type: Warp Text

The Warp Text command applies a *warp envelope* to the contents of a text layer, or a predefined characteristic that distorts the vector-based shapes. You're able to control the intensity and direction of the effects, enabling you to fine-tune a warp style to accommodate the quirks of a typeface, the image dimensions, or your tastes. Even after you've applied a warp, you're able to continue editing the text using the Type options and Character palette.

As long as the warped characters remain part of a text layer, you're able to edit them with the Type tool and Character palette. In the Layers palette, the text layer thumbnail displays a small Warp icon.

Issues to Consider

The Warp command affects the entire contents of a text layer. In other words, you can't warp a single highlighted character, or edit one line independently from the next. To produce this effect, you must remove the desired characters from the original layer, and use the Type tool to place them in a new layer. After warping, use the Move tool and the Edit: **Transform** commands place the type in the appropriate position.

Most Warp options distort the original spacing. For the best results, be prepared to adjust the tracking and kerning of the affected characters—especially if you intend to convert them to shapes or pixels.

Transferring warped type to Illustrator. The Warp command enables you to create several special effects that are not possible in Illustrator or FreeHand. You can't transfer live Photoshop type to another program, but you can convert warped type to paths, then copy/paste the paths into an Illustrator document. From there, you can add fill, stroke, and any other Illustrator-specific effects.

The Warp Text Dialog Box

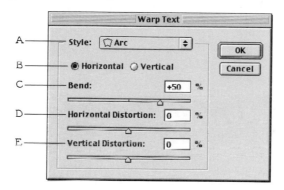

A. Style

To apply a warp effect, choose the desired item from this pop-up menu. There are 15 options—each one is accompanied by a small depiction of its shape. To remove an existing effect, choose None from the top of the list.

B. Horizontal/Vertical

When you choose the Horizontal option, the warp effect moves from left to right, matching the little icon in the Style pop-up menu. When you choose Vertical, the warp envelope is rotated 90°, and the effect runs from top to bottom.

C. Bend (-100 to 100%)

This slider controls the direction and intensity of the warp effect. At 0%, no distortion is applied (although the remaining sliders may still influence the characters). Moving the slider to the right applies the effect displayed in the small icon in the Style pop-up menu; moving it to the left applies the opposite effect. Higher values produce more extreme distortions.

D. Horizontal Distortion (-100 to 100%)

This slider enables you to add a level of perspective to the affected type, as if rotating it around the Y axis. The effect is not in true 3-D, however, and should only be used to bolster the appearance of a warp style. (If you don't need to preserve the characters as live type, you can add more realistic perspective by converting the text layer to shapes and using Edit: Transform: **Perspective**.)

E. **Vertical Distortion** (-100 to 100%)

This slider enables you to add a level of vertical perspective to the affected type, as if rotating it around the X axis. Like the Horizontal slider, however, this setting works best in small doses.

Related Topics

1.6   Move Tool
3.3   Type Tool
*9.16   Edit: **Transform***
*11.47 Layer: Type: **Convert to Shape***

11.54

Layer: Type: *Update All Text Layers*

When you open an image that contains live type, the fonts must be available to your system in order to display properly. You're able to open the image if the fonts aren't activated, but you're not you're not able to edit or output the type. One way or another, the font has to be activated.

If you activate the fonts while the image is open, Photoshop may or may not be aware that the information is now available. If you're using ATM Deluxe as a font management utility, Photoshop should recognize the data and allow you to continue working. If you're using Extensis Suitcase (or another utility, including the Fonts folder in your operating system), you may need to choose this command to direct the text layers to the necessary font information. If this doesn't work—and it often doesn't—quit and relaunch Photoshop.

11.55

Layer: Type: *Replace All Missing Fonts*

When you open an image that contains font information not currently available to your operating system, you have a choice: Activate the necessary fonts, or strip away the applied font and start over. Choose this command to remove the missing font tag from all text layers in the image. They're replaced with the program's default typeface, making them easier to identify. You can achieve similar results by activating each item in the Layers palette and choosing a new typeface in the Character palette.

11.56

Layer: *Rasterize*

The process of converting a vector-based object into editable pixels is known as *rasterizing.* The commands in this submenu address the different objects in Photoshop, enabling you to be selective about the information you convert. None of the Rasterize commands affect any existing transparent areas, applied layer styles, or group relationships.

Issues to Consider

Converting layer styles to editable pixels. None of the rasterize commands have any impact on layer styles, but it's possible to produce the same effect. Activate the layer and choose Layer: Layer Style: **Create Layer** to split the effect into its component layers. To reduce the different items to a single layer, hide all other items in the Layers palette, then choose Layer: **Merge Visible.** (If necessary, rasterize the main layer before applying this technique.)

Related Topics

11.4   *Content Layers*
11.18   *Layer:* **Layer Style**
11.35   *Layer: Layer Style:* **Create Layer**
11.104 *Layer:* **Merge Visible**
D.2   *Opening a Vector-Based File*

11.57

Layer: Rasterize: *Type*

Choose this command to convert a text layer to editable pixels. (If you actually intend to convert type to a shape, choose Layer: Type: **Convert to Shape** instead.)

Related Topics

11.47   *Layer: Type:* **Convert to Shape**

11.58

Layer: Rasterize: *Shape*

Choose this command to convert a shape layer to editable pixels.

11.59

Layer: Rasterize: Fill Content

Choose this command to convert the fill of a content layer to editable pixels. Any layer clipping paths are unaffected.

For example, if you rasterize a rectangular shape filled with a gradient, only the gradient data is converted to pixels; the item remains a shape, because the path comprising the layer clipping path still exists. Beyond that, any transparent areas, applied layer styles, or group relationships remain intact.

You must rasterize the content of a fill layer before you can apply any pixel-based commands such as color adjustments, brushstrokes, or filters.

11.60

Layer: Rasterize: Layer Clipping Path

Choose this command to convert a layer clipping path into a pixel-based layer mask. The element doesn't appear to change on screen, but the shape is no longer surrounded by a vector-based outline. This way, you're able to soften the edges of the mask, as well as apply any other pixel-specific command. Any transparent areas, applied layer styles, or group relationships remain intact.

If the masked item is a content layer, you must still rasterize the fill content if you intend to convert the entire layer to pixels. (For more information, see *11.59, Layer: Rasterize: Fill Content.*)

11.61

Layer: Rasterize: Layer

Choose this command to fully rasterize the contents of a layer. No masking is applied.

11.62

Layer: Rasterize: Linked Layers

Choose this command to fully rasterize the active layer, as well as any content or text layers currently linked to it. The effect is the same as activating and rasterizing the layers one-by-one.

11.63

Layer: Rasterize: *All Layers*

Choose this command to convert all content and text layers to pixels—it doesn't matter which item is active in the Layers palette, or if any of the items are linked. No masking is applied to the resulting layers.

11.64

Layer: *New Layer Based Slice*

Choose this command to create a new slice based on the contents of an image layer. Once created, the boundary of the slice is always based on a bounding box that surrounds the current contents of the layer. In other words, if the contents of the layer change (for example, if you add a layer style), the slice changes to accommodate it.

When you add slices this way, you must use the File: **Save for Web** command to export the graphic. You can't merge layers or flatten the image without changing the contents of the layer, which in turn changes the size of the slice.

Related Topics

8.9   File: *Save for Web*
1.12   Slice Tool
1.13   Slice Select Tool

11.65

Layer: *Add Layer Mask*

A layer mask uses the contents of a temporary channel to partially conceal the contents of a layer. Although this channel can be accessed in the Channels palette, it also appears as a thumbnail in the layer's item in the Layers palette. To edit the layer's contents, click the image thumbnail. To edit the layer mask, click the mask thumbnail.

This channel has the same properties of any other 8-bit color or mask channel. You can only add tones of gray, which dictate how the contents of the image layer are revealed. Black areas mask the image, and white areas expose the image. Gray values result in semi-opacity, depending on the value. For example, an area painted with 75% gray exposes 25% of the image layer's color values.

Mistakes to Avoid

Unintentionally breaking the layer mask link. The layer mask is linked to the image layer by default, as indicated by the three-link chain between the two thumbnails. If you click the icon to break the link, you can independently reposition the image and the mask.

Editing the image instead of the mask. It's easy to edit the image when you intend to work in the layer mask. The line around the thumbnails thickens to indicate whether the image or its mask is being edited. This line is black—the same color as our mask, making it difficult to see. Pay attention to the Status box for the selected layer in the Layers palette. If a paintbrush appears in the Status box, you can edit the image layer. If a dotted circle appears, you can edit the layer mask.

Issues to Consider

Deleting a layer mask. Besides choosing Layer: **Remove Layer Mask**, there are two ways to delete a layer containing a layer mask. In the Layers palette, dragging the image thumbnail to the Delete button removes the entire layer, mask and all. Dragging the mask thumbnail to the Delete button opens an alert, which gives you the option of removing the mask or permanently applying it to the image.

Adding a layer mask from the Layers palette. Clicking the Add Layer Mask button in the Layers palette has the same effect as choosing Layer: Add Layer Mask: **Reveal All**. If an active selection exists, it has the same effect as Layer: Add Layer Mask: **Reveal Selection**.

Related Topics

11.66

Layer: Add Layer Mask: *Reveal All*

This command adds a layer mask completely filled with white, which doesn't affect the contents of the layer. To gradually hide them, paint the mask thumbnail with black.

11.67

Layer: Add Layer Mask: *Hide All*

This command adds a layer mask completely filled with black, which completely hides the contents of the layer. To gradually reveal them, paint the mask thumbnail with white.

11.68

Layer: Add Layer Mask: *Reveal Selection*

This command creates a layer mask based on the active selection. In the mask channel, areas inside the active selection are filled with white (which reveals the layer contents); areas outside the active selection are filled with black (which hides the layer contents). Feathered or anti-aliased selection edges result in soft edges.

Related Topics

I.1   *Creating a Simple Silhouette*
I.2   *Creating a Vignette*
I.3   *"Painting" a Vignette by Hand*

11.69

Layer: Add Layer Mask: *Hide Selection*

This command creates a layer mask based on the inverse of the active selection. In the mask channel, areas inside the active selection are filled with black (which hides the layer contents); areas outside the active selection are filled with white (which reveals the layer contents). Feathered or anti-aliased selection edges result in soft edges.

11.70

Layer: *Remove Layer Mask*

This command removes a layer mask. An alert appears, asking, "Apply layer mask before discarding?" Select Apply to make the changes permanent. Select Discard to remove the layer mask without applying any changes. The command is available regardless of which thumbnail is selected in the Layers palette.

11.71

Layer: *Disable/Enable Layer Mask*

Choose this command to turn off the effects of the mask without discarding the layer. In the Layers palette, the mask thumbnail is crossed out by a red X. If the layer mask is disabled, selecting Enable activates it again.

11.72

Layer: *Add Layer Clipping Path*

A layer clipping path is similar to a layer mask. However, instead of using a temporary alpha channel as the basis for the mask, Photoshop uses a vector-based path. The path literally clips the layer contents—the result is a hard-edged mask that you can continue editing with the Pen tools.

Most often, this command is used to mask the contents of an image layer. You may not be aware that many tools and commands automatically create a layer clipping mask. For example, if you draw an object with one of the vector-based Shape tools, Photoshop applies a clipping path to a solid color fill layer. If an item is active in the Paths palette when you create a new content layer, Photoshop uses the path to clip the new element.

Regardless of the technique used, every clipped layer includes a temporary item in the Paths palette, labeled "clipping path." This item is only visible when you activate the layer in the Layers palette.

Issues to Consider

Don't confuse a layer clipping path with a print-oriented clipping path. Photoshop's terminology is a little unclear. The clipping paths produced here only apply to a layer. To produce the type of clipping path that you can import into a page layout document, you must use the Clipping Path command in the Paths palette submenu. You cannot use the same path for both techniques—at the very least, you must duplicate the layer clipping path, then use the copy as a print-oriented clipping item.

Supported layer types. You can apply a layer clipping path to every type of layer *except* the background layer. If the background layer is active in the Layers palette, these commands are dimmed. If you want to clip the contents of the background layer, you must first convert it to an image layer. (For more information, see *11.9, Layer: New: **Layer From Background**.*)

You can't edit a clipping path like a layer mask. Regardless of the information it clips, the path itself is a vector-based outline, and cannot be edited the same way as a layer mask. For example, you can't add soft edges or fades directly to a clipping path. If you desire these effects, you must either create a layer mask at the start, or convert the path to layer mask to continue editing. (For more information, see *11.60, Layer: Rasterize: **Layer Clipping Path**.*)

Applying a clipping path and a layer mask to the same layer. This way, you're able to mask an image with a crisp edge, but still apply pixel-based effects to the overall mask effect. For example, assume a layer already contains a clipping path. If you choose Layer: Add Layer Mask: **Reveal All**, a blank mask thumbnail appears in the layer's item in the Layers palette. As you apply black and gray data to the mask channel, you hide the information contained in the path. Use a black-to-white gradient to fade the contents to transparency.

Reversing the direction of a layer clipping path. To flip the mask effect of a clipping path—for example, to punch a hole into a layer rather than mask it—select the path with the Path Component Select tool (the black arrow). In the Options bar, click the Subtract From button in the Shape Blending controls. (For more information, see *3.1, Path Component Selection Tool.*)

Related Topics

11.73

Layer: Add Layer Clipping Path: Reveal All

This command adds a blank clipping path thumbnail to the active layer. At first, the image doesn't change on screen. However, as you draw with the Pen tool or one of the Shape tools, the resulting path masks the contents of the layer.

11.74

Layer: Add Layer Clipping Path: Hide All

This command adds a clipping path thumbnail to the active layer, but the entire layer is initially hidden. As you draw with the Pen tool or one of the Shape tools, the resulting path reveals the contents of the layer.

11.75

Layer: Add Layer Clipping Path: *Current Path*

This command is only available when a standard path is active in the Paths palette and visible onscreen. Choosing it converts the path to a layer clipping path. (Photoshop actually uses a copy of the path as a mask—the original item is not touched.)

11.76

Layer: *Delete Layer Clipping Path*

When the active layer contains a clipping path, this command replaces the Add Layer Path submenu. Choosing it removes the clipping path from the active layer, leaving the original contents untouched.

11.77

Layer: *Enable/Disable Layer Clipping Path*

When the active layer is clipped, choosing this command hides the effect of the path without deleting it. Choose this command again to re-apply the clipping path.

11.78

Layer: *Group With Previous/Group Linked* *(Command) [Control]-G*

A *clipping group* is a masking technique. Instead of using a temporary mask channel (like a layer mask does), a clipping group uses the contents of one layer to mask the contents of another. Photoshop uses the transparent pixels of the lower layer as the basis for masking the upper layer. When the layers are grouped, the information of the upper layer only appears wherever non-transparent pixels exist in the base layer.

To create a clipping group, select a layer in the Layers palette. If the layer is not linked to another, Group with Previous appears in the Layer menu. If the layer is linked to any adjacent layers, the Group Linked command appears in the Layers menu.

Layer: **Group with Previous** creates a clipping group between the active layer and the layer directly beneath it. Layer: **Group Linked** joins all adjacent linked layers into a linked Clipping Group. The bottom linked layer becomes the clipping layer, regardless of which layer was selected.

Issues to Consider

Applying this technique in the Layers palette. Duplicate the effect of this command in the Layers palette by holding down the (Option) [Alt] key and clicking the dotted line between two layers. (For more information, see *22.17, Grouping Layers.*)

Ungrouped layers dragged into clipping groups become part of the clipping group. Once part of the group, you can still rearrange the items by dragging them in the Layers palette. (For more information, see *22.15, Reordering Layers.*)

Clipping groups are not automatically linked. To maintain the relative position of the grouped layers, you must link them manually.

11.79

Layers: Ungroup *(Command-Shift) [Control-Shift]-G*

This command splits a clipping group into ordinary layers. All grouped items revert back to their unclipped state.

11.80

Layer: Arrange

Use the Arrange commands to change the order of layers in the Layers palette. These options are not available when the background layer is active.

11.81

Layer: Arrange: Bring to Front

(Command-Shift) [Control-Shift]-]

In the Layers palette, this command moves the active layer above the top layer. The following issues apply:

- If the active layer is an image or fill layer, its contents appear in front of the pixels in all other layers.

- If the active layer is an adjustment layer, all underlying layers are affected by its command.

- If the active layer is in a clipping group (and the topmost layer is not part of the group), the layer is removed from the clipping group. If the top layer is part of the clipping group, only the order of the grouped layers changes.

11.82

Layer: Arrange: **Bring Forward**   *(Command) [Control]-]*

In the Layers palette, this command moves the active layer over the item immediately above it. The following issues apply:

- If the active layer is an adjustment layer, the layer above it is then affected by this command.

- If the active layer is part of a clipping group (and the layer above it is not part of the group), it is removed.

- If the active layer is beneath a clipping group, it is added to the group.

11.83

Layer: Arrange: **Send Backward**   *(Command) [Control]-[*

In the Layers palette, this command places the active layer under the item directly beneath it. The following issues apply:

- If the active layer is the bottom layer of a clipping group, the entire group is moved.

- If the active layer is above a clipping group, it is added to the group.

- If the selected layer is an adjustment layer, the effects of the adjustment will be removed from the layer directly beneath it.

11.84

Layer: Arrange: **Send to Back**

(Command-Shift) [Control-Shift]-[

In the Layers palette, this command moves the active layer to the lowest position possible. The following issues apply:

- If the image has no background layer, the active layer becomes the bottom layer.

- If the image has a background layer, the active layer is placed immediately above it.

- If the active layer is the bottom layer of a clipping group, the entire group is moved.

- If the selected layer is an adjustment layer, its effects will only apply to the background layer. If there is no background layer, the adjustment layer will no longer apply to anything.

11.85

Layer: *Align Linked*

This command enables you to align multiple image layers to the contents of the currently active layer. After selecting the layer you want to use as a base (this information will not move), you must link the layers you wish to align by clicking their status box in the Layers palette.

Issues to Consider

These commands are only available when at least one layer is linked to the base. Since alignment involves a relationship between more than one layer, at least one must be linked to the active layer–otherwise, the commands are not available. Make sure you unlink any layers you want to leave untouched. You cannot use these commands to align different elements contained on the same layer.

11.86

Layer: *Align Linked: Top*

This command aligns the contents of all linked layers to the top edge of the information contained in the active layer.

11.87

Layer: *Align Linked: Vertical Center*

This command aligns the contents of all linked layers to the *vertical center* (the midpoint between the top and bottom edges) of the information contained in the active layer.

11.88

Layer: *Align Linked: Bottom*

This command aligns the contents of all linked layers to the bottom edge of the information contained in the active layer.

11.89

Layer: *Align Linked: Left*

This command aligns the contents of all linked layers to the left edge of the information contained in the active layer.

11.90

Layer: Align Linked: **Horizontal Center**

This command aligns the contents of all linked layers to the *horizontal center* (the midpoint between the left and right edges) of the information contained in the active layer.

11.91

Layer: Align Linked: **Right**

This command aligns the contents of all linked layers to the right edge of the information contained in the active layer.

11.92

Layer: **Distribute Linked**

This command enables you to evenly space multiple image layers between the contents of two base layers. Before distributing, you must link the layers you wish to affect by clicking their status box in the Layers palette. It doesn't matter which layer you select before choosing a command—each option is based on the layer elements placed farthest apart.

Issues to Consider

These commands are only available when at least two layer are linked to the base. Since distribution involves a relationship between more than two layers (the elements farthest apart do not move, and the elements in between are spaced evenly between them), at least two must be linked to the active layer—otherwise, the commands are not available. Make sure you unlink any layers you want to leave untouched. You cannot use these commands to space different elements contained on the same layer.

11.93

Layer: Distribute Linked: **Top**

This command vertically spaces the contents of all linked layers by measuring from the top edges of each layer.

11.94

Layer: Distribute Linked: **Vertical Center**

This command vertically spaces the contents of all linked layers by measuring from the *vertical center* (the midpoint between the top and bottom edge) of each layer.

11.95

Layer: Distribute Linked: *Bottom*

This command vertically spaces the contents of all linked layers by measuring from the bottom edges of each layer.

11.96

Layer: Distribute Linked: *Left*

This command horizontally spaces the contents of all linked layers by measuring from the left edges of each layer.

11.97

Layer: Distribute Linked: *Horizontal Center*

This command horizontally spaces the contents of all linked layers by measuring from the horizontal center (the midpoint between the left and right edge) of each layer.

11.98

Layer: Distribute Linked: *Right*

This command horizontally spaces the contents of all linked layers by measuring from the right edges of each layer.

11.99

Layer: *Lock All Linked Layers*

This command is only available when a linked layer is active in the Layers palette. It's a shortcut that enables you to apply the same lock settings to every linked item at once. The Lock All Layers in Set dialog box appears, listing the same options that appear across the top of the Layers palette. Check the desired boxes and click OK. (For more information, see *22.3, Lock Options.*)

11.100

Layer: *Merge*

This command combines multiple layers into a single image layer. Unlike Layer: **Flatten Image**, Merge only applies to specified layers. You can apply Merge to as few as two layers. Merged layers can still retain most of Photoshop-native attributes, such as transparent areas and adjustable opacity.

Common uses include the following:

Reducing file size. Although transparent areas of layers do not increase file size, the images do. Merging layers together reduces file size wherever images overlap each other.

Simplifying navigation. Problems with multiple layers include keeping track of them all, finding a specific layer, and scrolling through dozens of layers. Merging layers when editing is completed reduces confusion.

Restricting the effects of an adjustment layer. Adjustment layers apply to all layers beneath them. While this can be restricted to certain areas, you must avoid moving layers between Adjustment Layers and the layers you intend for them to affect. Merging adjustment layers with image layers applies the adjustments and then removes the Adjustment Layer, thus simplifying layer relationships.

Simplified editing. Many Photoshop functions, such as filters, can only be applied one layer at a time. To apply the same function to multiple layers, you must run the same function with the same settings to each layer—or, you can merge the layers and apply the command once.

Mistakes to Avoid

Merging prematurely. Before merging, ask yourself the following questions:
- Are the opacity settings exactly the way you want them?
- Are you finished editing any layer masks?
- Are the adjustment layers properly set?
- Are the blend modes properly set?
- Are the layers properly positioned?

Issues to Consider

Merging restrictions. Adjustment layers cannot be merged exclusively with other adjustment layers. Also, layers can't be merged when there is an adjustment layer as the bottom layer, unless Merge Linked is used. Since adjustment layers can only affect layers beneath them, Photoshop assumes you are making a mistake if you try to do this, and prevents you from doing so.

11.101

Layer: *Merge Down* *(Command) [Control]-E*

This command appears when the active layer is neither linked nor part of a clipping group. You can merge either two image layers or one adjustment layer and one image layer. The following issues apply:

- Hold down the (Option) [Alt] key when choosing this command to copy the contents of the selected layer into the layer below it, leaving the active layer unmerged and unchanged.

- This command cannot merge a layer outside a clipping group with one inside a clipping group.

- This command cannot merge an image layer with an adjustment layer if the adjustment layer is beneath the image layer.

11.102

Layer: *Merge Group* *(Command) [Control]-E*

This command appears when the active layer is part of a clipping group. The bottom layer of the group must be selected in order to merge. The following issues apply:

- Grouped layers will not merge if any layer inside the group is linked to a layer outside the group.

- Hold down the (Option) [Alt] key when choosing this command to copy the contents of all grouped layers into the bottom layer, leaving the upper layers untouched.

11.103

Layer: *Merge Linked* *(Command) [Control]-E*

This command appears when the active layer is linked to another, but is not part of a clipping group.

Hold down the (Option) [Alt] key when choosing this command to copy the contents of all linked layers into the selected layer, leaving the linked layers untouched.

11.104
Layer: *Merge Visible*   *(Command-Shift) [Control-Shift]-E*

This command merges all visible layers, regardless of which one is currently active. The following issues apply:

- Layers merge into the bottom-most visible layer.

- Layers will not merge if the bottom visible layer is an adjustment layer.

- Hold down the (Option) [Alt] key when choosing this command to copy the contents of all visible layers and merge them into the selected layer, leaving other layers untouched.

11.105
Layer: *Flatten Image*

This command converts all visible layers to a single background layer. All layer masks and adjustment layers are applied and discarded.

If any layers are hidden when the image is flattened, an alert appears, asking "Discard hidden layers?" Click Discard to eliminate the layers. Click Cancel to closes the alert, leaving the image unchanged.

11.106
Layer: *Matting*

Occasionally, when you place an anti-aliased selection into an image layer, the edge pixels retain color values from the original image. The matting commands can sometimes help this problem. They are often ineffective, though, because they only apply to anti-aliased edges that result from a solid background color. Also, they fill the edge pixels with sampled colors rather than making them semi-transparent, which would allow for true anti-aliasing with the underlying layers.

11.107
Layer: *Matting: Defringe*

This command replaces the pixels at the edge of a floating selection or image layer with pixels sampled from the adjacent pixels inside the selection or image layer.

Defringe should only be used when there is an obvious problem with the edge pixels of an image layer or floating selection. Otherwise, it will have no apparent effects on the image layer or floating selection.

11.108

Layer: Matting: *Remove Black Matte*

This command removes black edge pixels in a floating selection or image layer and fills them with colors sampled from adjacent pixels inside the selection or image layer.

This command is intended for images selected from a solid black background. Renderings from 3-D modeling programs are often created with such black backgrounds. Otherwise, it has little or no effect.

11.109

Layer: Matting: *Remove White Matte*

This command removes white edge pixels from a floating selection or image layer and fills them with colors sampled from adjacent pixels inside the selection or image layer.

This command is meant to be used exclusively on images selected from a solid white background. (Stock images on clip-art CD-ROMs are frequently shot this way.) Otherwise, it has little or no effect.

The Select Menu

Select: All

(Command) [Control]-A

This command creates a selection around the entire image window. The selection outline surrounds the border of the image, and every visible pixel is included. If an image only contains a background layer, this command selects all the available image information.

Issues to Consider

Be careful when using this command to select the contents of a layer. Only the visible pixels of the active layer are included in the selection—any image pixels positioned off the canvas are not included. If you move the selection, the visible pixels separate from the hidden portion. To move or change the contents of an entire layer, activate the layer (by clicking its item in the Layers palette), but don't make a selection.

Selecting only the colored pixels in a layer. To select all visible non-transparent pixels, hold down the (Command) [Control] key while clicking an item in the Layers palette. If the layer contains pixels that extend beyond the visible canvas, the new selection outline may appear to disappear off the edge of the image. Also note that this technique does not work on the background layer.

Related Topics

11.1 Layers Overview
Chapter 22, The Layers Palette

12.2

Select: *Deselect* *(Command) [Control]-D*

This command removes all active selections from an image. Select: **Deselect** enables you to remove a selection without touching the image, greatly reducing the possibility of human error.

Issues to Consider

Don't confuse this command with View: Show: Selection Edges. After making a selection and applying an adjustment, you might want to evaluate its effect by removing the selection from view. If you choose Select: **Deselect**, then you cannot undo the adjustment—the selection path simply appears again. View: Show: **Selection Edges** hides the selection edges while leaving the selection active.

Don't deactivate a selection simply by clicking on screen. Many users—particularly those who have used earlier versions of Photoshop—prefer clicking somewhere on screen to remove a selection, which poses the following problems:

- It only works if the Marquee tool or Lasso tool is selected. It works with the Magic Wand tool only if you click directly on the selection.

- If you accidentally drag while you click, you'll reposition the selection path. If you happen to be holding down the (Command) [Control] key, the contents of the selection move as well.

- If any other tool is active while you click—the Paintbrush tool, for example—you might accidentally edit the contents of the selection.

Keep an eye on your selections, especially when zooming around the image. While working with a series of small selections, you might attempt to use a Paint tool or filter only to find it has no affect on the image. This is common when working at high zoom ratios or on small monitors. If a selection remains active somewhere else in the image, no other tool can be used outside its boundaries. Choose Select: **Deselect** and try again.

Related Topics

*9.1 Edit: **Undo/Redo***
*12.1 Select: **All***
*14.27 View: Show: **Selection Edges***

12.3

Select: *Reselect*

Choose this command to restore the last selection you made. It does not matter how many commands are applied after deactivating the selection—as long as you do not change the width, height, or resolution.

12.4

Select: *Inverse*

This command creates the inverse of an active selection, or the exact opposite of the original. The effect of this command is the same as applying Image: Adjust: **Invert** to a mask channel before reloading it as a selection.

Issues to Consider

When you inverse a selection, the diminishing opacity values of a feathered edge are inverted as well. To determine the new value, Select: **Inverse** increases the current opacity value to the maximum (100%) and subtracts the original value. Therefore, if part of a feathered edge has an opacity value of 40%, it changes to 60% after applying this command.

12.5

Select: *Color Range*

This command creates selections based on a specified color range. Instead of manually drawn shapes, selections are based on targeted values. Common uses include the following:

- **Selecting fine details.** Good examples are hair, lace, or blades of grass— anything too complex to select by hand. This command is most successful when the colors surrounding the target image are in high contrast.

- **Selecting subtly varying tones and color.** This command excels at selecting a range of closely related colors, like fleshtones or the blue of a sky.

Issues to Consider

Avoid using Select: Color Range for standard selections. As a tool for assisting in delicate and subtle color adjustments, this command is unparalleled. As a tool for creating standard selections, it falters. It does not use anti-aliasing, so changes such as fills, extreme color adjustments, and filters can exaggerate the jagged selection edges.

This command can be applied to an entire image layer or to the contents of an active selection. If a selection is active when you choose this command, only the selected pixels appear in the dialog box. When you target colors in this area, the remaining pixels are removed from the active selection.

While the Color Range dialog box is open, you can still change the current image view. Hold down the spacebar and drag to scroll the image; hold down (Command) [Control]-spacebar to access the Zoom In tool; hold down (Option-Command) [Alt-Control]-spacebar to access the Zoom Out tool. When combined with different preview options, these shortcuts allow you to target colors with much more precision.

Switching between views. Press the (Command) [Control] key to toggle between thumbnail view options. For example, when the thumbnail is set to Selection, you can hold down the (Command) [Control] key to display the Image option. After using the eyedropper to affect the selected range, release the (Command) [Control] key to switch back.

The Color Range Dialog Box

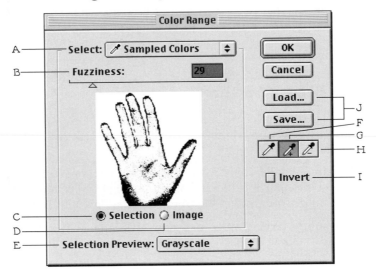

A. Select

Specify the range of colors you wish to target from this pop-up menu.

Sampled Colors

Photoshop defaults to this option. Here, the ultimate selection area depends on the color you initially sample, or target with the eyedropper tools. This range is increased or decreased using the Fuzziness slider and the plus/minus eyedroppers.

Predefined Colors

This option targets a range by measuring overall color intensity. For example, when you set Cyan in the pop-up, the Color Range command searches for any pixel where cyan is the dominant value. Wherever pixels are colored 100% cyan, it applies a total, non-transparent selection. Any pixels with a value of, say, 60% are surrounded by a semi-transparent selection. Pixels that contain no cyan are left untouched.

If you're editing an RGB image, the targeted colors are based on brightness values. Intensities of reds, for example, are compared to a value of R: 255. If a pixel contains R: 128 (50% of full intensity), it results in a 50% transparent selection.

When you set a predefined range that differs from the current color mode, Photoshop creates an average based on the RGB/CMY color wheel. For example, choosing Reds while editing a CMYK image affects pixels containing magenta and yellow. Likewise, choosing Cyans while editing an RGB image affects pixels containing green and blue.

Because these options are based on pre-existing color content, the eyedroppers and Fuzziness slider are not available. The selection preview cannot be edited. However, you can get a better feel for the component color values in the image by placing color samplers throughout the image. While the Color Range dialog box is open, Shift-click to add samplers, (Option-Shift) [Alt-Shift]-click to remove them. When you close the dialog box, the samplers are removed. (For more information, see *4.4, The Color Sampler Tool.*)

Tonal Range

These options base a selection on an image's tonal content. Highlights target the average tones from 0 to 25%, Midtones target average tones from 25% to 75%, and Shadows target average tones at more than 75%.

When you use the Color Range command on a Grayscale image, these options are the only items available (besides Sampled Colors); you cannot base a selection on a predefined color range.

Out of Gamut

This option is only available when an image is in RGB or Lab Color mode. When set, it targets all colors that fall outside the printable spectrum of CMYK inks. In theory, you can use this setting to select and adjust those colors before converting to CMYK, leaving in-gamut colors untouched. Unless the adjustments are very subtle, however, this technique quickly leads to a visible tonal shift between the two sets of colors.

B. Fuzziness Slider

Fuzziness determines the color range of a targeted area, based on the originally sampled color. Raising the value increases the range of colors throughout the image that will be included in the selection. In a continuous-tone image, this creates a more widespread and diffuse selection. Lowering the value decreases the range of colors, resulting in a smaller, more focused selection.

Fuzziness gets its name from the method it uses to include additional colors in a selection. Only the colors that you click or Shift-click with the eyedroppers are completely selected. The expanded range controlled by the Fuzziness slider is only partially selected, as evidenced by the gray values in the Selection preview. This creates a more evenly blended selection.

C. Selection

This option highlights the selected range of color. Similar to a masking channel, the selected areas are white, the unselected areas are black, and any gray areas represent semi-transparent selections. Whether you click on the actual image or directly on the thumbnail, the gray tones change to reflect the new selection area.

D. Image

This option displays a small preview of the actual image. If the Selection Preview is set to any option other than None, this provides the only full-color representation of the image. If you click on this thumbnail, the only way to preview the selection is to check the actual image, behind the dialog box.

E. Selection Preview

These options control how the selection is previewed in the original image. (Bear in mind that choosing between these options has no affect whatsoever on the actual image.)

None

This option displays the original image, with no indication of the selected range. Choose a preview of None when you need to target very precise details or colors with the Target Eyedropper.

Grayscale

This option matches the image thumbnail in Selection view. It is usually the intuitive choice for users familiar with masking channels.

Black Matte

Instead of previewing the selected areas, this option previews the selected colors. Before any colors are targeted, this preview fills the images with black. As colors are added to the selection, the black levels are reduced to display the selected colors on screen. The effect is the same as if the currently selected colors were copied and pasted onto a black background.

White Matte

The effect of this option is similar to Black matte, except that the preview image is filled with white before any colors are targeted. As colors are added to the selection, they are displayed on screen.

Quick Mask

Similar to the Quick Mask feature found in the Toolbar, this option previews a selection with a semi-transparent colored overlay. Uncolored areas indicate the currently selected range, while colored areas reflect unselected pixels. By default, the overlay is a 50% opaque red. If the default is too close to colors in the image, you can reset the color of the overlay. Double-click one of the Quick Mask buttons in the Toolbar and set a new color in the Quick Mask Options dialog box.

F. Target Eyedropper

Use this tool to target the initial color in a selection. Any color that you click with this eyedropper is ultimately included in the selected. The surrounding tones, as determined by the Fuzziness slider, are partially selected. With this eyedropper, only one color is targeted at a time. (Unless you use the shortcuts described under *"Add Eyedropper"* and *"Subtract Eyedropper,"* below.)

G. Add Eyedropper

To target more colors, use this eyedropper or hold down the Shift key while using the Target Eyedropper. Each additional color is 100% selected, and its surrounding ranges are also determined by the Fuzziness slider. To add a range of colors at once, drag the tool across the image or image preview.

H. Subtract Eyedropper

To remove colors from a selection, use this eyedropper or hold down the (Option) [Alt] key while using the Target Eyedropper. Remove a range of colors by dragging across the desired values.

I. Invert

Checking the Invert box reverses the currently targeted areas. The result is similar to applying Select: **Inverse** to an active selection.

J. Save and Load

These buttons allow you to save targeted color ranges into a separate file.

This is useful for targeting similar areas in a series of images. For example, an entire roll of film can be affected by the same problem, such as over-exposure or red-eye, which can be narrowed down to a specific range of color.

Target the colors for one image using Select: **Color Range**, then click the Save button to save the settings to your hard drive. When this file is loaded into the Color Range dialog box of another image, the same range of colors is targeted without using the eyedroppers.

Related Topics

12.4   Select: **Inverse**
B.17   Creating a Color Range Selection

12.6

Select: *Feather*
(Option-Shift) [Alt-Shift]-D

This command softens the edges of a selection. Rather than have a sharp distinction between selected and unselected pixels, feathering creates a fringe of increasing transparency. It's similar to anti-aliasing, which blends the contents of a selection with its surrounding pixels. There, however, the blend is only one pixel thick. By feathering a selection, you can increase the blend by up to 250 pixels.

The Feather Selection Dialog Box

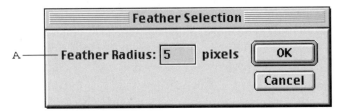

A. **Radius** (0.2 to 250.0)

This value determines the width of a feathered selection edge.

Although the Feather Radius is specified in pixels, that value does not accurately reflect the width of the feathered area. Photoshop uses a formula called the Gaussian Bell Curve to determine how the selection fades into the unselected areas. To prevent harsh transitions between the feathered and unfeathered portions, this formula slightly increases the distance of the blended area. The effect is more appealing to the eye—without this formula, the transitions appear mechanical and obvious. As a result, feathering affects about five times the number of pixels entered as the Feather Radius.

Issues to Consider

Don't attempt to use a low feather value in lieu of anti-aliasing. Anti-aliasing is intended to produce an invisible effect, creating a seamless blend between a selection and the remaining image. Even at its lowest values, feathering is a special effect, and its results are almost always visible to the eye.

When the Feather Radius is set high enough, you'll see an alert claiming that "No pixels are more than 50% selected." Don't be alarmed if this alert appears—even though you cannot see the selection outline, it's still there. In this case, it means the feathered edges have increased to the point of overlapping, and cover the entire selected area. Because Photoshop only displays selection paths when a selection is less than 50% transparent, this alert is telling you that the image will remain selected, but it will not display the outlines. To view the effect of the selection, try changing to Quick Mask mode and evaluate the colored overlay.

Setting a Feather value in other locations. Use the Select: **Feather** command to soften the edges of a selection that already exists. Many selection techniques enable you to enter a Feather value before you create the selection. For example, the Marquee and Lasso tools enable you to enter a value in the Options bar. Or, when you convert a path into a selection, the Make Selection dialog box contains an option for feathering.

12.7

Select: Modify

The Modify commands are used to edit the shape of an active selection. These changes are always based on the selection's original shape.

12.8

Select: Modify: Border

This command traces the edge of a selection outline with a new selection of a specified width. The original selection is discarded.

Like Select: **Feather**, this command creates a selection that fades into the surrounding pixels. Unlike Select: **Feather**, it does not use a Gaussian Bell Curve; the transitions are awkward and poorly executed, greatly reducing the usefulness of this command. Instead of using this command, consider the following techniques:

- **Creating a stroke.** Some users mistakenly use this command as the basis for applying a stroke. However, not only does it produce unsatisfactory results, a command such as Layer: Layer Style: **Stroke** produces an effect that you can edit and reset at will.

- **Creating a border selection.** If you want a border-shaped selection, its possible to create an anti-aliased version, as opposed to the awkward results produced by the Border command. First, create a standard selection, just as you would before using the Border command. Next, create a new alpha channel. (Don't save the selection; instead, choose the Create New Channel button in the Channels palette. Photoshop automatically activates the new channel.) Leaving the selection active, choose Edit:

Stroke and enter the width and position of the effect in the Stroke dialog box. This process should result in a stroked shape that matches the edges of the original selection. Because it exists as an alpha channel, you can reload it as a selection whenever you need it.

The Border Selection Dialog Box

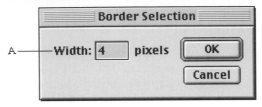

A. **Width** (1 to 200)

A value entered here represents the distance of the fade. Because the border is created both inward and outward from the original selection edge, the total width of the border is twice the entered pixel value. Only the two pixels on either side of the original selection edge are 100% selected.

Issues to Consider

This command can be applied to anti-aliased or feathered selections. However, those values are ignored. Photoshop simply traces the edge of the visible selection path.

12.9

Select: Modify: Smooth

This command enables you to reduce any jagged areas or sharp edges from a selection outline.

The Smooth Selection Dialog Box

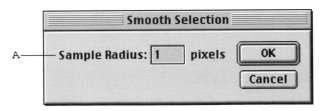

A. **Sample Radius** (1 to 100)

This command works by rounding off any corners that exist in a selection path. The Sample Radius determines the amount of rounding that occurs. Unlike Select: Modify: **Border**, this value does not affect any existing anti-aliasing or feathering.

12.10
Select: Modify: Expand

This command increases a selection by expanding its edges outward.

The Expand Selection Dialog Box

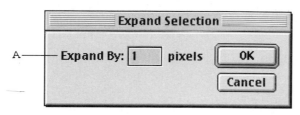

A. **Expand By** (1 to 100)

Enter a value to expand the selection by that amount. To increase the selection by more than 100 pixels, apply this command more than once. Anti-aliasing and feathering are unaffected by this value.

Issues to Consider

This command cannot increase the selected area beyond the canvas. When a selection outline reaches the edge of the image, it stops there.

12.11
Select: Modify: Contract

This command enables you to reduce the area of a selection outline by contracting its edges inward.

The Contract Dialog Box

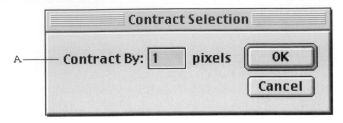

A. **Contract By** (1 to 100)

Enter a value to contract the selection by that amount. To decrease the selection by more than 100 pixels, apply this command more than once. Anti-aliasing and feathering are unaffected by this value.

Issues to Consider

Selected edge pixels are not affected by this command. It cannot contract selection edges that run along the edge of the canvas, but will contract the remainder of the selection.

12.12

Select: Grow

This command increases a selected area by including a wider range of similar colors. It only recognizes colors adjacent to the current selection.

Select: **Grow** bases its decisions on the Tolerance value in the Options bar for the Magic Wand tool. A value of 1 selects pixels identical to the colors of the selected area. A value of 255 selects every pixel in the active layer. Unfortunately, the only way to determine the exact number of colors affected is to simply apply the command. If necessary, choose Edit: **Undo** and enter a new value.

Issues to Consider

Adding similarly-colored pixels to a selection. This command is useful for expanding a selection to include pixels of subtly varying colors. Examples include a piece of fruit, or a high-contrast backdrop that surrounds a product shot. If you want to select colors that occur throughout an image, use Select: **Color Range** or Select: **Similar**.

Adding pixels to a selection. Apply this command more than once to continue adding pixels to the active selection. Each time, the tolerance increases by the value in the Options bar for the Magic Wand tool.

Related Topics
1.10   The Magic Wand Tool
12.5   Select: **Color Range**
12.13 Select: **Similar**

12.13

Select: Similar

This command is similar to Select: **Grow**, but colors from the whole image are added to a selection—they do not need to be adjacent. The range of colors affected by this command is determined by the Tolerance value of the Magic Wand tool.

12.14

Select: Transform Selection

The Select: **Transform Selection** command enables you to dynamically transform a selection outline. Only the outline itself is affected—the actual selected pixels are not touched. Choose this command after creating an initial selection (or transferring one from another image). Once the transform box appears around the selection, you can apply one of the following manual techniques:

- **Moving a selection outline.** Click inside the transform box and drag to reposition the selection.

- **Scaling a selection outline.** To scale disproportionately, drag any handle to change the height and width of the outline independently. To scale proportionately, hold down the Shift key and drag a corner handle. To scale disproportionately from the centerpoint, hold down the (Option) [Alt] key and drag a corner handle. To scale proportionately from the centerpoint, hold down the (Option-Shift) [Alt-Shift] keys and drag a corner handle.

- **Flipping a selection outline.** To flip the outline, drag one handle past another on the opposite side of the transform box. To flip horizontally, drag a handle on the left side past a handle on the right side. To flip vertically, drag a handle from the top past a handle on the bottom. To retain the original dimensions while flipping, hold the Shift key down while dragging a corner handle. To retain the dimensions while flipping from the center, hold down the Option and Shift keys while dragging a corner handle.

- **Rotating a selection outline.** Move the pointer outside of the transform box and drag clockwise or counter-clockwise to change its angle. Hold down the Shift key while dragging to constrain the rotation to 15° increments.

- **Distorting a selection outline.** Hold down the (Command) [Control] key and drag a corner handle in any direction to distort the outline. To distort from the centerpoint, hold down the (Option-Command) [Alt-Control] keys and drag any handle. To constrain a distortion to the current shape of the outline, (Command-Shift) [Control-Shift]-drag a corner handle.

- **Skewing a selection outline.** Hold down the (Command) [Control] key and drag any non-corner handle to skew the outline. To constrain the skew to the current shape of the outline, (Command-Shift) [Control-Shift]-drag a non-corner handle. To skew opposite sides of the outline simultaneously, (Option-Command-Shift) [Alt-Control-Shift]-drag a non-corner handle.

- **Adding perspective to a selection outline.** Hold down the (Option-Command-Shift) [Alt-Control-Shift] keys and drag a corner handle.

Issues to Consider

Applying a transformation. After manipulating the transform box, apply the changes by pressing Return, double-clicking inside the box, or clicking the checkmark button in the Options bar.

Canceling a transformation. To cancel a transformation in progress, press the Escape key or click the X button in the Options bar. The original selection is restored.

Use numerical transform values whenever possible. The techniques listed above are manual, and it can be difficult to note the precise values of your changes. (The upper right panel of the Info palette does offer some assistance.) If you have an idea of the numerical values you wish to impose—for example, if you know you want to rotate the outline by 40°— use the numerical fields that appear in the Options bar after you choose the Transform Selection command.

Reapplying transformation values. To reapply the last-used transformation values, choose Edit: Transform: **Again** after choosing Select: **Transform Selection**. (It's important to note that if you apply the Transform Again command without choosing Transform Selection first, you'll edit the contents of the selection, not the outline itself.)

Use the Edit: Transform commands to edit a selection. If you're uncomfortable using the key-activated transform commands described above, you can choose any of the Edit: **Transform** options after you choose Select: **Transform Selection**.

Related Topics

12.15

Select: *Load Selection*

This command creates an active selection based on currently existing image information. Common uses include the following:

- **Creating a selection based on a mask channel.** When a selection is saved, it's written to a mask channel. You can view and edit this channel by clicking its thumbnail in the Channels palette. This command allows you to reload the saved selection. If a second open image contains any mask channels, they can be loaded as selections in the first image—as long as the two images have identical pixel dimensions.

- **Creating a selection based on an image layer.** This effect is the same as holding down the (Command) [Control] key and clicking a layer in the Layers palette.

Issues to Consider

This command is not available unless the current image contains a mask channel or multiple layers. This command is also available when an image of the same width, height, and resolution is open and contains a mask channel or multiple layers.

Load Selection restrictions. Images in Bitmap mode cannot be loaded as a selection using this command, regardless of their dimensions. Neither can color channels from RGB, CMYK, and Lab images. A separate Grayscale image—because its structure is identical to a mask channel—can be loaded as a selection, as long as its width, height, and resolution match the current image.

Load Selection shortcuts. When you create selections based on channels or layers in the same image, the following shortcuts allow you to bypass the Load Selection dialog box:

- **New Selection.** Hold down the (Command) [Control] key and click the appropriate channel in the Channels palette. Or, hold down the (Option-Command) [Alt-Control] keys and type the number of the desired mask channel.

- **Add to Selection.** Hold down the (Command-Shift) [Control-Shift] keys and click the appropriate channel in the Channels palette.

- **Subtract from Selection.** Hold down the (Option-Shift) [Alt-Shift] keys and click the appropriate channel in the Channels palette.

- **Intersect with Selection.** Hold down the (Option-Command-Shift) [Alt-Control-Shift] keys and click the appropriate channel in the Channels palette.

The Load Selection Dialog Box

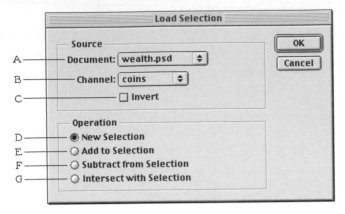

A. Document

Choose the source image from this pop-up. If no other image meets the Load Selection requirements, only the current image appears here.

B. Channel

This pop-up lists all available channels, depending on the image chosen in the Document pop-up. Mask channels are listed by their number. Matching Grayscale images are listed as Black.

If the currently active layer contains transparent pixels, it appears as a Transparency option (for example, Layer 1 Transparency or Layer 3 Transparency). Choose this option to create a selection based on the non-transparent layer pixels.

C. Name

Check this box to reverse the final selection. The effect is the same as applying a regular selection, then choosing Select: **Inverse**.

D. New Selection

This option replaces any existing selection with a new one, based on the Source information.

E. Add to Selection

This option adds the new selection to the current selection. The effect is similar to making a new selection while holding down the Shift key. Use this option to combine two saved selections into one active selection.

F. Subtract from Selection

This option removes the area of the new selection from the current selection. The effect is similar to using a selection tool while holding down the (Option) [Alt] key.

G. **Intersect with Selection**

This option results in a selection based on the overlapping areas of the current and new selections.

Related Topics

12.16

Select: Save Selection

This command enables you to save a selection for future use. This has nothing to do with saving the contents of a selection—rather, the outline and edge-softness of the selection itself are saved. The most efficient way to save this type of information is to make a mask, or a graphic representation of the selection outline. Photoshop does this by creating an additional item in the Channels palette that reflects the nature of the selection.

When the selection is made active again using Select: **Load Selection**, Photoshop refers to the information in this channel. White areas result in full selections, different levels of gray result in partial selections, and black areas are ignored.

Common uses of this command include the following:

• **Creating a selection you can load repeatedly.** It takes time to generate a complex selection. If there is a chance you might require that selection again, save it. This way, it can be restored with a single command, instead of creating the same selection again.

• **Graphically editing a selection.** Because a selection is saved graphically, it can be edited using Photoshop's tools, adjustment commands, and filters. This simply cannot be done with selection tools alone. A basic selection can be modified extensively before being reloaded. Photoshop simply bases the selection on the existing gray values.

• **Creating an alpha channel.** Certain types of graphics require an additional masking channel, such as transparent GIFs and PNG files. Also, many video editing suites use a masking channel to simulate a bluescreen effect.

• **Creating a layer mask.** This command can be used to create or replace a layer mask.

The Save Selection Dialog Box

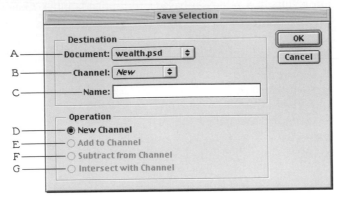

A. Document

The Document pull-down menu lists all possible images into which a selection can be saved:

Current Image

> By default, the name of the active image appears in this pop-up menu. Leave this option alone to save the selection as a new channel in the same image.

Open Images

> Only open images sharing the same width, height, and resolution as the current image are listed here. Choosing one of these saves the selection as a mask channel in the second image.

New

> This option saves the selection as a separate Grayscale image. The content is the same as if it had been saved as a mask channel. As long as the new image is open, it can easily be reloaded into the original image. This allows users with less-powerful workstations to save selections without increasing the file size of the current image.

B. Channel

This pop-up menu determines where a saved selection is placed within the destination image:

New

> This option saves a selection as a new channel, listed as a separate item in the Channels palette. Mask channels are always named numerically by their order of appearance in an image.

Existing Mask Channels

> If an image already contains one or more mask channels, they appear in the Channels pop-up menu. If you select an existing channel, you can replace it with the new selection or combine the two, depending on the chosen Operation setting.

Layer Mask

> If an image layer is active when you choose Select: **Save Selection**, this option appears in the Channels pop-up menu. It allows you to create a layer mask based on the current selection, similar to making a selection and choosing one of the Layer: **Add Layer Mask** options. If the active image layer already has a layer mask, you can replace it with the new selection or combine the two, depending on the chosen Operation setting.

C. **Name**

> If you want to name the new channel as you create it, enter it in this field. Otherwise, Photoshop automatically names it "Alpha." Note that you can always double-click an alpha channel's palette item to access the Channel Options dialog box, which enables you to rename the channel.

D. **New Channel**

> This option is the only one available when New or Layer Mask is selected in the Channel pop-up menu. The selection is either saved as a new channel without affecting any other image information or applied as a layer mask.

E. **Add to Channel**

> This option combines the contents of the existing and new mask channels.

F. **Subtract from Channel**

> This option removes any area in the existing channel that is overlapped by the new selection. This information is simply filled in with black, which prevents that area from becoming an active selection when the channel is reloaded.

G. **Intersect with Channel**

> This option modifies the existing channel so it displays only the areas that intersect with the current selection. The areas that do not overlap are filled with black, preventing them from loading as active selections.

Related Topics

The Filter Menu

Filters are automated image editing tools. They are named after photographic filters, the devices placed over a camera lens to correct bad lighting conditions or create special effects.

Like camera filters, Photoshop filters fall into two categories:

- **Production filters.** These filters prepare images for printing or for display in web or multimedia projects. They help correct deficiencies in the image, such as blurriness, film grain, noise, scratches, and other problems. When using Production filters, the goal is to create an image that appears in print or on screen as close to the original photograph as possible, or to enhance the quality of the image.

- **Creative filters.** These filters substantially alter the image in order to create a completely new and different result. Some creative filters recreate the image as though it were created using traditional media such as ink or charcoal. Others change the positions of pixels to make them appear as if they were distorted by glass. Others alter the image in ways that aren't easily classified. The goal of creative filters is to create a new image rather than to improve the quality of an existing image.

The Former Aldus Gallery Effects

The Artistic, Brush Strokes, and Sketch filters (as well as a few scattered throughout the remaining categories) are part of the former Aldus Gallery Effects suite. Adobe acquired these tools when it merged with Aldus. Even though some of these filters have barely changed since they debuted in Photoshop 2.0, they have been included as part of the standard filter set.

While these filters can certainly create some interesting effects, each one suffers from one or more of the following drawbacks:

- **Bad or nonexistent anti-aliasing.** Anti-aliasing blends the colors of pixels together to provide smooth transitions between colors. Without anti-aliasing, transitions are harsh, with the obvious square pixels clearly identifying an image as computer-generated. This defeats the Artistic, Brush Strokes, and Sketch filters' attempts to emulate natural media and typically produces images of unsatisfactory quality.

- **Meaningless values.** The Artistic, Brush Strokes, and Sketch strokes are all controlled by numerical values. However, these values are only relevant to the field itself—they do not relate to color values of the pixels, or to pixel distances. They don't even relate to values in other fields. A value of 0 that produces no effect in one field can produce a substantial effect in another. The only meaning they have is that a higher setting produces a different effect from a lower setting.

- **Incomplete options.** Nearly all the filters are missing a key element. Rough Pastels, for example, has settings for stroke length, stroke detail, texture, even for lighting, and yet it has no setting to change the angle of the brush stroke from 45°.

- **Superfluous functionality.** Many filters contain settings that blur, sharpen, adjust brightness and contrast, and perform other commands found in more useful forms elsewhere in the program.

- **Limited color modes.** These filters only function in RGB and Grayscale color modes.

13.1

Filter: Last Filter *(Command) [Control]-F*

This command applies the last filter used, repeating the same settings.

Issues to Consider

Access the last-applied filter settings. Hold down the (Option) [Alt] key when choosing this command to open the dialog box of the last filter used. The settings that you entered previously are retained, enabling you to make small adjustments before applying the filter again.

13.2

Filter: Artistic

These filters claim to reproduce an image as though it had been created using a traditional artistic technique. The Artistic filters all function on the same basic principle: they define areas of similar colors, then average or blur them together to form areas of solid color.

13.3

Filter: Artistic: Colored Pencil

This filter makes the image appear as if crosshatching were applied over the original image using a pencil the color of the background color. It also finds edges and blurs the image within the edges.

The Colored Pencil Dialog Box

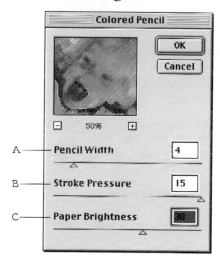

A. **Pencil Width** (1 to 24)

This setting controls the density of the crosshatching. A value of 1 covers the image with fine hatch marks. Higher settings produce large patches of solid foreground color and few hatch marks.

B. **Stroke Pressure** (1 to 15)

This setting controls the total quantity of the hatch marks. At 1, there are so many strokes that the resulting image is solid background color. At 15, the image is thoroughly crosshatched, but still retains enough of the original image to be identifiable.

C. **Paper Brightness** (1 to 50)

This setting darkens or brightens the crosshatching color. A value of 1 darkens the color to black. A value of 50 brightens the color substantially.

13.4

Filter: Artistic: Cutout

This filter recreates the image as though it were created from torn pieces of construction paper. Similar to an Image: Adjust: **Posterize** command with edge detection, it selects large areas of the image based on color similarity and reduces the color range within those areas. Unlike the Posterize command, edges are anti-aliased by the Cutout filter.

The Cutout Dialog Box

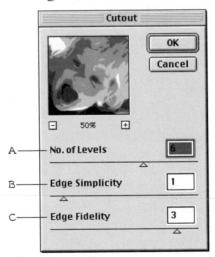

A. **No. of Levels** (2 to 8)

This value determines the number of color levels.

B. **Edge Simplicity** (0 to 10)

This setting determines the number of edges found by the filter. A value of 0 finds many edges, creating an image resembling the original image. Settings above 5 reduce detail to a point where only abstract shapes remain of the original image. A value of 10 reduces the image to a single solid color that is the average value of the selected colors.

C. **Edge Fidelity** (1 to 3)

This setting determines how closely the edges of the solid colors match the edges of the original image. A value of 1 follows the edges of the original image very loosely, and a value of 3 attempts to match the edges as closely as possible.

13.5

Filter: Artistic: *Dry Brush*

Traditional drybrush technique paints with liquid water colors without dipping the brush in water, producing dense areas of pure pigment. This filter attempts to reproduce this effect by repainting the image with small areas of solid color. It defines areas based on the similarity of the colors, then fills those areas with the average color values. It defines many more areas than other Artistic filters, creating a more detailed image.

The Dry Brush Dialog Box

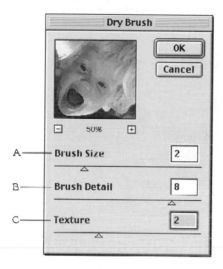

A. **Brush Size** (0 to 10)

This value sets the relative size of the area of color averaged into an area of solid color. 0 creates many small colored areas, and 10 defines fewer, larger areas.

B. **Brush Detail** (0 to 10)

This setting determines the quantity of edges found. A value of 0 captures the least detail, but it still captures enough detail information for the image to be recognizable as the original. A value of 10 finds the most edges, producing the highest number of colored areas and an image closely resembling the original.

C. **Texture** (1 to 3)

This setting determines the amount colored areas are lightened or darkened from their original colors. A value of 1 keeps the original, averaged values. A value of 3 darkens and lightens pixels to the point where there are many stray black-and-white pixels scattered over the image.

13.6

Filter: Artistic: Film Grain

Film grain often exists in enlarged photographs taken with high-speed film. Typically, it appears as a soft noise over the entire image. This filter attempts to recreate photographic film grain by randomly lightening and darkening pixels. Because the grain it adds is too blocky and pixelated, it produces nothing resembling film grain at any setting. The filter has the additional feature of lightening the image before applying the grain.

Issues to Consider

More effective grain filters are available. To create more realistic film grain effects, use the Noise: **Add Noise**, or the Texture: **Grain** filters.

The Film Grain Dialog Box

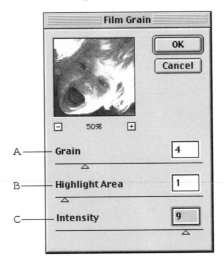

A. **Grain** (0 to 20)

This setting controls the amount pixels are randomly lightened or darkened. Low settings add slight noise to the image. Higher settings obliterate the image entirely.

B. **Highlight Area** (1 to 20)

This value defines areas to be made lighter. The higher the setting, the greater the range of colors lightened. A value of 1 lightens only the lightest areas of the image. A value of 20 lightens all colors.

C. **Intensity** (0 to 10)

This setting determines how much the range of colors defined by Highlight Area is lightened. A value of 0 does not lighten the image; 10 produces a very light image, with most colors lightened to white.

13.7

Filter: Artistic: Fresco

Fresco, a technique renowned for its beauty and durability, involves painting drying plaster with water color paints. This filter produces nothing remotely resembling a true fresco. Rather, it defines areas based on the similarity of the colors, then fills those areas with the averaged color values. It groups the new areas of solid color together based on a wider range of color similarity, and outlines them with thick black or gray lines. The effect is more reminiscent of coloring books than of frescos.

The Fresco Dialog Box

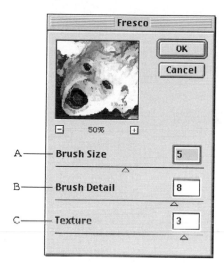

A. Brush Size (0 to 10)

This setting controls the size of the colored areas changed to the same color. A value of 10 produces the largest colored areas and the least detail in the resulting image.

B. Brush Detail (0 to 10)

This amount controls how many areas of similar color are defined before being averaged together. Higher settings define more areas, resulting in a more detailed image. This setting is virtually identical to Brush Size, only the values have the opposite effect. A value of 0 and a Brush Detail of 10 will produce the most detailed image.

C. Texture (1 to 3)

This value increases the contrast of the colors in the image. A value of 1 fills areas with the original, averaged values. Settings above 1 make fill colors darker or lighter.

13.8

Filter: Artistic: Neon Glow

This filter emulates the appearance of an object lit by the flash of a neon light at night. Neon Glow replaces shadows with the foreground color, midtones with the background color, and highlights with a third color specified in the Neon Glow dialog box. The Neon Glow filter produces the most realistic results when the foreground and background colors are set to the defaults.

The Neon Glow Dialog Box

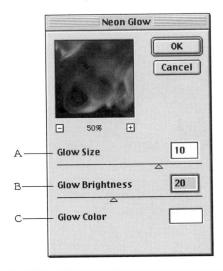

A. **Size** (–24 to 24)

Size is the range of colors considered to be highlights. These colors are changed to the color specified in the Color setting. Negative values invert the image. The closer the amount to 0, the greater the highlights.

B. **Brightness** (0 to 50)

Brightness determines if it is twilight or night. A value of 50 equals twilight, dark enough for colors to desaturate, but light enough so the glow from a neon light has no impact. At this setting, the image is defined completely by the foreground and background colors. Lower settings emulate darker night. More of the image is colored by the neon light, but the image is darker overall. At 0, it is too dark for the neon to light anything, producing an image of solid foreground.

C. **Color**

Clicking the Color box opens the Color Picker, where you choose the color of the neon light assigned to highlights.

13.9

Filter: Artistic: Paint Daubs

This filter creates nothing resembling daubs of paint. Rather, it defines an area based on color similarity, then blurs the area. The result is a blurry image that still retains edges where colors are substantially different. Additional blurring and sharpening effects can be performed using the Brush Type settings.

The Paint Daubs Dialog Box

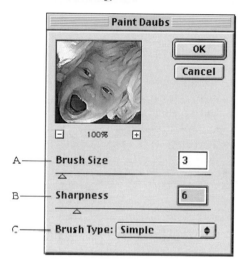

A. **Brush Size** (1 to 50)

This setting controls the relative size of colored areas. The lower the number, the greater the quantity, providing more color variations and more detail in the image.

B. **Sharpness** (0 to 40)

Sharpness determines how much sharpening is done to the image after the blurring has occurred (see *13.67, Filter: Sharpen* for details on sharpening).

C. **Brush Type**

Brush Types add additional blurring, lightening, darkening, or sharpening to the image:

Simple Brush

This option makes no additional changes.

Light Rough

This option lightens and sharpens the image after the initial blurring.

Dark Rough

This option darkens and sharpens the image after the initial blurring.

Wide Sharp
> This option sharpens the image after the initial blurring.

Wide Blurry
> This option blurs the image after the initial blurring.

Sparkle
> This option picks out the lightest of the highlights and lightens them even more, until they are substantially brighter than the rest of the image.

13.10

Filter: Artistic: **Palette Knife**

Traditional palette knife technique paints an image with a hard palette knife instead of a brush, producing, large, solid strokes of even color. This filter defines colored areas based on their similarity, averages the values, and fills the area with the averaged color. Colored areas are limited to roughly the same size and shape, as if created with a palette knife.

The Palette Knife Dialog Box

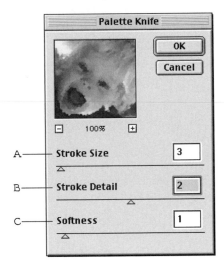

A. **Stroke Size** (1 to 50)
> This setting determines the size of the colored areas. The larger the size, the larger the area. A value of 1 produces a pixel-sized stroke, producing no change in the image. At 50, strokes are so large nothing is identifiable from the original image. Values from 2 to 5 substantially alter the image while retaining enough detail for the original image to be recognizable.

B. **Stroke Detail** (1 to 3)

This value sets the roughness of the colored areas. A value of 1 results in smooth, rounded areas, while 3 produces very rough edges.

C. **Softness** (0 to 10)

This setting determines how much blurring occurs at the edges where colors meet. At 0, there is no blurring. At 10, the edges blend together slightly.

13.11
Filter: Artistic: Plastic Wrap

This filter makes an image appear as though it were wrapped in heat-shrink plastic.

The Plastic Wrap Dialog Box

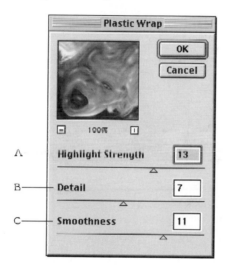

A. **Highlight Strength** (0 to 20)

This value represents the intensity of the light shining on the plastic, creating the reflection. A value of 0 is ambient light, producing no reflections. A value of 20 resembles a bright spotlight shining on the image.

B. **Detail** (1 to 15)

This setting determines how tightly the highlights follow the contours of the image. A value of 1 follows the contours loosely, while a value of 15 follows them closely.

C. **Smoothness** (1 to 15)

A better label for this setting would be *glossiness* or *shininess*. This setting determines how much light is reflected by the plastic. A value of 1 reflects very little light. A value of 15 hides the image almost completely, showing little but shiny plastic.

13.12

Filter: Artistic: *Poster Edges*

This filter reduces the number of tones, similar to Image: Adjust: **Posterize,** giving the image a flat, silk-screened appearance. The filter then traces the edges between more extreme differences in color with dark lines. It posterizes the colors more faithfully to the original colors than the **Posterize** command, and the colors are anti-aliased, as well. Unfortunately, there is no way to turn off the edge tracing, and no way to set a precise number of posterization levels, limiting the usefulness of the filter.

The Poster Edges Dialog Box

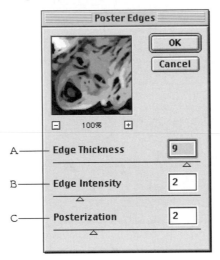

A. **Edge Thickness** (0 to 10)

This setting determines the thickness of the dark lines the filter draws between colored areas. A value of 0 produces a thin line, and a value of 10 produces a very thick line.

B. **Edge Intensity** (0 to 10)

This setting determines the number of edges that will be traced. A value of 0 only traces edges where colors are substantially different. A value of 10 traces the edge of nearly every area, producing an image thoroughly covered with black.

C. **Posterization** (0 to 6)

This setting determines the relative number of color levels. A value of 0 compresses the image into very few levels of color. A value of 6 produces an image with a color range almost identical to the original image.

13.13

Filter: Artistic: Rough Pastels

This filter streaks over the image with irregularly shaped clumps of color. The colors of the streaks are saturated colors sampled from the image. Strokes only occur at a 45% angle.

The Rough Pastels Dialog Box

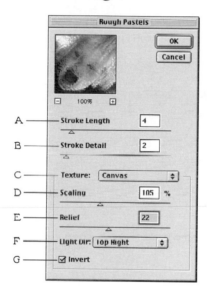

A. **Stroke Length** (0 to 40)

This setting determines how far the saturated sampled colors are smeared from their original colors. A value of 0 leaves the sampled colors in patches shaped by the selected texture over the original colors in the image. A value of 40 smears the colors over a distance long enough to produce obvious strokes.

B. **Stroke Detail** (1 to 20)

This setting is the amount that the filter saturates the sampled colors when it applies them to the image. A detail setting of 1 does not change the color values. A value of 20 pushes the saturation of the colors to their maximum values.

C. **Texture**

Strokes are roughened according to the pattern of the texture. Any file saved in the Photoshop format can be used as a texture by choosing Load Selection. An Open dialog box appears, allowing you to select a file. When the selected texture is smaller than the image, it is tiled to cover the entire image. When the selected texture is larger than the image, it crops to fit.

D. **Scaling** (50 to 200)

This setting changes the size of the texture before applying it to the image, from half to twice its original size.

E. **Relief** (0 to 50)

This setting determines how much of the texture is filled in. The higher the number, the more the texture is filled.

F. **Light Dir**

This setting makes the image appear to be lit from the specified direction.

G. **Invert**

Checking the Invert box inverts the lightness values of the texture before applying the filter, producing an inverted texture. It does not invert the image or the color values of the brush strokes.

13.14

Filter: Artistic: Smudge Stick

Smudge sticks are used to smear charcoal on paper. This filter considers the darkest pixels in the image to be charcoal and smears them over lighter pixels at a left diagonal, leaving lighter pixels unsmudged.

The Smudge Stick Dialog Box

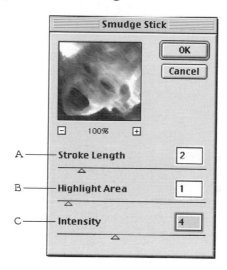

A. Stroke Length (0 to 10)

This setting controls the distance that dark pixels are smudged over light pixels. Higher settings result in longer smudges. A value of 0 still produces substantial smudging.

B. Highlight Area (0 to 20)

The filter can lighten pixels slightly before smudging occurs. Highlight Area determines the range of pixels to be lightened. A value of 0 produces no lightening of pixels. Low settings lighten only the lightest pixels. A value of 20 lightens all but the darkest pixels.

C. Intensity (0 to 10)

This setting determines how much the pixels in the Highlight Area will be lightened. A value of 0 does not lighten the image at all. A value of 10 lightens the image considerably.

13.15

Filter: Artistic: Sponge

This filter emulates the effect of applying a damp sponge to a painting. Detail disappears, and the colors are reduced to random, irregular shapes. Sponge defines large areas of color based on the similarities of color, then blurs the contents while preserving the edges. It varies the shape of the areas and the fill color more than other Artistic filters, so that the shapes and color follow the original image very loosely.

The Sponge Dialog Box

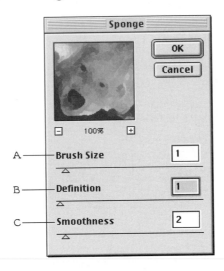

A. **Brush Size** (1 to 10)

This setting controls the size of the colored areas. The higher the size, the larger the areas. The filter blurs the image so much there is very little difference between 1 and 10, though 10 preserves slightly more detail from the original image and creates slightly smaller sponge pore shapes.

B. **Definition** (1 to 25)

This setting controls the darkness of sponge pore shading. A value of 1 produces slight mottling. A value of 25 looks like military camouflage painted over the image.

C. **Smoothness** (1 to 15)

This setting controls the amount of blending between the image and the sponge pore shadows. A value of 1 produces very rough-edged sponge pore shadows. A value of 10 blends the pores with the image, adding blurring to the image and creating large, diffused sponge pores.

13.16

Filter: Artistic: *Underpainting*

In traditional painting, underpainting roughs out the general colors and shape of the subject before detail information and shading are added.

This filter does a decent job of recreating the appearance of an underpainting. It lightens and blurs the image, destroying all detail information and producing a very diffused image.

Then it moves pixels and adds highlight and shadow detail based on a selected texture, giving the impression that the image was roughed out with oil paints on a textured canvas.

Issues to Consider

Try mimicking a conventional technique. Use an Undercolor filtered image just as you would a true undercolor painting, as the beginning of an image rather than the end. Run the filter, then add detail over the filtered image.

The Underpainting Dialog Box

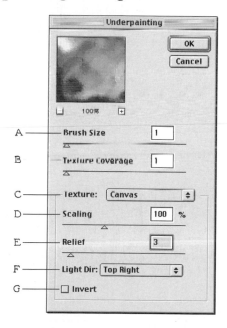

A. Brush Size (0 to 40)

This setting determines the amount of blurring the filter does before it applies the texture. A value of 0 obliterates all detail information from the image, but leaves enough of the original color information to resemble the original image. A value of 40 shifts colors and distorts shapes, leaving a vague outline of the original image.

B. **Texture Coverage** (0 to 40)

This setting determines the distance pixels are moved (displaced) into the shape of the texture. With a value of 0, pixels move very little. At 40, the image appears thoroughly mashed into the texture.

C. **Texture**

The filter uses the lightness values of the texture for adding highlight and detail information, and for displacing pixels. When you select Load Texture, an Open dialog box appears, prompting you to select a Photoshop file to use as a texture. The texture will be tiled if it is smaller than the image, or cropped if it is larger.

D. **Scaling** (50% to 200%)

This setting alters the size of the texture before it is applied to the image, from half to twice its original size.

E. **Relief** (0 to 50)

This setting determines the amount of highlight and shadow the texture adds to the image. This detail is based on the highlight and shadows of the texture file. A value of 0 adds no texture at all. At 50, all pixels are pure black or white. Settings from 3 to 7 produce the most realistic texture.

F. **Light Dir**

The options in this pop-up menu make the image appear to be lit from a specific direction.

G. **Invert**

Check this box to invert the values of the texture image.

13.17

Filter: Artistic: Watercolor

Watercolor paint dries from the edges, drawing more pigment to the edges of colored areas. This filter defines colored areas based on their similarity, averages the colors together, then fills the defined area with the new value. Then it darkens the edge pixels of those areas to produce a watercolor-like outline. Completely uncharacteristic of watercolors, the filter inexplicably saturates colors and adds dark shadows.

The Watercolor Dialog Box

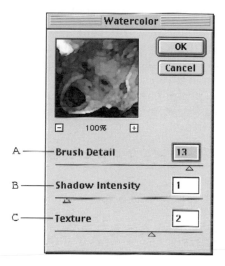

A. Brush Detail (1 to 14)

This setting defines the range of similar colors to be averaged together and turned into an area of solid color. The lower the number, the wider the range, resulting in larger areas and less detail. A value of 14 produces an image fairly close to the original. A value of 1 obliterates most information, leaving a rough outline of the original image.

B. Shadow Intensity (1 to 10)

This setting controls the amount edge pixels and shadows are darkened. Any setting above 1 darkens all but the very lightest pixels to the point where most of the image is black.

C. Texture (1 to 3)

The Texture setting increases the contrast of colors. Settings above 1 result in lighter lights and darker darks.

13.18

Filter: *Blur*

The Blur filters soften images. They work by analyzing the image and determining hard edges and areas of sharp color differences. Then, they average the colors of the pixels in those areas together to eliminate the sudden color differences.

Blur filters can be used as both production and creative filters. At low settings, they can hide noise and grain in an image. At higher settings, they can be used to create drop shadows and produce motion effects.

Issues to Consider

Blur filters produce significantly different results when used on a selected or unselected image layer. When the image layer is selected, pixels at the edge of the selection become partially transparent, but pixels outside the selection are unchanged. This leaves a sharp edge roughly 50% transparent at its most transparent point. When blur filters are applied to unselected image layers, transparent pixels at the edge of the image become semi-transparent, so the image fades into complete transparency. For most purposes, applying the filter to an unselected image layer produces much more satisfactory results than selecting the image layer.

13.19

Filter: *Blur: Blur*

This filter calculates areas in the image where color differences are most extreme, then averages the edge pixels between the areas of different color. Unlike Blur: **Gaussian Blur**, there is no way to determine the amount of blur and no way to preview the effect. This filter is only suitable for situations where speed is more important than image quality.

13.20

Filter: *Blur: Blur More*

This filter is identical to Blur, but has 4 to 5 times the effect.

13.21

Filter: Blur: *Gaussian Blur*

This filter averages the colors of adjacent pixels to reduce detail. Gaussian Blur is one of the most important Photoshop filters, used for everything from eliminating moiré patterns to creating drop shadows. The Gaussian Blur filter is superior to other Blur filters for two reasons: It can be set to precise values, and it blurs according to the Gaussian Bell Curve distribution. The Gaussian Bell Curve distribution fades the amount of blurring unevenly over a distance to create a more natural, aesthetically pleasing blur. The human eye is very sensitive to changes in color. When a blur fades steadily, it is noticeable and appears computer-generated. By varying the amount of blur, this filter emulates blurring found in nature, such as the edges of shadows.

Issues to Consider

This filter provides a dynamic full-image preview. To take full advantage of this preview, the view must be set to 100%, or Actual Pixels. This previews the image most accurately on screen. Other resolutions can blur the image preview slightly, which can lead to under-blurring.

Blurring channels, as opposed to the entire image. When blurring for corrective purposes, such as removing a moiré pattern, view each color channel individually before blurring. Moiré patterns and other flaws often exist only in one or two channels. Blurring one channel preserves more detail and results in a higher quality image.

The Gaussian Blur Dialog Box

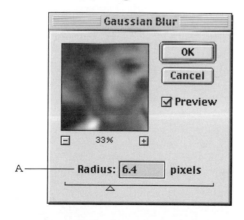

A. **Radius** (0.1 to 250 pixels)

This setting controls the amount of blurring. The higher the Radius, the greater the blur. A pixel radius of 0.1 produces little visible blurring. A value of 250 obliterates the image. Pixels bordering transparent areas are averaged with the transparency.

The exact amount that one pixel is averaged with another depends on the Gaussian Bell Curve distribution. Pixels within the first third of the radius closest to the center pixel are blurred the most. These pixels receive about 80% of their color from the pixel at the center of the radius.

The remaining 20% comes from the original pixel color. The amount of blurring fades about 60% across the next third of the radius. Over the last third, it fades 20%, until pixels are not blurred together.

The color from one pixel is actually averaged further than the radius specifies. For example, with a Radius value of 1, pixels immediately adjacent to the pixel at the center of the radius are averaged so that roughly 70% of their color comes from the center pixel and 30% from their original color value.

Adjacent pixels are blended with their new color, and so on. Even though the Radius is set to one pixel, color from a single pixel can be spread as far as five pixels.

13.22

Filter: Blur: Motion Blur

This filter creates the effect of an image in motion, blurring pixels in a specified direction over a specified distance. As with other Blur filters, Motion Blur is created by averaging the color values of pixels together. Colors are averaged not according to their differences, but according to the direction and distance of the blur. The amount colors fade increases farther from the original pixels.

Unfortunately, the Motion Blur occurs both in the direction specified and in the opposite direction, as if the image were vibrating back and forth very quickly, rather than moving quickly in the specified direction.

The Motion Blur Dialog Box

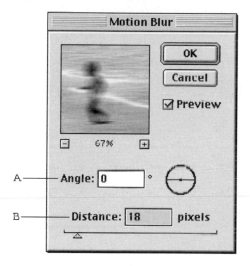

A. **Angle** (–90° to 90°)

This setting specifies the angle of the blur. The blur occurs in the direction specified and in the opposite direction.

B. **Distance** (1 to 999 pixels)

This setting determines the distance pixels are blurred.

13.23

Filter: Blur: Radial Blur

This filter blurs an image outward from a center point. The image is increasingly blurred from the image's center. This is useful for creating a feel of vertigo or focusing attention on a specific area. Radial Blur possesses no preview capabilities and is slow on even the most powerful computers.

The Radial Blur Dialog Box

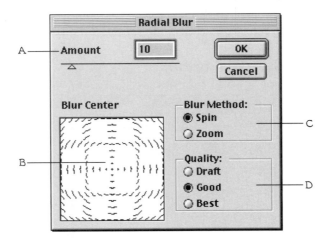

A. **Amount** (1 to 100)

This setting controls the intensity of the effect. A value of 1 produces slight blurring. A value of 100 obliterates the image, leaving only streaks of color, except for pixels at the center of the blur, which are only slightly changed.

B. **Blur Center**

The blur radiates from the blur center. Click within the square to position the blur center. The Blur Center box is always square regardless of the shape of the selection. Unless you have made a perfectly square selection, you must make an educated guess as to where the center of the blur is relative to your image.

C. **Blur Method**

Choose a blur method from this pop-up menu:

Spin

Spin applies the Radial Blur in concentric circles radiating from the center. The circles increase in frequency and blur more intensely the farther they are from the center.

Zoom

Zoom applies the Radial Blur in lines radiating from the center. The blur increases in intensity the farther it gets from the center.

D. **Quality**

Quality settings help compensate for the lack of an image preview. Preview the effects of the filter by running the filter at lower settings, by choosing Edit: **Undo**; then run the filter at its best setting.

Draft

This option applies the filter quickly, but produces a low quality blur with much noise and no smoothness. This is good for previewing the position of the Blur Center.

Good

This option takes a little longer to apply than Draft quality, but applies the blur more evenly with less noise. Use this to preview the Amount of the blur.

Best

Apply the filter in this mode only after determining the Blur Center and the Amount using Draft and Good quality settings.

Filter: Blur: *Smart Blur*

This filter is excellent for removing low-intensity noise from an image, such as film grain. It blurs while preserving edge detail. Smart Blur works by identifying areas of the image where substantially different colors meet. The filter protects these areas, while blurring areas of similar color. This filter works well for removing film grain, because the grain typically differs in color slightly from the surrounding areas. The grain can be blurred away, and detail is left unharmed because it substantially differs in color from the surrounding area.

The Smart Blur Dialog Box

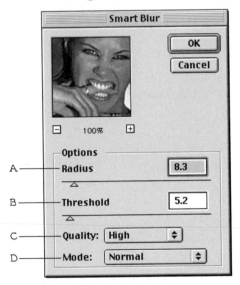

A. **Radius** (0.1 to 100 pixels)

This value determines the distance of the blur effect, as measured from the center of each targeted color. The higher the setting, the greater the amount of blur.

B. **Threshold** (0.1 to 100)

This setting determines the amount of difference between colors that the filter will define as an edge. Edge pixels are not blurred. At low settings, only pixels with very similar colors are blurred. At higher settings, substantially different colors are blurred together.

C. **Quality** (Low, Medium, or High)

Reducing quality speeds processing time, but produces less satisfactory results. Use lower quality settings when using the filter for artistic purposes, but use the High setting for production.

D. **Mode**

Mode provides different methods for applying the Smart Blur filter:

Normal

Normal applies blurring to the image without altering it further.

Edge Only

Instead of blurring the image, this option traces the center of areas the filter defines as edges with white, non–anti-aliased, single pixel lines, and fills the remaining image with black.

Overlay Edge

Instead of blurring the image, this option traces areas the filter defines as edges with white, non–anti-aliased, single pixel lines over the original image.

13.25

Filter: Brush Strokes

Brush Strokes function almost identically to the Artistic series of filters. They identify areas of similar colors. These areas are blurred, filled with the average of the colors within each area, or are altered in other ways. The Brush Strokes filters also add colors to the edges of the colored areas, or over the entire image.

13.26

Filter: Brush Strokes: Accented Edges

This filter traces the edges in the image, then darkens or lightens them. Low settings produce a slight glowing or an increase in shadows. At higher settings, the image appears massively darkened and grime-spattered, or glowing as if lit by a strange alien light. At highest settings, the image is distorted beyond recognition.

The Accented Edges Dialog Box

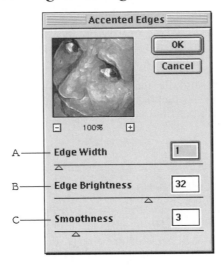

A. **Edge Width** (1 to 14)

This setting controls the width of the edges that are brightened or darkened. A value of 1 produces a thin line over the edges. A value of 14 creates very thick lines covering most of the image.

B. **Edge Brightness** (0 to 50)

This setting determines the amount edges are darkened or lightened. A value of 0 darkens edges to black. A value of 25, the neutral setting, retains the original lightness values of the image. A value of 50 makes edges almost white, eliminating most detail.

C. **Smoothness** (1 to 15)

This setting determines the amount of blurring done to the image after edges are found. With a high smoothness, major edges are still present, but most detail information is lost.

13.27

Filter: Brush Strokes: *Angled Strokes*

This filter identifies areas of similar colors and blurs within those areas, preserving the edges between different colors. It adds streaks to the areas by lightening or darkening the existing colors in narrow strokes. Strokes are rendered at left or right diagonals. Within a single area of color, all strokes are made in the same direction.

The Angled Strokes Dialog Box

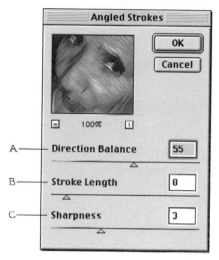

A. **Direction Balance** (0 to 100)

This setting determines if all areas are stroked at a right diagonal or a left diagonal, or if some areas are stroked at a left diagonal and others at a right diagonal. At 0, the strokes are entirely at a left diagonal. At 100, the strokes are entirely at a right diagonal. Numbers in between mix the two angles.

B. **Stroke Length** (3 to 50)

This setting determines the distance of the blurring and streaking. Lower settings preserve more of the image's original detail, while higher settings produce a more pronounced stroke.

C. **Sharpness** (0 to 10)

This setting controls the amount of sharpening done to the image after blurring and streaking. Sharpness intensifies highlights and shadows, creating more of a 3-D appearance. Too much sharpening produces artifacting (pixels with color obviously inconsistent with the rest of the image) and haloing (areas of light pixels surrounding dark areas).

13.28

Filter: Brush Strokes: Crosshatch

This filter is very similar to the Angled Strokes filter. It identifies areas of similar colors and blurs within those areas, preserving the edges between different colors. It adds streaks to the areas by lightening or darkening the existing colors in narrow strokes. Strokes are rendered at left or right diagonals. Unlike Angled Strokes, Crosshatch overlaps the strokes.

The Crosshatch Dialog Box

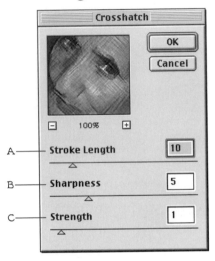

A. **Stroke Length** (3 to 50)

This setting controls the amount the image is blurred and the length of the shadow and highlight streaking. Higher settings result in more obvious crosshatching, but result in the loss of more detail information from the original image. A value of 0 does not change the image. A value of 50 retains only the largest colored areas.

B. **Sharpness** (0 to 20)

This setting determines the amount of sharpening done to the image after blurring and streaking. Sharpness increases the highlight and shadow detail, creating more of a 3-D appearance. Too much sharpening produces artifacting, haloing, and aberrantly bright pixels surrounding the dark areas.

C. **Strength** (1 to 3)

Strength increases the differences between colors in the image. Settings of 2 or 3 can cause substantial artifacting when all color values are pushed to their maximum values of 0 or 255.

13.29

Filter: Brush Strokes: *Dark Strokes*

This filter identifies areas of similar colors and blurs within those areas, preserving the edges between different colored areas. It then adds dark strokes over the areas at left or right diagonals. The darker the area, the darker the stroke. The darkest image areas are filled with black.

The Dark Strokes Dialog Box

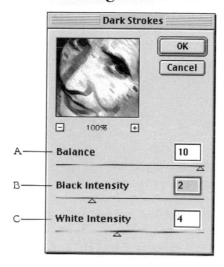

A. Balance (0 to 10)

This setting controls the quantity of strokes made at left or right diagonals. At 0, all strokes are at right diagonals. At 10, all strokes will be at left diagonals. Between 0 and 10, the strokes are a mixture of the two angles.

B. Black Intensity (0 to 10)

This setting determines the length and intensity of the dark strokes. At 0, the image is stroked lightly, with only the darkest areas of the image filled with black. At 10 all but the lightest pixels are filled with solid black. Settings above 5 cover most of the image with black strokes. A value of 1 or 2 substantially darkens the image while leaving recognizable detail from the original image.

C. White Intensity (0 to 10)

This setting controls the amount an image is lightened before being stroked. A value of 0 performs no lightening. A value of 10 obliterates most color variation, leaving large areas of very bright color.

13.30

Filter: Brush Strokes: *Ink Outlines*

This filter identifies areas of similar color and blurs within those areas, preserving the edges between different colors. Edges are outlined with black, and color areas covered with a dark haze, as if a black ink wash had puddled on the image and dried roughly in the shadow areas. Finally, light areas are lightly streaked over with black at a right diagonal.

The Ink Outlines Dialog Box

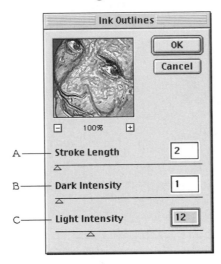

A. **Stroke Length** (1 to 50)

This setting determines the amount of blurring and streaking applied to the image. A value of 1 blurs and strokes the image very slightly, but still produces substantial puddling. A value of 50 leaves a vague blur of the original image.

B. **Dark Intensity** (0 to 50)

This setting controls the darkness of the strokes and puddles. A value of 0 produces pale, gray ink blotches over most of the image. A value of 50 darkens all but the lightest areas to black.

C. **Light Intensity** (0 to 50)

This setting determines how much the image is lightened beneath the added darkness. At 0, no lightening occurs; at 50, colors are intensely bright.

13.31

Filter: Brush Strokes: *Spatter*

This filter reproduces the image as though it were created with a clogged airbrush, with the image appearing to be spattered onto the canvas. It differs from other Brush Strokes filters in that it doesn't find edges or blur the image. Rather, it groups pixels into randomly sized and shaped groups, then randomly moves the groups. Pixels retain their original color values.

The Spatter Dialog Box

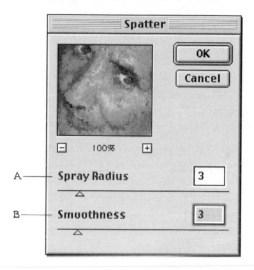

A. Spray Radius (0 to 25)

This value sets the distance pixels are moved from their original locations. A value of 0 does not move pixels. A value of 25 with a low Smoothness value reduces the image to a haze of pixels.

B. Smoothness (1 to 15)

This value sets the size limit of the grouped pixels. The larger the groups, the less the image is distorted. At 1, pixels are moved separately, with no grouping. At 50, the image is only slightly distorted, even when the spray radius is at its highest setting.

13.32

Filter: Brush Strokes: Sprayed Strokes

This filter is almost identical to Spatter, but it moves pixels less randomly. The Sprayed Strokes filter constrains pixels within specified distances. The resulting image appears tightly rippled.

The Sprayed Strokes Dialog Box

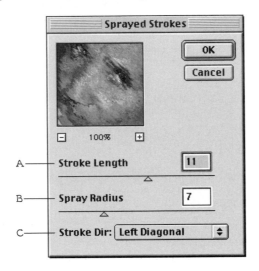

A. **Stroke Length** (0 to 20)

This setting determines the distance pixels are moved in the direction specified by the Stroke Dir setting. The higher the setting, the more apparent the stroke will be. At 0, the image is composed of jittery ripples. At 20, the ripples are longer and more obvious.

B. **Spray Radius** (0 to 25)

This setting determines the distance pixels are moved in any direction. When Stroke Length is low and a Spray Radius is high, pixels are moved very randomly. With a high stroke length and a high spray radius, pixels are moved very far along in the direction of the stroke.

C. **Stroke Dir**

The crests and troughs of the ripples point in the direction specified in this pop-up menu.

13.33

Filter: Brush Strokes: *Sumi-e*

This filter identifies areas of similar colors and blurs within those areas, preserving the edges between different colors. It then adds dark strokes over the edges and shadow areas at right diagonals. It is almost identical to the Dark Strokes filter. The difference is in the shape of the strokes—Dark Strokes uses fine strokes, while Sumi-e uses larger, roughly rectangular, blotches.

The Sumi-e Dialog Box

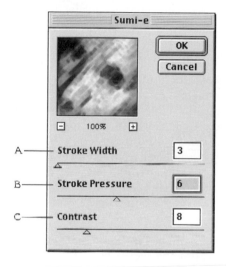

A. **Stroke Width** (3 to 15)

This setting controls the quantity and intensity of the semi-rectangular strokes. A value of three produces a few light gray strokes. A value of 15 produces many solid black strokes. In spite of the name of the setting, the actual width of the stroke changes little regardless of the setting.

B. **Stroke Pressure** (0 to 15)

This setting controls the darkness of the strokes. The higher the pressure, the darker the strokes. Stroke Width also increases and decreases the darkness of strokes.

C. **Contrast** (0 to 40)

This setting controls the darkening and lightening of colors in the original image. A value of 0 does not change values. Higher settings eliminate all detail, reducing the image to solid areas of black or very bright colors.

13.34

Filter: *Distort*

With the exception of Diffuse Glow, the Distort filters change the position of existing pixels without changing their color values. Some Distort filters emulate real-world effects, such as the appearance of an image reflected in rippling water or textured glass. They can also move pixels to match patterns in another image.

Issues to Consider

When the image layer does not contain a selection, most Distort filters move pixels into transparent areas. They also move transparency into vacated areas. Pixels can't be moved outside of an active selection, however, but transparency can still be moved into the selected area.

Some Distort filters base their effect from the center of the image or active selection. Examples of these filters include Twirl and Pinch. When there is no selection, the filter applies from the center of the canvas. When there is an active selection, the filter applies from the center of the selection. Selections can be used to position the center of the twirl. For example, to twirl an image layer from its upper right-hand corner, draw the selection so that the corner of the image layer is at the center of the selection, and the entire image layer is selected. This requires a selection marquee much larger than the target image, and may necessitate enlarging the canvas.

Some Distort filters base their effect on the height and width of the image or active selection. An example of this type of filter is Spherize. When no selection exists, the filter uses the height and width of the canvas. As with center distortions, use marquees larger than the image layer to position the distortion.

13.35

Filter: Distort: *Diffuse Glow*

This filter should be placed under the Artistic filters—it is not a Distort filter, because it does not move pixels, and has nothing in common with other Distort filters. Instead, it changes highlight areas to the background color. A light background color creates a glowing effect; a dark background color produces a grime layer over the image.

The Diffuse Glow Dialog Box

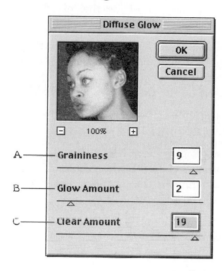

A. Graininess (0 to 10)

This setting determines whether the glow is a smooth haze or noise. A value of 0 produces a glow that is solid white over the highlight areas, and transitions smoothly to the non-highlighted areas. A value of 10 changes pixels randomly, adding monochrome noise over highlight areas.

B. Glow Amount (0 to 20)

This setting controls the range of colors identified as highlights that are replaced with the background color. A value of 0 produces no effect when the Graininess is also set to 0. A value of 0 with a Graininess of 1 or higher produces a light haze of noise evenly over the entire image, ignoring highlight values. Settings above 1 define a wider range of colors as the foreground color. At 20 the image fills with solid foreground color.

C. Clear Amount (0 to 20)

This setting determines to what extent non-highlighted areas of the image are filled with background color. A value of 20 produces no clearing. A value of 0 completely fills the image with the background color.

13.36

Filter: Distort: *Displace*

This filter distorts an image using the lightness values of another image (called the displacement map). One of the most useful Photoshop filters, it is vital for compositing images convincingly over texture, such as adding a shadow over rippling desert sands, or reflecting an image onto turbulent water.

Any image can be a displacement map, provided that the image is in RGB, CMYK, or Grayscale color mode, and if the image is saved in the native Photoshop format. The brightness values and color mode of the displacement map determine the distance and direction that pixels in the filtered image are moved.

When the displacement map is in Grayscale mode, black always moves pixels in the filtered image both down and to the right, and white always moves pixels up and to the left. If the displacement map is in RGB or CMYK Color mode, movement is based on the first two color channels:

- **The Red or Cyan channel.** Information in this channel controls horizontal movement. White in this channel moves pixels to the left, and black moves pixels to the right.

- **The Green or Magenta channel.** Information in this channel controls vertical movement. White in this channel moves pixels up, and black moves pixels down.

The end result of all this movement is that the image distorts to match the texture of the displacement map image.

The Displace Dialog Box

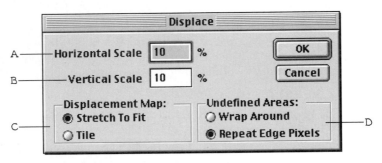

A. **Horizontal Scale** (–999% to 999%)

This setting controls the amount pixels move along the horizontal axis. At 100%, pixels move one pixel width for every level of brightness above or below neutral gray. At a 100% setting, pure white moves pixels to the right 127 pixel widths (128 subtracted from 255). The higher the setting, the farther pixels move. At 0, pixels do not move along this axis. Negative values move pixels in the opposite directions. Black moves pixels up and to the left instead of down and to the right and vice versa.

B. **Vertical Scale** (–999% to 999%)

This setting controls vertical movement using math identical to Horizontal Scale.

C. **Displacement Map**

When the pixel dimensions of the displacement map and the image differ, you must choose one of the following methods:

Stretch to Fit

This option resizes the displacement map while it is being applied to the proportions of the image.

Tile

This option repeats the displacement map to cover the entire image.

D. **Undefined Areas**

This option is only relevant when the filter is applied to a background layer. Pixel data must be generated to fill areas that can't be filled with transparency. The Undefined Areas options determine how this information is generated.

Wrap Around

This option fills in the empty areas with the pixels that were moved off the opposite edge of the displaced image.

Repeat Edge Pixels

This option duplicates pixels on the very edge of the image to fill in the empty areas. If the edge pixels are not one solid color, obvious streaking occurs as the filter repeats each pixel in a straight line out to the edge of the selection or canvas.

Filter: Distort: Glass

This filter distorts the image as though it were being viewed through textured glass. Similar to the Displace filter, it uses information from a second image to move pixels in the target image. The second image can be any of the four displacement maps built into the filter, or any file saved in the native Photoshop format. Unlike the Displace filter, there is far less control over how far the pixels are moved and in what direction. The Glass filter finds the edges of the displacement map, then duplicates pixels in the target image and moves them to match the edges of the displacement map.

Issues to Consider

The Glass filter does not automatically anti-alias displaced pixels. Anti-aliasing is done by the displacement map. If pixels in the displacement map are anti-aliased, the pixels it displaces will also be anti-aliased.

This filter does not wrap, repeat, or make any areas transparent when pixels are displaced. Instead, it fills the empty areas with the background color. Areas filled with the background color are not anti-aliased.

The Glass Dialog Box

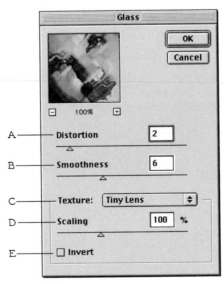

A. **Distortion** (0 to 20)

Distortion is the distance the filter offsets duplicated pixels from their original location. A value of 0 produces very little change. A value of 20 distorts the image heavily.

B. **Smoothness** (1 to 15)

Smoothness blurs the displacement map before applying the distortion. This produces distortions that occur gradually and over a wider area. Low settings produce extreme distortions. High settings produce more even distortions.

C. **Texture**

Textures are used as displacement maps to distort the image. The Glass filter comes with four built-in textures. Any image saved in the native Photoshop format can be selected as a displacement map by choosing Load Texture. An Open dialog box appears. Choose the Photoshop file and click OK.

D. **Scaling** (50% to 200%)

This setting controls the amount the displacement map is enlarged or reduced before displacing the target image. This creates a larger or smaller grain in the image.

E. **Invert**

Check the Invert box to invert the displacement map before distorting the image.

13.38

Filter: Distort: **Ocean Ripple**

This filter distorts an image according to the filter's built-in mathematics in order to create the impression that the image is under rippling water.

Issues to Consider

There is little to recommend about Ocean Ripple. It provides no control over the shape of the ripples, and it does a poor job of anti-aliasing the distorted image. To attain a quality ocean ripple effect, scan in a photograph of real ocean ripples, then use it as a displacement map for Distort: **Displace**, or use Distort: **Wave** or **Ripple**.

The Ocean Ripple Dialog Box

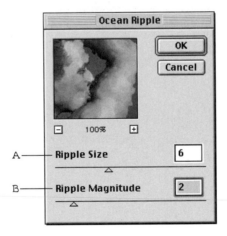

A. **Ripple Size** (1 to 15)

This controls the frequency of the ripples. The higher the number, the more ripples there are and the smaller they will be.

B. **Ripple Magnitude** (0 to 20)

This controls the amplitude of the ripples. The higher the amount, the greater the distortion.

13.39

Filter: Distort: *Pinch*

This filter shrinks or enlarges an image within a radius from the center of the filtered area. The size change diminishes farther from the center. At the edge of the affected area, there is no change at all. The effect makes the image appear to be sucking inward or swelling outward.

The Pinch Dialog Box

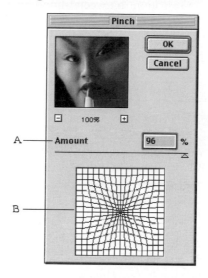

A. **Amount** (–100% to 100%)

This setting controls the amount the image pinches or swells. Settings below 0 bloat the image. Above 0, the image is pinched.

13.40

Filter: Distort: Polar Coordinates

This filter changes two-dimensional representations of three-dimensional spherical objects that distribute information according to the coordinates of the poles of the sphere. It is a very specific function: converting between Mercator projections (a method of displaying a map of the globe on a flat surface) to azimuthal equidistant projections (a method of applying a flat map onto the shape of a globe). In other words, these projections are different methods of translating information between three-dimensional and two dimensional space.

The Polar Coordinates Dialog Box

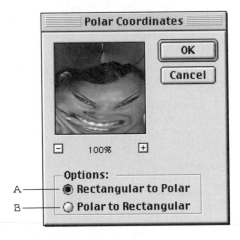

A. Rectangular to Polar

If the image is a Mercator projection, this option changes the image to an azimuthal equidistant projection. If the image is not a Mercator projection, the filter distorts the image. It takes the top of the image and compresses it to a single point in the middle of the selection, while stretching the bottom of the image in a circle until the left- and right-hand corners of the image meet. Then it redistributes all pixels proportionally.

B. Polar to Rectangular

If the image is an azimuthal equidistant projection, this option changes it to a Mercator projection. If the image is not a Mercator projection, the filter distorts the image. It takes the center pixel of the image and stretches it along the top of the rectangle. It pulls the left and right sides of the image down to form the bottom side, splits the center top-half of the image in two, and stretches the center out to form the new left- and right-hand sides of the image. Remaining pixels are distributed proportionally.

13.41

Filter: Distort: **Ripple**

This filter distorts an image to create the impression that the image is under rippling water.

Issues to Consider

For the most part, this filter is identical to Ocean Ripple. But there are three important differences:

- Ripples produced by this filter slant left, while Ocean Ripples are random.
- Ripple provides better anti-aliasing than the Ocean Ripple filter.
- The Ripple filter moves pixels into transparent areas and vice versa.

The Ripple Dialog Box

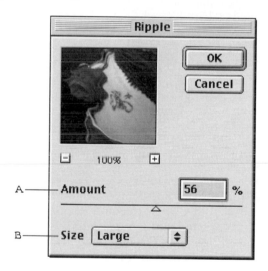

A. Amount (–999% to 999%)

This setting controls the amplitude of the ripples. A value of 0 produces no distortion; as the setting moves further from 0, the ripple size increases. The difference between positive and negative values is a slight shift in the ripple position (positive ripples go up-and-down, negative ripples go down-and-up).

B. Size (Small, Medium, or Large)

This setting controls the wavelength and frequency of ripples. The smaller the ripples, the more there are.

13.42

Filter: Distort: *Shear*

This filter distorts an image by pushing rows of pixels to the left or to the right along the horizontal axis.

Unlike most Distort filters, transparency won't be moved into an active selection by the Shear filter.

The Shear Dialog Box

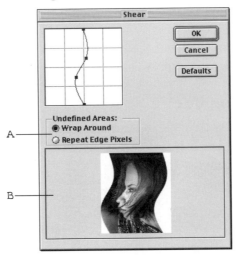

A. Distortion Grid

A grid with a line running vertically down the middle determines how the image is distorted. The line represents the center of the image. Distortion is controlled by dragging control points on the line. The line has control points on its top and bottom. Additional control points are added by clicking anywhere on the line. Drag the control points to the left or right to move the pixels at that relative height in that direction.

B. Undefined Areas

These options determine how empty areas left by displaced pixels are dealt with when transparency can't be moved into them. This happens inside active selections, and when pixels are moved at the edge of a background layer.

Wrap Around

This option puts the image information moved off the canvas on one side of the image or selection onto the opposite side.

Repeat Edge Pixels

For an unselected image layer, this cuts off any pixels moved off the canvas, but still allows transparency to be moved into the image. For a background layer or selected image, this removes pixels moved off the canvas or outside the selection, then fills the spaces with the sampled color of the edge pixels in a straight line to the edge.

13.43

Filter: Distort: Spherize

This filter makes a convex or concave distortion to the image, as though the image were reflected on the inside or the outside of a sphere. The distortion starts at the center of the selected area, and extends to its height and width. Spherize is very similar to Pinch. The only difference is that Pinch fades the amount of distortion as it gets to the edge, so the shrinking or enlarging blends with the image. Spherize increases distortion at the edges, creating a hemispheric appearance. Pinch is better suited for enlarging or shrinking parts of objects, while Spherize is best for turning objects into spheres.

Issues to Consider

Spherize creates hemispheres, based on the largest ellipse it can make within the selection. To avoid having unaffected areas within a selection, make the selection with an elliptical marquee.

The Spherize Dialog Box

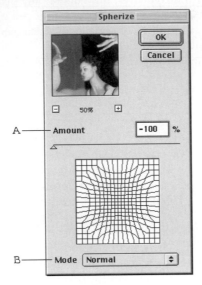

A. **Amount** (–100% to 100%)

This setting determines the amount of distortion. Negative values produce a concave sphere. Positive values produce a convex sphere. Settings of -100% and 100% produce a distortion equal to one hemisphere.

B. **Mode**

Normal distorts the image into the largest elliptical shape that can be fit within the selected area. Horizontal Only and Vertical Only distort the selected area along the horizontal or vertical axis, as if wrapping the image around a cylinder.

13.44

Filter: Distort: Twirl

This filter rotates the center of the selection while leaving the edges in place. The center of the image rotates the full amount specified by the Angle setting. The amount of rotation diminishes proportionally until it reaches the edge of the image.

The Twirl Dialog Box

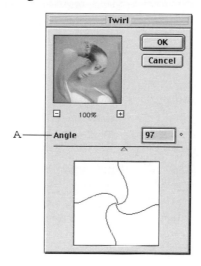

A. **Angle**

This setting ranges from –999° to 999°. This controls the number of degrees that the center rotates, and the direction of rotation. Negative values rotate the center counter-clockwise, while positive values rotate it clockwise. The center is rotated by the degree entered. A value of 999° rotates the center clockwise 2.775 times.

13.45

Filter: Distort: Wave

Similar to Ocean Ripple and Ripple, this filter distorts an image by rippling it as if it were beneath water. Wave provides much more control over the amount of variation between waves than Ocean Ripple or Ripple.

The Wave Dialog Box

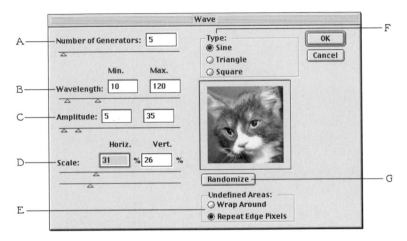

A. Number of Generators (1 to 999)

This setting controls the quantity of wave generators. A wave generator is anything that generates a wave, such as a rock thrown into the water. One or two wave generators is enough to produce substantial distortion; 999 creates waves as if produced by ultra-sonic noise.

B. Wavelength (Minimum: 1 to 999, Maximum: 1 to 999)

The Wavelength setting has two values: minimum and maximum. The length of the waves varies between these two values. The minimum setting controls how narrow the narrowest wavelengths will be. The maximum setting controls how wide the widest wavelengths will be. The wavelengths vary randomly between these two settings.

C. Amplitude (Minimum: 1 to 999, Maximum: 1 to 999)

Amplitude is the height of the waves. Like Wavelength, the amplitude setting has two values: minimum and maximum. The minimum setting controls how short the shortest wavelengths will be, and the maximum setting controls how tall the tallest wavelengths will be. The amplitudes vary randomly between these two settings

D. **Scale** (Horizontal: 0%; Vertical: 100%)

This setting reduces the total amount of distortion. At 100% the filter runs at the full settings. Lower percentages reduce the amount of distortion until at 0% the filter makes no change to the image.

E. **Undefined Areas**

These options determine how empty areas left when pixels are moved are dealt with when transparency can't be moved into them. This happens when pixels are moved at the edge of the canvas on a background layer.

Wrap Around

This option places the pixels moved off the canvas on one side to the opposite side of the image or selection.

Repeat Edge Pixels

For an unselected image layer, this cuts off any pixels moved off the canvas, but still allows transparency to be moved into the image. For a background layer or selected image, this removes pixels moved off the canvas or outside the selection, then fills the spaces with the sampled color of the edge pixels in a straight line to the edge.

F. **Type**

These options determine the shape of the waves:

Sine

This option produces the familiar sine wave, or bell-curve shape.

Triangle

This option produces jagged waves that move in straight diagonals.

Square

This option does not produce a wave form at all. The Square setting breaks the image into randomly sized rectangles. When Square is selected, the Amplitude setting controls the distance rectangles are moved from their original position. Unlike the Sine and Triangle setting, Square does not stretch pixels. It just moves them. Pixels maintain the same relative positions within the individual scales.

13.46

Filter: Distort: ZigZag

This filter ripples the image in concentric rings from the center, as if the image were underwater and a pebble were thrown into its center.

The ZigZag Dialog Box

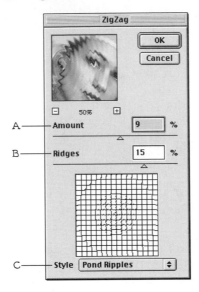

A. **Amount** (–100% to 100%)

This setting determines the amount of distortion the ripples create. The higher or lower the setting, the greater the distortion; 0 causes no distortion. Negative values produce crests where positive values produce troughs, and vice versa.

B. **Ridges** (1% to 20%)

This setting controls the quantity of ripples. The higher the percentage, the more ripples there are.

C. **Style**

These options produce ripple patterns of differing complexity.

Around Center

This option creates the simplest ripple pattern, producing ripples similar to those created by throwing a single pebble into still water; the rings are perfectly concentric, and the light source is directly overhead.

Pond Ripples

This option creates a slightly more complex pattern of ripple than Around center, as if the light source were moved off to the side, adding jagged distortions within the concentric circles.

Out from Center

This option creates ripples as if two pebbles were thrown into the pond very close together. Ripples emanate from a common center, but the concentric circles overlap each other in places, producing additional patterns of interference. This adds more jagged distortions to the image than Pond Ripples.

13.47
Filter: *Noise*

Noise is considered to be single stray pixels or small groups of pixels whose colors deviate noticeably from the colors of nearby pixels. The Noise filters are intended to create or eliminate this effect.

13.48

Filter: Noise: Add Noise

This filter randomly increases or decreases the color values of single pixels, adding noise to the image. At its lowest settings, it is useful for adding film grain to an image, or to prevent banding when using a large gradient in print.

The Add Noise Dialog Box

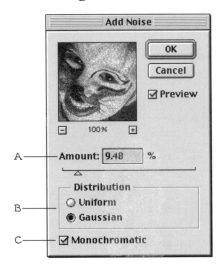

A. **Amount** (1 to 999)

This setting controls the range of the amount pixel colors are varied from their original color. At 255, the total amount of noise reaches a maximum. Pixels can possess any of the 16.7 million color values possible. However, enough pixels will remain similar to the original image to see a vague outline. Above 255 the quantity of noise can't increase, but the variation between the colors becomes more extreme. The higher the value, the more pixels will possess pure black, white, and the primary colors of whatever color mode the image is in. The lower the value below 255, the less noise there will be, and the more the original image is visible.

B. **Distribution**

These options determine how the noise is distributed over the image.

Uniform

This option spreads the noise randomly, but at the same density throughout the image, producing even randomness.

Gaussian

This option spreads the noise more randomly (using a Gaussian distribution, which is a mathematical theory that describes the "true" randomness occurring in nature). The Gaussian setting can produce single pixels of noise, clumps of noise, and areas of no noise.

C. Monochromatic

Check this box to produce noise that lightens or darkens existing pixels without changing their hue. At the highest setting, nearly all pixels will be black or white.

13.49

Filter: Noise: Despeckle

This filter reduces random light pixels, such as those resulting from grainy film, or dust on the scanner. It locates stray light pixels and very small groups of pixels, then fills them with the surrounding color.

Issues to Consider

Despeckle is a destructive filter. It destroys image data, resulting in a blurred, less detailed image and a narrowed tonal range. It provides no preview. It has no controllable settings, but arbitrarily decides what a "speckle" is. It should be used with caution; for example, apply it to individual channels instead of to all color channels at once.

Use the Smart Blur filter to remove film grain or other speckles. It provides both a preview and control over affected pixels, and is much less damaging than the Despeckle filter.

13.50

Filter: Noise: Dust & Scratches

This filter removes dust and scratches by blurring information over small or narrow areas of lighter or darker pixels. Unfortunately, the Dust & Scratches filter blurs the entire image as well, resulting in a less detailed, fuzzy image. This is only acceptable in situations where getting the job done quickly is more important than image quality. It is not a substitute for removing dust and scratches using the Clone tool.

Issues to Consider

Pay close attention to the image preview. The goal is to have the lowest Radius setting and the highest Threshold setting that still removes the dust and scratches you wish to remove. This produces the desired effect while retaining as much image information as possible.

The Dust and Scratches Dialog Box

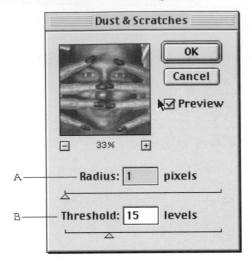

A. **Radius** (1 to 16)

This setting determines the size of the area considered to be dust or a scratch. A value of 1 will only affect single rows of pixels or solitary pixels. A value of 16 includes all areas of similar colors 16 pixels wide or less, that are different from the colors around them. The higher the setting, the blurrier the image will become overall.

B. **Threshold** (1 to 255)

This setting controls how much the color of the dust and scratches needs to vary from surrounding colors in order to be considered dust and scratches, and therefore become blurred. A value of 1 recognizes everything as a scratch, blurring the entire image. A value of 255 tolerates all color differences, producing no change.

13.51

Filter: Noise: Median

This filter eliminates noise by averaging pixel color values together. Unfortunately, this action is not restricted to noise. Even at its lowest setting, Median also eliminates detail information.

Issues to Consider

Median has little value in a production setting. As an artistic tool, it can produce interesting blurring effects different from Gaussian Blur because it's flatter and less detailed. The effect is more reminiscent of pastels than the Artistic: **Rough Pastels** filter.

The Median Dialog Box

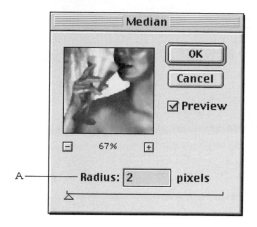

A. **Radius** (1 to 16)

This setting determines the number of pixels the filter will include when it averages pixels. With a Radius of 1, the filter only averages adjacent pixels. A value of 16 averages pixels within sixteen pixels of each other.

13.52

Filter: Pixelate

The Pixelate filters are intended for artistic purposes only. They work by breaking the image into shapes of solid color, generating heavily altered colors and destroying detail.

13.53

Filter: Pixelate: Color Halftone

This filter mimics the color halftone printing process. Halftone printing uses dots of CMYK ink. The dots vary in size to create tone, using smaller dots to create lighter colors and larger dots to create darker colors. Color Halftone recreates the image using dots of 100% values for each color channel. The dots are absurdly large. Real halftone dots can only be seen with the naked eye when you look very closely. The Color Halftone filter creates dots intentionally visible to the naked eye.

Issues to Consider

The Color Halftone filter works in RGB, Lab, and CMYK mode. However, a true color halftone emulation can only be created when the image is in CMYK mode, because color halftoning is a CMYK printing process.

The Color Halftone Dialog Box

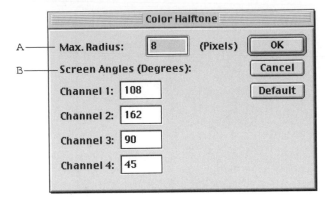

A. **Max. Radius** (4 to 127)

This setting determines the size, in pixels, of the largest halftone dot. A value of 4 produces dots visible to the naked eye. Settings above 20 look more like polka dots.

B. **Screen Angles** (0° to 360°)

In half-tone printing, screen angles are varied in order to avoid moiré patterns. In the Color Halftone filter, they are for strictly stylistic purposes. Color dots are placed in a separate grid pattern for each color. A separate setting exists to control the angle of each color channel. When the image is in RGB or Lab color mode, the setting for the fourth channel is ignored.

13.54

Filter: Pixelate: Crystallize

This filter converts the image into randomly shaped polygons of roughly the same size. The filter first defines the polygonal areas over the image. It then averages together the color values of pixels within those areas and fills them solidly with the averaged color.

The Crystallize Dialog Box

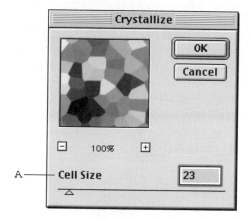

A. **Cell Size** (3 to 300)

This setting controls polygon size. At settings less than 10, the image is generally recognizable as the original image. At greater than 10, only a vague outline of the image remains. Greater than 20, the image consists solely of large, geometric shapes.

13.55

Filter: Pixelate: Facet

This one-step filter removes anti-aliasing from an image, as well as much image detail. It examines the image to find large colored areas. Then it replaces the anti-aliasing pixels between those colors, producing jagged, pixelated edges. This makes an image appear as though it were created using a primitive paint program such as Paintbrush or MacPaint, which were incapable of anti-aliasing.

13.56

Filter: Pixelate: Fragment

This one-step filter duplicates the image multiple times, reducing the opacity and offsetting the duplicated images in different directions. The resulting image appears to be vibrating.

Issues to Consider

Creating a controllable fragmenting effect. Duplicate the image layer multiple times using Layer: Duplicate Layer. Reduce the opacity of each layer using the Layers Palette, and offset them individually using the Move tool.

13.57

Filter: Pixelate: Mezzotint

Mezzotint is an artistic process that uses engraved metal plates to reproduce images. This filter bears little resemblance to this process, breaking the image into small groups of non–anti-aliased pixels over a white background. All color values are pushed to their absolute values. In an RGB image, blues are all converted to 255 in the blue channel, and 0 in the red and green channels. Reds are converted to 255 in the red channel, and so on.

The Mezzotint Dialog Box

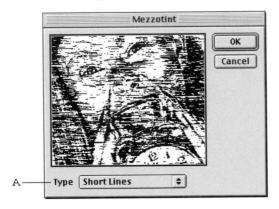

A. **Type**

The Type options control the shape and length of the colors that make the mezzotint pattern:

Fine, Medium, Grainy, or Coarse dots

Here, dots redraw the image in randomly sized and shaped groups of pixels.

Short, Medium, or Long lines

Here, lines are narrow, horizontal rows of pixels. The lines are of random length.

Short, Medium, or Long strokes

Here, strokes run horizontally, and are slightly wider than lines. Strokes are of random length.

13.58

Filter: Pixelate: Mosaic

Like images created with mosaic tiles, this filter recreates the image using nothing but squares of color. The filter places a grid over the image. It averages the colors within each square of the grid, then fills each square solidly with that color. The Mosaic filter is useful for obscuring parts of the image in a way that lets the viewer know that the area is deliberately hidden.

The Mosaic Dialog Box

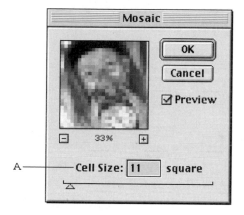

A. Cell Size

The Cell Size is the size, in pixels, of each square of the grid, and varies from 2 to 64. The higher the setting, the less recognizable the image.

13.59

Filter: Pixelate: Pointillize

Pointillism is an artistic technique popularized by such French impressionist painters as Georges Seurat. The technique creates images using points of pure color. Up close, the image appears to be nothing but points of color. From a distance, the points blend together and the image becomes apparent. This filter selects the image using many circles. The filter samples the color of the center pixel of each circle and fills the circle with that color. Each circle is offset slightly in a random direction. Areas around circles are filled with the background color.

The Pointillize Dialog Box

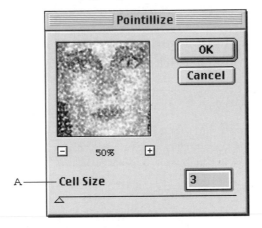

A. **Cell Size** (3 to 300)

This setting controls the diameter of the circles of color. This is roughly the pixel size of the points, though points vary slightly from each other. Higher settings require that the viewer be farther from the image in order for it to be recognizable. Settings higher than 50 generally produce images consisting of large, overlapping circles, with no discernible image. Settings from 3 to 6 create the most convincing recreations of the Pointillist technique.

13.60

Filter: Render

The Render filters add new information to the image based on the mathematics of the filter, rather than using data from the image itself. This data can be new detail placed over the existing image, such as the Clouds or Flare filters, or information altering the existing image, such as the Lighting Effects filter.

13.61

Filter: Render: 3-D Render

This filter is a rudimentary three-dimensional rendering program, allowing you to wrap an image around one or a series of simple shapes.

While capable of creating interesting effects, this toolset is quite limited, especially when compared to standalone rendering applications or more intensive third-party 3-D plug-ins:

- **You can only wrap images around simple outlines created within the filter's interface.** You can't import wireframes from other applications, nor can you use paths created with Photoshop's Pen tool. You can only use one or a combination of symmetrical shapes.

- **It doesn't affect the tonal values of the image it renders.** It won't darken or lighten pixels to create shadows and highlights. The image is simply distorted to match a particular shape.

- **The image only wraps around half of each wireframe.** When you rotate a shape more than 90°, its back side is filled with gray. When this happens, you must reposition the shape to conceal the inactive areas.

At its best, this filter is useful for creating simple distortions, or small specialized graphics such as buttons on a web page.

Issues to Consider

Duplicate the target Layer before applying this filter. 3-D Transform does not automatically place the results in a new layer—it only distorts the currently active layer. This poses three problems:

- You can no longer access the original image information.
- You can barely distinguish the resulting 3-D effect from the surrounding image pixels.
- It's considerably more difficult to edit the 3-D shape—for example, adding depth, isolating the result, or combining it with another image—when the shape doesn't exist in its own layer.

To place the new 3-D shape onto its own layer, duplicate the target layer before applying the filter. In the 3-D Transform dialog box, click the Options button and uncheck Display Background.

When applied to the background layer, this filter may introduce unwanted black pixels. If you apply this filter to the background layer after unchecking the Display Background option, the rendered shape is surrounded with black. This target color cannot be changed.

Use the filter's selection tools to move individual shapes. After drawing multiple shapes in the preview area, you can individually reposition them only along the X and Y axes (using the Selection tools). The Pan and Trackball tools will affect all shapes simultaneously.

Augment the 3-D effect with Layer Styles. To add depth and body to your 3-D shapes, use Layer Styles such as Inner Glow or Drop Shadow to apply simple highlights and shadows.

The 3-D Transform Dialog Box

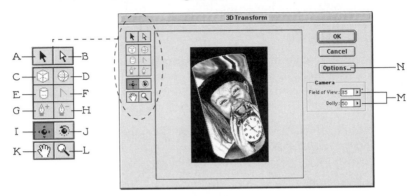

A. **Select Tool**   *Type "V"*

Use this tool to select and reposition existing shapes in the preview window. You cannot edit individual points.

B. **Direct Select Tool**   *Type "A"*

Use this tool to select, reposition, and edit existing shapes. To select, click anywhere on a segment or point.

When a shape is selected, it displays as bright green, and a series of vertex points appear around its contour. To reposition it, click-drag a segment and release. To edit the shape, click-drag a point. As long as the outline remains green, it can be rendered by the filter. If the shape turns red, it cannot exist in 3-D space, and the filter will have no effect.

Toggle between this tool and the Select tool by pressing (Command) [Control]-Tab. To temporarily select this tool while any other is selected, hold down the (Command) [Control] key.

C. **Cube Tool**   *Type "M"*

Click and drag with this tool to draw a six-sided cube. Initially, only three sides are visible—the image will only wrap around these sides. Over-rotating the shape using the Pan or Trackball tool will expose the rear sides, which fill with gray when you apply the filter.

D. **Sphere Tool**   *Type "N"*

Click and drag with this tool to draw a circular shape. The image will wrap around only its front face.

Two points appear around this shape—one on each side. Clicking and dragging one of them with the Direct Select tool only scales the shape—you cannot distort the sphere into an elliptical shape.

This tool is of limited use, because you cannot control the depth or intensity of the shape. If the effect you desire is simply to spherically distort part of an image, consider using the Elliptical Marquee tool to create a circular selection, choosing Layer: New: **Layer Via Copy** to copy its contents into a new layer, and then using Filter: Distort: **Spherize**.

E. Cylinder Tool   *Type "C"*

Click and drag with this tool to draw a cylindrical shape. The image will wrap around its front face and top end.

This shape is the most flexible, because you can add, delete, and further manipulate points along the outline. Editing a cylinder involves the following issues:

– Points can only be added to or deleted from the right-hand segment.

– Although new points are only added to one side, the edits are symmetrical. For example, when you place a point in the center of the segment then drag it to the center of the shape, the opposing segment mirrors the effect.

– Like the points that automatically appear when you draw a shape, the new points have no curve handles. Here, however, you can add smooth or corner points, as designated by the Convert Point tool.

– The point editing tools are only available when a cylindrical shape is selected.

F. Convert Point Tool

This tool can only be used on points that have been added using the Add Point tool. At first, these points are smooth, resulting in rounded connecting segments (these appear as a small circle). Convert these points to corner points by clicking once with this tool, which results in straight segments (these appear as a small diamond). Convert a corner point back to smooth by clicking again.

After converting a point, remember to choose the Direct Selection tool before continuing your edits. Otherwise, click-dragging will simply convert the point back to its previous form.

G. Add Point Tool   *Type "+"*

Add a point to the right-hand segment of a cylinder by clicking with this tool.

H. Delete Point Tool   *Type "-"*

Use this tool to delete any points that have been placed with the Add Point tool—it has no effect on the vertex points. When you delete a point, both sides of the shape reflect the change.

I. **Pan Tool** *Type "E"*

Use this tool to reposition the existing shapes in 3-D space. Unlike the simple linear repositioning offered by the Select tools, this effect is similar to moving a camera above, below, or to the side of a three-dimensional object.

When you select this tool, a simple rendering appears in the preview window.

J. **Trackball Tool** *Type "R"*

Use this tool to rotate a shape in 3-D space. You cannot define a different axis of rotation—you can only rotate around the center of the current shapes.

K. **Hand Tool** *Type "H"*

Use this tool to drag the image around, whenever it extends beyond the boundaries of the preview area. When the filter is first selected, the image (or the contents of the active selection) appears completely in the preview area, so this tool has no effect. As soon as you zoom in, you can manually scroll.

Temporarily access this tool by holding down the spacebar.

L. **Zoom Tool** *Type "Z"*

Click with this tool to zoom in. (Option) [Alt]-click to zoom out.

Temporarily access the Zoom In tool by holding down (Command) [Control]-spacebar. Access the Zoom Out tool by holding down (Option-Command) [Alt-Control]-spacebar.

M. **Camera**

These sliders act like different camera lenses, offering a degree of perspective to the rendered effects.

Field of View (1°–130°)

This control is similar to shooting an image with a wide-angle lens. It actually works in two separate stages:

When one of the select tools is active and wireframes are visible, this control affects vertical perspective. Low values simulate a high-angle view, higher values simulate a low-angle view.

When the Pan or Trackball tool is active and the preview is rendered, this control affects the amount of zoom. Low values zoom in, higher values zoom out.

Dolly (0–99)

This control is similar to a simple zoom lens, and is only available when the Pan or Trackball tool is active. Low values zoom in, higher values zoom out.

N. **Options**

Click this button to display the Options dialog box, which contains the following items:

Resolution

This pop-up menu controls the quality of the final rendered image. Low renders more quickly, but results in a poorer image. High offers the best quality, but takes considerably longer.

Anti-aliasing

This pop-up menu controls the level of anti-aliasing, or the edge-smoothing applied to the rendered shape. Although there are four choices, the only ones of any use are None, which may be desirable when creating certain web graphics, and High, which offers the best quality. The only time it makes sense to choose Low or Medium is when you want to preview the results on the actual image, before choosing Edit: **Undo**, setting the pop-up menu to High, and applying the filter for a final time.

Display Background

When this box is checked, the image pixels that are not wrapped around the 3-D shape remain after the filter is applied.

When the background layer is active and this box is unchecked, the rendered shape is surrounded by black pixels.

When an image layer is active and this box is unchecked, the rendered shape is surrounded by transparent pixels.

13.62

Filter: Render: *Clouds*

This one-step filter fills the selected area with clouds using the filter's own mathematics and the foreground and background colors. Data in the image does not influence the way the clouds are created, and the clouds completely replace the selected image.

Clouds and Difference Clouds are the only filters that can create new image information in an empty image layer.

13.63

Filter: Render: *Difference Clouds*

This filter generates clouds using its own mathematics and the foreground and background colors, just like the Clouds filter. Instead of replacing the selected image, however, Difference Clouds combines the clouds with the image using a Difference calculation.

Issues to Consider

To add a level of control to this effect, skip the Difference Clouds filter. Instead of using the Difference Clouds filter, apply the Clouds filter to an empty image layer. Then change the blend mode for the layer to Difference. This produces an effect identical to Difference Clouds, which enables you to continue adjusting the colors and layer contents.

13.64

Filter: Render: *Lens Flare*

Professional photographers take great pains to avoid lens flare, an accident in flash photography when too much light enters the lens and reflects off the various elements inside the lens. Using this filter, you can recreate these accidents.

Of all Photoshop filters, Lens Flare does the best job of emulating the traditional effect it is supposed to reproduce. Lens Flare is useful for creating starbursts and sunrises, and it can add a touch of realism to 3-D renderings by making the image appear to have been photographed rather than created on the computer.

For the best results, apply a lens flare to a layer filled with the neutral color of a blend mode. (For more information, see *11.8, Layer: New: **Layer**.*)

The Lens Flare Dialog Box

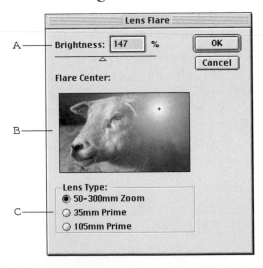

A. **Brightness** (10% to 300%)

This setting controls how bright the flare is, from a small flash at 10% to a blinding light that obliterates most of the image at 300%.

B. Flare Center

Use this option to position the center of the flare. Flare Center consists of a thumbnail of the selected image, a crosshair, and a preview of the flare. Position the crosshair to place the center of the flare on the image.

C. Lens Type

The difference among these options is primarily in refracted circles of light:

50–300mm Zoom

This option produces a greater number of smaller refractions.

35mm Prime

This option produces larger, darker refraction rings.

105mm Prime

This option produces a large, white flare with few refraction rings.

13.65

Filter: Render: *Lighting Effects*

This filter takes the lighting controls typically found in a 3-D modeling program and brings them into Photoshop. The Lighting Effects filter adds highlights and shadows, and shifts colors in the image as if there were light sources projecting onto the image. Up to 16 light sources can be added to the image.

Each light source can be one of three different styles of light and possess one of 16.7 million colors. There are ten additional settings that modify how each light source affects the image.

Lighting possibilities are virtually infinite, with effects ranging from subtle corrections to radical distortions. The filter can even use the lightness values of any color channel or mask channels to apply embossing effects.

Issues to Consider

Lighting Effects guidelines. The following items will assist you in using the Lighting Effects filter:

- The Lighting Effects filter only works on RGB images.

- For the best results, apply this filter to a layer filled with the neutral color of a blend mode.

- Shift-drag any control point to resize the light while preserving the current direction. (Command) [Control]-drag to change the direction while preserving the size.

- Duplicate a light by (Option) [Alt]-dragging it to a new location in the preview.

- Choosing a lighting style from the style submenu irretrievably eliminates any custom lights you have created unless they have been saved using the Save option located in the Style options.

The Lighting Effects Dialog Box

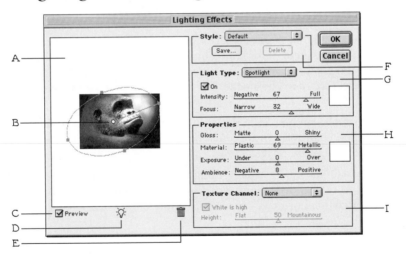

A. The Stage

The Stage previews the image, showing how the lighting will affect the image before the filter is applied. Lights are added, removed, and positioned on the stage.

Preview Image

The preview image shows the entire area of the image affected by the Lighting Effects filter. The image updates automatically every time lights or properties are changed, previewing how the image will look when the filter is applied.

Off Canvas

Lights can be placed off-canvas, represented by the white area surrounding the preview image. Lights placed off-canvas will be more diffused than those directly on the image.

B. Lights

Control the position of the light, as well as the size and shape of the area affected by the light, by clicking on the light's control points on the stage. Lights are represented by open circles filled with the color of the individual light. To make changes to the light, you must make it active by clicking on it. When the light is active, its control points are shown. There are three different styles of control points, corresponding to the item set in the Light Type submenu.

Directional

This type of light consists of a single control point with a line connecting it to the light. The distance between the control point and the light controls the intensity of the Directional light. The position of the light does not matter when there is no texture selected in the Texture Channel submenu. When no texture is selected, Directional lights light the image evenly. When a texture is selected, the direction the line makes from the control point to the light determines the direction of the highlights and shadows in the image.

Omni

When an Omni light is selected, there are four control points connected by a perfect circle around the light. Dragging any of these control points increases or decreases the radius of the Omni light. Omni lights are always circular, so their directions can't be changed.

Spot

The four Spot light control points are arranged in an ellipse, with a line from one control point to the light point. This line represents the direction of the Spot light. The control point at the end of the line represents the outside edge of the light. Change the direction and distance by dragging this point. Drag the adjacent control points to increase the width of the beam of light.

C. Preview

Click this button off to stop the lights from previewing. The unaltered image preview still appears, as do the light points, but changes are not previewed. This can speed up working with the filter on slower computers.

D. New Light

Click and drag from the light bulb at the bottom center of the stage to add additional lights. New lights are always small, white spotlights. After adding the light, change to a different type of light using the Light Type settings.

E. **Delete Light**

Drag any light to the trash can to permanently remove it.

F. **Style**

This section stores settings so that they can be reloaded. It includes a set of pre-saved lighting styles.

Style

This pop-up menu contains all lighting styles that came pre-saved with the program, and any additional styles you add. Choose any Style to load it, replacing any lights and their settings with the saved lights and settings.

Save

Save allows you to save the placement and settings of all lights on the stage as a Style. Reload saved settings using the Style submenu.

Delete

Choosing the Delete option permanently removes the currently selected Style from the Style submenu.

G. **Light Type**

These options control the individual lights on the stage. Set the brightness, color, and shape of the light here. Settings only apply to the currently selected light. There are five settings:

Light Type

This option determines the nature of the light.

Directional provides an even light to the entire image, as if from the sun or another distant, bright light source.

Omni creates a circular, omni-directional light, as if from a bare light bulb held close to the image.

Spot emulates a spot light, a projected beam of light that can be focused intensely on a single spot or widened into a broad beam.

Color

Clicking on the color square opens the default color picker. Here you can specify the color of the light.

On

Turn lights on or off individually using the On checkbox. This lets you eliminate the effects of a light without permanently removing it.

Intensity (−100 to 100)

This option controls how bright the light is. Unlike lights in real life, this filter can also absorb light. At 0, the light produces no light. If there are no other lights and Ambience is set to 0, the image will be black. Negative values darken the image. The lower the setting, the more the light absorbs other light. Positive values produce light. The higher the setting, the brighter the light.

Focus (Narrow: −100 to Wide: 100)

> This option only appears when Spot light is selected. The area a Spot light potentially affects is defined by its control points. The Focus setting determines how much of that area is actually changed by the light. A Narrow setting produces a small circle of light. A Wide setting affects all pixels within the control points.

H. Properties

These options control the way the image reflects light. They have a greater impact on the appearance of the filtered image when a texture is selected in the Texture Channel submenu. Properties apply to the entire image, not to individually selected lights.

Gloss (Matte: −100 to Gloss: 100)

> This option sets reflectivity of the surface. Matte is still reflective, but produces less overall lightening than Gloss. Matte preserves more detail information than Gloss. Gloss produces the most lightening, but can also eliminate much of the detail of the image.

Material (Plastic: −100 to Metallic: 100)

> This option affects the highlight areas, darkening or lightening the brightest areas of the image. Plastic produces the brightest highlights.

Exposure (Under: −100 to Over: 100)

> This option is virtually identical to Intensity, but it affects all lights simultaneously, not just the active light. A value of -100 produces a solid black image. A value of 100 makes all lights intensely bright.

Ambience (Negative. −100 to Positive: 100)

> This option lightens or darkens all pixels in the image with an even, non-directional light that produces no shadows. Pixels are lightened or darkened regardless of whether they are directly lit by lights.

Color

> Clicking on the Color square opens the default color picker. Here you can specify the color of the ambient light.

I. Texture Channel

Using Texture Channel, you can add texture and embossing to the image. Texture is based on the information in a color channel or mask channel within the image. The filter uses the channel's lightness values to add highlights and shadows to the image.

Texture Channel

> This submenu lists each color channel, the layer transparency, and all mask channels in the image. Select the channel to use as the texture channel from this menu. Choose "None" to prevent adding texture to the image.

White is high

When this option is selected, highlights are added where the texture channel is lightest, and shadows are added where the channel is darkest. When unselected, the opposite occurs.

Height (0 to 100)

This setting determines the amount of shading and highlighting added to the image by the texture channel. A value of 0 adds no extra highlighting or shading. A value of 100 creates a highly three-dimensional image.

13.66

Filter: Render: Texture Fill

This filter is designed to complement the Lighting Effects filter. In order to be used as a Texture Channel in the Lighting Effects Filter, textures must exist as channels in the image. Use Texture Fill to import a Grayscale image into a mask channel. Use this filter *before* running the Lighting Effects filter.

13.67

Filter: Sharpen

Sharpening is the opposite of blurring. Where the Blur filters make the colors of adjacent pixels more similar, the Sharpen filters increase the differences. This creates the impression that the image is more in focus and detailed.

The Sharpen filters can compensate for the loss of detail occurring when images are resized, rotated, or adjusted. They can also improve images that were scanned on a non-production–level scanner, or were scanned from out-of-focus photographs.

Issues to Consider

Sharpen filters only create the illusion of restored detail. After detail information has been lost through resizing or other adjustments to the image, it can't be restored. The Sharpen filters can restore the overall range of colors, but not the precise detail information.

13.68

Filter: Sharpen: Sharpen

This filter slightly increases the differences between the colors of adjacent pixels. This can be useful for removing the slight haze commonly associated with images scanned on low-end flatbed scanners.

Issues to Consider

Only consider this filter when you require the slightest amount of sharpening. Because there is no preview and no way to control the amount of sharpening, this filter is of limited use in a production environment.

13.69

Filter: Sharpen: Sharpen Edges

This filter identifies the larger areas of similar colors of pixels in an image and isolates the edges between these colored areas. It then increases the color differences between the edges.

Issues to Consider

Only consider this filter when you require the slightest amount of sharpening. Because there is no preview and no way to control the amount of sharpening, this filter is of limited use in a production environment.

13.70

Filter: Sharpen: Sharpen More

This filter sharpens the image approximately three times more than the Sharpen filter.

Issues to Consider

Unlike the Sharpen and Sharpen Edges filters, this filter produces a substantial difference in the image. There is no preview and no way to control the amount of sharpening. Additionally, the filter produces harsh and unrealistic sharpening. Use Sharpen: **Unsharp Mask** whenever more than a minute amount of sharpening is desired.

13.71

Filter: Sharpen: *Unsharp Mask*

This filter helps compensate for lack of detail, or blurriness, in an image by increasing the color differences between pixels. Unlike other Sharpen filters, Unsharp Mask allows you to precisely adjust the amount of sharpening. The effects can be restrained to edges, or applied evenly to the entire image. The effects can also be restrained within a range of color differences.

The Unsharp Mask filter duplicates the image and applies a Gaussian Blur to it. This second image is never visible, but is used as a mask that protects and exposes certain areas of the image.

The filter compares the original and the blurred image. The differences between the two images determine the amount of sharpening applied to each pixel in the image. The greatest amount of sharpening occurs where the two images are most different. Little sharpening occurs in areas that are most similar.

Issues to Consider

The Unsharp Mask dialog box provides a dynamic full-image preview. To take full advantage of it, view images at 100%, or Actual Pixels. This is the most accurate representation of the image on screen. Other view proportions can blur the preview image and lead to over-sharpening.

A potential adverse effect of the Unsharp Mask filter is artifacting. This occurs when the Amount value is set too high, resulting in pixels that stand out as obviously different from surrounding areas. When this happens, decrease the Amount value.

Another adverse effect is haloing, which appears when the Radius value is set too low. This results in a ring of noticeably light pixels around dark areas. Sharpening happens intensely around the edges, and the pixels don't blend with the rest of the image. Increasing the Radius spreads the sharpening farther into the image, allowing it to blend with the unsharpened areas of the image.

The Unsharp Mask Dialog Box

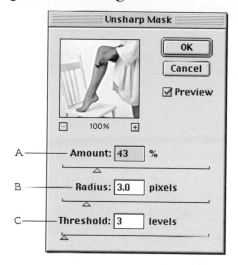

A. **Amount** (1% to 500%)

This setting determines the amount pixels are lightened or darkened. No pixel in an image will be sharpened by that precise amount, however. The exact amount of sharpening varies from pixel to pixel, and is affected by the Radius and Threshold settings.

The total amount of sharpening an image needs depends on the size and the content of the image. An image with a higher resolution may require a higher Amount setting than the same image at a lower resolution, because the effects of the filter are spread out over a wider range of pixels. Images with crisp details will require little or no sharpening.

B. **Radius** (0.1 to 250 pixels)

This setting controls the amount of blurring applied to the mask image. Low settings produce an image that is substantially different from the original image only along the edges. This sharpens edges the most, while areas in the original image where colors are similar are sharpened little. At high settings, the entire mask image differs from the original image, and sharpening occurs more evenly throughout the image.

C. **Threshold** (0 to 255 levels)

This setting constrains sharpening to pixels differing from each other above a certain level. Only pixels differing in color value from adjacent pixels by the Threshold amount or higher are sharpened. A value of 0 sharpens everything. A value of 255 prevents all sharpening.

Raising the Threshold level is useful to protect tones you don't want sharpened. Film grain, for example, consists of small patches of pixels that differ slightly from surrounding pixels. Sharpening film grain with a low Threshold setting turns the subtle grain into unwanted texture.

Similarly, sharpening areas of subtle tonal change, such as flesh tones, can destroy the subtle changes and create banding. Increasing the Threshold level protects such areas.

13.72

Filter: Sketch

The Sketch filters primarily emulate sketching techniques, creating rough outlines of the image using little detail and few colors. Most Sketch filters reduce all colors in an image to shades of the foreground and background colors.

While they work with any value as the foreground and background colors, the filters produce the most realistic results when these colors are set to the default black and white. Because the Sketch filters use such a limited range of specifiable colors, they are more controllable and predictable than the Artistic or Brush Strokes filters.

Issues to Consider

Set the foreground or the background to a neutral blend mode color, and apply a Sketch filter to an image layer. When the layer is set to the blend mode, the neutral color becomes transparent, leaving just the lines of the other color over the underlying image information.

13.73

Filter: Sketch: Bas Relief

Bas Relief is a technique of sculpting figures nearly flat to the surface from which they are created . This filter attempts to recreate the three-dimensional bas relief feel by reducing the image to shades of the foreground and background colors, then adding highlight and shadow detail to create a three-dimensional feel. It identifies areas of similar colored pixels, then performs an action similar to the Image: Adjust: **Threshold** command. Areas change to the foreground or the background color, depending on their lightness values and the Light Direction setting.

The Bas Relief Dialog Box

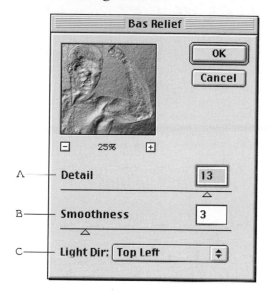

A. Detail (1 to 15)

Detail sets the amount pixels need to differ from each other to be considered an area. At low settings, pixels must differ from each other substantially in order to be considered separate colored areas. This produces an image consisting of a few large areas of foreground and background colors, with very little detail. Higher settings identify more areas, producing a more detailed and more recognizable image.

B. Smoothness (1 to 15)

Smoothness controls the amount of blurring done to the image after it is converted to the foreground and background colors. A value of 1 produces no blurring. At this setting all pixels in the image consist of the foreground or background color, except for anti-aliased pixels. At higher settings, the foreground and background colors blur together, eliminating detail information.

C. Light Dir

This option determines whether areas are assigned the foreground color or the background color. The filter assumes that the foreground color is lighter than the background color. Colors are assigned so that the image appears to be lit from the specified Light Direction.

Filter: Sketch: *Chalk & Charcoal*

This filter reproduces the image as though it were created using chalk and charcoal on gray construction paper. The filter uses the foreground color as Charcoal and the background color as Chalk. All Chalk strokes travel at a right diagonal, while all Charcoal strokes are made at a left diagonal. The textures of the strokes differ, emulating the media they represent. Chalk marks appear thick and powdery. Charcoal marks are rough and flat. Highlight areas are stroked with Chalk. Shadow areas are stroked with Charcoal. Mid-tone areas become neutral gray.

The Chalk & Charcoal Dialog Box

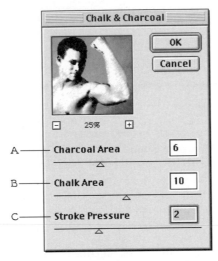

A. **Charcoal Area** (0 to 20)

This setting controls the range of color values considered to be shadow areas and stroked with Charcoal. The higher the number, the wider the range. At 0, only the darkest colors in the original image receive Charcoal strokes. At 20, all pixels darker than 50% are given a Charcoal stroke.

B. **Chalk Area** (0 to 20)

This setting controls the range of pixel colors considered highlight areas. The higher the number, the wider the range of colors. At 0, only the lightest colors in the original image receive Chalk strokes. At 20, all pixels lighter than 50% are given a Chalk stroke. When Charcoal Area and Chalk Area are both set to 20, there is no neutral gray in the image.

C. **Stroke Pressure** (0 to 5)

This setting controls the intensity of the color of the Chalk and Charcoal strokes. Settings of 0 and 1 produce rough, textured strokes, creating the most realistic chalk and charcoal feel. Settings higher than 1 produce solid strokes with no texture.

13.75

Filter: Sketch: Charcoal

This filter reproduces the image as though it were rendered with charcoal on paper. It uses the foreground color as the charcoal color and the background color as the paper color. Shadow information in the image receives charcoal strokes. Strokes are rough, irregularly sized, and always at a right diagonal. Midtone and highlight information are filled with the background color.

The Charcoal Dialog Box

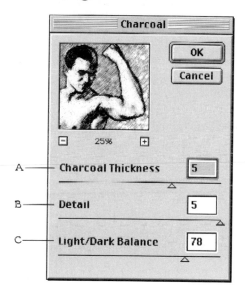

A. **Charcoal Thickness** (1 to 7)

This setting controls the stroke thickness: A value of 1 produces narrow strokes; a value of 7 produces wide strokes.

B. **Detail** (0 to 5)

Detail sets the range of colors defined as shadows and stroked with charcoal. A value of 1 defines only the darkest pixels as shadows. A value of 5 increases the range a little, but not substantially. Since highlight and midtone information convert to solid background color, it is generally best to leave the Detail setting at 5, so that there is enough information left to make the image recognizable.

C. **Light/Dark Balance** (0 to 100)

This setting controls the ratio of foreground to background color. At 0, the charcoal strokes appear very muted, blended with the background color throughout the image. At 100, most strokes consist of pure foreground color. A value of 50 produces a pleasing balance of dark and light charcoal strokes.

13.76
___

Filter: Sketch: Chrome

This filter recreates the image as though it were stamped into highly reflective metal. It does this by thoroughly distorting the image, blurring it, sharpening it, reducing the range of tones and converting it to Grayscale, until it appears to be made of bulging, shiny, silver metal.

The Chrome Dialog Box

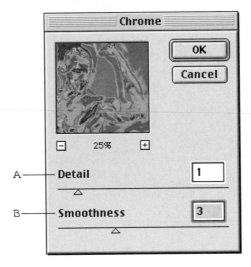

A. **Detail** (0 to 10)

Detail is the number of reflective surfaces the filter creates. The higher the number, the greater the amount of highlight and shadow areas.

B. **Smoothness** (0 to 10)

Smoothness controls the amount of midtone information between the shadows and highlights. At 0, the image consists of highlights and shadows with little midtone information to provide a transition between the two. At 10, there is much midtone information, and highlights and shadows are reduced, producing a much more fluid image.

13.77

Filter: Sketch: Conté Crayon

Conté crayons are hard, waxy, black or white sticks. This filter defines areas of similar colors and blurs within the areas, preserving the edge detail. Then it converts shadows to the foreground color, highlights to the background color, and midtones to neutral gray. The result is a soft-focused image with hard edges, much like conté crayons produce. It can also add texture to the image to create the impression that the image was created on textured paper.

The Conté Crayon Dialog Box

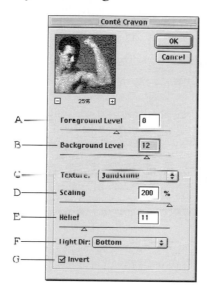

A. Foreground Level (1 to 15)

This setting controls the range of color values defined as shadow areas and stroked with the foreground color. The higher the number, the wider the range. At 1, only the darkest colors in the original image are stroked. At 15, all pixels darker than 50% in the original receive a conté crayon stroke.

B. Background Level (1 to 15)

This setting controls the range of color values defined as highlight areas and stroked with the background color. The higher the number, the wider the range. At 1, only the lightest colors in the original image are stroked. At 15, all pixels lighter than 50% are stroked. When both Foreground Level and Background Level are set to 15, there is no neutral gray in the image.

C. **Texture**

The lightness values of the texture are used for adding highlight and detail information. When "Load Selection" is selected, Photoshop prompts you to select a Photoshop file to use as a texture. The texture is tiled if it is smaller than the image, or cropped if it is larger than the image.

D. **Scaling** (50% to 200%)

This setting alters the size of the texture before it is applied to the image, from half its size to twice its size.

E. **Relief** (0 to 50)

This setting controls the amount of highlight and shadow the texture adds to the image. Highlight and shadow detail is based on highlights and shadows in the texture. A value of 0 adds no texture at all. A value of 50 makes most pixels solid black or white, destroying all tonal information and producing harsh, jagged, non–anti-aliased lines. Settings from 3 to 7 produce the most realistic texture.

F. **Light Dir**

This setting increases the shadows and highlights along the image detail at a specific angle, creating the appearance that the image is being lit from that direction.

G. **Invert**

Check the Invert box to invert the color values of the texture.

13.78

Filter: Sketch: Graphic Pen

This filter mimics images drawn with a Rapidograph-style pen. It only makes lines in one direction per image. All lines are single-pixel wide, non–anti-aliased lines. All lines are of roughly the same length as well.

The Graphic Pen uses the foreground color as the ink color, and the background color as the paper color. It strokes where shadow detail is in the original image. Midtones and highlights are filled with solid background color.

The Graphic Pen Dialog Box

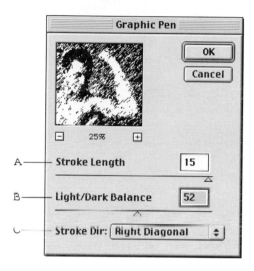

A. Stroke Length (1 to 15)

This setting determines the length of the pen stroke. A value of 1 produces single-pixel dots. A value of 15 produces short lines.

B. Light/Dark Balance (0 to 100)

This setting controls the range of colors defined as shadow and stroked. At 0, no shadows are defined, filling the image with solid background color. At 100, the entire range of colors is recognized as shadows, producing an image completely filled with the foreground color.

C. Stroke Dir

This setting determines the direction of the stroke marks.

13.79

Filter: Sketch: **Halftone Pattern**

This filter emulates the appearance of an image printed using halftone screens. The filter uses the foreground color as the ink color, and the background color as the paper color. It converts the image to two colors, using the foreground color to represent shadow and midtone information and the background color for highlight information.

The Halftone Pattern Dialog Box

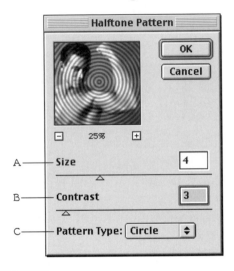

A. **Size** (1 to 12)

This option sets the size of the halftone pattern. A value of 0 applies fine lines or small dots. A value of 12 produces a large pattern that nearly obliterates the image.

B. **Contrast** (0 to 50)

This setting controls the amount of midtone information in the image. The higher the setting, the greater the number of pixels of pure foreground or background colors. At 0, the image emulates a tonal range similar to the original image. At 50, the image will be 100% foreground and background colors, with no midtone values.

C. **Pattern Type**

This setting determines the shape of the simulated screen:

Circle

This option produces a pattern of concentric circles starting at the center of the selected area.

Dot

This option produces a pattern similar to the traditional halftone screen.

Line

This option reproduces the image as a horizontal line pattern.

13.80

Filter: Sketch: Note Paper

This filter attempts to produce the appearance of an image sketched onto highly textured paper. Similar to Image: Adjust: **Threshold**, it converts all colors to foreground or background colors based on brightness values. It applies paper texture and embosses the image to create the impression that the image has been stamped into paper.

The Note Paper Dialog Box

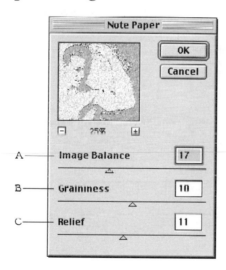

A. **Image Balance** (0 to 50)

This setting determines the point at which pixels change into foreground or background color. At 0, the entire image fills with the background color. At 50, the entire image fills with the foreground color. At 25, pixels with lightness values greater than 50% are filled with foreground color, and less than 50% with background color.

B. **Graininess** (0 to 20)

This setting controls the amount of simulated paper texture added to the image. A value of 0 adds no paper texture. A value of 20 adds rough texture over the entire image.

C. **Relief** (0 to 25)

This setting determines the number of black lines added to edges where foreground and background colors meet, and how much Graininess is darkened. A value of 0 adds no black lines. A value of 25 adds thick black lines.

13.81

Filter: Sketch: Photocopy

This filter makes the image appear as if it were photocopied. The foreground color is used as the toner color, and the background color is the paper color. The filter converts shadow and midtone information to the foreground color, and uses the background color for the highlights. Like a true photocopier, it also eliminates most detail.

The Photocopy Dialog Box

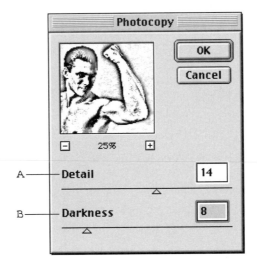

A. **Detail** (1 to 24)

This setting determines the amount of detail information the filter retains from the original image. The higher the setting, the more detail. At 24, the image retains much shadow and midtone detail, but changes highlights to solid background color. At 0, only thin edge outlines remain of the darkest areas of the image.

B. **Darkness** (1 to 50)

This setting emulates a photocopier's darkness setting. It controls how much toner (foreground color) replaces the detail information. A value of 1 produces a very light image. At 50, all lines are solid foreground color.

13.82

Filter: Sketch: *Plaster*

If wet plaster spilled on the ground and miraculously puddled in the shape of an image, it might look something like the results of this filter. It finds the major edges in the image, eliminating all detail information except for the shadows, which it fills with the foreground color. The remainder of the image is filled with the background color. It adds highlight and shadows around the edges, creating a loosely three-dimensional liquid impression. Finally, it runs a gradient across the background-colored areas. The gradient starts with the background color and ends with the foreground color.

The Plaster Dialog Box

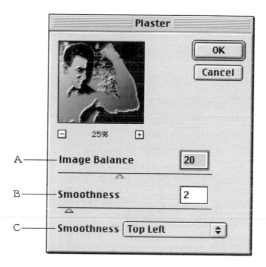

A. **Image Balance** (0 to 50)

This setting determines what is defined as shadow and filled with foreground color. At 50, the image fills solidly with the foreground color. At 0, the image is filled with the gradient. Recognizable images fall between the two values.

B. **Smoothness** (1 to 15)

This setting determines how closely the filter follows the edges of the image. The filter degrades the image so much, however, that a value of 1 differs little from a value of 15.

C. **Light Position/Smoothness**

Mistakenly labelled "Smoothness" on the Mac version of Photoshop 6, this pop-up enables you to establish the relative position of the light source. Highlights and shadows are added to the image to create the appearance of being lit from the direction set in this pop-up menu. Also, the gradient is drawn starting with the background color from the direction of the established position.

13.83

Filter: Sketch: **Reticulation**

Artistic reticulation represents images using web-like crisscrossing often seen in traditional Celtic art. This filter has nothing in common with reticulation, however. It makes the image appear as if it were printed with India ink on crepe paper: very distorted, textured, and with little detail information from the original image. It converts shadows to the foreground color, converts highlights and midtones to the background color, and applies texture according to mathematics built into the filter.

The Reticulation Dialog Box

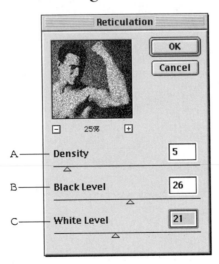

A. **Density** (0 to 50)

This setting controls the amount of texture added to the image. At 0, the image is created primarily with shades of the foreground color, and there is no texture. At 50, highlight areas are filled solidly with background color, and there is no texture. At settings between 0 and 50, the image is highly textured over all areas. The lower the setting, the greater the amount of foreground color appearing in the texture.

B. **Black Level** (0 to 50)

This setting determines the amount the foreground color blends with the background color. At lower settings, there is more background color texture in areas that are primarily foreground colors.

C. **White Level** (0 to 50)

This setting determines the amount the background color blends with the foreground color. At lower settings, there is more foreground color texture in areas that are primarily background colors.

13.84

Filter: Sketch: Stamp

This filter produces a fairly accurate reproduction of an image created with a rubber stamp. Stamp uses the foreground color as the ink color and the background color as the paper color. The filter finds edges and strokes them with the foreground color. Dark colors convert to the ink color, and light colors to the background color, with no tonal variation in between.

The Stamp Dialog Box

A. **Light/Dark Balance** (0 to 50)

This setting determines the threshold where dark colors become the foreground color and light colors become the background color. At 0, the entire image fills with solid background color. At 50, the entire image fills with solid foreground color. At 25, pixels darker than 50% change to the foreground color; pixels lighter than 50% become the background color.

B. **Smoothness** (1 to 50)

Smoothness is the amount of blurring done to the image before colors are changed. The higher the smoothness, the simpler the final image. A value of 1 typically produces the most realistic rubber stamp emulation.

13.85

Filter: Sketch: Torn Edges

This filter is similar to the Cutout filter, in that it recreates the image as though it were made from torn paper–however, it uses a single paper color. Colors are converted to the foreground or background color, then texture is applied to the edges to create a torn paper appearance.

The Torn Edges Dialog Box

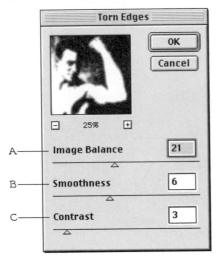

A. Image Balance (0 to 50)

This setting determines the threshold at which colors are changed to the foreground or background color, based on their lightness value. At 0, the image fills with background color. At 50, the image fills with foreground color. At 25, pixels darker than 50% become foreground color, while pixels lighter than 50% become background color.

B. Smoothness (1 to 15)

This setting controls the amount of texture applied to the edges. A value of 1 is the maximum amount of texture, reducing narrower lines to patches of rough texture over the background color. At 15, no roughening occurs, producing solid, non–anti-aliased areas of foreground or background color.

C. Contrast (1 to 25)

This setting determines the amount of difference between colors in the final image. At 25, all pixels are pure foreground or background color. At 1, blending occurs between the two colors.

13.86

Filter: Sketch: Water Paper

Traditional water paper technique involves soaking paper in water before painting on it with water color paints. Colors bleed together, and puddle into the grain of the paper because the paper itself can't absorb the paint. This filter produces a fairly convincing water paper emulation. It blurs the image in the direction of the paper grain, as if the colors ran along the paper grain before they dried. Brightness and contrast of the image can also be adjusted through the filter.

The Water Paper Dialog Box

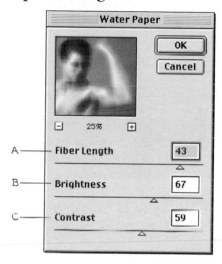

A. **Fiber Length** (3 to 50)

This setting controls the amount of blurring in the direction of the paper grain. A value of 3 produces slight mottling, while a value of 50 produces a greatly crosshatched image, as if paint were applied to a window screen instead of to textured paper. Values between 5 and 10 produce the most realistic water paper emulation.

B. **Brightness** (0 to 100)

This setting controls the amount pixels are brightened or darkened. A value of 0 darkens the entire image to black. A value of 100 brightens most pixels to white. Values between 50 and 60 come close to the brightness of the original image.

C. **Contrast** (0 to 100)

This setting increases or decreases the differences between colors in the image. At 0, colors are very close to the average of all colors in the image. At 100, color variations are extreme, anti-aliasing is totally eliminated, and many colors become totally black or white.

13.87

Filter: Stylize

With the exception of Solarize and Emboss, the Stylize filters do not attempt to emulate traditional artistic methods or styles. They create a very computer-generated feel.

13.88

Filter: Stylize: Diffuse

Diffuse randomly duplicates and offsets single pixels without changing their color values. The result is noise based only on colors that already exist in the image.

The Diffuse Dialog Box

A. **Normal**
Normal duplicates and offsets pixels randomly.

B. **Darken Only**
Darken Only duplicates and offsets pixels randomly, but only pixels lighter than the offset pixels are replaced.

C. **Lighten Only**
Lighten Only duplicates and offsets pixels randomly, but only pixels darker than the offset pixels are replaced.

13.89

Filter: Stylize: *Emboss*

This filter is a pre-filter used to prepare images for simulating the effect of pressing a three-dimensional shape into a flat surface. Embossed images are created in two ways:

- **Displacement Maps.** Emboss creates displacement maps to be used by Filter: Distort: **Displace**. That filter uses the neutral gray, black, white, red, and green colors into which Emboss converts an image to move pixels in specific directions. When used as a displacement map by the Displace filter, pixels are moved such that the final image appears to have the embossed image pressed into it.

- **Image Layers.** When the blend mode of an embossed image layer is set to Overlay, Hard Light, or Soft Light, it becomes transparent except for highlight and shadow detail. This creates the appearance that the image has been embossed into underlying layers.

Issues to Consider

If desired, eliminate the extra colors added by the filter. After applying Emboss to an image layer, use Image: Adjust: **Desaturate** to remove the red and green details the filter adds strictly for use in the Displace filter.

The Emboss Dialog Box

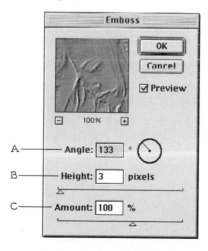

A. **Angle** (−180° to 180°)

Angle controls the direction of the highlights and shadows. Highlights are added around edges from the direction the light is coming. Shadows are added to the opposite edges.

B. **Height** (1 to 10)

This setting emulates the amount of force with which the image is embossed. The higher the setting, the greater the amount of shadows and highlight detail.

C. **Amount** (1% to 500%)

This setting controls the number of edges the filter finds. A value of 1% finds no edges in the image, and converts it to neutral gray. Higher settings define smaller and smaller colored areas as being different. The most realistic embossing effects happen between 100% and 200%.

13.90

Filter: Stylize: Extrude

This filter makes an image appear to be created using blocks or pyramids. The cubes or pyramids appear to project outward from the image, like an aerial view of a city.

When blocks are extruded, the image is defined as a grid, then squares are offset in different directions. Lines are drawn from the corners of the squares to their original location to define the sides of the cubes. The sides are then filled with color. The surface of the cube can be the offset image, or an average of the colors inside each square.

When extruding pyramids, the filter again defines a grid over the image, then creates a pyramid shape within each grid, using the averaged colors of the pixels in the original image.

Issues to Consider

Extrude is not available if an image layer is active *and* a selection outline is present. It will function within an active selection on the background layer, and it will also function on an active image layer if there is no active selection.

The Extrude Dialog Box

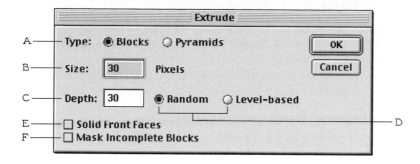

A. Type

This option determines whether the image will be extruded as blocks or as pyramids.

B. Size (2 to 255)

This option specifies in pixels the width of the face of each block, or of the base of each pyramid.

C. Depth (1 to 255 pixels)

This option sets the outer limit for how far a block face is moved from its original location, or how long the longest pyramid edges are. The actual distances they are moved vary based on the extrusion method.

D. Extrusion Method

These options determine how the distance of the extrusion is calculated:

Random

This option randomly varies the distance the faces are moved or the height of the pyramids.

Level-based

This option varies the distance based on the average lightness values of the pixels within each face or pyramid.

E. Solid Front Faces

Check this box to fill each face with the average color value for all pixels within that square, instead of using the image. This option is only available when Blocks are selected as the Type. When Pyramids is selected, the side of each pyramid is filled automatically with the average color value.

F. Mask Incomplete Blocks

When this option is checked, blocks or pyramids that would be extruded past the edges of the target area are not extruded. Pixel data in such areas is unchanged by the filter.

13.91

Filter: Stylize: *Find Edges*

This one-step filter outlines the edges between areas of similar colored pixels with lines that are the saturated color values of those pixels. Outlines are thick and solid when colors differ substantially, and are thin and light when there is little difference. Areas without edges are filled with white. The result is a highly stylized image that looks as though it has been outlined using colored pencils.

Issues to Consider

Find Edges is purely a special effect. You cannot control the number of edges it finds nor the thickness of the lines it traces. Glowing Edges performs functions identical to Find Edges, and has adjustable settings. That filter inverts the color values after tracing the edges, so if you choose Image: Adjust: **Invert** after applying it, you can simulate an adjustable Find Edges filter.

13.92

Filter: Stylize: *Glowing Edges*

This filter outlines the edges between areas of similarly colored pixels using lines of the saturated color values of those pixels. Outlines are thick and solid when colors differ substantially, and are thin and light when there is little difference. Areas without edges are filled with white. The filter then inverts the entire image. The resulting image looks as if it were created using colored neon lights.

The Glowing Edges Dialog Box

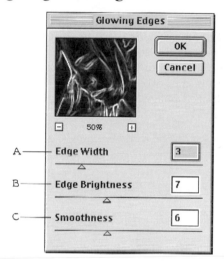

A. **Edge Width** (1 to 14)

This setting controls the line width of the edges that are traced. The widest lines are roughly double the pixel width of the setting.

B. **Edge Brightness** (0 to 20)

This setting controls how bright the lines are. At 0, all edges are completely black, producing a solid black image. At 20, edges glow brightly.

C. **Smoothness** (1 to 15)

Smoothness controls the number of edges the filter finds. A value of 1 finds the most edges, producing many edge lines. A value of 15 only traces the edges where colors vary the most, leaving the essential outlines of the image.

13.93

Filter: Stylize: *Solarize*

This filter is an homage to the Solarization technique popularized by Man Ray, who composited positive and negative film to achieve special effects. The Solarize filter inverts all color values above 128, or 50%.

Shadows and midtones below 50% are unchanged by the filter. Highlights become shadows, lighter midtones above 50% become darker midtones. Light colors become their opposites as well. Light magenta becomes dark green. Light blue becomes dark red. Dark colors are unchanged.

Issues to Consider

Man Ray rarely solarized an entire image. Instead, he would solarize a background, or part of the subject. For a most convincing solarizing effect, duplicate the image into another image layer. Solarize the duplicate, then composite the two by adding a layer mask and hiding portions of the solarized image. (See *11.65, Layer: **Add Layer Mask*** for more information.)

13.94

Filter: Stylize: *Tiles*

This filter breaks the image into squares, then randomly offsets them within a specified distance. It offers several options for filling the area of the image left empty when pixels are moved.

The Tiles Dialog Box

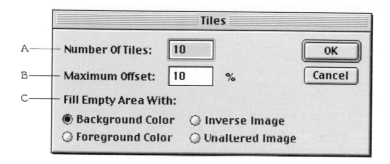

A. **Number of Tiles** (1 to 99)

This setting determines the number of full tiles per row. There can be any number of tiles per column. A partial tile may be added to allow the row to fill the entire width of the image.

B. **Maximum Offset** (1% to 99%)

This setting limits the maximum amount pixels can move from their original location. At 99%, any tile could be moved from 1% of its width to 99% of its width.

C. **Fill Empty Area With**

These options determine how areas of the image left empty when pixels are moved are dealt with.

Background Color

This option fills empty areas with the background color.

Foreground Color

This option fills empty areas with the foreground color.

Inverse Image

This option fills empty areas with the original image, inverted.

Unaltered Image

This option fills empty areas with the original image.

13.95

Filter: Stylize: Trace Contour

This filter finds edges between specific lightness values. For example, when a value of 150 is entered, the filter places a black (0 or 100% K) pixel between every point in the image where pixels darker than 150 are next to pixels lighter than 150. It does this for each color channel separately, then fills the image with white wherever no pixels are added. Because pixels are added in individual channels, the result is an image defined in pure cyan, magenta, and yellow. In CMYK images, black is used. The result is an image defined by single color, single pixel-width, non–anti-aliased lines over a white background.

Issues to Consider

The effects of Trace Contour are very different when the image is in Lab mode. Because lightness values occupy a separate channel, Trace Contour produces black lines over the image's color information.

The Trace Contour Dialog Box

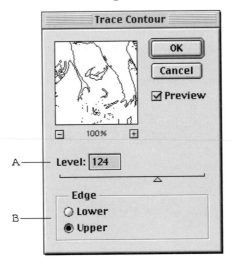

A. **Level** (0 to 255)

This value sets the lightness value that the filter finds edges around.

B. **Edge** (Lower or Upper)

This option specifies the side of the pixel edge to trace. Lower traces the darker side of the edge, Upper traces the lighter side.

13.96

Filter: Stylize: *Wind*

This filter randomly shifts entire rows of pixels to either the left or right.

The Wind Dialog Box

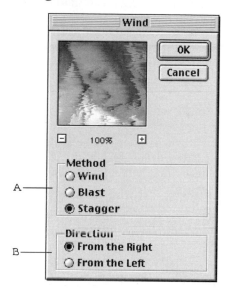

A. Method

The Method options determine how far pixels are shifted.

Wind

> This option shifts the pixels slightly.

Blast

> This option shifts the pixels approximately twice as far as Wind.

Stagger

> This option shifts the pixels approximately twice as far as Blast.

B. Direction

This setting determines the direction of the wind. From the Left moves pixels as if wind were blowing from the left of the image. From the Right moves pixels as if wind were blowing from the right of the image.

13.97

Filter: Texture

The Texture filters create the appearance of three-dimensional texture. They do this by generating a texture over the image based on mathematics built into the filter, or by altering existing color information. Texture filters are typically applied as the final step in an image creation to give the impression that it has been created on a textured surface.

13.98

Filter: Texture: Craquelure

This filter is intended to make the image appear to be an old, cracked, and decayed oil painting. It finds the edges of the image, blurs the contents slightly, and sharpens the edges. Then it emulates three-dimensional cracks by adding highlight and shadow details. Inside the cracks, the image is darkened and the contrast reduced to emulate the appearance of pigment left in the canvas after paint cracks off.

The Craquelure Dialog Box

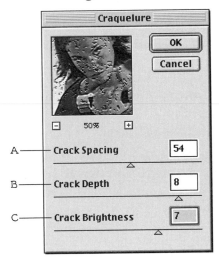

A. **Crack Spacing** (2 to 100)

This setting determines the quantity of cracks. Lower settings produce more cracks. At 2 all paint cracks off, leaving a dark, low contrast image. Settings between 50 and 100 produce the most believable effects. A value of 100 still produces significant cracking.

B. **Crack Depth** (0 to 10)

This setting controls the amount of highlight and shadow detail added to the edges of the cracks. Detail is added as if a light source were shining on the image from the top. Shadows are added along the top edges of the cracks, and highlights along the bottom, to create the illusion of depth. A value of 0 produces no depth. A value of 10 produces unrealistic solid black-and-white highlights. Settings between 2 and 5 produce the most realistic feelings of depth.

C. **Crack Brightness** (0 to 10)

This setting determines the amount areas inside cracks darken. At 0, the contents of the cracks are unrealistically dark. At 10, the contents are darkened very little from the original image. Middle settings produce the most convincing cracks.

13.99

Filter: Texture: Grain

This filter provides a variety of ways to add noise to an image, or to turn an image into noise. Noise is single pixels or small groups of pixels whose colors deviate substantially from adjacent pixels. Its effects range from subtle, such as adding a slight film grain to an image, to extreme, such as covering the image with a layer of black grime. Grain can also alter contrast before adding noise.

The Grain Dialog Box

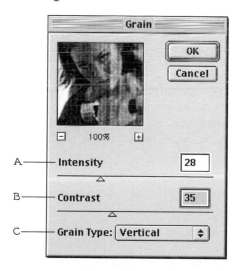

A. **Intensity** (0 to 100)

This setting controls how much grain is added to the image. The higher the intensity, the greater the effects of the filter. The exact effects of this setting depend on the selected Grain Type.

B. **Contrast** (0 to 100)

This setting reduces or exaggerates the difference between colors in the image. Settings below 50 bring all colors closer to neutral gray. Above 50, lights become lighter, darks become darker, and midtones are eliminated. At 50, there are no changes in contrast.

C. **Grain Type**

These options determine the style of grain added to the image.

Regular

This option is similar to Filter: Noise: **Add Noise**, set to uniform distribution. While Add Noise converts pixels to noise, Grain blends noise with existing pixels, producing a recognizable image even at the highest settings. At lower settings, Regular adds a light grain to the image very much like film grain. At higher settings, all pixels in the image are blended with noise.

Soft

This option is identical to Regular, except that it adds noise at half the opacity, so that more detail information from the image remains. This produces a much more subtle effect than Regular or the Add Noise filter.

Sprinkles

This option adds randomly placed pixels using the background color.

Clumped

This option adds noise at the Regular setting, then blurs the entire image. At low settings, it produces a mottled and blurred image. At high settings, it produces an image with many blurred patches of primary colors.

Contrast

This option adds noise at the Regular settings, then blurs the image and boosts the contrast. At low settings, the filter produces a high-contrast, blurred image. At high settings, it produces a high-contrast, mottled, textured image.

Enlarged

This option adds noise in small clumps of primary-colored pixels.

Stippled

This option recreates the image using single pixels, just as stippling uses single dots of ink. This option uses the current foreground color. Contrast is created by using more pixels in dark areas of the image, and fewer pixels in light areas.

Horizontal

This option covers the image with a layer of black, grimy noise that is streaked horizontally, as though India ink were applied to the image with a toothbrush.

Vertical

This option covers the image with a layer of black, grimy noise that is streaked vertically, as though India ink were applied to the image with a toothbrush.

Speckle

This option boosts the contrast of the image, then puts black specks over the shadows.

13.100

Filter: Texture: Mosaic Tiles

This filter is almost identical to Craquelure, only it adds cracks in a regular pattern instead of randomly.

The Mosaic Tiles Dialog Box

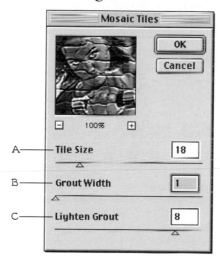

A. **Tile Size** (2 to 100)

This setting controls the width of the areas between cracks. Lower settings produce smaller areas, and more overall cracking. At 2, the entire image will be one big crack. At 100, tiles are so big that the image looks more like a weird quilt than a cracked painting. The most realistic looking cracking happens between 10 and 20.

B. **Grout Width** (1 to 15)

This setting controls the width of the cracks. A value of 1 produces hairline cracking. A value of 15 looks as though paint has been gouged off with a linoleum cutter. The size that works best for this setting depends on the Tile Size. Larger tiles look best with wide grout, smaller tiles with small grout.

C. **Lighten Grout** (0 to 10)

This setting controls how much the cracks are darkened. A value of 10 darkens the contents of the cracks slightly. A value of 0 turns the contents into dark gray.

13.101

Filter: Texture: Patchwork

This filter produces nothing resembling patchwork, but creates more convincing mosaic tiles than Mosaic or Mosaic Tiles. Like Mosaic, it breaks the image into a grid, then averages the colors of the pixels within each square of the grid individually, and fills the square with that color. It then adds shadows and highlights to each square to give a three-dimensional beveled-edge appearance to each tile.

The Patchwork Dialog Box

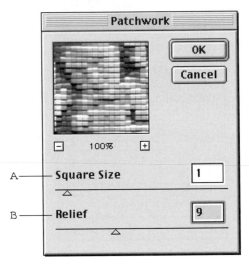

A. **Square Size** (0 to 10)

This setting determines the size of the squares. A value of 10 produces small squares. A value of 0 produces extremely small squares.

B. **Relief** (0 to 25)

This setting controls the appearance of the beveled edges of the image. Bevels are shaded as though a light were shining on the image from the top. A value of 0 adds very slight shadows to the edges. A value of 25 unrealistically blackens or whitens the sides. The most realistic shading occurs between 5 and 10.

13.102

Filter: Texture: Stained Glass

This filter defines the image with randomly shaped hexagons. It samples the color of the pixel at the center of each hexagon and fills the hexagon with that color. Then it borders each hexagon with the foreground color. Additionally, pixels can be lightened in a gradient from the center of the image, as if the sun were shining from behind.

The Stained Glass Dialog Box

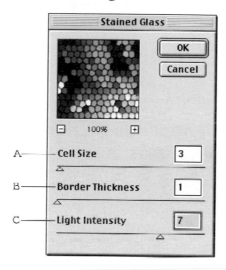

A. **Cell Size** (2 to 50)

This setting controls the relative size of each hexagon. Settings above 2 typically reduce the image to vague outlines of the original image. A value of 50 diagonally divides the image into two colors.

B. **Border Thickness** (1 to 20)

This setting determines the thickness of the line of foreground color hexagons are outlined with. A value of 1 produces a thin line. A value of 20 produces a line so thick that it will be larger than any hexagon under a 20 cell size.

C. **Light Intensity** (0 to 10)

This setting defines the intensity of the light shining from the center of the image. A value of 0 produces no lightening. A value of 20 produces a very beatific light.

13.103

Filter: Texture: Texturizer

This filter creates the impression that an image has been created on a surface that has three-dimensional texture. It does this by adding highlight and shadow detail based on the lightness values of a second image. Shadows in the second image become shadows in the target image, and highlights become highlights. The texture image can be selected from textures built into the filter, or from any image saved in the native Photoshop format.

Issues to Consider

Texturizer should be the last filter run on the image. If anything is added to the image after texture is applied, it will not be textured, thus destroying the illusion of the filter.

The Texturizer Dialog Box

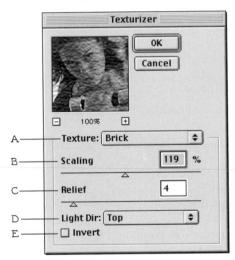

A. **Texture**

Textures resemble the substance they are named after. Select your own texture by choosing Load Texture. When you select Load Texture, an Open dialog box appears. Select the Photoshop file you wish to use as a texture and click OK.

B. **Scaling** (50% to 200%)

This setting controls the size of the selected texture as it is applied to the image, from half its size to twice its size.

C. **Relief** (0 to 50)

This setting determines the extent to which areas of the image are lightened or darkened according to the lightness values of the texture image.

A value of 0 produces no change. A value of 50 reduces the image to solid black-and-white pixels. Realistic texture occurs with settings from 2 to 6.

D. **Light Dir**

This setting adds shadows and highlights as though light were shining from a certain direction.

13.104
Filter: Video

The Video filters are created exclusively for images captured from video or destined for videotape. They're not useful for anything else.

13.105
Filter: Video: De-Interlace

Video is created by interlaced scan lines, or beams of light that alternate rows every time the screen is redrawn. This happens so quickly and the lines are so narrow that we perceive it as a constant image. When the video image is captured as a computer graphic, these scan lines can be out of synch, producing an image that is blurry or noisy. De-interlace can help compensate.

Issues to Consider

De-Interlace only works occasionally. The only way to find out if it works is to run it on the image. If the filter does not produce satisfactory results, you may need to recapture the video frame.

The De-Interlace Dialog Box

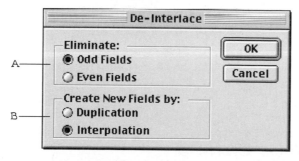

A. **Eliminate**

These options determine fields removed by the filter.

Odd Fields

This option eliminates every other row starting from the top row.

Even Fields
>This option eliminates every other row starting from the second row from the top.

B. **Create New Fields by**
>These options determine how new fields are added by the filter:

Duplication
>This option fills the empty rows by duplicating the immediately preceding row.

Interpolation
>This option averages the pixel values of the rows before and after the empty row to create the data for the empty row. Typically, Interpolation produces the best results.

13.106

Filter: Video: NTSC Colors

This one-step filter changes the colors of images to broadcastable colors. Just as with printing inks, television monitors use a different set of colors than a computer monitor. Not every color displayed on a computer monitor will display properly on a television monitor. NTSC Colors examines the values of every pixel in the image and changes it to the nearest displayable color.

Issues to Consider

NTSC Colors should be the last step before saving an image to video tape.
>While it eliminates non-displayable colors, it will not prevent new ones from being created if you do additional editing after applying the filter.

13.107

Filter: Other

The Other submenu collects all filters that can't be easily classified into other existing categories.

13.108

Filter: Other: Custom

This filter is the least intuitive part of Photoshop, and also one of the least useful, because it alters the image in ways that can be done more efficiently using other filters. It does provide interesting insight into the mathematics that filters use to calculate pixel changes.

Using the Custom filter successfully requires a certain amount of skill and luck. Literally millions of effects can be generated using the Custom filter. Fortunately, the filter previews the change to the image with every value entered. The best way to learn the filter is to open the filter and start entering values into the Matrix.

Follow these guidelines when entering values into the Custom filter:

- Enter values starting from the center field.

- If you like the general effect, but feel it is applied too strongly, increase the Scale value, because the total effect of the Matrix values is divided by the Scale value.

- If you like the effects of the Matrix and Scale values, but feel the image is too dark, enter positive values into the Offset field. If it is too light, enter negative values.

The Custom Dialog Box

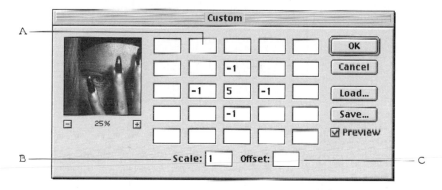

A. Matrix

The main part of the Custom filter is the Matrix, a grid of 25 fields. When the filter is applied to an image, it examines every pixel in the image. It multiplies the brightness value of the pixel by the value entered in the center field. Then it multiplies adjacent pixels by the numbers in the fields surrounding the center field.

B. Scale

The filter totals the products of pixels multiplied by the Matrix, then divides them by the value entered in the Scale field.

C. Offset

The value entered in the Offset field is added to the quotient of the Matrix divided by the Scale.

13.109

Filter: Other: *High Pass*

This filter changes areas of an image to neutral gray, based on the amount of difference between the colors of adjacent pixels. This is a valuable tool for finding edges between areas of different colors, because it allows you to eliminate all information in an image other than the highest contrasting areas. It is an excellent pre-filter for creating line art using Image: Adjust: **Threshold**, because it allows you to eliminate unwanted shading and detail.

The High Pass Dialog Box

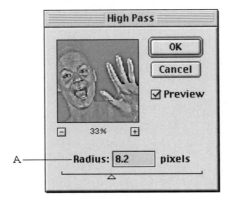

A. **Radius** (0.1 to 250)

This value determines how similar colors need to be in order to be changed to neutral gray. With a value of 25, for example, all adjacent pixels differing by 25 levels of brightness or less are changed to neutral gray.

13.110

Filter: Other: Maximum

This filter spreads areas of light pixels over areas of dark pixels. It dates back to before the Select: Modify: **Expand** command was added to Photoshop. Maximum was originally intended to increase the mask area of a saved selection, producing results similar to applying Expand to an active selection. Maximum can be applied to color channels for artistic effect.

The Maximum Dialog Box

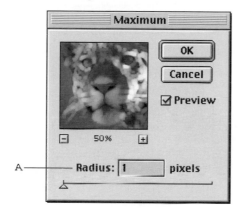

A. **Radius** (1 to 10)

This is the distance that light pixels are copied over dark pixels. This expands all light areas in the image.

13.111

Filter: Other: Minimum

This filter spreads areas of dark pixels over areas of light pixels. It dates back to before the Select: Modify: **Contract** command was added to Photoshop. Minimum was originally intended to decrease the mask area of a saved selection, producing results similar to applying Contract to an active selection. Minimum can be applied to color channels for artistic effect.

The Minimum Dialog Box

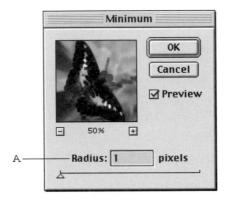

A. Radius (1 to 10)

This is the distance that dark pixels are copied over light pixels. This expands all dark areas in the image.

13.112

Filter: Other: Offset

This filter moves selected pixels in the specified direction. It is commonly used to create seamlessly tiling patterns. Depending on where this filter is applied, it has the following effects:

- **Offsetting a layer.** Here, its function is identical to the Move tool: It moves the layer a specified number of pixels.

- **Offsetting an active selection.** Here it moves only the contents of the selection. Offset is one of the only filters that can move pixel information into an active selection from outside the selection. When an area is offset, the area scrolls pixel data into the image from outside the selection to fill in areas left empty.

The Offset Dialog Box

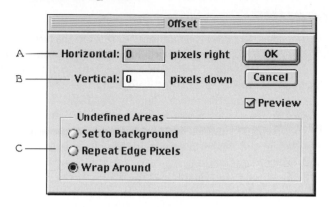

A. **Horizontal** (–30,000 pixels to 30,000 pixels)

This setting controls the amount the of horizontal offset. Negative values move the image to the left; positive values to the right.

B. **Vertical** (–30,000 pixels to 30,000 pixels)

This setting controls the amount of the vertical offset. Negative values move the image down; positive values up.

C. **Undefined Areas**

When there is no image data to move into the image—for example, when the entire background layer is offset—it leaves empty spaces. These options determine how to deal with these areas:

Set to Transparent

This option leaves the empty areas transparent.

Repeat Edge Pixels

This option fills the area by repeating the pixels on the very edge of the empty area. This produces obvious streaking when edge pixels are not one solid color.

Wrap Around

This option moves any part of the image moved outside the selected area or off the canvas to the opposite side.

13.113

Filter: **Digimarc**

The Digimarc filters are owned by the Digimarc Corporation, but are installed automatically with Photoshop. They are not fully functional unless an additional fee is paid to the Digimarc Corporation. They embed information into an image as background noise. Embedded information is only visible to the trained eye, but it can be interpreted as data by the Read Watermark filter. Embedded information provides a means to contact the original creator of the image, and theoretically hinders illegal usage of images. After the information is embedded in the image, it stays with that image through printing, re-scanning, and other manipulations. As of this writing, there have been no legal cases involving digital watermarks, so the effect of the Digimarc filters as a hindrance to copyright violation is purely theoretical.

13.114

Filter: Digimarc: **Embed Watermark**

This filter embeds specific information into the image: The Digimarc Locator Service ID Number, a content rating to specify adult content, and a URL for the Digimarc Locator Service.

The Digimarc Locator Service ID Number is a number that is embedded into the image. Anyone desiring to contact the creator of the image can scan in the image and obtain the Digimarc Locator Service ID Number using the Read Watermark filter. Then they can contact the Digimarc Corporation via phone or Internet to obtain creator contact information. In order for people to contact you, you must register with the Digimarc Corporation and pay a monthly fee.

Issues to Consider

Registering the service. You can register with Digimarc by selecting Embed Watermark, clicking Personalize, then clicking Register. This will launch your web browser and connect you directly to Digimarc's registration site. A toll-free number is provided if you do not have an Internet connection.

13.115

Filter: Digimarc: *Read Watermark*

This filter decodes the embedded information from a watermarked image. Scan or download the image and open it in Photoshop. If the creator of the image used the Embed Watermark filter on the image, a copyright symbol (©) appears before his name in the title bar of the image window. When this symbol appears, use the Read Watermark filter to obtain the creator ID. With the ID, you can call Digimarc's toll-free number (listed in the filter dialog box) or click the Web Lookup button to connect to Digimarc's database of artists and contact information. If the creator has paid his or her monthly dues to the Digimarc Corporation, creator and contact information are provided to you.

Issues to Consider

Use of the Embed Watermark filter is not yet widespread. It is likely that your time will be better spent contacting the publisher of the publication the image appears in, rather than taking the time to scan and run the Read Watermark filter on an image that might or might not have an embedded creator ID.

If you don't require the services of these filters, disable them. Many users notice that the Digimarc filters take a few seconds (more, on slower workstations) to evaluate each scan. When you're scanning a few dozen images, those seconds add up quickly. Disable the filters by removing them from Photoshop's Plug-ins folder, then restarting the program.

The View Menu

When Photoshop creates or opens a file, the information is displayed in an *image window*. The View menu commands affect how this window displays an image on screen. The image window itself contains another set of commands, as listed below.

Image Window: Magnification Box

Located in the lower left corner of the window, this box displays the current zoom percentage. If desired, you can enter a value by double-clicking on the box, typing a number between 1 and 1600, and pressing the Enter key. There is no need to add the percent symbol—Photoshop automatically interprets the number as a percentage.

Previous versions of Photoshop did not use percentages. Instead, they used a ratio that compared the size of the image pixels to the size of the monitor pixels. For optimal viewing, the relative size of each pixel had to be the same, or exist at a ratio of 1:1. Because images and monitors rarely share the same resolution, the results could be confusing. Images range from 72 ppi for onscreen graphics, to 300 ppi for high-resolution images, to 1200 ppi for line art scans. On the other hand, monitors rarely exceed 72–80 ppi. In order to make the pixels of a high-resolution image appear to be the same size as the monitor pixels, the magnification had to be significantly increased. At a 1:1 ratio, a 2 x 2–inch, 300-ppi image would appear to be 10 inches wide.

That same phenomenon exists, only now Photoshop calls the 1:1 ratio "100%." This style is different from page layout and illustration software, which refer to the actual print size as 100%. When Photoshop displays a high-resolution image at actual print size, it cannot display every pixel. Instead, it averages the onscreen pixel values, which obscures detail, making fine edits difficult at best. At 100%, every pixel is fully visible, giving you the best view of the image contents.

14.2

Image Window: *Image Data*

The Image Data field is located to the right of the Magnification Box. It displays information about the active image and the current status of Photoshop, based on the option currently set in the adjoining pop-up menu:

Document Sizes

This option is Photoshop's default. Here, the data field displays two numbers separated by a slash. The number on the left is the base file size, or the size of the image with no additional channels or layers (as if you flattened the image. The number on the right is the current file size, including any additional layers and channels.

You can use a simple formula to determine the base size of a Photoshop image. Measuring in pixels, multiply an image's width by its height. Then multiply that number by the depth of one pixel, or the number of bytes it uses to display color. For example, a Bitmap pixel uses 1 bit, or .125 bytes; a Grayscale pixel uses 8 bits, or 1 byte; an RGB pixel uses 24 bits, or 3 bytes; a CMYK pixel uses 32 bits, or 4 bytes. Therefore, a 500 x 500–pixel RGB image contains 750,000 bits (500 x 500 = 750,000). One byte contains 1,024 bits, so the image size is 733K (750,000 ÷ 1,024 = 733). This figure does not account for any compression that occurs after saving and closing the image.

Document Profile

This field displays the name of the color profile currently attached to the image. If no profile has been embedded, the image is listed as "untagged." It is quite easy to change the item that initially appears here. Most often, this occurs as a result of applying a new profile (for more information, see *10.17, Image: Mode: Assign Profile*), converting to a different profile (for more information, see *10.18, Image: Mode: Convert to Profile*), or changing color modes (for more information, see *10.1, Image Mode Overview*).

Scratch Sizes

Like Document Sizes, this option displays two numbers separated by a slash. The first represents the amount of RAM currently occupied by the active image. When you open an image, it initially demands a little more than three times its own size in RAM. As you apply commands, create layers, and retain history states, Photoshop is forced to access more RAM, which increases this value.

The second number is the total amount of RAM available to Photoshop. This number doesn't change unless you reset Photoshop's RAM allocation.

If the first number is greater than the second, it means Photoshop is using virtual memory, or space from your hard drive, as additional RAM. This process inevitably results in slower, less efficient performance. (For more information, see *9.53, Edit: Preferences: **Plug-ins & Scratch Disk**.*)

Efficiency

When this option reads 100%, Photoshop has more than enough RAM to process the active image. Lower values mean the program has begun using virtual memory. This makes Photoshop run more slowly, because instead of executing your commands in RAM, it must use space from your hard drive. The easiest solution to this problem is to allocate more RAM to Photoshop. If you've allocated all you can and the Efficiency percentage routinely dips below 80%, consider purchasing more RAM.

Timing

This option displays the amount of time Photoshop took to process the last-applied command.

Current Tool

This option displays the name of the item currently selected in the Toolbar.

Additional Image Data

Use the following keystrokes to display additional information:

- **Image dimensions.** Hold down the (Option) [Alt] key and click the field to display the current width, height, mode, and resolution.

- **Page position.** Hold down the (Command) [Control] key and click the field to see where the image will appear on the page when you print directly from Photoshop. If you've chosen any options in the File: **Page Setup** dialog box such as crop marks or color bars, they appear in the preview as well.

- **Tile info.** Hold down the (Command) [Control] key and click the field to display the size and number of image tiles. Photoshop breaks an image into a series of tiles to facilitate display and redraw. The only time you see these tiles is when you zoom in or out and the image refreshes, or if you apply a command to a large image and Photoshop applies the results one block at a time.

14.3

Image Window: **Scroll Bars**

Like any other window, a Photoshop image contains scroll bars. These, how-ever, are the least efficient method of scrolling. The most common technique is using the Hand tool, which you can access at any time by pressing the spacebar. Use the following shortcuts to scroll through an image window:

- **Up one entire screen.** Press the Page Up key or choose Control-K.

- **Down one entire screen.** Press the Page Down key or choose Control-L.

- **Up 10 pixels.** Hold down the Shift key and press Page Up, or choose Control-Shift-K.

- **Down 10 pixels.** Hold down the Shift key and press Page Down, or choose Control-Shift-L.

- **To upper-left corner.** Press the Home key or choose Control-A.

- **To bottom-right corner.** Press End or choose Control-D.

14.4

View: *New View*

This command opens a new window that displays exactly the same data as the active image. The second view enables you to create a *reference window*. Both images can scroll and magnify independently; the reference window reflects all the current edits, regardless of the other window's settings. You can create as many views as your available RAM will allow.

Don't confuse View: **New View** with Image: **Duplicate**, which creates a sepa-rate copy. To illustrate how both images read from the same source, make an edit in one window—as you do, the change instantly appears in the other.

14.5

View: **Proof Setup**

In an ICC-driven workflow, these options enable you to *soft-proof* an image, or view the colors closer to how they will appear when output to a specific device. In Photoshop 5, you could only proof an RGB image for a CMY device—the only profile you could reference was the current File: Color Settings: **CMYK Setup** item. In version 6, you're able to load a profile independently of the current RGB or CMYK workspaces (as established in the Edit: **Color Settings** dialog box). You can even proof the expected appearance of a Grayscale image, which you could not do in previous versions.

Issues to Consider

The Proof Setup options are intended for a linearized environment.
Unless you work in a rigidly controlled environment, soft-proofing in
Photoshop is a nearly pointless exercise. It may give you an indication of
what color or tonal ranges will ultimately shift, but you cannot assume
that what you see on screen is accurate.

Related Topics

9.37   Edit: *Color Settings*
14.6   View: Proof Setup: *Custom*
14.18 View: *Proof Colors*

14.6
_____

View: Proof Setup: *Custom*

Choose this command to create a new soft proofing setup for a color output
device. You can create as many setups as you have proofing conditions—
the information is saved as a standalone file, so you're able to distribute
them among in-house workstations or to clients, or receive them from
vendors, if necessary. Loaded setups appear in the bottom of the View: **Proof
Setup** submenu.

Issues to Consider

Simultaneously proofing for multiple devices. If you've defined the necessary setups, you're able to proof the same image for multiple output
methods. Use View: **New View** to create a series of reference windows,
then apply a proof setup to each window. This way, you can compare the
images side by side.

The Proof Setup Dialog Box

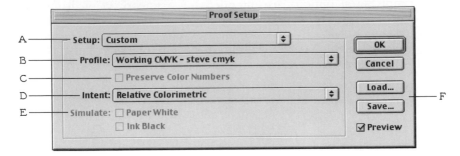

A. Setup

This pop-up menu displays the current soft proofing setup. If you haven't yet defined one, the pop-up displays Custom (you'll give it a name when you click the Save button). Otherwise, choose the setup you want to edit.

B. Profile

Set the profile you want to drive the proofing setup in this pop-up. Bear in mind that in order to create a setup for a particular output device, you have to create the actual profile.

C. Preserve Color Numbers

This option is only available when the target output device and the current image share the same color space. (For example, a CMYK image and a color printer set up to receive CMYK images.) When checked, it enables you to proof how the image will appear when output with no profile attached.

D. Intent

These options determine the method used to draw out-of-gamut colors back into the target color space. Most often, you'll choose Perceptual. (For full descriptions, see *9.37, Edit: **Color Settings**.*)

E. Simulate

When generating a soft proof, these options attempt to take certain printer-specific traits into account:

Paper White

When checked, the proof will compensate for how the colors produced by the target device are affected by the whiteness of its paper stock. When unchecked, image whites are displayed at the brightest possible monitor value.

Ink Black

When checked, the proof will simulate how the target device generates black (as determined by its ink or dye, in conjunction with the paper stock). When unchecked, image blacks are displayed at the darkest possible value.

F. **Load and Save**

Click the Save button to convert the current Proof Setup settings into a CSF file. By default, the dialog box will direct the file to the Application Support/Adobe/Color/Proofing folder in your operating system. When you save a setup, its name appears at the bottom of the View: **Proof Setup** submenu.

Click the Load button to access the settings of an existing setup, enabling you to either edit the contents (if you need to fine-tune it) or resave it to your system (if a vendor has given you a CSF file).

Related Topics

9.37   Edit: *Color Settings*
14.5   View: *Proof Setup*
14.18 View: *Proof Colors*

14.7

View: Proof Setup: Working CMYK

When editing a non-CMYK image, this command creates a soft proof based on the profile currently set as the CMYK working space. To base the soft proof on a different profile, you can either change the working space (in the Edit: **Color Settings** dialog box), or bypass the working space altogether and use a Custom setup.

You can continue editing an image with the Preview turned on. In theory, this enables you to see the final color results as you work. In practice, it may be confusing, because RGB or Lab adjustments will not produce the same results you've come to expect.

Related Topics

9.37   Edit: *Color Settings*
14.5   View: *Proof Setup*
14.6   View: Proof Setup: *Custom*

14.8

View: Proof Setup: Working Cyan Plate

When editing a non-CMYK image, this command displays the projected contents of the Cyan channel, as determined by the profile currently established as the CMYK working space. (For more information, see *9.37, Edit: Color Settings.*)

14.9

View: Proof Setup: Working Magenta Plate

When editing a non-CMYK image, this command displays the projected contents of the Magenta channel, as determined by the profile currently established as the CMYK working space. (For more information, see *9.37, Edit: Color Settings.*)

14.10

View: Proof Setup: Working Yellow Plate

When editing a non-CMYK image, this command displays the projected contents of the Yellow channel, as determined by the profile currently established as the CMYK working space. (For more information, see *9.37, Edit: Color Settings.*)

14.11

View: Proof Setup: Working Black Plate

When editing a non-CMYK image, this command displays the projected contents of the Black channel, as determined by the profile currently established as the CMYK working space. (For more information, see *9.37, Edit: Color Settings.*)

14.12

View: Proof Setup: Working CMY Plates

When editing a non-CMYK image, this command displays the projected contents of the Cyan, Magenta, and Yellow channels, as determined by the profile currently established as the CMYK working space. (For more information, see *9.37, Edit: Color Settings.*)

14.13

View: Proof Setup: Macintosh RGB

Choose this option to simulate the appearance of an uncalibrated Macintosh monitor. For example, it gives Windows-based designers a better indication of how a web graphic will appear when viewed on a Mac.

14.14

View: Proof Setup: Windows RGB

Choose this option to simulate the appearance of an uncalibrated Windows monitor. For example, it gives Mac-based designers a better indication of how a web graphic will appear when viewed on a PC.

14.15

View: Proof Setup: Monitor RGB

Choose this option to turn off the influence of any color profiles. Your monitor essentially displays uncalibrated color.

14.16

View: Proof Setup: Simulate Paper White

When you choose this command, your monitor attempts to compensate for how colors produced by the target device are affected by the whiteness of its paper stock. This information is determined by the profile established as the CMYK working space (in the Edit: **Color Settings** dialog box). To bypass the current working space, use the View: Proof Setup: **Custom** option.

14.17

View: Proof Setup: Simulate Ink Black

When you choose this command, your monitor attempts to simulate how the target device generates black (as determined by its ink or dye, in conjunction with the paper stock.) This information is determined by the profile established as the CMYK working space (in the Edit: **Color Settings** dialog box). To bypass the current working space, use the View: Proof Setup: **Custom** option.

14.18

View: *Proof Colors* *(Command) [Control]-Y*

Choose this command to activate the current Proof Setup option. For example, if Working CMYK is checked in the View: **Proof Setup** submenu, this command either activates or deactivates the viewing influence of the profile.

14.19

View: *Gamut Warning* *(Command-Shift) [Control-Shift]-Y*

This command highlights all color values that currently fall outside the CMYK gamut. It creates a sort of mask, concealing the out-of-gamut colors.

The effect is more obvious than one of the View: **Proof Colors** options, but it also makes this command less useful. You receive no indication of how the colors will appear in CMYK mode. Also, if enough pixels are concealed, continued editing is difficult at best.

Issues to Consider

The concealing color defaults to gray. Choose another color or lower its opacity in the Edit: Preferences: **Transparency & Gamut** dialog box. If you lower the opacity, the masking color combines with the underlying tones, creating new colors that simply do not exist in the image.

14.20

View: *Zoom In* *(Command) (Control)-+*

This command has the same effect as clicking on an image with the Zoom tool. The onscreen pixels enlarge, creating the impression of zooming in closer to the image. This allows you to edit an image in much finer detail.

Unlike the Zoom tool, you cannot specify the center of a zoom by clicking. Selecting View: **Zoom In** uses the center point of the current window.

Double-click the Zoom tool to reset the magnification to 100%.

14.21

View: *Zoom Out* *(Command) (Control)-minus sign*

This command has the same effect as holding down the (Option) [Alt] key and clicking with the Zoom tool. The onscreen pixels condense, creating the impression of moving away from the image. This allows you to see a larger image in its entirety.

Issues to Consider

Both View: Zoom In and Zoom Out resize the image window in an attempt to accommodate the larger onscreen image. This effect is the same as checking the Resize Windows to Fit box in the Zoom tool's Options bar. Override this option by holding down the (Option) [Alt] key when you select the command or shortcut.

14.22
View: *Fit on Screen*   *(Command) [Control]-Zero*

This command expands the edges of the window to the perimeter of the screen, displaying the entire image at the largest possible size.

14.23
View: *Actual Pixels*

This command sets the magnification to 100%. When an image is set to this view, the pixels are enlarged on screen to match the size of the monitor pixels. (For more information, see *14.1, Image Window: Magnification Box.*)

14.24
View: *Print Size*

Choose this command to evaluate the status of the image at the size it will ultimately print—it displays at its actual measured size, regardless of its resolution.

Because most web and multimedia graphics share the same resolution as your monitor, this command will appear to have no effect on them.

14.25
View: *Show Extras*   *(Command) [Control]-H*

Choose this command to reveal or hide every item currently checked under the View: **Show** submenu. For example, if **Grid** and **Annotations** are currently checked, this command hides them. Choose this command again, and only those items are revealed.

To prevent certain items from being affected by this command, uncheck their boxes in the View: Show: **Show Extras Options** dialog box.

14.26

View: *Show*

The options in this submenu enable you to determine which items are affected by the View: **Show Extras** command.

14.27

View: Show: *Selection Edges*

This command only affects the visible outline of an active selection, hiding it from view without deactivating it. Choose the same command to display the outline again.

Issues to Consider

Learn to hide frequently. After you become familiar with creating and working with selections, the outline quickly becomes intrusive. By hiding it, you can continue editing without having part of the image obscured.

14.28

View: Show: *Target Path*   (Command-Shift) [Control-Shift]-H

Similar to View: Show: **Selection Edges**, this option hides a the active item in the Paths palette. Choose the same command to display the path. As long as the path is turned off, it doesn't appear on screen when you click the path in the Paths palette. You must select the path and choose this command again.

14.29

View: Show: *Grid*   (Option-Command) [Alt-Control]-apostrophe

The grid is a criss-crossing series of guides, used to facilitate a rigid and highly structured work environment. The increments, line type, and color are set in the Edit: Preferences: **Guides & Grid** dialog box. (For more information, see *14.38, View: Snap To.*)

14.30

View: Show: *Guides*

A guide is a non-printing horizontal or vertical line, similar to a blue-line drawn in a conventional page design. (This feature is identical to guides found in page layout and illustration software.) This command hides and reveals all existing guides. It does not remove them from the image. (For more information, see *14.38, View: Snap To.*)

Issues to Consider

The rulers must be visible in order to place a guide. Create a horizontal guide by clicking and dragging from the horizontal ruler; create a vertical guide by clicking and dragging from the vertical ruler. Constrain the guides to the ruler tickmarks by holding down the Shift key while dragging.

Repositioning a guide. After placing a guide, you can move it again by dragging with the Move tool. If you're using another tool, hold down the (Command) [Control] key and drag. To remove all guides (as opposed to hiding them), choose View: **Clear Guides**.

Changing the appearance of guides. Set the guide color and line type in the Edit: Preferences: **Guides & Grid** dialog box. If desired, open the preference by double-clicking one of the guides.

14.31

View: Show: *Slices*

Choose this command to hide all slices from view. Choose it again to display the slices. Note that every image contains at least one slice. If the slices are set to Show, its tiny tag appears in the upper left corner of the image.

14.32

View: Show: *Annotations*

Choose this command to hide all notes and audio annotations from view. Choose it again to display the annotations.

14.33

View: Show: *All*

Choose this command to reveal all available options in the View: **Show** submenu, even those items that have been protected in the View: Show: **Show Extras Options** dialog box.

14.34

View: Show: *None*

Choose this command to hide all available options in the View: **Show** submenu.

14.35

View: Show: *Show Extras Options*

This command enables you to pick and choose the items that are affected by the Show Extras command. It exists because of the popular keyboard short-cut for showing and hiding: (Command) [Control]-H. This way, when you apply the shortcut, you can control the number of items hidden or revealed, leaving others untouched. When an item is protected, its name appears in brackets in the View: **Show** submenu.

The Show Extras Options Dialog Box

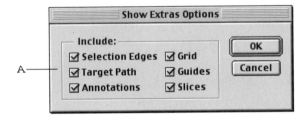

A. **Include**

To protect an item from the Show Extras command, uncheck its box. For example, if an active selection and the grid are both showing, choosing Show Extras affects both items. However, if you've unchecked the Grid box, the Show Extras command only affects the selection. (You can still affect the grid by choosing it directly from the View: **Show** submenu.)

14.36

View: *Show Rulers*

This command reveals and hides the horizontal and vertical rulers. The rulers measure in pixels, inches, centimeters, points, or picas. Establish these units in the Edit: Preferences: **Units & Rulers** dialog box, accessed by double-clicking the ruler. Or, change the values on-the-fly from the pop-up menu in the lower left of the Info palette. Common uses for the rulers include the following:

- **Positioning items across the width or height of an image.** In Photoshop, the position of an item is based on the coordinates of its upper left corner. When moving an element across an image, this appears as the ΔX and ΔY values in the upper-right panel of the Info palette.

- **Repositioning the zero origin.** Click and drag from the criss-cross icon in the upper left of the image, where the two rulers meet. Two crosshairs representing the X axis and Y axis converge on the cursor. Using the rulers or image contents as a guide, release the crosshairs at the desired position. The rulers reflect the change. (See *Issues to Consider*, below.)

- **Creating accurate selections.** Use the rulers to target the starting point of a selection. This value appears as the X,Y anchor in the upper-right panel of the Info palette.

- **Creating guides.** Non-printing guide lines can be dragged from the rulers onto an image.

Issues to Consider

Using the ruler increments. Constrain the crosshairs to the ruler tickmarks by holding down the Shift key while dragging.

Reading from the zero origin. Regardless of the specified unit, the rulers always measure from the zero origin, or the point where the horizontal plane (X) crosses the vertical plane (Y). After you reposition the zero origin, Photoshop displays its measurement values slightly differently. If you remember your high school algebra, you'll recall the Cartesian plane, which measures the position of a point based on X and Y coordinates. By moving the zero origin and exposing the two axes, you divide the plane into four quadrants. Photoshop mixes positive and negative values to display precise X and Y measurements:

  - Lower-right quadrant: positive X and Y values.
  - Lower-left quadrant: negative X and positive Y values.
  - Upper-left quadrant: negative X and Y values.
  - Upper-right quadrant: positive X and negative Y values.

You do not encounter negative measurement values until you move the zero origin. Because it defaults to the upper-left corner, the image exists entirely in the lower-right quadrant, which displays only positive X and Y values.

Related Topics

14.37

View: *Snap*

Photoshop enables you to *snap* to different placement aids in an image, including ruler guides, the grid, and the edge of the image. This way, as you drag or position a part of the image, one of two things occurs:

- **The edges snap.** For example, assume the Snap To option is set for the ruler guides. When you drag an element close enough to a guide (about 8 screen pixels), the item appears to leap to it. This makes it easier to align elements to a particular location.

- **The center snaps.** For example, assume you're dragging the same element over the same guide. When it gets close enough, the element's geographical center will leap to the guide. This makes it easier to pinpoint the center of an image layer or selection.

On a Macintosh, you can override the Snap To option by holding down the Control key *after* you start dragging. (There is no Windows equivalent.)

14.38

View: *Snap To*

When you choose an item from this submenu, Photoshop regards it as a snapping item. In other words, any guide or element that you drag will snap to it.

14.39

View: *Lock Guides*   *(Option-Command) [Alt-Control]-semicolon*

This command disables your ability to reposition a guide. You can still place new guides (as well as hide and show them), but they are locked as soon as you release the mouse button. Choose the same command to unlock the guides.

14.40

View: *Clear Guides*

Choose this command to remove all existing guides. This is the only command in the View Menu that can be reversed by selecting Edit: **Undo**.

14.41

View: New Guide

Choose this command to place a new guide at a precise coordinate, as opposed to dragging manually. It is useful when creating an image template, or a rigidly structured series of guide.

The New Guide Dialog Box

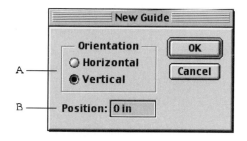

A. **Orientation**

Here, specify whether you want a horizontal or vertical guide.

B. **Position**

Enter the desired position of the guide in this field. For example, when placing a vertical guide, enter the desired location along the horizontal ruler. This field defaults to the current measurement unit assigned to the rulers. Override the setting by adding the correct abbreviation after the value.

14.42

View: Lock Slices

Choose this command to lock all of the slices in an image, which prevents you from using the Slice or Slice Select tools. Choose the command again to unlock the slices.

14.43

View: Clear Slices

Choose this command to remove all slices from the image, even when View: **Lock Slices** is enabled. Bear in mind that a single slice will remain that encompasses the entire image.

Navigator Palette

15.1
Navigator Palette Overview

The Navigator palette offers a way to easily access different areas of an image. Rather than pan and zoom using separate tools or keyboard shortcuts, you can use the palette's controls.

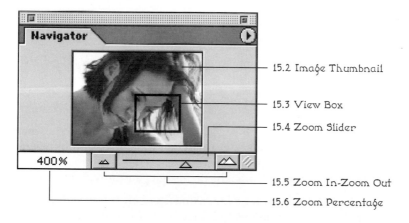

15.2 Image Thumbnail

15.3 View Box

15.4 Zoom Slider

15.5 Zoom In-Zoom Out

15.6 Zoom Percentage

Depending on the images you work with, however, the Navigator palette may not be necessary. Photoshop redraws onscreen images faster than ever—especially on PowerPC and Pentium workstations—and it might be more intuitive to use traditional keyboard shortcuts for panning and zooming. Most often, the users who benefit from the Navigator palette have small monitors (12–15 inches) that cannot display the entire image at a useful size, or work with exceptionally large high-resolution files, such as poster-sized images for large-format output.

Issues to Consider

Bypassing the Navigator palette. Use the following shortcuts at any time to pan and zoom without the Navigator palette:

- **Panning.** Hold down the spacebar to access the Hand tool.

- **Zooming in.** Hold down the (Command) [Control] key with the spacebar to access the Zoom tool.

- **Zooming out.** Hold down the (Option) [Alt] and (Command) [Control] keys with the spacebar.

15.2

Image Thumbnail

The Image Thumbnail is a low-resolution preview of the entire image. Although it defaults to 1 x 1.25 inches, its overall size depends on the size of the Navigator palette. Resize the palette by dragging the Resize Window button in the lower-right corner. Click the Original Size button in the upper-right corner to return to the default size.

15.3

View Box

The shape of the View box mimics the current dimensions of the active image window. If the window is altered, the View box immediately changes to match it. The contents are proportional as well; the information inside the View box equals the contents of the image window. Use the following techniques:

- **Panning.** Drag the View box across the thumbnail to pan the image. The image dynamically redraws in the window, as if you were manipulating the two scroll bars simultaneously. If your computer is fast enough—or if the image size is small enough—the image pans in real-time.

- **Zooming.** Hold down the (Command) [Control] key and drag to create a new box in the thumbnail. When you release the mouse button, the selected area fills the image window.

Issues to Consider

Changing the View box color. The color of the View box is of little consequence, unless an image contains an abundance of the same color. Change the box's color by choosing Palette Options from the palette submenu. This provides three different methods of setting a new color: choose a color from the pop-up menu, click on the color swatch to access the Color Picker, or click on any color in the open image.

15.4

Zoom Percentage

Enter a new zoom percentage in the lower-left corner of the palette. This feature is identical to the box in the lower left of the image window—double-click the value to highlight it, type in a new number, and press the Enter key to apply the zoom. The maximum value is 1600%, but the smallest value depends on the width, height, and resolution of the open image—each Zoom Out command can reduce the onscreen image until it's either one pixel high or one pixel wide.

Issues to Consider

Rapidly entering a series of scale values. If you hold down the Shift key while applying a new percentage, the number remains highlighted. This way, you can enter a series of zoom percentages in quick succession by typing new values and pressing Enter

15.5

Zoom Slider

The least precise tool in the palette, the Zoom slider is used to dynamically zoom in or out. Photoshop centers the zoom on the point in the middle of the View box. Drag to the right, toward the Zoom In button, to zoom in. Drag to the left, toward the Zoom Out button, to zoom out. (You can always double-click the Zoom tool icon to automatically zoom to 100%.)

15.6

Zoom In/Zoom Out

Zoom incrementally by clicking the Zoom Out and Zoom In buttons, on the left and right of the Zoom Slider. This method uses the same percentages as the standard Zoom tool. These buttons never resize the image window, as the Zoom tool does when the Resize Windows to Fit box is checked in the Zoom Options palette.

The Info Palette

Info Palette Overview

Use the Info palette to evaluate the contents of an image. It displays two essential values: the color of the image pixels beneath your cursor and information on the currently selected tool.

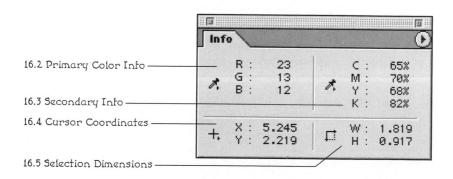

16.2 Primary Color Info

16.3 Secondary Info

16.4 Cursor Coordinates

16.5 Selection Dimensions

The most common uses for the Info palette include the following:

- **Reading color values.** The Info palette displays color values in two different ways. When it shows the values of the current color mode, it can display the relative values of any other color mode. For example, while you edit an RGB image, you can also read the colors as CMYK percentages. This way, you know what the values will be before you convert to another mode.

- **Plotting cursor coordinates.** Regardless of the tool currently in use, the Info palette always displays the X and Y coordinates of the cursor. These values are based on the zero-points of the horizontal and vertical rulers (For more informations, see *14.36, View: **Show Rulers**).

- **Gauging the effect of tools in use.** As certain tools are utilized, the Info palette displays their status, including any appropriate sizes, angles, and distances.

- **Predicting image adjustments.** When the dialog box for any Image: **Adjust** command is open, the Info palette displays two different color values. The first is the original color value, and the second shows the change that will take place when the command is applied. This way, you can monitor the range of each adjustment before making any final decisions.

- **Tracking transformations.** When transformations such as scaling or rotation are manually applied, the degree of change is reflected in the Info palette. This allows for very precise adjustments without having to make the changes using numerical dialog boxes.

Issues to Consider

Although this information appears on an easily hidden palette, always display it. If your work involves any color adjusting, complex selections, precise measurements, or transformations, the Info palette proves an invaluable tool.

Read color values before converting modes. The Info palette is the only place in Photoshop where you can read the converted color values in an image before you change from one mode to another.

The Info palette is divided into four panels. Each one displays a particular form of information. However, when you add color samplers (using the Color Sampler tool), up to four additional panels may appear, displaying the values of the targeted pixels. In the sampler panels, you can choose the same information as Panel One and Panel Two, with the exception of Opacity.

16.2

Panel One: Primary Color Info

The upper-left panel always displays color values. There are two methods of determining the type of values it displays: select Palette Options from the Info palette submenu, or click on the small eyedropper icon in the first panel to access its pop-up menu.

Issues to Consider

For the most accurate readings, leave this section set to Actual Color. Set Section Two to the target color mode, which indicates how the colors convert when you change color modes.

Color channels are based on Grayscale values. Whenever one particular color channel is chosen—regardless of the color mode—the Actual Color setting switches to Grayscale percentages.

HSB is not based on a color mode. Because HSB is based on the traditional color theory taught for years in art classes, this model is often more intuitive for those trained in traditional painting and other artistic techniques.

Displaying out-of-gamut colors. If the palette is set to CMYK values while editing an RGB or Lab Color image, the Info palette displays colors that fall out of gamut. When this occurs, Photoshop replaces the percent symbols with exclamation points (!). The remaining numerical values represent the closest color in the CMYK gamut.

The Info Options Dialog Box

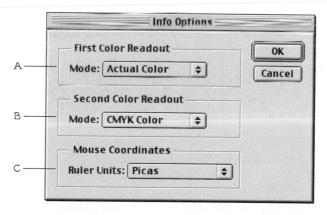

A. First Color Readout

Actual Color

> This is the default setting. Its color values are based on the current color mode of the image.

Grayscale

This value is labeled with a K, which stands for the amount of black ink required to print the image as a halftone. If the current image is in color, it displays the values that result when the image is converted to Grayscale. Tones are displayed as output values, which range from 0% (white) to 100% (black).

RGB Color

This displays color as brightness values, or the 256 tones of the Grayscale spectrum. When the open image is RGB, it displays the tonal values of the red, green, and blue channels for each pixel. If the image is Grayscale, the three values are always equal. If the image is in Lab Color, then these values display what the exact colors will be when the image is converted to RGB. If the image is CMYK, however, these values are of little use—the converted values are affected by the Edit: **Color Settings** dialog box.

HSB Color

This option displays color values in terms of Hue, Saturation, and Brightness. Hue values, or a pixel's particular color, range from 0° to 360°. This number represents the location of the color on the RGB/CMY color wheel. Saturation values, or color intensity, range from 0% (gray) to 100% (full color intensity). Not to be confused with RGB's brightness values, Brightness here is a measure of how light or dark a color is. Values range from 0% (black) to 100% (full brightness).

Web Color

This option displays values using hexidecimal ("hex") color code, the system referenced by HTML. When an image is in RGB mode, each component color is tagged with a value between 0 and 255. For example, dark orange might appear as R: 220, G: 80, B: 8. In hexadecimal, each color is represented by six characters: two each for red, green, and blue. Hex colors are generated by inserting the values 0 through 255 into a graph plotted horizontally and vertically with the following characters: 0, 1, 2, 3, 4, 5, 6, 7, 8, 9, A, B, C, D, E, F. By locating each brightness value on the graph, then pairing the matching characters, you can determine the hex value for each component color. Referring to the dark orange example cited earlier, the red component reads as DC; the green as 50; the blue as 09. Therefore, the hex color value is DC5009. (For more information, see *5.7, The Adobe Color Picker.*)

When you choose this option, a readout labeled "Idx" appears beneath the RGB items. This stands for Index, and refers to the Indexed Color mode used by many web graphic types. When you measure a color in an Indexed Color image, the readout will display the number assigned to that particular value in the file's built-in color table. If an image is in any other color mode, no value will appear.

CMYK Color

These values are based on the four individual Grayscale channels of a CMYK image that control the cyan, magenta, yellow, and black ink densities. Because CMYK images are always destined for printing, the colors display as output percentages.

Lab Color

These display the values found in the three Lab channels. The L value is the Lightness value, similar to HSB's Brightness, and ranges from 0 (black) to 100 (full lightness). The values of the a and b channels are positions in Lab Color space, and range from -128 to 127. The a value represents a color's location between magenta and green, and the b value represents its location between yellow and blue.

Total Ink

This displays the total ink density of a particular color, or its combined CMYK percentages. If this option is selected for a non-CMYK image, the value represents the ink density that would result if it were converted to CMYK.

The Total Ink Limit, or the maximum amount of CMYK percentages, is determined using the Edit: **Color Settings** controls. This amount is applied when an image is converted from RGB or Lab Color to CMYK. When in CMYK mode, it's possible to increase the Total Ink value beyond the specified limit, so this option provides a way to keep track of your darkest colors.

Opacity

This gives the combined opacity levels of all layers in a particular area. If the background layer is visible, it always will read 100%. Hide the background layer to get an accurate reading.

B. **Second Color Readout**

This pop-up menu lists the same items as First Color Readout. Choosing an option here determines the color values that display in Panel Two.

C. **Mouse Coordinates**

From this pop-up menu, select the desired unit of measurement. Choosing an option here determines the values that display in Panel Three.

Related Topics

16.3

Panel Two: Secondary Info

The upper right panel displays two types of information. If no tool or Edit: **Transform** command is being used, it displays color values. As with Panel One, options are selected in two ways: select Palette Options from the Info palette submenu, or click on the small eyedropper icon in the second panel to access its pop-up menu. When a tool or transformation is in progress, it displays a variety of other data. The most common uses include the following:

- **Marquee tool status.** The second panel displays the X and Y coordinates of the origin, or anchor point, of the selection. When you drag an active selection, the values change to the distance moved along the horizontal and vertical axes (ΔX and ΔY), the angle of its direction (A), and the distance from its original location (D).

- **Crop tool status.** When you draw a crop marquee, the Info palette displays the XY coordinates of its origin point. When the mouse button is released, the Info palette displays the marquee's angle of rotation.

- **Move tool status.** Dragging the contents of a layer is similar to dragging a selection: The values change to the distance moved along the horizontal and vertical axes (ΔX and ΔY), the angle of its direction (A), and the distance from its original location (D).

- **Pen tool status.** The values of this panel only change when you manipulate a curve handle or reposition a point with the one of the arrow tools. The Info palette displays the change in XY coordinates (ΔX and ΔY), the angle (A), and the distance of the handle from the point (D).

- **Line tool status.** When you draw a line, this panel displays the distance moved along the horizontal and vertical axes (ΔX and ΔY), the angle of its direction (A), and the distance from its original location (D).

- **Gradient tool status.** While a gradient is being drawn, this panel displays the distance moved along the horizontal and vertical axes (ΔX and ΔY), the angle of its direction (A), and the distance from its original location (D). The distance value also tells the width of the active gradient.

- **Zoom tool status.** When you drag with the Zoom tool to zoom in on an image, this panel displays the XY coordinates of the anchor point.

- **Layer: Transform status.** This panel displays percentage change in width (W) and height (H), the angle of rotation (A), and the angle of horizontal or vertical skew (H or V).

Issues to Consider

You can use the Line tool to measure the width, height, or angle of specific image areas. Under Line Tool Options, set the pixel width to 0. By drawing a line and holding the mouse button, you can use the values in the second panel to measure distance (D) and angle (A).

Related Topics
3.14   *The Line Tool*
9.16   *Edit: Transform*

16.4

Panel Three: Cursor Coordinates

The lower-left panel displays the XY coordinates of whatever pixel the cursor is over. The units of measurement for these values are in pixels, inches, centimeters, points, or picas. Specify a new unit in three places: under Edit: Preferences: **Units and Rulers**, by selecting Palette Options from the Info palette submenu, or by clicking the axis icon in the third panel to access its pop-up menu. Whatever method is used changes the default unit of measurement throughout the entire program.

16.5

Panel Four: Selection Dimensions

The fourth section of the Info palette only displays information when there is an active selection or crop marquee. If the selection is a rectangular selection, it displays the width (W) and height (H). For irregular selections, it displays the height and width of the selection at its tallest and widest points.

16.6

The Info Palette Submenu

The following commands (16.7–16.8) enable you to refine the appearance and function of the Info palette.

16.7

Palette Options

Choose this command to open the Info Options dialog box. (For more information, see *16.2, Panel One: Primary Color Info.*)

16.8

Show/Hide Color Samplers

Choose this command to show or hide any color samplers that have been placed with the Color Sampler Tool. When you display color samplers, up to four additional panels appear in the Info palette. (For more information, see *4.4, Color Sampler Tool.*)

The Color Palette

The Color palette contains options similar to the color picker. Rather than define colors using an extensive dialog box, you can enter specific numerical values or manipulate sliders on-the-fly. While this palette lacks the picker's precision, it offers a certain degree of speed and efficiency—and can still be used to access the Picker, if necessary. On the whole, it offers no new capabilities; indeed, on small monitors its usefulness may be outweighed by the amount of on screen space it occupies.

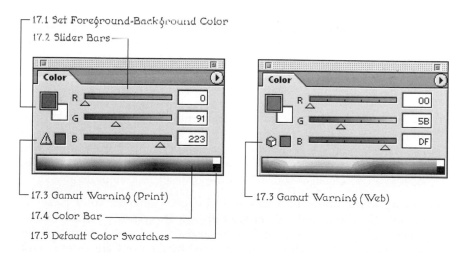

The Color palette is often used in conjunction with the Swatches palette, which is used to contain custom color values. After you've taken the time to define a specific color, add it to the Swatches palette to save your work. (For more information, see Chapter 18, *The Swatches Palette.*)

17.1

Set Foreground/Background Color

The overlapping squares in the upper left of the palette represent foreground and background color. These items are identical to the swatches found in the Toolbar—in fact, changes made in one tool are automatically reflected in the other.

The active swatch is surrounded by a double border, indicating the one that changes when a new value is specified in the palette. Click once on the inactive swatch to make it the active color. Click once on the active color to open the color picker.

Related Topics

5.2, Set Foreground Color
5.3, Set Background Color

17.2

Slider Bar

Using the sliders, you can define new colors in two ways:

- **Move the sliders back and forth.** This is useful for onscreen colors only.

- **Enter specific values in the numerical fields.** This is useful when you know the exact values of the colors you require.

The color sliders default to the current mode of the active image. In addition to Grayscale values, you can reset them to represent any of Photoshop's supported color models. (For more information, see *17.7, Slider Options.*)

Issues to Consider

The Color palette does not let you apply out-of-gamut colors. Although you can *define* values using different color models, the actual colors you can *apply* are still restricted by the available gamut. For example, even though you can define RGB colors at any time, you cannot apply them as such to a CMYK image—you still get the closest CMYK equivalent.

Specifying black values in a Grayscale image. Using the color picker to define values in a Grayscale image can be a frustrating process. Because there is no place to enter black percentages, the closest substitute is the K value under CMYK. This value is affected by the Dot Gain setting in the

Edit: **Color Settings** dialog box, so the color you define does not match the color you apply. This is Photoshop's attempt to compensate for on-press darkening. Using the Color palette to define black percentages overrides that setting and gives you the precise values.

Each slider possesses a colored band. If nothing else, these bands illustrate the cause-and-effect relationship that exists between the different sliders. As one is moved, the other bands change to reflect the available colors.

17.3

Gamut Warning

The same gamut warning symbols that appear in the Adobe color picker can be found in the Color palette.

When defining colors using the RGB, HSB, or Lab Sliders, you are warned when you select a color outside the range of printable CMYK colors. If such a color is chosen, two things appear in the lower left of the palette:

- **An exclamation point.** This symbol is Photoshop's standard CMYK out-of-gamut symbol.

- **A small color swatch.** This box displays the CMYK value that exists most closely to the current color.

When the palette submenu is set to Web Color Sliders, the Gamut Warning feature reverts to Photoshop's web-safe options:

- **A cube.** This is Photoshop's standard symbol for out-of-gamut web colors.

- **A small color swatch.** This box displays the "browser-safe" value that exists most closely to the current color.

Issues to Consider

Reining in any out-of-gamut colors. If you click any of the out-of-gamut symbols, the current color is replaced with the in-gamut variation. Ignore the CMYK warning when creating on-screen images.

Related Topics

17.4

Color Bar

The color bar is found at the bottom of the palette. If desired, define foreground or background colors by clicking anywhere on the bar—bearing in mind that this technique is wildly inaccurate, given the tiny size of the color range. To specify the color of the currently active swatch, simply click anywhere on the bar. To specify the color of the inactive swatch, hold down the (Option) [Alt] key while clicking.

There are two ways to display a new color range. First, you can select the color bar from the Color palette submenu and choose a new option from the pop-up menu. Or, Shift-click the bar to cycle through the options. (For more information, see *17.7, Slider Options.*)

17.5

White/Default Black Swatches

The tiny swatches to the right of the color bar enable you to quickly specify black or white as the target color. The effect is similar to using the Toolbar's default color swatches to reset the foreground and background colors, but with a little more precision. There, you change the color of both swatches. Here, you only change whatever swatch is active in the Color palette; the remaining swatch is not affected.

Issues to Consider

This option only sets to the available default black. This can be misleading, especially when the ramp is set to a color model different than the current image mode. For example, if you're working on a CMYK image and the ramp is set to Grayscale, it's easy to assume that clicking the black swatch specifies a value of C:0, M:0, Y:0, K:100, just as it would in a Grayscale image. However, regardless of what the palette states, it actually specifies the default CMYK black, as determined by the settings in the Edit: **Color Settings** dialog box.

Related Topics

5.5   *Default Foreground and Background Colors*
9.37   *Edit:* **Color Settings**

17.6

The Color Palette Submenu

The following commands (17.7–17.10) enable you to refine the appearance and function of the Color palette.

17.7

Slider Options

The options in the first section of the palette submenu determine the type of sliders that appear in the Color palette.

Grayscale Slider

This option offers one slider, ranging from 0% to 100% black. The values are misleading, however. If a black percentage is applied to a CMYK image, the resulting gray depends on the Black Generation setting established in the Edit: **Color Settings** dialog box.

RGB Sliders

This option offers three sliders, one each for the red, green, and blue content. Enter RGB brightness values in the fields to define specific colors.

CMYK Sliders

This option offers four sliders, one each for the cyan, magenta, yellow, and black components. Enter output percentages in the fields to define specific colors.

HSB Sliders

This option offers three sliders, one each for the Hue, Saturation, and Brightness levels. The H slider, ranging from 0° to 360°, sets the color. The S slider, ranging from 0 to 100%, controls its intensity. The B slider, also ranging from 0 to 100%, controls the amount of brightness.

Lab Sliders

This option offers three sliders, one each for Lightness, Lab's a channel and b channel. The L slider, ranging from 0 to 100, controls the amount of Lightness. The a slider repositions a color in the spectrum between green and magenta. The b slider repositions a color in the spectrum between blue and yellow.

Web Color Sliders

This option offers three RGB sliders, but the values that appear for each one are hexadecimal. Additionally, each slider is segmented to indicate the position of the 216 browser-safe web colors. By default, when you drag the sliders, they snap to these tick marks, enabling you to pinpoint such a color more easily. To override the snap-to command, hold down the (Option) [Alt] key while dragging.

17.8

Copy Color as HTML

When you choose this command, it copies the current color value as HTML. This enables you to paste the proper hexadecimal code into your HTML editing program, bypassing the need to enter the information by hand. There are two ways to approach this command:

- **Use the Color palette to define the value first.** Here, you can use values you're more familiar with before choosing this command. For example, you can use the Web Color or RGB sliders to specify the color, then choose Copy Color as HTML.

- **Bypass the palette and choose a color directly from the image.** Here, you can use the Eyedropper tool to sample any color value from an open image. When the desired value appears in the active swatch in the Color palette, choose the Copy Color as HTML command.

17.9

Color Bar Options

The options in the last section of the palette submenu determine the range of colors that appears in the bar at the bottom of the palette.

RGB Spectrum

This option displays all the values of the RGB spectrum. The values that normally appear in a clockwise fashion around the RGB/CMY color wheel are instead distributed from left to right. Lighter values appear at the top of the box, darker values toward the bottom. (For more information, see *10.10, Image: Mode: RGB Color.*)

CMYK Spectrum

This option appears to display the same range of colors as RGB Spectrum, but the gamut is reduced to the CMYK limitation. In fact, when you switch back and forth between the two, you can see that the CMYK option is dimmer and darker, suggesting the limited color range. (For more information, see *10.11, Image: Mode: CMYK Color.*)

Grayscale Ramp

This option displays a gray ramp, enabling you to choose any output value between 0% and 100% black. (For more information, see *10.7, Image: Mode: Grayscale.*)

Current Colors

As you manipulate the sliders in the Color palette, the thin bars beneath each one change to reflect the currently available range of colors. When you choose this option in the palette submenu, the color bar displays the same range of possibilities. As you continue to move the sliders, the bar changes as well.

17.10

Make Ramp Web Safe

When you choose this command, the bar displays only the 216 browser-safe options. As you click the bar to specify a color, you are restricted to that particular palette. The effect is the same as checking the Only Web Colors box in the Adobe color picker, with one difference. There, you're restricted to browser-safe colors regardless of the values you enter; here, you can manipulate any of the sliders to specify a non-safe color.

The Swatches Palette

18.1

Swatches Palette Overview

The Swatches palette displays a set of *swatches*, or blocks of pre-defined color. These items are used to redefine the foreground or background color at the click of a button. By creating a swatch, you save yourself the repetitive task of defining colors manually. By saving a series of swatches, you can easily use a large range of preset values in the future.

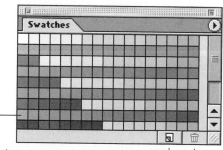

18.2 Specifying Color with Swatches ———

18.3 Create New Swatch of Foreground Color ———

18.4 Delete Swatch ———

The Swatches palette is closely related to the Color palette. Although the two palettes are grouped together by default, separating them provides quicker access to both sets of commands.

You don't use the Swatches palette to *define* colors. Instead, it's a way to store and retrieve values that already have been created with the color picker or Color palette. From there, you can use the palette controls to add, delete, or replace swatches, or use them as a reference for the foreground and background color.

18.2

Specifying Color with Swatches

When you simply move the cursor over the swatches, it becomes an eyedropper. Clicking on any swatch applies that color to the foreground or background color.

The Swatches palette pays close attention to the foreground and background swatches of the Color palette. If the foreground swatch is selected, then clicking on a swatch automatically sets the foreground color. If the background swatch is selected, then clicking on a swatch automatically sets the background color. To override whichever color is selected in the Color palette, hold down the (Option) [Alt] key while clicking a swatch.

18.3

Create New Swatch of Foreground Color

Click this button to add the current foreground color value to the Swatches palette (the effect is the same as choosing New Swatch from the palette submenu). By default, the new item simply appears in the palette. However, if you (Option) [Alt]-click the button, the Color Swatch Name dialog box appears, enabling you to name the new item more descriptively.

There are two other ways to add a color to the Swatches palette:

- **Add a new swatch.** Move the cursor to the white space at the bottom of the palette and click. The Color Swatch Name dialog box appears, enabling you to name the new item. To bypass this dialog box, hold down the (Option) [Alt] key while clicking. (You can rename the item later by double-clicking it.)

- **Replace an existing swatch.** Move the cursor over an existing swatch, hold down the Shift key, and click. The swatch is replaced with the new color.

18.4

Delete Swatch

To remove a particular swatch, drag it directly onto this button. Or delete a swatch on-the-fly by (Command) [Control]-clicking it.

Issues to Consider

There is no command to clear the entire contents of the Swatches palette.
However, you can achieve the same effect by clearing the palette manually and saving it as a swatch called "Clear Palette." This way, whenever you want to add a unique set of colors to the palette, you can choose the Clear option from the palette submenu. (For more information, see *9.36, Preset Manager.*)

Note that you cannot save a swatch if the entire palette has been cleared. Therefore, some people save only a single white or gray swatch; others save a large number of same-colored items, such as white, neutral gray, or black.

18.5

The Swatches Palette Submenu

The following commands (18.6–18.12) enable you to refine the appearance and function of the Swatches palette.

18.6

New Swatch

Choose this command to add the current foreground color to the Swatches palette. When you do, the Color Swatch Name dialog box appears, enabling you to enter a descriptive color name.

18.7

Reset Swatches

When you choose this command, an alert appears that gives you two options. If you click OK, the current contents of the palette are replaced with Photoshop's default swatches. If you click Append, the default list is added to the existing palette.

18.8

Load Swatches

This command enables you to load a previously saved list of swatches. Typically, they come from three sources:

- Any swatches saved from the Swatches palette.

- Any color table saved from the Image: Mode: **Color Table** dialog box.

- Any saved swatch that appears at the bottom of the Swatches palette sub-menu. (For more information, see *9.x, Edit: **Preset Manager**.*)

When you choose this command, the new swatches are appended to the current list, or added to the bottom, or added to the current list.

Issues to Consider

Check the current color mode before loading a swatch. You can load a swatch based on any color mode, whether or not it matches the current image. Therefore, it's easy to choose a color that doesn't translate accurately to your target medium. For example, if you use the Mac OS or Web Safe Colors swatch to define a value for an image in CMYK Color mode, there is no way to predict how it will appear when printed. Similarly, if you use a PANTONE Process or Trumatch swatch in a web graphic, you have far less control over how it will appear on screen. For the best results, match the swatch types with an image's intended use.

Be careful when loading a swatch while editing in Indexed Color mode. When importing a specific color palette using the Load Swatches or Replace Swatches commands, make sure the active image is not currently in Indexed Color mode. If so, the imported swatches will only display the colors of the current palette. (This can be confusing, because the new swatches will only display the colors of the current palette—for example, if the current palette contains 16 colors and the imported palette contains 216, the same 16 values will simply appear over and over again. In fact, if the Info palette is visible, you can read the different values of the imported colors as you move the cursor over the palette.) If you convert the image to RGB after importing the palette, the swatches change to display their actual color values.

18.9

Save Swatches

This command saves the current list of swatches into an external file. These files are used in three ways:

- To create an easy way to distribute color schemes to coworkers or other users.

- To save a group of colors as a loadable swatch, which you can access in the future with one-click ease. (For more information, see *9.36, Preset Manager.*)

- To save the list of colors used in a specific project. Typically, these colors are chosen from libraries such as Trumatch or PANTONE Process.

18.10
Replace Swatches

This command is the same as Load Swatches, except the current color items are completely replaced by the new swatch.

18.11
Small Thumbnail

When you choose this display option, the items in the Swatches palette appear as tiny colored squares. To see the name of a particular color, briefly position the cursor over it.

Use this setting when the items in the swatch are placed in a particular arrangement (the Visibone options, for example), or you're simply familiar with viewing the colors in that order (as with the Web Safe Color option, which appears similarly in many other programs).

18.12
Small List

When you choose this display option, the items in the Swatches palette appear as an alphabetical or numerical list, depending on how the individual colors are named.

Use this setting when the swatch contains large numbers of items, especially if they're based on a catalog, such as the PANTONE or Trumatch libraries. However, you'll quickly discover that you can't jump to a palette item by typing the first few characters of its name, like you can in other programs (or even the custom color picker). If you need quick access to a color from a long list, avoid the Swatches palette and use the color picker. Better yet, if you know you're going to use a particular sequence of colors, create your own custom swatch.

The Styles Palette

Styles Palette Overview

When you create a *style*, you save a combination of settings established in the Layer: **Layer Style** dialog box. This way, you're able to apply the same effect to an image layer with a single mouse-click. Saved styles reside in the Styles palette.

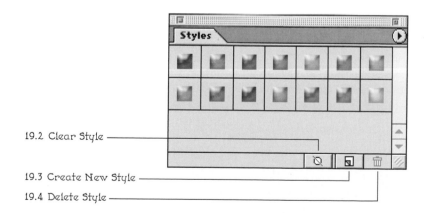

19.2 Clear Style

19.3 Create New Style

19.4 Delete Style

To apply an existing style, activate the desired image layer and click an item in the Styles palette. Because they're a direct extension of the Layer Styles commands, any effect applied from the Styles palette is subject to the same rules and restrictions. (For more information, see *11.18, Layer: **Layer Style**.*)

19.2
Clear Style Button

Click this button to remove any styles from the active layer. It doesn't matter if they were initially applied from the Styles palette or the Layer Style dialog box—all styles and blending options are removed, leaving the original layer information intact. (This button produces the same results as choosing Layer: Layer Styles: *Clear Layer Style.*)

19.3
Create New Style Button

Click this button to create a new style based on the attributes of the active layer. The New Style dialog box is bypassed, as an item is immediately placed in the palette. To give the style a name, double-click its palette item. To access the New Style dialog box, (Option) [Alt]-click the button, or choose New Style from the palette submenu. (For more information, see *19.6, New Style.*)

This button is not available if you haven't applied a layer effect to the active layer, or if you haven't changed its blend mode or opacity value in the Layers palette.

19.4
Delete Style Button

To remove a particular item from the Styles palette, drag it directly onto this button. You can only delete one style at a time this way—unlike other palettes, you can't select an item then click the Delete button. If you do, you simply apply the style, then discover that the button isn't available. To remove a style without dragging, (Option) [Alt]-click it. Deleting a style has no effect on any layers to which you already have applied a style.

19.5

Styles Palette Submenu

The following commands (19.6–19.16) enable you to refine the appearance and function of the Styles palette.

19.6

New Style

Choose this command to create a new style based on the attributes of the active layer. The effect is the same as clicking the Create New Style button—with the exception that the New Style dialog box appears, giving you access to more options.

Issues to Consider

Additional style creation methods. There are three additional ways to add a new item to the Styles palette (each one triggers the New Styles dialog box):

- **Click the New Style button in the Layer Styles dialog box.** This way, you can create a style as soon as you establish the desired values.

- **Click an empty area inside the Styles palette.** Not an incredible time-saver, but it does free you from bothering with the palette submenu.

- **Drag a layer directly onto the Styles palette.** Here, you can drag an item from the Layers palette, or you can use the Move tool to drag the layer directly from the image.

You cannot edit a style. There is no way to directly access the settings of an existing style—therefore, you can't edit one. The closest you can get is the following technique: Apply the style you want to change to a new, blank item in the Layers palette. Choose Layer: **Layer Style** and make the desired edits. Create a new style based on these settings, and delete the old style, if necessary.

Renaming an existing style. To change the name of an existing style, double-click its palette item. The Style Name dialog box appears, enabling you to enter a new name.

The New Style Dialog Box

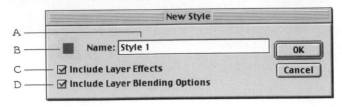

A. **Name**

Enter the desired style name in this field. Be descriptive—the thumbnails don't display information such as semi-opacity or blend modes.

B. **Preview Icon**

This non-editable thumbnail illustrates how the new style would appear when applied to a 16 x 16-pixel gray square. When the icon appears a blank box, it's telling you that the current settings in the New Style dialog box will result in a style that produces no effect.

C. **Include Layer Effects**

When this box is checked, the new style includes any settings that have been established in the Layer Style dialog box. When unchecked, the style only includes the current blend mode and opacity value.

D. **Include Layer Blending Options**

When this box is checked, the new style includes the current blend mode and opacity value. When unchecked, only layer style settings are included. (Note that at least one of the two boxes must be checked—if not, you cannot create a new style.)

19.7

Reset Styles

When you choose this command, an alert appears that gives you two options. If you click OK, the current contents of the palette are replaced with the default set of styles, as established in the Preset Manager. If you click Append, the default set is added to the existing palette. (For more information, see *9.36, Edit: Preset Manager.*)

19.8

Load Styles

This command enables you to add a saved list of styles to the palette.

19.9

Save Styles

This command saves the current list of styles into an external file. Most often, these files are used for the following:

- Distributing special effects or specific treatments to other users.

- Saving a group of styles as a loadable set, which you can access in the future with one-click ease. (For more information, see *19.16, Style Presets.*)

19.10

Replace Styles

This command is the same as Load Styles, except the current palette items are completely replaced by the new set.

19.11

Text Only

When you choose this command, only the style names are listed in the palette. Select this option when thumbnails are not important, or if you must conserve palette space.

19.12

Small Thumbnail

When you choose this command, the styles are listed as small, 16-pixel square thumbnails. Select this option when the style names are not as important as their appearance.

19.13

Large Thumbnail

When you choose this command, the styles are listed as 32-pixel square thumbnails embedded within 64-pixel square buttons. Choose this option when you need to visually discern between subtly-varying styles, or if your monitor is set to an extremely high resolution.

19.14

Small List

When you choose this command, palette items are listed as small thumbnails, followed by the style name.

19.15

Large List

When you choose this command, palette items are listed as larger thumbnails, followed by the style name.

19.16

Style Presets

The bottom of the submenu lists a group of styles that you can load into the palette by choosing the desired item. To add your own to the list, save a series of styles, then place the file in the following location: The Adobe Photoshop 6 folder/Presets folder/Styles folder.

The History Palette

History Palette Overview

The History palette temporarily keeps a record of each command you apply to an image, enabling you to access the contents of an earlier editing stage. It works by saving each edit as a separate palette item called a *history state*. When you need to access a previous image state, you can target the state that contains the desired information.

Another way to view this palette is as Photoshop's most comprehensive *selective reversion* tool. The remaining reversion tools are as follows:

- **Choosing File: Revert.** This command restores the entire image to the last saved version.

- **Choosing Edit: Undo.** This command removes the last single command.

- **Using the History Brush.** This tool allows you to paint the image using the information in the active history state as a source. By selecting different states in the History palette, you can partially re-apply previous incarnations of the image.

- **Using the Eraser tool.** By holding down the (Option) [Alt] key while painting with this tool, you apply the information contained in the active history state–similar to using the History Brush. However, the History Brush is slightly more effective, because you have the option of utilizing different brush modes as you work.

- **Using Edit: Fill.** In the Fill dialog box, you can choose History from the Use pop-up menu, which fills the current selection or layer with the contents of the active snapshot or history state.

Most often, the History palette is used for the following:

- **Simulating multiple Undo levels.** Like Adobe Illustrator or Macromedia FreeHand, the History palette allows you to step backward and forward through your edits. Instead of choosing (Command) [Control]-Z, which performs a single undo, choose (Option-Command) [Alt-Shift]-Z to cycle back through the history states, or (Command-Shift) [Control-Shift]-Z to cycle forward. (Of course, if you change the shortcuts in the Edit: Preferences: **General** dialog box, these keystrokes do not apply.)

- **Specifying a source for the History Brush.** Before you can use this tool (or any other selective reversion command), you must activate the desired state or snapshot.

- **Toggling between effects.** To view the image before and after any of the commands you've applied, first select the desired state. Choose (Option-Command) [Alt-Shift]-Z to hide the effect of the active state; choose (Command-Shift) [Control-Shift]-Z to reveal the effect again. For example, this is useful if you need to go back and double-check the amount of sharpening you applied to the image.

- **Taking multiple snapshots.** In earlier versions of Photoshop, you could only save one snapshot at a time. The History palette allows you to create a snapshot any time you want to save a version of the image separate from the history states. This way, you can always revert back to a specific version of the image, even if the correlating history state has disappeared. There is no numerical limit to the number you can save—you can continue creating snapshots until all the RAM allocated to the program is filled.

- **Testing a series of commands.** Instead of duplicating the image in order to test the effect of multiple commands, you can simply apply the commands to the original image, and choose (Option-Command) [Alt-Shift]-Z to undo the series if you don't want to keep it. If desired, you can create a snapshot before undoing the commands for later use.

- **Restoring the image to its original state.** When you choose File: **Revert**, you restore the last saved version of the image. To restore the image to the way it was when you first opened it—regardless of how many times you've saved—activate the top snapshot in the palette. (Note that in order for this snapshot to appear, the Automatically Create First Snapshot box must be checked in the History Options dialog box.)

Mistakes to Avoid

Assuming that history states save with the image. The contents of the History palette are only available while an image is open. As soon as the image is saved and closed, the palette contents are purged. However, you do have the option of preserving a state as an individual image. Before closing, select the desired state and choose New Document from the History palette submenu. The state is opened in a new image window, which you can then save as needed. Additionally, when you duplicate an image by choosing Image: **Duplicate**, the history states do not carry over.

Attempting to access states that were generated before changing the image's dimensions, resolution, or color mode. When you apply these types of commands, you cannot utilize any of the states that existed beforehand. However, if you later change the image back to its original status, you can access the original states. For example, if you convert an image from RGB to CMYK, you cannot restore any state created while the image was in RGB mode. If you change the image back to RGB, you can then access the states—but then, you cannot access any state created while the image was in CMYK.

Accidentally deleting hidden states. When you activate an earlier state, the subsequent items are dimmed, indicating that they're hidden. If you apply an edit at this point, the hidden items are removed from the palette. Unless you immediately choose Edit: **Undo**, you cannot restore the deleted history states. (Note that this does not occur when the Allow Non-Linear History box is checked in the History Options dialog box.)

Incorrectly clicking a snapshot or state. One of the more confusing aspects of the History palette is the difference between *targeting* an item and *activating* it. When you click the small paint box to the left of a snapshot or state, you *target* it, which enables you to refer to its contents through a different part of Photoshop (for example, with the History Brush tool). When you click directly on a snapshot or state, you *activate* it, or display its contents on screen. This can produce unexpected results; for example, if you're trying to target a snapshot and activate it by accident, the entire image will change. If this happens, choose Edit: **Undo** immediately, and try again.

Issues to Consider

Higher maximum numbers of history states require more RAM. Although the palette can contain up to 100 history states, the number you can successfully work with ultimately depends on the amount of RAM allocated to Photoshop, the intensity of your edits, and the size of the image. If your workstation has a smaller amount of RAM (96 MB or below), you might want to set a lower number of histories—say, between 20 and 40—when working with larger images.

Purge history states if you run low on memory. To free up the RAM occupied by unneeded states, choose Edit: Purge: **Histories** (or, if desired, Edit: Purge: **All**). You can also choose Clear History from the palette submenu, which gives you the option of choosing Edit: **Undo** immediately afterwards. Make sure you won't require the deleted states before performing either of these commands. Conversely, if you never use the History palette, avoid the need to purge its contents by setting the maximum number of states to 1. (For more information, see *9.47, Edit: Preferences: **General**.*)

It's possible to remove the effect of a single command applied to an image by deleting its history state. By default, if you delete a state, you also delete all states that were generated after it. However, if you check the Allow Non-Linear History box in the History Options dialog box, you can remove a state while leaving the subsequent items untouched.

Add the contents of a history state to another image. If you drag a state onto another image, the contents of the palette item replace the contents of the second image. Unlike copying a layer or channel, the entire contents are replaced—even the width, height, resolution, and color mode change to accommodate the new information.

However, if you drag a snapshot onto an image, only the snapshot's palette item is carried over. This allows you to access the snapshot as if it were created in the current image. Note that if the copied snapshot's width, height, resolution, or color mode is different than the current image, you will not be able to access its contents with any selective reversion commands.

20.2

The History Palette Controls

The History palette contains the following options.

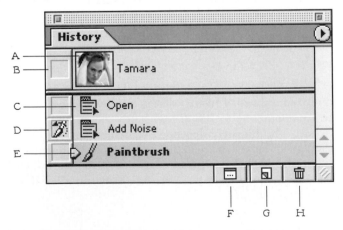

A. **Snapshot**

This thumbnail represents a *snapshot*, or a temporary copy of the image. Snapshots are not based on a specific edit, like the history states. Rather, you take a snapshot to preserve a version of the image that you can access later. Unlike history states, you can rename snapshots to recognize them more easily.

B. **Snapshot Activation Box**

To access the contents of a particular snapshot when selectively reverting, you must click this box next to the desired item.

C. **History State**

Every time you edit an image, a new state appears in the palette. These items appear chronologically—the first edit appears at the top, and subsequent edits are inserted below.

The name of each state is based on the edit it represents.

By default, 20 history states can be displayed. After you exceed this number of edits, these items are removed from the palette: the original state first, then the second, the third, and so on. To prevent this from occurring, raise the maximum number of history items in the History Options dialog box.

D. **State Activation Box**

To access the contents of a particular state when selectively reverting, you must click this box next to the desired item.

E. **History State Slider**

When a state is highlighted, this triangular tab appears between the activation box and the palette item. Drag this slider up or down to simultaneously activate and highlight palette items. Make sure you drag straight up and down—if the cursor falls off to either side, the slider won't behave as expected.

F. **Create New Document from Current State Button**

Because you cannot save the contents of the History palette, it gives you the option of saving a state or snapshot as a separate image. To do this, activate the desired state and click this button. The item opens in a new image window, which you can save as needed.

You can achieve the same effect by dragging a palette item onto this button, or by activating an item and choosing New Document from the palette submenu.

G. **Create New Snapshot Button**

Click this button to create a new snapshot. This is the same as choosing New Snapshot from the palette submenu. (See "New Snapshot," later in this chapter, for more information.)

H. Delete Button

To remove a snapshot or state, highlight it and click this button. You can also delete an item by dragging it onto this button, or by highlighting it and choosing Delete from the palette submenu.

20.3
The History Palette Submenu

The following commands (20.4–20.10) enable you to refine the appearance and function of the History palette.

20.4
Step Forward *(Command-Shift) [Control-Shift]-Z*

Choose this command to activate the next state down in the History palette. If the last state is currently highlighted, this command is not available. Most often, this command is chosen after choosing Step Backward. (Note that this command and Edit: **Step Forward** are exactly the same.)

20.5
Step Backward *(Option-Command) [Alt-Control]-Z*

Choose this command to activate the next state up in the History palette. Repeatedly stepping back to previous states creates the effect of multiple undo levels. (Note that this command and Edit: **Step Backward** are exactly the same.)

20.6
New Snapshot

Choose this command to add a new snapshot to the History palette. By default, the effect is the same as (Option) [Alt]-clicking the palette's New button.

This command cannot be undone, nor does choosing it appear as a state in the History palette. To remove a snapshot, you must highlight it and choose Delete from the palette submenu (or click the Delete button).

The New Snapshot Dialog Box

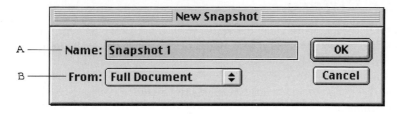

A. Name

Enter the desired name for the new snapshot in this field. Be descriptive; because you only have a small thumbnail to refer to, the name should allow you to quickly identify its contents.

B. From

The options of this pop-up menu determine the information included in the new snapshot:

Full Document

This option results in a snapshot of the entire image, maintaining the individual layers.

Merged Layers

This option also takes a snapshot of the entire image, but the individual layers are merged. This only pertains to the contents of the snapshot—the actual image layers are untouched.

Current Layer

This option results in a snapshot of only the currently active image layer.

20.7

Delete

Choose this command to remove the highlighted snapshot or state from the History palette. When you delete a state, its effect on the remaining states depends on whether the Allow Non-Linear History option is checked in the History Options dialog box:

- If it's unchecked, deleting a state also removes all states that follow it (and their effect on the image).

- If it's checked, you can delete a single state without affecting the states that follow.

20.8

Clear History

Choose this command to clear the states from the History palette. One state remains, however—the currently highlighted item. So if you want to leave the image completely untouched when the palette is cleared, make sure the last state is highlighted before choosing this command. To clear the palette while reverting the image to an earlier state, activate the desired state before choosing this command.

20.9

New Document

Choose this command to place the contents of the currently active snapshot or state into a new document. The new image initially contains the same title as the original palette item, but you can change the filename when you choose File: **Save**.

20.10

History Options

The options in this dialog box determine the overall behavior of the History palette.

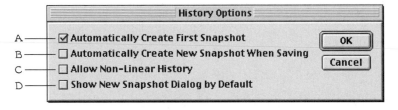

A. Automatically Create First Snapshot

When this box is checked, Photoshop adds a snapshot of an image as soon as it is opened. This enables you to revert to the image's original form, regardless of how many times it has been saved. When unchecked, no snapshot is added when you open the image (although, if desired, you can create one before performing any additional edits).

B. Automatically Create New Snapshot When Saving

When this box is checked, Photoshop adds a new snapshot every time you save an image. You don't have the option to name the snapshot; instead, each new item is labeled with the time the save occurred. Only enable this option when it is essential that you have access to previously saved iterations of the file. (For example, some illustrators apply lengthy sequences of effects and filters to their images, saving after each step to produce a snapshot, then use selective reversion techniques to blend the different versions together.) If you don't require this option, leave it off; otherwise, you may find the additional snapshots devouring your available RAM.

Remember that as soon as you close the image, the snapshots are discarded. Regardless of how many there were, Photoshop only retains the one most recently created. If you need to save any snapshots in particular, use the New Document command (in the palette submenu) to place them into separate files before closing the original.

C. **Allow Non-Linear History**

When this box is unchecked, you cannot edit your states non-sequentially. For example, if you delete a state from the middle of the list, all the undone states (or, the states that follow the highlighted item) are removed as well. When this box is checked, however, you can remove a state while leaving the edits that followed intact.

D. **Show New Snapshot Dialog By Default**

This option only pertains to the New Snapshot button in the History palette. When checked, the New Snapshot dialog box appears when you click the button; to bypass it, hold down the (Option) [Alt] key as you click. When unchecked, clicking the New Snapshot button automatically bypasses the dialog box; to access it, hold down the (Option) [Alt] key as you click.

Whether this option is enabled or not, the New Snapshot dialog box is accessed when you choose New Snapshot from the History palette submenu. To bypass it, hold down the (Option) [Alt] key while choosing the command.

The Actions Palette

Actions Palette Overview

A Photoshop action is a *script*, or a recorded series of commands that you can apply to an image with a single mouse-click or keystroke. The result is similar to a macro created with AppleScript or a program like CE Software's *QuicKeys*. Actions they can be simple or complex. Simple actions only apply one command, such as filling with semi-opaque white or rotating a selection by a specific value. Complex actions can involve multiple layer, channel, and filter-based adjustments.

Most often, actions are used to ease the tedium of applying the same string of commands over and over again. For example, this book contains about 500 screenshots that were captured with Snapz Pro, a popular utility from Ambrosia Software. Before applying any specific edits, you'd have to perform the following on each image: convert to Grayscale, open the Image Size dialog box, open the Save As dialog box, and close the image. These commands only take about a minute to apply, but the fact that you'd otherwise be required to spend almost 500 minutes (8+ hours) repeating yourself make this sequence a perfect candidate for a script. An action would enable you to record the steps, then press the assigned keystroke whenever you open a new screenshot in Photoshop.

Actions are also commonly used for the following:

- **Standardized corporate procedures.** When a large corporation maintains a graphics department, its employees can number in the hundreds, and they can be spread out in branches all over the country. To ensure that the most important techniques are executed consistently, they will distribute a series of actions that contain the necessary commands.

- **Training materials.** By inserting informative dialogs that describe every step of a technique, tech support staff or IS personnel can use an action to teach a new or updated technique to Photoshop users. (For more information, see *A.18, Including Special Notes or Instructions.*)

- **Canned special effects.** Many Web sites and after-market books distribute special effects such as custom frames, 3-D effects, and the creation of specialized images as actions. By copying them to your hard drive and loading them into your Actions palette, you can apply these effects without necessarily understanding the steps that comprise them.

- **Batch processing.** You can use Photoshop's Batch dialog to automatically apply the same action to any number of images. (For more information, see *A.24, Preparing to Batch Process* and *A.25, Executing a Batch.*)

The controls for recording, duplicating, arranging, and running your actions are found in the Actions palette.

21.2

Actions Palette Controls

The Control Buttons are found at the bottom of the Actions palette, when the palette is in List view. The first three are labeled with the same symbols for Stop, Record, and Play found on most tape recorders and vcrs. In fact, their function is almost identical.

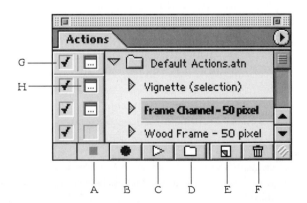

A. Stop Playing/Recording

This button is only available when an action is recording or playing. Click it to stop the current function. The Stop button has the same effect as choosing Stop Recording or Stop Playing from the palette submenu. Key equivalents include pressing the Escape key or (Command) [Control]-Period.

B. Begin Recording

Click this button to record additional commands into an existing action. New commands are inserted after the currently selected item. If the action itself is selected, new additions are placed at the end of the current list of commands. The Record button has the same effect as choosing Start Recording from the palette submenu.

C. Play Selection

The effect of this button depends on the selected item. If an action is selected, it executes its sequence of commands. If a single command is selected from within an action, it executes the sequence from that point onward. In both cases, clicking this button is the same as choosing Play from the palette submenu.

To play only the selected command, hold down the (Command) [Control] key while clicking this button. Or, hold down the (Command) [Control] key while double-clicking the command. (Be aware that double-clicking on a command in the Actions palette opens its dialog box. You can enter new settings and click OK to apply the command, but watch out—the new settings are recorded in the action, and the old settings are discarded.)

D Create New Set

Click this button to add a new set to the Actions palette. Doing so produces the same result as choosing New Set from the palette submenu.

E. Create New Action

Click this button to access the New Action dialog box, similar to choosing New Action from the palette submenu. (For more information, see "New Action," later in this chapter.)

F. Delete

Click this button to permanently remove the currently selected item. An alert appears, asking if you want to delete the action or command. Click OK to continue. To bypass the alert, hold down the (Option) [Alt] key while clicking Delete, or drag the item and drop it on the button.

G. Enable/Disable Checkbox

When the Actions palette is in List mode, each action (and its component commands) is preceded by either one or two checkboxes.

When a checkmark is visible in the first box, it indicates that an action is enabled, and can be played at any time. If there is no checkmark, the action is disabled—selecting it and clicking the Play button has no effect. By default, this box is checked when an action is created.

To disable an individual command within the action, click the Open triangle next to the action's title and click the appropriate checkbox. The next time you play the action, Photoshop skips any disabled commands. The primary checkmark for the entire action appears red when any of its commands are disabled. Clicking this checkmark again enables all disabled commands.

H. **Open Dialog Checkbox**

The second checkbox is only available to commands controlled by a dialog box. Commands without a dialog box, such as Image: Mode: **Invert**, display a blank space instead.

This box determines whether or not the dialog box appears while the action is running. By default, Photoshop retains the settings that you applied while recording an action. With Open Dialog off, the action simply uses all the recorded settings without opening the dialog box. With Open Dialog on, the command's dialog box is opened the next time you play the action. This way, you can enter different settings for a command without the need to record a new action. Click OK to close the dialog box and continue the sequence.

When one command within an action has Open Dialog turned on, a red mark appears in the box next to the action's title. Clicking this mark once turns on all the Open Dialog marks; clicking it again turns them all off.

21.3
Actions Palette Submenu

The following commands (21.4–21.21) enable you to refine the appearance and function of the Actions palette.

21.4
New Action

This command is the equivalent of the New Action control button. Two things happen when you choose this command. It opens the New Action dialog box, where you name the action and assign a keystroke. After you close the dialog box, it immediately starts recording an action.

Issues to Consider

F-key assignments are only visible when the Actions palette is in Button mode. To see the keyboard shortcut while in List mode, include the name of the F-key in the title of the action.

The New Action Dialog Box

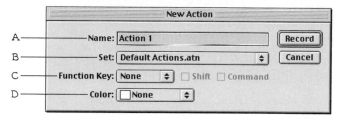

A. Name

Name the new action in this field. Be as descriptive as possible, so the action is quickly identifiable. The name can be up to 32 characters long.

B. Set

This pop-up menu displays all sets currently available in the Actions palette. If more than one set exists, the one that is currently active appears in the pop-up menu by default. If you want the new action to be placed into a different set, specify the desired item here.

C. Shortcut Keys

The only key equivalent you can assign to an action is one of the 15 Function keys of your keyboard. The pop-up menu lists all currently available keys, or the ones that have not been assigned to an action. Even though Photoshop defaults to its own set of F-key shortcuts, they are overridden by an action using the same key. In the future, pressing the assigned F-key executes the action, similar to selecting an action from the palette and pressing the Play button.

After assigning an F-key, you can add modifier keys to the shortcut by checking the Shift or (Command) [Control] boxes, or both. For example, if you set F5 in the pop-up menu and check the Shift box, pressing Shift-F5 will trigger the action in the future; if you set F9 and check Shift and (Command) [Control], you'll press (Command-Shift) [Control-Shift]-F9.

Adding modifier keys to the F-key shortcuts increases the possible number of key equivalents to 90.

D. Color

This option colors the action when the Actions palette is in Button view.

21.5

New Set

This command creates a new folder (or set) in the Actions palette. Sets are simply a way to organize multiple scripts in the Actions palette. Acting like ordinary folders, they can have up to 24 scripts in each set. There is no realistic limit on the number of sets you can create.

21.6

Duplicate

This command makes an exact copy of the current selection, similar to holding down the (Option) [Alt] key and dragging.

21.7

Delete

This command permanently removes the current selection from the Actions palette, similar to pressing the Delete button.

Issues to Consider

The Delete command cannot be reversed by choosing Edit: Undo. When an action or command is removed, it can only be restored if it was saved using Save Actions.

21.8

Play

When an action is selected, this command executes its sequence of commands. When a single command within an action is selected, it runs the action from that command onward. This command is the equivalent of pressing the Play button.

21.9

Start Recording

This allows you to add commands to an existing action, similar to pressing the Record button. If the action's title is selected, the new commands are placed at the bottom of the list. If a specific command is selected, the new commands are inserted immediately after it.

Issues to Consider

You cannot record Edit: Undo as part of an action. Not only does it reverse the last command, it erases it from the recording. This allows you to undo erroneous commands and continue recording an action without stopping. If you must add Edit: **Undo** to an action, use the Insert Menu Item command after you've stopped recording. (For more information, see *21.10, Insert Menu Item.*)

21.10

Record Again

When a script is selected in the Actions palette, this item allows you to replace all the operations, while leaving its name, F-key, and color untouched. When a single operation is selected, it allows you to replace a single, selected item within an action.

21.11

Insert Menu Item

Certain menu items may not be remembered when you record an action. This command allows you to insert them after the action is defined.

When you insert a menu item that uses an editable dialog box, it will always appear when the action is run. Because no Open Dialog checkbox is available for inserted commands, you cannot turn this feature off. When you enter the desired settings in the dialog box and click OK, the action executes the remaining commands. Click the Cancel button in the dialog box to stop the action at its next command.

21.12

Insert Stop

Although this command claims to insert a *stop*, it does not stop an action from running. Rather, it pauses the action in progress and displays a dialog box containing a user-defined message. Common uses include the following:

- **Manually executing commands.** Certain commands cannot be included in an action, such as painting or manipulating a transformation box. By inserting a stop, you pause the action long enough to perform the necessary work by hand. When you click the Play button again, the action resumes.

- **Sending a message to the user.** If desired, you can set your own message to appear when the action reaches a Stop. For example, a Stop dialog box inserted at the beginning of an action could thoroughly describe the action and any special preparations it requires. Messages inserted in the middle of an action usually contain special instructions.

Issues to Consider

Enabling or disabling a Stop dialog box. Like other commands, the dialog box of an inserted Stop is controlled by the Open Dialog checkbox in the Actions palette. To have the dialog box appear, check the box. To ignore the dialog box and only pause the action, uncheck the box. Disable the Stop completely by unchecking the Enable box.

The Record Stop Dialog Box

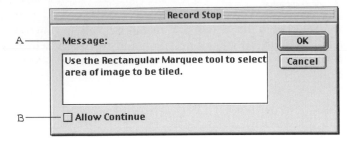

A. **Message Box**

Here, you can enter a message up to 200 characters long. It should clearly communicate the purpose for stopping. For example, a Stop dialog box at the beginning of an action could say, "This action creates embossed text—create text using Type Mask tool before continuing." A Stop inserted in the middle might say, "Action stopped because original image window must be made active before continuing."

B. **Allow Continue**

Checking this box allows the user to choose between continuing or stopping an action from the Stop dialog box. If this button is left unchecked, the only available option is stopping.

21.13

Insert Path

Use this command to insert a path created using one of the Pen tools. In order for the command to be available in the palette submenu, you must select a path that already exists in the Paths palette.

After a path is added to a script, the coordinates of each anchor point (as well as each curve handle) appear in the new operation. This way, Photoshop knows the precise information required to reproduce the path when the action is run on future images.

To insert the path in the appropriate sequence, select the operation that appears *before* the desired location. In other words, when you run the script, the path will appear *after* the operation that was selected when you chose the Insert Path command.

Issues to Consider

Inserted paths are not automatically saved. When you run an action that includes an inserted path, the new path is not saved, even if the original was. Instead, it appears as a work path.

An inserted path retains its original position, even if the currenty image is too small. When running the script on a smaller image than the one that contained the original path, the inserted path may fall completely outside the image boundaries. If this occurs, the path is still built into the file. If you select the path in the Paths palette, then choose View: **Zoom Out** until the image is smaller than the image window; you can usually locate the path in the gray area that surrounds the image. If desired, you can reposition it with one of the the path selection tools. Be aware that if the path falls completely outside the image boundaries, it cannot be used to edit the image.

21.14

Action Options

This command allows you to change the name, F-key, and color of the selected action. The Action Options dialog box is identical to the New Action dialog box, but it only changes the appearance of an action's palette item.

21.15

Playback Options

The items in this dialog box determine the method Photoshop uses to run a script from the Actions palette.

The Playback Options Dialog Box

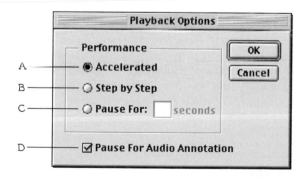

A. **Accelerated**

When this option is selected, the script plays as fast as Photoshop can apply the commands. This is the preferred setting for everyday work.

B. **Step by Step**

When this option is selected, Photoshop refreshes the screen after each operation in the script.

C. **Pause For** (1–60 seconds)

This option enables you to insert a specific amount of time between each operation.

D. **Pause for Audio Annotation**

When this option is checked, the action will pause long enough for any embedded audio annotations to play completely before continuing. When unchecked, the action will continue running while an audio annotation plays.

21.16

Clear Actions

This permanently removes all current actions from the Actions palette. You cannot Undo this command—after the actions are cleared, there is no way to bring them back. The only actions you can recover are the Photoshop defaults and any actions that you have already saved.

21.17

Reset Actions

This replaces all current actions with the Photoshop defaults. If you have custom-tailored some of those defaults or do not want to replace your current actions, click Append in the alert. The defaults are added to the end of the palette.

Issues to Consider

You don't have to retain the Default Actions set. Because they were not tailored to your specific work, they're probably of little use. They do illustrate the basic functions of the Actions palette, however, so consider hanging on to them while you become more familiar with the palette. Then delete them to make room for your own actions.

21.18

Load Actions

Use this command to add a pre-existing set of actions to the palette. When loaded, it appears at the end of the current list.

21.19

Replace Actions

Use this command to remove the current list of actions and replace them with a saved set.

21.20

Save Actions

Use this command to save the currently selected set of actions into a separate file. You can only save a set—if you select multiple sets or a single action, this command is not available.

21.21

Button Mode

Although only Button mode is listed at the bottom of the palette submenu, repeatedly selecting it toggles between the two views of the Actions palette.

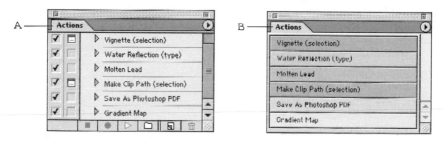

A. **List View**

This option is indicated by the lack of a checkmark next to Button mode in the submenu. Here, the actions are arranged vertically. Each one has a Show arrow. Turn the arrow to display an action's commands; turn the arrow next to a command to display its settings and values.

Actions and commands can only be recorded, rearranged, and edited in List view. It also provides a status report while the action is running—when the commands are shown, each one highlights while it is being applied. If the list is too long to display completely in the Actions palette, it automatically scrolls.

The List view displays the control buttons at the bottom of the Actions palette, giving you quick access to the New, Record, Stop, Play, and Delete commands.

B. **Button View**

This view strips the Actions palette to its barest essentials, making it easier to use. Actions are reduced to single buttons labeled only with the name of the action and its assigned F-key. Simply click a button to run an action.

Actions can only be played in this view—they cannot be created or edited. You must change back to List view to edit actions. All control buttons are hidden.

Since Button mode does not show commands, provides no feedback, and prohibits editing, its usefulness is extremely limited. Button view is most useful for emulating the Commands palette, an ancestor of the Actions palette found in earlier versions of Photoshop.

The Layers Palette

The Layers palette enables you to store, position, and arrange the different types of layers available in Photoshop. All items are listed in hierarchical order—layers at the top of the list appear in front of layers at the bottom.

22.1 Set the Opacity

22.2 Set Blending Mode

22.3 Lock Options

22.4 View, Hide Layer

22.5 Layer Status

22.6 Add a Layer Style

22.7 Add a Mask

22.8 Create a Layer Set

22.9 Create New Fill or Adjustment Layer

22.10 Create New Layer

22.11 Delete Layer

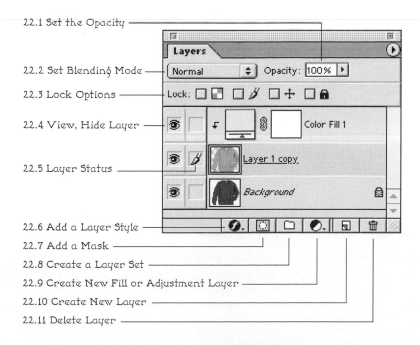

There are three types of layers: background layers, image layers, and content layers (which include fill and adjustment layers). Although each type is used for different purposes, they are treated identically by the tools of the Layers palette. (For more information, see *11.1, Layers Overview.*)

22.1

Set the Opacity

This slider allows you to change the opacity setting of the active image or adjustment layer. Depending on the type of layer selected, manipulating the opacity slider produces different effects:

- **Image and content layers.** Reducing the opacity of an image layer creates the appearance of semi-transparency. Actually, Photoshop combines the color values of the active layer with the values of the underlying image information. For example, if the opacity is reduced to 70%, then 30% of the visible color values are based on the underlying colors.

- **Adjustment layers.** Reducing the opacity of an adjustment layer lessens the effect of its adjustment command. For example, if an adjustment layer darkens the underlying pixels by 20%, lowering its opacity to 50% reduces the impact of the command by half—the underlying pixels are only darkened by 10%.

- **Background layers.** The opacity slider is not available when the background layer is selected in the Layers palette.

Issues to Consider

Shortcuts for setting opacity. If desired, enter opacity values by typing numbers on the keyboard. Opacity values for single numbers register in multiples of 10. For example, type 1 for a value of 10%, 8 for a value of 80%, and so on. Type 0 to set the opacity to 100%. To enter a precise two-digit value, enter the numbers in rapid succession.

Related Topics

11.5   Transparency
11.6   Opacity

22.2

Set the Blending Mode

Multiple layers enable multiple pixels to share the same XY coordinates in the image window. For display and print purposes, however, only one pixel can appear at each coordinate. This pop-up menu contains a list of *blending modes,* which affect how the contents of one layer combine with the color values of the underlying info.

When you apply a blending mode, every non-transparent pixel in the active layer is recalculated and changed to a new value. Therefore, layering involves three values:

- **Blend colors.** The blend colors are the values contained in the layer receiving the change in blending modes.

- **Base colors.** The base colors are the values contained in the underlying layers.

- **Result colors.** The result colors are the values ultimately produced by a blending mode. These values change whenever you select a new blending mode, but they become permanent when the layer is merged or the image is flattened.

At first, blending modes seem like just another way to create bizarre special effects, like certain filters or color adjustment commands. While some of them do produce off-the-wall color changes, it's important to remember that every one of them was created to be a production aid. When used most successfully, blending modes are usually part of a larger, more focused technique.

Issues to Consider

Blending modes base their calculations on brightness values, not color mode. To better understand how blending modes work, go straight to an image's color channels. No matter what the current color mode is, the contents of each channel are the same: Every pixel is one of 256 possible tones, just like a Grayscale image. Ultimately, the color modes apply a different meaning to those channel values (CMYK Color converts them to output values, Lab Color converts them to coordinates within a color model, and RGB Color continues to regard them as brightness values). Blending modes, on the other hand, refer directly to the gray levels in the color channels to calculate new values. (For more information, see *10.1, Image: Mode Overview.*)

Assume you're working on an RGB image. The base color is R: 50, G: 50, B: 200 (royal blue), and the blend color is R: 240, G: 200, B: 90 (gold). A blending mode compares the two brightness values for each channel, then applies a calculation to produce a third value. For example, if the blending mode is Multiply, it calculates R: 50 and R: 240 to produce R: 47; G: 50 and G: 200 to produce G: 39; and B: 200 and B: 90 to produce B: 71. The result color, therefore, is R: 47, G: 39, B: 71 (navy blue). If you change the blending mode, a different formula is applied to the same numbers, which produces a new range of color values. (For more information on these calculations, see "Multiply," later in this section.)

Now assume you're working on a CMYK image. Even though Photoshop presents color values as output percentages, the individual channels are still based on 256 levels of gray. When you apply a blending mode here, it ignores the values that you see in the Info palette and refers directly to the brightness levels of the color channels. Because each color mode ultimately applies a different meaning to the channel data, the result colors typically vary from mode to mode. However, the math used to generate them is identical.

Blending modes work on Grayscale images, too. The use of blending modes is not restricted to full-color images. In fact, you can create some surprisingly subtle montage effects when you apply these modes to a layered Grayscale image. Because the range of possible colors is reduced to 256 levels of gray, you eliminate the possibility of wild, unpredictable result colors. Instead, the affected elements appear to become seamlessly intertwined.

Most blending modes have a neutral color. A neutral color is a value that results in no color change when you apply the blending mode. For example, Multiply's neutral color is white. If you apply that mode to a layer that contains white pixels, they simply become transparent; the underlying colors remain unaltered. You can set a neutral color when you first create a layer (it appears as an option in the New: **New Layer** dialog box), or you can simply fill or paint the desired neutral value into an existing layer. There are three neutral colors:

- **Black.** The neutral color for Screen, Color Dodge, Lighten, Difference, and Exclusion.
- **White.** The neutral color for Multiply, Color Burn, and Darken.
- **50% Gray.** The neutral color for Overlay, Soft Light, and Hard Light.

The Normal, Dissolve, Hue, Saturation, Color, and Luminosity modes have no neutral colors.

Utilizing the blending modes' neutral colors. A neutral color is a natural by-product of a blending mode's calculations—most often, you don't even have to think of them when choosing a mode. However, by deliberately using the influence of a neutral color, you can execute some reasonably efficient (and sometimes unique) techniques. Consider these examples:

- Some filters, such as Filter: Render: **Lens Flare** or **Lighting Effects**, cannot be applied to a transparent, empty image layer. Many users assume that the only option is to apply the filter directly to the target layer, which profoundly limits your ability to make additional tweaks or edits. By choosing a blending mode and filling a layer with its neutral color, you apply the effect of these filters without permanently altering the actual image.

  Moving artwork from a Grayscale scan (such as a pencil or charcoal sketch) into a color image is tricky. Some people drag-and-drop the layer, then try to delete the white pixels that carry over; others try to select only the anti-aliased artwork, then transfer it to the color image. Try dragging the entire layer into the color image, then setting the new layer to Multiply. The white pixels surrounding the artwork disappear (because white is Multiply's neutral color), leaving the black and gray tones to overprint the underlying colors.

"Remembering" the keyboard shortcuts for applying blending modes.
After activating an item in the Layers palette, you can apply a keystroke to trigger the desired mode. Some shortcuts are obvious (for example, (Option-Shift) [Alt-Shift]-N for Normal, or (Option-Shift) [Alt-Shift]-M for Multiply); some aren't (for example, (Option-Shift) [Alt-Shift]-I for Dissolve, or (Option-Shift) [Alt-Shift]-F for Soft Light). There is no need to memorize all the shortcuts. Instead, hold down the (Option-Shift) [Alt-Shift] keys with one hand, and start typing the name of the desired mode with the other. The shortcut for each mode is based on the first available letter in its name.

Blending **modes are not quite the same as** *brush* **modes.** Don't confuse blending modes with the brush modes found in the Options bar settings for each Paint tool. Although the options of both lists are largely the same, the techniques required to apply them are different. Blending modes affect the contents of an entire layer. By using the Paint tools, you can affect a smaller portion of a layer with brush modes.

Normal *(Option-Shift) [Alt-Shift]-N*

This mode displays the full values of the blend colors (if the opacity is set to 100%). Any non-transparent pixels conceal any underlying information.

When working on an image in Bitmap or Indexed Color mode, this item appears as Threshold in the pop-up menu.

Dissolve *(Option-Shift) [Alt-Shift]-I*

This mode only affects semi-transparent pixels. Here, a layer's contents do not blend with the underlying pixels. Instead, certain pixels are made transparent while the rest remain at 100% opacity, resulting in a diffused, scattered effect.

The amount of scattered pixels is determined by the transparency value of the layer. If its opacity slider is set to 60%, then 60% of the pixels in the layer remain fully opaque, and 40% of the pixels become fully transparent. Even if a layer's opacity is set to 100%, this mode still affects semi-transparent pixels such as soft-edged brushstrokes or anti-aliased shapes.

Multiply *(Option-Shift) [Alt-Shift]-M*

The resulting color produced by this mode is always darker than the blend and base colors.

Multiplying brightness values is exactly the same as multiplying fractions. For a moment, imagine that the 256 potential brightness values of a color channel are a range extending from 0 to 1. Zero is black, or a brightness value of 0. One is white, or a brightness value of 255. If you treat the remaining values as fractions, you can regard a brightness value of 100 as 100/255, and a value of 200 as 200/255.

If you apply one value to the other using Multiply, the resulting color value is the product of the two fractions, or 78 (78/255). Because multiplying two fractions always results in a smaller fraction (here, a lower brightness value), the resulting color is always darker.

Issues to Consider

Try a calculation shortcut. An easier method of calculating the result color is to multiply the brightness values of each component values of the base and blend color, then divide that number by 255. In other words, 100 x 200 ÷ 255 = 78.431, which rounds down to 78.

This mode is used almost exclusively when creating realistic shadows. The most useful feature of Multiply is the way it handles gray tones. When the blend colors are gray or black, this mode uses them to naturally darken the underlying colors.

Screen   *(Option-Shift) [Alt-Shift]-S*

The effect of this mode is the opposite of Multiply. The result colors it produces are always lighter than the blend and base colors.

To create screened values, Photoshop multiplies the inverted values of the base colors and blend colors. It then inverts the new brightness values, creating lighter tones.

For example, if you apply a value of 100 to a value of 200 (similar to the example described under Multiply), Photoshop inverts the values and multiplies 155/255 and 55/255. The product is 33, which is inverted to create the result value of 222. (See *Issues to Consider*, below.)

Issues to Consider

Inverting brightness values. To invert a tone, subtract its value from 255. For example, inverting a value of 50 results in 205. (For more information, see *10.31, Image: Adjust: Invert.*)

Creating a monotone effect. One of the more useful features of this mode is its ability to simulate a one-color halftone. In a color image, the base colors must consist entirely of gray tones—for example, when you've applied Image: Adjust: **Desaturate** to an image layer. If you create a new layer filled with a solid color and set the blending mode to Screen, the underlying gray values appear to be replaced with the blend color. (For more information, see *H.2, Creating an RGB Monotone.*)

Overlay
(Option-Shift) [Alt-Shift]-O

The effect of this mode is the same as either Multiply or Screen, depending on the values of the base colors. Brightness values lower than 128 (the midpoint) are *multiplied* by the blend colors. Brightness values higher than 128 are *screened* by the blend colors.

Depending on the blend and base colors, the Overlay mode produces the following results:

* **Blend and Base elements: full color.** Here, the effect of the Overlay mode is similar to reducing the opacity of the blending layer, with exaggerated highlights and shadows.

* **Blend: gray tones; Base: full color.** Here, the Overlay mode uses the gray information in the blending layer to lighten or darken the tone of the underlying colors.

* **Blend: solid color; Base: desaturated gray tones.** Here, the Overlay mode uses the blend color to colorize the underlying tonal information, similar to using the Colorize option in the Hue/Saturation command.

Soft Light
(Option-Shift) [Alt-Shift]-F

The effect of this mode is similar to Overlay, only less intense.

Hard Light
(Option-Shift) [Alt-Shift]-H

The effect of this mode is similar to Overlay, only more intense.

Color Dodge
(Option-Shift) [Alt-Shift]-D

This mode lightens the base colors. The resulting hues are shifted toward the blend colors. Lighter blend colors cause more intense changes, while darker colors produce a more subtle effect.

Color Burn
(Option-Shift) [Alt-Shift]-B

This mode lightens the base colors. The resulting hues are shifted toward the blend colors. Lighter blend colors cause more intense changes, while darker colors produce a more subtle effect.

Darken
(Option-Shift) [Alt-Shift]-K

This mode compares the component brightness values of the base colors and blend colors. The result colors are formed by the darkest brightness values of each channel. For example, if a blend color is R: 160, G: 70, B: 220 and a base color is R: 80, G: 120, B: 155, the result color is R: 80, G: 70, B: 155.

Lighten
(Option-Shift) [Alt-Shift]-L

This mode compares the component brightness values of the base colors and blend colors. The resulting colors are formed by the lightest brightness values of each channel. For example, if a blend color is R: 160, G: 70, B: 220 and a base color is R: 80, G: 120, B: 155, the result color is R: 160, G: 120, B: 220.

Difference   *(Option-Shift) [Alt-Shift]-E*

This mode compares the component brightness values of the base colors and blend colors. The resulting colors are formed by subtracting the smaller values from the larger values. For example, if a blend color is R: 160, G: 70, B: 220 and a base color is R: 80, G: 120, B: 155, the result color is R: 80, G: 50, B: 65.

Exclusion
(Option-Shift) [Alt-Shift]-X

The effect of this mode is similar to Difference, but the resulting colors tend to contain neutral grays.

Hue
(Option-Shift) [Alt-Shift]-U

This mode replaces the hue values of the base colors with the values of the blend colors. The saturation and lightness levels of the base colors are not affected. (For more information, see *10.1, Image: **Mode** Overview.*)

Saturation
(Option-Shift) [Alt-Shift]-T

This mode replaces the saturation values of the base colors with the values of the blend colors. The hue and lightness levels of the base colors are not affected. (For more information, see *10.1, Image: **Mode** Overview.*)

Color
(Option-Shift) [Alt-Shift]-C

This mode replaces the hue and saturation values of the base colors with the values of the blend colors. The lightness levels of the base colors are not affected. (For more information, see *10.1, Image: **Mode** Overview.*)

Luminosity
(Option-Shift) [Alt-Shift]-Y

This mode replaces the lightness values of the base colors with the values of the blend colors. The hue and saturation levels of the base colors are not affected. (For more information, see *10.1, Image: **Mode** Overview.*)

22.3

Lock Options

The Layers palette enables you to lock all or part of a layer, which restricts your ability to edit the information. From left to right, the options are as follows:

Lock Transparent Pixels

When this box is unchecked, you can add color to the transparent areas of an image layer. When checked, the transparent areas are protected, enabling you to edit only the pixels that contain color information. Semi-transparent pixels retain their level of transparency, regardless of the commands you apply.

Note that this option does not restrict the effect of the Layer: **Transform** commands.

Lock Image Pixels

When this box is checked, you cannot edit the individual pixels of a layer—for example, you cannot apply any brushstrokes, filters, or color adjustment commands. However, you can still reposition the layer contents with the Move tool, and change blending modes and Opacity levels.

Because transparent pixels are locked along with colored pixels, the Lock Transparent Pixels option is dimmed whenever this box is checked.

Lock Position

When this box is checked, you cannot reposition the layer contents with the Move tool or arrow keys. Interestingly, while you can't move the layer contents directly, you're still able to reposition parts of the image by (Command) [Control]-dragging a selected area.

Lock All

Check this box to completely lock the contents of a layer, as if you've checked the previous three options.

Issues to Consider

Using a common shortcut. To simultaneously lock or unlock the transparent pixels *and* the position of a layer, press the backslash key ("/"). (Of course, you can always check the boxes manually.)

22.4

View/Hide Layer

Click this box to hide or reveal the contents of a layer. When a layer is visible, an eyeball icon appears in the box.

- **Hiding a layer.** Hide a layer by clicking the eyeball in its view box. This allows you to preview an image without the contents of that layer.

- **Revealing a layer.** Reveal a layer by clicking its empty view box.

- **Hiding or revealing multiple layers.** Click and drag over multiple view boxes to affect several layers at a time.

- **Hiding all other layers.** Hold down the (Option) [Alt] key and click the view box to hide every other layer. (Option) [Alt]-click the box again to reveal all layers.

Issues to Consider

Working with hidden layers. Hidden layers possess the following characteristics:

- They do not affect the appearance of an image. When you hide an adjustment layer or an image layer set to a blending mode other than Normal, its impact on underlying layers is turned off.

- You can create a selection based on the contents of a hidden layer (by (Command) [Control]-clicking its palette item), but you cannot edit the pixels in any way.

- If a hidden layer contains no active selections, you can reposition its contents with the Move tool.

- They cannot be printed.

22.5

Layer Status

The status box always displays one of the following items:

Paintbrush

This symbol indicates that the layer is active, and any edits will affect its contents.

Dotted Circle

This symbol applies to adjustment layers and the mask thumbnail of a layer mask. It indicates that a mask item is selected, and any edits will affect this temporary channel.

Three-link Chain

This symbol indicates that a layer is linked to the active layer. This is the only status icon that appears when a layer is not selected.

Empty Square

No symbol indicates that the layer is not selected and it is not linked to the selected layer (although it might be linked to an unselected layer).

22.6

Add a Layer Style

This button is actually a pop-up menu, giving you quick access to the options in the Layer Style dialog box. (For more information, see *11.18, Layer: Layer Style*.)

22.7

Add a Mask

This button adds a mask to the active layer. If there are no active selections, choose from the following options:

- **Add a layer mask that reveals the entire layer.** Click the Add a Mask button.

- **Add a layer mask that hides the entire layer.** (Option) [Alt]-click the button.

- **Add a layer clipping path.** (Option-Command) [Alt-Control]-click the button. If you draw a shape or path immediately afterward, Photoshop uses the outline to mask the layer contents.

If a selection is present, choose from the following options:

- **Add a layer mask that reveals the selected area.** Click the Add a Mask button.

- **Add a layer mask that hides the selected area.** (Option) [Alt]-click the button.

- **Create a blank layer mask.** (Command-Shift) [Control-Shift]-click the button. Here, Photoshop simply ignores the selection.

- **Add a layer clipping path.** (Option-Command-Shift) [Alt-Control-Shift]-click the button. The selection is ignored, but if you draw a shape or path immediately afterward, Photoshop uses the outline to mask the layer contents.

Note that every one of these options has an equivalent item under the Layers menu.

Issues to Consider

Applying two mask types to the same layer. Photoshop 6 enables you to apply a layer mask *and* a clipping path to the same layer. While this can produce a variety of interesting masking effects, it often results in some confusion. For example, if a item that already contains a layer mask is active in the Layers palette, clicking the Add a Mask button automatically adds a blank layer clipping path. If you're not anticipating it, you may wind up wondering why three thumbnails now appear across the layer item. Should this occur, either choose Edit: **Undo** immediately after clicking the button, or drag the unwanted mask thumbnail directly onto the palette's Delete Layer button.

Related Topics

11.66   Layer: Add Layer Mask: **Reveal All**
11.67   Layer: Add Layer Mask: **Hide All**
11.68   Layer: Add Layer Mask: **Reveal Selection**
11.69   Layer: Add Layer Mask: **Hide Selection**
11.73   Layer: Add Layer Clipping Path: **Reveal All**

22.8

Create a Layer Set

Click this button to add a new layer set to the Layers palette. (Option) [Alt]-click the button to access the New Layer Set dialog box, which enables you to enter a name, set a blending mode, or set a new opacity level. (For a full description of layer sets, see *11.11, Layer: New:* **Layer Set**.)

22.9

Create New Fill or Adjustment Layer

This button is actually a pop-up menu, giving you quick access to the options in the Layer: **New Fill Layer** and **New Adjustment Layer** submenus. (For more information, see *11.38, Layer: New Fill Layer*, and *11.42, Layer: New Adjustment Layer*.)

22.10

Create New Layer

Click this button to create a new layer. There are two ways to use this button:

* **Creating an empty image layer.** Simply click this button to create a new, empty image layer. The layer is fully transparent, and based on the default settings of the New Layer dialog box. Hold down the (Option) [Alt] key while clicking to access the New Layer dialog box before the new layer appears. (For more information, see *11.8, Layer: New:* **Layer**.)

* **Duplicating a layer.** Drag an existing layer onto this button to create a copy. The new layer is placed directly above the original in the Layers palette. (For more information, see *11.15, Layer:* **Duplicate Layer**.)

22.11

Delete Layer

Click this button to permanently remove the active layer from the Layers palette. An alert appears, giving you the option of canceling the command. To avoid the alert, hold down the (Option) [Alt] key while clicking.

22.12

Renaming a Layer

To rename an existing layer, hold down the (Option) [Alt] key and double-click its palette item. When the Layer Properties dialog box appears, enter a new name and click OK.

22.13

Activating a Layer

Before you can edit any layer, you must select it in the Layers palette. You can only activate one layer at a time. To activate a layer, click once on its name or its image thumbnail.

To activate a layer mask, you must click its individual thumbnail. The layer highlights and the thumbnail's border thickens, but the border and the mask are often the same color (black), making it difficult to see if the mask is selected. If you wish to edit the layer mask, make sure the dotted circle icon appears in the status box.

22.14

Moving the Contents of a Layer

After activating a layer, you can reposition its contents by dragging with the Move tool. Unlike earlier versions of Photoshop, elements in an image layer are not deleted if they are moved off the canvas. At any time, you can reveal the hidden contents by dragging with the Move tool again.

Issues to Consider

Be careful when moving the contents of a selection. If the contents of a layer are contained in an active selection outline, the rule changes. As long as the selection remains active, you can move it off the canvas and back again. If you move part of it off the canvas and deactivate the selection, the hidden contents are clipped.

22.15

Reordering Layers

Change the ordering of a layer by dragging it into a new position (click-dragging directly from the palette item's name works best). When the item is between two other layers, the line between them highlights, representing the layer's new position when the mouse button is released.

Changing the order of an image layer directly affects the onscreen appearance of the image—the contents are layered in a different order.

If any Blending mode other than Normal has been applied to an image layer, it affects a new series of underlying layers. If you move an adjustment layer, its built-in commands only apply to the new series of underlying layers.

Issues to Consider

Reordering shortcuts. Use the following shortcuts to reorder items in the Layers palette:

– **Move the active layer up one level.** Hold down (Command) [Control] and press the close-bracket key (]).

– **Move the active layer down one level.** Hold down (Command) [Control] and press the open-bracket key ([).

– **Move the active layer to the top.** Hold down (Command-Shift) [Control-Shift] and press the close-bracket key (]).

– **Move the active layer to the bottom.** Hold down (Command-Shift) [Control-Shift] and press the open-bracket key ([). If the image contains a background layer, the active layer is placed directly in front of it.

22.16

Linking Layers

Typically, you can only edit layers one at a time. By linking two or more layers, you create a connection that results in one of the following:

• When multiple layers are linked, you can reposition their contents simultaneously with the Move tool.

• The Layer: **Transform** commands affect all layers linked to the active item. For example, you're able to rotate or scale the contents of more than one layer at once.

To create a link between two layers, activate one layer and click the empty status box of another. The three-link chain symbol appears. To link additional layers, click the appropriate status boxes. Unlink a layer by clicking its status box again, which removes the chain symbol.

Issues to Consider

Linking and unlinking layer masks. By default, new layer masks are linked to their image layer. When linked, the contents of the layer mask move and transform with the image layer. Unlink a layer mask using the three-link chain between the two thumbnails. You can then move or transform the image or its layer independently by clicking on the appropriate thumbnail and applying the desired command. Restore the link by clicking the empty space between the two thumbnails.

22.17

Grouping Layers

A *clipping group* is another masking technique performed in the Layers palette. Instead of using a mask channel (like a layer mask) or a vector-based path (like a layer clipping path), a clipping group uses the contents of one layer to mask the contents of another. Photoshop uses the transparent pixels of the lower layer as the basis for masking the upper layer. When the layers are grouped, the contents of the upper layer only appear wherever non-transparent pixels exist in the base layer.

It's important to note that the upper layer can contain pixels, specialized fill data (such as a pattern or gradient), or an adjustment layer. Grouping it restricts what appears to the shape and opacity of the lower layer.

Although you can use the Layer: **Group with Previous** and Layer: **Group Linked** commands to create a clipping group, you can do it much more efficiently using the Layers palette. After making sure your layers are properly ordered in the Layers palette, hold down the (Option) [Alt] key and click the line that divides the two palette items.

Issues to Consider

Adding layers to an existing group. To add multiple layers to the group, make sure the Layers palette is positioned above the group and (Option) [Alt]-click the dotted dividing line. Or, in the Layers palette, you can drag an ungrouped item between the layers in an existing group.

22.18

Layers Palette Submenu

The following commands (22.19–22.31) enable you to refine the appearance and function of the Layers palette.

22.19

New Layer

Choose this command to open the New Layer dialog box. Hold down the (Option) [Alt] key to bypass the dialog box and create a new layer based on Photoshop's default settings. (For more information, see *11.8, Layer: New: Layer.*)

22.20

Duplicate Layer

Choose this command to create a duplicate of the currently active layer. (For more information, see *11.15, Layer: Duplicate Layer.*)

22.21

Delete Layer

Choose this command to permanently remove the active layer from the Layers palette. (For more information, see *11.16, Layer: Delete Layer.*)

22.22

New Layer Set

Choose this command to add a new set to the Layers palette. By default, the New Layer Set dialog box appears, enabling you to name the set and establish the blend mode and opacity. To bypass the dialog box, hold down the (Option) [Alt] key while choosing the command. (For more information, see For more information, see *11.11, Layer: New: Layer Set.*)

22.23

New Set From Linked

Choose this command to move the active layer (and every layer currently linked to it) into a new set.

This is particularly useful when adding a series of grouped layers into a set. If you try to drag a clipping group into an existing set, you'll quickly discover that you can only drag one layer at a time. As soon as you do, the group is broken; it takes a little work to finish adding the layers, rearrange them, and re-establish the group. As long you've linked the items in the group, however—which doesn't happen automatically—this command places them all into a new set without disabling the group.

By default, this command automatically accesses the New Layer Set dialog box. To bypass these controls, hold down the (Option) [Alt] key when choosing the command.

Related Topics

11.11   Layer: New: **Layer Set**
22.16   Linking Layers
22.17   Grouping Layers

22.24

Lock All Layers in Set

This menu item is only available when a set is active in the Layers palette. It's a shortcut that enables you to apply the same lock settings to every item in the set at once. The Lock All Layers in Set dialog box appears, listing the same options that appear across the top of the Layers palette. Check the desired boxes and click OK. (For more information, see *22.3, Lock Options.*)

22.25

Lock All Linked Layers

This command is only available when a linked layer is active in the Layers palette. It's a shortcut that enables you to apply the same lock settings to every linked item at once. The Lock All Layers in Set dialog box appears, listing the same options that appear across the top of the Layers palette. Check the desired boxes and click OK. (For more information, see *22.3, Lock Options.*)

22.26

Layer Properties

This command enables you to establish two settings that pertain only the appearance of a item in the Layers palette: name and color. (For more information, see *11.17, Layer:* **Layer Properties**.)

22.27

Blending Options

This command open the Layer Style dialog box, activating the first item in the list of effects. If desired, you can adjust the settings of any layer style along with the basic blending options. (For more information, see *11.19, Layer: Layer Style:* **Blending Options**.)

22.28

Merge Down/Grouped/Linked

Choose this command to merge the contents of the active layer with one or more of the remaining items in the Layers palette. The command that appears in the submenu depends on whether or not the active layer is part of a clipping group or linked to other layers. (See *11.100, Layer: Merge* for more information.)

22.29

Merge Visible

Choose this command to merge the contents of all visible layers into a single item in the Layers palette. (For more information, see *11.104, Layer: Merge Visible.*)

22.30

Flatten Image

Choose this command to reduce the contents of all visible layers into a single non-transparent background layer. (For more information, see *11.105, Layer: Flatten Image.*)

22.31

Palette Options

Choose this command to open the Palette Options dialog box. Here, you can change the size of the item thumbnails in the Layers palette.

The Channels Palette

Channels Palette Overview

Channels are one of the fundamental components of any Photoshop image. Although they're used for different things, they exist in exactly the same form—an 8-bit, 256-level Grayscale image. There are five types:

- **Color channels.** Every color image contains multiple channels. Each channel represents the values of one specific color. To facilitate editing, Photoshop offers a composite channel that combines the different values on screen to present a full-color image.

- **Alpha channels for internal use.** When you save a selection outline using Select: **Save Selection**, its shape is saved as an additional 8-bit channel, or *mask*. This information can be edited and reloaded as a selection later. It also can be combined with other saved selections or brought into different images.

- **Alpha channels for external use.** You can define an additional channel to achieve a specific effect in separate software packages:

  - Alpha channels allow web browsers like Netscape Navigator and Microsoft Internet Explorer to utilize transparent pixels.

  - PICT files containing an alpha channel can be masked in multimedia software like Adobe After Effects, and can form the basis for an additionally imported masking image in Macromedia Director.

- Alpha channels are used by video editing software for chroma-key, or bluescreen editing.

- **Quick Mask channels.** When you access the Quick Mask Mode using the Toolbox, a special, temporary channel is created. You can view, activate, delete, duplicate, and change the options of this channel just as you can with any other mask channel. As soon as Quick Mask Mode is deactivated, however, the Quick Mask channel disappears.

- **Layer mask channels.** If an image layer with a layer mask is active in the Layers palette, it appears as a channel in the Channels palette. Here the layer mask can be viewed, activated, deleted, and duplicated and its channel options changed, just as with any other mask channel. This channel does not appear when the image layer is not selected in the Layers palette.

23.2
Using the Channels Palette

Whether you realize it or not, you work with channels every time you apply the simplest color change or brushstroke to an image. In order to work with channels most flexibly, you must use the tools of the Channels palette.

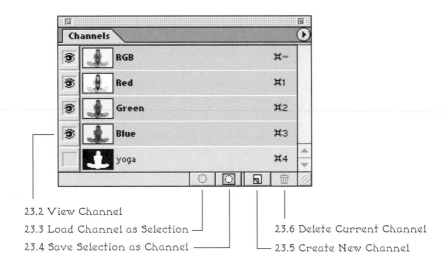

23.2 View Channel

23.3 Load Channel as Selection

23.4 Save Selection as Channel

23.6 Delete Current Channel

23.5 Create New Channel

By default, all color channels are active; any additional spot or alpha channels are not. To select a specific channel, perform one of the following:

- Click the appropriate item in the Channels palette.

- Hold down the (Command) [Control] key and type the number of the channel. Use this technique to select the first nine channels. (Command) [Control]-~ (tilde) displays Photoshop's composite view.

- Click the top item of the Channels palette to activate all color channels.

- Shift-click to activate multiple channels.

23.3

View Channel Box

Use the following commands to view the contents of a channel:

- **Displaying a channel.** Click its View box to make the eyeball icon appear.

- **Activating and viewing a channel.** Click on the name of the channel in the Channels palette. All other channels will be hidden and deactivated.

- **Hiding a channel.** Click the eyeball icon in its View box.

- **Editing a single color channel.** It is often useful to view the color composite while editing a single color channel, such as when you wish to edit a single color channel while viewing the effect on the overall image. To do this, activate a channel, then click on the color composite View box.

- **Simultaneously viewing color and mask channels.** Activate the mask channel and click its View box. The mask channel appears as a 50% transparent red, overlaying the color composite. This approach is useful when you're editing the alpha channel, and you want to keep an eye on how it relates to the rest of the image.

Issues to Consider

Viewing individual channels is a vital part of high-end image editing. Due to deficiencies in scanning hardware, different color channels can be scanned with varying quality. Fuzziness in an image can be attributable to fuzziness in a single channel. While other channels need no adjustment, the appearance of the whole image can be affected by the imperfections of a single channel. Before editing the entire image, view each channel individually by clicking on it in the Channels palette.

23.4

Load Channel as Selection

Clicking the Load Channel button creates a selection based on the active channel. Use the following shortcuts when loading selections from the Channels palette:

- **Load channel as selection.** (Command) [Control]-click the item in the Channels palette. Or, hold down (Option-Command) [Alt-Control] and press the number of the channel you want made into a selection.

- **Add channel to active selection.** (Command-Shift) [Control-Shift]-click the item in the Channels palette to add to an active selection.

- **Subtract channel from active selection.** (Option-Command-Shift) [Alt-Control-Shift]-click the channel in the Channels palette to subtract from an active selection.

- **Intersect channel with active selection.** (Option-Command-Shift) [Alt-Control-Shift]-click the item in the Channels palette to subtract any selected area that is not included in both the active selection and the mask channel.

Related Topics

23.5

Save Selection as Channel

Click this button to save the current selection as an alpha channel. The effect is the same as choosing Select: **Save Selection**.

If desired, (Option) [Alt]-click the button to bring up the New Channel dialog box. This way, you can determine the behavior of the mask channel as you create it.

Related Topics

23.6

Create New Channel

Click this button to create a new channel, similar to choosing New Channel from the palette submenu. The new channel is positioned as the next available bottom-most item in the palette, regardless of which channel is active. To access the New Channel dialog box, (Option) [Alt]-click the Create New Channel button.

Issues to Consider

Duplicating a channel. To create a duplicate of a color or alpha channel, drag its palette item directly onto the Create New Channel button. This technique also enables you to convert a temporary Quick Mask or layer mask channel into a permanent alpha channel.

New channels must be edited before they impact the image. The new channel will be a total mask, solid black or solid white, depending on the most recent setting in the Channel Options dialog box. You must edit it further—for example, by applying one of the Paint tools—to achieve a visible effect.

23.7

Delete Current Channel

Click this button to permanently remove the active channel. An alert appears when you do, asking if you really want to delete the channel. Click OK to eliminate the channel.

Issues to Consider

The effect of this button is affected by channel type and color mode. For example:

- If the active channel in the Channels palette is a layer mask, an alert appears, asking if you wish to apply the mask before discarding. Click Apply to make the effects of the channel permanent to its associated image layer before discarding the layer mask. Click discard to eliminate the channel without changing the image layer.

- Deleting a color channel from an image automatically converts the image to Multichannel mode.

- (Option) [Alt] click the Delete button to bypass the alert and remove the channel. If the item was a layer mask, it is removed without being applied.

23.8

Arranging Channels

Generally, only mask channels can be rearranged in the Channels palette. Do so by dragging the appropriate item. A thick black line appears between channels, indicating the new position of the channel when you release the mouse button.

Issues to Consider

A color channel can't be replaced with a mask channel in Grayscale, RGB, CMYK, and Lab Color images. Also, the order of the color channels can't be rearranged by dragging. Doing so would alter output/brightness settings by substituting the color values in one channel for the values of another.

Rearranging mask channels does not alter the appearance or function of the image or its mask channels. The only time the order of these channels matters is when you save into a file format capable of containing only one additional channel. Saving into such a format discards all mask channels but the first. Move the channel you wish to keep into the alpha position (Alpha 2 for a Grayscale image, Alpha 4 for an RGB or Lab image, and Alpha 5 for a CMYK image) before saving into these formats.

23.9

The Channels Palette Submenu

The following commands (23.10–23.18) enable you to refine the appearance and function of the Channels palette.

23.10

New Channel

This command creates a new mask channel, placing it after all existing channels. You cannot use this command to create new color channels.

Issues to Consider

Bypass the New Channel dialog box. Ordinarily, choosing this command accesses the New Channel dialog box, where you can determine the behavior of the new channel as you create it. To bypass the dialog box, hold down the (Option) [Alt] key while selecting while choosing this command. The new channel is created using the last-applied settings in the New Channel (or Channel Options) dialog box.

The New Channel Dialog Box

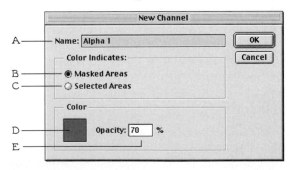

A. Name

Enter a name for the channel in this field. Always name channels if you're planning to use more than one additional channel. If you choose not to name a channel, Photoshop applies the next available number in the sequence of channels. For instance, the first channel added to an RGB file is named "Alpha 1" by default. If you add another channel, it's named "Alpha 2," and so forth.

B. **Masked Areas**

When this is chosen, black areas in the mask channel or color in the Quick Mask indicate the parts of an image that are masked, or protected. White indicates unmasked, unprotected areas. This is the default setting when you create a new channel via Select: **Save Selection**.

C. **Selected Areas**

This is the opposite of Masked Areas. When this is chosen, white areas in the mask channel or the fully transparent parts of the Quick Mask indicate parts of the image that are protected or unselected. Black indicates unmasked, or unprotected areas.

D. **Color**

Change the color of the Quick Mask by clicking this box. The standard color picker appears.

E. **Opacity**

This determines the opacity of the mask when it's viewed in the Quick Mask mode. This only affects the way it appears, not the way it functions. Vary the opacity to make the Quick Mask easier to discern from other channels.

23.11

Duplicate Channel

This command duplicates the active channel. This applies to color channels as well as mask channels. Common uses for this command include the following:

- **Reducing file size.** Multiple channels can significantly increase file size and slow the performance of Photoshop. This problem may be solved by duplicating channels into new files, then deleting them from the source image. If necessary, the duplicated channels can be reloaded from the new files.

- **Creating new masks based on old masks.** This way, you can combine the masks of two individual channels into one.

- **Creating Grayscale images from color images.** Because each color channel is actually a Grayscale image, you can sometimes use them to create separate, usable halftone images.

- **Making mask channels out of image channels.** Creating masks by duplicating and modifying color channels is often an effective way to create complex masks.

Issues to Consider

Be careful when drag-copying a channel between images of different dimensions. If any part of the channel falls off the canvas when you release the mouse button, it's automatically cropped.

Bypassing the Duplicate Channel dialog box. Hold down the (Option) [Alt] key while selecting this command to bypass the Duplicate Channel dialog box. This duplicates the active channel as the next available channel in the active image, based on the last-applied settings of the Channel Options dialog box. Or, you can bypass this command altogether by dragging a channel onto the Create New Channel button at the bottom of the palette.

The Duplicate Channel Dialog Box

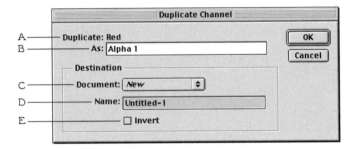

A. Duplicate

This field displays the name of the active channel.

B. As

Name the duplicate channel in this field. If the selected channel has no name, then Photoshop names the duplicate channel numerically.

C. Destination Document

Using this pull-down menu, choose the destination of the new channel:

Same Document

This is the default setting. If you wish to duplicate the active channel as a new channel in the same document, do not change this option.

Different Document

Channels can be duplicated from one Photoshop image into another, but two requirements must be met: Both images must have identical pixel dimensions, and both images must be open. They do not have to be in the same color mode. Select the appropriate image title.

New

This option uses the duplicate channel as the basis for a new Grayscale document.

D. **Name**

The Name field is dimmed unless New is selected in the Destination Document field. If it's available, you can title the new image. It still must be saved.

E. **Invert**

Check this box to invert the color values of the duplicate channel.

23.12

Delete Channel

This command permanently removes a channel or layer mask. Use it to discard unnecessary channels, reduce file size, or improve system performance.

Issues to Consider

Deleting can change the color mode. Deleting a color channel automatically converts the image from its original color mode to Multichannel.

Mask channels and image channels are discarded without any alert or prompt. When you delete a layer mask, an alert appears, asking "Apply layer mask before discarding?" Click Apply to retain the effects of the layer mask before the mask itself is deleted. Click Discard to eliminate the layer mask without changing the image layer.

23.13

New Spot Channel

Use this command to add spot color information to an image. Most often, a spot color is added when you wish to reproduce a color that falls outside the CMYK gamut. Instead of using a combination of process inks, a custom ink is mixed and applied during the press run. Common uses for this technique include matching the custom ink of a corporate logo, or incorporating an ink used throughout the rest of a page layout document.

When specifying a spot color, be aware that additional plates will result when the image is separated. If unsure that your project has been budgeted for a five-color press run (or more), double-check before using this command. Running additional colors adds considerable expense to a project.

Spot colors are represented by a new channel. No specific color values are included here, because an alpha channel can only display 8-bit Grayscale information. Instead, the channel is tagged with the desired spot ink name. When the image is imported and later separated, the tones contained in the channel output onto the color plate bearing the ink's name, just as if the information were defined in your page layout program.

There are two ways to create a spot color channel:

- **Start with an empty channel.** Choose New Spot Channel from the palette submenu, or (Command) [Control]-click the New Channel button. Any information you add or paint into this channel will output as a spot color.

- **Start with a selection.** Here, you define the area you want to reproduce with a spot ink with a selection, then choose New Spot Channel. When a selection is active when you create the channel, its parameters automatically appear in the channel.

Issues to Consider

Saving a spot color image in the correct file format. In order to output spot separations, you must save the image in the Photoshop DCS 2.0 format. If you save as a TIFF, two things will occur: The colored area will not appear in the imported image, and no spot plates will result during output.

Don't confuse adding a spot color with a custom ink with CMYK values. Often, designers will attempt to reproduce a spot ink using the closest CMYK equivalent. When this is the case, you can do the following:

- Choose the desired color from the color picker and apply it like any other color.

- Add the desired color using the New Spot Channel command, but remember to merge the channel before saving and importing the image.

Be aware that only a small percentage of spot inks can be reproduced with process inks.

Don't try to add a spot color simply by using the color picker. On the other hand, users will occasionally choose a custom ink from the color picker and apply it like a CMYK value. When this occurs, no spot ink plate appears when the image is separated.

Make sure you add the correct spot color name. Like defining spot colors in an illustration program, you must ensure that the channel name is consistent with the naming convention supported by the destination program. For example, if the color in question is Pantone 287 CV, make sure it appears as the channel name. If you name the channel "Blue" and import the image into a document containing Pantone 287 CV, an additional plate titled "Blue" appears during separation.

Trapping a spot color channel. Most trapping software packages (aside from some standalone trapping applications) have no effect on Photoshop's spot color information. For the best results, you might need to trap the spot channel before saving and importing the image. (For more information, see *10.54, Image: **Trap**.*)

Basing a spot color channel on an existing alpha channel. You can convert an existing alpha channel to a spot color channel by double-clicking the item in the Channels palette and selecting the Spot Color button in the Channel Options dialog box.

New Spot Channel Dialog Box

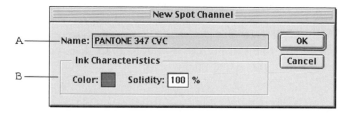

A. **Name**

This field contains the name of the desired spot ink. If you choose a custom color using the color picker, the name automatically appears here. If desired, you can change the color name at any time. It won't change the appearance of the onscreen color, but that's not important—it's the name that determines the plate destination of the channel's contents.

B. **Ink Characteristics**

These options determine the appearance of the selected ink.

Color

Click this swatch to access the color picker. For the best results, click the Custom button in the color picker, which enables you to choose from a long list of custom inks. After selecting a color, its name automatically appears in the Name field.

If you simply choose a value from the color picker's color field, the name will appear as "Spot Color 1." This may give you more control over the on-screen appearance of the color, but you must make sure the spot channel name matches the desired ink name.

Solidity (0–100%)

This value controls the opacity of the onscreen color. It has no effect on the final printed result. By reducing the solidity, you can mimic the appearance of transparent inks or varnishes. It defaults to 100%, which conceals all underlying inks.

Related Topics

5.8, The Custom Color Picker
10.54, Image: Trap

23.14

Merge Spot Channels

This command is only available after selecting a spot color channel in the Channels palette. When applied, three things happen:

- If the image contains multiple layers, it is flattened (you will be prompted).

- The selected channel is removed.

- The on-screen color (including the Solidity value) that represented the spot ink is added to the actual image.

The final value of the color varies, depending on the current color mode and the spot color you originally defined. Expect unpredictable color shifts.

23.15

Channel Options

This command is only available when an alpha channel or spot color channel is active in the Channels palette. It brings up the Channel Options dialog box, which controls the behavior of the target channel. This dialog box is nearly identical to the New Channel dialog box. The only difference is the addition of the Spot Color button under the Color Indicates controls, which enables you to convert an existing alpha channel into a spot color channel. (Use the Color swatch in the dialog box to specify the desired spot color.)

You can also access the Channel Options dialog box by double-clicking the desired alpha or spot channel.

23.16

Split Channels

This command separates all color and mask channels into individual Grayscale images. The filename of each new image is the name of the original file and its channel name, separated with a dot (such as "House.Red" or "House.Green").

This command is not available when an image contains multiple layers. If necessary, choose Layer: **Flatten Image** before splitting the channels.

Issues to Consider

Large images were once split for easier transport. Splitting an image into channels was popular when the only form of removable storage media was the 44 MB SyQuest drive. To transport a color image larger than 44 MB to the service bureau, you had to split the image into separate files, copy the files onto separate SyQuest cartridges, copy the files from the SyQuest cartridges onto the service bureau's hard drive, and merge the channels into one image again.

23.17

Merge Channels

This command was originally created to reverse the effects of the Split Channels command. However, it can combine any open files to create a single image, provided they meet the following requirements:

- **They have identical pixel dimensions.** If the width, height, or resolution of the images are different by even one pixel, they can't be merged.

- **They are in Grayscale mode.** Images in any other mode can't be merged.

- **They possess no image layers.** Images with layers other than the background layer can't be merged.

- **They have only one channel.** Images possessing channels other than the Black image channel can't be merged.

When you apply this command, you'll encounter two dialog boxes with deceptively similar names. First, you see Merge Channels, where you specify the color mode and number of channels that the merged image will contain. As soon as you click through, you see the Merge [Color Mode] Channels dialog box (for example, "Merge RGB Channels" or "Merge Lab Channels," depending on what you select in the first dialog box). There, you designate each open file to be a particular color channel.

Issues to Consider

Pay attention to the tags applied by the Split Channels command. If the images possess channel tags, such as the ".red," ".green," and ".blue," that the Split Channels command gives them by default, they appear in their proper order by default in their respective Specify Channels pulldown menus.

This command will not merge additional images as alpha channels. For example, if you try to merge four images into a single RGB file, you can only include three channels. To add the alpha channel, merge the channels into a Multichannel image, making sure the first three or four channels are merged in their proper color channel order. Then use one of the Image: **Mode** options to convert the image into your desired color mode. The first three or four channels are converted into their respective color channels, and the remaining channels become mask channels.

The Merge Channels Dialog Box

A. Channels

Enter the number of channels you intend to merge. Selecting any number other than 3 or 4 when merging as an RGB, Lab Color, or CMYK file automatically sets the mode to Multichannel.

B. Mode

Here, you set the color mode of the merged images:

Multichannel

Two or more images can become Multichannel images, regardless of whether they began as mask channels or not.

RGB & Lab

Three channels are required for RGB and Lab Color mode. Mask channels can't be added when merging an RGB or Lab image.

CMYK

Four channels are required for a CMYK image. Mask channels can't be added when merging an RGB or Lab Color image.

The Merge [Color Mode] Channels Dialog Box

A. Specify Channels

Here, you assign the available Grayscale files to the desired color channels of the new image. Sometimes, this is a straightforward process. For example, if you split an RGB image into three files, the Split Channels command automatically tags each new image with the channel that produced it: .Red, .Green, and .Blue. If these files are open when you merge, they are automatically placed in the corresponding pop-up menus in this dialog box. At other times, the process is more complex:

- **You can use this command to re-order the contents of the color channels.** For example, you can quickly replace the red channel with the green channel, the green with the blue, and the blue with the red. The result is typically a radical color shift, along the lines of a special effect.

- **You cannot create a four-channel image (such as CMYK) out of three available Grayscale images.** If you try, the option is unavailable. On the other hand, you can create a three-channel image out of four (or more) available images. When you do, the leftover file remains open and untouched.

- **You cannot use the same image for more than one channel.** For example, you cannot use the contents of the original red channel for both the red and green channels of the merged image. If you desire such an effect, copy and paste the contents of one file into the other before merging. If you desire the effect, choose Image: **Duplicate** to create an open copy of the current image, and split them both. Close the files that contain the unwanted channels, then merge them into a single color file.

- **You cannot merge an image in Bitmap mode.** For example, some users convert a split channel into Bitmap mode to take advantage of the Dither or Halftone Screen options, only to be stopped when they try to merge. Avoid this problem by converting the Bitmap file back to Grayscale mode.

B. **Mode**

Click this button to return to the previous Merge Channels dialog box, in case you need to change the target color mode of the new image.

23.18

Palette Options

The only option available in the Palette Options dialog box is whether or not to change the size of the little thumbnails that appear next to each item in the Channels palette. Select a different size by clicking the radio button beside the desired choice.

Thumbnails enable you to identify different channels more efficiently than if the channels were listed by name alone, because the eye recognizes graphic shapes more quickly than it does text. Larger graphics allow you to identify individual channels more quickly. Unfortunately, larger thumbnails use up more of your monitor's real estate. Choose the largest thumbnail that still allows you to work efficiently.

The Paths Palette

Paths Palette Overview

Like Adobe Illustrator and Macromedia FreeHand, Photoshop features a toolset for drawing paths based on Bézier curves. For the most part, Photoshop's paths are the same as the ones in a vector-based graphics program. You still use a Pen tool to place points and segments, and in certain situations, Photoshop 6 even enables you to output clean, resolution-independent shapes. Most often, however, you'll force a path to interact with the image somehow, most often as a clipping path or selection. (In fact, once you become proficient with the Pen tool, you'll find it one of the most powerful and flexible selection tools Photoshop has to offer.)

When you create a path, the Paths palette contains the path management commands required to save, manipulate, and utilize paths. (The tools used to create and edit paths are located in the Toolbar. See Chapter 3, *Vector Tools* for more information.)

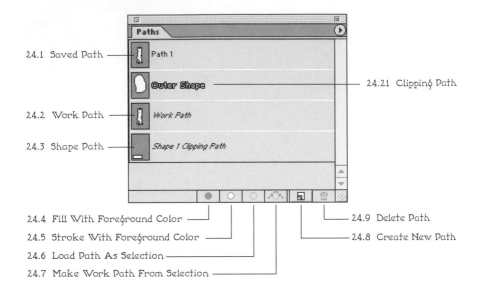

24.1 Saved Path — Path 1

24.21 Clipping Path — Outer Shape

24.2 Work Path — Work Path

24.3 Shape Path — Shape 1 Clipping Path

24.4 Fill With Foreground Color

24.5 Stroke With Foreground Color

24.6 Load Path As Selection

24.7 Make Work Path From Selection

24.9 Delete Path

24.8 Create New Path

Issues to Consider

Understanding Photoshop's definition of "path." Each path appears as a clickable item in the Paths palette, similar to a layer or a channel. Because so many programs use the term "path," Photoshop's system seems misleading at first. The following terms are used:

- **Subpath.** Other programs refer to an individual object-oriented shape as a path. Photoshop refers to them as subpaths, because each item in the Paths palette can contain multiple shapes.

- **Path.** Each item in the Paths palette is referred to as a path, even if it contains a grouping of subpaths.

24.2

Saved Path

You can identify a saved item in the Paths palette by its name—it appears in plain, black text. You can change the name at any time (by double-clicking the palette item), and re-order them at will (among other saved paths). It's important to note that once you save a path, you must still save the image before the item is "permanent."

Related Topics

24.3
___

Work Path

When you add a path to the Paths palette, it initially appears as a work path, or a temporary, unsaved item. The palette item is always titled *"work path"*, and the name is always italicized.

In earlier versions of Photoshop, you could not deactivate an unsaved path. The path would simply disappear, and you'd have to start over from scratch. Now, you can hide, re-activate, and save a work path along with the image. You can even convert it to selections or export it to an Illustrator file. Despite their seeming flexibility, work paths are still of limited use—above all else, they're unstable: If you start creating a new path while a work path is deactivated, it is discarded.

The only path creation technique that doesn't start off with a work path is when you duplicate a new path. Here, the new item appears as a saved path.

Issues to Consider

Stepping around the work path. If desired, avoid the step of dealing with a work path altogether by choosing New Path from the palette submenu before creating any subpaths.

There is no tangible reason to leave a path as a work path. Lower the risk of losing your work by saving a path soon after its creation. Use one of the following techniques:

– Activate the work path palette item and choose Save Path from the Paths palette submenu.

– Double-click the work path palette item to access the Save Path dialog box.

– Drag the work path palette item onto the New Path control button.

Related Topics

24.4

Shape Path

When you create a vector-based shape (using the Geometric Shape, Line, or Custom Shape tools), it is listed in the Paths palette as a clipping path. It is a temporary item, and its name always appears in italicized type.

Don't be confused by the use of the term "clipping path." Many users are familiar with the print-oriented clipping paths that you define from the Paths palette submenu (For more information, see *24.22, Clipping Path.*) In Photoshop 6, a path can also clip the contents of a single layer, producing a behavior much like a layer mask. Most often, this effect is generated by the following:

- Choosing the Layer: **Add Layer Clipping Path** command (which uses a path to mask an image layer).

- Drawing with one of the shape tools (which use paths to mask a content layer).

- Creating a new fill layer while an item is currently activated in the Paths palette.

Because these paths are literally *clipping* image information—exactly the way a traditional clipping path behaves in a layout document—the term is simply applied to every path that possesses this attribute. If you want such a path to behave as a print-oriented clipping path, you still must define the option manually.

Related Topics

24.5

Fill With Foreground Color

Click this button to fill the shape of the active path with the most recent settings in the Fill Path dialog box. If you desire different fill specs, access the Fill Path dialog box by (Option) [Alt]-clicking the button or choosing Fill Path from the palette submenu.

Issues to Consider

This command doesn't produce a new shape layer. When you click this button (or apply the Fill Path command), it doesn't convert the path into a new shape layer—rather, it applies the color change directly to the current layer. The effect is exactly the same as if you converted the path to a selection, then chose Edit: **Fill**. If you want to be able to change the path's fill content at will *and* treat it as a separate layer, click the target path and choose the desired Layer: **New Fill Layer** option.

24.6

Stroke With Foreground Color Path

Click this button to stroke the outline of the active path with the most recent settings in the Stroke Path dialog box. If you desire different stroke specs, access the Stroke Path dialog box by (Option) [Alt]-clicking the button or choosing Stroke Path from the palette submenu.

Issues to Consider

This command doesn't apply the Stroke layer style. When you click this button (or apply the Stroke Path command), it doesn't convert the path to a shape or tag it with the Stroke layer style—rather, it applies the color change directly to the current layer. The effect is exactly the same as if you converted the path to a selection, then chose Edit: **Stroke**.

To use a path to create a stroke that exists as an independent layer item, avoid this command entirely. Try this instead: activate the target path and choose Layer: New Fill Layer: **Solid Color**. When the color picker appears, set it to white and click OK. In the Layers palette, click the fill layer and set the blend mode to Multiply. The white fill disappears. Choose Layer: Layer Style: **Stroke**, and set the desired stroke color. The stroke's blend mode defaults to Normal, which prevents it from being affected by the layer's Multiply setting. The stroke color appears exactly as you define it, and you can continue editing the shape at will.

24.7

Load Path As Selection

Click this button to convert the active path to a selection outline, based on the most recent settings in the Make Selection dialog box. If you desire different selection specs, (Option) [Alt]-click the button or choose Make Selection from the palette submenu. (For more information, see *24.19, Make Selection.*)

24.8

Make Work Path From Selection

Click this button to convert an active selection to a path, based on the most recent setting in the Make Work Path dialog box. If you desire a different path tolerance, (Option) [Alt]-click the button or choose Make Work Path from the palette submenu. (For more information, see *24.18, Make Work Path.*)

24.9

Create New Path

Click this button to add a new, pre-saved path item to the Paths palette. You can also duplicate an existing path by dragging it onto this button.

24.10

Delete Path

Click this button to permanently remove the active path. When you do, an alert appears, double-checking your decision to remove the path. Avoid this alert by (Option) [Alt]-clicking the button. You can also delete a path by dragging its palette item directly onto this button (which avoids the alert).

24.11

Viewing a Path

Use the following techniques to control how a path displays in an image:

- **Activate a path.** Click an item in the Paths palette to activate it and display its subpaths on screen.

- **Deactivate a path.** Click the blank space at the bottom of the Paths palette to deactivate it and hide its subpaths.

- **Hide a path.** When you hide a path, it remains hidden from view, even when you activate it and apply path-based editing commands. Activate a path and choose View: Show: **Target Path** (the checkmark beside the menu item disappears). To show the path again, activate it and choose View: Show: **Target Path**.

Issues to Consider

You can only display the contents of one path at a time. Therefore, the only way to simultaneously view two subpaths is when they're part of the same path. To combine the contents of two paths, you must cut from one and paste into the other.

24.12

Reordering Paths

When an image contains multiple paths, you can reorder them in the Paths palette by clicking and dragging an item. When the item is between two other Paths, the line between them highlights, representing the paths' new position when the mouse button is released. Changing the order of the paths only affects the appearance of the palette. It does not alter the function of the paths in any way.

When the Paths palette contains more than one path type, you'll discover that your ability to reorder them is restricted. For example, work paths always appear below any saved paths, and cannot be positioned above them; shape paths always appear at the bottom of the palette, and cannot be positioned above any other path type.

24.13

Renaming a Path

Double-click an item in the Paths palette to rename a path. When the Rename Path dialog box appears, enter a new name and click OK.

24.14

Paths Palette Submenu

The following commands (24.15–24.23) enable you to refine the appearance and function of the Layers palette.

Certain listings in the submenu depend on whether or not a specific subpath is selected. For example, if you activate a path in the Paths palette, the fill command appears as Fill Path. If you select a subpath with an arrow tool, the same command appears as Fill Subpath.

24.15

New Path/Save Path

When no paths are active, this command creates a new, pre-saved path. Choosing it from the submenu opens the New Path dialog box, allowing you to name the path. This is recommended, but not necessary—if you don't enter a name, Photoshop automatically enters Path 1, Path 2, Path 3, and so on.

Issues to Consider

When a work path is active, this command appears as Save Path. The Save Path dialog box appears, allowing you to name the path. You can also double-click the work path's palette item to achieve the same effect.

24.16

Duplicate Path

This command creates a copy of the currently active path. Choosing it from the submenu opens the Duplicate Path dialog box, allowing you to rename the path. This is recommended, but not necessary—if you don't enter a name, Photoshop automatically enters the name of the original path with "copy" tagged at the end.

24.17

Delete Path

Choose this command to remove the currently active item from the Paths palette.

24.18

Make Work Path

This command converts an active selection to an object-oriented path.

Issues to Consider

Unless it consists only of straight lines, this command never matches a selection perfectly. Low-tolerance paths are jagged and distorted. High-tolerance paths are loose and unruly. To create your desired path, you have two options: Use the Pen tool to create the path manually, or edit the automatically generated path. Often, properly editing the automatic path takes longer than creating a path by hand.

The Make Work Path Dialog Box

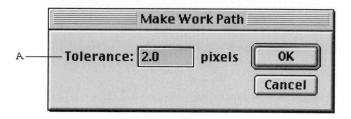

A. **Tolerance** (0.5–10)

The Tolerance value determines how closely the new path adheres to the selection outline. Lower values create a path that follows the selection more tightly, but result in a greater number of points. Higher values create a smoother path that follows the selection more loosely.

24.19

Make Selection

This command converts the currently active path into a selection. If desired, use the following keyboard shortcuts to apply the Operation options, bypassing the Make Selection dialog box:

- **New Selection.** Activate a path and press the Enter key. Or, (Command) [Control]-click the desired item in the Paths palette.

- **Add to Selection.** Activate a path, hold down the Shift key, and press Enter. Or, (Command-Shift) [Control-Shift]-click the desired item.

- **Subtract from Selection.** Activate a path, hold down the (Option) [Alt] key, and press Enter. Or, (Option-Command) [Alt-Control]-click the desired item.

- **Intersect with Selection.** Activate a path, hold down the (Option-Shift) [Alt-Shift] keys, and press Enter. Or, (Option-Command-Shift) [Alt-Control-Shift]-click the desired item.

The Make Selection Dialog Box

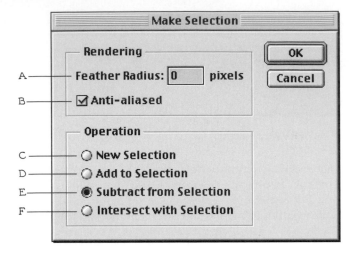

A. Feather Radius

This value applies a feathered edge to the new selection. (For more information, see *12.6, Select: Feather.*)

B. Anti-aliased

Check this box to anti-alias the edge of the next selection, or apply a one-pixel transition into the surrounding image information. Unless you have a reason for not doing so, leave this box checked.

C. New Selection

This replaces the current selection with the new selection.

D. Add to Selection

This adds the new selection to the current selection.

E. Subtract from Selection

This subtracts the new selection from the current selection.

F. Intersect with Selection

This removes the intersecting areas of the two outlines from the current selection.

24.20

Fill Path/Fill Subpath

This command fills the contents of a path or subpath. The path itself is not filled—rather, it is used as a guide for applying a colored fill to the currently active layer. (For more information, see *24.5, Fill With Foreground Color.*)

The Fill Subpath Dialog Box

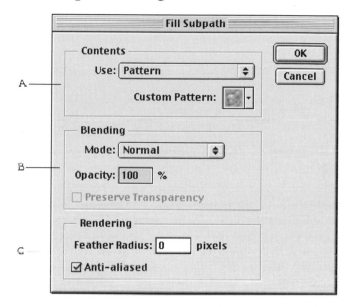

A. Contents and Blending

These options are identical to Photoshop's standard Fill dialog box. (See *9.11, Edit: Fill* for full descriptions.)

B. Feather Radius

This value applies a feathered edge to the new selection. (For more information, see *12.6, Select: Feather.*)

C. Anti-aliased

Check this box to anti-alias the edge of the next selection, or apply a one-pixel transition into the surrounding image information. Unless you have a reason for not doing so, leave this box checked.

Related Topics

24.21

Stroke Path/Stroke Subpath

This command allows you to trace a path using any of the Paint tools. This way, you can apply specific, detailed brushstrokes without attempting to apply them by hand. This is helpful if you use a mouse—which quickly appears clunky and primitive when you begin painting—instead using of a drawing tablet and stylus.

The Stroke Path Dialog Box

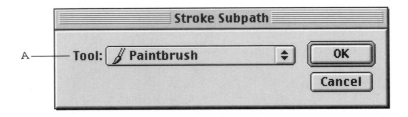

A. **Tools**

Select one of the 11 Paint tools from this pop-up. When you click OK, Photoshop traces the path using the current brush shape and Options bar settings of the selected tool. However, you must adjust your desired tool settings before opening the Stroke Path dialog box. If you stroke with the Rubber Stamp tool, you must (Option) [Alt]-click to define a starting point.

Related Topics

24.22

Clipping Path

The only way to successfully import *part* of an image is to use a *clipping path,* or an object-oriented mask. After tracing an image with the Pen tool, you can create an output command that tells other programs and printing devices to ignore the pixels that fall outside the mask.

Don't confuse these clipping paths with the ones that Photoshop refers to in the Layer menu and Paths palette. This command only defines a clipping path that comes into play when you import the image into another application. (For more information, see *24.4, Shape Path.*)

You must create and save a path before choosing this command. After a path is designated as the clipping path, its name displays in outlined text. This enables you to identify the clipping path when an image contains multiple paths.

The Clipping Path Dialog Box

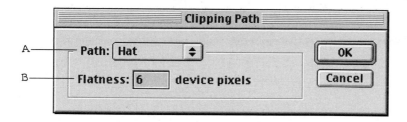

A. Path

Choose the name of the path you want to use as the clipping path from this pop-up menu.

B. Flatness

This value allows you to print the curves of the clipping path as a tiny series of straight lines. It is not necessary to enter a value here—the only reason to do so is to shorten output times. Values range from 0.2 to 100, which represent the length of the tiny lines in terms of printer dots. For example, if a Flatness value of 33 is output to a 2400 dpi imagesetter, each line segment is 1/72 of an inch, or one point long. Use a value of 5 or below to avoid visible lines.

Related Topics

24.23

Palette Options

This dialog box enables you to change the size of the item thumbnails in the Paths palette.

The Character Palette

Character Palette Overview

The Character palette enables you to apply precise typographical values to the contents of a type layer. Along with the Paragraph palette, these tools offer the kind of control usually associated with layout and illustration programs, such as tracking, kerning, unconstrained scaling, and the use of ligatures. These features are Adobe's response to frequent complaints that the type options in Photoshop 5 were too feeble to be of any use. Indeed, when you pair the new tools with the powerful text and type options of Illustrator—which is likely Adobe's intention, because each program lacks rather prominent features offered by the other—you can cover a surprising range of stylistic ground.

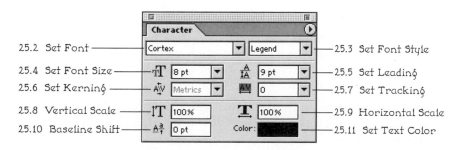

25.2 Set Font
25.3 Set Font Style
25.4 Set Font Size
25.5 Set Leading
25.6 Set Kerning
25.7 Set Tracking
25.8 Vertical Scale
25.9 Horizontal Scale
25.10 Baseline Shift
25.11 Set Text Color

Issues to Consider

Ask yourself how much typesetting you really want to perform in Photoshop. To be sure, the program now offers the kind of control and finesse that users have demanded for years. However, the fact that these tools exist doesn't necessarily mean you start setting the majority of your type in Photoshop. Consider the following:

- **Photoshop has no real page construction features**, which makes it inappropriate for the tasks normally handled by a layout program.

- **Sooner or later, the type you work with must be converted to pixels.** In a print environment, this kind of type does not output as cleanly as the vector-based characters created in an illustration or layout program. (Granted, it's possible to embed live type outlines in a Photoshop file, but this technique is rarely appropriate for most environments. See *11.45, Layer: Type* for more information.)

- **Other programs still have more robust toolsets**, and their object-oriented environments makes it much easier to handle type. However, this doesn't mean you're forced to choose one set of controls over another. For example, you can set type in Adobe Illustrator, then export the information into a Photoshop document. When you open the new image, you can continue editing the type using Photoshop's formatting tools. (For more information, see *D.4, Retaining Layers in a Rasterized Illustrator File.*)

Just like the earlier versions of Photoshop, the new type features work best when they augment another stronger, more powerful set of tools. The type you produce in Photoshop should be handled there for a reason: For example, if you intend to apply Photoshop-specific filters or effects, or if you plan to convert it to outlines to edit further in Illustrator.

Focusing the range of your edits. The effect of the Character palette's options depend on how you've addressed the target type layer:

- If a range of text is highlighted with the Type tool, setting a new value only affects the selected characters.

- If you're not using the Type tool, setting a new value affects the entire contents of the type layer.

- If you're using the Type tool but you haven't highlighted any text, establishing a new value might produce confusing results. In this situation, the flashing text cursor is usually visible somewhere in the type layer. If you set a new size, it has no effect on any existing text. However, if you immediately begin typing, the new text will appear at the new font size.

The Character palette only affects live type. Once you've converted a type layer to shapes, paths or pixels, you can no longer use the Character palette to edit the information.

25.2

Set Font

This pop-up menu displays all typefaces currently available to your operating system. (The same list also appears in the Options bar when the Type tool is active.)

Most other programs enable you to choose from the different members of a font family from an available submenu, but here, you can only choose the overall font name. By default, the Regular or Plain version of the typeface is set. To choose a more refined option, you must use the Set Font Style pop-up menu.

Issues to Consider

Fonts must be properly installed before you can use them in Photoshop.
Font files simply copied to your hard drive are not recognized by the program. There are two ways to install fonts on your system:

– **Install all fonts.** On a Mac, drag all font files into the Fonts folder, located in the System Folder. On Windows, use the Windows Explorer to drag-and-drop font files from a disk into the Fonts folder. When you re-launch Photoshop, the new fonts are available.

– **Use a font management utility,** such as Adobe Type Manager Deluxe or Extensis Suitcase. This software enables you to turn fonts off and on, without having to manually relocate files on your hard drive. Use this method when you routinely accept fonts from clients, turn projects over to a vendor for further processing, or maintain type libraries of over 100 fonts.

25.3

Set Font Style

This pop-up menu lists the different members of the current typeface family. For example, when Futura appears in the Set Font pop-up menu, the options here might include Light, Light Oblique, Regular, Oblique, Bold, Bold Oblique, and so forth. The choices ultimately depend on the current typeface—some fonts ship with a large assortment of styles, some with only one.

If the typeface you're using doesn't have a bold or italic variation, the Character palette enables you to simulate the appearance of either style. (For more information, see *25.13, Faux Bold* and *25.14, Faux Italic.*)

25.4

Set Font Size

This option enables you to set the size of your type. There are three ways to establish a value:

- **Enter a value manually.** Do this by highlighting the entire contents of the field, then entering a value between 0.1 and 1296 pt. By default, Photoshop measures type size in points—if desired, you can use another unit of measurement. (See *Issues to Consider*, below.)

- **Choose a preset size.** The pop-up menu to the right of the field contains a list of 14 standard sizes, from 6 to 72 pt. Another value will appear at the very top of the pop-up—the last non-standard size that was entered manually in the Font Size field.

- **Sizing shortcuts.** You're not limited to manually entering size values. To change the point size on-the-fly, highlight a range of text and use the following shortcuts:

  - **Increase size in 2-pt increments.** Press (Command-Shift) [Control-Shift]-period.

  - **Decrease size in 2-pt increments.** Press (Command-Shift) [Control-Shift]-comma.

  - **Increase size in 10-pt increments.** Press (Option-Command-Shift) [Alt-Control-Shift]-period.

  - **Decrease size in 10-pt increments.** Press (Option-Command-Shift) [Alt-Control-Shift]-comma.

  For an easy way to remember these shortcuts, check out the keyboard characters above the comma and period: Less Than (which *decreases*) and Greater Than (which *increases*).

Issues to Consider

Changing the default measurement unit. The Character palette is able to base the type size on millimeters and pixels, as well as points. To change the current setting, choose Edit: Preferences: **Units & Rulers** and set the desired item in the Type pop-up menu. The new setting will remain until you manually change it.

Overriding the current measurement unit. The Character palette is able base the type size on any other unit supported by Photoshop. To override the current setting, enter the appropriate abbreviation after each value: px = pixels, in = inches, cm = centimeters, pt = points, picas = picas. The palette automatically converts your entry into the measurement standard currently in use. (To resize based on percentages, use Edit: Transform: **Scale**.)

Increasing type size beyond the palette limit. If you enter a value above 1296 pt in the Font Size field, an alert appears that tells you it isn't possible. However, you can use the Edit: Transform: **Scale** command to set type size beyond the limit imposed by the Set Font Size field. For example, if you scale 1000-pt type by 200%, the palette indicates that the results are indeed 2000 pts. Additionally, you're now able to set any size between 1296 and 2000 pt.

Changing the image size may change the font size. If you resample an image up or down, the type size will increase or decrease the changes. If you resize the image by cropping or trimming, the size is untouched.

25.5

Set Leading

Leading (pronounced "ledding") refers to the amount of space between the rows of text in a type layer. It measures the vertical distance between *base-lines*, or the imaginary line that a row of characters appears to rest upon. As with the Set Font Size option, there are three ways to set a leading value:

- **Enter a value manually.** Do this by highlighting the entire contents of the field, then entering a value between 0.1 and 1296 pt. By default, Photoshop measures type size in points—if desired, you can use another unit of measurement. (See *Issues to Consider*, below.)

- **Choose a preset size.** The pop-up menu to the right of the field contains a list of 14 standard sizes, from 6 to 72 pt. Another value will appear at the very top of the pop-up—the last non-standard size that was entered manually in the Font Size field.

- **Leading shortcuts.** You're not limited to manually entering size values. To change the point size on-the-fly, highlight a range of text and use the following shortcuts:

  - **Increase size in 2 pt increments.** Press (Command-Shift) [Control-Shift]-period.

  - **Decrease size in 2 pt increments.** Press (Command-Shift) [Control-Shift]-comma.

  - **Increase size in 10 pt increments.** Press (Option-Command-Shift) [Alt-Control-Shift]-period.

  - **Decrease size in 10 pt increments.** Press (Option-Command-Shift) [Alt-Control-Shift]-comma.

For an easy way to remember these shortcuts, check out the keyboard characters above the comma and period: Less Than (which *decreases*) and Greater Than (which *increases*).

25.6

Set Kerning

In conventional typesetting, *kerning* refers to the process of decreasing the space between two characters (sometimes called a *kern pair*). In digital graphics, it involves increasing or decreasing the space. Here, it enables you to fine-tune the letter-spacing of any type set in a Photoshop image.

This option defaults to Metrics, or the kern information built into a font file by its developer. (Don't confuse this setting with 0, which turns off any built-in spacing values.) To adjust the spacing of a specific pair, insert the cursor between the characters and enter a new value. Positive values increase the space; negative values decrease the space. Enter a value between –1000 and 1000.

This option is only available when the flashing text cursor appears between two characters. Otherwise, you only have access to the Metrics and 0 setting in the pop-up (See *Issues to Consider*, below).

Issues to Consider

Clearing all kerning values. To reset all manually adjusted kern pairs to the default setting, choose 0 from the Set Kerning pop-up menu, then Metrics. (If using the Type tool, you'll need to highlight all of the adjusted text.)

A single kern unit measures 1/1000 em. Kerning values are based on the active typeface's em space, or the current width of its capital M. This way, the kerning retains its relative spacing as you increase or decrease the point size or change the typeface.

Kerning shortcuts. To kern on-the-fly, insert the cursor between two characters and use the following shortcuts:

- **Decrease in increments of 20.** Press (Option) [Alt]-left arrow.
- **Increase in increments of 20.** Press (Option) [Alt]-right arrow.
- **Decrease in increments of 100.** Press (Option-Command) [Alt-Control]-left arrow.
- **Increase in increments of 100.** Press (Option-Command) [Alt-Command]-right arrow.

25.7

Set Tracking

Tracking enables you to increase or decrease the character spacing of a range of text. Here, track values affect the spacing to the right of each character. This option is very similar to kerning—even the keyboard shortcuts are the same. However, kerning is only available when targeting the space between two characters. When text is highlighted (or you've activated a type layer in the Layers palette) tracking is the only option.

Issues to Consider

High tracking values are often applied as a typographical effect. When adding considerable character spaces, don't enter spaces with the space-bar. You'll quickly find the spacing difficult to predict and control. Instead, use a high tracking setting.

Targeting a single word. To change the tracking of a single word without affecting the space after it, highlight every letter except the last one.

25.8

Vertically Scale

This option increases the height of the selected type, without affecting the width. Enter a value between 0% (which renders the type invisible) and 1000%. To reset the original scale, enter 100%.

Note that this field does not reflect the results of a transformation. For example, if you use Edit: Transform: **Scale** to vertically stretch the contents of a type layer, the scale setting does not change, and setting it to 100% will not.

25.9

Horizontally Scale

This option increases the height of the selected type, without affecting the width. Enter a value between 0% (which renders the type invisible) and 1000%. To reset the original scale, enter 100%.

Typically, there are two reasons to use this effect. You can create compressed or expanded versions of a typeface by setting a horizontal value between 85% and 130%. Also, to preserve line space at the end of a paragraph, many designers highlight the entire paragraph and setting a horizontal value of 97–98%—enough to squeeze the text into place, but not enough to cause visible shift in character shape. Like the Vertical Scale setting, this field does not reflect the results of a transformation.

25.10

Set Baseline Shift

This command raises or lowers text from the *baseline*, or the invisible line upon which a row of characters rests. Adjusting the Baseline Shift is similar to applying the Superscript and Subscript type styles, but with an important difference: Those effects can only be set to one offset value, whereas this command can set multiple characters to different offset values.

Enter a value between −1296 and 1296 pt. Positive values raise text above the baseline; negative values drop text below the baseline. If you increase or decrease the size of the type, the baseline shift changes to maintain proportional offset values.

When text is highlighted, this command only affects the current selection; when the flashing cursor is present, it affects the subsequently entered text.

Issues to Consider

Baseline shift shortcuts. To adjust the baseline shift on-the-fly, use the following shortcuts:

- **Decrease in increments of 2.** Press (Option-Shift) [Alt-Shift]-down arrow.
- **Increase in increments of 2.** Press (Option-Shift) [Alt-Shift]-up arrow.
- **Decrease in increments of 10.** Press (Option-Command-Shift) [Alt-Control-Shift]-down arrow.
- **Increase in increments of 10.** Press (Option-Command-Shift) [Alt-Control-Shift]-up arrow.

25.11

Set Text Color

Click this swatch to access the color picker, which enables you to apply a new color to the selected type. (For more information, see *5.7, The Adobe Color Picker.*)

To edit a specific range of characters (including a single character), highlight the desired items before clicking the swatch. To edit the entire contents of a type layer, highlight all of the characters, or choose an item other than the Type tool before clicking the swatch.

25.12

Character Palette Submenu

The following items (25.13–25.26) enable you to refine the function of the Character palette. Most of them aren't commands—they're options that toggle on and off. When an item is on, it is tagged with a checkmark; when off, there is no indicator. When a selected text range contains both options, the item is tagged with a dash.

25.13

Faux Bold

This option thickens the selected character shapes, in an attempt to simulate a boldfaced type style. Whenever possible, ignore this option in favor of an actual Bold font variation.

25.14

Faux Italic

This option skews the selected character shapes, in an attempt to simulate an italicized type style. Whenever possible, ignore this option in favor of an actual Italic font variation.

25.15

Rotate Character

This option enables you to affect the orientation of vertical type characters. By default, it's turned on—this way, the characters remain in a right-reading orientation, even though they flow vertically. When turned off, the individual characters snap 90°clockwise, as if horizontal type has simply been rotated. This option is only available when vertical type is present or active in the image. (For more information, see *11.49, Layer: Type: **Vertical**.)

25.16

All Caps   *(Command-Shift) [Control-Shift]-K*

This option converts all lowercase characters to uppercase. The effect is not the same as typing with the Caps Lock key depressed. That way, you can't change uppercase back to lowercase. Using All Caps, you can always convert text back to lowercase by turning it off. This type style has no effect on upper-case characters created by holding down the Shift key.

25.17

Small Caps

This type style converts all lowercase characters to scaled-down uppercase characters. The default small-cap size is roughly 75% of the current point size. There is no way to change this setting. If you want more control over the ratio between the small cap characters and the caps, set the type in a program like Illustrator or QuarkXPress, then import it into Photoshop. (For more information, see *D.2, Opening a Vector-Based File* and *D.7, Opening a QuarkXPress File.*)

25.18

Superscript

This option reduces the size of a character and adds a positive baseline shift. It is commonly used for instances such as the numerator in a fraction, exponents, and footnote numbers. There is no way to adjust the default values; if not satisfied with the automatic sizing or spacing, fine-tune the baseline shift and point size manually.

25.19

Subscript

This option reduces the size of a character and adds a negative baseline shift. It is commonly used for instances such as the numerals in a chemical equation. There is no way to adjust the default values; if not satisfied with the automatic sizing or spacing, fine-tune the baseline shift and point size manually.

25.20

Strikethrough

This type style applies a line through all affected characters. The width of the line is the same as that produced by the Underline option. Strikethrough is used most often as an editorial device, indicating text to be removed from a story.

25.21

Underline

This type style underlines all characters and spaces. Tab spaces are not affected. The underline thickness is always one-fifteenth the current point size. For example, 60 pt type receives a 5 pt underline; 12 pt type receives a .8 pt underline. The space between the baseline and the underline is always the same as the line thickness.

Underline is rarely used for design purposes. You can't edit for thickness or position, and the underline unattractively overlaps the descenders of lower-case characters. If your intention is to add emphasis in your text, use an Italic type style (even the Faux Italic option is better than this one). If you must create an underline, consider using the Line tool, which enables you to edit the effect independently of the characters.

25.22

Ligatures

This option is only available when you've selected an OpenType font—it will not work on Type 1 or TrueType fonts, the platforms used by the vast majority of designers.

A ligature is a single type character that replaces two or more letters with conflicting shapes. The most common examples are "fi", "fl", "ffi", and "ffl". With many typefaces—especially those containing serifs—the ascender of the letter "f" overlaps the dot of the "i" or the top of the "l", resulting in an awkward artifact. Most typefaces have ligature characters built in, so this problem can be avoided (in fact, look for those letter combinations in this book, which uses ligatures). When this option is enabled, all occurrences of these combinations are replaced with the appropriate ligature. When unchecked, the individual letters are left alone, and the remaining options are not available.

If you do not use OpenType fonts, you can still enter ligatures manually, as long as you have the Expert character set of the typeface in question.

25.23

Old Style

Like Ligatures, this option is only available when you've selected an OpenType font—it will not work on Type 1 or TrueType fonts. Assuming that the font in question contains the necessary characters, this option will replace all numerals with their Old Style counterparts.

If you do not use OpenType fonts, you can still enter ligatures manually, as long as you have the typeface's Expert or Old Style character set.

25.24

Fractional Widths

When this option is enabled, the space between two characters can be based on fractions of a pixel width. Photoshop must decide how the extra width is distributed, and as a result, the spaces may be unequal. At larger sizes (18 points and up), the effect is typically unnoticeable. At smaller sizes, the effect can be staggered and obvious. In these cases, you may need to turn off this option to even out the spacing. This way, the spaces are based on whole-pixel increments.

Note that this option applies to the entire contents of a type layer. You cannot pick and choose the characters that receive it.

25.25

No Break

This option enables you to prevent two or more specific characters from breaking to the next line. Do this by highlighting the desired items and choosing this option from the palette submenu. Be aware that if you include *too* many characters in your selection, the text may break awkwardly out of necessity.

25.26

Reset Character

Choose this option to remove any value that deviates from the default type settings—the only settings that won't change are the typeface and point size. To reset a specific range of characters, highlight them with the Type tool. To reset the entire contents of a type layer, choose any other tool and activate the item in the Layers palette before choosing this option.

Note that this item doesn't toggle. You must manually choose it every time you want to remove the additional settings from the active type.

The Paragraph Palette

26.1
Paragraph Palette Overview

The Paragraph palette offers a series of formatting options usually associated with page layout programs. Unlike the Character palette—which enables you to edit the characteristics of a highlighted range of type—these settings only affect text on the *paragraph level.* As far as Photoshop is concerned, a paragraph is any range of text separated by pressing the Return key, even if it's only a single word.

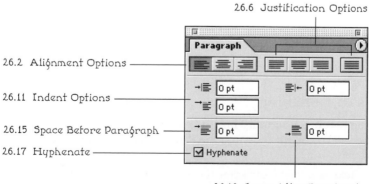

26.6 Justification Options

26.2 Alignment Options

26.11 Indent Options

26.15 Space Before Paragraph

26.17 Hyphenate

26.16 Space After Paragraph

Issues to Consider

Use a bounding text box for more formatting control. When you draw a text box with the Type tool, you apply a boundary to your text, similar to drawing a box or field in a page layout program. If you simply click the image to place the text cursor, your formatting values are based on more intangible margins.

Formatting different paragraphs within the same text layer. You don't have to highlight a range of text to apply a paragraph-level option—just insert the cursor before changing the desired setting. To select more than one paragraph in a type layer, highlight a text range that includes at least one character in each target paragraph.

Ask yourself if you really need to format in Photoshop. The Paragraph palette offers the most powerful formatting tools in the history of the pro-gram—but that doesn't mean you should suddenly start handling all of your text in a new program. As with any other feature, make sure you have a good reason for doing so. For example, some users in a web-based environment may not possess the most robust text-editing tools, and will benefit from these options. In certain situations, even print professionals can put these features to good use. For example, assume you wanted to apply a Photoshop effect to a range of type (such as semi-transparency, or placing it behind a finely-detailed silhouette). After formatting it as desired, you can embed the type outlines in the image to ensure crisp output.

Hyphenating manually. If you decide to format a lengthy range of text in Photoshop, you don't necessarily have to fuss with the automatic hyphen-ation settings. Enter *point type* (created by clicking on screen) instead of dragging a text box, and add line breaks by entering the cursor and pressing Return.

26.2

Alignment Options

These buttons determine the horizontal alignment of a range of text. By default, text is aligned between the left and right edge of a type layer (or the edges of a text box, if you've dragged one with the Type tool).

Issues to Consider

Aligning text in a bounding box. If you enter new values for the Left Indent, First Line, or Right Indent in the Paragraph palette, alignment is based on the following:

– Text is aligned between the values entered in the Left Indent and Right Indent fields.

– The First Line value offsets the first line of Left, Centered, Justified, and Forced aligned text. (It has no effect on Right aligned text.) When applied to Center aligned text, any First Line value prevents the text from being truly centered.

Aligning point text. When you align point text, the alignment is based on the location of the initial click-point.

26.3

Left Align Text *(Command-Shift) [Control-Shift]-L*

Click this button to align text to the left indent. Conventionally, it is known as "ragged-right" alignment, because while the left edge is flush, the right edge is determined by hyphenation and line breaks.

26.4

Center Text *(Command Shift) [Control-Shift]-C*

Click this button to evenly align text between the left and right indents.

26.5

Right Align Text *(Command-Shift) [Control-Shift]-R*

Click this button to align text to the right indent. Conventionally, this is known as "ragged-left" alignment, because while the right edge is flush, the left edge is determined by hyphenation and line breaks.

26.6

Justification Options

These buttons distribute text evenly across each line, avoiding the ragged edges that result from the Alignment options. This is accomplished by expanding or compressing the spaces between words—and, if necessary, characters. The settings that control this effect are found in the Justification dialog box. (For more information, see *26.20, Justification*).

26.7

Justify Last Left

This option distributes text to the left and right indents. The last line in each paragraph is not justified—it remains aligned to the left margin.

26.8

Justify Last Centered

This option produces the same effect as Justify Last Left, except the last line is centered between the left and right margins.

26.9

Justify Last Right

This option produces the same effect as Justify Last Left, except the last line is aligned to the right margin.

26.10

Justify All

This option produces the same effect as Justify Last Left, except the last line in each paragraph extends from the left to the right indent—even if the last line only contains a single word.

26.11

Indent Options

These settings enable you to add space between the text and the edges of a text box or type layer. Note that values you set will linger and affect the next type sample, unless you change them or reset the palette.

26.12

Indent Left Margin

This value specifies the distance of the left edge of the text from the left edge of the text box or click-point.

26.13

Indent Right Margin

This value specifies the distance of the right edge of the text from the right edge of a text box. This option has no effect on point type.

26.14
Indent First Line

This value determines the distance of the first line of a paragraph from the left indent. If Indent Left Margin is set to zero, you can only enter positive values, which indent the first line to the right. If you enter a Indent Left Margin value, you can enter negative values here—this indents the first line to the left, resulting in a hanging indent. Here, the distance specified in the Indent First Line field cannot exceed the distance in the Indent Left Margin field.

26.15
Add Space Before Paragraph

This item adds a space before any paragraph, except the first paragraph in a text box. Enter a value between 0 and 1296 pt.

26.16
Add Space After Paragraph

This item adds a space after any paragraph, except the last paragraph in a text box. Enter a value between 0 and 1296 pt.

26.17
Hyphenate

Check this box to activate Photoshop's Auto Hyphenation feature. Checking it here is the same as checking the Hyphenation box in the Hyphenation dialog box. (For more information, see 26.21, *Hyphenation*.)

26.18
Paragraph Palette Submenu

The following commands (26.19–26.24) enable you to refine the function of the Paragraph palette.

26.19

Roman Hanging Punctuation

This option determines the placement of any punctuation that falls against the edge of a bounding text box. When turned on, the punctuation falls just outside the edge, producing an effect that is more typographically "correct." When unchecked, the punctuation is included in the box, producing the same results as QuarkXPress, Photoshop or Adobe PageMaker.

26.20

Justification

The settings in the Justification dialog box enable you to fine-tune the overall word and character spacing of any text tagged with one of the Justify options.

Justification Dialog Box

A. **Word Spacing** (Min: 0–1000%; Des: Min–Max; Max: Min–1000%)

These values determine the amount of space Photoshop allows between the words of justified text.

The percentages are based on the standard *space width* of the applied typeface (created by pressing the spacebar), which tends to vary from font to font. 100% equals the space width built into the typeface.

Photoshop initially applies the Opt value to word spaces. If the results are insufficient, it adjusts the spaces to fit within the range defined by the Min and Max values. Although spacing may vary from line to line, the same spacing is used on a single line.

For tighter overall spacing, set the Desired value to a lower number, such as 88–92%. For looser overall spacing, set the value to a higher number, such as 105–115%. To prevent the spaces from becoming awkwardly narrow or wide, keep the Min and Max values at a reasonable range, such as 80% and 150%.

Although Photoshop never creates a word space below the Min value, it may exceed the Max value if necessary.

B. **Letter Spacing** (Min: -100–0%, Des: Min–Max; Max: 0–500%)

These values determine the amount of letter spacing allowed by Photoshop. That these values appear as percentages is somewhat misleading. Each percentage point is actually the same as a kerning or tracking unit: 1/200 of an em space.

Photoshop initially applies the Desired value. If the results are insufficient, it adjusts the spaces to fit within the range defined by the Min and Max values. Although letter spacing may vary from line to line, the same values are used on a single line.

When any alignment other than Justified is used, Photoshop only applies the Desired value.

To turn off letter spacing, enter 0% in all three fields. This way, spaces are only applied between words (as defined by the Word Spacing values, above), instead of characters.

C. **Glyph Spacing** (Min: 50–100%, Des: Min to Max; Max: 100–200%)

These values enable Photoshop to squeeze or stretch the actual character shapes when justifying text. Most often, this setting is used to gently tweak a range of text to make fit a desired space. Although you can set a wide range, it is not intended as a special effect. To apply consistent horizontal or vertical scale values, use the settings in the Character palette. Otherwise, these settings may affect each line of text in a paragraph differently, depending on the space requirements.

D. **Auto Leading** (0 to 500%)

This value determines the line spacing of text tagged with a leading value of *auto*. Here, leading is based on a percentage of the current point size of the text. For example, if you set type at 100 points and the Auto Leading value is 120% (the default), the result leading is 120 points. Reducing that type to 10 points changes the leading to 12 points. (For more information, see *25.5, Set Leading*.)

Note that the auto leading of a line of text is determined by the largest point size that appears. For example, if a paragraph is set at 12 points but a letter or word is set at 24, the line containing the larger characters has a leading of 28.8 points (assuming the Auto Leading value is set to 120%). To avoid this, apply a numerical leading value, instead of the Auto setting.

26.21

Hyphenation

Hyphenation determines how words break (or hyphenate) at the end of a line. The hyphenation values apply to all text, regardless of its alignment.

The Hyphenation settings help create a satisfying visual flow of words, characters, and spacing throughout columns of text. Inappropriate values result in awkward spacing, such as *rivers* (large gaps between words occurring on several lines in succession), single words stretching across an entire column, or lines too "loose" to read easily.

Hyphenation Dialog Box

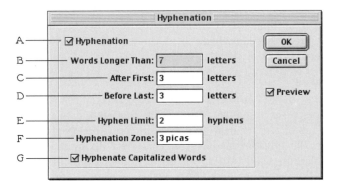

A. **Hyphenation**

When this box is checked, all image text is subject to the following hyphenation settings. When unchecked, no words are broken.

B. **Words Longer Than** (2 to 25 letters)

This value determines the minimum number of letters a word can contain and still be hyphenated. The default is 7.

C. **After First** (1 to 15 letters)

This value determines the minimum number of letters allowed to exist before an automatic hyphen. The default is 3.

D. **Before Last** (1 to 15 letters)

This value determines the minimum number of letters allowed to exist after an automatic hyphen. The default is 3.

E. **Hyphen Limit** (2 to 25 hyphens)

This value determines the maximum number of consecutive lines that can end with a hyphen. Short-turnaround, high-volume publications (such as newspapers) tend to increase the setting to maximize space. Producers of higher-quality publications keep this number to a minimum, and then add any further hyphens that are required manually.

F. **Hyphenation Zone** (0 to 720 picas)

The hyphenation zone is a defined space, measured from the right margin, which allows you to partially limit the occurrence of automatic hyphens. For example, assume this value is set to 3 picas (the default). Photoshop now hyphenates the last word in a line only if one of the following is true:

–   The previous word ends before this 3-pica zone. If the previous word falls partially within the zone, the last word is bumped to the next line.

–   A point where Photoshop wants to break the word falls within this zone. If not, the word remains unbroken.

The hyphenation zone only applies to left-, right-, and center-aligned text. It has no effect on justified or forced-aligned text, controlled by the justification settings on the right of this dialog box.

G. **Hyphenate Capitalized Words**

When this box is checked, Photoshop will hyphenate words starting with a capital letter, such as names and words at the start of sentences. When unchecked, these words will not be broken.

This option only applies when you capitalize the first letter of a word by holding down the Shift key as you type. Text entered with the Caps Lock key depressed or formatted with the All Caps style is not affected.

26.22

Adobe Single-Line Composer

When you choose this option, Photoshop addresses a range of text on a line-by-line basis when hyphenating. A single line is scrutinized and spaced—and if necessary, the word at the end is broken—before Photoshop moves to the next line. The Paragraph palette defaults to this option, but it typically does not produce the best results. (For more information, see *26.23, Adobe Every-Line Composer.*)

26.23

Adobe Every-Line Composer

Unlike the Single-Line Composer, this option scrutinizes every line of text before making any spacing or word-breaking decisions. It generally results in more appealing spacing and fewer hyphens.

26.24

Reset Paragraph

Choose this option to remove any value that deviates from the default palette settings—the only settings that won't change are the typeface and point size. Note that this item doesn't toggle. You must manually choose it every time you want to remove the additional settings from the active type.

Automation Techniques

Working with Sets

Sets were added to the Actions palette as a way of keeping the potentially large number of actions under some kind of organizational control. Appearing as a folder, each set can contain virtually unlimited actions. They are utilized as follows:

- **Creating a new set.** Choose New Set from the Actions palette submenu, or click the New Set button at the bottom of the palette. The New Set dialog box appears, allowing you to enter a name.

- **Selecting a set.** Click the desired folder in the Actions palette.

- **Renaming a set.** Double-click the palette item to access the Rename Set dialog box.

- **Repositioning a set.** Click-drag its name and move it to a new position. When you move the item between two other actions, the line between them highlights, representing the new position when you release the mouse button.

- **Deleting a set.** Select the item and either choose Delete Set from the palette submenu or click the trash can icon. Note that deleting a set also deletes any actions it contains—if you want to preserve any actions, move them to another set before deleting.

- **Displaying a set.** Turn down the Show arrow situated to the left of the set to reveal its contents.

- **Executing a set.** To apply every action contained within a set, select the set and click the Play button. The actions are applied in their order of appearance.

- **Saving/Loading sets.** (For more information, see *A.21, Saving Actions* and *A.22, Loading Actions.*)

Every action must reside in a set. Even if you delete all the sets in the Actions palette, the next action you record is automatically placed in a new set.

A.2

Selecting Actions and Commands

Before an Action or any of its components can be executed, edited, moved, or deleted, you must select an item in the Actions palette:

- **Selecting an action.** Turn down the set's Show arrow to display the actions, then click the desired item.

- **Selecting a command.** Turn down the action's Show arrow to display the commands, then click the desired item.

You cannot select sets and actions simultaneously, nor can you select commands and actions simultaneously. You can only select multiple actions when they are in the same set. Likewise, you can only select multiple commands when they are part of the same action.

A.3

Organizing Actions and Commands

You can change the order of actions and commands, similar to repositioning layers or channels in their respective palettes:

- **Moving an action.** Click-drag its name and move it to a new position. When you move the item between two other actions, the line between them highlights, representing the new position when you release the mouse button. Changing the order of the actions only affects the appearance of the palette—it doesn't alter their function in any way.

- **Moving a command.** Click-drag its name and move it to a new position, similar to moving an Action. However, moving a command changes the order of its execution in the action, which may pose problems if you aren't careful.

Issues to Consider

Move a copy of an action or command. You can drag a command out of one action and place it into another. It's no longer part of the original action, but it maintains the same settings when its applied by the new one. Hold down the (Option) [Alt] key while moving an action or command to place a duplicate in the new position. (The original item is untouched.)

A.4

Clearing the Actions Palette

To permanently remove all current items from the Actions palette, choose Clear Actions from the palette submenu. You cannot undo this command— once the actions are cleared, there's no way to bring them back. If necessary, save any actions you want to keep before applying this command. The only actions you can recover are any you have already saved.

A.5

Executing an Action

There are two ways to run an action. You can key the shortcut that was assigned in the New Action dialog box, or select the item in the Actions palette and click the Play button.

A.6

Executing Single Commands

To apply just one command contained in an action, double-click its item in the Actions palette. To apply a series of commands one at a time, follow these steps:

1. Select the first command you want to apply.

2. Hold down the (Command) [Control] key.

3. Click the Action palette's Play button. Each time you click, the next command in the list is applied.

A.7

Undoing an Action

Since most actions consist of more than one command, choosing Undo won't reverse the effect—instead, it reverses only the last-applied command. To remove the effect of an entire action, do one of the following:

- **Choose File: Revert.** Because this command restores the image to its last-saved state, it's only effective if you save the image immediately prior to executing the action.

- **Use a snapshot.** Before executing the action, choose New Snapshot from the History palette submenu. This way, you can restore the original image by clicking the snapshot at the top of the History palette, avoiding the need to revert. (For more information, see *20.6, New Snapshot.*)

- **Use a history state.** In the History palette, select the state that existed just before you applied the action. It may seem confusing at first, since the History palette only lists applied commands—it doesn't display action names. If unsure which state to select, go back to the Actions palette and look up the first command of the executed action. Back in the History palette, find this command and select the state that immediately precedes it. If desired, choose Clear History from the palette submenu to remove the unwanted states. (For more information, see *20.5, Step Backward.*)

A.8

Disabling an Action

By default, an action is enabled when you first create it, as indicated by a checkmark in a box on its left. This means it can be executed at any time. To disable the action, click the checkmark to remove it. The action is still visible, but selecting it and clicking the Play button has no effect. This is typically done to prevent the accidental execution of actions that either don't apply to the work at hand, or that haven't yet been refined.

A.9

Disabling Commands Within an Action

By default, a component command is enabled when you first insert it, as indicated by a checkmark in a box on its left. This means that whenever the action is executed, the command will be applied. To disable a command, click the checkmark. The next time you play the action, Photoshop will skip any disabled commands. Note that the primary checkmark for the entire action is red when any commands are disabled. Click this checkmark again to enable all commands.

A.10

Recording an Action in Real Time

Follow these steps to record an action:

1. Prepare your image for recording. For example, if the action requires a blank RGB image, create one before starting to record; if the action will produce a shadow-style effect, make sure the appropriate starting layer exists.

2. Choose New Action from the Actions palette submenu, or press the New Action button. The New Action dialog box appears.

3. Name the action, determine its location in the palette, and assign a keystroke, if desired. Click Record to continue.

4. Perform the commands that will comprise the action.

5. Click the Stop Recording button to complete the Action. If necessary, edit the Action using the remaining commands of the palette submenu.

Issues to Consider

Rehearse before recording. For complex sequences, duplicate the image using Image: **Duplicate** and run a test before recording. Write down the commands and dialog box settings if necessary.

Take your time when recording the steps. Actions are not time-sensitive. When recording, it doesn't matter if you move slowly or quickly, so you can take your time and make sure you get it right.

A.11

Recording into an Existing Action

To insert a series of real-time commands into an action, follow these steps:

1. Select an action or command. If you select an action, the new items are inserted after the last existing command. If you select a command, the new items are inserted immediately after it.

2. Choose Start Recording from the palette submenu, or click the Record button.

3. Apply the commands you want to insert.

4. Click the Stop button. The new commands are added to the location you specified.

A.12

Editing a Single Command

If a command has editable settings, such as the Unsharp Mask filter, you can change them after you've recorded the action—there's no need to re-record the command. Follow these steps:

1. Double-click the command in the Actions palette.

2. When the command's dialog box appears, change the settings as desired.

3. Click OK to apply the command. Be aware that doing so applies the command to the current image.

4. If necessary, choose Edit: **Undo** to remove the effect of the command. The altered dialog box settings are not affected.

A.13

Replacing a Single Command

To change the values of a single existing command, follow these steps:

1. Click the target action's Show arrow to view the component commands.

2. Select the desired command.

3. Choose Record Again from the palette submenu.

4. Perform the command you wish to re-record.

5. Click the Stop button. The newly recorded command replaces the original item.

A.14

Replacing the Entire Contents of an Action

To re-record an entire action, you don't have to delete the action, and then create and name a new one. Instead, follow these steps:

1. Select the appropriate action.

2. Choose Record Again from the palette submenu.

3. Execute the series of commands that comprise the new action.

4. Click the Stop button. The former list of commands is replaced with the newly recorded sequence.

A.15

Inserting New Commands into an Action

A common action-editing technique is to insert a menu item into an existing action. This is different than inserting real-time commands (as described in *A.12, Recording into an Existing Action*). Here, you determine where you need an additional command, then simply plug it in. Since you're not recording, you don't have to apply any commands to the active image. Follow these steps:

1. Record a new action or select an existing action.

2. Click the action's Show arrow to view the component commands.

3. Select the command just above the desired position of the new item.

4. Choose Insert Menu Item from the palette submenu. The Insert Menu Item dialog box appears. **A**

5. Set the desired item by choosing the actual command, just as if you were applying it to an image. This doesn't affect the open image—its name is simply entered in the Menu Item field.

6. Click OK to insert the new item into the action.

A *The Insert Menu Item dialog box.*

Issues to Consider

Command dialog boxes will always appear. When you use Insert Menu Item to plug in a command that uses an editable dialog box (such as Levels or Gaussian Blur), it will always appear when you run the action. Since no Open Dialog checkbox is available for commands inserted this way, you cannot turn this feature off—whenever the action is run, the user will have to examine the dialog box settings and click OK to continue. However, it's possible to re-record an inserted command, which enables you to access the action's Open Dialog option. (For more information, see *A.16, Accessing Dialog Boxes During an Action.*)

Use Insert Menu Item while recording on-the-fly. You can use the Insert Menu Item command while recording an Action in real-time. When you reach a point in the recording where you wish to have a command open its dialog box instead of applying recorded settings, select Insert Menu and choose the desired command. Click OK to add the command and resume recording.

A.16

Accessing Dialog Boxes During an Action

When a component command involves a dialog box, you can determine whether or not it appears when you run the action. These commands display a box to the immediate left of the action name, which indicates the dialog box's status. Commands without a dialog box, such as Image: Mode: **Invert**, lack this box.

When Open Dialog is turned on (a small icon is visible), the command's dialog box appears when you play the action. This way, you can enter different values for a command without the need to record a new action. When Open Dialog is turned off, the dialog box is ignored, and the action uses the values that were entered when it was first recorded.

When you plug a command into an action using Insert Menu Item, it will always open any relevant dialog box. The palette offers no option to turn the dialog box off. Instead, follow these steps:

1. Delete the inserted item.

2. Select the command that immediately preceded the inserted item.

3. Choose Start Recording from the palette submenu.

4. Record the same command you just deleted.

5. Click Stop. The command will now have a dialog status box. **A**

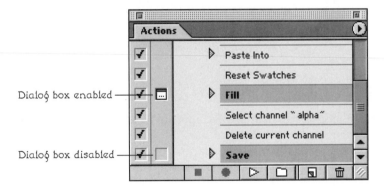

A *Determining whether a command's dialog box will open while running an action.*

Issues to Consider

Activate or deactivate all action dialog boxes at once. When one command within an action has Open Dialog turned on, a red mark appears in the action's dialog status box. Click this mark once to turn on all the Open Dialog marks; click it again to turn them all off.

A.17

Assigning a Keystroke to a Commonly-Used Command

You can use the Actions palette to assign a keyboard shortcut to a command that lacks one. For example, the Threshold command doesn't have a short-cut—you must manually choose it from the Image: **Adjust** submenu. Add a shortcut by creating a one-command action. Follow these steps:

1. Choose New Action from the Actions palette submenu, or press the New Action button. The New Action dialog box appears.

2. Enter the target command in the name field.

3. Choose a Function Key shortcut. Between the 15 F-keys, the Shift key, and the (Command) [Control] keys, you have 60 variations to choose from. Click Record to continue.

4. Choose the single command that you want the action to represent. For example, Image: Adjust: **Threshold**.

5. Click the Stop Record button.

Note that F-key assignments are only visible when the Actions palette is in Button Mode. To see the keyboard shortcut while in List Mode, include the name of the F-key in the title of the Action.

A.18

Including Special Notes or Instructions

Use the Insert Stop command to pause an action. There are two reasons to do so:

- **Allowing the user to apply manual edits.** You cannot include certain commands in an action, such as adding brushstrokes or manipulating a transformation box. By inserting a stop, you pause the action long enough to perform the necessary work by hand. You can press the Play button again to resume the action.

- **Sending a message to the user.** You can set your own message to appear when the action reaches a Stop. For example, a Stop dialog box inserted at the beginning of an action could thoroughly describe a technique and any special preparations it requires. Messages inserted in the middle of an action typically contain special instructions such as recommended settings.

To insert a stop, follow these steps:

1. Record a new action or select an existing action.

2. Click the action's Show arrow to view all the commands in the action.

3. Select the command just above the desired position of the Stop.

4. Select Insert Stop from the palette submenu. The Record Stop dialog box appears.

5. Enter a message in the Record Stop dialog box, if desired.

6. Check the Allow Continue box, if desired. When checked, the user executing the action will have the option of either stopping or continuing the action. If you leave this option unchecked, the user will only be able to stop the action.

7. Click OK to close the dialog box.

A.19

Inserting a Path into an Action

Use the Insert Path command when you want an action to enter a vector-based path that was created using one of the Pen tools. This option is available in the palette submenu only after selecting an item in the Paths palette. Once a path is added to a script, the coordinates of each anchor point (as well as each curve handle) appear in the new operation. This way, Photoshop knows the precise information required to reproduce the path when the action is run on future images.

To insert the path in the appropriate sequence, select the operation that appears *before* the desired location. In other words, when you run the script, the path will appear *after* the operation that was selected when you chose the Insert Path command.

When you use this command, there is no need to store a path in a separate file. The action actually contains the coordinates necessary to reproduce the path from scratch every time it runs. Any new path produced by an action appears in the Paths palette.

Issues to Consider

Inserted paths are not automatically saved in the Paths palette. When running an action that includes an inserted path, the new path is not saved, even if the original was. It appears as a work path. If necessary, add the Save Path command to the action directly after inserting the path.

Inserted paths do not automatically scale to fit. When running the script on a smaller image than the one in which you created the original path, the inserted path may fall completely outside the image boundaries. If this occurs, the path is still built into the file. If you select the path in the Paths palette, then choose View: **Zoom Out** until the image is smaller than the image window; you can usually locate the path in the gray area that surrounds the image. If desired, you can reposition it with one of the arrow tools. Be aware that if the path falls completely outside the image boundaries, it cannot be used to edit the image.

A.20

Troubleshooting a New Action

It's possible to record an action that only works on the image that was open during its creation. Perhaps one of the steps referred to a specific layer name, or maybe a filter's settings are too steep for future images. Before putting an action into widespread use, test the effectiveness of every command that comprises it. Follow these steps:

1. Record the desired action.

2. Open a test image, preferably one that was not open when you created the action.

3. In the Actions palette, expand the action item by turning down the small triangle located beside it. Every command should be visible.

4. Click the first command in the list.

5. Hold down the (Command) [Control] key and click the Play button to execute only the selected command.

6. Examine the image to ensure the command is applied correctly. Keep an eye on all the necessary palettes, too.

7. If everything appears as it should, (Command) [Control]-click the Play button again to apply the next command. Again, examine the image and palettes.

8. If something unexpected occurs, such as selecting the wrong layer or improperly naming a channel, stop what you're doing and either edit the command (see *A.12, Editing a Single Command*) or replace it entirely (see *A.13, Replacing a Single Command*).

9. If you've made adjustments to the action, choose File: **Revert** and start the troubleshooting process from the beginning.

10. Repeat steps 4 through 9 until the action is correct.

A.21

Saving Actions

You cannot save a single action—you can only save a set that contains at least one action. Users save sets for two reasons: To keep actions on their own hard drive for future loading, and to distribute actions to other users. Once saved, the set and all of its actions will appear in a single file, which you can later add to the Actions palette using one of the Load Actions commands. To save a set, follow these steps:

1. Select the single set you wish to save. (If you select multiple sets or a single action, the Save Actions command is not available.)

2. Choose Save Actions from the palette submenu.

3. In the navigational window that appears, determine the location of the new set file.

4. Click Save.

A.22

Loading Actions

Use the load commands to add saved action sets to your Actions palette. You have two options:

Adding to the current palette. To add a set of saved actions to the end of the current list, choose Load Actions from the palette submenu.

Replacing the current palette. To replace the current contents of the Actions palette with a saved set, choose Replace Actions from the palette submenu.

Issues to Consider

Actions are not fully backward-compatible. Saved actions are not fully compatible between Photoshop versions. Photoshop 6.0, 5.5, and 5.0 can read files from all other versions, but Photoshop 4 cannot read files from later versions. This can be problematic if you intend to distribute actions to a wider audience. Also be aware that if an action utilizes a command not found in an earlier version of the software, they cannot be used.

A.23

Creating Reloadable Actions

Photoshop 6 enables you to load saved actions directly from the Actions palette submenu. In fact, a list of default items already appears there. To add your own, follow these steps:

1. Create a set that contains at least one action that you'll need to access in the future.

2. Click the set in the Actions palette.

3. Choose Save Actions from the palette submenu.

4. In the window that appears, navigate to the Photoshop Actions folder, located inside the Presets folder, inside the Photoshop application folder.

5. Click Save. (If a set has already been saved, you can drag the file directly into the Photoshop Actions folder.)

6. Before the set appears in the palette submenu, you must quit and relaunch Photoshop.

7. In the future, you can load the set at any time by choosing it from the Actions palette submenu.

It should be noted that Photoshop 5.5 and 5.0 don't handle reloadable actions this way. Instead, these versions ship with a single default set named Default Actions, located in Photoshop's Required folder. Photoshop refers to this file whenever you choose Reset Actions from the palette submenu. You're not required to use these actions, or even keep them around; in fact, many users find that they get in the way. To establish one of your own sets as the new default, follow these steps:

1. Create and organize the new set as desired.

2. Choose Save Actions from the palette submenu.

3. In the window that appears, navigate to the Required folder, inside the Photoshop application folder.

4. Name the new file Default Actions. If you intend to refer to the original defaults in the future, remove the file from the required folder, renaming it as necessary. If you know you won't need them, you can overwrite the file.

5. Click Save.

From now on, choosing Reset Actions will replace the current palette with your new default set.

A.24

Preparing to Batch Process

When you batch process, you automatically edit multiple images, instead of just one. In Photoshop, it refers to applying the same action to a series of images. The images do not even have to be opened—they only need to be stored in the same folder. Batch processing is a valuable time-saver whenever you have a series of images that need to share the same characteristics. Successful processing will require using the Actions palette as well as the File: Automate: **Batch** command.

Before selecting this command to start a batch process, you must prepare your actions and files. Follow these steps:

1. Record the action that the Batch command will apply to your images.

2. If you need to set the file format of the images, include a Save As command at the end of the action. When you record this part of the action, the only thing that matters is the option in the File Format pop-up menu. The file name and destination are overridden by the Batch command. If you do not need to set a new file format, ignore this step.

3. Create a Source Folder, or a single folder to contain all the images you wish to process.

4. Create a Destination Folder, or an empty folder to contain the new images after batch processing. You could use any existing folder, but with a new folder you can quickly compare the new and original files to make sure they were processed correctly. If the Source folder is used as the Destination folder, the original images will be overwritten.

Issues to Consider

Use aliases (or shortcuts) to access images in multiple folders. If you want to include images contained in multiple folders in the batch, you can place them into one folder and check the Include All Subfolders box in the Batch dialog box. If moving large image folders around is too unwieldy, you can place aliases/shortcuts for the folders into the source folder, and the effect is the same.

A.25

Executing a Batch

After recording the action and collecting your files (as described in *A.24, Preparing to Batch Process*), you're ready to batch a series of images. Follow these steps:

1. Choose File: Automate: **Batch**. The Batch dialog box appears.

2. From the Source pop-up menu, select Folder or Import. If you've defined a Source Folder, select Folder and click the Choose button to point it out to the command. If you are importing images, select Import and choose a Plug-in from the From pop-up menu.

3. Set the desired action in the Action pop-up menu.

4. Choose Folder from the Destination pop-up menu. Click the choose button to target the right folder.

5. Check the Override Action "Save In" Commands box.

6. Click OK to run the batch. Keep an eye on the first image to make sure the action runs properly.

A.26

Strategic Action Techniques

The following items offer guidelines for creating and applying your actions more efficiently.

Using Paint Tools

You cannot include the use of any painting tools in an action—if you attempt to do so, the action will only include the selection of the tool, not any brush-strokes you apply. As a solution, insert a stop at the point you wish to use such a tool. This way, you can run an action, have it pause while you make manual edits, then continue the action.

Using View and Zoom Commands

These commands include zooming in and out, opening an image in a new window, panning and activating other images. Most can be added using Insert Menu Item from the Actions palette menu. If they cannot, you must insert a stop and apply the command manually.

Using Layer: Transform Commands

The Scale, Skew, Rotate, Distort, Perspective, and Free Transform all involve using a transform box, which needs to be adjusted manually. When an action contains a Transform command, it inserts a transform box, but doesn't apply any changes. It attempts to run the remaining commands without removing the box, which brings up an alert stating, "The selected command is not available." As a solution, insert these commands using Insert Menu Item from the palette submenu. After inserting a Transform command, insert a stop immediately afterward, which gives you the opportunity to make manual adjustments.

Adding Incremental Movement

You cannot record movements made with the Move tool or the arrow keys. As a solution, use Edit: Transform: **Numeric Transform** to add the movement while recording the action.

Selecting Layers

If a specific layer is selected while recording, the Action looks for that layer when it's run on another image. Problems arise when the action cannot find a layer of the same name. When this happens, either part or none of the Action is performed. As a solution, use menu commands or keyboard shortcuts whenever possible. For example, instead of manually selecting the bottom layer in the Layers palette, type (Option-Shift) [Alt-Shift]-[, the keyboard shortcut for selecting the bottom layer.

Resetting Image Dimensions

When you enter unit-based measurements in the Image Size or Canvas Size dialog boxes, the values are absolute. When you apply the action to another image, the exact same values are applied, regardless of the current image's dimensions. This can result in unintended cropping, or images that are too large or small to accommodate the action. As a solution, use percentages when including a resize command, to keep the changes proportional.

Including Save Commands

When an action includes a Save As or Save a Copy command, do not enter a new file name. If you do, that act is recorded, and every future image the action is applied to is saved under that name. If applied to a batch process, you could reduce hundreds of images to a single file—the last one processed. As a solution, leave the file name untouched when recording a Save command, saving the file under its current name. Future images affected by the action will retain their original name, too.

Creating Self-Cleaning Actions

If some of your action items involve creating new layers or channels, it is wise to include commands that remove them. For example, if an action involves creating multiple layers, include Layer: **Flatten Image** at the end, if appropriate. If an action involves creating a series of additional channels, include commands that select and delete them. Otherwise, each image will contain information that will only get in the way of future edits.

Name New Channels and Layers

Naming is an important issue when an action creates new channels. Include a command that selects and renames new channels immediately after they appear. Use a specific name, such as "Shadow Mask Channel," instead of the default numbers. This way, the channels can be added to images of different color modes, with no conflict or confusion.

Selection Techniques

Determining Selection Edge Transition

Before you create any selection, you have to anticipate how its edges will inter-act with the surrounding pixels. Think about it: The selection outline is the starting point for a particular edit. Maybe you're lifting an element into a new layer, or applying a focused tonal adjustment, or copying and pasting part of the background to conceal a flaw. Sometimes the boundaries should be unde-tectable; sometimes they're distorted to produce a special effect. Whatever the case, the selection will contain new information, and its edges determine how well that information transitions into the remaining image. There are two edge types: hard and partially-selected.

Understanding Hard Edges

The least-used edge type, a hard-edged selection does not transition into the surrounding information. Any edits take place solely within the precise boundaries of the outline. The problem is that hard edges produce a jagged appearance. For example, if you use a hard selection to create a silhouette, the isolated element doesn't possess a soft, smooth edge. Instead, you can see the tiny stair-steps of each pixel. It doesn't matter if it's a low-res web graphic or a CMYK image reproduced at 150 lpi; the pixelization is easily detected by the viewer. **A**

A *The effect of a hard-edged selection, as represented by an alpha channel (left), and a silhouette (center). On the right is a close-up of the edge detail.*

The majority of hard-edged selections are produced in two ways:

- **When you draw a selection after specifically turning off any edge-softening options,** such as anti-aliasing or feathering. As you'll see in the following items, the need to do this rarely arises.

- **When you create a complex selection based on the contents of a color channel,** the editing required to optimize the effect unavoidably produces a hard-edged outline. As you'll see in such techniques listed in this chapter, however, there are ways to add a level of softness to the edges.

Of course, there are instances when a hard-edged selection is desired. For example, you may want to use the Magic Wand tool to select a contiguous area of a single color, without lifting any other values along the edge. And at other times, hard edges occur automatically. For example, selections made with the Rectangular Marquee tool are automatically hard, because no transition is required along horizontal or vertical edges. Unless you have a specific need for a hard-edged selection, assume that you'll use an anti-aliased or partially-selected edge.

Understanding Partially-Selected Edges

It's easy to assume that when you create a selection, the image pixels are either completely selected or completely protected. For example, if you simply draw a selection with the Rectangular Marquee tool, its contents are *completely* selected, and fully affected by any subsequent command. If you fill the selection with black, all the pixels are uniformly recolored, obliterating any pre-existing detail. When an area is *partially* selected, the impact of your edits is reduced, resulting in a semi-transparent effect. It's similar to lowering the opacity of a layer, but here, the semi-opacity is built directly into the selection. For example, if a partial selection exists at 60% of full intensity, the subsequent command appears as if were applied to a layer with its opacity value reduced to 60%.

Partial selections appear in the following circumstances:

- **Anti-aliased edges.** By far the most commonly used selection edge, anti-aliasing provides a one-pixel transition into the surrounding image information. The effect is slight, but it provides a world of difference. The thin blend is just enough to obscure the jagged pixels, making the final result appear smooth to the eye. Nearly every selection option in Photoshop defaults to having anti-aliasing turned on. Unless you have a specific reason for turning it off, leave it alone. **B**

B *The effect of anti-aliasing on a selection, as represented by an alpha channel (left), and a silhouette (center). On the right is a close-up of the edge detail.*

- **Soft (or feathered) edges.** The edges of any selection can be softened, or made to gradually increase in semi-transparency. When you apply a command, soft edges result in a wider transition between the selected and unselected pixels. Unlike anti-aliasing, which strives to be invisible, soft edges are usually used to produce visible effects, such as an old-style portrait that fades to white. The most common occurrence is feathering, which enables you to numerically determine the width of transition. **C**

C *The effect of feathering on a selection, as represented by an alpha channel (left), and a silhouette (center). On the right is a close-up of the edge detail.*

- **Alpha channel selections.** When Photoshop loads a saved selection, it refers to the alpha channel information: 0% black areas are completely selected, and 100% black areas are ignored. Gray pixels result in partial selections. The same values apply when you make a selection by (Command) [Control]-clicking on a color channel.

- **Quick Mask selections.** If you use a soft-edged or semi-opaque brush while in Quick Mask mode, or apply a blur filter to the temporary Quick Mask channel, the resulting outline is partially selected.

- **Color Range selections.** When you tell the Color Range dialog box to make a selection based on a predefined range, only full color intensities are 100% selected. The remaining values result in partial selections, as determined by the Fuzziness setting.

Although they remain active, pixels less than 50% selected are not surrounded by an outline.

B.2

Constraining a Marquee to an Aspect Ratio

To constrain a marquee with unequal width and height values, you must determine the appropriate *aspect ratio*, or the relationship between the width and height. Follow these steps:

1. Conceive of a model for the relative dimensions. For example, assume you want to mimic the proportions of an image 3 inches wide and 2 inches high.

2. Use a calculator to divide the larger number by the smaller. In this example, 3 divided by 2 is 1.5. The aspect ratio is therefore 1.5 to 1.

3. Write this value down for future reference.

To create the constrained marquee, follow these steps:

1. Choose the desired marquee tool.

2. In the Options bar, choose Constrained Aspect Ratio from the Style pop-up menu.

3. Using the same example described above, enter 1.5 in the Width field. Enter 1 in the Height field. (If the target dimensions were based on a tall image instead of wide, you would enter 1.5 in the Height field, and 1 in the Width field.)

4. Create a selection using the desired marquee tool. The outline retains its uneven proportions, regardless of its size.

Issues to Consider

Using a constrained aspect ratio to create a series of uniformly-sized images. Here's another instance of using the Rectangular Marquee tool as a specialized crop tool. By using a constrained aspect ratio, you can select the desired part of an image, then choose Image: **Crop** to change the dimensions without affecting the resolution.

Such technique were used in the production of this book. A large number of images are 1.667 by 2.125 inches, or an aspect ratio of 1.227 to 1. However, most of the source files were much larger, typically around 9 x 6 inches, at 300 ppi. The designer needed to select and crop the focus of the image, but wanted to leave the resolution untouched until editing was complete. A constrained selection was used to crop the image to the *relative* dimensions needed. When editing was finished, the Image: **Image Size** command was used to resample the file to the desired size. This way, an abundance of image data was available to work with while creating an effect; the extra information was reduced only at the very end, when it was no longer necessary. (The Crop tool can be used to a similar end, but in this scenario, many find that tool's controls unnecessarily complex.)

B.3

Using Marquee Tool Variations

The following table lists the different types of selections you can create with the Rectangular and Elliptical Marquee tools. Although you can duplicate some by using the Operations buttons in the Options bar, many more variations are available when you use a series of modifier keys and drag techniques. (For more information, see *1.2, Rectangular Marquee Tool.*)

Creating a New Selection	Marquee Tool Technique
New unconstrained shape	Click-drag with a Marquee tool.
New constrained shape	Hold down Shift key while dragging marquee.
New free-form shape that radiates from a centerpoint	Hold down (Option) [Alt] key while dragging marquee.
New constrained shape that radiates from a centerpoint	Hold down (Option-Shift) [Alt-Shift] key while dragging marquee.

Adding to an Existing Selection	Marquee Tool Techniques
Add a free-form shape	Hold down Shift key, then drag marquee.
Add a constrained shape	Hold down Shift key and begin dragging marquee (do not release mouse button). Release Shift key. Press Shift key again—the preview outline snaps to a constrained shape—and continue dragging.

Add a free-form shape that radiates from a centerpoint	Hold down Shift key and begin dragging marquee (do not release mouse button). Release Shift key. Press (Option) [Alt] key—the preview snaps to a radiating marquee—and continue dragging.
Add a constrained shape that radiates from a centerpoint	Hold down Shift key and begin dragging marquee (do not release mouse button). Press (Option) [Alt] in addition to Shift—the preview snaps to a radiating, constrained shape—and continue dragging.

Subtracting from an Existing Selection	Marquee Tool Techniques
Add a free-form shape	Hold down (Option) [Alt] key, then drag marquee.
Add a constrained shape	Hold down (Option) [Alt] key and begin dragging marquee (do not release mouse button). Press Shift key in addition to (Option) [Alt]—the preview snaps to a constrained shape—and continue dragging.
Add a free-form shape that radiates from a centerpoint	Hold down (Option) [Alt] key and begin dragging marquee (do not release mouse button). Release (Option) [Alt] key. Hold down the (Option) [Alt] key again—the preview snaps to a radiating marquee—and continue dragging.
Add a constrained shape that radiates from a centerpoint	Hold down (Option) [Alt] key and begin dragging marquee (do not release mouse button). Release (Option) [Alt] key. Hold down (Option) [Alt] key again. The preview snaps to a radiating marquee. Hold down the Shift key as well—the preview snaps to a constrained shape—and continue dragging.

B.4

Repositioning a Selection Outline

After creating a selection—regardless of the tools or methods used—you can change its position at any time. As long as any selection tool is active in the toolbar, you can drag a selection outline without affecting the underlying image. You can also use the arrow keys to nudge the outline in 1-pixel increments (holding down the Shift key to move in 10-pixel increments). Be aware that if any non-selection tool is active, you won't be able to move the outline. For example, if you drag with the Move tool, you'll reposition the selected pixels; if you drag with the Gradient tool, you'll fill the outline with a gradient.

B.5

Including Edge Pixels in a Lasso Tool Selection

To include pixels at the very edge of the image in a selection, don't bother trying to drag a Lasso tool along the side of the image area—you're bound to drag a crooked line. Instead, move the cursor beyond the edge of the image boundary. The selection outline traces the edge pixels until you move the cursor back onto the image. (Note that if the image window is smaller than the image, the actual edge pixels may not be visible. When you drag beyond the window's edge, the image automatically scrolls.)

B.6

Including Polygonal Edges in a Lasso Tool Selection

As you draw a free-form selection outline, you can use a simple technique to include straight lines (essentially, you're temporarily imitating the Polygon Lasso tool):

1. Begin drawing a selection with the Lasso tool.

2. When you want to begin adding a straight edge, hold down the (Option) [Alt] key.

3. Release the mouse button. As you continue moving the cursor, you don't add to the selection. Instead, a line extends from the click-point to the cursor.

4. Place the cursor wherever you want the straight line to end.

5. Click to add the straight segment to the preview outline. **A**

6. At this point, you can do three things: Move the cursor and click again to add more straight segments, press the mouse button and release the (Option) [Alt] key to continue drawing a free-form shape, or release all the buttons to convert the preview to a selection.

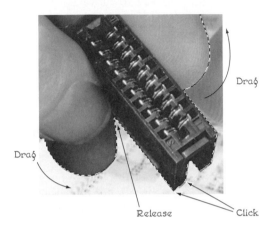

A *Adding straight edges to a Lasso selection.*

B.7

Including Edge Pixels in a Polygon Tool Selection

To include the pixels that appear along the edge of the image in a polygon selection, you must be able to click just outside the image. If you click along the image itself, you'll probably miss the edge-most pixels. If you click outside the image window, you'll activate an application running in the background. There are three ways to capture the edge pixels:

- Choose View: **Show Rulers**. This way, you can click along the rulers and scroll bars to extend the selection to the image edges.

- If the image is small enough, resize the window until it's larger than the image. When you extend the selection into the gray area surrounding the image, the edge pixels are automatically included. **A**

- Press the "F" key to change the viewing mode to Full Screen View. If the image is sized small enough on screen, it will be surrounded by the same gray area mentioned above. If necessary, zoom out to achieve this effect. (For more information, see *7.3 Full Screen View [with Menu Bar].*)

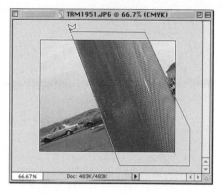

A   *Extending the polygon selection.*

B.8

Including Free-Form Outlines in a Straight-Edge Selection

As you draw a polygon selection, you can use a simple technique to include free-form edges (essentially, you're temporarily imitating the Lasso tool):

1. Begin drawing a selection with the Polygon Lasso tool.

2. When you want to begin adding a free-form edge, stop and hold down the mouse button.

3. Hold down the (Option) [Alt] key.

4. Draw the free-form outline as you would using the Lasso tool.

5. To click straight lines again, release both the mouse button and (Option) [Alt] key.

6. Complete the selection.

B.9

Using Quick Mask to "Paint" a Selection Area

A Quick Mask enables you to create a selection by coloring the desired area with one of Photoshop's paint tools. Although you apply brushstrokes directly onto the image, you don't change any pixel values. Instead, when you switch to Quick Mask mode, the edits are applied to a temporary alpha channel that appears in the Channels palette. When you switch back from Quick Mask mode, the channel is converted to a selection, then removed from the Channels palette. People familiar with conventional prepress techniques will find this technique similar to using rubilith tape to mask part of an image.

To create a new selection using painting techniques, follow these steps:

1. Click the "Edit in Quick Mask Mode" button in the toolbar. The image doesn't change (although "Quick Mask" appears after the file name in the image's title bar).

2. Choose a paint tool and select a brush from the Brushes palette.

3. Set the foreground color to black.

4. Paint the area you want to select. If necessary, you can change brush types on the fly. **A**

5. To remove part of the overlay—for example, if you painted beyond the edges of what you wanted to select—switch the foreground color to white. The paint tool now acts as an eraser, enabling you to refine the overlay as needed.

6. When you're finished, click the "Edit in Standard Mode" button. The overlay is replaced with an active selection. **B**

A *Painting a Quick Mask (see color insert).*

B *Quick Mask converted to selection (see color insert).*

Issues to Consider

Preview the selection before applying it. Sometimes, it doesn't matter how strongly the colored overlay contrasts with the image. It's easy to miss a few pixels in your Quick Mask, particularly when you're painting solid areas with a soft-edged brush. You can sneak a peek at your selection by hiding all the color channels in the Channels palette, leaving only the item titled "Quick Mask" visible. If necessary, you can continue editing the Quick Mask by painting the channel (which is useful for filling the last of those solid areas). Return to the full-color image by clicking the Show Channel box to the left of the topmost item in the Channels palette.

Reverse the selection, if necessary. If the wrong Color Indicates option was set in the Quick Mask Options dialog box, the new selection may appear to be the opposite of what you intended. If so, choose Select: **Inverse** to reverse the selection area.

Pay attention to the current brush settings. Even though you're painting in Quick Mask mode, Photoshop retains the last-used settings of the brush you use. For example, if the last time you used the Paintbrush tool you used a reduced Opacity value or a brush mode, those settings will affect your Quick Mask if you don't change them beforehand.

Be careful not to paint the image by accident. Photoshop doesn't loudly announce when you're in Quick Mask mode, which makes it easy to start painting the actual image by mistake. (A friend of mine, forgetting that his Paintbrush tool was set to apply a semi-opaque red, once spent several minutes applying red all over his image, assuming he was in Quick Mask mode.) The moment this occurs, choose Edit: **Undo** (or use the History palette to remove the brush strokes), click the Edit in Quick Mask Mode button, and start again.

B.10

Using Quick Mask to Edit an Existing Selection

You can switch to Quick Mask mode to refine a selection that you've already created using any other tool. Follow these steps:

1. Create an initial selection. **A**

2. Click the "Edit in Quick Mask Mode" button. The active selection is temporarily converted to a semi-transparent overlay. **B**

3. Edit the overlay as needed, using the appropriate paint tool and brush size.

4. When finished, click the "Edit in Standard Mode" button to convert the overlay back to a selection. **C**

A *Original selection.*   **B** *Edited using Quick Mask tools.*   **C** *New selection.*

B.11

Creating a Hard-Edged Quick Mask

To create a selection with no anti-aliasing or feathering, use the Pencil tool in Quick Mask mode. (The Pencil tool only applies hard-edged brushstrokes—for more informationrmation, see *2.9, Pencil Tool.*)

B.12

Creating an Anti-Aliased Quick Mask

To create a selection with a thin, transitional edge, use the Paintbrush tool and choose one of the standard anti-aliased brush shapes. If these brushes are not currently available in the Options bar, choose Reset Brushes from the fly-out palette submenu. (For more information, see *2.8, Paintbrush Tool.*)

B.13

Creating a Feathered Quick Mask

To create a feathered selection, use the Paintbrush tool and choose one of the soft-edged brush shapes. If desired, you can paint a hard-edged or anti-aliased selection, then apply a Select: **Feather** value after you convert the Quick Mask to a selection. However, Photoshop's Feather values are not analogous to a brush shape's Hardness value. It will be difficult to predict the final outcome of the Quick Mask unless you use a soft-edged brush.

B.14

Inverting a Quick Mask

To reverse the overlay while in Quick Mask mode, choose Image: Adjust: **Invert**. To reverse the selection after you've exited Quick Mask mode, choose Select: **Inverse**.

B.15

Canceling a Quick Mask

If you don't like the way a selection is working out, don't bother trying to erase everything. Instead, click the "Edit in Standard Mode" button to create a selection, then choose Select: **Deselect**. If desired, click the "Edit in Quick Mask Mode" button and try again.

B.16

Saving a Quick Mask

Ordinarily, Quick Mask selections are temporary—to access the same selection later on, you'd have to paint it again from scratch. To save the selection for future use, choose Select: **Save Selection** immediately after clicking the "Edit in Standard Mode" button. (For more information, see *B.18, Saving a Selection.*) or, if desired, go to the Channels palette while in Quick Mask mode. Drag the temporary Quick Mask channel directly onto the Create New Channel button.

B.17

Creating a Color Range Selection

The Color Range command is the best way to make a selection based on a particular range of tones and colors. Most often, this command is used for selecting details too fine to select by hand, such as hair or lace. It's also a superior tool for targeting a range of closely-related colors, such as fleshtones, sky, or fabric.

It has limitations, like any other tool. For the best results, the information you want to select should stand out in high contrast from the surrounding pixels. For example, it's easier to select the branches of a tree if it stands against a clear sky, than if it stands in front of another tree. Also, this command cannot produce anti-aliased selections; using it for techniques like solid-color fills, extreme color adjustments, and certain filter effects will only exaggerate the selection edges.

To make the actual selection, start with the following approach, changing the dialog box settings when necessary:

1. Evaluate the original image to determine the targeted colors. In this example, I want to change the color of the man's shirt from blue to green. **A**

2. Choose Select: **Color Range**. Move the Color Range dialog box to the side, so you can see the image as well as the controls.

3. Start with these settings: Set the Select pop-up menu to Sampled Colors, so you can target your own selection; set the Selection Preview to None; click the Selection button so the dialog box thumbnail displays the selection preview. **B**

4. Set the Fuzziness slider to 30.

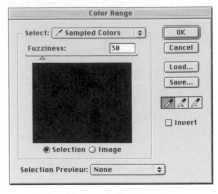

A *Original image (see color insert).*   **B** *Color Range dialog box.*

5. In the actual image, click the range you want to select. The targeted pixels appear as white areas in the preview. **C**

6. To expand the range, click the image with the Add eyedropper (the one with the "+"), or Shift-click with the standard eyedropper. To remove colors from the range, click with the Subtract eyedropper (the one with the "-"), or (Option) [Alt]-click with the standard eyedropper.

7. Once you've targeted the desired range, increase or decrease the Fuzziness value, keeping an eye on the preview. If you're selecting a specific element, use a lower value. If you're targeting pixels for a color adjustment, use a higher value.

8. Click OK to create the selection. **D**

C *Targeted color range.*   **D** *New selection.*

9. Edit the selection as desired. In this example, I changed the hue of the selected element. (For more information, see *H.5, Recoloring an Element, Retaining Original Tone.*) **E**

E *The edited selection (see color insert).*

Issues to Consider

Refining a Color Range selection. Since the Color Range command is based on numerical color values, your selection may include pixels that you don't want to affect. For example, if you're targeting red-eye in a bad photograph, the selection will include any similar colors pixels throughout the image. Don't try to select one range of red over another in the Color Range dialog box—instead, complete the selection, then manually deselect any unwanted areas. If you used a lower Fuzziness value, use the Lasso tool. If you used a higher Fuzziness value, use the Quick Mask tools.

Focusing the effect of the command. The Color Range command has the ability to limit its own behavior. For example, maybe you've already done some work selecting an element from the background, and now you want to desaturate a specific color in the selected area only. If you create a selection before opening the Color Range dialog box, the command will only affect the contents of the current outline.

Using a larger selection preview area. If you have difficulty referring to the tiny thumbnail in the Color Range dialog box, try swapping the preview functions of the thumbnail and actual image. Click the Image button to display the image as the thumbnail, and choose Grayscale from the Selection Preview pop-up menu. Now, you can use the eyedropper to click the small preview, and see the targeted results in the larger image.

Softening the edges of a Color Range selection. When using a Color Range selection to make a drastic color change, apply a Feather value to it before applying your edits. After clicking OK to close the Color Range dialog box, choose Select: **Feather** and enter a value of 1. This will further conceal the edges of the selection.

Be cautious with Color Range's auto-select options. In the above technique, I used the "Sample Colors" option in the Select pop-up menu. The remaining options are presets, which target a specific color group or tonal range. For example, if you choose Cyans, the command hunts down every color that has cyan as a primary component. It then examines the secondary and tertiary color components to determine how "pure" the color is. The purer the color, the more selected it becomes. The results are difficult to predict.

The tonal ranges are a little more useful, and enable you to target the image's highlights, midtones, or shadows. These presets compare the Luminance value of each pixel's equivalent Lab color. Photoshop consults an internal chart to determine what represents a highlight, midtone, or shadow, and it works reasonably well. Unfortunately, you can't access the Fuzziness slider when using these options, which limits your ability to refine the edges of the selection.

B.18

Saving a Selection

Creating a complex selection is hard work. When you spend a certain amount of time drawing and refining a selection, ask yourself if you'll need to access it again before completing the image. If you don't like the thought of reproducing a selection from scratch, save it.

Saving a selection has nothing to do with saving the pixels it surrounds; instead, you save the outline itself, including any partially selected areas that have been added via feathering, Quick Masking, or Fuzziness values. Photoshop does this by creating an *alpha channel*, or a graphical representation of the selection outline. An alpha channel appears as a new item in the Channels palette, below the existing color channels. You can reload it at any time, and even edit its contents to change the appearance of the resulting selection.

There are two ways to save an existing selection. First, you can use the Channels palette. Follow these steps:

1. Use any selection technique to create the initial outline. **A**

2. In the Channels palette, click the "Save Selection as Channel" button. A new item titled "Alpha 1" appears below the existing color channels.

3. To view the contents of the new channel, click its item in the Channels palette. Selected areas are converted into white pixels, and unselected areas are black. Partially selected areas appear as gray tones (see ***Issues to Consider***, below). **B**

If desired, you can bypass the Channels palette by choosing Select: **Save Selection**. The Save Selection dialog box appears—its default settings produce the same effect as clicking the "Save Selection as Channel" button. However, the controls offer a little more flexibility when creating the alpha channel (see ***Issues to Consider***, below).

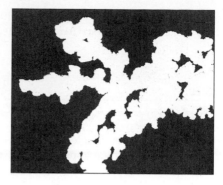

A *Original selection*

B *A selection outline saved as an 8-bit alpha channel*

Issues to Consider

Determine whether color indicates a masked or selected area in the new channel. Photoshop can use white or black pixels to indicate the selected area in an alpha channel. By default, it uses white pixels to represent selected areas, and black pixels to represent unselected areas. To change this setting, hold down the (Option) [Alt] key when clicking the Channels palette's "Save Selection as Channel" button. The New Channel dialog box will appear, enabling you to choose a different Color Indicates option. Also note that these settings can be changed in different locations, such as the Quick Mask Options dialog box, or when creating a new empty alpha channel. Whenever and wherever this option is changed, it will affect the appearance of every subsequently saved selection. Regardless of the setting, the alpha channel will behave the same.

Name your alpha channels clearly. When working with multiple alpha channels, name them as clearly as you can. Otherwise, you'll be forced to browse through items titled "Alpha 1", "Alpha 2", and so forth, looking for the appropriate one. To rename an existing alpha channel, double-click its item in the Channels palette. The Channel Options dialog box appears, enabling to to enter a new name.

Deactivate the selection after saving it, if necessary. Saving a selection does not deactivate the current outline. Before you continue editing, you still have to choose Select: **None** to remove the original selection.

Discard unnecessary channels when editing is complete. Saved selections should only hang around during the editing stage of the image. As soon as the image is ready for print, delete any alpha channels (unless you need them for a specific effect, such as saving a spot color channel). If you don't, you'll likely experience difficulties when saving or importing the file. For example, you can't save a file containing any extra channels as a Photoshop EPS file. If a TIFF image contains a mask channel, it may not separate properly from your page layout program. Delete a channel by clicking its item in the Channels palette, then choosing Delete Channel from the Channels palette submenu (or clicking the palette's trash can button).

B.19

Editing a Saved Selection

You can edit a saved selection just as you would any other Grayscale image. Any changes become apparent when the channel is re-loaded as a selection. Follow these steps:

1. Create and save the initial selection. **A**

2. To view only the contents of the alpha channel, click its item in the Channels palette. To view the contents as an overlay superimposed over the image, only click the view button beside the alpha channel's palette item.

3. Apply the desired edits. For example, you can apply tonal adjustments, brushstrokes with the paint tools, or filters. **B**

4. Re-load the alpha channel as a selection. The new outline embodies whatever changes were made. **C**

A *Original selection.* **B** *Editing the alpha channel.* **C** *Reloading the edited selection.*

While editing an alpha channel, it often helps to view it as a semi-transparent overlay, as opposed to viewing only the channel contents. This way, you can see the position of the selection boundary in relation to the image, making it easier to judge the impact of your edits. The effect is similar to editing a selection in Quick Mask mode. Follow these steps:

1. Create and save the initial selection.

2. Click the alpha channel's new item in the Channels palette. Only the contents of the alpha channel are visible.

3. Click the View box next to the composite channel item. (For example, in a CMYK image, click the View box next to the CMYK item.) **D**

4. The image becomes visible, and the contents of the alpha channel appear as an overlay. Because the new channel is still active, any edits you apply only affect the selection information. **E**

5. To hide the overlay, click the View box again to hide the eyeball icon. The alpha channel is still activated.

6. To edit the entire image again, click the composite channel item.

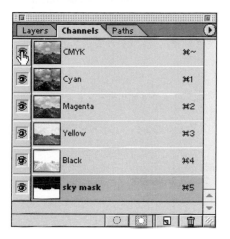

D *Activating the composite channel after clicking the alpha channel.*

E *Viewing the alpha channel as an overlay.*

Issues to Consider

It's easy to edit the composite image when you really want to edit the alpha channel. It's quite easy to click the wrong item in the Channels palette, and wind up painting over valuable image information by mistake. As soon as something like this occurs, stop immediately, choose Edit: **Undo**, and double-check the palette. If necessary, use the Edit: **Step Forward/Step Backward** commands to revert appropriately.

Retain the original alpha channel, if necessary. When you edit an alpha channel, you can no longer access the originally saved selection. Before applying any changes, you may want to create a copy of the initial mask channel, and edit that one. That way, if you make a mistake or change your mind, you can readily access the original selection. Duplicate an alpha channel by clicking its item in the Channels palette and choosing "Duplicate Channel" from the palette submenu. (Or, in the Channels palette, drag the alpha channel directly onto the New Channel button.)

Loading a saved selection. To convert an alpha channel to an active selection outline, use the Select: Load Selection command. (For more information, see *12.15, Select: **Load Selection**.*)

B.20

Transferring a Selection to Another Image

You don't have to use the Save Selection or Load Selection commands to transfer a selection outline to another image. (In fact, unless the two images share the same width, height, and resolution, those commands won't let you.) However, it's possible to move an outline from one image to another, without creating additional channels. Follow these steps:

1. In the first image, create the desired selection.

2. Open a second image, positioning it so both images are visible.

3. In the first image, make sure one of the selection tools is chosen in the toolbar.

4. Drag the selection outline from the first image onto the second. When the second image highlights, release the mouse button.

5. Continue editing the selection outline. (In the first image, the position of the selection is unchanged.)

Issues to Consider

The size of the selection outline may change. If the two images have different resolutions, the shape of the outline will remain constant, but its size will change. Remember that a selection contains a specific number of pixels; when you transfer it to another image, it will adjust itself to contain the same amount of information. For example, if you drag a selection from a 300 ppi image to a 200 ppi image, the outline will appear to grow larger. Likewise, if you drag an outline from a 72 ppi image to a 300 ppi image, it will appear to grow smaller. If necessary, you can use the Transform Selection command to adjust the size of the new outline. (For more information, see *12.14, Select: **Transform Selection**.*)

B.21

Creating a Complex Mask: Extract Command

Sometimes a simple selection isn't enough. Often, you'll need to target part of an image for additional color correcting, or protect it as you adjust the surrounding pixels. If it has clear, crisp edges, you can use one of the regular selection tools. If it has finely detailed edges, your only option may be to create a complex mask channel, based on the existing image information. This will enable you to load a selection that precisely matches the shape of the element.

If the element appears in high contrast against the surrounding pixels, you can use the Extract command to create the alpha channel, using steps similar to creating a silhouette. Follow these steps:

1. Open the image that contains the element you want to mask. In this example, I want to mask the woman and desaturate the surrounding colors. **A**

2. Duplicate the layer. **B**

A *Original image (See color insert)*   **B** *Duplicating the background layer*

3. Following the steps described in *I.5, Creating a Complex Silhouette (Hair)* and *I.6, Cleaning an Extracted Silhouette,* use the Extract command to isolate the element, then refine it as necessary.

4. Convert the isolated element to a selection by (Command) [Control]-clicking its item in the Layers palette.

5. Choose Select: **Save Selection** to convert the selection outline to an alpha channel. **C**

6. Choose Select: **Deselect** to deactivate the selection.

7. Delete the layer that contains the isolated element.

8. In the Channels palette, click the new mask channel. It should display the shape of the targeted element.

9. If any stray pixels appear inside the white shape, remove them with the Paintbrush tool.

10. Return to the full-color image by clicking the composite item in the Channels palette.

11. Load the selection by (Command) [Control]-clicking the mask item in the Channels palette. **D**

C   *Saving the selection as an alpha channel*

D   *Re-loading the selection*

12. If you need to adjust the targeted image, apply the commands now. If you need to adjust the surrounding pixels, reverse the selection by choosing Select: **Inverse**, then apply the commands. **E**

13. When finished with the mask channel, delete it by clicking it in the Channels palette and choosing Delete Channel from the palette submenu.

E   *Final image (see color insert).*

B.22

Creating a Complex Mask: Color Channels

If the image you need to target is too complex for the Extract command, you can usually create a mask based on one of the existing color channels. In this example, I want to isolate a detailed tree, so I can edit the color of the sky. Follow these steps:

1. Open an image you want to mask. For the best results, the edge detail should appear in high contrast against the background pixels. **A**

2. Click through the items in the Channels palette, examining the contents of each color channel. Look for the one that has the most contrast between the targeted image and the surrounding pixels. **B**

A *Original image (see color insert).*

B *Color channels (clockwise from upper left: C, M, Y, K).*

3. Convert the color channel to a mask channel by dragging it directly onto the Create New Channel button in the Channels palette. **C**

4. In the new channel—making sure you don't edit the color channel by mistake—refine the masking element by removing any pixels that aren't part of the targeted image. Start by applying the Unsharp Mask filter to better define the edge detail. (In this example, the Unsharp Mask values are A: 100%, R: 4, and T: 18.) **D**

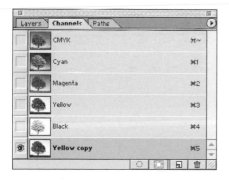

C *Copying the Yellow channel.*

D *Alpha channel detail before (left) and after sharpening.*

5. Use the Levels command to reduce the amount of gray in the mask channel. The goal is to end up with as much white in the background and black in the image as possible. For best results, move both the shadow and highlight slider toward the center of the histogram. Pay attention to

the edge detail, making sure they stay consistent with the targeted image. Click OK when finished. **E**

6. Touch up the mask channel with the Lasso, Pencil, and Eraser tools, removing any lingering gray ranges and stray pixels. **F**

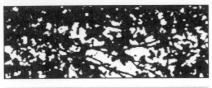

E   *Using Levels to add contrast.*

F   *Alpha channel detail before (left) and after touching up.*

7. Return to the full-color image by clicking the composite item in the Channels palette.

8. Load the selection by (Command) [Control]-clicking the mask item in the Channels palette. In my example, the tree and ground are masked, leaving the sky selected. If you need to reverse the selection, choose Select: **Inverse**. **G**

9. Apply the desired adjustment. (To make your edits easier to see, choose Select: **Hide Edges** to hide the active outline.) **H**

10. When through with the mask channel, delete it by clicking it in the Channels palette and choosing Delete Channel from the palette submenu.

G   *Alpha channel converted to selection.*

H   *Adjusted image—note that only the sky is affected (see color insert).*

Issues to Consider

Anticipate this technique by starting with an image size larger than you actually need. This technique only produces a hard-edged selection. However, if you know you'll be using these steps before you receive the image, you can simulate the effect of anti-aliasing. If possible, start with an image larger than you actually need. For example, if your sending out an original to be scanned, increase the scale by 20–30% (if the details are particularly fine, add another 50 ppi to the target resolution). After you've produced and saved the selection—but before you've used it to adjust the image—use the Image: **Image Size** command to downsample the file to the desired specifications. The interpolation process used by Photoshop will add a slight level of softness to the alpha channel. When you load the selection again, that softness acts like anti-aliasing, making the edges of your adjustments much smoother and harder to detect.

Cropping & Resizing Techniques

C.1

Applying a Simple Crop

Conventionally cropping a photo involved physically marking the item to designate the rectangular portion you wanted to use. That way, the operator processing the image knew the appropriate area to shoot to lithographic film. Photoshop uses the Crop tool to do the same thing. Follow these steps:

1. Choose the Crop tool.

2. Click-drag to draw a marquee around the image area you want to keep. The information outside the marquee is temporarily shaded. **A**

3. Fine-tune the crop marquee by dragging any of the handles that surround its outline.

4. To apply the crop, click the checkmark in the Options bar (or press the Return or Enter key). When you do, the information outside the marquee is discarded, and the image is resized to the specified width and height. **B**

A *Dragging the crop marquee.*   **B** *The cropped image.*

Issues to Consider

Cropping in Photoshop versus your layout document. Page layout programs offer their own tools for cropping imported images. Unlike cropping in Photoshop, however, they only hide portions of the image from view. The hidden information must still be processed when the file is output, which may cause printing problems. At the very least, the document takes longer to output; in extreme cases (for example, cropping a series of 8 x 11-inch CMYK images to the size of postage stamps), the document may not print at all. Avoid any potential problems by cropping your images in Photoshop whenever possible.

Overriding the snap-to option. The crop marquee automatically snaps to the image edge when you drag it to within 8 or 10 screen pixels. Disable this effect by holding down the (Command-Shift) [Control-Shift] keys while dragging.

Adjusting the crop marquee. A crop marquee can be scaled and repositioned just like a standard selection marquee. To drag the entire outline, click-drag anywhere inside. To create a perfectly square marquee, hold down the Shift key before initially dragging with the Crop tool. To proportionately scale an existing marquee, hold down the Shift key and drag a corner handle. To cancel a marquee and start again, press the Escape key.

Shielding the cropped area. When you initially drag the crop marquee, the image information outside of it is shaded with a semi-transparent overlay. Photoshop does this to better indicate the information it will discard when you apply the crop. To turn off this feature (making it more similar to the Crop tool of earlier Photoshop versions), uncheck the Shield Cropped Area box in the Options bar, after you've dragged the marquee. To change the color of the overlay (for example, if it conflicts with the underlying image), click the Color swatch in the Options bar, then set a new value in the Color Picker dialog box. To reduce or increase the overlay's level of transparency, set a value in the Opacity field, in the Options bar.

C.2

Using a Selection to Crop an Image

It's possible to crop an image based on an active selection. Follow these steps:

1. Choose the desired selection tool.

2. Draw a selection around the desired area. **A**

3. Choose Image: **Crop**. If the selection is perfectly rectangular, the effect is the same as using the Crop tool. If the selection is irregular—for example, if you used the Elliptical Marquee or Lasso tool—the image boundaries are reduced to match the highest and widest points of the outline. **B**

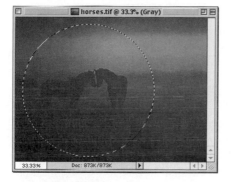

A *Creating a selection for cropping.*   **B** *The cropped image.*

Issues to Consider

Cropping does not deactivate the selection. When you use this technique to crop an image, the selection remains active. If necessary, you may have to choose Select: **None** before continuing.

Crops based on an irregular selection still produce a rectangular image. When you crop a non-rectangular selection, you don't discard all the pixels outside the outline. Any pixels between the new image boundaries and the selection edge will remain intact. However, it's easy to eliminate those pixels after cropping to a selection. Immediately after cropping, choose Layer: New: **Layer Via Copy** to lift the contents of the selection into a new image layer. Then delete the original layer in the Layers palette. The image is now cropped to the size of the selection, and the selected information is surrounded by transparent pixels.

Using the Crop command to apply all cropping methods. Many people use the Actions palette to assign a keyboard shortcut to the Image: **Crop** command. This way, whether you're using a Crop tool marquee or a selection outline, you can trigger the crop using the same keystroke. (For more information, see *A.17, Assigning a Keystroke to a Commonly Used Command.*)

C.3

Cropping and Rotating Simultaneously

It's possible to rotate a Crop tool marquee. When the crop is applied, the marquee reverts back to its original orientation, rotating the contents. Most often, this technique is used to straighten a crooked scan. Because it is difficult to position artwork in a scanning device—particularly when placing irregularly-edged material on a flatbed scanner—this technique enables you to quickly compensate for any misalignment. (For more information, see *1.11, Crop Tool.*) Follow these steps:

1. Choose the Crop tool.

2. Drag the desired marquee. **A**

3. Place the cursor just outside the marquee edge. The cursor shape will appear as a double-sided arrow. (The orientation of the cursor will change as you move it around the marquee, but that's just for show.)

4. Click-drag to rotate the marquee around its centerpoint. You can reposition, rotate, and resize the marquee as often as you need to. **B**

5. Click the checkmark button in the Options bar to apply the crop. **C**

A *Dragging a crop marquee.*

B *Rotating the marquee.*

C *The cropped, rotated result.*

Issues to Consider

Using a flat edge to align the crop marquee. When straightening an image, it helps to have some sort of reference when rotating the crop marquee. Often, the original artwork will contain a flat area somewhere along its edge; if so, use it to align the marquee. If it doesn't, try to add one to the original before scanning it. It can be a pencil line, the bottom edge of a page, or a piece of low-stick tape. As long as it can be used to produce the proper orientation, you'll eliminate the need to further rotate the image in Photoshop.

Rotating the marquee past the image edges. When you initially draw the crop marquee, you cannot drag it past the image boundary. When you rotate it, though, you can easily move a corner beyond the edge of the image. After you apply the crop, the information contained in this "negative" space depends on the current contents of the image:

- If the image only exists as a background layer, the space will be filled with the current background color. To avoid the background color, convert the background layer to an image layer before cropping.

- If the image contains multiple image layers, the space will be filled with transparent pixels. However, if any layer contains hidden data— that is, information that extends beyond the image boundaries— those pixels will be revealed.

Determining the final orientation of the cropped image. It's easy to assume that wherever you position the bottom edge of the marquee will automatically become the bottom edge of the cropped image. That's not necessarily the case. For example, if you rotate the marquee 180°, the cropped result does not appear upside-down. Instead, Photoshop will snap the cropped image to the closest horizontal or vertical orientation. You may need to apply one of the Image: **Rotate Canvas** commands to further orient the image.

Repositioning the centerpoint. By default, the crop marquee rotates around the center of the outline. To rotate around a more specific point, drag the small centerpoint icon to the desired location. For example, you might drag the centerpoint to a corner, to make it easier to align the marquee to a flat edge.

C.4

Correcting Perspective While Cropping

Sometimes, the perspective of an image is slightly off. Perhaps the photographer was standing off-center, and a rectangular image element doesn't appear flush on all sides. Perhaps a camera unit was improperly positioned, adding an element of *keystone distortion*, or the appearance of oblique, off-kilter perspective. As long as the flaw is not too severe, you can use the Crop tool to compensate for it. Essentially, you perform a transformation similar to using the Edit: Transform: **Perspective** command, but you're able to use the Crop marquee as a flexible guide. Follow these steps:

1. Choose the Crop tool.

2. Drag the desired crop marquee.

3. In the Options bar, check the Perspective box. (When you do, you'll notice that the centerpoint moves from the center of the marquee to the center of the image. For the best results, don't attempt to reposition the icon.)

4. Adjust the corner handles until the marquee edges match the skewed perspective of the image. **A**

5. To apply the crop, click the checkmark button in the Options bar. The corners of the cropped image are "stretched" back onto a rectangular plane, compensating for the distortion. **B**

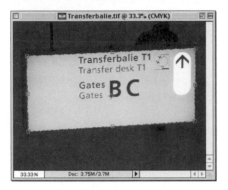

A *Adjusting the crop marquee.*

B *The cropped image.*

Issues to Consider

Encountering the error dialog box. If Photoshop cannot process the way you've adjusted the crop marquee, it displays an alert that states, "Could not use the cropping tool. The centerpoint is not correctly placed or the corners are not properly selected." From there, you can choose Don't Crop, which removes the marquee, or Cancel, which takes you back to the current marquee for further adjustments. The alert appears when your adjustments are too extreme, or if you've dragged the centerpoint. It also appears if you don't follow the basic guidelines of perspective. For example, if you drag a corner point perfectly horizontally or vertically, the resulting perspective would be harsh and unnatural, so Photoshop rejects it. Unfortunately, this option doesn't automatically inform you when adjustments are unacceptable, or prevent you from dragging erroneously. For most images, a single approach will suffice: when placing an upper corner handle, drag it slightly downward; When placing a lower corner handle, drag it slightly upward. From there, drag toward the center of the box until you've aligned the edge to your reference point in the image.

C.5

Cropping to a Specific Width and Height

The Crop tool enables you to determine the width and height of a cropped image. This accomplishes two things. First, it constrains the crop marquee to the desired aspect ratio, so you know exactly the image information that will be preserved or discarded. Second, it automatically resizes the image when you apply the crop, freeing you from having to use the Image Size command to change the dimensions in the future. This technique is particularly useful when creating a series of images to fit predetermined requirements. For example, a magazine or newspaper may have specific column-based measurements for its photographs. By cropping the scans to fit, you ensure that the final images are appropriately sized. Follow these steps:

1. Choose the Crop tool.

2. Before dragging a crop marquee, refer to the Options bar. Enter the desired dimensions in the Width and Height fields. If cropping to a particular resolution, enter the value in the Resolution field. (See **Issues to Consider**.)

3. Drag the crop marquee. You can rotate and reposition the outline, but the ratio between the width and height is locked.

4. Apply the crop. Regardless of the original dimensions, the cropped image is resized to the targeted width and height.

Issues to Consider

Setting the resolution of the resized image. If you leave the resolution field blank, the image is resized without interpolation. This means that the resolution will automatically change, depending on the final size of the cropped image. If the dimensions you've plugged into the Options bar produce a smaller image, then the resolution will increase. If they produce a larger image, then the resolution will decrease. On one hand, resizing an image this way ensures that no detail is lost due to upsampling or downsampling. On the other, if you don't keep an eye on the final resolution, it may be too high or low for the image's intended use. Unless you're prepared to make any resolution-based manipulations in the future, enter an appropriate value in the Resolution field when resizing a crop. For example, if using the image for print purposes, enter 300 pixels/inch.

Using different measurement units. When you enter numbers in the Width and Height fields, the units default to the current Rulers setting in the Edit: Preferences: **Units & Rulers** dialog box. To enter a value based on a different unit, change the current setting.

C.6

Using Fixed Target Size Variations While Cropping

You can achieve additional resizing effects by leaving one or more of the fields in the Options bar blank:

- **Blank Width.** The crop marquee is not constrained. The cropped image is resized to accommodate the Height value, regardless of the crop marquee's width.

- **Blank Height.** The crop marquee is not constrained. The cropped image is resized to accommodate the Width value, regardless of the crop marquee's height.

- **Blank Width and Height.** The crop marquee is not constrained. The cropped image is reduced or enlarged to match the specified resolution without resampling the pixels.

C.7

Resampling an Image

When you scale an image in a layout document, you simply enlarge or reduce its width and height, stretching or squeezing it to fit a particular area. Both actions directly affect the image's resolution. For example, if you increase the scale, you force the same number of pixels to accommodate a larger space; the pixels become larger, thereby decreasing the resolution. When you decrease the scale, you force the same number of pixels to accommodate a smaller space; the pixels become smaller, thereby increasing the resolution. Because the number of image pixels never changes, no information is added or removed from the file.

However, scaling in a separate program is not always the best approach. For example, you may need to reduce a 9 x 6-inch image to fit a 3 x 2-inch space. (If the original resolution is 300 ppi, scaling it down in a layout document effectively increases the resolution to 900 ppi—far more than necessary for halftoning purposes.) Or you may need to repurpose a print-oriented image for display on a web site. (The size difference between a 3 x 5-inch CMYK image at 300 ppi and the same image optimized for the Web at 72 ppi is over 5 MB.) In cases like these, you need to resample the image, or use Photoshop to change the resolution.

There are many ways to resize all or part of an image, but the most flexible tool is the Image: **Image Size** command. As you'll see, there are two types of resampling. When you resize in a way that decreases the resolution, you downsample the file. When you resize in a way that increases the resolution, you upsample the file. In both cases, you need to specify how Photoshop interpolates the image information, or how it determines the appearance of the new arrangement of pixels.

C.8

Downsampling an Image

Downsampling is a common technique, used to reduce image resolution to an acceptable value. Because Photoshop is essentially throwing away redundant pixels, downsampling generally results in very little loss of overall detail. Many users scan their images at a higher resolution than necessary, because the extra data enables them to apply techniques such as layering and extracting more successfully—when their editing is complete, they can safely discard the extra resolution, reducing the file size enough to accommodate their target output method. Also, minor flaws such as rough transitions between combined elements can be softened somewhat by the interpolation process. **A B**

A *300 ppi image.*

B *Downsampled to 72 ppi.*

There are three ways to downsample an image. The right method depends on whether you want to change only the resolution value, change only the width and height, or change the width, height, and resolution simultaneously.

Reducing the Resolution (Same Width and Height)

To reduce the image resolution while maintaining the current width and height, follow these steps:

1. Choose Image: **Image Size** to access the Image Size dialog box. **c**

2. Check the Resample Image box (making sure Bicubic is set in the neighboring pop-up menu).

3. Enter the desired value in the Resolution field. In this example, I reduce a 300 ppi image to 72 ppi. (Note the difference in size at the top of the dialog box.)

4. Click OK to downsample the image.

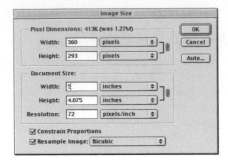

C *Reducing only the resolution.*

Reducing the Width and Height (Same Resolution)

To reduce the width and height while maintaining the current resolution, follow these steps:

1. Choose Image: **Image Size** to access the Image Size dialog box. **D**

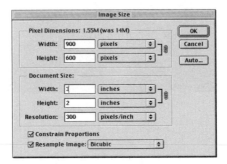

D *Reducing only the width and height.*

2. Check the Resample Image box (making sure Bicubic is set in the neighboring pop-up menu).

3. Check the Constrain Proportions box.

4. Enter the desired values in the Width and Height fields. For example, if you want the image to be a specific width, enter the value in the Width field. The Height value will change automatically. In this example, I reduce a 9 x 6-inch image to 3 x 2 inches. (Note the difference in size at the top of the dialog box.) Remember that in order to downsample the image, the width and height must be *lower* than the original values.

5. Click OK to downsample the image.

Reducing the Width, Height, and Resolution at Once

To reduce an image's width, height, and resolution at the same time, follow these steps:

1. Choose Image: **Image Size** to access the Image Size dialog box. **E**

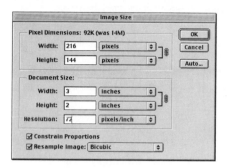

E   *Reducing width, height, and resolution simultaneously*

2. Check the Resample Image box (making sure Bicubic is set in the neighboring pop-up.)

3. Check the Constrain Proportions box.

4. Enter the desired width and height. In this example, I reduce a 9 x 6-inch image to 3 x 2 inches.

5. Enter the desired resolution. In this example, I reduce the resolution from 300 ppi to 72 ppi.

6. Click OK to downsample the image.

Issues to Consider

Downsampling at the appropriate stage of the editing process. These techniques should be employed at the very end of the editing cycle, after you've applied any corrections, sharpening, layering, and so forth. If the resampling was extensive—for example, if you reduced the resolution from 300 ppi to 72 ppi, or if you drastically reduced the width and height—the image may benefit from a small boost from the Unsharp Mask filter.

C.9

Upsampling an Image

When you upsample an image, you increase its resolution. At first, this may seem like a way to cross-purpose a low-res image for high-res uses, such as converting a web or FPO graphic for output at a high linescreen value.

However, upsampling is rarely employed in a production workflow, especially using the Image Size dialog box. When you increase the resolution of an image, Photoshop can only add more pixels—it cannot add a higher level of detail. The end result is invariably blurred and mottled. **A B C**

A *150 ppi scan.*   **B** *Upsampled to 300 ppi.*   **C** *Upsampled to 300 ppi, scaled 300%.*

One of the only places where Photoshop can upsample successfully is when converting a Grayscale image to a higher-resolution Bitmap file. (For more information, see *E.8, Creating a 1-bit Halftone.*)

Resizing Without Interpolation

When you resize an image without interpolating the pixels, you do not resample the data at all. Instead, you constrain the width, height, and resolution. This way, the size of the pixels are enlarged or reduced on the fly, with no recalculation. It's as if you were able to change the size of a brick wall by directly affecting the size of the bricks—no bricks would be added or deleted from the wall, so no additional effort would be required from the bricklayer. Follow these steps:

1. Choose Image: **Image Size**. The Image Size dialog box appears. **A**

2. Uncheck the Resample Image box. (Notice that the Width, Height, and Resolution fields are linked, and the Constrain Proportions box is checked and hidden.)

3. Enter the desired width, height, or resolution. Enter a higher width or height, and the resolution decreases; enter a lower width or height, and the resolution increases. Conversely, enter a higher resolution, and the width and height decreases; enter a lower resolution, and the width and height increases.

4. Click OK to apply the change.

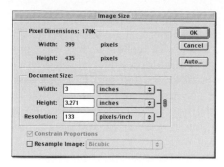

A *Resizing an image without resampling the pixels.*

On screen, the image may not appear to change at all. The command is applied instantaneously, and the image detail is completely retained. However, if you check the document information, you'll notice two important things. First, the file size has not changed—the image still contains the same number of pixels. Second, the width and height are different. By resizing the pixels (or changing the resolution), the image bounds simply shift to accommodate the change.

Issues to Consider

Anticipating the final resolution. When using this technique to adjust width and height, the final resolution will depend on the extent of scaling. For example, if you change a 5 x 7-inch, 300 ppi image to 2 x 2.8 inches, the new resolution is 750 ppi. If you change a 5 x 7-inch, 72 ppi image to 2 x 2.8 inches, the new resolution is 180 ppi. On the other hand, if you change a 2 x 3-inch, 300 ppi image to 6 x 9 inches, the resolution is now 100 ppi. When resizing images destined for print, you must make sure that the final resolution does not fall below the target linescreen value. Similarly, if the final resolution is far too high for print purposes—for instance, the 750 ppi version mentioned above—you may have to resize the image again, down-sampling the resolution while retaining the current width and height. (For more information, see *C.8, Downsampling an Image.*)

Resizing screenshots. Consider all the screenshots included in this book. Most dialog boxes are actually four to eight inches wide, far too large to fit comfortably on the inner column of each page. If these images were resampled, the crisp, clean information that comprises each dialog box would suffer; the text would become slightly anti-aliased, the lines would soften, the screenshots would just look *wrong.* By not resampling, the effect is the same as if the images were scaled in a page layout program. However, because the images were sized correctly in Photoshop, no additional scaling was necessary in the layout documents.

Granted, this task was made easier by the fact that nearly all of the dialog boxes had to appear at a single width: 2.125 inches. So, after taking each screenshot, the above technique was used to set the width to that value. The final resolution depended on the original size of each image: the Image Size dialog box became 222 ppi; the Extract dialog box became 450 ppi; the Unsharp Mask dialog box became 114 ppi. The varying resolutions didn't really matter. Some were a little too high, some were a little too low, but all in all, the printed results were consistent enough to let it slide.

C.11

Scaling by Percentages

Many users prefer to scale an image by percentages, similar to the method used in a page layout program. This is especially true when you're in the habit of using a proportion wheel to determine the target size. For example, if you know that your 5 x 7-inch image must ultimately appear at 2.25 x 3.15 inches, such a device will tell you that the necessary scale is 45%. To use percentages in the Image Size dialog box, follow these steps:

1. Choose Image: **Image Size**. The Image Size dialog box appears. **A**

2. To change the width and height simultaneously, check the Constrain Proportions box.

3. To retain the current resolution value, check the Resample Image box. To scale the image without resampling (as described under *C.10, Resizing Without Interpolation*), uncheck the resample Image box.

4. Under the Document Size portion of the dialog box, set the pop-up menus beside the Width and Height fields to Percent.

5. Enter the desired scale percentage in the Width and Height fields.

6. Click OK to resize the image.

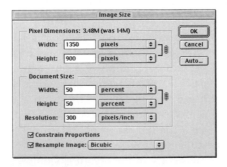

A *Scaling an image down to 50%.*

C.12

Scaling Disproportionately

The techniques presented so far focus on proportional scaling, or retaining the ratio between the width and height. Occasionally, you may need to alter one value independently of the other, producing the same effect as horizontally or vertically scaling in your layout program. Unchecking the Constrain Proportions box in the Image Size dialog box enables you to edit the width, height, and resolution values separately. Just be aware that the box will still be unchecked the next time you open the Image Size dialog box, which may cause some confusion if you attempt to use a different resizing technique. **A**

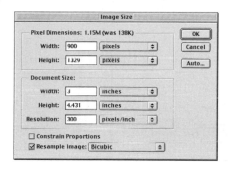

A *Setting width and height independently.*

C.13

Increasing the Canvas Size

There's a difference between resizing the entire image and increasing the canvas size. When you resize, you force all of the pixels to accommodate a new space. When you increase the canvas, you add new pixels around one or more of the image edges, without affecting the existing information. Most often, this is done when you realize that the current image size is too short or too narrow for the image information you need to work with.

Figure out two things before you begin. First, determine where you want the new pixels to appear. Across the top? To the left edge? All the way around the image? Next, determine how much new information you need. An inch? Two picas? 300 pixels? From there, follow these steps:

1. Choose Image: **Canvas Size**. The Canvas Size dialog box appears, displaying the current size of the image. **A**

2. In the Anchor grid, determine where you want the existing image information to appear in relation to the new pixels. For example, if you want

the new data to appear all the way around the current image, click the middle box. If you want the new info to appear above the image, click the box in the bottom center. (The small arrows indicate where the new pixels will appear.) **B**

3. In the Width and Height fields, enter the increased image dimensions. You're not entering the amount of extra information; Instead, you must add the desired amount to the existing value. For example, if the image is 4 inches wide and you want to add another inch of working space, enter 5 in the Width field.

4. Click OK to increase the canvas size. **C**

A *Original image.*

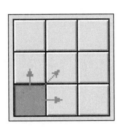

B *Postioning the expanded area.*

C *The increased canvas.*

Issues to Consider

Anticipating the contents of the new image information. When Photoshop increases the canvas, the new pixels will contain one of three things. If the image consists only of a background layer, the new pixels are filled with the current background color value. If the image consists of image layers, the new pixels are transparent. If any image layer contains information that extends beyond the image boundaries, the new pixels may reveal the hidden data. (Note that a single image can contain all of the above layer types—here, when you increase the canvas, the new pixels will be transparent, filled with the background color, or reveal hidden information, depending on each layer.)

C.14

Decreasing the Canvas Size

Decreasing the canvas size produces the same effect as using the Crop tool to discard unwanted pixels from an image. On one hand, this technique is not as flexible as the Crop tool—you cannot place a precise crop marquee, and it can be difficult to see exactly what information is being cut. On the other hand, you can use this technique to quickly trim an image to precise numerical dimensions, especially if you can afford to be flexible with the range of data that it discards. You can also automate this approach with an action, which you cannot do with the Crop tool. Follow these steps:

1. Assess the image to determine the extent and location of the trimmed pixels. **A**

2. Choose Image: **Canvas Size**. The Canvas Size dialog box appears, displaying the current size of the image.

3. In the Anchor grid, determine the area of the image you want to preserve. For example, if you want to trim pixels all the way around the image, click the center square. To trim from the left edge only, click the right center square. To trim from the right and bottom edges, click the upper left square. **B**

4. In the Width and Height fields, enter the reduced dimensions.

5. Click OK to decrease the canvas size. An alert will appear, informing you that "some clipping will occur." Click the Proceed button to continue. **c**

A *Original image.*

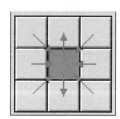

B *Determining the area to protect.*

c *The reduced canvas size.*

File Conversion Techniques

Opening Other Pixel-Based Images

Photoshop can read just about any type of pixel-based image file. However, you usually aren't able to open a non-Photoshop file by double-clicking its icon. For example, if you double-click a JPEG image you downloaded from a web site, it will probably open up in one of your OS's basic utilities, such as PicViewer or JPEGView. If you try to open a BMP image created in Windows on a Mac, you'll likely get a message stating that the file cannot be opened because the application that created it could not be found. If you use dedicated scanning software to acquire images (as opposed to using a Photoshop plug-in), double-clicking the file will simply open it up in the original program.

To open such images in Photoshop, you need to direct the file to the program's attention. Follow these steps:

1. In Photoshop, choose File: **Open**. The Open dialog box appears.

2. In the Show pop-up menu, choose All Readable Documents.

3. Use the dialog box's navigational controls to locate the desired file.

4. Select the file and click Open.

If the file is pixel-based, it will open directly into Photoshop. If the file contains vector-based information—such as PostScript-defined shapes or active fonts—the Rasterize Generic EPS Format dialog box appears, requesting additional data (for more information, see *D.2, Opening a Vector-Based File*).

Issues to Consider

Photoshop does not recognize all file types. The target file may not be available in the Open dialog box, even after setting the Show pop-up menu to All Readable Documents. For example, Photoshop cannot translate page layout documents or text files, so they are ignored. When this occurs, try setting the Show pop-up menu to All Documents. This way, every file on your drive is displayed, whether or not Photoshop is able to read it. All you can do is try to open it; if it can't be done, Photoshop will quickly let you know, and you can start employing another technique. Most often, using the original application to convert the file to a PDF will do the trick (for more information, see *D.6, Opening a PDF File*).

Drag-and-drop to quicken the process. You can bypass the Open dialog box by placing an Alias (or Shortcut, for Windows users) of the Photoshop application file on your Desktop. To open any non-Photoshop file, drag its icon directly onto the Alias (or Shortcut)—if the file can be translated, it will happen automatically.

D.2

Opening a Vector-Based File

To edit a file created in a vector-based editing program (such as Adobe Illustrator, Macromedia FreeHand, CorelDraw, or a page layout application), you must translate the artwork into information that Photoshop can read. The process of converting object-oriented shapes into editable pixels is known as *rasterizing*. To rasterize a vector-based file, follow these steps:

1. In Photoshop, choose File: **Open**. The Open dialog box appears.

2. Use the dialog box's navigational controls to locate the file, then click Open. The Rasterize Generic EPS Format dialog box appears. **A**

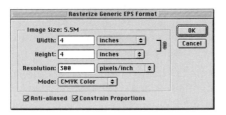

A *The Rasterize Generic EPS Format dialog box.*

3. Enter the desired width and height of the converted image. (To retain the original proportions as you change the size, check the Constrain Proportions option.)

4. Enter the target resolution. Vectors have no resolution until they are output or converted; pixel-based images are defined in large part by the size of their pixels. You must establish the resolution at which you want the new shapes to exist. (See *Issues to Consider*, below.)

5. Set the desired color mode in the Mode pop-up menu. Choose the option that dovetails with the requirements of your project. (See *Issues to Consider*, below.)

6. Check the Anti-aliased box, unless you know for sure that you don't want a thin, edge-smoothing transition between your converted shapes.

7. Click OK to rasterize the file. It may take several seconds or longer, depending on the complexity of the original image, the dimensions you entered, and the speed of your computer.

Issues to Consider

Understanding the difference between pixels and vectors. Paint programs (like Photoshop) use pixels, or tiny colored squares, to construct an image. The effect is similar to painting on a piece of graph paper, filling each cell with a single color. The *resolution*, or the exact size of the pixels, depends on the intended use of the image. For this reason, pixel-based images are *resolution dependent*. Successfully displaying or outputting such an image depends largely on its fixed pixel size.

On the other hand, vector-based graphics have no resolution. They don't use pixels. Instead, their shapes are comprised of points and segments, like a connect-the-dots puzzle. Only here, you can reposition the points, curve the segments, and create a series of overlapping shapes virtually at will. These graphics are *resolution independent*—they have no resolution until they're printed, and the final value depends on the output device used. For example, assume you have a 300 pixel-per-inch Photoshop image of a black circle. If you output it to a 300 dpi printer, of course, it reproduces at 300 dpi. If you send the same image to a 2400 dpi imagesetter, its resolution doesn't change—it still outputs at 300 dpi. The resolution is fixed. Now assume you have an Illustrator image that contains a vector-based circle. On a 300 dpi printer, it outputs at 300 dpi; on a 600 dpi printer, it outputs at 600 dpi; on a 2400 dpi imagesetter, it outputs at 2400 dpi. The resolution depends solely on the output device used to reproduce the image.

Understanding the rasterizing process. The term "rasterize" may seem new, but you've been exposed to the basic concept ever since the first time you printed a document. Every output device uses a RIP to process image information prior to printing. RIP stands for *Raster* Image Processor. Similar to converting multi-layered objects into a flat canvas of pixels, a printer's RIP changes the multiple elements of a page layout into two-dimensional composites or color separations.

Determining when to convert vector-based data. As with any conversion, you should rasterize artwork only when you have a specific reason. Most often, people rasterize objects when they want to apply pixel-specific effects such as semi-opacity, soft drop shadows, or Photoshop filters. I know several artists who prefer to perform complex typesetting in a program like Illustrator or XPress, as opposed to using Photoshop's rather clunky toolset. When they need to incorporate the type into an image, they rasterize the file and continue editing.

Attempting to blend images of different resolutions. If the resolution of the converted file does not meet your editing requirements, you could be in for a surprise when you add the new data to another image. For example, if you rasterize an Illustrator graphic at 72 ppi and drop it into a 300 ppi scan, the graphic appears disproportionately tiny. Since the Rasterize dialog box always retains the last-applied resolution value, you should always double-check it. Or, you can bypass the Rasterize dialog box and import the image using File: **Place** (for more information, see *D.3, Importing Vector-Based Artwork*).

Rasterizing in other applications. Illustrator and FreeHand both feature rasterizing commands, but you should refrain from using them whenever possible. Since the new pixels will reside only in the vector-based file, your editing options are extremely limited. You're able to apply some filters and a few other effects, but for the most part, you're limited to the results of the command. The only time you should rasterize in Illustrator or FreeHand is when you don't have access to Photoshop—easily, the most powerful pixel-editing program.

Rasterizing vectors and pixels simultaneously. If the original file contains images of different resolutions (for example, a 300 ppi halftone and 1200 ppi line art), both images are interpolated to whatever resolution is entered in the Rasterize dialog box.

Rasterizing color information. If the original graphic contains images of different color modes (for example, a CMYK TIFF, a Grayscale TIFF, and line art), they are all converted to the option set in the Rasterize dialog box's Mode pop-up menu. This can lead to altered color values, particularly if the graphic is translated into RGB mode first, then converted to CMYK.

D.3

Importing Vector-Based Artwork

To add vector-based artwork directly to an open image (without creating a separate file), you can import it, which bypasses the Rasterize Generic EPS Format dialog box. The file is converted to match the resolution and color mode of the master image. Follow these steps:

1. In Photoshop, open the image that you want to receive the converted artwork.

2. Choose File: **Place**. The Place dialog box appears. **A**

3. Use the dialog box's navigational controls to locate the target file.

4. Click Place to import the image. A preview of the converted artwork appears in a bounding box. **B**

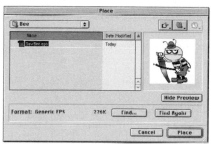

A   *The Place dialog box.*   **B**   *Imported image preview.*

5. Position the artwork as needed. Scale the preview by dragging the corner points of the box, rotate it by dragging the cursor outside the box, and move it by dragging the box or nudging with the arrow keys. **C**

6. To rasterize the artwork, double-click the bounding box or press the Return key. The converted information appears in a new image layer. **D**

C   *Scaled and positioned preview.*   **D**   *Editing the rasterized image layer.*

D.4

Retaining Layers in a Rasterized Illustrator File

To open an Adobe Illustrator file in Photoshop, simply follow the steps described under *D.2, Opening a Vector-Based File*. For the best results, convert any type in the document to outlines and save the file as an EPS.

When you use Photoshop to rasterize the image, all the separate shapes and colors appear on a single image layer, making it extremely difficult to edit any individual items. Illustrator 9.0, on the other hand, enables you to produce a Photoshop file that retains multiple layer information. You don't rasterize such a file in Photoshop. Instead, follow these steps:

1. In Illustrator 9.0, produce a multi-layered document. **A**

2. Choose File: **Export**. The Export dialog box appears. **B**

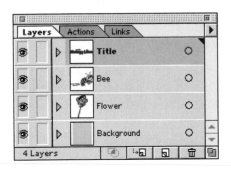

A *Multi-layered Illustrator file.*

B *Illustrator's Export dialog box.*

3. In the dialog box's Format pop-up, choose Photoshop 5 (PSD).

4. Click OK. The Photoshop Options dialog box appears. **c**

5. Set the target color mode in the Color Model pop-up menu.

6. Set the target resolution.

7. Check the Write Layers box. If you don't, the converted file will only contain one image layer.

8. Click OK to produce the new file.

9. Open the converted file in Photoshop. You're able to continue editing the individual layers. **D**

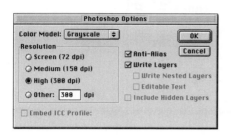

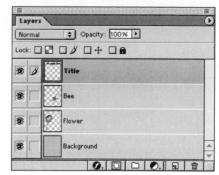

C *Illustrator's Photoshop Options dialog box.*

D *Separate layers retained in Photoshop.*

Issues to Consider

The Rasterize command recognizes the artwork bounds. When you convert an Illustrator file using the Rasterize Generic EPS Format dialog box, the width and height fields automatically reflect the current width and height of the shapes themselves—the document edges are ignored. You can increase or decrease the scale of the shapes without compromising their converted quality. However, you should make sure that no unwanted shapes or points exist in the EPS file. For example, if a small shape was placed beyond the page boundaries in Illustrator—for testing purposes, perhaps—it is included in the conversion, and will likely skew the dimensions of the new image.

D.5

Opening a Macromedia FreeHand File

Unlike Illustrator files, Photoshop cannot convert a native FreeHand document. You must first save the artwork as an EPS file. There are two ways to do this:

- When saving the document, set Editable EPS in the Save As dialog box's Format pop-up menu.

- To export the artwork as an EPS file, choose File: **Export**. In the Export dialog box, set Macintosh EPS or MS-DOS EPS, depending on your platform. (When using a version of FreeHand earlier than 8.0, this is the only available option.) **A**

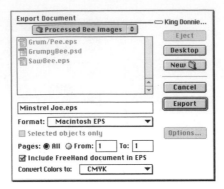

A *FreeHand's Export dialog box.*

Once you've created the EPS file, the steps for converting it to pixels are the same as described under *D.2, Opening a Vector-Based File* and *D.4, Opening an Adobe Illustrator File.*

D.6

Opening a PDF *File*

Photoshop is able to convert any PDF file to editable pixels. This technique is particularly useful when you need to open any of a wide variety of unsupported file types, such as Microsoft Excel graphs, page layout documents, or even text files. As long as the person providing the file is able to distill a PDF, you can access the information. The technique you use will depend on whether you're converting a single-page or multi-page PDF file.

Single-Page PDF

To convert a single-page PDF file, follow these steps:

1. In Photoshop, choose File: **Open**. The Open dialog box appears.

2. Set the Show pop-up menu to All Readable Documents.

3. Use the dialog box's navigational controls to locate the desired PDF file.

4. Click Open. The Rasterize Generic PDF Format dialog box appears. **A**

5. Enter the desired dimensions of the converted image, following the same guidelines listed under *D.2, Opening a Vector-Based File.*

6. Click OK to convert the file. The new information appears on a single image layer.

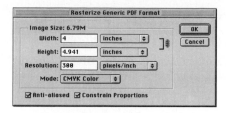

A *The Rasterize Generic PDF Format dialog box.*

A Single Page from a Multi-Page PDF

To convert a single page from within a multi-page PDF file, follow these steps:

1. In Photoshop, choose File: **Open**. The Open dialog box appears.

2. Set the Show pop-up menu to All Readable Documents.

3. Use the dialog box's navigational controls to locate the desired PDF file.

4. Click Open. The Generic PDF Parser dialog box appears. **B**

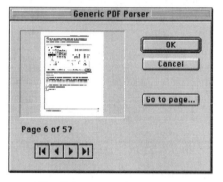

B *The Generic PDF Parser dialog box.*

5. Use the dialog box's navigational controls to target the desired page within the PDF file.

6. Click OK to convert the file. The Rasterize Generic PDF Format dialog box appears.

7. Enter the desired dimensions of the converted image, following the same guidelines listed under *D.2, Opening a Vector-Based File.*

8. Click OK to convert the file. The new information appears on a single image layer.

Multi-Page PDF

To convert a number of pages from a multi-page PDF file, follow these steps:

1. Choose File: Automate: **Multi-Page PDF to PSD**. The Convert Multi-Page PDF to PSD dialog box appears. **C**

2. Under Source PDF, click the Choose button. The Select PDF File to Convert dialog box appears. **D**

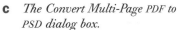
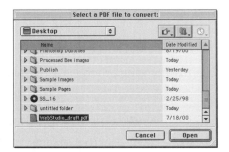

C *The Convert Multi-Page PDF to PSD dialog box.*

D *The Select PDF File to Convert dialog box.*

3. Use the dialog box's navigational controls to locate the desired multi-page PDF file. Click Open to revert to the previous dialog box.

4. Under Page Range, enter the PDF pages you want to convert. You can only choose All or a range sequential page numbers; to convert non-sequential pages, either include some pages you don't want and delete them later, or apply this command more than once.

5. Set the target resolution.

6. Choose the desired color mode from the Mode pop-up menu.

7. Under destination, enter a base name. For example, if you enter "SamplePDF", the converted pages are named "SamplePDF0001.psd", SamplePDF0002.psd", and so forth. By default, the root name of the targeted PDF appears here.

8. Under destination, click the Choose button to determine a folder that will receive the converted pages. Create a new folder, if necessary.

9. Click OK to convert the pages. After each page is rasterized, it is saved, placed into the destination folder, and closed.

10. Re-open the images in Photoshop to continue editing. Each converted page appears on a single image layer.

Issues to Consider

Converted pages may contain transparency. If the original PDF file contained blank page information—such as white space surrounding text or graphics—it will appear as transparent pixels. Flattening the image will convert the transparent pixels to white.

Converting a PDF removes any PostScript-based data. Many PDF files are constructed to output successfully to a PostScript printer. However, as soon as they are rasterized, the entire file exists as a pixel-based image. When employing the above techniques, make sure you intend to use the file as an image element, and not a standalone high-res document.

Convert to a larger width and height, then scale down when needed. It can be difficult to predict the actual file size you need, particularly if you only intend to use part of a page layout as an image element. When converting a single PDF page, start with a larger size, then use the Image: **Image Size** command to resize the final product more accurately. (Note that when you convert a multi-page PDF, you can only rasterize using the original page dimensions.)

If possible, make sure the fonts have been included in the PDF file. If the person who created the original PDF file did not subset the font information, the document fonts will need to be acquired and installed before you convert the file. Otherwise, Photoshop will use the default system font.

You cannot compensate for incorrect compression options. Photoshop can only work with the image information that resides in the PDF file. For example, if the person who created the original PDF downsampled all of the images to 72 ppi, you cannot regain any of the lost information, even if you rasterize using a higher resolution. If possible, request that the PDF be distilled again, using settings that produce a more desirable result.

D.7

Opening a QuarkXPress File

To convert a single page of a QuarkXPress document to editable pixels, follow these steps:

1. In XPress, navigate to the desired document page.

2. Choose File: **Save Page as EPS**. The Save Page as EPS dialog box appears. Use the following settings: **A**

    - Make sure the desired page number appears in the Page field.

    - To include any information that extends beyond the page boundaries, enter a value in the Bleed field.

    - Choose Color from the Format pop-up menu.

- Choose Binary from the data pop-up menu.
- Choose Include Images from the OPI pop-up menu.

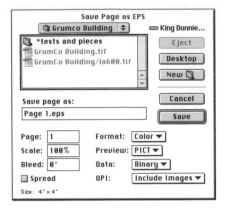

A *XPress' Save Page as* EPS
dialog box

3. Use the dialog box's navigational controls to determine the location of the saved file.

4. Click Save to create the EPS file.

5. In Photoshop, choose File: **Open**. The Open dialog box appears.

6. Set the Show pop-up menu to All Readable Documents.

7. Use the dialog box's navigational controls to locate the Quark EPS file.

8. Click Open. The Rasterize Generic EPS Format dialog box appears.

9. Enter the desired dimensions of the converted image, following the same guidelines listed under *D.2, Opening a Vector-Based File.*

You can only save one page at a time as an EPS file. To open a multi-page XPress document in Photoshop, convert the entire document to a PDF file (using either Adobe Acrobat Distiller or PDFWriter). Then follow the steps listed in *D.6, Opening a PDF File.*

Issues to Consider

Photoshop only recognizes page dimensions. When you convert an XPress page, the dimensions that appear in the Rasterize Generic EPS Format dialog box reflect the page edges, not the artwork that it contains. For example, if you attempt to rasterize a single 4 x 4-inch text block on an 8.5 x 11-inch page, Photoshop will rasterize the entire page. If you try to reduce the dimensions to 4 x 4 inches to match the original size of the artwork, you only succeed in shrinking the entire page. There are three ways to work with this phenomenon. First, rasterize the entire page, then crop it immediately after it opens in Photoshop. Second, reduce the page dimensions in XPress so they match the size of the target artwork. Finally, if you have Adobe Illustrator, open the saved EPS there first. The page bounds will appear as a white box encircling the artwork. Delete the box, resave the file as an Illustrator EPS, and convert it to pixels.

D.8

Opening an Adobe InDesign File

To open an Adobe InDesign page in Photoshop, you must save it as a PDF file. Follow these steps:

1. If you only want to save a single InDesign page (for example, if you are working on a very large document), save a copy of the file and delete any unnecessary pages. Otherwise, skip this step.

2. Choose File: **Export**. The Export dialog box appears. **A**

3. Choose Adobe PDF from the Formats pop-up menu.

4. Click OK. The Export PDF Options dialog box appears. **B**

5. Set the desired font and compression options, then click OK to create the PDF.

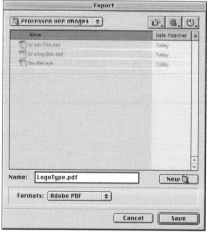

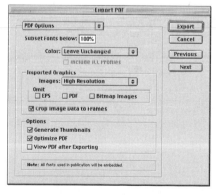

A *InDesign's Export dialog box.*

B *InDesign's Export PDF Options dialog box.*

6. To rasterize the PDF pages, follow the steps listed in *D.6, Opening a PDF File.*

Although InDesign enables you to export a document as an EPS, avoid using this option. Photoshop has difficulty reading single-page EPS files saved from InDesign, and it cannot read multi-page EPS files at all.

D.9
Opening an Adobe PageMaker File

The only way to access PageMaker information in Photoshop is to convert the document to a PDF file. For the best results, use Adobe Acrobat Distiller or PDFWriter. Once the PDF file exists, follow the steps listed in *D.6, Opening a PDF File.*

D.10
Converting an Image to Editable Paths

The process of producing vector-based outlines from a pixel-based image is known as *tracing.* You trace an image because you want to be able to edit it with the tools of a vector-based editing program like Illustrator or FreeHand. Perhaps you need to create a crisp, scalable version of a company logo that only exists in a printed form. Perhaps you want to apply a black stroke and gradient fill to a sketch that you've made. Once they hear about this technique, many users feel they have to trace *every* image they scan, and this simply isn't required. For example, if you just want to incorporate a hand-drawn image into a page layout, there is no reason to trace it. Just scan it at the right size and resolution, then import it like any other graphic. Once you've determined the need for tracing an image, you must determine the appropriate method.

To manually trace an image element, follow these steps:

1. In Photoshop, open the image that contains the target element.

2. Use the Pen tool to create the desired vector-based shapes. **A**

3. Refine the path as necessary and save it. **B**

A *Tracing an element with the Pen tool.*

B *The completed path.*

Once you have created the desired paths, there are two ways to edit them in a vector-based application. To bring the paths directly into an Illustrator file, follow these steps:

1. In Photoshop, select the target path with the Path Component Selection tool.

2. Choose Edit: **Copy**.

3. In an Illustrator document, choose Edit: **Paste**. The new shapes appear with no applied fill or stroke.

4. Continue editing the path using Illustrator's toolset. **c**

c *Editing the paths in Illustrator.*

To export the paths into a file that can be read by additional programs (such as FreeHand), follow these steps:

1. Choose File: Export: **Paths to Illustrator**. The Save dialog box appears.

2. Choose the target path name from the Write pop-up menu.

3. Name the file as necessary ("untitled" appears in the Name field by default).

4. Use the dialog box's navigational controls to determine the location of the new file.

5. Click Save to create the new file. The path—and only the path—is saved in an Adobe Illustrator file, which can be opened by other applications.

Manually tracing an image is adequate for simpler shapes. For more complex items, you may want to invest in an auto-tracing program such as Adobe Streamline 4.0, available for under $150. You can use it to convert black and white, grayscale, or color images to vectors, and it features several commands that control the frequency of points, the number of included shades, and overall smoothness. After converting, you can save the paths in a variety of formats, including Illustrator and FreeHand.

However, Streamline does not produce the flawless results that you may be hoping for. Even simple tracings usually require further tweaking in your preferred graphics program.

Line Art Editing Techniques

Setting Resolution for Scanned Line Art

Line art scans are the only type of image that isn't *screened* during output, or converted to halftone dots. Instead, the pixels output exactly they way they appear in the image—as a series of tiny, solid black squares. Therefore, when you set the resolution of a line art scan, you must make sure the pixels are small enough to avoid detection by the human eye.

Many users hear the term "300 ppi" tossed around, not realizing that it only pertains to Grayscale and full-color images. If line art exists at any resolution less than 900 ppi, the black pixels are visible as a series of tiny, jagged lines. The lower the resolution, the more visible they become, and the less detail the scan can contain. The industry standard value is 1200 ppi, and there's really no reason to deviate from that setting. Higher values won't tangibly increase image quality—they just produce larger files that take longer to process. **A B C**

A *100 ppi line art.*

B *300 ppi line art.*

C *1200 ppi line art.*

E.2

Testing Your Scanner Before Acquiring Line Art

Don't assume that your scanner is capable of acquiring perfect artwork straight off the glass, even with something as basic as line art. Different scanners have varying levels of sensitivity to light and dark information, and your software's default settings may not produce optimal results. Before scanning live jobs, try a simple test to determine the amount of pre-adjustment needed for future work. Use a clean, clear sample of finely-detailed black-and-white artwork. Follow these steps:

1. Acquire the image at the appropriate resolution, using your scanner software's default Line Art setting.

2. Immediately after scanning, output the image to your laser printer. (The printer should be at least 600 dpi. For the most accurate results, output the scan to a high-res imagesetter.)

3. Compare the printout to the original artwork. Any lost detail will appear in two forms: Areas filled in with black or burned out to white. **A B C**

If the printout closely matches the original, you're ready to move on. If it's cluttered with stray pixels, your scanner may have faulty (or low-quality) CCDs or a fading light source. If the printout is too light or dark, you may be able to compensate for it by adjusting some settings in your scanner software. (See *E.3, Optimizing Your Scanning Software for Line Art.*)

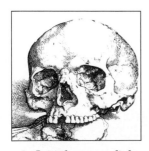

A *Initial scan too light.*

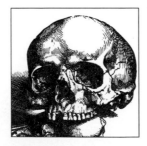

B *Initial scan too dark.*

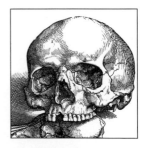

C *Balanced scan.*

Issues to Consider

Use a resolution tester. Companies with in-house imagesetters often output test strips to gauge the performance of their output devices. Most of them involve a *resolution tester,* or a group of starbursts constructed of super-thin lines. It's unlikely that you'll be scanning any detail finer than this, which makes it well-suited for testing the sensitivity of your scanner. If you don't have immediate access to a test target, ask your vendor to make a positive of their test film. If they regularly output to RC paper, they'll probably find a recent round of strips sitting in their recycling bin.

E.3

Optimizing Your Scanning Software for Line Art

When scanning line art, its easy to assume that you're only working with two tones: black and white. That's not necessarily so. Before creating the 1-bit file, the scanner initially sees the artwork as a Grayscale image. It then applies a *threshold,* or a line that determines which pixels become black or white.

Most often, the default threshold is placed at the halfway point—any tones over 50% black are converted to full black, and any tones under 50% are converted to pure white. However, the scanner's not smart enough to know what's *supposed* to be black and what's *supposed* to be white. When light is reflected off the artwork and detected by the CCDs, the very edges of the black data may possess a slightly blurred fringe. If these "gray" tones appear dark enough to your scanner, they're converted to black pixels, which may result in clogged details. If the tones appear light enough, they're converted to white pixels, which may result in a loss of detail.

Your software should produce an acceptable off-the-glass scan of any simple to medium-detailed original. The trick is to reposition the threshold so it preserves enough detail in the lightest and darkest areas. Most scanner software contains a setting called "Threshold" or "Brightness/Contrast," available whenever you set Line Art as a scanning option. Most often, you'll be able to either set a new threshold percentage or manipulate a slider that ranges from 0 to 255. (The slider refers to the 256 brightness levels of a Grayscale image. Most often, the starting position is 128, the midpoint between black and white.)

To find the optimal Threshold setting, follow these steps:

1. Choose a piece of reasonably detailed artwork, such as a turn-of-the-century engraving.

2. Scan the artwork as Line Art, using your software's default Threshold setting.

3. Print the scanned image and compare it to the original.

4. If the test scan is too dark, increase the threshold percentage (or move the slider closer to 0), which specifies that more of the gray fringe converts to white. If the scan is too light, decrease the percentage (or move the slider closer to 255), which converts more of the fringe pixels to black. Work in small amounts—for example, adjust the percentage in 5% increments.

5. Rescan the image at the new setting and compare it to the original.

6. Repeat steps 4 and 5 until you pass the point of optimal quality.

7. Work backwards in 1% increments until you nail the best balance between black and white.

8. Save the scanner settings (if your software has this feature), and load them whenever you scan line art in the future. At the very least, jot down the optimal setting for future reference.

Issues to Consider

The default threshold value may vary from scanner to scanner. Many manufacturers are aware of their devices' different sensitivities, and will attempt to set the threshold accordingly. Some may default to 30%, some as high as 60–70%. More often than not, you should regard the initial setting as a starting point, not a value set in stone. As you test different amounts, move in small increments from the original threshold.

Most scanners cannot capture the finest detail. It's unfair to assume that any scanner is sensitive enough to capture the most complex and difficult line art scans. In these cases, you're almost always better off employing some additional scanning techniques (for more information, see *E.7, Optimizing Finely Detailed Line Art*). When setting the optimal threshold, you just need to get as close as possible, which should give you acceptable results for most scans.

Further examples of Threshold in action. Your scanning software is not the only place where a threshold can be applied. When you convert an image from Grayscale to Bitmap mode, Photoshop enables you to apply a "50% Threshold" option, which produces the same result as described above. Also, the Image: Adjust: **Threshold** command enables you to convert any image to black and white by manually setting the threshold level.

E.4

Establishing a Line Art Scanning Strategy

Once you've tested your scanner's ability to interpret black-and-white artwork, you can follow the same step-by-step process whenever you scan line art:

1. Set the scanning mode to Line Art.

2. Set the appropriate resolution. (For more information, see *E.1, Setting Resolution for Scanned Line Art.*)

3. Preview the scan.

4. Acquire the scan.

5. Evaluate the image. (For more information, see *E.5, Evaluating a Line Art Scan.*)

6. Crop and clean up the image. (For more information, see *E.6, Cleaning Up a Line Art Scan.*)

7. Save the file. Unless you have a specific reason for doing otherwise, save every line art image as a TIFF, using the LZW compression option.

E.5

Evaluating a Line Art Scan

Before editing your line art, evaluate the image to make sure the initial scan was successful. There are two ways to check scan quality: Print a copy to compare to the original, and examine the individual pixels.

Printing a Test Copy

Immediately after the scan opens in Photoshop, print it to your laser printer and compare it to the original artwork. Even if your output device is only 600 dpi—half the resolution of the typical line art scan—it will give you a reasonable impression of its overall quality. If the shapes appear jagged, the resolution is probably too low. If the fine details are clogged or blown out, you may need to use a different scanning technique (for more information, see *E.7, Optimizing Finely Detailed Line Art*). If the printout compares favorably, you're ready to move on.

Examining the Pixels

When you print a test copy to a lower-res output device, it may not fully display the results of any scanner noise or ultra-fine detail. To examine every last detail, set the view percentage to 100%, by choosing View: **Actual Pixels** or double-clicking the Zoom tool (see *Issues to Consider*, below). You're only able to examine a small segment of the image at a time. It will be tempting to scroll around or reposition the contents of the window using the Hand tool, but doing so makes it too easy to miss part of the image. Instead, follow these steps: **A B**

1. Set the View to 100%.

2. Press the Home key on your keyboard to automatically scroll to the upper left corner of the image. Check the contents of the window for any random pixels or noise.

3. Press the Page Down key, which scrolls down the height of one window. Again, check the contents of the window.

4. When you reach the bottom of the image, click once in the scroll bar on the bottom of the window, to the right of the page icon. This scrolls the width of the image window to the right.

5. Press the Page Up key to scroll to the top of the image. When you get there, click the bottom scroll bar again, as described in the previous step.

6. Repeat steps 3–5 until you've covered every square inch of the image.

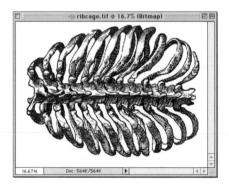

A *Viewing at a lower percentage may obscure flaws.*

B *Viewing at 100% displays the slightest noise.*

Issues to Consider

Anticipating the effect of viewing at 100%. When you set the view percentage to 100%, Photoshop does not display the image at the size it will print. Rather, it increases its onscreen size until the pixels comprising the image are the same size as the pixels used by your monitor. When you set a percentage lower than 100%, Photoshop is unable to display every pixel, and essentially displays its best educated guess. The program even anti-aliases the onscreen display, creating the illusion of smooth, detailed artwork. At 100%, Photoshop is able to display the precise contents of every pixel, giving you the best indication of how the final image will print. Just be aware that the image will appear to dramatically increase in size; the pixels of a typical line art scan are extremely tiny, so they must be enlarged all the more to create that one-to-one relationship with the size of your monitor pixels.

Stray pixels and "dirt" are usually invisible at low view percentages. Unwanted noise can be as small as a single pixel, rendered invisible at any zoom percentage under 100%. The tiny pixel size may make this seem an unimportant issue, but your clients may disagree if such data makes it into the final printed result. Years ago, when I produced my very first line art scans, I didn't understand the relationship between image and monitor pixels. I evaluated my scans on screen at their print size, assumed they were acceptable, and handed over the files. After the project was run on-press, an angry client appeared at my desk and jabbed a finger at one printed scan after another. They were covered with thousands of miniscule spots, the unfortunate result of dust and scanner noise. If I'd inspected the image at a 100% view, I could have seen this data and removed it during the clean-up stage. As it was, the dirty images only announced to the world that I had no idea what I was doing.

E.6

Cleaning Up a Line Art Scan

Cleaning up a line art scan is a straightforward process: Change any unwanted black pixels to white; change any unwanted white pixels to black. Most people use the Pencil tool, which enables you to paint with black or white information using a variety of brush sizes. As you scroll through the image (following the steps listed in *E.5, Evaluating a Line Art Scan*), use the following techniques:

- After selecting the Pencil tool, choose a brush from the pop-up palette in the Options bar. Use a size appropriate for the level of detail you're addressing. If you're removing black pixels from an expansive field of white, use a large brush. If you're working close to the actual artwork, choose a smaller brush.

- To paint with black pixels, set black as the foreground color. To paint with white pixels, set white as the foreground color. Set these values automatically by pressing the "D" key. Toggle between them by pressing the "X" key.

- If desired, use the Pencil tool's Auto Erase function (available in the Options bar). Here, instead of toggling between black and white, the color is applied automatically: If you click on black pixels, the Pencil tool applies white; if you click on white pixels, the tool applies black.

- Use any of the selection tools to draw an outline around unwanted information. For example, you might use the Lasso tool to encircle a larger range of stray pixels, then fill the selection with black or white, as needed.

- If you make a mistake—for example, if you accidentally erase an important part of the image—immediately press (Command) [Control]-Z to reverse it. This keystroke will only undo the most recent edit. If you happen to apply another edit before undoing, you won't get the results you want. Fortunately, Photoshop's History palette enables you to simulate the effect of multiple undo levels: Press (Option-Command) [Alt-Control]-Z to cycle backwards through your past edits, and (Command-Shift) [Control-Shift]-Z to cycle forward again.

Issues to Consider

Make the shape of your brush visible as you edit. For the best results, your cursor should display the size of the currently selected brush. If it doesn't, choose Edit: Preferences: **Display & Cursors**. In the Preferences dialog box, under the Painting Cursor controls, choose the Brush Size option.

Don't obsess when cleaning line art. When you view a 1200 ppi line art image at 100%, the pixels appear enormous. Many users dwell on the smallest details, adjusting the shape of a fine line just so, not realizing that the pixels are so small that many such edits have no effect on the image's printed appearance. When a few pixels cling to the edge of an otherwise straight line, remember that they're only 1/1200 of an inch across. Focus your efforts on the obvious flaws: stray pixels, large blotches, any information that shouldn't be included with the artwork.

E.7
Optimizing Finely Detailed Line Art

Most flatbed scanners do a poor-to-fair job of capturing finely-detailed line art, such as complex engravings or delicate pen-and-ink drawings. Depending on the sensitivity and Threshold setting of your scanner, details are invariably filled in with black or blown out to white. Once a 1-bit image is opened in Photoshop, there's nothing you can do to recapture any lost information. Fortunately, you can work around this limitation by scanning the line art as a Grayscale file. From there, you can use Photoshop's tools to accentuate the necessary detail before converting the image to a 1-bit file, retaining far more data than your scanner alone ever could. Follow these steps:

1. Use your scanning software's Grayscale setting. By working with a series of tones (instead of absolute black and white), you'll be able to exaggerate the differences between light and dark pixels before converting the image to a Bitmap file.

2. Set the desired resolution. Although you're initially scanning Grayscale information, the image will ultimately become black-and-white artwork. Therefore, you must scan at a resolution appropriate for line art: 800 to

1200 ppi. If you don't, the final resolution will be too low for accurate reproduction.

3. Scan the image. **A**

4. Choose View: **Actual Pixels** to set the view percentage to 100%.

5. Choose Filter: Sharpen: **Unsharp Mask**. This command will accentuate the detail areas.

6. In the Unsharp Mask dialog box, enter Amount: 400%, Radius: 5, and Threshold: 1, then click OK. Choose (Command) [Control]-F to apply the filter again, using the same settings. **B**

A *The original Grayscale scan.*

B *The gray tones before (left) and after sharpening.*

7. Choose Image: Adjust: **Threshold**. This command will convert the image tones to pure black and white.

8. In the Threshold dialog box, the slider's position determines the break point between black and white. Low values produce a lighter, more"open" image; higher values produce darker line art. The best approach is to move the slider back and forth, as you preview the effect onscreen. Pinpoint the setting where fine detail is nice and open, but solid black areas aren't speckled with white pixels. Click OK to apply the Threshold. **C**

9. Choose Image: Mode: **Bitmap**. This command will convert the Grayscale image to a 1-bit line art file.

10. In the Bitmap dialog box, make sure the Output resolution is the same as the Input value, and set "50% Threshold" in the Use pop-up menu. Click OK. **D**

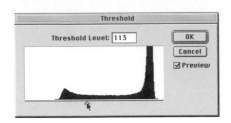
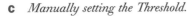

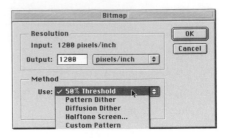

C *Manually setting the Threshold.*

D *The Bitmap dialog box, set to 50% Threshold.*

11. Scroll through the image and clean up any stray pixels (following the steps listed in *E.5, Evaluating a Line Art Scan.* and *E.6, Cleaning Up a Line Art Scan*).

12. Save the image as a TIFF. **E F**

E *Original artwork, scanned as straight line art.*

F *The optimized line art image.*

Issues to Consider

Be prepared for a large Grayscale image. When you initially scan the line art as Grayscale, it produces an exceptionally large file. For example, when you scan a 3 x 5-inch Grayscale image at 300 ppi (the standard for halftoning), its size is roughly 1.3 MB. At 1200 ppi, the same image exceeds 20 MB. The inflated size is only temporary. Once you convert it to 1-bit color and save it as an LZW-compressed TIFF, the file size is reduces to as little as a couple hundred kilobytes.

This technique is appropriate for a wide variety of line art. Although it takes more time, many users employ this technique for the vast majority of their line art scans. It invariably produces a higher quality result than scanning straight off the glass, and you have more control over the final image every step of the way.

E.8

Creating a 1-bit Halftone

The vast majority of one-color halftones are based on a Grayscale image. During output, the printer reviews the contents of the file, calculates the equivalent halftone dot sizes, and converts the continuous tones to spots. However, certain workflows and techniques require the generation of halftone dots in Photoshop, before the image is imported into another application. This is most often done in two situations:

- **When creating a low-screen special effect.** Here, the image is converted to large, visible halftone dots. Instead of reproducing the appearance of a traditionally screened image, you're creating an obvious visual effect.

- **When a proprietary workflow system cannot accommodate Grayscale images.** Many older publishing systems (usually those deeply entrenched in a custom-programmed pagination system) cannot accurately screen 8-bit files. In order to include screened images, they are converted to 1-bit halftones.

To create a 1-bit halftone, follow these steps:

1. Open the desired Grayscale image. For the best results, adjust it for sharpness, contrast, and press conditions just like any other halftone. **A**

2. Make sure the image exists at the precise width and height demanded by your project. Use the Image: **Image Size** command to make any necessary adjustments.

3. Choose Image: Mode: **Bitmap**. The Bitmap dialog box appears.

4. If your screen frequency will be 110 lpi or less, enter 1200 ppi in the Output resolution field. If the frequency will be between 110 and 150 lpi, enter 2400 ppi. **B**

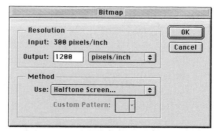

A *Original Grayscale image.*

B *The Bitmap dialog box, set to generate a halftone.*

5. Set Halftone Screen in the Use pop-up menu.

6. Click OK. The Halftone Screen dialog box appears.

7. Enter the desired lines-per-inch value in the Frequency field.

8. Enter the desired screen angle in the Angle field. The optimal value is 45°, the angle preferred for black ink and one-color halftones.

9. Set the desired option in the Shape field, which determines the shape of the individual halftone dots. (See *Issues to Consider*, below.)

10. Click OK to convert the image to a 1-bit halftone. **C D**

11. Save the image as a TIFF.

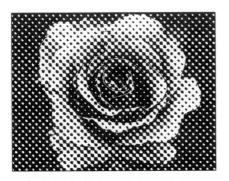

C *1-bit halftone (20 lpi, 1200 ppi).*   **D** *1-bit halftone (120 lpi, 2400 ppi).*

Essentially, this technique simulates the output process. By increasing the target resolution, you ensure that the file can reproduce subtle variations between the tiny halftone dots. By saving the file as line art, you ensure that every pixel in the image is printed exactly as it appears in the file, and no additional screening is applied.

Issues to Consider

Avoid halftoning filters, unless looking for a specific effect. Photoshop offers two "halftoning" filters, but you should avoid them when producing a 1-bit halftone. The Filter: Pixelate: **Color Halftone** option produces the effect of round, anti-aliased dots. However, it doesn't allow you to determine a screen frequency—you can only specify a dot size in terms of pixels, which makes it quite difficult to calculate a particular lines-per-inch value. The Filter: Sketch: **Halftone Pattern** option applies a screen-like pattern to the image, based on the current foreground and background color settings. Similarly, it offers only vague control over dot size, and you cannot change the angle. Also, unless you apply either of these filters to an image of at least 1,200 ppi, the resolution will not be high enough to display a wide range of tones.

Don't be alarmed by onscreen moiré. When you view the halftoned image at percentages under 100%, it will appear to suffer an extensive moiré pattern. The problem is not with the file—it's just the result of your monitor's low-res pixel grid failing to accurately display the high-res halftone dots. As soon as you set the view to 100%, any moiré will disappear.

Choosing the appropriate dot shape. When choosing a dot shape for a low-frequency special effect, the options are obvious: Round, Diamond, Ellipse, Line, Square, and Cross each perfectly describe the resulting halftone dot shapes, and it only takes a few minutes of experimentation to pinpoint the effect you want. When creating a higher-frequency halftone (65 lpi and above), the choice isn't as clear. One limitation to this technique is that it doesn't emulate the halftoning method used by PostScript printers. There, the dot shapes are round in the highlights and shadows, but become squared in the midtones, to add more contrast. The closest Photoshop gets to that effect is the Ellipse option, which offers slight squaring in the midtone dot shapes. However, after printing a round of samples under their target press conditions, many people have settled on the Round or Square options, as well.

Do not scale or rotate 1-bit halftones. Consider the width, height, and angle of a 1-bit halftone set in stone. If you scale the image after importing it into your page layout, you effectively increase or decrease the screen frequency. If you rotate it, you change the screen angle. Scaling and rotation may also confuse the layout program during the output stage, resulting in a moiré pattern after printing. If the image must be resized or rotated, do it in Photoshop while still in Grayscale mode.

Be wary of converting back to Grayscale or color. This technique assumes that you intend to save and output the halftoned image as a standalone file. If you convert the file back to Grayscale, RGB, or CMYK Color mode—for example, to add colors or additional effects—the halftoning effect is destroyed, and because the file resolution is so high, it probably won't print successfully. If you intend to convert an image to simulated halftone dots and then combine it with other images, don't increase the resolution to 1,200 ppi. Instead, set it to the same value as the other images.

E.9

Creating a 1-bit Random-Screened Image

A random-screened image reproduces the appearance of continuous tones using scattered (or *dithered*) pixels. Unlike creating a 1-bit halftone, you don't have to increase the file's resolution to imagesetter-like levels. Instead, you'll set a lower value when you convert the image to a Bitmap file. The exact value will depend on the effect you're trying to achieve. Follow these steps:

1. Open the desired Grayscale image. For the best results, adjust it for sharpness and contrast, just like any other halftone. (See *Issues to Consider*, below.) **A**

2. Choose Image: Mode: **Bitmap**. The Bitmap dialog box appears. **B**

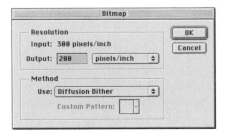

A *Original Grayscale image.*

B *The Bitmap dialog box, set to generate a random screen.*

3. Enter the target resolution in the Output field. For print purposes, a value between 150 and 250 ppi usually suffices; any higher, and the pixels may be too small for accurate reproduction.

4. Set Diffusion Dither in the Use pop-up menu.

5. Click OK to convert the image. The former continuous tones are now represented by randomly scattered pixels. In darker areas, the pixels are closer together; in lighter areas, they're placed farther apart.

6. Save the image as a TIFF. **C D E**

C *72 ppi dither.*

D *200 ppi dither.*

E *300 ppi dither.*

Issues to Consider

Dithered images often benefit from increased contrast. A Grayscale image with sufficient contrast may appear flat and indistinct after you convert it to dithered line art. You may have to print a sample of the image, just to be sure. When this happens, undo the conversion and use Levels or Curves to increase the contrast. Also, if the image contains fine details, try applying the Unsharp Mask filter a couple of times, to exaggerate the tonal differences (start with the following settings: A: 200%, R: 2.0, T: 32). It doesn't matter if the adjustments make the Grayscale image unfit for printing; they're intended to optimize the dithered results.

The target paper stock will determine the smallest tolerable dot size. When I recommended a resolution of 100 to 200 ppi, it was to accommodate the majority of paper stocks. You can expect the tiny dots of the dithered image to expand slightly during printing; if they're small enough, the dots in the darker image areas will run together, filling in to solid black. If you know that you're going to be printing onto paper stock that results in extremely low dot gain—for example, high-quality coated stock—it's possible to increase the resolution up to 300 ppi. (In these cases, you may need to lighten the midtones and shadows of the Grayscale image before you convert it.) On the other hand, if you're going to print onto cheap stock or newsprint, you may not want to exceed 100-120 ppi.

Avoid scaling a dithered image. When you adjust the scale of a 1-bit dithered image in your layout program, you change the size of the component pixels. Reduce the scale too much, and the dots will likely become too small for the target paper stock. Increase the scale too much, and the image is comprised of large, pixelated blocks. When you need a smaller image, use the Image: **Image Size** command to reduce the dimensions before converting to Bitmap mode. Fortunately, when you need to create a much larger dithered image, this technique is extremely forgiving to over-sampled files. For example, assume you're working with a 3 x 5-inch, 300 ppi Grayscale file, but you want to reproduce it as a 9 x 15-inch, 150 ppi dither. In this case, use the Image Size command to increase the width and height, without changing the resolution. The larger, upsampled file will appear to lose a fair degree of sharpness and detail, as usually happens when you increase its size that way. However, as soon as you convert the image to a Bitmap, any image degradation will disappear.

E.10

Creating a 1-bit Mezzotint

Mezzotints are similar to random-screened images. Instead of using a scattering of individual pixels, though, the effect is traditionally based on a *stippled* pattern, or a series of randomized blotches. This technique centers around Photoshop's Mezzotint filter, but as you'll see, a quality mezzotint may require a little more work than pointing and clicking. Follow these steps:

1. Open the desired Grayscale image. For the best results, adjust it for sharpness and contrast, just like any other halftone. (See *Issues to Consider*, below.) **A**

2. If necessary, use the Image: **Image Size** command to increase the image's resolution without affecting the file size. (See *Issues to Consider*, below.)

3. Choose Filter: Pixelate: **Mezzotint**. The Mezzotint dialog box appears. **B**

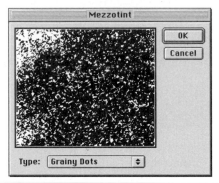

A   *Original Grayscale image.*   **B**   *The Mezzotint dialog box.*

4. Set the desired screening method in the Type pop-up. There are three methods: Dots (which use small stippled blotches), Lines (which a series of thinner lines), and Strokes (which use thicker lines).

5. Click OK to apply the effect. If unsatisfied with the results, choose Edit: **Undo**, re-open the filter, and try a new setting.

6. When satisfied with the image, choose Image: Mode: **Bitmap**. The Bitmap dialog box appears.

7. Make sure the Output resolution matches the Input value. (Because the image tones have already been converted to black and white, increasing the resolution of the Bitmap file will have no noticeable effect.)

8. Set 50% Threshold in the Use pop-up menu.

9. Click OK to convert the image.

10. Save the image as a TIFF. **C D**

C *300 ppi Grainy Dots mezzotint.*

D *600 ppi Grainy Dots mezzotint.*

Issues to Consider

Image resolution directly affects the dot sizes. While the Mezzotint filter enables you to choose from a series of dot sizes, their actual size is dictated by the image resolution. The higher the resolution of the original image, the smaller the dot size of the applied mezzotint. For example, if you apply the Coarse Dots option to a 200 ppi image, the dots are so big that most of the image details are obliterated. If you apply the same setting to a 300 ppi image, the resulting dots are 50% smaller. You may need to create a few image duplicates at different resolutions to find the setting that works best.

E.11

Scanning Pre-Screened Line Art

In a perfect world, every line art original that appeared on your desk would possess clear, well-defined detail. Of course, that's not always the case. The most problematic originals are printed samples that were partially screened by the initial designer. When you scan such an image, the details are polluted by an abundance of halftone dots, making it extremely difficult to convert to quality line art.

Many users, unable to find a better-quality original for their project, resign themselves to painting away the halftone dots one by one, essentially recreating the artwork from scratch. However, it's possible to manipulate the image to reduce the prominence of the screen pattern, enabling you to salvage all but the most horrendous samples. Follow these steps:

1. Choose the desired pre-screened line art. For the best results, it should exist at 110 lpi or above—otherwise the halftone dots may be too big to remove.

    For this example, I used a reprint of a Renaissance-era engraving, pulled from the yellowed, uncoated stock of a bargain-bin paperback. The art-work was placed on a tinted background, so halftone dots appear throughout all the detail areas, and add a visible texture to the edges of the lines.

2. In your scanning software, acquire the image as a Grayscale file. **A**

3. Set the resolution 50% higher than the value you normally use for line art, plus 10 pixels. For example, if you usually scan at 1200 ppi, scan at 1810.

4. If your scanner has a Brightness/Contrast option, reduce the contrast by 20%. This will reduce the initial prominence of the halftone dots.

5. Scan the image. When it opens in Photoshop, choose View: **Actual Pixels** to set the view to 100%. **B**

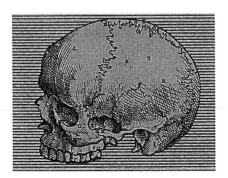

A *Original pre-screened image.*   **B** *Halftone pattern, viewed at 100%.*

6. Use the Info palette to examine the tonal values of the detail areas. The artwork should appear well above 50% black. The halftone dots, already softened somewhat by the lower scanning contrast, should appear closer to (if not below) 50%.

7. Choose Filter: Blur: **Gaussian Blur**. Enter a value between 2.0 and 3.5, making sure you don't obliterate any detail you want to retain. This will further soften the dot pattern, bringing most of their values below 50% black. **C**

8. Choose Image: **Image Size**. The Image Size dialog box appears.

9. Check the Resample Image box, which enables you to change the image's resolution separately from the width and height.

10. Enter your standard resolution value in the Resolution field. For example, if you normally scan line art at 1200 ppi, enter 1200.

11. Click OK to downsample the image. This process will further soften the dots, forcing most (if not all) of their values below 50% black. (The fact that the initial resolution was 50% more plus 10 pixels prevents Photoshop from taking any shortcuts when re-interpolating the image.)

12. Choose Image: Adjust: **Threshold**. In the Threshold dialog box, move the slider until the majority of the halftone dot pattern disappears, but the target artwork is retained.

13. Choose Image: Mode: **Bitmap**. In the Bitmap dialog box, set 50% Threshold in the Use pop-up menu. Click OK to convert the image to a 1-bit line art file.

14. If necessary, use the Pencil tool to touch up the image, removing any lingering halftone dots or solidifying any of the remaining black data.

15. Save the image as a TIFF. **D**

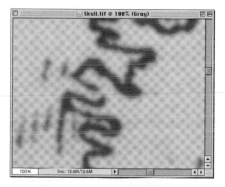

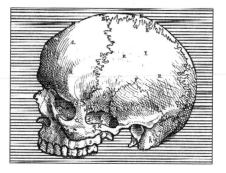

C *Blurring the image (Radius: 3.0).*   **D** *1-bit halftone (120 lpi, 2400 ppi).*

Granted, this technique is a little heavy-handed; the initial file can be dozens of megabytes in size, and the blurring can blow out some of the finer details. But these steps take only a few minutes to apply, as opposed to the several hours it can take to restore black-and-white artwork manually. At the very least, it will remove most of the offending pattern, reducing the time it takes to refine the image by hand.

E.12

Retaining White Pixels in a Line Art Image

The white pixels of an image in Bitmap mode are transparent once you import the file into a layout document. Normally, this phenomenon doesn't pose a problem—most artists are aware of it, and simply design around it as needed. In certain cases, though, this trait is a limitation. There is no automatic way to retain the interior white—the white pixels that actually appear to be part of the artwork—while rendering the outside white transparent.

Produce this effect by drawing a clipping path along the outside edge of the artwork. This way, when you import the image, the black-and-white pixels inside the path are visible, and the pixels outside the path are ignored. Because the image still exists as a high-resolution Bitmap file, black pixels will output smoothly.

Realistically, drawing a clipping path by hand is only appropriate for simple images. When the artwork consists of intricate lines and finer details, the time required to create a form-fitting path may not be worth the effort. Line art is also quite unforgiving when it comes to clipping paths—wherever the path doesn't precisely overlap the edge of the black artwork, slivers of white are visible when you place the image over another page element.

With the right preparation, you can apply a quick series of commands that automatically produce an intricate clipping path and ensure it overlaps black pixels. Follow these steps:

1. Scan, optimize, and clean the desired line art. Make sure there are no stray pixels in the white space surrounding the image. **A**

2. For this technique to work, there can be no "open" spots along the outer edge of the artwork. Scroll through the image and examine the edges, using the Pencil tool (and an appropriately-sized brush) to close them. **B**

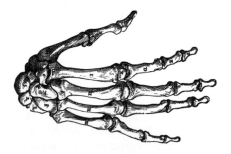

A *Original line art.*   **B** *"Closing" the artwork edges.*

3. Choose Image: Mode: **Grayscale**.

4. Choose the Magic Wand tool. In the Options bar, uncheck the Anti-Aliased box, and check the Continuous box.

5. Click the white area surrounding the artwork. The selection outline should conform to the outer edge of the black lines; if any white pixels inside the artwork are included, you need to close any remaining open spots along the outer edge, as described in Step 2.

6. If you need to "punch out" any white areas inside the artwork, hold down the Shift key and click them with the Magic Wand tool.

7. At this point, everything but the target artwork is selected. Choose Select: **Inverse** to reverse the selection. **C**

8. Choose Make Work Path from the Paths palette submenu. In the Make Work Path dialog box, enter a value of 2.0 in the Tolerance field.

9. Click OK to convert the selection to a path. Upon closer examination, you'll see that the new path comes close to adhering to the edges, but it doesn't go all the way. (Don't bother lowering the Tolerance value—the path will be just as inaccurate, but will contain a huge number of points.) **D**

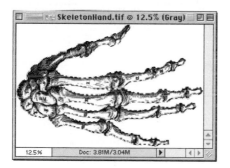

C *Properly selected artwork.*

D *The new path doesn't precisely match the edges.*

10. Save the new path and designate it as a clipping path. (For more information, see *I.10, Creating a Clipping Path.*)

At this point, you've added a complex clipping path around the artwork. You still need to address the areas where the path doesn't quite touch the artwork, which exposes those white slivers. Instead of editing the path—which can take just as long as creating one from scratch—add some black information directly underneath it. Follow these steps:

1. Convert the path back into a selection by (Command) [Control]-clicking its item in the Paths palette.

2. Choose Edit: **Stroke**.

3. In the Stroke dialog box, set a width between 3 and 6 pixels. Use a lower value when the resolution of the file is under 900 ppi; use a higher value for 1200 ppi files.

4. Under the dialog box's Location options, choose Center.

5. Click OK to apply the stroke. It straddles the exact position of the path. **E**

6. Choose Image: Mode: **Bitmap** to convert the image back to a 1-bit line art file.

7. Save the image as a Photoshop EPS file. **F**

In the vast majority of cases, the expanded artwork edge is too thin to detect. For example, if you add an six-pixel stroke to a 1200 ppi image, you increase the edge by less than half a point—just enough to conceal any unwanted white.

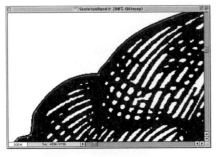

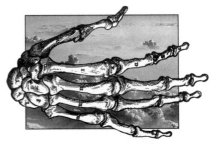

E *Applying a black stroke (note the position of the path).*

F *The clipped line art, imported into an XPress document.*

Issues to Consider

You cannot recolor Photoshop EPS line art in your layout document. Line art saved as a TIFF automatically overprints in your layout document, and you can recolor and trap it at will. Line art saved as an EPS file automatically knocks out, and you cannot recolor or trap it using your layout program's tools. If you need to apply a spot color to line art saved with a clipping path, you must convert it into a monotone, a variation of a duotone image. (For more information, see *J.2, Creating a PMS Monotone.*)

Duplicate your artwork before applying this technique. Although it only adjusts the shape of the artwork very slightly, the changes are pretty much irreversible. If you need to use the image again in the future, play it safe and create a duplicate before creating the clipping path.

Halftone Editing Techniques

Establishing a Halftone Editing Strategy

In a perfect world, you could simply shoot, scan, and print. Images would require no additional adjustments to reproduce successfully on-press. However, the very act of scanning and printing prevents that from happening:

- Scanning flattens the tonal depth and slightly blurs the detail of any image. This is a natural by-product of the process—the extent of it depends on the sensitivity of your device.

- Halftone dots expand slightly as ink is absorbed by the target paper stock, a phenomenon known as dot gain. Unless you anticipate this change during the editing stage, your images reproduce more darkly than expected.

- No printing press can reproduce every tone between 0% and 100% black. Each press has its own limit, and you must compress the range of image tones to make them fit.

- Every time you adjust an image to compensate for the above issues, you reduce the number of available tones and obliterate detail. It's all too easy to over-adjust a scan, which results in a thin, washed-out appearance.

The impulse to adjust an image until it looks good on your monitor (or a laser printout) is natural. Unfortunately, you can't depend on either of these methods. The values displayed by your monitor bear only a passing relationship to the values that actually print. Also, when an image is properly adjusted for press, a printed proof will appear lighter and thinner than you expect. If a proof looks perfect, especially if you've output it to RC paper or made a contact proof, the on-press result is always too dark.

Instead of editing on the fly, follow a systematic plan for scanning and adjusting your halftones. (You can use the same approach on all scans, but the exact number of steps may vary, depending on the content of each image.) Use the following steps as a starting point:

1. Assess the original image and determine its purpose. (For more information, see *F.3, Evaluating an Original Before Scanning.*)

2. Preview, measure, and adjust your scan, applying any necessary settings in your scanning software.

3. Set the appropriate scanning resolution. (For more information, see *F.4, Setting Resolution for Scanned Halftones.*)

4. Acquire the scan.

5. Assess the scan, rescan if necessary, and save. (For more information, see *F.5, Evaluating Detail in a New Grayscale Scan.*)

6. Crop the image to the desired dimensions. (For more information, see *C.1, Applying a Simple Crop.*)

7. Repair or retouch any large, glaring problems.

8. Sharpen the image. (For more information, see *13.71 Filter: Sharpen:* **Unsharp Mask**.)

9. Check and adjust the endpoints for press. (For more information, see *F.6, Targeting Endpoints for Press* and *F.8, Resetting Endpoints for Press.*)

10. Adjust for contrast. (For more information, see *F.10, Using Curves to Add Contrast.*)

11. Retouch any small flaws, such as dust specks or scratches. (See *K.1, Retouching with Brushstrokes.*)

12. Compensate for dot gain. (See *F.13, Anticipating Dot Gain.*)

13. Review, proof and refine as needed.

Issues to Consider

Halftoning is a process of managed loss. When you consider the amount of information that is discarded by scanning, adjusting, and printing an image, it's a wonder that we can do it at all. You start with an original possessing a full, rich tonal range and an ultra-fine photographic grain. Scanning reduces it to 256 levels of gray. Adjusting the endpoints, adding contrast, compensating for dot gain, and sharpening the detail discards anywhere from 20 to 40% of the tones. Outputting the image converts the remaining continuous tones to a series of black halftone dots. Finally, a printing press can only reproduce 50 to 60 tones per ink color; the rest is lost to spreading ink, lightened highlights, and other imperfections of the process. Fortunately, the halftoning process is quite forgiving, as long as you stick to the editing guidelines presented in this chapter.

F.2

Mapping Your Scanner Bed

As a rule, flatbed scanners don't read information consistently across the glass. Light leaks under the cover, light sources age, the hardware contains imperfections, all of which introduces variables that negatively impact image quality. To find your scanner's "sweet spot"—the area on the glass that produces the most accurate image—create a *scanner map*. Follow these steps:

1. Place a large sheet of highly reflective white paper in your scanner, covering the entire glass. The resin-coated (RC) paper used by some imagesetters works best.

2. Scan the entire bed as a 72 ppi RGB image. Leave the remaining scanner settings at their defaults.

3. Open the image in Photoshop. In theory, the image pixels should be entirely white. However, any imperfections in your scanner will introduce light areas of tone throughout the image.

4. Choose Image: Adjust: **Equalize** to exaggerate any errant tones. This command completely expands the existing tonal range, boosting the darkest pixel value in each color channel to full intensity; any areas that didn't scan as completely white appear dark and splotchy. **A**

5. In the future, avoid placing artwork on the parts of the scanner bed that resulted in blotchy areas.

Optimally, this technique should only produce a few dark pixels. If light is leaking under the cover, blotches will appear around the image edges. When your scanner's light source starts to wear out, the entire image will turn dark. If a brand new scanner produces an image full of dark pixels, you may have a defective (or simply low-quality) unit.

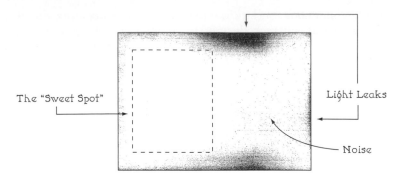

The "Sweet Spot"

Light Leaks

Noise

A *Placing materials on your flatbed scanner's "sweet spot" will ensure the most consistent results.*

Issues to Consider

Using the scanner map as a mask. If you're able to output the scan at actual size, consider trimming away the white areas, placing the rest back on the scanner, and taping it down. This way, it acts as a permanent mask that blocks the lesser-quality scanning areas.

Keeping the glass clean. This technique makes you aware of any noise introduced by your scanner; you can't do anything about that but avoid the problem areas. What you can do something about is dust, fingerprints, and smudges, which impact your scans just as badly. Clean your scanner at least once a day. (High-volume users should do it as many as 10 times a day.) Pull together a cleaning kit that includes the following: an anti-static brush; glass cleaner (some scanners require non-ammonia cleaners); scanner wipes; photo wipes; film cleaner; and a can of compressed air. Most of these items are available at your local photographic supply store. Use the brush, glass cleaner and scanner wipes to clean the scanner plate. Use the photo wipes and film cleaner to get clear fingerprints and gunk from the face of your photographic originals. Use the compressed air to spray the dust from the scanner glass or artwork.

F.3

Evaluating an Original Before Scanning

Study every original before scanning it. A thorough appraisal will identify potential problem areas, prevent you from scanning dirty artwork, and otherwise base your future edits on realistic information. Look for the following:

• **The distribution of tones throughout the image.** Pinpoint the location of the highlight and shadow areas.

• **The overall image composition.** Try to estimate the values you'll read when you measure the image in Photoshop.

- **Potential trouble spots.** Determine the parts of the image you feel will be most difficult to correct, such as deep shadow detail, thinly varying highlights, or midtones flattened by diffuse overall lighting. You may be able to compensate for them at the time of the scan.

- **The most important part of the image.** Successful adjustment often involves some sort of compromise; To properly focus on the subject, you may have to sacrifice the quality of less important areas. Identify the area that requires the best results and strive to protect it.

As pressing as these issues seem, they're even more important when scanning color images.

F.4

Setting Resolution for Scanned Halftones

The resolution setting of a halftone scan depends on how it will be reproduced on-press. Before scanning, you must know the linescreen at which your project will be output. For example, images reproduced on newsprint typically output at 85 lines per inch; Images intended for glossy, coated paper typically output at 150 lpi. The industry-standard approach is this: After determining the linescreen value, double the number and scan at that resolution. Therefore, you would scan the above newsprint image at 170 pixels per inch, and the coated paper image at 300 ppi.

Issues to Consider

A resolution/linescreen ratio of 2:1 is recommended, but not required. Most people assume that the resolution of their halftones must be twice the linescreen value. That's not the case. Actually, most halftones can successfully reproduce at a ppi/lpi ratio of 1:1. For example, when output at 150 lpi, a 150 ppi image can reproduce just as well as a 300 ppi image. However, as I mentioned above, it's not a *requirement*, it's an *industry-standard methodology*. The increased resolution gives you a little wiggle-room when adjusting the image. The impact of your edits is less extreme, you can resample the image without obliterating detail, and you can even increase the scale of the image in your page layout. If you scanned every image at a 1:1 ratio, your editing options would be limited.

Consider using a single resolution setting for all halftones. The vast majority of halftones are screened between 85 and 150 lpi. However, many users apply a uniform resolution setting for all of their print-oriented Grayscale images: 300 ppi. This way, the impact of your edits is consistent from image to image—for example, the effect of the Gaussian Blur or Unsharp Mask increase or decrease, depending on the current resolution. The extra resolution has no effect on lower-screened images, but its enough to accommodate higher values. The only time you really need to raise the resolution above 300 ppi is when working with super-fine image detail, to be screened at 150 lpi or above. In this case, raise the setting to 350 ppi.

Evaluating Detail in a New Grayscale Scan

When a scan first opens in Photoshop, you must make a choice: Keep it and continue editing, or discard it and scan again. The best way to assess the quality of a new scan is to check the contents of the lightest and darkest image areas. Follow these steps:

1. Zoom into the image's shadow information.

2. Without clicking, move the cursor over the darkest pixels. In the Info palette, you should see the K value flash through a changing series of percentages. This indicates that subtle tonal variances have been captured by the scanner, which is necessary to reproduce detail. If the percentages don't change—or if the area exists as a two-toned blotch—you have a problem. The shadows have been averaged to a single value, and will reproduce as a solid patch. (See *Issues to Consider*, below.)

3. Zoom into the highlight areas. Look for the same varying pixel values, and make sure no areas are blown out to 0% black.

4. When a scan doesn't contain the necessary detail, acquire it again with a different round of settings.

5. As you assess the image for detail and tone, keep an eye out for any defects. If there's an excess of dust or hair, clean the glass and/or the original and scan again. Rescanning almost always takes less time than manually repairing such defects in Photoshop.

Before moving on, make a mental list of an image's potential trouble spots and where they're located. This will act as a checklist to review after you've adjusted the image for press conditions.

Issues to Consider

Scanned photographs shouldn't contain broad areas of the same value.
For example, you shouldn't see large patches of 35% black in a photo of a landscape. Even image elements that appear solid, such as white snow or a clear sky, should be composed of pixel values that vary subtly. Nature doesn't contain "solid" colors—everything you see is affected by light, shadow, and texture. When patches of tone appear in a halftone, they're usually the result of a bad scan or over-adjustment, which posterizes the tonal range. These areas are picked up by the eye, and

recognized as unnatural. Minor pixel variations produce ever-so-slight differences in halftone dot sizes, which gives the printed image a much more organic feel.

Targeting Endpoints for Press

An image's lightest and darkest pixel values are referred to as the *endpoints*. However, no printing press can successfully reproduce all the tones that Photoshop can display. When editing a Grayscale image, you work with dot sizes that range from 1% and 99% (0% and 100%, white and black, are not made of halftone dots). The average press can tolerate dots between 8% and 90%. In this case, values lower than 8% burn out to white, and values higher than 90% fill in to solid black. You must *target* the endpoints, or locate the diffuse highlight and shadow values, and make sure they fit within the printable range of the press. If they don't, you must reposition the endpoints, compressing the tonal range to accommodate the limitation.

Targeting is as easy as finding the lightest and darkest image pixels. If desired, you could move the cursor across the image, reading every value in the Info palette. However, there's an easier method, using the Levels command. Follow these steps:

1. Open the image you want to target.

2. Choose Image: Adjust: **Levels**. The Levels dialog box appears.

3. Make sure the Preview box is checked.

4. Hold down the (Option) [Alt] key and grab the white slider just beneath the histogram. The image appears to turn black.

5. Move the slider to the left. As soon as the you reach the point in the histogram that represents the lightest tones, those pixels in the image appear to turn white. These are the lightest image pixels, or the current highlight endpoint. **A**

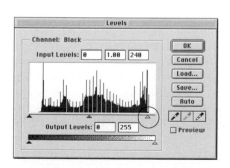

A *(Option) [Alt]-drag the white Levels slider to reveal the highlight area.*

6. Move the white slider back to its original position.

7. Hold down the (Option) [Alt] key and grab the black slider. The image appears to turn white.

8. Move the slider to the right. As soon as you reach the point in the histogram that represents the darkest tones, those pixels in the image appear to turn black. These are the darkest image pixels, or the current shadow endpoint. **B**

9. Move the black slider back to its original position and click Cancel to close the dialog box.

Armed with this information, you'll know where to go to measure the endpoints using the Info palette.

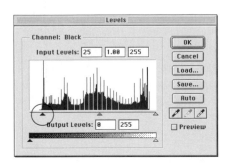

B   *(Option) [Alt]-drag the black Levels slider to reveal the shadow area.*

Issues to Consider

Understanding specular and diffuse highlights. In the case of an image's lightest value, you must make a further distinction. An area with no tonal information—which results in pure white paper after printing—is the *specular highlight*. Most often, a specular highlight is a small, intensely bright part of an image, such as a flash on gleaming metal or light caught by the rim of a glass. The lightest part of an image that actually carries detail is the *diffuse highlight*. The difference between the two is important. For the most part, a specular highlight is a unique and focused effect, and only appears when a particular scan requires it. The diffuse highlight determines the value of the lightest information in any image. If it falls outside the range of the press, the dot structure breaks down, resulting in irregular patches of pure white. Even a picture of snow or a white cloud doesn't appear as white paper; examine it closely, and you'll see a fine screen of halftone dots.

F.7

Specifying Endpoint Source Values

Before you can remap the endpoints of a scan, you must make Photoshop aware of your target press' reproducible range. For this example, assume you've already determined that the press will tolerate a range from 8% to 90%. Follow these steps:

1. Choose Image: Adjust: **Curves**. The Curves dialog box appears.

2. To set the shadow dot, double-click the black Eyedropper button. The color picker appears.

3. In the CMYK fields, enter C:0, M:0, Y:0, K:90. Click OK. **A**

4. To set the highlight dot, double-click the white Eyedropper button. The color picker appears again.

5. In the CMYK fields, enter C:0, M:0, Y:0, K:8. Click OK. **B**

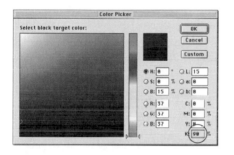

A *Specifying the shadow dot.*   **B** *Specifying the diffuse highlight.*

Once these values are entered, they remain there until you manually change them. If your press requirements will never change, you can set this value once and leave it. If you routinely adjust images for different printing methods, you'll have to set the right values for each round of scans.

The endpoint controls covered in this technique are also available in the Levels dialog box. However, because you'll likely use Curves to apply the majority of your tonal edits, it pays to become more familiar with this command.

F.8

Resetting Endpoints for Press

There are three ways to remap endpoints to the range of the target press. The first two are automatic: Clicking the Auto button in the Curves dialog box, or choosing Image: Adjust: **Auto Levels**. Avoid the automatic options. They simply hunt down the lightest and darkest pixels in the entire file, then arbitrarily apply the new endpoint values. You have no control over the targeted values—specifically, Photoshop doesn't know the difference between a specular and a diffuse highlight. If the image contains a small, bright flash that you want to reduce to 0% black, the Auto Levels command will set those pixels to 8%, which skews the remaining tonal range. For the best results, set the endpoints manually. Follow these steps:

1. Choose Image: Adjust: **Curves** to access the Curves dialog box. If necessary, move it to the side of the screen so you can see the entire image.

2. To set the shadow dot, click once on the black Eyedropper in the Curves dialog box.

3. Using the Info palette as a guide, move the cursor over the image until you find the darkest value. (You've already pinpointed its general location, using the technique described under *Fx, Targeting Endpoints for Press.*)

4. Click the darkest pixel.

5. To set the highlight dot, select the white Eyedropper.

6. Using the Info Palette as a guide, move the cursor over the image until you find the diffuse highlight.

7. Click the lightest pixel. **A B**

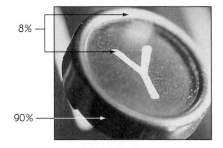

A *Image reproduced without adjusting endpoints.*

B *Image reproduced after setting endpoints for press.*

Issues to Consider

Undoing an endpoint value. If you feel you've clicked in error, hold down the (Option) [Alt] key. The dialog box's Cancel button changes to Reset, and clicking it removes any edits you've made while the command was open.

Anticipating how the image will appear after remapping the endpoints. After you reset the endpoints, an image usually appears to flatten considerably. This is natural, and you'll soon compensate for it by adding contrast. Also, you may notice that an occasional pixel falls outside the established limits. Unless it occurs in a wide area, it won't impact the final print quality.

F.9

Using Levels to Set Endpoints

You can use the Levels dialog box to reduce the range of image tones, essentially resetting the highlight and shadow endpoints. Follow these steps:

1. To establish the restricted shadow dot, enter a value in the left Output Levels field, or move the black slider at the bottom of the dialog box to the right.

2. To establish the diffuse highlight, enter a value in the right Output Levels field or move the white slider to the left. **A**

3. When you click OK to apply the adjustment, the tonal range is compressed to fit within the new endpoints. **B**

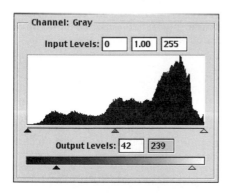
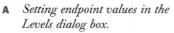
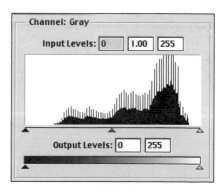

A *Setting endpoint values in the Levels dialog box.*

B *Compressing the range.*

This technique only enables you to use brightness levels when setting the endpoints. Refer to the following table for a list of common endpoint values:

%	Level	%	Level	%	Level	%	Level
5%	245	11%	233	85%	57	91%	38
6%	243	12%	230	86%	54	92%	34
7%	241	13%	229	87%	51	93%	32
8%	239	14%	226	88%	48	94%	28
9%	237	15%	225	89%	44	95%	25
10%	235	16%	222	90%	42	96%	16

Issues to Consider

The difference between this method and using the highlight and shadow Eyedroppers is an important one. There, the endpoints are based on actual image data; you're able to choose the pixels that map to the target values. Here, you simply define the highest and lowest possible values, and if necessary, squeeze the existing tones to fit inside. It's done with little finesse, and the results will likely be less accurate. However, the ability to include this technique in an action makes it appealing to automated workflows where accuracy isn't as high a priority as speed.

F.10

Using Curves to Add Contrast

This technique demonstrates the most commonly applied contrast curve. It's a straightforward adjustment, suitable for a wide range of image types. Follow these steps:

1. Choose Image: Adjust: **Curves**. The Curves dialog box appears.

2. Make sure the Input/Output values display output percentages. If not, click the values gradient.

3. Move the cursor to the three-quarter tones portion of the curve. When the Input/Output fields read 75%, click to add a point.

4. Drag this point straight up until the Output value reads 80%. (The Input value should still read 75%.)

5. Move the cursor to the quarter tones portion of the curve. When both Input/Output fields read 25%, click to add a point.

6. Drag this point straight down until the Output value reads 20%. The Input value should still read 25%.

7. Click OK. **A B C**

Consider these values a starting point. Let the content of the image determine your actual edits. For example, one image may require a lesser adjustment in the quarter tones than the three-quarter tones; another may need a greater adjustment in the shadows. Whatever the case, you won't know until you inspect the image.

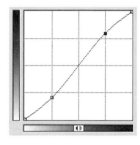

A *Original image.*   **B** *Contrast curve.*   **C** *Adjusted image.*

F.11

Applying Targeted Curve Adjustments

Adjustment points have two uses. They can adjust tone and color, which happens when you drag a point from one spot to another, remapping the values. You can also use them to anchor the curve, allowing you to target one part of the tonal range. For example, if you only want to edit the highlights, click to add points at 25%, 50%, and 75%. Now, when you edit the lightest values, you don't affect the remaining tones. **A B C**

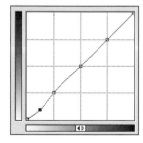
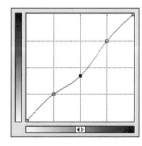
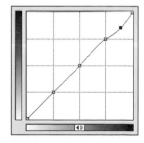

A *Targeting only the highlight tones.*

B *Targeting only the midtones, leaving the highlights and shadows untouched.*

C *Targeting only the shadow tones.*

F.12

Using Levels for Simple Enhancements

Although not as powerful or precise as the Curves dialog box, it's possible to create rough-and-ready tonal adjustments using the Levels controls:

1. Open the Levels dialog box.

2. Expand the tonal range by (Option) [Alt]-dragging the highlight and shadow sliders to the beginning and end of the histogram. This distributes the tones over the widest possible range, compensating for the limited sensitivity of your scanner. (For more information, see *F.6, Targeting Endpoints for Press.*)

3. Click OK and re-open the dialog box. This way, you continue editing with a more accurate histogram. (If desired, however, you can adjust all three sliders at the same time.)

4. If necessary, adjust the endpoints for print (for more information, see *F.9, Using Levels to Set Endpoints*). Images destined for multimedia or the Web do not require this step.

5. Move the gray slider left or right to lighten or darken the midtones. Usually, dragging toward the apparent gravitational center of the mass of vertical bars provides the best results.

6. Click OK to apply the changes. **A B C**

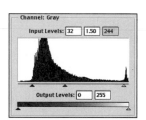

A   *Original image.*

B   *Setting the Levels sliders to redistribute the tones.*

C   *Enhanced image.*

F.13

Anticipating Dot Gain

After you've tweaked, adjusted, and retouched a halftone, only one task remains. You must lighten the overall image to compensate for the dot gain that will occur when the image is run on-press. The idea is simple: Since dot gain results in a darker halftone, printing a deliberately lightened image should enable the tones to fall right into place.

Before you apply the adjustment, you must know how much dot gain to expect. It all depends on the printing method and the type of paper stock used. The more absorbent the paper, the higher dot gain you can expect. Because dot gain affects the midtones more than any other part of an image, you'll focus the adjustment on the 50% value.

Dot gain is measured as a percentage, which can sound confusing. For example, when your printer says you can expect a 25% dot gain, it doesn't mean that your 50% dot will jump to 75%. Instead, it means that the 50% dot will expand by 25% of its original size, to roughly 62%. The following table lists four printing options, their typical dot gain amounts, and the degree you should adjust the midtones to compensate for it:

Printing Method	Anticipated Dot Gain	Reduce 50% to:
Web/coated stock	15 to 25%	44 to 40%
Sheetfed/coated stock	10 to 15%	46 to 44%
Sheetfed/uncoated stock	18 to 25%	43 to 40%
Newsprint	30 to 45%	39 to 35%

You can apply the dot gain compensation manually or automatically. As you'll see, the method you choose depends on whether you want to change the actual contents of the image.

Issues to Consider

Adjusting for dot gain is a halftone-only requirement. You only have to manually adjust for dot gain when editing a Grayscale image. When you convert a full color image to CMYK mode, Photoshop accounts for dot gain automatically.

F.14

Manually Compensating for Dot Gain

In this example, the midtones are lightened to accommodate an expected 15% dot gain (following the chart listed in *Fx, Addressing Dot Gain*). Follow these steps:

1. Open a Grayscale image that you've already adjusted for press limitations and contrast.

2. Choose Image: Adjust: **Curves.**

3. Move the cursor to the midtones and click to add a point at 50%.

4. Drag this point straight down until the Output value reads 44%.

5. Click OK and save. **A B**

The image will appear much lighter than you want to be, especially when you proof it on a laser printer. This is supposed to happen; rest assured, it will darken when you run it on-press.

A *Image without dot gain compensation.*   **B** *Image with dot gain compensation.*

Issues to Consider

Dot gain curves alter the image contents. When you manually apply a dot gain curve, you irreversibly editing the image's tonal range, making it much more difficult to repurpose the same image for other printing methods. For example, assume you've already adjusted an image for newsprint. If you print the same image in the future on high-quality coated paper, the image will reproduce too lightly on-press. If necessary, save a copy of the original image, including the dot gain adjustment in the file name.

Compensating for dot gain during output. If you need to retain the original image values (and you don't want to produce different copies of the same image), your only option is to embed a *transfer curve*, or a tonal adjustment that affects the image only during output. This option does have some limitations. You have to save it as an EPS file, which are larger than TIFFs, and you won't be able to recolor the halftone in a page layout program.

F.15

Removing Moiré from a Pre-Screened Halftone

When you acquire an image that's already been printed (for example, a photo in a magazine or newspaper), you're not scanning the same continuous tone information found in a photograph or film transparency—you're scanning halftone dots. The scanner partially recognizes the spaces between the dots, but not well enough to reproduce them identically or convert them to continuous tones. As a result, the image contains a moiré pattern. To eliminate the pattern, follow these steps:

1. Scan the image at twice the normal resolution, minus 10 pixels. For example, if you would normally scan a halftone at 300 ppi, scan the pre-screened sample at 590 ppi. **A**

2. In Photoshop, choose Filter: Blur: **Gaussian Blur**. This filter is quite damaging to the image, so only apply low values. A radius of .7 to 1.2 pixels should suffice. **B**

A *Original scan, with moiré pattern.*   **B** *Blurring the halftone dots.*

3. Choose Image: **Image Size**.

4. In the Image Size dialog box, check the Constrain Proportions and Resample Images boxes. This allows you to change the resolution without affecting the width and height. Also, make sure the Interpolation is set to Bicubic.

5. Enter 300 in the Resolution field.

6. Click OK. By cutting the resolution in half, you remove three-quarters of the image pixels. Often, this removes most of the pattern as well.

7. Evaluate the image. If the dots have been sufficiently reduced, continue editing as normal. If not, move on to the next step.

8. Evaluate the image again. If a slight dot pattern still exists, apply the Filter: Noise: **Despeckle** command.

9. Continue adjusting the scan for its intended purpose. **c**

c *Reduced levels of moiré.*

Issues to Consider

Subtracting 10 after doubling the resolution is not an absolute amount. It's just a way of preventing you from scanning at exactly twice the target resolution. When that happens, Photoshop uses an algorithmic "shortcut" when you downsample the file, which doesn't produce the necessary softening effect. Since you'll want Photoshop to re-interpolate the value of every last pixel, subtracting 10 after doubling the resolution creates the desired effect.

Using your scanner's Descreen option. Some scanning software packages feature a "descreening" command, which attempts to convert halftone dots to continuous tones. Some work very well; many cause as many problems as they attempt to solve. Before applying any moiré-removal techniques, it doesn't hurt to see what your scanner offers. Most often, you have to determine the linescreen of the original artwork, then choose the closest value from a "Descreen" pop-up in the scanner interface. (If you have difficulty recognizing the value on sight—as many people do—you can purchase a linescreen gauge at your local graphic arts supply shop, which enables you to determine the ruling of a printed image by placing an escalating screen over it.) Once you've determined the linescreen, choose the next-highest value from the Descreen pop-up and scan away. If the moiré is significantly reduced, continue editing as usual. If not, refer to the steps mentioned above.

Color Adjusting Techniques

Color Scanning and Adjusting Checklist

The following list is a typical approach for color scanning and correction. You may find that it varies, depending on your particular workflow and personal style. Except where noted, feel free to make alterations. The important thing is to attend to the image in a systematic fashion that makes the most intuitive sense to you and the needs of your production environment:

1. **Evaluate the original material and determine its purpose.** How will it be printed? What's the target linescreen and paper stock? Are the colors critical, or do they just need to be balanced and appealing? This usually requires meeting with the client or art director of a project.

2. **Preview, measure, and adjust the image using your scanner's software.** These options ultimately depend on the make and quality of your scanner and its software.

3. **Acquire the image.** After you scan the image, open it in Photoshop (if your scanning software doesn't do it automatically).

4. **Evaluate the scan.** Make sure the range of colors and tones were captured adequately by the scanner, by examining the Histogram or Levels dialog boxes. If not, scan again. If so, save the image.

5. **Prepare the RGB to CMYK separation settings, if necessary.** If you intend to convert an image to CMYK color, the proper conversion settings must be established in the Edit: **Color Settings** dialog box.

6. **Repair any obvious image defects.** These are the big ones, like a tear in the original material, an element that must be removed, or any image compositing.

7. **Sharpen the image.** Always use the Unsharp Mask filter to enhance the level of image detail.

8. **Retouch the smaller image flaws.** Use the Clone Stamp tool to remove scratches, dirt, and other small imperfections.

9. **Evaluate and adjust the endpoints for press.** This prevents the highlight areas from burning out and the shadows from filling in during printing. It will also enable you to ensure the endpoints are neutral, removing the possibility of a color cast.

10. **Adjust the tones.** This refers to the image's overall lightness, darkness, and contrast.

11. **Adjust the overall color content of the image.** Here, you tweak the image colors to either match the original material as closely as possible, or emphasize a particular element.

12. **Review and massage.** Proof the image, making any necessary corrections, and save the file for further use.

Issues to Consider

Converting print-destined images from RGB to CMYK. You may have noticed that the above list doesn't contain an item for converting from RGB to CMYK color. This step will depend on whether you scan an image yourself, the type of scanning equipment used, and other workflow considerations. Most people find themselves correcting images in RGB and CMYK mode. The advantages to correcting in RGB include faster processing times, a greater variety of available tools in Photoshop, and of course, its wider color gamut. The advantages to correcting in CMYK are fewer unexpected color shifts and more intuitive, print-oriented color values.

Ideally, the bulk of correcting should take place in RGB. Convert to CMYK only after the most intensive adjustments are made, and it's time to generate a proof. In the adjustment checklist, this step would appear between steps 11 and 12. If the image requires any subtle tweaks after proofing, make the corrections in CMYK. (Of course, this approach assumes that you have an RGB image to begin with, and that you actually want to convert it. Many high-end scanners convert the image to CMYK color on-the-fly, using internal, customized settings.)

G.2

Common CMYK Conversion Setups

The following tables describe a widely-accepted series of RGB-to-CMYK conversion settings. Your print shop should be able to assist you with any uncertainly concerning your particular requirements.

Coated Stock

Ink Colors	SWOP (Coated)
Dot Gain	15–25%
Separation Type	GCR
Black Generation	Light
Black Limit	90–100%
Total Ink	290–340% (less for web press, more for sheet-fed)
UCA	0–10% (typically 0%)

Uncoated Stock

Ink Colors	SWOP (Uncoated)
Dot Gain	18–25%
Separation Type	GCR
Black Generation	Light
Black Limit	90–100%
Total Ink	270–300% (less for web press, more for sheet-fed)
UCA	0–10% (typically 0%)

Newsprint (GCR)

Ink Colors	SWOP (Newsprint)
Dot Gain	30–40%
Separation Type	GCR
Black Generation	Medium
Black Limit	90–100%
Total Ink	250–280% (less for web press, more for sheet-fed)
UCA	0–10% (typically 0%)

Newsprint (UCR)

Ink Colors	SWOP (Newsprint)
Dot Gain	30–40%
Separation Type	UCR
Black Generation	N/A
Black Limit	70–80%
Total Ink	250–280% (less for web press, more for sheet-fed)
UCA	N/A

Adjusting RGB *vs.* CMYK *Color*

Using the Curves command to adjust a CMYK image is similar to adjusting a Grayscale image for print. Always make sure the dialog box displays output values, or percentages from 0% to 100%. If the Input/Output fields are showing brightness levels, click the Values Gradient at the bottom of the graph.

When editing an RGB image, though, you don't want to use output values. If you do, the numbers you read in the dialog box don't relate to the values displayed in the Info palette. Remember, an RGB image is based on transmitted light, not reflected light. Therefore, the output values that describe halftone dot sizes have no bearing here. There is no such thing as "50% red" or "75% blue." By basing your adjustments on brightness levels, which range from 0 to 255, you use the same values referred to by your monitor to display the image. If the Input/Output fields are showing output values, click the Values Gradient at the bottom of the graph.

The most important thing to remember is that RGB is the inverse of CMYK. The tonal values mapped in the Curves dialog box are opposite, as well. For example, to lighten the midtones of a CMYK image, place a point in the center of the curve and drag downward. To lighten the midtones of an RGB image, place a point in the center of the curve and drag upward. In a CMYK image, like a Grayscale, the highlight information is found in the lower left of the graph; the shadows are found in the upper right. In an RGB image, the highlights are in the upper right and the shadows in the lower left. **A**

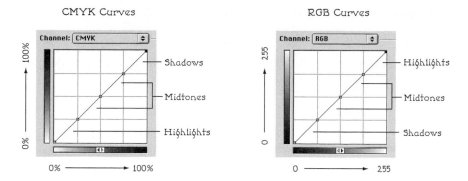

A *When you move between RGB and CMYK images, the Curves command may seem awkward at first. Just as RGB and CMYK are inverse color models, their curves share an inverse relationship, as well.*

Keep this inverse relationship in mind when adjusting colors, too. The following table illustrates the basic relationships you'll encounter when editing RGB and CMYK images, and provides a starting point for your adjustments.

Adjustment	RGB Image	CMYK Image
Subtract red	Pull down red curve (or pull up green and blue curves)	Pull up cyan curve (or pull down magenta and yellow curves)
Subtract green	Pull down green curve (or pull up red and blue curves)	Pull up magenta curve (or pull down cyan and yellow curves)
Subtract blue	Pull down blue curve (or pull up red and green curves)	Pull up yellow curve (or pull down cyan and magenta curves)
Add red	Pull up red curve (or pull down green and blue curves)	Pull down cyan curve (or pull up magenta and yellow curves)
Add green	Pull up green curve (or pull down red and blue curves)	Pull down magenta curve (or pull up cyan and yellow curves)
Add blue	Pull up blue curve (or pull down red and green curves)	Pull down yellow curve (or pull up cyan and magenta curves)
Subtract cyan	Pull up red curve or pull down green and blue curves	Pull down cyan curve (or pull up magenta and yellow curves)

(Continued)

Subtract magenta	Pull up green curve (or pull down red and blue curves)	Pull down magenta curve (or pull up cyan and yellow curves)
Subtract yellow	Pull up blue curve (or pull down red and green curves)	Pull down yellow curve (or pull up cyan and magenta curves)
Add cyan	Pull down red curve (or pull up green and blue curves)	Pull up cyan curve (or pull down magenta and yellow curves)
Add magenta	Pull down green curve (or pull up red and blue curves)	Pull up yellow curve (or pull down cyan and magenta curves)
Add yellow	Pull down blue curve (or pull up red and green curves)	Pull up cyan curve (or pull down magenta and yellow curves)

G.4

Sharpening Full-Color Images

The best way to approach sharpening is to make a distinction between *fine* detail and *subtle* detail. Fine detail is clearly visible: Tree branches interwoven against the sky, hair blowing in the wind, and the criss-cross pattern of plaid fabric are all good examples. Subtle detail is less obvious: Fleshtones, the skin of an apple, and blades of grass in a manicured lawn are all based on the slightest tonal and color variations. Of course, some images possess neither fine nor subtle detail. For example, a product shot of a telephone primarily consists of well-defined, simple shapes. Unsharp Mask settings that work well on one type of detail will either obliterate or have no effect on the other.

It's impossible to recommend only one or two Unsharp Mask settings for a wide variety of color images. However, you can start with a basic strategy:

- **Normal detail.** When the image detail consists of bold, clean lines against a reasonably contrasting background, start with a higher Radius (between 1.5 and 3 pixels, depending on the image resolution) and a lower Threshold (between 2 and 5 levels). These values produce a more pronounced effect that includes most of the image pixels. **A**

- **Fine detail.** Areas of fine detail typically require a low Radius (between .5 and 1.5 pixels) and low Threshold (between 2 and 5 levels). This way, no detail is obliterated by the halo produced by a large Radius, and more pixels are included in the overall effect. **B**

- **Subtle detail.** Areas of subtle detail typically require a higher Radius value (between 1 and 3 pixels) and a higher Threshold (between 6 and 15 levels). These values emphasize the more contrasting ranges, while ensuring that slightly varying values are unaffected. **C**

These relationships are only starting points—the content of each image will determine the final settings. Also, notice I didn't include an Amount setting. That value simply determines the degree of lightening and darkening applied by the Unsharp Mask filter. Since detail is most affected by the Radius and Threshold, establish those settings before setting the Amount.

Original   A: 120 R: 2.0 T: 3   Radius too high (4.0)

A   *Normal detail (consisting of bold, clearly-defined shapes) can tolerate a higher Radius and lower Threshold, with less possibility of artifacting or lost detail (see color insert).*

Original   A: 150 R: 1.0 T: 3   Radius too high (3.0)

B   *Fine detail (like branches against the sky) requires a lower Radius. Higher settings may obliterate the vital information (see color insert).*

Original   A: 170 R: 1.5 T: 10   Threshold too low (3)

C   *Subtle detail (like this apple skin) requires a higher Threshold. If every pixel is sharpened, the image appears textured and unnatural (see color insert).*

G.5

Sharpening Individual Color Channels

Some images are difficult (if not impossible) to sharpen in one even-handed pass. This is especially true in two cases: Images produced by a lower-end RGB scanner, and fleshtones. If you can't get balanced, satisfying results by sharpening the composite channel, you'll likely do better by sharpening one or more of the color channels.

The trick is to sharpen the channels that contain the *least* amount of detail. In most RGB scans, the blue channel contains most of the detail, as well as a little bit of scanner noise. If you oversharpen this channel, you can quickly introduce visible artifacts and halos to the image. By sharpening only the red and green channels, you can emphasize the image detail without exaggerating these aberrant pixels.

If the image has already been converted to CMYK, you'll have to examine the channels more closely. If the original image contained blue channel noise, most of it will carry over to the yellow channel—avoid sharpening this one. However, the content of the remaining channels will determine your next actions. If the subject matter is predominantly green, the cyan channel will contain considerable detail. In this case, sharpen the magenta and black plates. If it's predominantly red, the magenta channel will contain considerable detail. Here, sharpen the cyan and black plates.

Issues to Consider

There are no recommended settings for channel-based sharpening. The best results will require some trial and error, but you can do two things to make it easier on yourself. First, always work from a duplicate of the original image. Second, before sharpening, create a preview image by choosing View: **New View**. This command appears to duplicate the image, but it doesn't—the window enables you to see the same image using different view settings. Set its view to 100%, reduce the window size, and position the image so the most important detail is visible. This way, when you select a channel in the first copy and manipulate the sliders in the Unsharp Mask dialog box, you can preview the effect on the overall image.

G.6

Sharpening Fleshtones

Fleshtones have their own sharpening requirements. If these details are overexaggerated, the subject picks up an unsightly pattern, as if he had an unfortunate skin condition. (Also, glossy red lips tend to look unnatural when you sharpen them, regardless of the settings used.)

Printed fleshtones are mostly composed of magenta and yellow. In an RGB image, this means the details are contained in the green and blue channels. Here, you can focus the bulk of your sharpening on the red channel.

An image comprised mostly of fleshtones—for example, a close-up head shot—is one of the few occasions where it is preferable to sharpen after converting to CMYK color. Here, it's easier to ignore the magenta and yellow channels completely, focusing your edits on the cyan and black information. Because details such as wrinkles, acne scars, pores, and gleaming lips are far less likely to appear on these channels, you can typically use more intensive Unsharp Mask settings. **A**

| Original | Globally sharpened | Only cyan and black channels sharpened |

A *Globally-sharpened fleshtones often suffer from an over-accentuated, sickly appearance. By sharpening the channels that contain the least amount of fleshtone data, you emphasize important detail without adding texture to the skin (see color insert).*

Issues to Consider

Sharpening selected areas. Many users attempt to use different Unsharp Mask settings on different parts of an image, working with either selections or complex masks. They may want to apply softer settings to the subject's face, then apply higher, crisper settings to hair and other details. If you've found that you can do this successfully, congratulations—but it's not recommended. It's far too easy to introduce a noticeable imbalance, where it's clear to the viewer that portions of the image have been singled out. Whenever something appears to be wrong with the focus, your Unsharp Masking efforts have failed. It's usually better to sacrifice one part of the image for another—for example, losing a little detail in the hair to better accentuate the face—than to force the image to give you something it isn't willing to hand over without a fight.

G.7

Evaluating Shadows and Highlights

Before you spend any time adjusting color, make sure the image is worth the effort. Just like assessing a Grayscale image, the highlights should not blow out to white, and the shadows should not fill in to black. Highlights are easier to examine—if any patches are solid white, it's likely a fair amount of detail has been lost. The shadows may be trickier, because it's more difficult for the eye to discern any subtle differences. To see if there is an acceptable level of shadow detail, move the cursor over the image areas and keep an eye on the Info palette. If the values change, it indicates the existence of a certain level of detail. If the palette shows a constant value, the area exists as a solid color, containing no detail. **A**

A   *If an image initially suffers from blown-out highlights or plugged shadows, no amount of correcting can save it. The colors are reasonably balanced in the scan on the left, but the shadows are plugged in, and the highlights are almost solid white. The colors are also balanced on the right, but the shadow and highlight areas carry significantly more detail (see color insert).*

The next step is to evaluate the overall tone of the shadows and highlights. Here, you must refer to the original material. If the original contains very light information—for example, snow or a white shirt—the image highlights should contain similar values. If the image values are initially too dark, the overall contrast is thrown off balance, making the image more difficult to correct. Likewise, if the shadows initially appear as a sort of dark, washed-out gray, you may be fighting a losing battle. You can correct these imbalances, true, but doing so will expand the tonal content of the color channels. This causes two problems. First, it reduces the flexibility you have in applying future color adjustments, since less information will be available in the file. Second, if the expansion is too great, your colors will look washed-out or posterized.

Issues to Consider

Bad color endpoints are usually the result of improper scanning—or worse, an incapable scanner. Most midrange and high-end devices give you the ability to manually target the endpoints, or the lightest and darkest image values. This way, the tones and colors are better distributed during the time of the scan. As you evaluate the image, make sure the image endpoints match what you see in the original. When these values are set incorrectly (or not at all) during the prescan stage, the final scan will suffer from lost detail or bad contrast. You're better off scanning again, paying closer attention to the endpoints.

G.8

Assessing Gray Balance and Color Cast

Some unbalanced colors are easy to spot—you can simply look at the screen and see that something is off. Maybe the clouds have a pinkish tinge, or someone's flesh looks more jaundiced than rosy. Others are less visible, and cannot be identified until you evaluate a laminate proof. Here, you can assess something that isn't supposed to have any color bias whatsoever: neutral grays.

Every image contains neutral values. They may be obvious, like a gray sweater, a slab of granite, or a concrete wall. Or they may be subtle, appearing only in the diffuse highlight, or in the edge of a shadow stretching across a white tablecloth. However they occur, they provide one of the most important color adjustment benchmarks. Most scanners introduce a slight cast into each image, or a bias toward one color or another. If you can identify the values that are supposed to be neutral, you can determine the extent of the cast and take measures to remove it.

Issues to Consider

Most color casts appear during the scanning stage. To determine the extent introduced by your specific device, scan a *gray wedge* (available at a photographic supply shop), a thin strip that contains perfectly neutral shadow, midtone, and highlight information. When you assess the image in Photoshop, you can identify the predominant casts, as well as the tones they affect most. For example, you might see that a red cast consistently appears in the midtones and highlights.

This accomplishes two things. First, whenever you generate a scan, you'll know how and where to begin your adjustments. Second, you can use this information to create a pre-adjustment curve in your scanning software, which compensates for the cast at the time of the scan. (If you're using a midrange to high-end flatbed, try positioning the gray wedge next to the original as you scan. This will give you some easy neutral values to evaluate, before you crop away and continue your edits.)

G.9

Reading RGB Neutrals

It's easy to identify neutrals in an RGB image: Equal amounts of red, green, and blue produce a neutral gray. Therefore, when you evaluate what you presume to be a neutral color, the values should be the same. If any of the values are off, you've identified a cast. For example, assume a gray midtone reads as R:127, G:127, B:135 in the Info palette; the neutral contains too much blue data, which indicates that the image contains a slight blue cast. On the other hand, if the same midtone reads as R:127, G:127, B:120, the neutral doesn't contain enough blue data, which indicates a slight yellow cast. Therein lies the beauty of using neutral values to identify color casts—if a neutral contains a bias, you can be sure the remaining colors are affected by it, as well. **A**

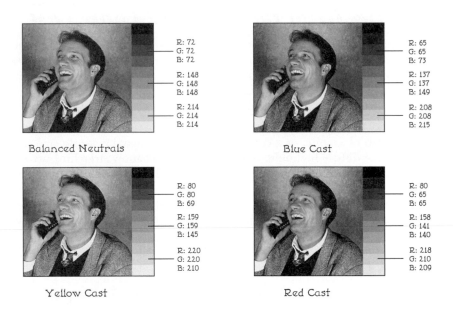

Balanced Neutrals

R: 72
G: 72
B: 72

R: 148
G: 148
B: 148

R: 214
G: 214
B: 214

Blue Cast

R: 65
G: 65
B: 73

R: 137
G: 137
B: 149

R: 208
G: 208
B: 215

Yellow Cast

R: 80
G: 80
B: 69

R: 159
G: 159
B: 145

R: 220
G: 220
B: 210

Red Cast

R: 80
G: 65
B: 65

R: 158
G: 141
B: 140

R: 218
G: 210
B: 209

A *If an image has a color cast, it quickly becomes apparent when you assess a value that is supposed to be neutral. To better illustrate the effect of a cast, a gray ramp has been added next to each image (see color insert).*

G.10

Reading CMYK Neutrals

Reading neutrals in a CMYK image is more difficult. In theory, equal amounts of cyan, magenta, and yellow produce a neutral gray. In reality, this cannot happen, due to impurities in the printing inks. If you do the bulk of your corrections in RGB, Photoshop automatically maintains the status of any neutral values when you convert to CMYK color. (The exact percentages will depend on the current settings in the CMYK Setup dialog box.) If you have to compensate for a color cast in a CMYK image, you must become familiar with the basic relationships between the inks. Put simply, neutral values must contain more cyan than magenta and yellow. How much more depends on whether the neutral is a shadow, midtone, or highlight. **A**

C	M	Y	CMY	K		C	M	Y	CMY	K
5%	3%	3%		5%		60%	46%	46%		60%
10	6	6		10		75	64	64		75
25	16	16		25		80	71	71		80
30	21	21		30		90	82	82		90
40	29	29		40		95	87	87		95
50	37	37		50						

A *Once colors exist as CMYK values, neutrality requires a special relationship. Due to impurities found in all process inks, each neutral gray requires more cyan than magenta and yellow. When determining the equivalent black value of a neutral, let the cyan percentage be your guide (see color insert).*

Think of the charted values as a guide, not gospel. The main issue is the relationship between cyan and the remaining inks. As you can see, a neutral value contains equal amounts of magenta and yellow, but the amount of additional cyan changes as you move along the gray ramp:

Tone	Additional Cyan
Highlights	2–3%
Quarter tones	7–10%
Midtones	12–15%
Three-quarter tones	8–12%
Shadows	7–10%

Don't worry if a value is off by a point or two. For example, the magenta and yellow may differ by 1%, or the cyan value may appear a notch above or below the recommended amount. The effect of such subtle variations is usually negligible when the image runs on-press.

G.11

Identifying Endpoints in a Color Image

Before you can properly map the extreme shadow and diffuse highlight values for print, you need to identify their location in the image. You'll ultimately pinpoint these areas by examining the image with the cursor and Info palette, but you need some way to narrow down the field.

Although you can use the levels command to display the shadow and highlight values of a halftone, that technique is of little use with color images. When the image is in RGB color, (Option) [Alt]-dragging the sliders in the Levels dialog box produces a confusing rainbow effect. When the image is in CMYK color, it produces no effect at all. Follow these steps instead (they work equally well on RGB and CMYK images):

1. Open the image you want to target.

2. Choose Image: Adjust: **Threshold**.

3. In the Threshold dialog box, make sure the Preview option is checked and move the slider all the way to the right (the image appears to turn white).

4. Slowly increase the Threshold value (highlight the Threshold Value field and press your keyboard's up arrow to raise the value in increments of 1.) The first pixels to appear as black are the image's darkest shadows. **A**

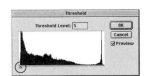

A *To locate an image's darkest shadow areas, move the Threshold slider all the way to the left and gradually increase the value. The first pixels to turn black are the shadows.*

5. Move the slider all the way to the right (the image appears to turn black).

6. Slowly decrease the Threshold value. The first pixels to turn white are the image's lightest highlights. **B**

7. Click Cancel to close the Threshold command.

Take note of the shadow and highlight locations. You'll soon return to them, using the Curves command to set their values for printing.

B *To locate an image's diffuse highlight, move the Threshold slider all the way to the right and gradually decrease the value. The first pixels that turn white are the lightest values. (Be sure to ignore the specular highlight–it will appear to turn white first.)*

G.12

Establishing Neutral Endpoint Values

When setting the endpoints of a Grayscale image for print, you have one concern: Making sure the lightest and darkest pixel values fit within the reproducible range of the target press. The endpoints in a color image involve two issues. First, like a Grayscale image, they must fit the range of the printing press. Second, they must exist as neutral values. When the extreme shadow and diffuse highlight are unbalanced, the resulting cast more than likely affects the entire image. By remapping the endpoints to neutral values (that also match the press requirements), the changes impact the entire image; the remaining gray levels are automatically drawn one step closer to neutrality. Before you can reset an image's endpoints, however, you must enter the desired values in the Curves dialog box.

Normally, Photoshop sets the shadow dot value automatically. You can see this when you double-click the shadow Eyedropper in the Curves dialog box—the CMYK fields in the Color Picker are already filled with the default black percentages. However, if you already set the shadow dot for Grayscale images, you'll notice that those values still exist (most likely, only a K percentage appears in the CMYK fields). Don't bother figuring out the CMYK shadow values in your head. Instead, follow these steps:

1. Open the Curves dialog box.

2. Double-click the black Eyedropper.

3. In the color picker, move the cursor to the colored field in the left half of the dialog box.

4. Click-drag, moving the cursor all the way to the lower left of the field. The default black values are automatically entered in the CMYK fields. **A**

6. Click OK to close the color picker.

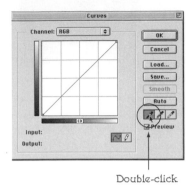 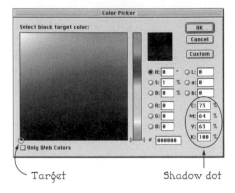

Double-click   Target   Shadow dot

A *When setting the desired shadow dot value, enter Photoshop's default black value. (Note the indicator in the lower left of the color field.)*

To set the diffuse highlight value, double-click the white Eyedropper to access the Color Picker again. Here, you must enter a neutral value that retains its dot structure on-press. When printing onto coated paper, the best place to start is C:5, M:3, Y:3, K:0, which produces the visual equivalent of a 5% gray dot. As the quality of your paper (and the tolerance of your printing method) decreases, you may need to raise this value, based on the advice of your printer. **B**

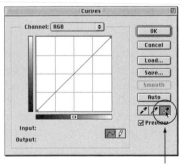 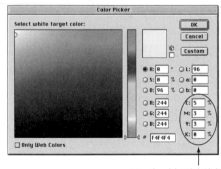

Double-click   Neutral highlight

B *The diffuse highlight value requires a light neutral gray. The exact value depends on the printable tolerance of your target press. In this example, the value is C:5, M:3, Y:3, K:0, a common standard for coated paper.*

Issues to Consider

Remember the difference between diffuse and specular highlights. The diffuse highlight represents the lightest printed tone. The specular highlight represents any information that you want reduced to pure white on-press. Common examples include a glint in someone's eye, or a bright flash on a metallic object. Speculars are almost always small pinpoints, and should be ignored when applying your endpoints (and they're not found in every image). When targeting the desired spot, look for the lightest printable dot, such as a white shirt collar, a light patch of snow, or the shiniest tooth in a smile. If you map a specular highlight to a gray tone, it will slightly darken the rest of the image, reducing the overall contrast.

Re-establishing endpoint values. If you work in a closed-loop environment, producing color images for a single printing method, you can set these values once and leave them—they'll remain until you manually change them again. If you routinely produce images for a variety of printing methods, you'll have to evaluate the press requirements and enter appropriate endpoint values for every project.

Photoshop automatically converts neutral RGB gray into its CMYK equivalent. If unsure of the exact percentages involved in a neutral highlight, try entering a series of identical values in the RGB fields of the color picker. Photoshop knows to preserve the neutral relationship between RGB's brightness levels and CMYK's output percentages. For example, assume you've optimized the CMYK Setup dialog box for sheetfed printing onto uncoated paper. If you enter 244 in each of the RGB fields, C:5, M:3, Y:3, K:0 automatically appears in the CMYK fields. If you enter 238 in the RGB fields, the CMYK values change to C:8, M:5, Y:5, K:0—a neutral value that equals an 8% gray dot. Set them to 233, and the CMYK values change to C:10, M:6, Y:7, K:0.

Don't assume that every diffuse highlight should be set at the lightest printable value. The ultimate value depends on the content of the original image, as well as any art direction provided by the client. For example, instead of setting the neutral highlight to the equivalent of a 5% dot (C:5, M:3, Y:3, K:0), the original may require a highlight of 20% (C:20, M:13, Y:13, K:0). If you remap a quarter-tone down to a highlight, the entire tonal range of the image is expanded. True, a greater disparity between lights and darks increases the overall contrast. That's generally a good thing, but not if the photographer intended otherwise. Among other things, unnatural contrast can destroy the impact of specular highlights.

G.13

Applying Neutral Endpoint Values

Most images require a neutral highlight (see *Issues to Consider*, below). Most often, the current highlight will be close to neutral, but will either contain a slight cast, or be too light for the target press. If you're adjusting an image with a non-neutral highlight, you can still attack a scanner-induced cast using a different round of techniques. **A**

R:248
G:239
B:242

C:1
M:8
Y:1
K:0

R:244
G:244
B:244

C:5
M:3
Y:3
K:0

A *Above and beyond ensuring printable shadows and highlights, neutral endpoints will correct a large part of any existing color casts. In this example, the highlights are too light for printing and contain a red bias. After remapping the endpoints, the highlights are neutralized—affecting the red cast all the way up to the midtones—and contain satisfactory dot sizes for printing (see color insert).*

Assuming you've already targeted the image's highlight and shadow, follow these steps to remap the endpoints:

1. Open the Curves dialog box.

2. Click the white Eyedropper.

3. Move the cursor over the actual image, referring to the Info palette, until you locate the lightest pixel value.

4. Click with the Eyedropper.

To set the shadow endpoint, leave the Curves dialog box open and follow these steps:

1. Click the black Eyedropper.

2. Move the cursor over the actual image, referring to the Info palette, until you locate the darkest pixel value.

3. Click with the Eyedropper.

Issues to Consider

Before applying neutral endpoints, double-check the original. Pay particular attention to the diffuse highlight—you must be sure that this part of the image is *supposed* to be neutral. For example, if the original photo was taken using colored gels or filters, the highlights will have a deliberate cast. If you remap a non-neutral color to a neutral gray, the resulting color shifts will likely be too extreme in the rest of the image.

New endpoints are far more predictable when they're applied to an RGB image. This is mainly due to the fact that the black plate hasn't yet been generated, giving Photoshop much more flexibility in remapping the overall image tones. If you're adjusting a CMYK image, ask yourself if you need to reset the endpoints. If the scan was made using a high-end flatbed or drum scanner, a savvy operator will have set the endpoints during the prescan stage. If the endpoints (especially in the highlights) are off by only a couple of points, you may be better off applying small curve adjustments, as opposed to using the Eyedroppers.

For example, if the diffuse highlight in a CMYK image is currently C:5, M:5, Y:3, K:0, it will appear to have a pinkish cast. If you use the Eyedroppers in the Curves dialog box to reset the endpoint, you'll likely wind up with a value such as C:5, M:4, Y:2, K:0, which is close, but not the precise neutral you seek. Instead, you can ease the magenta cast by applying a slight reduction in the magenta highlights.

G.14
___

Addressing Neutral Midtones

Neutralizing the endpoints will affect the color and tone of the remaining image. Adjustments to the shadow dot tend to impact values all the way *down* to the midtones; adjustments to the diffuse highlight tend to impact values all the way *up* to the midtones. The human eye is most sensitive to the latter part of the tonal range—therefore, identifying and correcting casts in this region requires delicate work on your part. Base your decisions on a thoughtful, systematic examination of both the original material and the current image values.

After you apply neutral endpoints, re-assess the remaining neutrals. If a slight cast still exists, use the Curves command to selectively compensate for the additional color. For example, after setting neutral endpoints, the midtones may still possess a magenta bias. If the image is RGB, you can compensate by increasing the level of green in the affected areas. If the image is CMYK, you can reduce the level of magenta. **A**

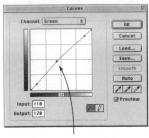

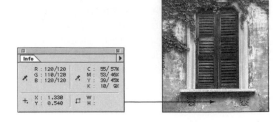

110 Green increased to 120

A *The endpoints of this image are neutral, but a slight magenta cast persists in the midtones. In this RGB image, I protected the highlights and shadows, attacking the cast directly in the midtones of the green channel.*

Issues to Consider

It's easy to pay too much attention to neutral grays. Neutrals are an undeniably useful benchmark, but your adjustments must be tempered by the variables introduced by each color image. You can't expect every gray to be neutral. A common mistake is to go into overdrive, neutralizing every gray value in sight. A better approach is to neutralize only the values that you know for certain are neutral, and be more circumspect about the rest. The neutral model is a solid guide, but your decisions must be rooted in the original materials. Keep the following issues in mind:

– **Every scanner introduces a slight cast of one color or another.** Transmissive originals tend to suffer more than reflective. However, a color corrector shouldn't be burdened with the entire responsibility for removing them. The scanner operator should be able to avoid most casts by targeting neutrals during the prescan process, using a series of curves similar to those in Photoshop. In fact, you can use your Photoshop adjustments as a sort of template for the prescan stage. Some scanning software even enables you to load a set of curves you created and saved in Photoshop.

– **When neutralizing, you often have a choice between adding and subtracting color.** Removing color is generally a safer move than adding color, particularly where higher ink densities are involved. For example, when removing a red cast in an RGB image, it's better to decrease the level of red, as opposed to increasing the levels of green and blue. The only exception to this rule is if the colored area is rather washed–out or weak, and rescanning is not an option. In this case, increasing the amount of the remaining colors may add body to the overall image, and neutralize the cast. (For more information, see *G.3, Adjusting RGB vs. CMYK Color.*)

– **Photographic subjects illuminated with different light sources may suffer from multiple casts.** It will be extremely difficult to fix them with a single global correction. Focus your efforts on the predominant cast. In extreme cases, use the Color Range selection command to isolate one of the biased areas, make a subtle adjustment, then invert the selection to adjust the remaining tones.

G.15

Applying a Half-Cast Removal

Completely neutralizing a color cast may move the overall values too far away from their intended appearance. This frequently occurs when the image does not contain obvious neutrals to use as a reference. Your screen (or more often, your proofs) will display an apparent cast, but if you totally remove it, the remaining colors look too clean, even unnatural. These cases are best addressed by a *half-cast removal.* Here, as the name implies, you determine the degree of change required for a full-cast correction, then remove half the necessary amount.

For example, if a neutral value reads as R:130, G:130, B:125, it's easy to identify and compensate for the cast: Increase the level of blue in the midtones. However, if the same area reads as R:140, G:130, B:106, the strategy isn't as clear. Granted, it indicates that a yellowish cast exists, but completely neutralizing it would have an extreme affect on the surrounding colors. The optimal correction will depend on the image at hand, but this example is well suited for a half-cast correction: Determine the adjustments required for full neutralization, then cut them in half. In this example, this means reducing the level of red by 5, and increasing the level of blue by 12. A value of R:135, G:130, B:118 will still have a slight cast, but the results will be more appealing than a full correction. **A**

 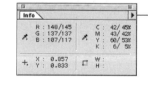 

Casted Image   Half-Cast Removal

A *When a cast is too dominant, completely neutralizing it may adversely affect the remaining image colors. Applying a half-cast removal brings the cast halfway to neutral, clearing up the most offensive aspect of the cast without compromising the remaining colors (see color insert).*

When adjusting a CMYK image, your correction strategy will depend on your ability to identify neutrals. The following table illustrates two examples based on cyan, magenta, and yellow inks:

Cast Color	Closest Neutral Value	Difference	Corrected Values
C:25	C:25	0%	C:25 (no change)
M:18	M:16	2%	M:17 (16+1)
Y:12	Y:16	4%	Y:14 (12+2)
C:84	C:80	4%	C:82 (80+2)
M:71	M:71	0%	M:71 (no change)
Y:69	Y:71	2%	Y:70 (69+1)

G.16

Adjusting Non-Neutral Colors

The secret to color correcting is understanding how cyan, magenta, yellow, and black inks work together. Even if you routinely adjust RGB images, you must learn to "think" in terms of CMYK. Why? Because most people can visualize a color based on CMYK percentages; far fewer have the same intuitive grasp of RGB. For example, if you're interested in a color consisting of 50% magenta and 100% yellow, it's relatively easy to envision how it might appear. If you ask for 218 red, 155 green, and 35 blue, few people automatically think "orange."

Neutral gray relationships are easy to follow, but non-neutral colors will never be so organized. It's impossible to provide targeted values for every color you'll encounter—there are simply too many. However, by knowing how your inks behave—by understanding what happens when they combine to create colors—you can approach your adjustments more intuitively.

The relationship between CMYK inks is as follows:

- **Primary component.** This component is the dominant ink, or the one with the highest percentage. In the above example (M:50, Y:100), yellow is the primary. This ink drives the color's hue, or its starting position along the RGB/CMY color wheel.

- **Secondary component.** This component refines the first color, deepening its tone and adding depth. In the same example, the lesser amount of magenta gives the yellow its orange color.

- **Tertiary component.** This component reduces the overall purity of the color, adding an element of gray into the mix. For example, if you add 20% cyan to the sample orange, the result is a less intense version of the same basic hue. (If you hear a color described as too "dirty," the tertiary component is probably too high.) Although this value is sometimes called the "unwanted" color, it's of utmost importance to image reproduction—it adds detail and texture, and a level of control over the color's saturation.

- **Black.** In full-color imaging, black generally isn't used to create colors; instead, it helps the tertiary component carry detail, and adds strength to the shadows. It's also used to replace CMY inks on-press (via UCR or GCR), and printers occasionally use it to replace a certain amount of the tertiary color, depending on the reproduction method. In the vast majority of images, the black plate carries the least amount of information. (For more information, see *9.40, Color Settings: CMYK Working Space.*) **A**

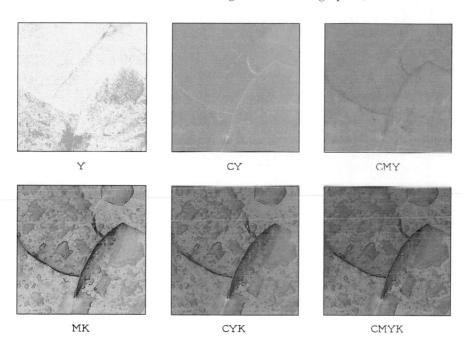

| Y | CY | CMY |
| MK | CYK | CMYK |

A *In the greens of this image, yellow is the primary component, and cyan is the secondary. Magenta, the tertiary component, adds tone and detail, and black carries the shadows. Here, these relationships are illustrated by printing one or more inks at a time (see color insert).*

If you can identify a color's primary and secondary components, you can base your initial adjustments on the tertiary. Consider these brief examples:

- **Flesh.** The primary component of Caucasian flesh is yellow, and the secondary is magenta—start by evaluating the cyan levels.

- **Sky.** The primary component of sky is cyan, and the secondary is magenta—start by evaluating the yellow content.

- **Leaves.** The primary component of green leaves is yellow, and the secondary is cyan—start by evaluating the magenta.

The exact adjustments depend on the image. If the amount of the tertiary component is too high, the colors will look dingy and gray. If the levels are too low, the colors will appear oversaturated and lack detail.

G.17
_____

Correcting Fleshtones

The primary fleshtone component, regardless of race, is usually yellow. Magenta is secondary, typically lagging behind yellow by up to 10%. This makes cyan the tertiary, with values often consisting of one-third to one-half of the magenta dot. Of course, these values will vary, depending on the person, the lighting, even the curves of someone's face. The important thing is the relationship between the colors. When it's unbalanced, the flesh will appear off somehow to the viewer. Too much yellow, and a jaundiced look sets in. Too much magenta, and the subject looks sunburned. Too much cyan, and the colors lose their vitality. The following table illustrates the basic CMYK relationships between the predominant fleshtones:

	Cyan	**Magenta**	**Yellow**	**Black**
African	35%	45%	50%	Up to 30%
Asian	15	43	53	0
Causasian	10	40	50	0

Refer to this chart as you learn to identify and correct these colors. By no means should you try to map any fleshtones to these particular settings. The values you encounter will change from image to image. For example, in the fair skin of a blonde, the relationship between yellow and magenta may change places, due to the nature of her complexion—but the distance between the two values should remain fairly constant. A lighter-skinned African-American will contain less cyan than someone with darker-toned flesh. You must be able to identify any aberrant component values, based in part on the above relationships, and in part on the image at hand.

Take a look at these ideas at work. The first image is a fair-skinned woman. By taking several samples of her face, you can see that it contains too much magenta, which makes her appear too ruddy and flushed. In the Curves command, apply a midtone adjustment to the magenta channel, drawing the ink closer to the yellow/magenta relationship appropriate for Caucasian flesh. In the corrected example, you can see that the aberrant redness has been removed, but enough still exists to give her face a natural glow. **A**

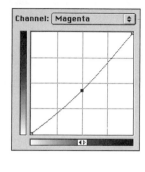

C: 5	C: 2	C: 5
M: 48	M: 32	M: 49
Y: 27	Y: 24	Y: 33
K: 0	K: 0	K: 0

C: 5	C: 2	C: 5
M: 40	M: 29	M: 43
Y: 27	Y: 24	Y: 33
K: 0	K: 0	K: 0

A *Here, most of the magenta data exists in the midtones. Reducing the overall level takes the "sunburn" out of the subject's skin (see color insert).*

In the second image, the background colors are acceptable, but the skin contains a yellow cast in the three-quarter tones. Because I know the yellow content shouldn't be much more than 10% greater than the magenta, I draw a curve for the yellow channel that reduces the level of yellow in the three-quarter tones and shadows, but preserves the content of the highlights and midtones. **B**

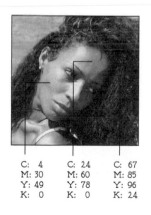
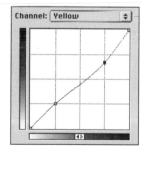
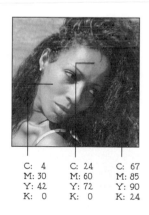

C: 4	C: 24	C: 67
M: 30	M: 60	M: 85
Y: 49	Y: 78	Y: 96
K: 0	K: 0	K: 24

C: 4	C: 24	C: 67
M: 30	M: 60	M: 85
Y: 42	Y: 72	Y: 90
K: 0	K: 0	K: 24

B *In the original image, the yellow cast appears primarily in the darker areas of the subject's skin. By limiting the adjustment to the tones most severely affected, you can preserve the color content of the rest of the image (see color insert).*

Issues to Consider

Always keep an eye on the surrounding image pixels. For example, if you find yourself removing magenta to balance the flesh, you may be pulling important color from another part of the image. When this is the case, try using the Color Range selection command to isolate the fleshtones. This is one of the few cases where correcting the colors of a selected area is advisable; fortunately, flesh tends to stand out in reasonably high contrast from the surrounding colors, making it easier to create a clean selection. Again, it's better to work with small, incremental adjustments. If you over-adjust the selected area, it eventually won't fit in with the surrounding colors, and it will appear to be cut and pasted from another image.

G.18

Correcting Blue Sky

Like correcting fleshtones, you can develop a strategy to adjust sky blues if you have an idea of how they're composed. As you might expect, the primary component of sky blue is cyan. The secondary is magenta, which adds richness. You should avoid yellow altogether—it tends to move blue closer to an unnatural teal. If you need to deepen the overall tone, you're much better off adding black as the tertiary component.

The relationship between cyan and magenta shapes the tone and hue of the sky—or as some viewers would claim, its overall mood. In a standard blue, the ratio between cyan and magenta is about 2:1. To create a cooler sky, reduce the level of magenta to as low as 20% of the cyan content—any less than that, and the sky develops an obviously cyan bias. To create a warmer sky, increase the level of magenta to as high as 75% of the cyan content—any more than that, and the sky becomes purple. **A**

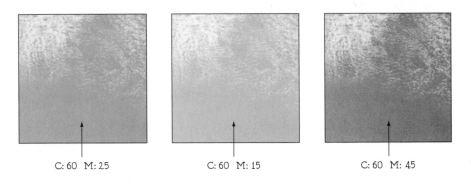

C: 60 M: 25   C: 60 M: 15   C: 60 M: 45

A *The same sky can be subject to different "moods," depending on the level of the secondary component: magenta (see color insert).*

The following table illustrates the basic CMY relationships:

	Cyan	Magenta	Yellow	Black
Sky blue	60%	25%	0%	0%
Warmer	60	45	0	0
Cooler	60	15	0	0

Issues to Consider

As with fleshtones, use this chart as a guide, not gospel. Again, the original materials will provide the strongest basis for your decisions. For example, do the clouds contain a reddish cast? This often occurs in nature—if the original contains such a bias, don't attempt to remove it from the image. If the original contains fluffy white clouds, you'll definitely want to reduce the level of magenta—but not so much that the sky becomes unnaturally cool. Remember, it's rare that the sky needs to match the original perfectly; more important is that it looks natural to the viewer, that it matches his expectation of how a sky should appear.

G.19
___

Targeting Common Color Components

The following figure provides a starting point for some common color combinations. Take note of the primary, secondary, and tertiary components of each one. Create the same colors in Photoshop, then reduce or increase the individual levels, and assess the resulting changes. Produce a four-color proof of the same values and compare them to the color sample provided in this book.

The list of possible color combinations could go on forever. However, the following examples should provide a solid basis for evaluating many of the values you'll encounter in a color adjusting workflow. **A**

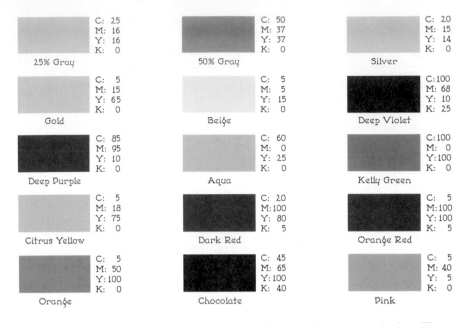

25% Gray — C: 25, M: 16, Y: 16, K: 0	**50% Gray** — C: 50, M: 37, Y: 37, K: 0	**Silver** — C: 20, M: 15, Y: 14, K: 0
Gold — C: 5, M: 15, Y: 65, K: 0	**Beige** — C: 5, M: 5, Y: 15, K: 0	**Deep Violet** — C:100, M: 68, Y: 10, K: 25
Deep Purple — C: 85, M: 95, Y: 10, K: 0	**Aqua** — C: 60, M: 0, Y: 25, K: 0	**Kelly Green** — C:100, M: 0, Y:100, K: 0
Citrus Yellow — C: 5, M: 18, Y: 75, K: 0	**Dark Red** — C: 20, M:100, Y: 80, K: 5	**Orange Red** — C: 5, M:100, Y:100, K: 5
Orange — C: 5, M: 50, Y:100, K: 0	**Chocolate** — C: 45, M: 65, Y:100, K: 40	**Pink** — C: 5, M: 40, Y: 5, K: 0

A *This chart lists the CMYK values for a series of commonly encountered colors. These values are not absolutes; use them as a benchmark for understanding the relationships between the primary, secondary, and tertiary components (see color insert).*

Issues to Consider

Learn to make notes as you work. As you work with color, keep extensive notes about the values you see and the CMYK percentages that comprise them. This will help inform you of the colors to expect, given the unique considerations of your workstation, monitor, proofing devices, and printing conditions. You'll eventually learn to apprise colors numerically, instead of allowing yourself to be seduced by what you see on screen. It's easy to think to yourself, "something doesn't look right." It takes considerable effort on your part to make the jump to thinking, "there is about 5% too much magenta in this sky."

Printed samples are the best resource. The color relationships described in this section are useful, but you can also rely on a wide variety of printed samples. Create your own series of target swatches, proofing them out under the conditions specific to your workplace. Even swatchbooks like Trumatch or PANTONE Process are helpful—they display hundreds of printed samples, and each one lists its CMYK components. Whatever you can evaluate that compares output percentages to actual, printed colors will only enrich your ability to identify them intuitively.

Colorizing Techniques

Colorizing with Duotone Mode

Converting an image to a duotone colorizes it in a way that's often difficult to achieve using other methods. If desired, you can temporarily convert an image to duotone, then discard the spot color designations. Follow these steps:

1. Open or create the desired Grayscale image.

2. Convert the image to Duotone mode. If desired, specify a CMYK value in the color picker, instead of spot inks. (For more information, see *J.2 Creating a PMS Monotone* and *J.3 Creating a Black/PMS Duotone*.)

3. After closing the Duotone Options dialog box, choose Image: Mode: RGB or **CMYK Color**. The duotone information is discarded, leaving a colorized image ready for further editing.

Issues to Consider

Using the Tritone and Quadtone options to colorize an image. You can load up to four color values in the Duotone Options dialog box, and manipulate the curves to produce effects that are difficult to achieve with the Image: **Adjust** commands. You're not committed to keeping the image in Duotone mode (especially when colorizing with four randomly-selected PANTONE inks). If desired, convert the image to RGB or CMYK Color mode. This way, you can continue editing the image using more flexible commands. Note that this approach may require considerable proofing to check and double-check the values, especially if the image will be reproduced on-press.

H.2

Creating an RGB Monotone

This technique replaces the tones of an image with a single hue. The effect is the same as importing a Grayscale TIFF into a layout document, and tagging it with a process color. Follow these steps:

1. Open the image you want to colorize. **A**

2. If the image is in Grayscale mode, convert it to RGB Color. If the image is already in full color, choose Image: Adjust: **Desaturate**.

3. Choose Layer: New Fill Layer: **Solid Color**.

4. In the New Layer dialog box, set Screen in the Mode pop-up menu and click OK. The color picker appears.

5. Enter the desired color value and click OK. **B C**

Grayscale tones (or their desaturated equivalent) tend to flatten when colorized. For more balanced results, boost the contrast before adjusting. **D E F**

A *Normal contrast.*   **B** *Purple monotone (see color insert).*   **C** *Deep red monotone (see color insert).*

D *High contrast.*   **E** *High contrast: Purple.*   **F** *High contrast: Deep red.*

Issues to Consider

This technique may not produce dead-on accurate colors for print purposes. The colors produced by this technique may not translate successfully from RGB to CMYK mode. For example, assume you've based the coloring on Pantone Process 155-1 (C:20, M:100, Y:0, K:40). It's easy to assume that converting the image to CMYK color will retain the intended values, because they're based on process values. In practice, the converted values depend on your RGB-to-CMYK separation settings. (Setting your Black Generation value to Maximum before converting will produce the closest translation, but it'll still be off by a point or two.) If you're just looking to get close to a particular color, this technique does the trick most of the time. To nail a particular swatchbook value in a printed piece, you need to use a CMYK-based technique. (For more information, see *H.3, Creating a CMYK Monotone.*)

An unflattened image provides greater editing flexibility. When you start with a flattened image, this technique results in two layers: the desaturated background layer, and the solid color fill. As long as the image remains unflattened, you can specify new color values by double-clicking the Solid Fill thumbnail in the Layers palette. (On the other hand, if you use traditional Fill or Hue/Saturation techniques, you must use a copy of the original image to recolor with a different value. Otherwise, recoloring the same image more than once throws the tonal distribution off-balance.)

Reading the values of a colorized image. When an image is colorized by a solid color fill layer, you cannot read the new color values in the Info palette while that layer is active. To read the new values, activate the desaturated layer and move the cursor around the image.

Creating an action for this technique. This technique is perfectly suited for automation. For example, if you need to recolor 50 images for a website or print project, you don't want to muddle through the same five or six steps over and over again. You want to be able to click a button, specify a color, then move on to the next file. Before creating the action, determine whether you want it open-ended (which leaves the image unflattened) or closed (which flattens the image).

Keeping an eye on the blend mode. It's all too easy to forget to set the blend mode in the New Layer dialog box. If this technique results in your image being completely obscured by a solid color, you don't have to start over. In the Layers palette, click the Solid Color layer and set the blend mode to Screen.

H.3

Creating a CMYK Monotone

The steps listed in *H.2, Creating an RGB Monotone* are reasonably straightforward, but they are less successful when applied to a CMYK image. The Screen blend mode interacts differently with four channels than it does with three, and the resulting colors tend to be lighter than expected. There are two reasons to use the following technique:

- **You aren't able to edit an image while it's still in RGB mode.** Although its preferable to make color edits to an RGB image, it's not always possible—and you gain nothing by converting back and forth between the two color modes.

- **When your workflow demands recolored images based on precise values,** with no unexpected variations or unwanted components. For example, a newsprint publication may sell two process inks as spot colors for their advertising. Here, you must base any colorized images on the available inks—otherwise they may not separate properly (or worse, they could be rejected by a proprietary pagination system).

Follow these steps:

1. Open the image you want to colorize. **A**

2. If the image is in Grayscale or RGB mode, convert it to CMYK. If the image is already in CMYK Color mode, choose Image: Adjust: **Desaturate**.

3. In the Channels palette, (Command) [Control]-click the CMYK item to create a channel-based selection. **B**

A *Original image.*

B *Creating a selection based on the CMYK channel.*

4. Choose Select: **Inverse** to reverse the selection outline.

5. In the Layers palette, click the Create New Layer button. Make sure the new layer is active. **c**

6. In the Toolbar, click the foreground color swatch to access the color picker. Define the desired color and click OK.

7. Press (Option) [Alt]-Delete to fill the selection with the foreground color.

8. Delete the background layer and flatten the image. **D**

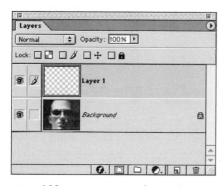

c *Adding a new target layer above the existing image.*

D *A C:100, Y:100 monotone (see color insert).*

H.4

Colorizing an Image, Retaining Deep Tones

Unlike the previous techniques—which replaced all of the image tones with the target color—the following steps enable you to retain the existing light and dark image data, while affecting the color of the midtones. The resulting images possess shadows that deepen to black. As you'll see, though, there are three ways to apply the color to the existing tonal range. Follow these steps:

1. Open the image you want to colorize.

2. If the image is in Grayscale mode, convert it to RGB or CMYK. If the image is already in full color, choose Image: Adjust: **Desaturate**.

3. Choose Layer: New Fill Layer: **Solid Color**.

4. In the New Layer dialog box, set Overlay in the Mode pop-up menu and click OK. The color picker appears.

5. Enter the desired color value and click OK.

6. If unsatisfied with the distribution of the new color, try resetting the blend mode to Soft Light (which tends to produce a less pronounced effect) or Color (which tends to produce more saturated colors). **A B C**

A *Colorized using Overlay mode (see color insert).*

B *Colorized using Soft Light mode (see color insert).*

C *Colorized using Color mode (see color insert).*

H.5

Recoloring an Element: Maintaining Original Tone

The following technique enables you to recolor an isolated image element. For example, if you need to create a series of different-colored versions of the same product for a company website, the following steps enable you to quickly generate the images you need from a single source.

This technique is suitable for color changes that produce minimal tonal shifts. For example, changing a medium gray sweater to a similar shade of green or brown, or a maroon coat to navy blue. You have a considerable amount of latitude, but extreme color shifts will require a different approach. (For more information, see *H.6, Recoloring a White Original* and *H.7, Converting a Darker Element to White.*) Follow these steps:

1. Draw a selection around the element you want to recolor. (See *Issues to Consider*, below.) **A**

2. Choose Layer: New: **Layer Via Copy**.

3. Choose Image: Adjust: **Desaturate**. The desaturated product sits in a layer above the rest of the image.

4. Choose Layer: New Fill Layer: **Solid Color**.

5. In the New Layer dialog box, check the Group With Previous Layer box and set the blend mode to Overlay. Click OK to access the color picker.

6. Set the desired values and click OK. (See *Issues to Consider*, below.) **B C**

A *Original image*
   (see color insert).

B *Recolored green*
   (see color insert).

C *Recolored purple*
   (see color insert).

Issues to Consider

Double-check the image before continuing your edits. Did the isolated element fill with a solid color? If so, set the correct blend mode in the Layers palette. Was the entire image affected by the new color? If so, click the solid color item in the Layers palette, then choose Layer: **Group With Previous**.

When recoloring parts of an image, use paths whenever possible. Most users claim that the majority of items they recolor have reasonably clear, hard edges. When this is the case, the Pen tool is by far the most appropriate selection tool. Not only does a path give you an easily-editable, crisp-edged selection outline, it enables you to load and re-load a selection as many times as you need it. Armed with the right techniques, you can create a surprisingly precise selection template. (For more information, see *L.7, Drawing Objects with an Adjacent Edge.*)

Adjusting the new color's tonal depth using Levels. The crux of this technique is the relationship between the solid color layer (which supplies the initial color values) and the desaturated layer (which carries the tone). As long as the image remains unflattened, you can change the tonal depth of the element separately from the new color. For the best results, activate the desaturated layer and use the Levels command. (For more information, see *10.20, Image: Adjust: Levels.*)

Adjusting the saturation of the new color. Depending on the element in question, the Overlay mode may not be quite what you're looking for. The wrong blend mode can appear to change the texture of the recolored element. Before trying to adjust the desaturated layer, try setting the solid color's blend mode to Soft Light or Color.

Sampling colors from another image. As long as another image is open and visible while you're adding the solid color layer, you can click to sample a value from a separate source. For example, if you're creating colored variations of a single product shot, you can leave open a scan that displays all of the necessary color swatches. This way, you can click the scanned image until you grab a satisfactory value, rather than try to determine the values by sight and guesswork alone. For the best results, set the Eyedropper tool's Sample Size pop-up to 3-by-3 Average before recoloring.

Get more consistent results by converting to Lab Color before desaturating, then back again. When you desaturate an image, you essentially average the brightness values of each color channel. If an image is predominantly colored with one of the primaries—for example, a bright yellow raincoat—most of the detail is lost when you desaturate the selected element. (This is because the contents of at least one of the color channels is mostly black, which is enough to obscure the detail carried by the remaining channels.)

When this occurs, convert the image to Lab Color mode before choosing Image: Adjust: **Desaturate**, and convert back to the original color mode immediately afterward. This way, the gray levels are based on a single channel, instead of three or four.

H.6

Recoloring an Element: White Original

To apply a darker color to a white original—for example, turning a white shirt red—follow these steps:

1. Select the element you want to recolor. **A**

2. Choose Layer: New: **Layer Via Copy**.

3. Choose Image: Adjust: **Desaturate**. The desaturated product sits in a layer above the rest of the image.

4. Choose Layer: New Fill Layer: **Solid Color**.

5. In the New Layer dialog box, check the Group With Previous Layer box and set the blend mode to Multiply. Click OK to access the color picker.

6. Choose the desired color and click OK. **B**

A *Original image (see color insert).*   **B** *Recolored image (see color insert).*

Depending on the amount of tonal detail in the original element, you may need to give the shadows a boost. If so, follow these steps:

1. Duplicate the layer that contains the desaturated element.

2. Of the two desaturated items in the Layers palette, move the lower one (the one not grouped with the solid color layer) all the way to the top.

3. Set the blend mode of the top-most layer to Multiply.

4. Adjust the Opacity of the top layer until you've attained the desired level of shadow detail. **C D**

C *Shadows layer set to 35% Opacity (see color insert).*

D *Shadows layer set to 70% Opacity (see color insert).*

H.7

Converting a Darker Element to White

One of the most difficult colorizing tasks is to convert a colored element to white. You can't simply desaturate it, because the gray values will look unnatural. You can't ghost the original with a semi-transparent white layer, because you'll obscure the shadows. And you can't make the image too "white," or else you can't place it against a solid white background. Follow these steps:

1. Select the element that you want to recolor. **A**

2. Choose Layer: New: **Layer Via Copy**.

3. Choose Image: Adjust: **Desaturate**. The desaturated product sits in a layer above the rest of the image.

4. In the Layers palette, create two additional copies of the desaturated layer item. **B**

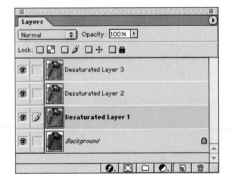

A *The original element*
    (see color insert).

B *Creating three copies of the*
    desaturated element.

5. Activate the desaturated layer on the bottom.

6. Choose Layer: New Fill Layer: **Solid Color**.

7. In the New Layer dialog box, check the Group With Previous Layer box and set the blend mode to Hard Light. Click OK to access the color picker.

8. Enter the following values in the RGB fields: R:230, G:230, B:235. Click OK.

9. Activate the desaturated layer in the middle and set its blend mode to Overlay.

10. Activate the top-most desaturated layer. Set its blend mode to Overlay and its Opacity to 25%. **c**

11. Hide the top-most layer and evaluate the image. If satisfied with the conversion, flatten or merge the layers and continue editing. If the shadows need a boost, reveal the topmost layer and adjust the Opacity until the shadows are acceptable. **D**

As you might imagine, a thoughtfully recorded action makes this technique much easier to handle. (For more information, see *A.10, Recording an Action in Real Time.*)

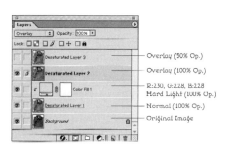

Overlay (50% Op.)
Overlay (100% Op.)
R:230, G:228, B:228
Hard Light (100% Op.)
Normal (100% Op.)
Original Image

c *Setting the necessary blend modes.*

D *Recolored to simulate white (see color insert).*

Issues to Consider

You still have to fine-tune the image. It's impossible to create a single technique that converts every tonal and color combination to realistic white. This technique brings an element *close,* but you'll almost always have to apply a couple of tweaks. For example, you may want a slightly different cast, or you may need to deepen the shadows (by revealing the top-most layer and adjusting its Opacity). For more troublesome conversions, use the following guidelines:

– If you need to deepen the shadow detail more than the available layers allow, duplicate the top-most layer. Fine-tune by adjusting the new copy's Opacity.

– To sharpen the element before flattening, focus on one of the desaturated layers.

H.8

Adding Multiple Colors to B&W Artwork

A popular technique is to use a line art scan as a template for full-color painting. The initial line art scan provides the bold, black lines of the image; the artist adds color using a variety of brushstrokes and painting techniques. As you'll see, the heart of this technique is the ability to convert a flattened, 1-bit line art scan into a full-color file, replacing the original white pixels with transparent space. In this example, I retain the crisp, hard edges of the original line art.

It's best to approach this technique in two phases: Prepping the file for color, and applying the color. To prepare a line art scan to receive color data, follow these steps:

1. Choose a line art original appropriate for colorizing. For the best results, use an image with firmly-defined lines and clean, open spaces. **A**

2. Scan the image at 400 to 450 ppi. This is enough to capture the most important details; the larger pixel sizes will be concealed by the halftoning process when the colored image is output.

3. Prepare the image following the steps listed under *E.7, Optimizing Finely Detailed Line Art.* Make sure the image exists in Bitmap mode before continuing.

4. Choose Image: Mode: **Grayscale**.

5. If preparing the image for print, choose Image: Mode: **CMYK Color**. For an on-screen or web graphic, choose Image: Mode: **RGB Color**.

6. Choose the Magic Eraser tool. In the Options bar, enter 0 in the Tolerance field, and uncheck the Anti-Aliased and Continuous options. 7

7. Click a white image area. Two things happen: First, every white pixel becomes transparent. At the same time, the background layer is converted to an image layer. The image is now ready to receive color. **B**

A *Original line art image.*

B *Making white pixels transparent.*

When adding color, you won't even touch the artwork layer. Instead, add a series of new image layers, one for each color. This approach offers two advantages. First, you can use the artwork as a template while you work, without the possibility of erasing or painting over it. More importantly, you'll be able to edit each color area independently, until you flatten and save the image. Follow these steps:

1. Determine the first area to color. For this example, I'll start with the face and neck.

2. In the Layers palette, click the Create New Layer button to add a blank image layer. Reposition the layer so it sits below the item containing the artwork.

3. Rename the new layer (by holding down the (Option) [Alt] key and double-clicking the layer's palette item). When the Layer Properties dialog box appears, enter a descriptive name, such as "Flesh". **c**

4. In the toolbar, click the Foreground Color swatch. When the Color Picker appears, enter the desired color value. For the best results, choose a CMYK value from a printed swatchbook.

5. Choose the Paintbrush tool. In the Options bar, set the Mode pop-up to Normal and select a brush shape.

6. Paint the target area, using the artwork as a guide. (Make sure the correct layer is active in the Layers palette—if you accidentally paint the artwork layer, stop and immediately choose Edit: **Undo.**) Zoom in as close as needed, overlapping the black lines to create a solid transition. **D**

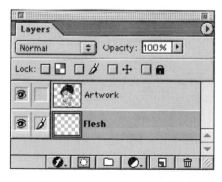

c *A new layer for the new color.*

D *Painting the desired area.*

7. Repeat steps 2 through 6 for each colored area. **E**

8. When editing is complete, choose Layer: **Flatten Image**.

9. Convert the image to CMYK Color (if necessary) and save it as a TIFF. **F**

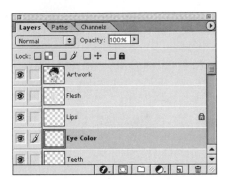

E *Layers used for the remaining colors.*

F *Final colorized image (see color insert).*

This example used solid colors only. (For more information on adding soft shadows and highlights to your brushstrokes, see *2.21, Dodge, Burn & Sponge Tools.*)

Issues to Consider

Create a new layer for every colored area. You should have as many separate layers as you do colored areas, all stacked beneath the original line art. The example contained the following items: "Flesh" (painted with C:5, M:15, Y:20, K:0); "Lips" (C:5, M:25, Y:15, K:0); "Hair" (C:40, M:65, Y:70, K:20); "Eye Color" (C:85, M:0, Y:100, K:0); "Eye Whites" (C:5, M:3, Y:3, K:0); "Teeth" (C:5, M:3, Y:3, K:0); "Shirt" (C:80, M:50, Y:15, K:30). there is also a layer called "Background Info", which contains a graphic element. Because the layers are separate, it is much easier to make and color changes. For example, to change the shirt from blue to red, you can click the "Shirt" layer, check the Preserve Transparency box, and replace the color with an entirely new value. Or, use the Image: Adjust: **Hue/Saturation** command to alter the existing color. In both cases, none of the remaining image information is affected.

H.9
___

Colorizing Line Art: Using Flat vs. Process Black

Whenever you colorize line art (as described under *H.8, Adding Multiple Colors to B&W Artwork*), you must determine the composition of the black lines. You have two choices: *Process black*, which uses at least one additional ink to produce heavier coverage, or *flat black*, which uses only 100% black ink. Both options have strengths and weaknesses.

Process black produces the heaviest black, and the CMY components eliminate any need for trapping. However, the ink coverage may be too high for your target paper stock, particularly if the image contains large black ranges. Also, any on-press misregistration may produce a soft, colored "fringe" around the edges of the black lines. Flat black produces thinner coverage, since only one ink is used. As a result, any underlying brushstrokes may show though, as well as any grain inherent in the paper stock. However, the lighter ink density is far less likely to cause drying or bleed-through problems. Most often, the quality of your paper stock will determine the appropriate black type. If unsure, consult your printer.

Generating Process Black

When you convert a line art image to CMYK Color, Photoshop automatically produces a process black—the black artwork appears as a combination of CMYK inks, with no further adjustments necessary.

The exact component values, however, depend on your color separation settings, as established in the Color Settings dialog box. For example, if your current CMYK settings are Black Generation: Light, Black Ink Limit: 100%, and Total Ink Limit: 300% (Photoshop's default), the default black values are C:73, C:62, Y:61, K:100. If the Total Ink Limit is reduced to 270%, the default black is C:65, M:53, Y:52, K:100. If you need to use a different process black value for your line art, don't try to produce it by adjusting the Color Settings dialog box. Instead, use the techniques listed in the next section to reapply a new value.

B. Generating Flat Black

When recoloring your line work 100% black, you can wait until the very end of the editing stage. Before flattening the image, follow these steps:

1. In the toolbar, click the foreground color swatch. When the Color Picker appears, enter the following values: C:0, M:0, Y:0, K:100. Click OK to close the dialog box.

2. In the Layers palette, click the item that contains the original artwork.

3. Hold down the (Command) [Control] key and click the same layer item. The black information is surrounded with a selection.

4. Press (Option) [Alt]-Delete to fill the selection with the foreground color.

At this point, the black lines knock out the underlying colors. Only 100% black will be used to reproduce the lines, which may result in visible gaps if the color plates misregister on-press (especially if the colors used in the surrounding areas contain no black components). To avoid this, many users force the 100% black to overprint. This way, wherever the underlying brush-strokes fall beneath the black lines, a trap is produced; where there is no underlying color—such as the middle of a larger black range—it remains flat. Follow these steps:

1. In the Layers palette, activate the artwork layer.

2. Choose Multiply from the palette's Mode pop-up. **A B**

The artwork will not appear to change on screen; however, if you examine the values in the Info palette, you're able to detect the underlying components.

A *Flat black artwork, knocking out underlying colors (see color insert).*

B *Flat black artwork, overprinting (see color insert).*

H.10

Colorizing Line Art: Using an Anti-Aliased Template

The steps of *H.8, Adding Multiple Colors to B&W Artwork* describe how to add color to a line art file while keeping the edges of the artwork hard and crisp. Depending on the intended use of the image, however, you may benefit from a different approach. Instead of keeping the edges hard—which requires a higher image resolution—you can anti-alias the edges before colorizing it. This way, you can edit the file at lower resolutions, retain the essence of the original line art, and add a smooth transition between the black information and the new colors. Follow these steps:

1. Choose a line art original appropriate for colorizing. For the best results, use an image with firmly-defined lines and clean, open spaces. **A**

2. Scan the image at the standard line art resolution: 800-1200 ppi.

3. Optimize the image following the steps described under *E.7, Optimizing Finely Detailed Line Art.* Make sure the image exists in Bitmap mode before continuing.

4. Choose Image: Mode: **Grayscale**.

5. Choose the Magic Eraser tool. In the Options bar, enter 0 in the Tolerance field, and uncheck the Anti-Aliased and Continuous options.

6. Click a white image area. When you do, two things happen. First, every white pixel becomes transparent. At the same time, the background layer is converted to an image layer. **B**

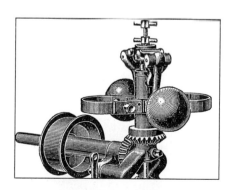

A *Original line art image.*

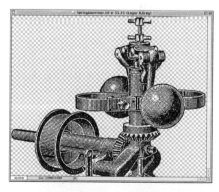

B *Converting white pixels to transparency.*

7. Choose Image: **Image Size**.

8. In the Image Size dialog box, check the Resample Image box, which enables you to change the resolution without affecting Width and Height.

9. In the Resolution field, enter the desired value. For example, change 1200 ppi to 300 ppi, the standard resolution used for full-color print-oriented images. **C**

10. Click OK to downsample the image. As the pixels are re-interpolated, Photoshop automatically adds a degree of anti-aliasing to the artwork edges. Because the artwork is surrounded by transparent pixels, the semi-transparent transition is not polluted by any other color information. This way, when you add new layers beneath the artwork and use the Paintbrush tool to apply new color values, the edges blend smoothly. **D**

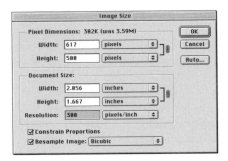

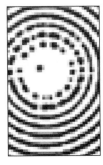

C *Re-interpolating the image.*

D *Artwork edges before (left) and after anti-aliasing.*

11. Choose Image: Mode: CMYK **Color**.

12. Continue colorizing the image, following the steps described in the second portion of *H.8, Adding Multiple Colors to B&W Artwork*. **E F**

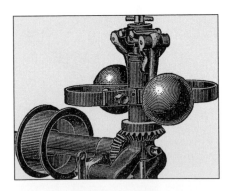

E *Colorized line art with hard edges (see color insert).*

F *Colorized line art with anti-aliased edges (see color insert).*

Issues to Consider

Don't worry about reducing the resolution. Ordinarily, line art must exist at a high resolution in order to output properly. When using this technique, some people hesitate to reduce the resolution, fearing that they'll lose important image detail. For the most part, they shouldn't be concerned. True, the resolution is lowered, but the artwork no longer exists as a 1-bit file. Just like the edges, the rest of the image will be anti-aliased during re-interpolation, retaining the appearance of fine detail. If necessary, you can apply the Unsharp Mask filter to the artwork layer after reducing the resolution. Use relatively low values (for example, A:75%, R:1.0, T:8), and keep an eye on the edges. If you sharpen the image too much, the anti-aliasing will degrade.

This technique prepares a line art scan for blending with other images. Normally, adding line art to a full-color image poses certain problems. The resolutions are quite different, which results in sizing discrepancies. Line art is not automatically anti-aliased, which may cause jagged transitions along the edges. Some people simply convert the image to Grayscale mode and drag the layer into an existing color file, only to grapple with the white pixels that carry over. By using the above technique, you can scan and optimize a line art original, add transparent pixels, match the resolution to the target file, and produce a smooth, anti-aliased edge, all before you add the artwork to another image.

H.11

Using Spot Inks to Colorize Line Art

You can use spot channels to apply custom inks to a line art image, similar to coloring shapes in Illustrator or FreeHand. Instead of clicking a shape to color, however, you must use one of two techniques: Apply the spot color using brushstrokes, or fill a series of selections. Either way, it requires interaction between the black artwork and the spot color channel.

If the artwork does not consist of solid, firmly defined lines, you're better off painting in the color. Follow these steps:

1. Open the image that contains the artwork. For the best results, it should start as an optimized line art scan. (For more information, see *E.7, Optimizing Finely Detailed Line Art.*) ▲

2. If necessary, use the Image Size command to reduce the resolution to 300 ppi. (For more information, see *C.8, Downsampling an Image.*)

3. Choose Image: Mode: **Grayscale**.

4. Choose New Spot Channel from the Channels palette submenu. In the New Spot Channel dialog box, specify the ink required for your project.

5. Choose the Paintbrush tool. In the Options bar, select an appropriately sized anti-aliased brush shape.

6. Press the "D" key to set the foreground color to black. (Even though you're applying spot color information, understand that you're painting a channel. Therefore, applying 100% black is the same as applying 100% of the spot ink.)

7. In the Channels palette, click the spot color channel.

8. Paint the desired area, using the artwork as a guide. (You're not restricted to applying a 100% value of the ink. To apply a tint, use the Color palette to reduce the level of black to the desired screen value.) **B**

9. When finished, save the image as a Photoshop DCS 2.0 file. **C**

A *Original image.*

B *Painting the spot channel to add color*

C *The final image: two inks, multiple tints*

When the artwork consists of heavy, solid lines, you don't have to use the Paintbrush tool. Instead, follow these steps:

1. Open the desired image and convert it to a Grayscale file. **D**

2. Create the necessary spot color channel.

3. Choose the Magic Wand tool. In the Options bar, check the Anti-aliased and Contiguous boxes.

4. In the Channels palette, click the Gray item.

5. In the image, click the white areas you want to color. **E**

6. Because the Magic Wand tool may not include all of the edge information (and because you want to underprint the black lines just a little bit, to add a level of trapping), choose Select: Modify: **Expand**. In the Expand dialog box, enter a value of 1 and click OK. The selection outline expands into the artwork by one pixel.

7. In the Color palette, specify the desired tint.

8. In the Channels palette, click the spot ink channel.

9. Fill the selection. (As a shortcut, press (Option) [Alt]-Delete.)

10. Repeat steps 4 through 9 until the image is fully colorized. When finished, save the image as a Photoshop DCS 2.0 file. **F**

D *Original image.*

E *Selecting the areas to color.*

F *The final image: two inks, multiple tints*

Issues to Consider

Working around a DCS 2.0-unfriendly workflow. If your workflow cannot successfully separate DCS 2.0 files, you can still use this technique. After creating and adjusting the spot color channels, copy the data of each one, pasting it into a channel in a CMYK Color image. If done properly, you can output the image just like any other CMYK file, and provide the necessary stripping instructions to your printer. (For more information, see *J.12 Converting a Spot Channel Duotone into a Process-Plate Duotone.*)

H.12
Creating a Ghosted Image

When you ghost an image, you fill all or part of it with semi-opaque white. A popular technique involves ghosting part of a Grayscale or color image, then laying text over it in your page layout program. The faded area appears to be part of the image—you can still see the pixels that comprise the overall graphic—but they're light enough so the text remains legible.

Most often, a ghost is described by the amount of information that remains in the image. For example, a "20% ghost," uses a white area with an opacity value of 80%. Ghosts usually range from 30% to 10%, and the value you use depends on the underlying image. Darker images require a ghost around 10%–15%. If you're ghosting a lighter image, high opacity values tend to blow out highlight detail—set a ghost to 20%–30%. **A**

    30% Ghost   20% Ghost   10% Ghost

A   *Ghosts are defined by how much underlying information shows through the semi-opaque white area. For example, a "20% ghost" uses an opacity value of 80%.*

To create a ghost, follow these steps:

1. Open the image you want to ghost.

2. Create an empty image layer by choosing Layer: New: **Layer** (or by clicking the "Create New Layer" button in the Layers palette).

3. Select the area you want to ghost by dragging a rectangle with the Marquee tool (or drag a vector-based shape with the Rectangle tool). The ghost's dimensions are often determined ahead of time; if so, choose View: **Show Rulers** and refer to the values in the Info palette as you create the selection. If you intend to ghost the entire image, don't make a selection.

4. Fill the selection with white. The quickest way to do this is to reset the default colors (by pressing "D"), then press (Command-Delete) [Control-Backspace].

5. In the Layers palette, set the Opacity slider to the desired value.

6. Use the Info palette to examine the ghosted area, making sure that no values have blown out to 0%.

7. Flatten the image and save.

H.13

Creating a Resizable Ghost

Once you've created a ghost, the only way to change its position in the image is to produce the effect all over again. If you want the ability to change the orientation of a ghosted area after you've imported the image into a page layout, follow these steps:

1. In Photoshop, open the image you want to ghost.

2. Duplicate the image by choosing Image: **Duplicate**.

3. Close the original image.

4. In the duplicate, apply a ghost to the entire image, following the steps described in the previous technique.

5. Save the ghosted image. Add "ghost" or "gh" to the file name to make sure you don't overwrite the original image.

6. In your page layout program, place and position the original, unghosted image.

7. Import the ghosted image, placing it exactly on top of the original. In QuarkXPress, apply the Item: **Step and Repeat** command to the original image (using no vertical or horizontal offsets), and import the ghosted image into the new picture box. In PageMaker, place the ghosted image, then align the two using the Element: **Align** command. In InDesign, place the image and align the two using the Align palette.

8. Crop the ghosted image to the desired dimensions. As long as you don't move the image, you can change its orientation by using your layout program's cropping functions to manipulate the image edges.

9. When gathering files for final output, make sure you supply both the original and the ghosted image. Many people fail to supply the ghost—if this happens, you'll either get a call from the service bureau, or the image will output at 72 ppi.

Silhouetting Techniques

The following techniques describe the most popular methods of isolating part of an image into its own layer. Unless stated otherwise, they're not industry-specific—you can safely apply the steps no matter how you intend to use the image. Once an element is extracted, though, the next move depends on your plans for the image:

- If preparing a standard silhouette for print purposes, choose Image: **Flatten Image** to convert the transparent pixels to white, then save the image as a TIFF. (If preparing a clipping path, save the image as a Photoshop EPS.)

- If preparing the image as a Web graphic, use the File: **Save For Web** command to create a transparent GIF or PNG.

- If planning to combine the element with other image information, leave the layer alone and continue editing.

One piece of advice: When creating any kind of silhouette, it's always best to work on a high-resolution image. Isolate the desired element at 300 ppi whenever possible, even if you ultimately downsample an image to a 72 ppi web graphic. This way, you're able to work with as much detail as possible, ensuring the best results.

I.1

Creating a Simple Silhouette

Most often, a silhouette (or "silo") is a simple shape with hard edges, such as a boat, a wagon-wheel, or a product shot for a catalog. Lifting the element from the surrounding pixels is as easy as drawing a decent selection. Follow these steps:

1. Open the image that contains the desired element. If the image is a new scan, make sure it is already corrected and adjusted for the target printing method. **A**

2. Use the Crop tool to trim away as much of the unwanted surrounding area as possible, making sure you don't clip the element. **B**

A *Original image.*

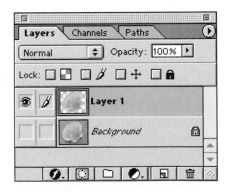

B *Cropped image.*

3. Create a selection outline around the desired element. (See ***Issues to Consider***, below.) **C**

4. Once the selection is complete, choose Layer: New: **Layer Via Copy** to lift the element into a new image layer. **D**

C *Selected element.*

D *Element in new layer.*

5. Preview the silhouette by hiding the underlying layer that contained the original image. You should see only the isolated element, surrounded by transparent pixels. (See *Issues to Consider*, below.) **E**

6. If the selection wasn't perfect—if it included any of the surrounding pixels or shaved off any information you wanted to use—delete the new image layer and try again.

7. If the silhouette is satisfactory, delete the hidden original layer.

8. Continue preparing the image for its target destination. (See *Issues to Consider*, below.) **F**

E *Previewing the silo.*   **F** *Final silhouette.*

Issues to Consider

Use a path to outline the element. When creating a simple silo, many people use the Lasso tool to draw the selection. However, success with this tool relies a little too much on patience, hand-eye coordination, and plain luck. For the most flexible selections, use the Pen tool: You can refine the shape of your outlines as needed, and reload them at will. When using a path, convert it to a selection by (Command) [Control]-clicking its item in the Paths palette.

Try using a vector mask. Photoshop 6 offers new flexibility when you outline the targeted element with a path. Instead of converting the path to a selection (as described above), choose Layer: Add Vector Mask: **Current Path**. The element is masked, rather like a real-time clipping path, and its edges are hidden or revealed as you refine the outline.

Understand paths versus clipping paths. If you use a path while creating a silo, don't attempt to re-use it later as a clipping path. If you do, the anti-aliased edge of the isolated element will be visible along the edge of the vector-based mask. To use the same element as a silhouette and a clipping path, save a copy of the image after creating the path, but before creating the silo. (For more information, see *I.10 Creating a Clipping Path.*)

Updating your methods. Many users still apply silhouetting techniques that date back to Photoshop 2.5 and earlier. First, they select the element using the Lasso tool, choose Select: **Inverse** to activate the surrounding pixels, then fill the background with white. Or, they use the same tool to select part of the surrounding pixels, press the Delete key to fill the selection with white, and continue all the way around the element. While these methods can indeed produce a viable silhouette, they provide precious little room for error. By using the above techniques, you can instantly review a silo's quality without compromising the original image. It also becomes much easier to apply additional effects, such as a drop shadow.

I.2
___

Creating a Vignette

A *vignette* is a silhouette with at least one edge that fades to white. (In conventional prepress, the term also applied to a simple gradient that fades to white.) The most popular example is a soft-edged, oval-shaped portrait, similar to a late-19th century photographic technique. Although there are several ways to produce this effect in Photoshop, the most successful use layer masks. Follow these steps:

1. Open an image with adequate space around the desired element. If the image is cropped too closely, you may cut off part of the soft edge. **A**

2. If the image exists as a background layer, convert it to an image layer. Double-click its item in the Layers palette, then click OK in the Make Layer dialog box. **B**

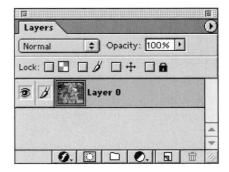

A *Original image.*

B *Converted background layer.*

3. Draw a selection around the subject. In this example, I used the Elliptical Marquee tool. **C**

4. Choose Layer: Add Layer Mask: **Reveal Selection**. The contents of the selection are masked with a hard edge. **D**

C *Selected element.*   **D** *New layer mask.*

5. In the Layers palette, click the layer mask thumbnail (it should be selected by default immediately after creating the layer mask).

6. Choose Filter: Blur: **Gaussian Blur**. This command softens the edges of the layer mask, producing the vignette effect. Higher blur values produce softer edges, but the exact value will depend on your personal preference and the image's resolution. **E**

7. Continue preparing the image for its target destination. **F**

E *Blurred layer mask.*   **F** *Final vignette.*

Issues to Consider

Fine-tune the image's position. After creating the layer mask and applying the blur, you may decide that the subject isn't positioned exactly the way you want within the soft edges. To move the image independently, unlink the mask by off-clicking the Link icon in the Layers palette. Select the Move tool and either drag the image or nudge it with the arrow keys.

Update your methods. When many users create a vignette, they simply draw a selection, apply a Select: **Feather** value, then lift the selection into a new layer (or invert the selection and fill it with white). True, the effect is often identical to the technique described, but the process is much less flexible. You cannot preview different levels of edge softness, and if you're unsatisfied with the result, you have to discard your efforts and start over. The layer mask enables you to edit the effect separate from the image, then combine the two at the very end.

Flexographic concerns. Vignettes are not usually appropriate for flexo-graphic printing, the process used by packaging manufacturers and many newspapers. Flexo tends to suffer from strong dot gain in the highlight areas, making it difficult to create a soft fade without a harsh break appearing along the edge. For the best results, don't fade to white. Use a hard-edged silo, fade off the edge of the page, or fade into at least a 10% tint. Otherwise, plan to use a different effect.

I.3

"Painting" a Vignette by Hand

You don't have to base a vignette on a selection outline. Many users prefer to use manual brushstrokes to shape the edges, using the Paintbrush tool on a layer mask. Follow these steps:

1. Open the image you want to vignette. **A**

2. Convert the background layer to an image layer by double-clicking it in the Layers palette.

3. Choose Layer: Add Layer Mask: **Reveal All**. The image doesn't appear to change, but a blank layer mask is now visible in the Layers palette.

4. Choose the Paintbrush tool.

5. Select a soft-edged brush in the brush picker—larger and softer brushes produce softer edges in the vignette.

6. Press the D key to set the foreground color to black.

7. Paint away the image areas that you want to remove. Doing so replaces them with transparent pixels. (To reveal a hidden part of the image, switch the foreground color to white—by pressing the X key—and paint over the area.) **B**

8. Continue preparing the image for its target destination. **C**

A *Original image.*

B *Hiding unwanted image pixels.*

C *Final vignette.*

Issues to Consider

Don't accidentally paint the image When painting a layer mask, make sure the layer mask thumbnail is highlighted. Otherwise, you'll apply the foreground color directly to the image.

For the best results, use the same brush shape. Using different brush sizes on the same vignette—especially if you're hiding and revealing different parts of the image—may result in irregular, uneven edges.

Add an underlying white layer for contrast. The checkerboard pattern that appears as you add the transparent areas makes it a little hard to evaluate your work. Before you start painting the layer mask, try the following: Create a new layer, fill it with white, and position it underneath the vignette layer. This way, as you create the vignette, you reveal only white pixels. (If necessary, change the color of the underlying layer for better contrast.) When finished, delete the underlying layer and continue editing.

This method is not appropriate for hard-edged silhouettes. This approach only works when adding soft edges. Although it's possible to paint a hard-edged silo, it's much easier in the long run to base the effect on a selection technique.

I.4

Creating a Silhouette with Hard and Soft Edges

To create a silhouette that involves hard- and soft-edge detail, follow these steps:

1. Open the image you want to silhouette. If it has been flattened, convert the background layer to an image layer. **A**

2. Draw an anti-aliased selection around the desired element. (Leave extra space around the areas that will receive the soft edge.)

3. Choose Layer: Add Layer Lask: **Reveal Selection**. The selected element appears as a hard-edged silhouette. **B**

A *Original image.*   **B** *Creating the hard-edged silo.*

4. Choose the Paintbrush tool.

5. Select a soft-edged brush and set the foreground color to black.

6. Making sure the layer mask thumbnail is active in the Layers palette, paint away the unwanted image information. **C**

7. Continue preparing the image for its target destination. **D**

C *Adding the soft edge.*   **D** *Final silhouette.*

I.5

Creating a Complex Silhouette (Hair)

When an image element contains fine edge detail, such as hair or the nap of a sweater, it may be impossible to include them in a simple selection outline. Here, you have three choices. First, if the details aren't essential, exclude them from the selection and follow the steps described in the previous technique. Second, you can use a mask channel to select the element with a complex outline. (For more information, see *I.7, Creating a Complex Silhouette: Tree.*) Third, you can use the Image: **Extract** command, which does a reasonable job of isolating detailed edges. Follow these steps:

1. Open an image already scanned and adjusted for print. For the best results, the edge detail should appear in high contrast against the background pixels. **A**

2. Choose Image: **Extract**.

3. In the Extract dialog box, use the Edge Highlighter tool to target the edge of the element. Don't try to paint the exact details. Instead, for wispy details (like the fur in this example), use a larger brush size to include the detail area as well as the surrounding pixels. For harder edges (like the dog's ears and nose), use a smaller brush size to define the area more precisely. Change the brush size on-the-fly by moving the Brush Size slider in the dialog box. **B**

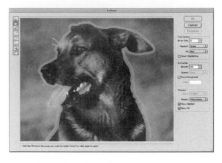

A *Original image.*   **B** *Highlighting the edges.*

4. After highlighting the entire outer edge, choose the Paint Bucket tool in the dialog box and click inside the highlighted area. This defines the primary element of the silhouette. **C**

5. Under the Extraction controls, set a value using the Smooth slider. This determines how accurately the edge details are lifted from the surrounding pixels. Start with a low value, gradually increasing it if necessary.

6. Click the Preview button to evaluate the extraction. If any pixels are being excluded, or if the edge detail is retaining too much of the background pixels, increase the Smooth value or edit the mask. You can edit and preview the image as many times as needed. **D**

C *Filling the highlighted element.*   **D** *Previewing the extraction.*

7. When the silhouette is satisfactory, click OK to apply the Extract command. The element appears in the same layer, but is now surrounded by transparent pixels. **E**

8. Examine the element at 100% magnification to see if the edges require additional refining. If they do, refer to *I.4, Cleaning an Extracted Silhouette.* If not, continue preparing the image for its target destination. **F**

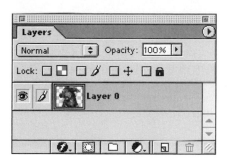

E *Extracted element in new layer.*   **F** *Final silhouette.*

Issues to Consider

Extract command tips. Successfully executing this technique depends on how well you can manipulate the tools in the Extract dialog box. Keep the following techniques in mind:

- Always use a smaller brush size to define hard edges. If you don't, the edges may drop out or include fringe pixels when you apply the command. Use larger brush sizes only when highlighting complex, highly-detailed edges.

- When extracting a clearly-defined element, always make sure it is completely enclosed by the Edge Highlighter tool. When an element touches the image boundaries, you don't have to highlight the edges—you only have to highlight to the edge.

- To remove highlighted edge pixels, paint them with the Eraser tool. You can also erase the highlight by (Option) [Alt]-painting with the Edge Highlighter tool.

- Use Photoshop's standard zoom and scroll shortcuts in the Extract dialog box. To zoom in, hold down the (Control) [Command] key and the spacebar, and click the image. To zoom out, hold down the (Option-Command) [Alt-Control] keys and the spacebar, and click the image. To scroll around, hold down the spacebar and drag.

- To preview the extraction against a colored background, set a color in the Show pop-up, in the Preview section of the dialog box. To see how the image will appear as a silhouette, choose White Matte. If the pixels are too light to see clearly, choose Gray Matte or Black Matte.

Preserve the original layer. The Extract command edits the contents of the currently active image layer. If you want to preserve this data for future edits, duplicate the layer before choosing Image: **Extract**.

I.6

Cleaning an Extracted Silhouette

More often than not, the Extract command gets close, but doesn't go all the way. For example, if the element colors share any similar values to the background pixels—particularly in the harder edges—the command may exclude them. Also, if the Smooth value was set too low, it may have included fringe pixels that you need to erase. After examining the extraction, use the following techniques, depending on what you find.

Restoring Excluded Pixels

The most common problem with an extraction is that parts of the image are dropped out. The easiest way to restore them is to use the History Brush tool. By default, the History palette retains a snapshot of the image in its original form. The History Brush tool enables you to re-apply this information, painting it onto the current layer like any other color. Follow these steps:

1. Zoom in and target the area you want to restore. A magnification of 200–400% usually works best. **A**

2. Choose the History Brush tool.

3. In the Options bar, choose a brush type that matches the information you're trying to restore. If you're refining a hard edge, choose an anti-aliased brush. If you're refining a softer edge, choose a feathered brush.

4. Paint in small strokes from the existing image outward, making sure you don't include any of the original background pixels. As you paint over the excluded areas, their original content is restored. **B**

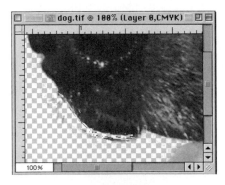
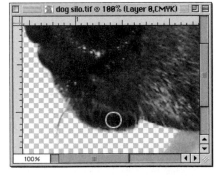

A *Targeting excluded pixels.*　　　　　**B** *Restoring the pixels.*

Issues to Consider

Preparing for the History Brush. If you've changed an image's color mode, dimensions, or resolution since it was opened, you won't be able to use the default snapshot in the History palette. When this is the case, you must create a new snapshot before extracting the silhouette. Do two things: Choose New Snapshot from the History palette submenu, then immediately click the paint box next to its palette item. This way, you can use the History Brush tool to restore any missing pixels from the extracted image. If desired, give yourself an extra layer of flexibility by taking another snapshot immediately after creating the extraction. This way, you're able to target both versions in the History palette.

Be ready to undo your brushstrokes. You'll find it all too easy to expose some of the original background colors when using the History Brush. When this happens, choose Edit: **Undo** immediately, keep an eye on the desired boundary, and try again. This is the most important reason to use small, quick brushstrokes. If you paint in long lines, a single undo may negate several inches of delicate work.

Erasing Unwanted Pixels

Perhaps using the Exclude command included some of the background pixels; maybe it masked some of the detailed edges poorly, and you simply want to remove parts of it altogether. Whatever the case, you'll probably need to remove unwanted information from an extraction. Follow these steps:

1. Zoom in and target the area you want to edit. A magnification of 200–400% usually works best. **A**

2. Choose the Eraser tool.

3. In the Options bar, set Paintbrush in the Mode pop-up menu.

4. To produce a hard edge, choose an anti-aliased brush. To produce a feathered edge, choose a soft-edged brush.

5. Paint in small strokes, moving toward the existing image, making sure you don't accidentally erase any part of the silhouette you want to keep. **B**

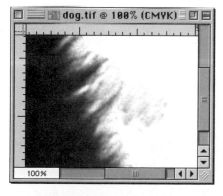

A *Targeting unwanted pixels.*

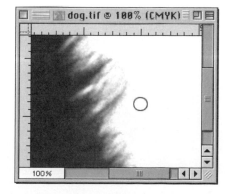

B *Erasing the pixels.*

Issues to Consider

Use a temporary high-contrast background. Some stray pixels may be too light to see on screen, but will be visible after the image is imported and printed. If necessary, create a new image layer, positioning it underneath the silhouette. Fill it with black to emphasize the errant pixels. Delete this layer when your editing is complete.

Try the Background Eraser tool. The standard Eraser tool works best when the unwanted information stands out clearly from the desired extraction. When the unwanted pixels are intermingled with the extraction, making it more difficult to retain the edge detail, use the Background Eraser to remove pixels of a specific color range.

I.7

Creating a Complex Silhouette (Tree)

When an element is too complex for the Extract command, you can usually isolate it using the information found in one or more of its color channels. In this example, I want to remove a detailed tree from its background. This technique is similar to *B.22 Creating a Complex Mask*, but with a couple of twists. Follow these steps:

1. Open the image that contains the desired element. For the best results, it should appear on a high-contrast background. It also helps if the colors of the element differ considerably from the surrounding pixels. (For example, it's easier to isolate a predominantly red element from a blue background, as opposed to a light blue element.) **A**

2. In the Channels palette, examine the contents of each color channel. Locate the one with the greatest contrast between the targeted element and the surrounding pixels. In this example, it's the yellow channel. **B**

A   *Original image.*

B   *Color channels (clockwise from upper left: C, M, Y, K).*

3. Convert the color channel to an alpha channel (drag it directly onto the Create New Channel button in the Channels palette).

4. Make sure the new alpha channel is active in the Channels palette—it's easy to edit the original color channel by mistake.

5. Choose Filter: Sharpen: **Unsharp Mask**. This command will better define the edges of the masking element. Enter a value high enough to create a slight halo around the element, but not so high that detail is obliterated. (In this example, the values were A: 120%, R: 5, T: 18.) **C**

6. Choose Image: Adjust: **Levels** to reduce the number of gray levels in the alpha channel. The goal is to produce as much white in the background and black in the image as possible. For best results, move the shadow and highlight sliders toward the center of the histogram. Pay attention to the edge detail, making sure it stays consistent with the targeted image. Click OK when finished. **D**

C *Alpha channel detail before (l) and after sharpening*

D *Adding contrast using Levels.*

7. Use the Lasso and Eraser tools to touch up the mask channel, removing any lingering gray ranges or stray pixels. **E**

8. Click the composite item in the Channels palette to return to the full-color image.

9. Convert the alpha channel to a selection by (Command) [Control]-clicking the item in the Channels palette. **F**

10. In my example, the tree and ground are masked, leaving the sky selected. If you need to reverse the selection, choose Select: **Inverse**.

11. Choose Layer: New: **Layer Via Copy** to lift the selected element into a new image layer.

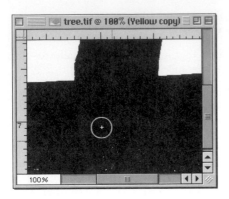

E *Touching up the alpha channel.*

F *Alpha channel converted to selection.*

12. Hide or delete the layer that contained the original image. **G**

14. Assess the silo and perform any additional edits. (For example, I may have wanted to remove the grass from around the base of the tree, or apply a Layer Style.)

15. Delete the alpha channel when you've finished with it (click it in the Channels palette and choose Delete Channel from the palette submenu).

16. Continue preparing the image for its target destination. **H**

G *Isolated element.*

H *Final silhouette.*

Issues to Consider

Test the silo on screen before flattening. When assessing the quality of your silhouette, it helps to compare it to the original image layer. Of course, when the new silo layer sits above the original, you can't really tell the difference between the two. Try inserting a new layer filled with white beneath the silo. This way, when you view the silo and white layers, they appear the same as a flattened image. When you hide them, you can view the original image. You don't have to delete any new layers before flattening the image—just make sure the silo sits above a white or transparent background before applying the flatten command.

Using the Clone tool to avoid fringe pixels. Depending on the type of image detail (and the contrast of the target color channel), this technique may result in a thin, colored fringe around the edge of the silhouette. When this happens, step back to before the element was lifted to a new layer. Before loading the selection, use the Clone tool to expand the colors of the target element into the surrounding pixels. (Be heavy-handed; if silhouetting thin strands of hair, cover the wisps entirely with samples of the model's head.) It may look bad at first, but when you load the selection and copy it to a new layer, the thin details will blend more successfully.

Downsample the image to anti-alias the edges. One of the drawbacks to this technique is that it's based on a hard-edged selection. Therefore, the edges of the silhouette are jagged and pixelated, instead of smooth and anti-aliased. If you reproduce the image at a high enough linescreen, the edges will likely be visible. You can add a degree of anti-aliasing by using the Image Size command to re-interpolate the image pixels, which slightly blurs the edge detail. For the best results, reduce the image dimensions (if possible) while maintaining the same resolution. If you can't reduce the size, reduce the resolution by 30 or 40 ppi while maintaining the same dimensions. Depending on the degree of resizing, you may need to add a small Unsharp Mask adjustment. (For more information, see *C.8, Downsampling an Image.*)

I.8

Overprinting a Grayscale Silhouette

A common technique involves forcing a grayscale silhouette to overprint a solid colored area (the effect is sort of a low-end duotone). Many people try to specify the overprint in their layout program by applying a trap command to either the silo or a colored box. However, the results are unpredictable at best:

- You can't preview the effect on screen. You have to output proofs to a high-end color printer, and even then, it may not give you an accurate representation of how the image will appear on-press.

- If the underlying color contains black, the silo will not overprint completely. It will overprint the cyan, magenta, and yellow inks, but knock out the underlying black information, producing an obvious color shift.

- Many proprietary pagination workflows are not designed to handle this type of trapping manipulation. If the command is discarded by your dedicated software, the entire silhouette knocks out.

Most often, the image overprints a tint of one process ink (such as Y:30) or two (such as C:20, M:20). Although you'll convert the Grayscale image to CMYK, it is important that the gray tones exist solely on the black channel—if you simply convert by choosing Image: Mode: CMYK **Color**, the tones are distributed through all four channels, which results in problematic color shifts. Follow these steps:

1. Open the Grayscale image that contains the desired element. If the image is a new scan, make sure it is corrected and adjusted for the target printing method before continuing. **A**

2. Silhouette the element, lifting it into a new image layer. (Depending on the image, follow the steps listed in *I.1, I.2,* or *I.3.*) **B**

A *Original image.*   **B** *Element in new layer.*

3. Choose Layer: **Flatten Image**. **C**

4. In the toolbar, set the foreground/background colors to the default values (press the D key).

5. Choose Select: **All**.

6. Choose Edit: **Cut**.

7. Choose Image: Mode: CMYK **Color**.

8. In the Channels palette, click the black channel.

9. Choose Edit: **Paste**. This way, the tonal information appears only on the black plate. **D**

10. In the Channels palette, click the composite CMYK channel.

11. In the Toolbar, click the foreground color swatch to open the color picker.

12. In this example, the silo will overprint a 30% yellow screen. In the CMYK fields, enter C:0, M:0, Y:30, K:0. Click OK.

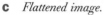

C *Flattened image.*

D *Pasting into the black channel.*

13. Choose Edit: Fill. In the Fill dialog box, set the Use pop-up to Foreground Color, and the Mode pop-up to Multiply. Click OK. **E**

14 Save the image as a TIFF. **F**

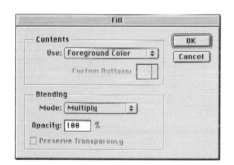

E *Fill dialog box settings.*

F *The overprinting silhouette (see color insert).*

Issues to Consider

A common newsprint technique. This effect is often found in publications that use "colored" stock, such as telephone directories or special newspaper inserts. The stock itself is actually white; it's cheaper to color the paper by laying down a light screen during the press run, especially during high-volume jobs. Here, it's particularly important to place the Grayscale data entirely on the black plate. First, many of these publications are printed using only two inks: the stock color and black. Second, if the halftone is converted to CMYK data, the ink density may be too much for the target stock, resulting in bleed-through or overlong drying times.

Keep an eye on the channels palette. If you don't target the black channel before pasting the silhouette, Photoshop distributes the tonal data over all four channels. If you see any information appear in the cyan, magenta, or yellow channel thumbnails, choose Undo, click the black channel, and paste again.

Handling large numbers of images. If you need to apply this technique to a large number of images—say, 20 or more—it's possible to streamline the process by creating a temporary CMYK conversion table. In the Edit: **Color Settings** dialog box, choose Custom from the CMYK pop-up (under Working Spaces). When the Custom CMYK dialog box appears, set the Black Generation pop-up to Maximum. This way, whenever you convert a Grayscale silhouette to CMYK, all the tonal data automatically appears in the black channel. Remember to restore the original CMYK setting when you've finished.

Add the color using a separate layer. To add a level of editing flexibility, don't use the Fill command to add the color. Instead, create a new layer above the silhouette and fill it with the desired CMYK values. In the Layers palette, set the blend mode to Multiply. The initial effect is the same, but you're able to independently adjust the silhouette's layer. When your editing is complete, flatten the image and save it as a TIFF.

Overprinting a clipped element. It's easy to apply this technique to an image masked with a clipping path. Instead of isolating the Grayscale element in a new layer (steps 1–3, above), surround it with a vector-based outline, and set the item as a clipping path. Follow steps 4–12 to convert the image to CMYK and add the background color, then save the file as a Photoshop EPS.

Make sure the background colors are the same. The entire point of this technique is to keep the background color consistent from image to layout document. Unless they're identical, the differences will be quite apparent after the press run. If the background color changes in the layout document, there's no way to automatically update the image. If the possibility of change exists, save a copy of the original Grayscale silhouette without the added color.

I.9

Adding a Drop Shadow to a Silhouette

Silhouettes often receive a drop shadow, which adds a bit of depth to the element on the printed page. Structurally speaking, a shadowed silhouette is the same as a vignette; both contain soft edges, both are subject to the same positioning limitations. The only difference is how and when you apply the soft edge.

Follow these steps:

1. Open the image that will cast the shadow.

2. Silhouette the element, lifting it into a new image layer.

3. Delete the original layer.

4. Choose Layer: Layer Style: **Drop Shadow**.

5. Add the desired drop shadow beneath the image. **A**

6. If the shadow is unsatisfactory, double-click the silo's item in the Layers palette to re-access the Layer Style dialog box. If you're happy with the shadow, continue editing. **B**

A *Extracted layer with shadow.*   **B** *Final silhouette.*

I.10

Creating a Clipping Path

If you intend to stack an imported image over other items in a page layout, silhouettes pose a problem. Because you've surrounded the image with white pixels, they obscure any information that sits underneath. If you want to produce the *effect* of a silhouette, but be able to place the image over a colored background in your layout document, you must use a vector-based mask called a *clipping path*. By encircling the desired element with a Photoshop path, your layout program will only recognize the pixels inside the path, and ignore any other information. Follow these steps:

1. Use the Pen tool to trace the desired element with a path (For more information, see *L.1, Drawing a Basic Path*.) **A**

2. Save the path. (Double-click its item in the Paths palette to access the Save Path dialog box.)

3. Choose Clipping Path from the Paths palette submenu.

4. In the Clipping Path dialog box, set the saved item in the Path pop-up menu. **B**

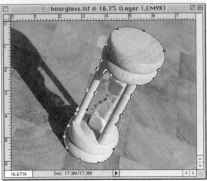

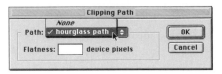

A *Element traced with path.*   **B** *Setting the clipping path.*

5. Save the image as a Photoshop EPS file. (If you save it as a TIFF, the clipping path command will not take effect.)

6. Import the image into your page layout. **c**

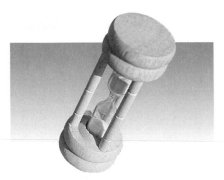

c *The clipped element placed over a gradient (in an XPress document).*

Issues to Consider

Crop the image. Even though your output device will only print the info inside the path, it still has to process any masked pixels. Crop the unwanted image info before creating the path, making sure you don't trim the edges of the targeted element. If you need to retain the entire image for future use, save a copy of it before cropping.

Use a closed path. If you define an open path as a clipping path, the two endpoints are automatically connected by a straight line, which will likely exclude part of the image you want to use. For the best results, start and finish your path on the same point.

Avoid fringe pixels. If the path falls beyond the shape of the target image, the background colors will be visible when you print the file. Avoid this problem by cutting the path at least two or three pixels into the element you're masking.

Use simple paths. Paths that contain an extremely large number of points take longer to output, and in certain environments—particularly in work-flows using older laser printers—they may not print at all. A common mistake is to draw a selection, then convert it to an outline using the Paths palette's Make Work Path command. Far more often than not, a manually-drawn path contains fewer points (and causes fewer output-oriented problems) than any path created using automatic commands.

Clipping multiple items. It's possible to clip more than one element in a single image. If the clipping path you designate contains more than one separate subpath, each one acts as a separate masking item. However, once you import a file containing multiple clips, you're unable to position them independently of each other. To achieve this effect, you must select, copy, and paste one of the elements into a new image, create separate clipping paths, then import the individual files into your layout.

Intersecting subpaths. When a clipping path contains overlapping subpaths, the intersecting areas are masked. For example, assume you're isolating a donut: A small circular subpath appears inside a larger circular subpath. The information inside the larger path displays and prints, but the information inside the smaller circle does not appear.

Setting Flatness. The Clipping Path dialog box contains a field for a Flatness value. You don't have to enter a value here—the only reason to do so is to shorten output times. By default, your output device reproduces the curves of the path using the highest detail possible. By entering a Flatness value, you reduce the curves to a series of tiny straight lines. Values can range from 0.2 to 100 device pixels, which represents the length of each line, as measured in printer dots. For example, if you output a Flatness value of 16 to a 2400 dpi imagesetter, each line segment is 1/144 of an inch (16/2400), or a half-point long. If you must enter a Flatness amount, use a value of 6 or below to avoid visible segments.

I.11

Shadowing a Clipped Element

When you import an image that contains a soft drop shadow into a page lay-out document, it has certain limitations. The obvious is that you can't place the shadow over other colored information, such as a neighboring high-res image, or any object you've created in the layout program. This is compounded by the fact that you can't include a soft shadow edge as part of a clipping path.

The best way to add a soft-edged shadow over a full color image is to combine the elements in Photoshop. However, this method may prove too cumbersome. A large high-res image may be to big for some workstations to handle, and once you apply the shadow, the only way you can change its position is to re-edit the original file. Fortunately, you can apply a rough and ready workaround: Create the image and shadow separately, then combine them in your layout. The results may not be as superlative as a true drop shadow, but it usually does the trick. Follow these steps:

1. Open the image that will cast the shadow. **A**

2. Surround the desired element with a vector-based path. Convert it to a clipping path and save the image as a Photoshop EPS (for more information, see *I.10 Creating a Clipping Path*). Leave the image open.

3. Choose Image: **Duplicate** to create a copy of the image. Close the original file.

4. Convert the clipping path into a selection by (Command) [Control]-clicking its item in the Paths palette. **B**

5. Choose Layer: New: **Layer Via Copy** to lift the selected element into a new image layer. **c**

A *Original image.*   **B** *Selected element.*

6. Delete the original layer.

7. Choose Layer: Layer Style: **Drop Shadow**.

8. Add the desired drop shadow beneath the image. (See *Issues to Consider*, below.) **D**

9. Choose Layer: Layer Style: **Create Layer**. Although the image doesn't appear to change, the drop shadow Layer Style has been split into its component layers.

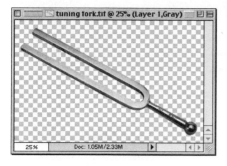

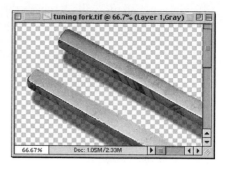

C *Element in new layer.*

D *Adding the shadow.*

10. In the Layers palette, hide every layer except the one that contains the drop shadow. **E**

11. Convert the image to Bitmap mode. If the image is in color, you must first choose Image: Mode: **Grayscale**, then **Bitmap**. When Photoshop asks to merge or flatten any layers, click OK.

12. In the Bitmap dialog box, set the target resolution and choose the Diffusion Dither option. When you click OK, the soft-edged shadow is converted to its 1-bit equivalent. Because the tones are dithered, they still maintain the appearance of soft edges. (See *Issues to Consider*, below.) **F**

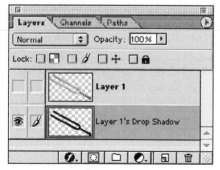

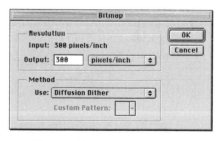

E *Targeting the shadow layer.*

F *Bitmap dialog box settings.*

13. Save the image as a TIFF, being careful to use a different file name than the image that contains the clipping path. **G**

14. Import both images into your layout document.

15. Place the shadow file beneath the image with the clipping path. If possible, group the two images together. The shadow now exists as a separate file, so you can position it as needed, at any time. Since it exists as 1-bit artwork, the black pixels will automatically overprint any underlying information, mimicking the appearance of a true drop shadow. **H**

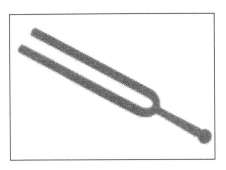

G *Shadow image.*

H *Image and shadow combined (placed over text in an XPress document).*

Issues to Consider

Use a thinner shadow edge. The edges of a true drop shadow consist of ever-lightening tones. In a 1-bit shadow element, however, this effect is produced by a random scattering of black pixels. If the shadow's edge is too wide (or too soft), the black dithering will extend farther than you expect, and look awkward when you combine the elements in your layout. For the best results, define a thinner (or harder-edged) shadow in the Layer Style dialog box.

Set the proper shadow resolution. The value you set in the Bitmap dialog box's Resolution field should divide evenly into resolution of your target output device. For example, if you're outputting to a 2,400 dpi imagesetter, use a value of 150, 300, 600, 800, or 1,200 ppi. Otherwise, a moiré-like pattern may result during output.

Try the Halftone Screen option. If you're not satisfied with the appearance of a dithered shadow, try the Halftone Screens option in the Bitmap dialog box. Instead of randomized black pixels, the shadow is reproduced by a 1-bit halftone pattern. (For more information, see *E.8, Creating a 1-bit Halftone.*) This technique produces a more realistic shadow effect, but be careful. If you place the shadow over another halftoned image, a moiré pattern may result during output, particularly if one of the elements is rotated in the layout document. This method works best when the shadow is placed over unscreened ink values, such as solid black text or 100% spot ink coverage. (Note that the moiré issue only exists when the image will be reproduced on-press.)

I.12

Clipping with an Adobe Illustrator Path

It's possible to use an Adobe Illustrator path as a Photoshop clipping path. This isn't done to trace a particular image element (a task better done in Photoshop using the Pen tool). Instead, many people prefer to use Illustrator's tools to craft a detailed path, then import it into Photoshop to use as a customized mask. Follow these steps:

1. Create the desired path in Illustrator. **A**

2. Select the entire path.

3. Choose Edit: **Copy**.

4. Back in your Photoshop image, choose Edit: **Paste**. When the Paste dialog box appears, choose the "Paste as Paths" option. The path is inserted as a new item in the Paths palette. **B**

5. Save the path. (Double-click its item in the Paths palette to access the Save Path dialog box.)

6. Use Photoshop's path editing tools to scale and position the outline as needed.

7. Choose Clipping Path from the Paths palette submenu.

8. In the Clipping Path dialog box, set the saved item in the Path pop-up menu.

9. Save the image as a Photoshop EPS. **C**

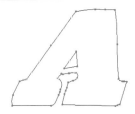

A *Original Adobe Illustrator path.*   **B** *Paste dialog box settings.*   **C** *Path used as clipping path.*

Issues to Consider

Masking in Illustrator. Of course, you can perform a similar technique in Illustrator: Import the image, draw the path, then combine the two by creating a mask. However, this method adds an unnecessary level of complexity. If the image is linked to the Illustrator document, then both files must be present during output. If you import the image without a link, it becomes considerably more difficult to perform any last-minute edits (and some workflows have experienced difficulty outputting these files successfully).

Using Macromedia FreeHand paths. Unfortunately, you can't paste FreeHand paths into Photoshop. You're able to access the Paste dialog box, but Photoshop can only convert the information to rasterized pixels. The only way to use a FreeHand path is if you export it to an EPS or Illustrator file, open it in Illustrator, and copy/paste from there.

Working with low memory. If your workstation doesn't have enough memory to open Photoshop and Illustrator at the same time, don't despair. After creating and copying the path in Illustrator, simply quit the program, launch Photoshop, open the target image, and paste.

Custom Ink Techniques

Using Predefined Duotone Curves

The easiest way to make a quality duotone is to use the predefined settings that ship with Photoshop. These files contain curve combinations that have already been proofed for optimal reproduction, relieving you from having to draw and test your own curves.

Access these values by clicking the Load button in the Duotone Options dialog box. They are located in the Photoshop application folder, inside the Presets folder, inside the Duotones folder. There, you'll find three folders, one each for duotones, tritones, and quadtones. The presets for each type are split into three categories:

- **Gray/Black.** These presets are combinations of black and one or more gray PANTONE ink. These combinations reproduce the greatest range of grays without adding any colored bias to the halftone.

- **PANTONE.** These presets represent combinations of different PANTONE inks. Each uses black as Ink 1, but not every PANTONE ink appears as an option. Instead, colors representing a wide and uniform range of the PANTONE spectrum are listed—if necessary, you can re-specify the desired PANTONE ink.

- **Process.** These presets are combinations of CMYK inks. Again, each one uses black as Ink 1.

When you load a preset, the inks and curves automatically appear in the Duotone Options palette, as if you defined them yourself. You can continue to edit the values, if desired.

J.2

Creating a PMS Monotone

When you create a monotone, you specify that a halftone is based on a single custom ink, as opposed to black. Because the Grayscale image has already been adjusted for optimal printing, there is no need to load any preset values, or adjust any tonal curves in the Duotone Options dialog box. The only thing you need to know is the name of the target ink. Follow these steps:

1. Open or acquire the Grayscale image you wish to convert to a duotone. **A**

2. Adjust the image for contrast and sharpness, and perform any retouching.

3. Choose Image: Mode: **Duotone**. The Duotone Options dialog box appears. (See *Issues to Consider*, below.)

4. Set Monotone in the Type pop-up.

5. Click the color swatch for Ink 1. The Color Picker dialog box appears. (If necessary, click the color picker's Custom button to display the Custom Colors dialog box.)

6. Choose the desired PANTONE library from the Book pop-up. (See *Issues to Consider*, below.)

7. Click the desired ink. (Instead of scrolling through the list, type the catalog number on your keypad to jump to the swatch.)

8. Click OK to return to the Duotone Options dialog box. Double-check the ink name, to make sure you've chosen the correct color. (See *Issues to Consider*, below.)

9. Click OK to close the Duotone Options dialog box.

10. Save the image as a Photoshop EPS file. **B**

A *The original image.*   **B** *A PANTONE 485 monotone.*

Issues to Consider

Resetting the Duotone Options dialog box. If you've recently created a duotone—especially if you've been defining your own curves, or loading Photoshop's predefined settings—you may need to reset the dialog box when it first appears. Otherwise, the curve that affects Ink 1 may retain any adjustments that were applied to another image. To reset the dialog box, hold down the (Command) [Control] key; the Cancel button temporarily changes to Reset. Click this button to clear any previous settings.

Converting a monotone into an RGB or CMYK image. When you convert an image to a monotone, it colorizes it in a way that is difficult to achieve using other methods. If desired, you can temporarily convert an image to a monotone to create this effect, then discard the spot color designation. If you're just looking to get close to a particular color, this technique will usually do the trick. To nail a particular swatchbook value, you need to use a different technique. (For more information, see *H.3, Creating a CMYK Monotone.*)

J.3

Creating a Black/PMS Duotone

The quickest way to create a two-color duotone is to start with one of the predefined settings that ship with Photoshop. As you browse through the presets, though, don't be put off by the fact that not all the PANTONE inks are available—if they were, you'd have to search through thousands of files to find the necessary preset. Instead, Photoshop includes a broad sampling from the library, enabling you to choose the color that most closely matches the ink you want. (Of course, this assumes you have a printed PANTONE swatchbook to refer to.) Follow these steps:

1. Open or acquire the Grayscale image you wish to convert to a duotone. **A**

2. Adjust the image for contrast and sharpness, and perform any required retouching.

3. Choose Image: Mode: **Duotone**. The Duotone Options dialog box appears. **B**

4. Click the Load button. Navigate to the PANTONE Duotones folder (in the Photoshop application folder, in the Presets folder).

5. Locate the preset based on the ink that best approximates the one you want. In this case, it's "red 485 bl".

6. From the four available presets, choose the one that produces the desired level of color bias. Click Open. (See *Issues to Consider*, below.) **C D E F**

7. To assign a new spot color to the setting, click the PANTONE swatch in the Duotone Options dialog box.

8. Click OK to close the Duotone Options dialog box. If not satisfied with the blend of inks, select Image: Mode: **Duotone** again and choose another preset.

9. Save the image as a Photoshop EPS file. In the EPS Options dialog box, make sure the Include Halftone Screens box is checked.

A *The original image.*

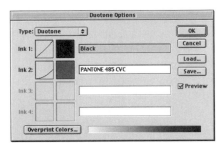

B *The Duotone options dialog box, set to a black/PMS 485 duotone.*

C *Duotone preset #1.*

D *Duotone preset #2.*

E *Duotone preset #3.*

F *Duotone preset #4.*

Issues to Consider

Understanding the ramped values of each preset series. Each duotone and tritone preset has four variations. They range from a warmer, higher color bias (#1) to a cooler lower bias (#4). The quadtone presets cover the same range, but offer fewer options.

Editing the values of a duotone. Once you create a duotone, it's more difficult to adjust its tonal range. This is mainly due to the following:

- The colors you defined do not appear in the Info palette, as if they were comprised of RGB or CMYK values. Instead, choose Actual Color from the Palette Options submenu. This way, the different inks are listed as they appeared in the Duotone Options dialog box: Ink 1, Ink 2, Ink 3, and Ink 4.

- Regardless of how many inks you defined, the image has only one channel. You cannot use Image: Adjust: **Curves** to edit an individual ink. Only one curve exists for the entire image, and that controls the overall brightness values. To adjust individual colors, you must edit their curves in the Duotones dialog box, or load a new preset. (However, it is possible to convert a duotone to an image with two spot color channels, which would enable you to address individual values. For more information, see *J.11, Converting a Duotone Data into Spot Color Channels.*)

J.4

Inspecting Duotone Data

Since duotones only have one channel, the only way you can read the different ink densities is to check the Actual Color values in the Info palette. If you have a question about how each ink is affecting a certain part of the image, however, you can temporarily convert the duotone data into individual channels. Follow these steps:

1. Choose Image: Mode: **Multichannel**. This creates a file containing one channel for each ink.

2. Inspect the ink percentages by choosing individual channels in the Channels palette, moving the cursor over the image, and reading the Info Palette. It is imperative that you do not make any edits to the Multichannel image.

3. Choose Edit: **Undo** to switch the image back to Duotone mode.

J.5

Adding a Gray Ramp to Evaluate Duotone Edits

If your goal is to expand the tonal range of an image without adding an inappropriate color shift, it helps to temporarily include a gray ramp in the duotone. This way, you can evaluate the effect of your adjustments across a full range readily-identifiable tones. Follow these steps:

1. After creating your initial duotone, create a new Grayscale image. Make it the same width as the duotone, but only a quarter-inch high.

2. Using the Gradient tool, create a horizontal black-to-white gradient the exact width of the new file. (Uncheck the Dither box in the Options bar to keep the transitions between tones hard and smooth.)

3. Apply Image: Adjust: **Posterize**, set to 21 levels. This produces a gray ramp from 0% to 100%, in 5% increments.

4. In your duotone, use Image: **Canvas Size** to add a half-inch to the bottom of the image.

5. Copy and paste the gray ramp into the duotone, placing it in the new space.

6. Keep both images open and visible. As you edit the duotone, compare the values of the two gray ramps. The values should remain consistent as you work.

7. When you've finished editing the duotone, use the Crop tool to discard the gray ramp.

J.6

Setting Screen Angles for a Duotone

A duotone consists of two overprinting inks. Unless the separated information is output at the appropriate screen angles, it will not reproduce successfully on-press. Photoshop attempts to resolve this issue by automatically setting each ink to a different angle, similar to the requirements imposed on a CMYK image. For example, if you create a duotone based on black and a single PANTONE ink, the black plate is set to output at 45°, the standard value for the darkest ink. The second ink, whether you create your own curves or load a preset value, is set to output at 108.4°. The assumption is that this angle is the optimal value to avoid conflicting screens on-press, which produce moiré.

In practice, it doesn't always work. As any pressmen will tell you, most print shops with experience printing duotones have discovered their own angles that work best with their in-house equipment. It may depend on their platemaking technology, or the type of press used to run the job. Whatever the case, if you plan to include duotones in a project, ask your printer for the optimal screen angles. At the very least, be prepared to make some last-minute changes if the default angles produce unwanted patterning—many printers, especially those using a digital press, are prepared to make such edits.

To change the screen angles of a duotone, follow these steps:

1. Choose File: **Page Setup**. The Page Setup dialog box appears.

2. The dialog box may default to display the options specific to your print driver. If necessary, set it to display the Adobe Photoshop 6.0 options.

3. Click the Screens button. The Halftone Screens dialog box appears.

4. Uncheck the Use Printer's Default Screens box. The remaining controls become available.

5. The Ink pop-up menu defaults to display the Ink 1 values, which are already set to 45°. To reset the angle for the second ink, choose it from this pop-up.

6. Enter the desired value in the Angle field.

7. Because you're overriding the default printer settings, you must manually enter the target linescreen value for each ink. Otherwise, the image will output at the setting that initially appears: 53 lpi. Enter the target value in the Frequency field for each ink. (See *Issues to Consider*, below.)

8. Click OK to close the dialog box.

Issues to Consider

Embedding halftone screen values. Whenever you make any internal changes to an image's screen values, you must embed the information in the file. Otherwise, your output device will not recognize the new behavior. Fortunately, this requires that you save the image as a Photoshop EPS file—the format already used to reproduce duotone data. As you save the file, the EPS Options dialog box appears. To embed the screen information, make sure the Include Halftone Screen box is checked.

The Include Halftone Screens option should be enabled whenever you create a duotone, whether or not you re-address the screen information. If it isn't, all inks will output at the default angle used for black (45°), and the printed result will be murky and muddled.

Understanding the default screen settings. If you don't specify new screen angles for a duotone, the image will output at the default settings. The angles will appear at 45° and 108.4°, and the image will output at the linescreen value specified in your layout document. However, as soon as you override the default settings, the image reverts to the linescreen values that initially appear in the dialog box. Unless you set the frequency of each ink to the target lpi, you won't get the results you expect on-press.

Monotones and images converted to CMYK do not require this treatment. The reason you reset the screen angles is to accommodate the overprinting spot inks. When you create a monotone, you're only dealing with one ink; it's angle defaults to 45°, the recommended value, regardless of the color. If you convert any duotone to CMYK color (to achieve a particular colorizing effect), you don't need to address the angles, even if you originally specified spot inks. The angles will revert to the optimal values required for cyan, magenta, yellow, and black.

J.7

Determining the Need for a Spot Color Channel

Photoshop 5, 5.5, and 6 enable you build custom ink information directly into an image, in the form of an additional channel. When you output the image from a layout program, the contents of each extra channel appear on a separate film plate, titled with the spot ink name. Spot channels aren't always the right way to add a custom ink to an image. Before using this feature, consider the following questions:

- **Have you already planned to use spot inks in your project?** Spot ink channels produce additional color plates when your document is output, and you must make sure your project can accommodate them. For example, if you add a spot ink to a CMYK image, you must prepared for the extra cost and effort of a five-color print job. If you're only trying to generate a CMYK equivalent of a spot color, skip this feature, define it using the color picker, and apply it like any other color.

- **Do you want to add the color to a simple shape?** If you're using this feature to color a box, circle, or even type, you're better off creating the object in another application, such as Illustrator, FreeHand, or your page layout software. Those programs produce crisp PostScript outlines that you can easily position over the imported image.

- **Do you want to create a standard duotone?** If you're simply enhancing the tonal range of a halftone by supplementing it with a custom ink, convert it to a duotone instead. (However, as you'll see, it's possible to use spot channels to produce a variety of specialized duotone effects.)

- **Do you want to recolor the entire image with a spot ink?** The easiest way to recolor an entire halftone is to import it into your layout document as a Grayscale TIFF, and recolor it there. Or, if necessary, convert the image to a monotone.

Most often, people define a spot color channel for one of three reasons: First, to add the color to a specialized shape that you can only create using Photoshop's tools. Second, to add a spot varnish to part of the image, or a clear coating that is applied on press. Third, to add a bump plate, which uses a spot ink to intensify a particular color in a CMYK image.

J.8

Basing a New Spot Channel on a Selection

The most intuitive way to add a spot channel is to select the area you want to color with the custom ink. Follow these steps:

1. Create the desired selection, using any of Photoshop's selection techniques. (If you're creating a bump plate, use the Color Range command to isolate the color you want to supplement.)

2. Choose New Spot Channel from the Channels palette submenu. The New Spot Channel dialog box appears.

3. To define the spot ink, click the small color swatch to access the color picker—if the standard color picker appears, click the Custom button. Choose the desired color library from the Book pop-up menu (usually, it will be PANTONE Coated) and select the color you need from the scrolling list.

4. Click OK to close the dialog box and create the new channel.

5. Save the image as a DCS 2.0 file. This file format is a variant of EPS, and it's the only one that can communicate the spot channel to your page layout program. In the DCS 2.0 dialog box, set the Preview pop-up to 8-bit Macintosh or 8-bit TIFF (for Windows users). Set the DCS pop-up to Single File DCS, and the Encoding pop-up to Binary.

For more information, see *H.11, Using Spot Inks to Colorize Line Art.*

Issues to Consider

The color you choose only affects the onscreen appearance of the spot color. You can choose any color you like, as long as the correct name appears in the New Spot Channel dialog box. Although you can always change the name later on, it's best to stay on the safe side and select the actual spot ink you'll use on press. This reduces the possibility of the spot channel info appearing on the wrong plate when the image is separated. Note that all of this means nothing if you decide to apply the Merge Spot Channel command, which applies the overlay color to the actual image pixels. This is never recommended. (For more information, see *23.14, Merge Spot Channels.*)

Although the colored information initially appears on screen, it doesn't exist on an image layer. If you need to edit the contents of the spot channel, you have to click the item in the Channels palette (hiding the remaining channels from view, if necessary).

Viewing a spot channel along with the rest of the image. To view the spot channel in addition to the image, click its view box in the Channels palette. To hide the channel, click the box again to hide the eyeball icon. To view only the spot channel, hide the remaining color channels.

Controlling the on-screen display of a spot channel. The Solidity value in the New Spot Channel dialog box controls the on-screen opacity of the spot color. It has no affect on the printed results. If you set it to 100%, you can't see any underlying pixels when you view the spot color channel; if it's set to 0%, you can't see the spot color at all. Choose a value that works best for the specific color you've defined.

Changing or renaming an existing spot color channel. To change the current spot color, double-click its item in the Channels palette. The Spot Channel Options dialog box appears, displaying the same controls as the New Spot Channel dialog box. To select a new color, click the color swatch. To only change the name, enter a new one in the Name field.

J.9
Painting with a Spot Ink

You don't have to base a spot channel on a selection. Instead, you can create a blank spot channel, then apply the color using any of Photoshop's paint tools. Follow these steps:

1. Without creating a selection, choose New Spot Channel from the Channels palette submenu.

2. Set the desired color in the New Spot Channel dialog box, and click OK.

3. Make sure the new channel is active in the Channels palette.

4. Choose one of the paint tools. To paint with the spot color, set the foreground color to black. To erase the spot color, set the foreground color to white and paint with the same tool.

You can also use this technique to edit a spot channel that was initially based on a selection. (For more information, see *H.11, Using Spot Inks to Colorize Line Art.*)

J.10

Trapping the Contents of a Spot Channel

Unless you use dedicated trapping software that can edit the contents of a DCS 2.0 file, you must trap your own spot colors in a Photoshop image. Of course, if you intend to overprint the color, you don't have to trap it. However, spot inks don't conceal underlying inks very well, and overprinting them produces muddy results. Before trapping a color, you'll have to manually knock out the underlying information. (In a layout or illustration program, spot colors are spread or choked, depending on how much darker or lighter it is than the surrounding pixels. However, spreading in Photoshop tends to obscure the edge detail of the spot channel; for most purposes, choking will suffice.) Follow these steps:

1. Complete all your edits and flatten the image before performing the remaining steps.

2. Create a selection based on the spot channel, by (Command) [Control]-clicking its item in the Channels palette.

3. Choose Select: Modify: **Contract**. In the Contract dialog box, enter a value of 1 pixel and click OK. (Contracting the selection produces the choke effect.)

4. Set the background color to white.

5. Press the Delete key to fill the selection with white, removing the underlying pixels. (You should still see the spot color—if it disappears, undo the command and make sure the composite channel is clicked in the Channels palette.)

J.11

Converting Duotone Data into Spot Color Channels

As long as a duotone exists in duotone mode, you'll find it fairly difficult to apply changes to one specific ink. The only way you can redistribute the tones affected by each ink is to return to the Duotone Options dialog box, and use the limited toolset of each ink curve. If you need to add new information to the file, especially if you want to add a range of one specific ink, the Duotone Options dialog box makes it extremely difficult. You can add a considerable level of editing flexibility by converting the duotone information into separate spot color channels. This way, unlike temporarily converting a duotone to Multichannel mode (as described under *J.4, Inspecting Duotone Data*), you're able to edit individual inks without affecting the entire image. You're also able to edit the duotone with more control, using layers and temporary channels to incorporate new information to the image. Follow these steps:

1. Open or create the Grayscale image you want to convert to a duotone.

2. Choose Image: Mode: **Duotone** and specify the target inks, as described under *J.3, Creating a Black/PMS Duotone*. In this example, I use black and PANTONE 485. **A**

3. Choose Image: Mode: **Multichannel**. The component data of the duotone is split into two separate channels, each named with the ink it represents. **B**

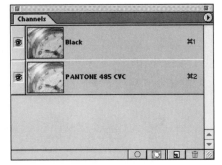

A *The original black/PMS 485 duotone.*

B *The Channels palette, after converting the duotone to a Multichannel image.*

4. In the Channels palette, click the item that represents the Black ink.

5. Choose Select: **All**.

6. Choose Edit: **Cut**.

7. Choose File: **New**. In the new dialog box, the Width, Height, and Resolution automatically match the information you've copied. The mode is automatically set to Grayscale.

8. Click OK to create the new image.

9. In the new image, choose Edit: **Paste**. The black data you cut from the duotone is placed into the Gray channel.

10. Return to the duotone. In the Channels palette, click the item that represents the spot ink information.

11. Choose Select: **All**.

12. Choose Edit: **Cut**.

13. Return to the new image. Choose New Spot Channel from the Channels palette submenu. When the New Spot Channel dialog box appears, click the color swatch to designate the spot ink. Make sure you specify the same second ink used in the original duotone.

14. Click OK to close the New Spot Color dialog box. A new item appears in the Channels palette.

15. In the Channels palette, click the new spot channel item.

16. Choose Edit: **Paste.** The data you cut from the original duotone is placed into the spot channel, and the image now displays the combined ink values. **c**

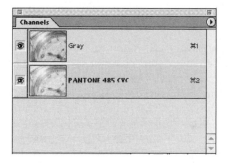

c *The Channels palette of a Grayscale image, displaying a Gray and spot color channel.*

You're now able to edit the component inks individually, by clicking the desired item in the Channels palette. (For more information, see *J.x, Adding Information to a Spot Channel Duotone.*) However, before you save and import the image, you must consider a couple of additional issues. (See *Issues to Consider*, below.)

Issues to Consider

Setting screen angles for a spot channel duotone. When you use this technique, Photoshop discards the default halftone screen settings that affected the original duotone. Before you save the image, you must manually set the target screen angles and linescreen frequency. Otherwise, the inks will output at the same angle when you separate the image. (For more information, see *J.6, Setting Screen Angles for a Duotone.*)

Saving a spot channel duotone. Ordinarily, you save a duotone as a Photoshop EPS file. However, because you've converted the duotone data into spot color channels, you must save the image in the only file format that successfully communicates that information to an output device: Photoshop DCS 2.0. Because this format is a variation of an EPS file, it is capable of containing the embedded screen information described in the previous discussion item. In fact, as you save, you'll encounter the EPS Options dialog box, where you'll set the same options as a standard duotone.

Creating a spot channel duotone using two custom inks. In the above example, I used a duotone based on black and a single PANTONE ink. When converting a duotone based on two PANTONE inks, you only need to make a couple of adjustments. Instead of cutting and pasting the black information into the Gray channel of the new image, ignore the Gray channel completely. Simply create a new spot channel, specifying the appropriate ink. When you transfer the second color, create a new spot channel for it as well. This way, the new image will contain three channels: the two spot items, and a blank Gray channel. Delete the Gray channel, then continue editing the image.

Adding one-color data to a spot-channel duotone. One of the most prominent reasons to create a spot channel duotone is the ability to include areas of one specific ink. For example, assume you've created a duotone based on black and PANTONE 286. If you want to add an image element colored only with a tint of the blue ink, the Duotone Options dialog box doesn't make it easy. There, you'd have to create exaggerated, spiking curves in an attempt to prevent the black ink from being applied to a particular tonal range. The effect of such a curve on the rest of the image is unpredictable at best, and it fails to accommodate such information as soft edges or anti-aliasing. By converting the duotone to spot color channels, you can add the new information to one channel, then manually remove any areas of the second ink that overprint.

J.12

Converting a Spot Channel Duotone into a Process-Plate Duotone

Some workflows cannot process DCS 2.0 files, forcing users to seek other methods to handle Photoshop images with spot channels. One of the more successful workarounds is a simple trick: Convert the image to a CMYK file, and transfer the contents of each spot channel to a cyan, magenta, yellow, or black channel. This way, the spot color data will separate properly during output, and your printer (assuming they're informed of the image requirements) can correctly impose the films.

Bear in mind that this technique is not as simple as choosing Image: Mode: CMYK **Color**—in fact, doing so will quickly destroy your spot color information. You're not creating a CMYK equivalent of the image—you're manipulating Photoshop's ability to produce process color separations. Follow these steps:

1. Open the spot color duotone you need to convert. **A**

2. In the Channels palette, click the spot color channel that represents the darkest custom ink.

3. Choose Select: **All**.

4. Choose Edit: **Copy**.

5. Choose File: **New**. The New dialog box appears. The correct Width, Height, and Resolution are automatically entered. Set CMYK Color in the Mode pop-up menu and click OK.

6. In the new image, click the Black item in the Channels palette.

7. Choose Edit: **Paste**. The spot color information appears as black data.

8. Return to the original image. In the Channels palette, click the second spot color item.

9. Choose Select: **All**.

10. Choose Edit: **Copy**.

11. In the new image, click the Cyan item in the Channels palette.

12. Choose Edit: **Paste**. The spot color information appears as cyan data.

13. Click the CMYK item in the Channels palette to preview the duotone. (See *Issues to Consider*, below.) **B**

14. Save the image as a TIFF or Photoshop EPS.

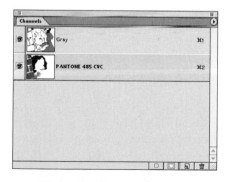

A *The original two-color spot channel duotone.*

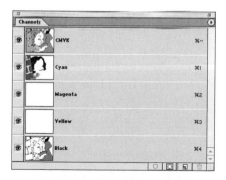

B *Spot color channels, transferred to the cyan and black plates of a CMYK image.*

Issues to Consider

The CMYK image will not display the correct values. When you follow the steps above, it will always display a cyan/black image. This does not matter. When you separate the file, the spot color data will appear on completely independent plates—exactly what you need to reproduce the image. Just make sure your vendor knows how the plates are supposed to be arranged.

Setting screen values. Normally, you don't have to set custom screen angles when you use this approach. When you separate a CMYK image, the black plate always outputs at 45° and the cyan plate always outputs at 105°. These angles should be sufficient. If unsure, double-check with your print vendor. If they suggest different angles, use the File: Page Setup: **Screens** controls to set new values. (For more information, see *J.6, Setting Screen Angles for a Duotone.*)

J.13

Combining Two Monotones in a Single Duotone

In the duotone techniques described so far, two inks are used to enhance the tonal range of the entire image. However, once you start using spot channels to reproduce a duotone, you can create an effect that is patently impossible using the Duotone Options dialog box: combining two spot ink monotones in a single image. This way, the tones of each part of the image are generated using only a single ink, rather than a mix of both.

First, I use basic selection techniques to apply spot inks to different parts of the same image. For this example, assume you want to tag the roses with PANTONE 485 (red), and color the surrounding pixels with PANTONE 419 (dark gray). Follow these steps:

1. Before you begin, press the "D" key to set the foreground and background colors to black and white.

2. Open or create the Grayscale image you want to edit as a spot channel duotone. For the best results, adjust it for contrast and sharpness before continuing. **A**

3. Choose New Spot Channel from the Channels palette submenu to add the first spot color channel, which will contain the roses. Here, PANTONE 485 is specified.

4. Choose New Spot Channel again to add the second spot channel, which will contain the background. Here, PANTONE 419 is specified. **B**

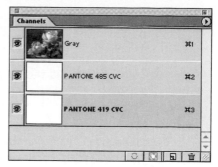

A *Original Grayscale image.*   **B** *Adding two blank spot channels.*

5. In the Channels palette, click the Gray item.

6. Choose Select: **All**.

7. Choose Edit: **Cut**.

8. In the Channels palette, click the PANTONE 419 item.

9. Choose Edit: **Paste**. The entire image appears on the black channel. **c**

10. Draw a selection around the image element you want to add to the other spot channel. **D**

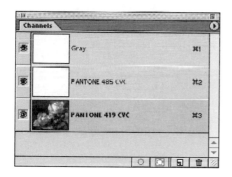

c *Moving the Gray data to the*   **D** *Selecting the element that will*
   PANTONE 419 channel.   *receive the second color.*

11. Choose Edit: **Copy**.

12. Leave the selection active, and click the PANTONE 485 item in the Channels palette.

13. Choose Edit: **Paste**. The selection is filled with a copy of the roses. (At this point, the roses are based on a red/black duotone, and the background is only based on black ink. If you desire this effect, skip to step 17.) **E**

14. In the Channels palette, click the PANTONE 419 item.

15. Choose Select: Modify: **Contract**. In the Contract dialog box, enter a value of 1 and click OK. The selection outline is restricted by one pixel. (This will satisfy the need for trapping the two spot inks on-press.)

16. Press the Delete key. The overprinting red data is removed, leaving pure red roses above a black background. **F**

17. Set new halftone screen values if necessary, then save the image as a Photoshop DCS 2.0 file. (For more information, see *J.6, Setting Screen Angles for a Duotone*, and *J.11, Converting Duotone Data into Spot Color Channels*.)

E   *Pasting a copy of the roses into the PMS 485 spot channel.*

F   *Deleting the roses data from the PMS 419 spot channel.*

Retouching & Pattern Techniques

K.1

Retouching with Brushstrokes

Sampling and cloning to retouch an image is a two-step process. When you *sample*, you specify the pixels that you'll use to conceal the defect. When you *clone*, you apply the sampled pixels. When done correctly, it appears as if the flaw never existed. Follow these steps:

1. Set your view percentage to 100% and choose the Clone Stamp tool.

2. In the Options bar, choose a brush that best accommodates the amount of data you need to sample and clone. If you're retouching a small flaw, choose a small brush. For the best results, use a brush with either a thin, anti-aliased edge or a higher Hardness value (as defined in the Edit Brush pop-up). The broad, soft-edged brushes tend to produce muddy results.

3. Pinpoint and evaluate the area you need to retouch. In this example, it's a small speck.

4. To sample, hold down the (Option) [Alt] key and click the image. Don't click on the flaw, and don't click on some random spot. Rather, click near the defect, on an area that contains similar pixel values.

5. Release the (Option) [Alt] key. (If you don't, you'll just create a new sample the next time you click the image.)

6. Click directly on the defect. Two things happen: A small crosshair appears from where you originally sampled, and the defect is concealed by the source pixels. **A B**

If retouching a longer flaw—a scratch for example—use a zig-zag pattern when sampling and cloning. (See *Issues to Consider*, below.) **C D**

7. If you are not satisfied with the results, choose Edit: **Undo** and try again. Otherwise, move on to the next sample.

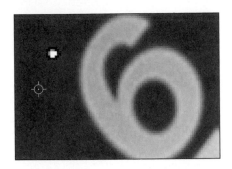

A *(Option) [Alt-click to sample.*

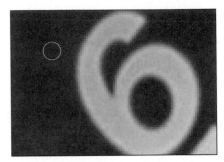

B *(Option) [Alt-click to sample.*

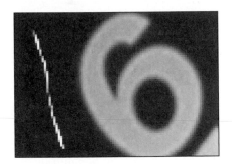

C *Lengthy defect.*

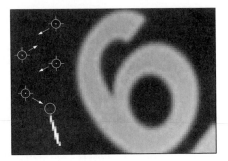

D *Following a "zipper" pattern.*

Issues to Consider

Clone into a new layer. Most users instinctively apply the Clone Stamp tool directly to the background layer of a flattened image. However, this limits your ability to make small tweaks and adjustments to your work. (In fact, the only way to selectively restore the original pixels is with the History Brush tool. Unfortunately, if you convert color modes, crop the image, or change the resolution before you finish retouching, the History Brush does you no good.) Avoid this problem by creating a new, blank image layer before you start (make sure the Use All Layers box is checked in the Clone Stamp Options bar). The results look the same on screen, but the new pixels remain separate from the background, enabling you to evaluate or erase them much more efficiently. When finished, flatten or merge the layers.

Clone Stamp tool versus Dust & Scratches filter. Photoshop includes a "Dust & Scratches" filter, which theoretically removes any minor specks and flaws from the image. Some people apply this command to the entire image, attempting to repair it in a single pass, which is a mistake. By blurring the information between narrow areas of lighter or darker pixels, the filter will indeed remove minor flaws. Unfortunately, it affects the entire image, producing slightly fuzzy, less detailed results. This filter is only acceptable in situations where getting the job done quickly is more important than image quality. It's not a substitute for using the Clone tool removing to dust and scratches.

Resist the temptation to paint with the Clone Stamp tool, or clone in sweeping brushstrokes. For example, if you're retouching a long scratch or errant hair, don't create a single sample then drag the length of the flaw. It may seem easier, but it will more than likely produce noticeable streaking or tonal variations. For the best results, follow a zipper-style pattern, sampling pixels on either side of the scratch as you move along. Take a piece from here and a piece from there, carefully dabbing them into place.

Don't sample too close to the flaw. Depending on the size of your brush, you may include the flaw in the sampled area. When this happens, it creates the effect of the flaw jumping around on screen as you re-apply it click after click.

Reading information from a separate image. Sample from a separate file by opening both images at once. (Option-click) [Alt-click] to define a sample area in the first image, then click in the second to apply the pixels.

The Clone Stamp tool is not well-suited for cloning a specific image element, such as a tree or rock. To create multiple copies of an existing element, you're much better off using one of the Selection tools to isolate the desired pixels, and copying it to a new layer. From there, it's much easier to duplicate and reposition the item. However, if your intent is to remove the rock or tree, the Clone Stamp tool is often the most effective option.

K.2

Retouching with Irregular Samples

Sampling and cloning is an effective retouching method, but it's not your only option. One of the biggest drawbacks of the Clone Stamp tool is that you're restricted by the brush shape. Elliptical brushes tend to leave recognizable patterns in some areas, such as the subtle detail found in fleshtones, or any smooth surface in a high-grain image. Avoid this problem by retouching with a series of amorphous Lasso tool selections. With some minor changes to your approach, you can achieve the same control over edge transition and layering as the Clone Stamp tool. Follow these steps:

1. Choose the Lasso tool.

2. To simulate the effect of cloning with an anti-aliased brush, check the Anti-Aliased box in the Lasso Options bar. To simulate the effect of a soft-edged brush, enter a Feather value. (The feathering radius is influenced by the current resolution; you may have to test a few values to pinpoint the desired results.)

3. Zoom in close to the element you want to retouch. In this example, it's a mole on a model's face. **A**

4. Focusing on the neighboring pixels, draw a small, irregularly-shaped selection. **B**

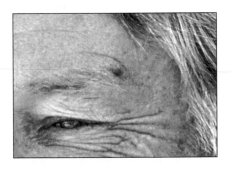

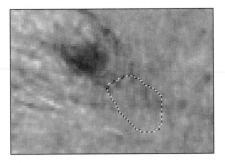

A *Targeting the flaw.*   **B** *Drawing an irregular selection.*

5. Move the cursor directly over the selection and (Option) [Alt]-drag to create a floating clone. **C**

6. Drag the clone over the flaw until it is concealed. As long as the selection is floating, you don't need to hold down the modifier keys. If desired, use the arrow keys to nudge the selection. Uncheck the View: **Show Extras** command to hide the selection edges.

7. When satisfied with the placement of the cloned pixels, choose Select: **Deselect. D**

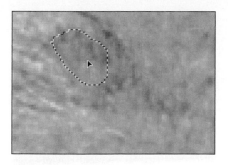

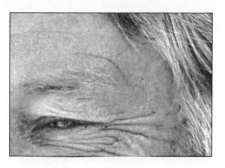

C *Moving the cloned pixels over the flaw.*

D *The retouched image.*

Issues to Consider

It often pays to work in small parts, even with minor edits. If you're not careful, this technique produces artifacts and visible transitions just as easily as the Clone Stamp tool. Avoid this problem by working with very small selections. Don't try to cover a flaw with one giant outline. Instead, use two or three small selections, cloned from different areas around the flaw.

K.3

Defining a Pattern with Non-Adjacent Edges

This pattern consists of an image surrounded by a solid color. Since different colors don't touch the edge of the tile, there is no risk of an obvious seam appearing when you apply the pattern. Follow these steps:

1. Isolate the image that you want to tile, surrounding it with a solid color.

2. Using the Rectangular Marquee tool, draw a selection around the image. Keep in mind that the amount of space left between the image and the selection edge determines the space between the tiled images: If the selection edge is close to the image, it tiles closer together; if the edge is farther away, it tiles farther apart. (If desired, you can use the selection to crop the image, then define the pattern with no active selection.) **A**

3. Choose Edit: **Define Pattern**.

4. Apply the pattern as desired. **B**

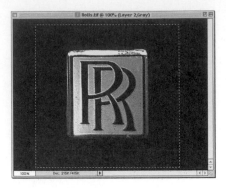

A *Determining the tile contents.*   **B** *Applying the pattern.*

K.4

Defining a Staggered Pattern with Non-Adjacent Edges

This pattern is similar to the one described above, but the results are staggered, instead of linear. This technique only works on a perfectly square image.

1. Isolate the image you want to tile. **A**

2. Using the Rectangular Marquee tool, drag a selection closely around the image.

3. Choose Edit: **Copy**.

4. Choose Select: **None**.

5. Choose Filter: Other: **Offset**. Click the Wrap Around button and enter half the width and height of the image. Since this filter only measures in pixels, you must determine the precise measurements. Open the Image: **Image Size** dialog box, read the first two values, and choose Cancel. When you offset by half the width and height, the image appears in the four corners of the window. **B**

A *Original pattern tile.*   **B** *Offsetting the image.*

6. Choose Edit: **Paste**. The copied image appears in the center. **c**

7. Choose Layer: **Merge Down** to combine the two layers.

8. Choose Edit: **Define Pattern**.

9. Apply the pattern as necessary. **d**

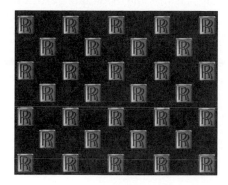

c *Pasting the copy into the center of the tile.*

d *Applying the staggered pattern.*

K.5

Defining a Non-Continuous Pattern

These patterns are perhaps the simplest to create—just draw a rectangular selection in an image and choose Edit: **Define Pattern**. Once the pattern is applied, you see distinct edges between the tiles. **A B**

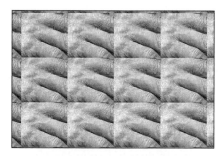

A *Selecting the desired tile shape with the Marquee tool.*

B *Applying the non-continuous pattern.*

K.6

Creating a Seamless Pattern

Use the following technique to conceal the edges of a pattern as it tiles across a layer. Follow these steps:

1. Choose File: **New** and create a square document. Since this image will be used as a repeating tile, it doesn't need to be very large.

2. Create a texture using a series of filters or Paint tools.

3. Choose Filter: Other: **Offset** to examine the tile's edges. For best results, click the Wrap Around button, and enter half the width and height of the image. **A**

4. Wherever the edges are visible, use the Clone Stamp tool to conceal the seam.

5. Apply Filter: Other: **Offset** again to make sure no new seams were accidentally generated.

6. Choose Edit: **Define Pattern**.

7. Apply the pattern as desired. **B**

A *Offsetting the texture to reveal seams.*

B *Final pattern.*

Issues to Consider

Creating automatically seamless filter-based patterns. If you use a 128 by 128-pixel image as a template, you may not have to perform any additional edits to make a seamless pattern. This becomes apparent when you apply Filter: Other: **Offset**—if there are no visible seams, you're free to define the pattern. This is true for at least two commonly used patterns: A cloud pattern using Filter: Render: **Clouds**, and a raised, grainy texture using Filter: Noise: **Add Noise**, then Filter: Stylize: **Emboss**.

K.7

Creating a Seamless Image Pattern

Creating a seamless pattern from a scanned or PhotoCD image is more complex than creating a simple texture. The information is more varied, and sloppy retouching is more pronounced when you apply the pattern. Therefore, the technique described above probably isn't enough. Follow these steps:

1. Draw a rectangular selection around part of the target image. This method works best if you define a fixed-size square selection in the Marquee tool's Options bar. In this example, the outline is 350 by 350 pixels. (Note: to restrict the image pattern to the target element—including no surrounding pixels—make sure the first selection doesn't go beyond the element's edges.) **A**

2. Choose Edit: **Define Pattern**.

3. Choose File: **New** to create a new image window. Set the width and height to three times the size of the original selection (in this case, 1050 by 1050 pixels). Make sure the color mode and resolution are the same as the original image.

4. Choose Edit: **Fill** and fill the entire image with the pattern. (Don't bother creating a Pattern Fill layer.) **B**

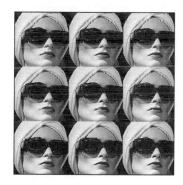

A *Selecting the partial tile.*

B *Filling the new image with the initial pattern tile.*

5. Choose the Clone Stamp tool. In the Options bar, check the Clone (Aligned) box.

6. Return to the original image.

7. (Option) [Alt]-click to define the sample point. (For the best results, choose a tiny, easily identifiable spot, such as a small specular highlight. This way, when you return to the second image, you're able to clone from the exact same location.)

8. Focus on one seam, cloning pixels from the original image to fill in the spaces. In this example, the tile's top seam is blended.

9. Place another fixed-size marquee that straddles the new seam. **c**

10. Choose Edit: **Define Pattern**.

11. Apply the new pattern to the entire image.

12. Repeat steps 5-9 for the next seam. As you can see, you only need to blend one horizontal seam and one vertical seam to complete this effect. **D**

c *Creating a tile that includes the first continuous seam.*

D *Creating a tile that includes both continuous seams.*

13. After the last seam is edited, place a fixed-size marquee that straddles both blended seams and choose Edit: **Define Pattern**. **E**

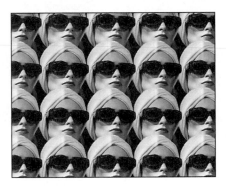

E *Applying the completed seamless pattern.*

Issues to Consider

Protecting the target image. To protect certain areas of your pattern from being cloned over, select them with the Lasso or Pen tool and choose Select: **Inverse** before cloning.

Clone into a new layer. This technique is much easier to execute when you clone the original image pixels into a new layer. For example, if your click-point was slightly off when using the Clone Stamp tool, you're able to nudge the cloned pixels into place. Also, you can use the Eraser tool (set to the Paintbrush setting) to refine the cloned area. Whenever you've finished cloning, merge or flatten the layers before continuing.

K.8

Defining a Pattern that Includes Transparent Pixels

If more than one image layer is visible when you define a pattern, all of the visible information is included. To make a pattern that includes transparent or semi-transparent pixels, follow these steps:

1. Create a new image layer. This will not work on a background layer.

2. Create the pattern, surrounding the desired element or elements with transparent pixels.

3. Hide any other layers from view.

4. Draw a rectangular selection. Just like patterns with non-adjacent edges (described above), the amount of space left between the image and the selection edge determines the space between the tiled images. **A**

5. Choose Edit: **Define Pattern**. (To restrict the area included in the tile, draw a rectangular selection first.)

6. Apply the pattern as desired. **B**

A *Determining the tile contents.*

B *Applying the partially transparent pattern.*

Path Editing Techniques

Drawing a Basic Path

The easiest path to create is made entirely out of straight lines—just click around the image without dragging. Most paths require a little curving, though, but many people try to get around that by clicking hundreds of tiny straight lines, hoping they're small enough to escape detection (a technique that never works as well as you hope). Getting the most out of Photoshop's Bézier toolset does require a bit of experience, but you can use the following technique to start drawing simple curves with a minimum of effort. In this example, the Pen tool is used to trace a basic shape:

1. To start the path, click once with the Pen tool (without dragging) to place a single point.

2. Move the cursor a small distance along the shape you're tracing, making sure the next segment you place won't have to curve too steeply.

3. As you click to place the next point, hold the mouse button down and drag in the same direction as the path. This reveals the handles, enabling you to curve the segment.

4. Move the handle until the segment matches the edge of the shape. (Take your time; as you get accustomed to the handles, it may take a moment or two to get it right.) Release the mouse button.

5. Hold down the (Option) [Alt] key and click the point you just placed. This hides the second curve handle, preventing it from adding curve to the next segment.

6. Repeat steps 2 through 5 until you complete the path. **A**

The advantage of this technique is that each segment is controlled by only one curve handle, making it much easier to shape the path as you create it.

Click to place
first point.

Click-drag to
place next point
and curve segment.

(Option) [Alt]-click
point to hide
second handle

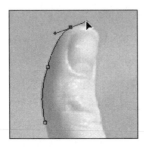

Click-drag to
place next point.

(Option) [Alt]-click
point to hide
second handle.

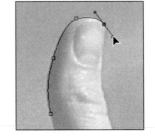

Continue until
path is complete.

A   *This simple path-editing technique will satisfy most of your needs in Photoshop, at least until you become more comfortable with the Pen tool.*

Issues to Consider

Closing a path. If you've determined that you need a closed path, remember to end on the first point you placed.

Editing a path. Don't try to get the path *perfect* the first time around. Just try to get as close as you can. When you've completed the path, you can always tweak it as necessary with the Direct Selection tool.

Be ready to Undo. If you click in error, don't try to repair the path on-the-fly (if you're new to the Pen tool, your path can quickly spin out of control). Instead, press (Command-Z) [Control-Z] to undo the last action, then try again.

Placing the path when tracing an image element. When tracing an element for a clipping path, try to place the path *just inside* the element's edge, shaving off a couple of pixels. This way, you reduce the chances of including any unwanted background pixels in the outline. When intending to use the path as a selection (for example, to recolor an element), try to place the path precisely along the edge of the element. This way, your edits won't be surrounded by an unsightly fringe.

L.2
Continuing an Existing Open Path

It's possible for a path to become deselected as you're creating it. Usually, this happens as a result of accessing the Direct Selection tool while using the Pen tool (which happens when you hold down the (Command) [Control] key). If you try to continue an unselected path, you actually create two separate subpaths instead, and the shape likely won't behave the way you expect. To reactivate a deselected path, click either end of it with the Pen tool. From there, continue placing new points.

L.3
Creating Multiple Open Subpaths

To create more than one open subpath in a single Paths palette item, you must deselect one completed subpath before starting the next—otherwise, the two will be connected by a segment. Follow these steps:

1. Create the first subpath.

2. Hold down the (Command) [Control] key to access the Direct Selection tool.

3. Deselect the path by clicking anywhere else on the image.

4. Create the next path.

L.4
Joining Two Open Subpaths

Unlike Illustrator and FreeHand, Photoshop doesn't have a command to automatically join two points with a segment. You have to do it manually: Click one point with the Pen tool, then click the other.

L.5

Transferring a Path to Another Palette Item

To transfer a path from one item to another in the Paths palette, follow these steps:

1. Select the entire subpath (by clicking once with the black arrow tool, or (Option) [Alt]-clicking with the white arrow).

2. Choose Edit: **Cut**. The subpath is removed.

3. Activate the palette item that you want to contain the subpath. If necessary, click the Create New Path button to add a blank palette item.

4. Choose Edit: **Paste**. The subpath appears in the palette item at the same position as before.

Issues to Consider

Changing the image dimensions may change the path's position. Note that if you change the width, height, or resolution before pasting the path, Photoshop places it in the center of the image window.

Make sure you select the entire shape. If you only select part of the path—for example, if you click a single point with the white arrow tool—you'll only transfer a segment or two. When this occurs, choose Edit: **Undo**, make sure the original path is completely selected, and try again.

L.6

Transferring a Path to Another Image

There are three ways to transfer a path or subpath between images:

Copy and paste. When you paste a path into a second image of the same width, height, and resolution, it retains its original position. When any dimensions are different, Photoshop places it in the center of the image. The new path always appears as a Work Path, even if it was saved in the original file.

Drag-and-drop a palette item. When you drag an item directly from the Paths palette onto another image, Photoshop treats it the same as a pasted path (see previous item), with one difference: if the path was saved, it appears in the second image as a saved item.

Drag-and-drop a subpath. If desired, use the black arrow tool to drag a subpath directly into another image. If another path is currently active in the second image, the new subpath is added to it. If no path is active, a new item appears in the Paths palette.

L.7

Drawing Objects with an Adjacent Edge

Using manual techniques, it is virtually impossible to draw two shapes that share an adjacent edge. For example, assume that you're creating a *selection template* for an article of clothing, or a series of paths that enable you to target certain areas consistently. The problem is that you can't view a path you've already drawn while drawing a new one. For example, the line between the sleeve and the body may appear to be obvious, but the two paths won't precisely match. They'll overlap slightly in some places, and not quite touch in others. When you apply tonal or color adjustments (especially any that involve blend modes, such as the recoloring techniques listed in Appendix H, *Colorizing Techniques*), any edge discrepancies will quickly produce incorrect colors and artifacting. Avoid this problem by using identical edge information for both shapes. Follow these steps:

1. Evaluate the image to determine the necessary paths.

2. Choose the Pen tool.

3. Click the Create New Path button to add a blank item to the Paths palette.

4. Draw and refine the first shape.

5. Determine which part of the path will abut the neighboring shape. (See *Issues to Consider*, below.)

6. Use the white arrow tool to select only the adjacent edge. For the best results, don't include the points on either end of the targeted portion. (See *Issues to Consider*, below.) **A**

7. Choose Edit: **Copy**.

8. In the Paths palette, click the Create New Path button. **B**

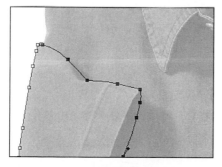

A *Selecting the adjacent edge.*

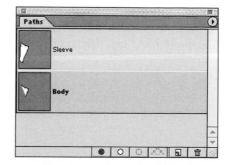

B *Creating a new palette item before drawing the path.*

9. Choose Edit: **Paste**. The copied portion appears in the same position as the original. **c**

10. Choose the Pen tool.

11. Click one of the endpoints of the new path and continue drawing the next shape. **D**

12. Repeat steps 4-11 for all shapes with adjacent edges.

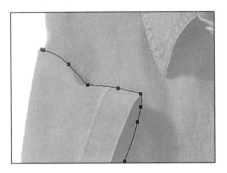

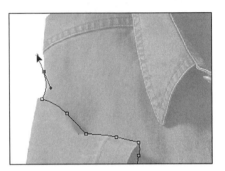

c *Copying the adjacent edge.*   **D** *Continuing the next shape.*

Issues to Consider

You may need to add points that specify the beginning and end of the adjacent edge. If necessary, use the Add Anchor Point tool to insert the points, then continue selecting.

Don't select the endpoints of the adjacent edge. When you copy and paste a point, you also include any segments attached to it. Photoshop places another point to close the segment. If possible, select all points along the adjacent edge *except* the endpoints. This way, when you copy and paste, the endpoints automatically fall into place. If you happen to include the endpoints, just delete the unwanted segments before continuing the path.

Two shapes may have more than one adjacent edge. Complex shapes may abut along more than one edge. When this occurs, copy and paste all of the edges first. Then use the Pen tool to connect the endpoints.

L.8

Converting a Path into a Shape

To convert a path into a colored-vector shape, follow these steps:

1. Activate the desired item in the Paths palette.

2. Choose Layer: New Fill Layer: **Solid Color**. The path is used to mask the contents of the new layer, creating the appearance of a vector shape.

3. Continue editing the shape.

Note that the original path remains untouched in the Paths palette. Delete it if necessary.

L.9

Converting a Shape into a Path

To convert a vector shape into a path, follow these steps:

1. Activate the desired shape in the Paths palette (where it is listed as a "Clipping Path").

2. Drag the palette item onto the Create New Path button. A new path appears, containing only the vector-based information used in the shape.

3. Continue editing the path.

Note that the original shape remains untouched in the Layers palette. Delete it if necessary.

Keyboard Shortcuts

Selection Tools

Action	Mac OS	Windows
Choose current Marquee tool	M (Shift-M to cycle)	M (Shift-M to cycle)
Draw marquee from centerpoint	Option-drag	Alt-drag
Constrain marquee to square or circle	Press Shift while drawing shape	Press Shift while drawing shape
Reposition marquee while drawing	Spacebar	Spacebar
Choose current Lasso tool	L (Shift-L to cycle)	L (Shift-L to cycle)
Switch from Lasso to Polygon Lasso	Option-click tool	Alt-click tool
Add point to a magnetic selection	Click with Magnetic Lasso	Click with Magnetic Lasso
Delete last-added point of magnetic selection	Delete	Backspace
Increase or reduce magnetic selection width	Press bracket keys	Press bracket keys
Close Polygon or Magnetic selection	Double-click with tool or press Return	Double-click with tool or press Return
Close Magnetic selection with straight segment	Option-double-click or Option-Return	Alt-double-click or Alt-Enter

Action	Mac OS	Windows
Cancel Polygon or Magnetic outline	Esc	Esc
Add to selection	Shift-drag with tool (or Shift-click palette item)	Shift-drag with tool (or Shift-click palette item)
Subtract from selection	Option-drag with tool (or Option-click	Alt-drag with tool (or Alt-click
Retain intersected area of selection outlines	Option-Shift drag with tool	Alt-Shift drag with tool
Choose Crop tool	C	C
Reposition crop marquee while drawing	Spacebar	Spacebar
Move crop marquee	Drag inside boundary	Drag inside boundary
Resize crop marquee	Drag boundary handle	Drag boundary handle
Resize crop marquee to origin	Option-drag boundary handle	Alt-drag boundary handle
Scale crop marquee proportionally	Shift-drag corner handle	Shift-drag corner handle
Scale crop marquee with respect to centerpoint	Option-drag corner handle	Alt-drag corner handle
Skew crop marquee	Command-drag side handle	Ctrl-drag side handle
Skew crop marquee along constrained axis	Command-Shift-drag side handle	Ctrl-Shift-drag side handle
Distort crop marquee	Command-Option drag side handle	Ctrl-Alt-drag side handle
Symmetrically distort crop marquee's opposite corners	Command-Option-drag corner handle	Ctrl-Alt-drag corner handle
Constrain-distort crop marquee for perspective effect	Command-Shift-drag corner handle	Ctrl-Shift-drag corner handle
Constrain-distort crop marquee for symmetrical perspective effect	Command-Option-Shift-drag corner handle	Ctrl-Alt-Shift-drag corner handle
Apply crop marquee	Double-click inside boundary or press Return	Double-click inside boundary or press Enter
Cancel crop marquee	Esc	Esc
Choose Move tool while in another tool (except Pen)	Type "V" or press and hold Command	Type "V" or press and hold Ctrl
Constrain movement to 45° angles	Shift-drag selection	Shift-drag selection

Action	Mac OS	Windows
Nudge selection in 1-pixel increments	Command-arrow key	Ctrl-arrow key
Nudge selection in 10-pixel increments	Command-Shift-arrow key	Ctrl-Shift-arrow key
Clone selection	Option-drag with Move tool	Alt-drag with Move tool
Clone selection in 1-pixel increments	Command-Option-arrow key	Ctrl-Alt-arrow key
Clone selection in 10-pixel increments	Command-Option-Shift-arrow key	Ctrl-Alt-Shift-arrow key
Move selection (outline only) in 1-pixel increments	Arrow-key while selection tool is active	Arrow-key while selection tool is active
Move selection (outline only) in 10-pixel increments	Shift-arrow-key while selection tool is active	Shift-arrow-key while selection tool is active
Set opacity of floating selection	Command-Shift-F	Ctrl-Shift-F
Enter or exit Quick Mask mode	Q	Q
Create inverted Quick Mask	Option-click Quick Mask icon	Alt-click Quick Mask icon
Change Quick Mask overlay color	Double-click Quick Mask icon	Double-click Quick Mask icon
View Quick Mask channel	Tilde (~)	Tilde (~)

Paint Tools

Action	Mac OS	Windows
Display cursor as crosshair	Caps Lock	Caps Lock
Choose Airbrush tool	J	J
Choose Pencil or Paintbrush tool	B (Shift-B to cycle)	B (Shift-B to cycle)
Choose Eraser tool	E (Shift-E to cycle)	E (Shift-E to cycle)
Choose History or Art History Brush	Y (Shift-Y to cycle)	Y (Shift-Y to cycle)
Choose Stamp tool	S (Shift-S to cycle)	S (Shift-S to cycle)
Choose Gradient or Paint Bucket	G (Shift-G to cycle)	G (Shift-G to cycle)
Choose Focus tool	R (Shift-R to cycle)	R (Shift-R to cycle)
Choose Toning tool	D (Shift-D to cycle)	D (Shift-D to cycle)
Revert image with Magic Eraser tool	Option-drag with Eraser tool	Alt-drag with Eraser tool
Specify an area to clone	Option-click with Clone Stamp tool	Alt-click with Clone Stamp tool

Action	Mac OS	Windows
Sharpen with Blur tool or blur with Sharpen tool	Option-drag	Alt-drag
Add foreground color while Smudging	Option-drag with Smudge tool	Alt-drag with Smudge tool
Darken with Dodge tool or Lighten with Burn tool	Option-drag	Alt-drag
Paint or Edit in a Straight Line	Click and then Shift Click	Click and then Shift Click
Change Opacity, Pressure or Exposure in 10% increments	Press number (1 through 0)	Press number (1 through 0)
Change Opacity, Pressure or Exposure to exact value	Press two numbers in a row	Press two numbers in a row
Increase or decrease brush size	Press bracket keys	Press bracket keys
Change brush hardness in increments of 25%	Press Shift-bracket key	Press Shift-bracket keys
Delete shape from brush picker	Option-click brush shape	Alt-click brush shape
Create new shape in brush picker	Click empty area in picker	Click empty area in picker
Edit brush shape	Click brush icon in Options bar	Click brush icon in Options bar
Set brush mode	*See "Blend Mode" under Layers palette shortcuts*	*See "Blend Mode" under Layers palette shortcuts*

Vector Tools

Action	Mac OS	Windows
Select Pen tool	P (Shift-P to cycle)	P (Shift-P to cycle)
Add corner to path	Click with Pen tool or Option-click with Freeform Pen tool	Click with Pen tool or Alt-click with Freeform Pen tool
Add smooth curve to path	Drag with Pen tool	Drag with Pen tool
Redirect second curve handle before placing next point	Option-click, then drag with Pen tool	Alt-click, then drag with Pen tool
Add point to magnetic path	Click with Magnetic Pen tool	Click with Magnetic Pen tool
Delete last point added with standard or Magnetic Pen tool	Delete	Delete
Draw freehand path segment	Option-drag with Freeform Pen tool	Alt-drag with Freeform Pen tool

Action	Mac OS	Windows
Toggle to convert direction tool from direct select tool	Command-Option-over anchor point	Ctrl-Alt-over anchor point
Increase or decrease magnetic pen width	Press bracket keys	Press bracket keys
Close magnetic selection	Double-click with Magnetic Pen tool or click first point	Double-click with Magnetic Pen tool or click first point
Close magnetic selection with straight segment	Option-double-click or Option-Return	Alt-double-click or Alt-Return
Cancel magnetic or freeform path	Esc	Esc
Choose path selection tool (black or white arrow)	A, or press and hold Command when a Pen tool is active	A, or press and hold Ctrl when a Pen tool is active
Access path selection tool while drawing	Press and hold Command while a Pen tool is active	Press and hold Ctrl while a Pen tool is active
Toggle between path selection tools	Shift-A, or Option-click item in Toolbar	Shift-A, or Alt-click item in Toolbar
Choose insert or remove point tool	Plus (+) or minus (−) while Pen tool is active	Plus (+) or minus (−) while Pen tool is active
Nudge selected points	Press arrow keys	Press arrow keys
Select multiple points in a path	Shift-click points with white arrow or	Shift-click points with white arrow
Select entire path	Click with black arrow or Option-click with white arrow	Click with black arrow or Option-click with white arrow
Clone path	Option-drag path with arrow	Alt-drag path with arrow
Convert corner or cusp to smooth arc	Command-Option-drag	Ctrl-Alt-drag
Convert arc to corner	Command-Option-click	Ctrl-Alt-click
Convert arc to cusp	Command-Option-drag with arrow or Option-drag with Pen tool	Ctrl-Alt-drag with arrow or Alt-drag with Pen tool
Insert point in path	Click segment with Pen tool or Option-click with Remove Point tool	Click segment with Pen tool or Alt-click with Remove Point tool

Action	Mac OS	Windows
Remove point from path	Click point with Remove Point tool or Option-click with Insert Point tool	Click point with Remove Point tool or Alt-click with Insert Point tool
Select all text on a text layer	Double-click "T" in Layers palette	Double-click "T" in Layers palette
Select all text (while editing text)	Command-A	Control-A
Select a single word	Double-click word with Type tool	Double-click word with Type tool
Select word to left or right	Command-Shift left or right arrow	Ctrl-Shift left or right arrow
Show/Hide text highlight while editing	Command-H	Ctrl-H
Add character outlines to a selection	Shift-click with Type tool (in tool's Mask mode)	Shift-click with Type tool (in tool's Mask mode)
Cut letter-shaped holes into a selection	Option-click with Type tool (in tool's Mask mode)	Alt-click with Type tool (in tool's Mask mode)
Retain areas where character outlines and selection intersect	Shift-Option-click with Type tool (in tool's Mask mode)	Shift-Alt-click with Type tool (in tool's Mask mode)

Special Tools

Action	Mac OS	Windows
Choose Eyedropper, Color Sampler, or Measure tool	I (Shift-I to cycle)	I (Shift-I to cycle)
Sample foreground color	Option-click with Paint tool	Alt-click with Paint tool
Sample background color	Option-click with Eyedropper	Alt-click with Eyedropper
Place color sampler	Shift-click with Eyedropper	Shift-click with Eyedropper
Delete color sample	Option-click with color sampler tool, or Option-Shift-click with Eyedropper	Alt-click with color sampler tool, or Alt-Shift-click with Eyedropper
Measure angle between two lines (Protractor option)	Option-drag endpoint	Alt-drag endpoint

View Tools

Action	Mac OS	Windows
Choose View mode	F (Shift-F to cycle)	F (Shift-F to cycle)

Color Controls

Action	Mac OS	Windows
Reset foreground/background color to black and white	D	D
Switch foreground/background colors	X	X

File Menu

Action	Mac OS	Windows
New image	Command-N	Ctrl-N
New image with default settings	Command-Option-N	Ctrl-Alt-N
Open	Command-O	Ctrl-O
Close	Command-W	Ctrl-W or Ctrl-F4
Close All	Command-Shift-W	Ctrl-Shift-W or Ctrl-Shift-F4
Activate No button when closing image	N	N
Activate Don't Save or Don't Flatten button when closing	D	D
Save	Command-S	Ctrl-S
Save As	Command-Shift-S	Ctrl-Shift-S
Save a Copy As	Command-Option-S	Ctrl-Alt-S
Save for Web	Command-Option-Shift-S	Ctrl-Alt-Shift-S
Save flattened copy of layered image	Command-Option-S	Ctrl-Alt-S
Page Setup	Command-Shift-P	Ctrl-Alt-O
Print Options	Command-Option-P	Ctrl-Alt-P
Print Setup	Command-Shift-P	Ctrl-Shift-P
Print	Command-P	Ctrl-P
Quit/Exit	Command-Q	Ctrl-Q

Edit Menu

Action	Mac OS	Windows
Undo or redo last operation	Command-Z	Ctrl-Z
Undo operation prior to last one	Command-Option-Z	Ctrl-Alt-Z
Redo undone operation	Command-Shift-Z	Ctrl-Shift-Z
Step Backward	Command-Option-Z	Ctrl-Alt-Z
Step Forward	Command-Shift-Z	Ctrl-Shift-Z
Fade Last Operation	Command-Shift-F	Ctrl-Shift-F
Copy	Command-C	Ctrl-C
Copy Merged	Command-Shift-C	Ctrl-Shift-C
Cut	Command-X	Ctrl-X or F2
Paste	Command-V or F4	Ctrl-V or F4
Paste image into selection	Command-Shift-V	Ctrl-Shift-V
Paste image behind selection	Command-Option-Shift-V	Ctrl-Alt-Shift-V
Clear	Delete	Delete
Fill	Shift-Delete or Shift F5	Shift-Backspace or Shift F5
Fill from History	Command-Option-Delete	Ctrl-Alt-Backspace
Fill selection or layer with foreground color	Option-Delete	Alt-Backspace
Fill layer with foreground color but preserve transparency	Shift-Option-Delete	Shift-Alt-Backspace
Fill selection on background layer with background color	Delete	Backspace Or Delete
Fill selection on any layer with background color	Command-Delete	Ctrl-Backspace
Fill layer with background color but preserve transparency	Command-Shift-Delete	Ctrl-Shift-Backspace
Fill selection with source state in History palette	Command-Option-Delete	Ctrl-Alt-Backspace
Display Fill dialog box	Shift-Delete or Shift F5	Shift-Backspace or Shift F5
Free Transform	Command-T	Ctrl-T
Transform Again	Command-Shift-T	Ctrl-Shift-T
Transform Again (with copy)	Command-Option-Shift-T	Ctrl-Alt-Shift-T

Action	Mac OS	Windows
Freely transform selection, layer or path	Command-T	Command-T
Duplicate selection and freely transform	Command-Option-T	Ctrl-Alt-T
Move transformation origin	Drag crosshair target	Drag crosshair target
Resize image	Drag boundary handle	Drag boundary handle
Resize with respect to origin	Option-drag boundary handle	Alt-drag boundary handle
Scale proportionally	Shift-drag corner	Shift-drag corner
Scale with respect to center point	Option-drag corner	Alt-drag corner
Scale proportionally with respect to center point	Option-Shift-drag corner	Alt-Shift-drag corner
Skew image	Command-drag side handle	Ctrl-drag side handle
Skew image along constrained axis	Command-Shift-drag side handle	Ctrl-Shift-drag side handle
Skew image with respect to origin	Command-Option-drag side handle	Ctrl-Alt-drag side handle
Skew image along constrained axis with respect to origin	Command-Option-Shift-drag side handle	Ctrl-Alt-Shift-Shift-drag side handle
Distort image	Command-drag corner handle	Ctrl-drag corner handle
Symmetrically distort opposite corners	Command-Option-drag side handle	Ctrl-Alt-drag side handle
Constrained distort for perspective effect	Command-Shift-drag corner handle	Ctrl-Shift-drag corner handle
Constrained distort for symmetrical perspective effect	Command-Option-Shift-drag corner handle	Ctrl-Alt-Shift-drag corner handle
Apply specific transformation Transform mode	Ctrl-click in image window	Right-click in in Free image window
Accept transformation	Double-click inside boundary or press Return	Double-click inside boundary or press Enter
Replay last transformation	Command-Shift-T	Ctrl-Shift-T
Cancel transformation	Esc	Esc
Duplicate selection and apply last transformation	Command-Option-Shift-T	Ctrl-Alt-Shift-T

Action	Mac OS	Windows
Color Settings	Command-Shift-K	Ctrl-Shift-K
Preferences	Command-K	Ctrl-K
Preferences (most recent panel)	Command-Option-K	Ctrl-Option-K

Image Menu

Action	Mac OS	Windows
Access dialog box with last-used settings	Option-choose Image: **Adjust** command	Alt-choose Image: **Adjust** command
Levels	Command-L	Ctrl-L
Auto Levels	Command-Shift-L	Ctrl -Shift-L
Auto Contrast	Command-Option-Shift-L	Ctrl-Alt-Shift-L
Curves	Command-M	Ctrl-M
Curves: Add point to curve	Click graph line	Click graph line
Curves: Add specific color as a new point on composite curve	Command-click in image window	Ctrl-click in image window
Curves: Add color as new point on independent channel curves	Command-Shift-click image window	Ctrl-Shift-click in in image window
Curves: Nudge selected curve point	Press arrow key	Press arrow key
Curves: Select next curve point	Command-Tab	Ctrl-Tab
Curves: Select previous curve point	Command-Shift-Tab	Ctrl-Shift-Tab
Curves: Delete curve point	Command-click point	Ctrl-click point
Curves: Select multiple curve points	Shift-click point	Shift-click point
Curves: Deselect all points	Command-D	Ctrl-D
Color Balance	Command-B	Ctrl-B
Hue/Saturation	Command-U	Ctrl-U
Hue/Saturation: Move range to new location	Command-drag color bar in dialog box	Ctrl-drag color bar in dialog box
Hue/Saturation: Add colors to range	Shift-click or drag in image window	Shift-click or drag in image window
Hue/Saturation: Subtract colors from color range	Option-click or drag in image window	Alt-click or drag in image window
Hue/Saturation: Edit all colors	Command-tilde (~)	Ctrl-tilde (~)
Hue/Saturation: Edit predefined color range	Command-1 through Command-6	Ctrl-1 through Ctrl-6
Duplicate image, bypassing dialog box	Option-choose Image: **Duplicate**	Alt-choose Image: **Duplicate**

Action	Mac OS	Windows
Invert	Command-I	Ctrl-I
Desaturate	Command-Shift-U	Ctrl-Shift-U
Extract	Command-Option-X	Ctrl-Alt-X
Liquify	Command-Shift-X	Ctrl-Shift-X

Layer Menu

Action	Mac OS	Windows
New Layer	Command-Option-Shift-N	Ctrl-Alt-Shift-N
New Layer (with options)	Command-Shift-N	Ctrl-Shift-N
New Layer Via Copy	Command-J	Ctrl-J
New Layer Via Cut	Command-Shift-J	Ctrl-Shift-J
New Layer via Copy (no dialog box)	Command-J	Ctrl-J
New Layer via Copy (with dialog box)	Command-Option-J	Ctrl-Alt-J
New Layer via Cut (no dialog box)	Command-Shift-J	Ctrl-Shift-J
New Layer via Cut (with dialog box)	Command-Option-Shift-J	Ctrl-Alt-Shift-J
New Layer from Floating Selection	Command-Shift-J	Ctrl-Shift-J
Group with Previous Layer	Command-G	Ctrl-C
Bring Layer Forward	Command-]	Ctrl-]
Bring Layer to Front	Command-Shift-]	Ctrl-Shift-]
Send Layer Backward	Command-[	Ctrl-[
Send Layer to Back	Command-Shift-[	Ctrl-Shift-[
Ungroup Layers	Command-Shift-G	Ctrl-Shift-G
Adjust "fuzziness" in Layer Styles dialog box	Option-drag Blend If slider triangle	Alt-drag Blend If slider triangle
Clone contents of layer into next layer down	Command-Option-E	Ctrl-Alt-E
Clone contents of linked layers to active layer	Command-Option-E	Ctrl-Alt-E
Clone contents of all visible layers to active layer	Command-Option-Shift-E	Ctrl-Alt-Shift-E
Merge Down	Command-E	Ctrl-E
Merge Group	Command-E	Ctrl-E
Merge layer set	Command-E	Ctrl-E

Action	Mac OS	Windows
Merge Linked	Command-E	Ctrl-E
Merge Visible	Command-Shift-E	Ctrl-Shift-E
Merge grouped layers	Command-E	Ctrl-E
Edit Layer Style	Double-click layer	Double-click layer
Switch between layer styles in Layer Styles dialog box	Command-1 through Command-0	Ctrl-1 through Ctrl-0

Select Menu

Action	Mac OS	Windows
Select All	Command-A	Ctrl-A
Deselect	Command-D	Ctrl-D
Reselect	Command-Shift-D	Ctrl-Shift-D
Inverse selection	Command-Shift-I or Shift-F7	Ctrl-Shift-I or Shift-F7
Feather selection	Command-Option-D or Shift-F6	Ctrl-Alt-D or Shift-F6
Hide or Show Selection	Command-H	Ctrl-H

Filter Menu

Action	Mac OS	Windows
Repeat filter with last-used settings	Command-F	Ctrl-F
Apply last filter (access dialog box)	Command-Option-F	Ctrl-Alt-F
Scroll preview in Filter dialog box	Drag in preview box or click in image window	Drag in preview box or click in image window
Zoom preview in Filter dialog box	Command-click and Option-click	Ctrl-click and Alt-click
Increase selected value by 1 (or 0.1, in low end of range)	Up arrow	Up arrow
Decrease value by 1 (or 0.1, in low end of range)	Down arrow	Down arrow
Increase value by 10 (or 1, in low end of range)	Shift-up arrow	Shift-up arrow
Decrease value by 10 (or 1, in low end of range)	Shift-down arrow	Shift-down arrow
Adjust Angle value in 15°- increments	Shift-drag in Angle wheel	Shift-drag in Angle wheel

Action	Mac OS	Windows
Reset options inside dialog box	Option-click Cancel button or Option-Esc	Alt-click Cancel button or Alt-Esc
Lighting Effects: Duplicate light source in dialog box	Option-drag light	Alt-drag light
Lighting Effects: Remove light source	Delete	Delete
Lighting Effects: Adjust footprint size and light angle	Shift-drag handle	Shift-drag handle
Lighting Effects: Adjust light angle without affecting footprint	Command-drag handle	Ctrl-drag handle
3D Transform: Switch between arrow tools	V, A or Command-Tab	V, A or Ctrl-Tab
3D Transform: Select Cube, Sphere or Cylinder tool	M, N or C	M, N or C
3D Transform: Edit shape with pan camera or trackball	E or R	E or R
3D Transform: Delete selected 3D transform shape	Delete	Delete

View Menu

Action	Mac OS	Windows
Preview how image sits on printed page	Click Document Info box in status bar	Click Document Info box in status bar
View size and resolution of image	Option-click Document Info box in status bar	Alt-click Document Info box in status bar
View image tile information	Command-click Document Info box in status bar	Ctrl-click Document Info box in status bar
Proof Colors	Command-Y	Ctrl-Y
Gamut Warning	Command-Shift-Y	Ctrl-Shift-Y
Zoom In	Command-plus (+)	Ctrl-plus (+)
Zoom Out	Command-minus (-)	Ctrl-minus (-)
Zoom In without changing window size	Command-Spacebar-click or Command-Option-plus (+)	Ctrl-Spacebar-click or Ctrl-Alt-plus (+)
Zoom in and change window size to fit	Command-plus (+)	Ctrl-plus (+)

Action	Mac OS	Windows
Zoom out without changing window size	Option-Spacebar-click or Command-Option-minus (-)	Alt-Spacebar-click or Ctrl-minus (-)
Zoom out and change window size to fit	Command-minus (-)	Ctrl-Alt-minus (-)
Apply Zoom value but keep magnification box active	Shift-Return	Shift-Enter
Fit On Screen	Command-Zero (0)	Ctrl-Zero (0)
Actual Pixels (100%)	Command-Option-Zero (0)	Ctrl-Alt-Zero (0)
Show/Hide Rulers	Command-R	Ctrl-R
Show Extras (Selection Edges, Grids, Guides)	Command-H	Ctrl-H
Show/Hide Grid	Command-Option-"	Ctrl-Alt-"
Show/Hide Guides	Command-"	Ctrl-"
Show/Hide Path	Command-Shift-H	Ctrl-Shift-H
Snap (to Grids, Guides or document boundaries)	Command-semicolon (;)	Ctrl-semicolon (;)
Scroll image with Hand tool	Spacebar-drag, or drag in Navigator palette	Spacebar-drag, or drag in Navigator palette
Scroll up or down one screen	Page Up or Page Down	Page Up or Page Down
Scroll up or down (smaller increments)	Shift-Page Up or Shift-Page Down	Shift-Page Up or Shift-Page Down
Scroll up or down one frame in a Filmstrip file	Shift-Page Up or Shift-Page Down	Shift-Page Up or Shift-Page Down
Scroll left or right one screen	Command-Page Up or Command-Page Down	Ctrl-Page Up or Ctrl-Page Down
Scroll left or right (smaller increments)	Command-Shift-Page Up or Command-Shift-Page Down	Ctrl-Shift-Page Up or Ctrl-Shift-Page Down
Jump to upper left corner	Press Home	Press Home
Switch to lower right corner	Press End	Press End
Magnify to custom zoom ratio	Command-Spacebar-Drag or Command-Drag in Navigator palette	Ctrl-Spacebar-drag or Ctrl-drag in Navigator drag or Ctrl-
Lock Guides	Command-Option-semicolon (;)	Ctrl-Alt-semicolon (;)

Action	Mac OS	Windows
Create guide	Drag from ruler	Drag from ruler
Move guide	Drag guide with Move tool or Command-drag with other tool	Drag guide with Move tool or Ctrl-drag with other tool
Snap guide to ruler tick marks	Press Shift while dragging guide	Press Shift while dragging guide
Toggle snapping guides	Command-semicolon (;)	Ctrl-semicolon (;)
Lock or unlock guides	Command-Option-semicolon (;)	Ctrl-Alt-semicolon (;)
Toggle snapping grid	Command-semicolon (;)	Ctrl-semicolon (;)
Edit guide color and grid increments	Command-double-click guide	Ctrl-double-click guide
Toggle guide between horizontal and vertical	Press Option while dragging guide	Press Alt while dragging guide

Palettes

Action	Mac OS	Windows
Display or hide all palettes and Toolbar	Tab	Tab
Display or hide palettes except Toolbar and Options bar	Shift-tab	Shift-tab
Hide Toolbar	Tab, then Shift-tab	Tab, then Shift-tab
Separate palettes	Drag panel tab	Drag panel tab
Snap palette to edge of screen	Shift-click palette title bar	Shift-click palette title bar
Fully collapse palette	Option-click collapse box or double-click panel tab	Alt-click collapse box or double-click panel tab
Permanently delete item from palette	Option-click trash can	Alt-click trash can

Info Palette

Action	Mac OS	Windows
Display or hide Info palette	F8	F8
Change unit of measure	Ctrl-click ruler	Right-click ruler

Color Palette

Action	Mac OS	Windows
Show or Hide Color palette	F6	F6
Set foreground color from palette's color bar	Click bar	Click bar
Set Background color from palette's color bar	Option-click bar	Alt-click bar
Cycle through color bars	Shift-click bar	Shift-click bar
Specify new color bar	Control-click bar	Right-click bar

Swatches Palette

Action	Mac OS	Windows
Set foreground color from Swatches palette	Click swatch	Click swatch
Set background color from Swatches palette	Option-Click swatch	Alt-Click swatch
Delete swatch from palette	Command-click swatch	Ctrl-click swatch
Replace swatch with foreground color	Shift-click swatch	Shift-click swatch
Add new swatch to palette	Click in empty area of palette or Shift-Option-click swatch	Click in empty area of palette or Shift-Alt-click swatch

History Palette

Action	Mac OS	Windows
Revert to a specific editing state	Click item in History palette	Click item in History palette
Duplicate previously performed operation	Option-click item in History palette	Option-click item in History palette
Target state for selective reversion techniques	Click Source box for that state	Click Source box for that state
Create snapshot from active state	Click New Snapshot button	Click New Snapshot button
Create new image from active state	Click New Document button	Click New Document button

Actions Palette

Action	Mac OS	Windows
Display or hide Actions palette	F9	F9
Play script	Command-double-click item in Actions palette	Ctrl-double-click item in Actions palette

Layers Palette

Action	Mac OS	Windows
Show/Hide Layers palette	F7	F7
View single layer, hiding all other layers	Option-click view box beside layer	Alt-click view box beside layer
Add new layer above current layer (no dialog box)	Command-Shift-N or click New Layer button	Ctrl-Shift-N or click New Layer button
Create new layer below current layer (no dialog box)	Command-click New Layer button	Ctrl-click New Layer button
Create new layer above current layer (with dialog box)	Command-Option-Shift-N, or Option-click New Layer button	Ctrl-Alt-Shift-N or Alt-click New Layer button
Create new layer below current layer (with dialog box)	Command-Option-click New Layer button	Ctrl-Alt-click New Layer button
New adjustment layer (with options)	Option-click New Adjustment Layer button	Alt-click New Adjustment Layer button
Duplicate layer	Drag palette item onto New Layer button, or press Command-A, then Command-J	Drag palette item onto New Layer button, or press Ctrl-A, then Ctrl-J
Activate layer above current layer	Option-]	Alt-]
Activate layer below current layer	Option-[	Alt-[
Activate top layer	Option-Shift-[	Alt-Shift-]
Activate bottom layer	Option-Shift-[	Alt-Shift-[
Bring layer forward one level	Command-]	Ctrl-]
Send layer backward one level	Command-[	Ctrl-[
Bring layer to front	Command-Shift-]	Ctrl-Shift-]
Send layer to back	Command-Shift-[	Ctrl-Shift-]
Target layer by clicking image (with Move tool)	Command-click or Option-Ctrl–click with Move tool	Ctrl-click or Alt-right-click with Move tool

Action	Mac OS	Windows
Target layer by clicking image (with any tool)	Command-Option-Ctrl–click with tool	Ctrl-Alt-right click with tool
Select from overlapping layers (with Move tool)	Ctrl-click image	Right-click image
Select from overlapping layers (with any tool)	Command-Ctrl-click image with tool	Ctrl-right click image with tool
Toggle between current lock setting and no locks	Backslash (/)	Backslash (/)
Convert layer contents to selection outline	Command-click layer in palette	Ctrl-click layer in palette
Add layer-based selection to current selection	Command-Shift-click layer in palette	Ctrl-Shift-click layer in palette
Subtract layer-based selection from current selection	Command-Option-click layer in palette	Ctrl-Alt-click layer in palette
Intersect transparency mask with selection	Command-Option-Shift-click layer in palette	Ctrl-Alt-Shift-click layer in palette
Move contents of entire layer	Drag with Move tool or Command-drag with any tool	Drag with Move tool or Ctrl-drag with any tool
Move entire layer in 1-pixel increments	Command-arrow key	Ctrl-arrow key
Move entire layer in 10-pixel increments	Command-Shift-arrow key	Ctrl-Shift-arrow key
Link layer to active layer	Command-Option-Ctrl-Shift-click layer	Ctrl-Alt-Shift-right click layer
Unlink layer from active layer	Command-Option-Ctrl-Shift-click layer	Ctrl-Alt-Shift-right click layer
Unlink all layers from active layer	Command-Option-Ctrl-Shift-click active layer	Ctrl-Alt-Shift-right click active layer
Delete linked layers or sets	Command-click Delete button	Ctrl-click trash Delete button
Add Layer Set	Click Folder icon in Layers palette	Click Folder icon in Layers palette
Set opacity of active layer in 10% increments	Press number (1 through 0) when selection tool is active	Press number (1 through 0) when selection tool is active
Set opacity of active layer to any percentage	Press two numbers when selection tool is active	Press two numbers when selection tool is active

Action	Mac OS	Windows
Edit layer's Blend options	Double-click layer in palette	Double-click layer in palette
Edit Layer Style	Double-click style symbol on layer	Double-click style symbol on layer
Set blend mode	Option-Shift-letter	Alt-Shift-letter
Cycle through blend modes	Shift-plus (+) or Shift-minus (-)	Shift-plus (+) or Shift-minus (-)
Blend mode: Normal	Option-Shift-N or Option-Shift-L	Alt-Shift-N or Alt-Shift-L
Blend mode: Dissolve	Option-Shift-I	Alt-Shift-I
Blend mode: Clear	Option-Shift-R	Alt-Shift-R
Blend mode: Multiply	Option-Shift-M	Alt-Shift-M
Blend mode: Screen	Option-Shift-S	Alt-Shift-S
Blend mode: Overlay	Option-Shift-O	Alt-Shift-O
Blend mode: Soft Light	Option-Shift-F	Alt-Shift-F
Blend mode: Hard Light	Option-Shift-H	Alt-Shift-H
Blend mode: Color Dodge	Option-Shift-D	Alt-Shift-D
Blend mode: Color Burn	Option-Shift-B	Alt-Shift-B
Blend mode: Darken	Option-Shift-K	Alt-Shift-K
Blend mode: Lighten	Option-Shift-G	Alt-Shift-G
Blend mode: Difference	Option-Shift-E	Alt-Shift-E
Blend mode: Exclusion	Option-Shift-X	Alt-Shift-X
Blend mode: Hue	Option-Shift-U	Alt-Shift-U
Blend mode: Saturation	Option-Shift-T	Alt-Shift-T
Blend mode: Color blend	Option-Shift-C	Alt-Shift-C
Blend mode: Luminosity	Option-Shift-Y	Alt-Shift-Y
Blend mode: Pass Through (layer set)	Option-Shift-P	Alt-Shift-P
Group layers	Option-click line between layers	Alt-click line between layers
Ungroup layers	Option-click dotted line between layers in palette	Alt-click dotted line between layers in palette
Add layer set (with naming and blending options)	Option-click Folder icon in palette	Alt-click Folder icon in palette
Layer Mask: Switch view from mask to image	Command-tilde (~)	Ctrl-tilde (~)
Layer Mask: Switch view from image to layer mask	Command-backslash (/)	Ctrl-backslash (/)

Action	Mac OS	Windows
Layer Mask: View mask as colored overlay	Option-Shift-click layer mask thumbnail or press backslash (/)	Alt-Shift-click layer mask thumbnail or press backslash (/)
Layer Mask: Disable mask	Shift-click layer mask thumbnail	Shift-click layer mask thumbnail
Layer Mask: Convert mask to selection	Command-click layer mask thumbnail, or Command-Option-backslash (/)	Ctrl-click layer mask thumbnail, or Ctrl-Alt-backslash (/)
Layer Mask: Add mask to selection	Command-Shift-click layer mask thumbnail	Ctrl-Shift-click layer mask thumbnail
Layer Mask: Subtract mask from selection	Command-Option-click layer mask thumbnail	Ctrl-Alt-click layer mask thumbnail
Layer Mask: Intersect mask with selection	Command-Option-Shift-click layer Mask thumbnail	Ctrl-Alt-Shift-click layer Mask thumbnail
Layer Clipping Path: Add clipping path	Command-click Mask button in palette	Ctrl-click Mask button in palette
Layer Clipping Path: Add clipping path using current path	Command-click Mask icon in Layers palette with path active	Ctrl-click Mask icon in Layers palette with path active
Layer Clipping Path: Disable path	Shift-click Layer Clipping Path thumbnail	Shift-click Layer Clipping Path thumbnail
Layer Clipping Path: Toggle path for editing	Option-click Layer Clipping Path thumbnail	Alt-click Layer Clipping Path thumbnail

Channels Palette

Action	Mac OS	Windows
Activate or deactivate color channel	Shift-click channel name in Channels palette	Shift-click channel name in Channels palette
Switch to composite color view	Command-tilde (~)	Ctrl-tilde (~)
Switch between individual color and mask channels	Command-1 through Command-9	Ctrl-1 through Ctrl-9
Create alpha channel filled with black	Click New Channel button	Click New Channel button
Save selection as a channel	Click Save Selection button	Click Save Selection button

Action	Mac OS	Windows
Save selection as a channel and set options	Option-click Save Selection button	Option-click Save Selection button
View channel as colored overlay	Tilde (~)	Tilde (~)
Convert channel to selection	Command-click channel in palette or Command-Option-channel number	Ctrl-click channel in palette or Ctrl-Alt-channel number
Add channel-based selection to current selection	Command-Shift-click channel name	Ctrl-Shift-click channel name
Subtract channel-based selection from current selection	Command-Option-click channel name	Ctrl-Alt-click channel name
Intersect channel-based selection with current selection	Command-Option-Shift-click channel name	Ctrl-Alt-Shift-click channel name
Add spot color channel from selection	Option-Command-click New Channel button	Alt-Ctrl-click New Channel button

Paths Palette

Action	Mac OS	Windows
Show or hide path	Command-Shift-H	Ctrl-Shift-H
Save and name path for future use	Double-click Work Path item in palette	Double-click Work Path item in palette
Deactivate path	Click in empty portion of palette	Click in empty portion of palette
Convert path to selection outline	Command-click path name in Paths palette	Ctrl click path name in Paths palette
Add path-based selection to current selection	Command-Shift-click path in palette, or Shift-Enter	Ctrl-Shift-click path in palette, or Shift-Enter
Subtract path-based selection from current selection	Command-Option-click path name or Option-Enter	Ctrl-Alt-click path name or Alt-Enter
Intersect path-based selection to current selection	Command-Option-Shift-click path name or Shift-Option-Enter	Ctrl-Alt-Shift-click path name or Shift-Alt-Enter
Apply brushstroke around perimeter of path	Press Enter while Paint tool is active	Press Enter while Paint tool is active

Action	Mac OS	Windows
Revert around perimeter of path	Press Option-Enter when Eraser tool is active	Press Alt-Enter when Eraser tool is active

Character Palette

Action	Mac OS	Windows
Increase type size two pixels (or points)	Command-Shift-greater than (>)	Ctrl-Shift-greater than (>)
Decrease type size two pixels (or points)	Command-Shift-less than (<)	Ctrl-Shift-less than (<)
Increase type size 10 pixels	Command-Option-Shift-greater than (>)	Ctrl-Alt-Shift-greater than (>)
Decrease type size 10 pixels	Command-Option-Shift-less than (<)	Ctrl-Alt-Shift-less than (<)
Reduce kerning 1/10 em	Command-Option-left arrow	Ctrl-Alt-left arrow
Increase kerning 1/10 em	Command-Option-right arrow	Ctrl-Alt-right arrow
Reduce kerning 1/50 em	Option-left arrow	Alt-left arrow
Increase kerning 1/50 em	Option-right arrow	Alt-right arrow
Bold/unbold text	Command-Shift-B	Ctrl-Shift-B
Italicize or unitalicize text	Command-Shift-I	Ctrl-Shift-I
Remove all text styles	Command-Shift-Y	Ctrl-Shift-Y
Underline text	Command-Shift-U	Ctrl-Shift-U
Strikethrough text	Command-Shift-backslash (/)	Ctrl-Shift-backslash (/)
Make all text uppercase or lowercase	Command-Shift-K	Ctrl-Shift-K
Small caps text	Command-Shift-H	Ctrl-Shift-H
Superscript text	Command-Shift-(+)	Ctrl-Shift-(+)
Subscript text	Command-Shift-Option-plus (+)	Ctrl-Shift-Alt-plus (+)
Set horizontal scale to 100%	Command-Shift-X	Ctrl-Shift-X
Set vertical scale to 100%	Command-Shift-Option-X	Ctrl-Shift-Alt-X
Increase leading 2 pixels	Option-down arrow	Alt-down arrow
Decrease leading 2 pixels	Option-up arrow	Alt-up arrow
Increase leading 10 pixels	Command-Option-down arrow	Ctrl-Alt-down arrow

Action	Mac OS	Windows
Decrease leading 10 pixels	Command-Option-up arrow	Ctrl-Alt-up arrow
Set leading to Auto	Command-Option-Shift-A	Ctrl-Alt-Shift-A
Increase baseline shift 2 pixels	Option-Shift-up arrow	Alt-Shift-up arrow
Decrease baseline shift 2 pixels	Option-Shift-down arrow	Alt-Shift-down arrow
Increase baseline shift 10 pixels	Command-Option-Shift-up arrow	Ctrl-Alt-Shift-up arrow
Decrease baseline shift 10 pixels	Command-Option-Shift-down arrow	Ctrl-Alt-Shift-down arrow

Paragraph Palette

Action	Mac OS	Windows
Left-align text	Command-Shift-L	Ctrl-Shift-L
Center-align text	Command-Shift-C	Ctrl-Shift-C
Right-align text	Command-Shift-R	Ctrl-Shift-R
Justify all text	Command-Shift-F	Ctrl-Shift-F
Justify all text (except last line)	Command-Shift-J	Ctrl-Shift-J
Insert non-breaking space	Option-spacebar	Ctrl-Alt-X

Color Plates

10.2 The RGB/CMY Model

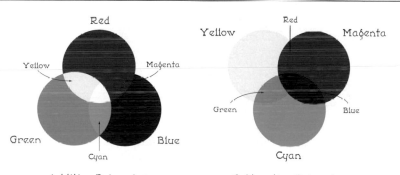

Additive Primaries   Subtractive Primaries

A *When you combine full intensities of the additive primaries (the basis of transmitted light), the result is white. When you combine full intensities of the subtractive primaries (the basis of reflected light), the result is black. Note how combining two primaries of one model produces a primary of the other.*

10.2   The RGB/CMY Model

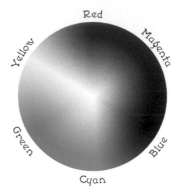

B *The RGB/CMY color wheel alternates between the additive and subtractive primaries. To determine a color's complement, look for the value directly across the wheel.*

10.5   The HSB Model

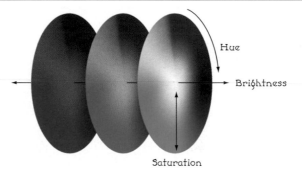

A *The HSB color space is cylindrically shaped. Hue refers to a color's position around the RGB/CMY color wheel. Saturation determines the intensity of a color, or its position between the center of the wheel and the outer edge. Brightness determines how light or dark a color appears, or its position between the front and back of the cylinder.*

B.9 Using Quick Mask to "Paint" a Selection Area

A *Painting a Quick Mask.*   **B** *Quick Mask converted to selection.*

B.17 Creating a Color Range Selection

A *Original image.*   **E** *The edited selection.*

B.21 Creating a Complex Mask: Extract Command

A *Original image.*   **E** *Mask used to desaturate background.*

B.22   Creating a Complex Mask: Color Channels

A   *Original image.*

H   *Adjusted image—note that only the sky is affected.*

G.4   Sharpening Full-Color Images

Original   A: 120 R: 2.0 T: 3   Radius too high (4.0)

A   *Normal detail (consisting of bold, clearly-defined shapes) can tolerate a higher Radius and lower Threshold, with less possibility of artifacting or lost detail.*

Original   A: 150 R: 1.0 T: 3   Radius too high (3.0)

B   *Fine detail (like branches against the sky) requires a lower Radius. Higher settings may obliterate the vital info.*

G.4   Sharpening Full-Color Images (continued)

| Original | A: 170 R: 1.5 T: 10 | Threshold too low (3) |

c *Subtle detail (like this apple skin) requires a higher Threshold. If every pixel is sharpened, the image appears textured and unnatural.*

G.6   Sharpening Fleshtones

| Original | Globally sharpened | Only cyan and black channels sharpened |

A *Globally-sharpened fleshtones often suffer from an over-accentuated, sickly appearance. By sharpening the channels that contain the least amount of fleshtone data, you emphasize important detail without adding texture to the skin.*

G.7   Evaluating Shadows and Highlights

A *If an image initially suffers from blown-out highlights or plugged shadows, no amount of correcting can save it. The colors are reasonably balanced in the scan on the left, but the shadows are plugged in, and the highlights are almost solid white. The colors are also balanced on the right, but the shadow and highlight areas carry significantly more detail.*

G.9   Reading RGB Neutrals

R: 72
G: 72
B: 72

R: 148
G: 148
B: 148

R: 214
G: 214
B: 214

Balanced Neutrals

R: 65
G: 65
B: 73

R: 137
G: 137
B: 149

R: 208
G: 208
B: 215

Blue Cast

R: 80
G: 80
B: 69

R: 159
G: 159
B: 145

R: 220
G: 220
B: 210

Yellow Cast

R: 80
G: 65
B: 65

R: 158
G: 141
B: 140

R: 218
G: 210
B: 209

Red Cast

A *If an image has a color cast, it quickly becomes apparent when you assess a value that's supposed to be neutral. To better illustrate the effect of a cast, a gray ramp has been added next to each image.*

G.10   Reading CMYK Neutrals

C	M	Y	CMY	K		C	M	Y	CMY	K
5%	3%	3%		5%		60%	46%	46%		60%
10	6	6		10		75	64	64		75
25	16	16		25		80	71	71		80
30	21	21		30		90	82	82		90
40	29	29		40		95	87	87		95
50	37	37		50						

A *Once colors exist as CMYK values, neutrality requires a special relationship. Due to impurities found in all process inks, each neutral gray requires more cyan than magenta and yellow. When determining the equivalent black value of a neutral, let the cyan percentage be your guide.*

G.13   Applying Neutral Endpoint Values

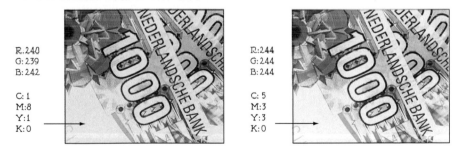

R:240
G:239
B:242

C:1
M:8
Y:1
K:0

R:244
G:244
B:244

C:5
M:3
Y:3
K:0

A *Above and beyond ensuring printable shadows and highlights, neutral endpoints will correct a large part of any existing color casts. Here, the highlights are too light for printing and contain a red bias. After remapping the endpoints, the highlights are neutralized—affecting the red cast all the way up to the midtones—and contain satisfactory dot sizes for printing.*

G.15   Applying a Half-Cast Removal

Casted Image   Half-Cast Removal

A *When a cast is too dominant, completely neutralizing it may adversely affect the remaining image colors. Applying a half-cast removal brings the cast halfway to neutral, clearing up the most offensive aspect of the cast without compromising the remaining colors.*

G.16   Adjusting Non-Neutral Colors

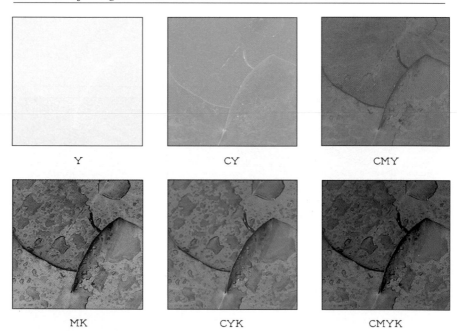

Y   CY   CMY

MK   CYK   CMYK

A *In the greens of this image, yellow is the primary component, and cyan is the secondary. Magenta, the tertiary component, adds tone and detail, and black carries the shadows. Here, these relationships are illustrated by printing one or more inks at a time.*

G.17 Correcting Fleshtones

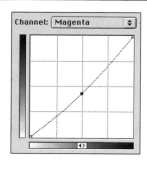

C: 5	C: 2	C: 5
M: 48	M: 32	M: 49
Y: 27	Y: 24	Y: 33
K: 0	K: 0	K: 0

C: 5	C: 2	C: 5
M: 40	M: 29	M: 43
Y: 27	Y: 24	Y: 33
K: 0	K: 0	K: 0

A *Here, most of the magenta data exists in the midtones. Reducing the overall level takes the "sunburn" out of the subject's skin.*

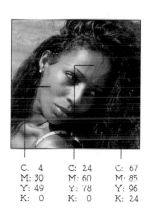
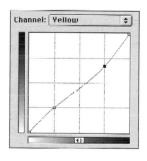

C: 4	C: 24	C: 67
M: 30	M: 60	M: 85
Y: 49	Y: 78	Y: 96
K: 0	K: 0	K: 24

C: 4	C: 24	C: 67
M: 30	M: 60	M: 85
Y: 42	Y: 72	Y: 90
K: 0	K: 0	K: 24

B *In the original image, the yellow cast appears primarily in the darker areas of the subject's skin. By limiting the adjustment to the tones most severely affected, you can preserve the color content of the rest of the image.*

G.18   Correcting Blue Sky

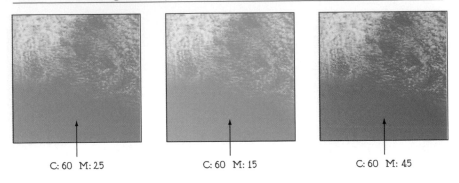

C: 60 M: 25   C: 60 M: 15   C: 60 M: 45

A *The same sky can be subject to different "moods", depending on the level of the secondary component: magenta.*

G.19   Targeting Common Color Components

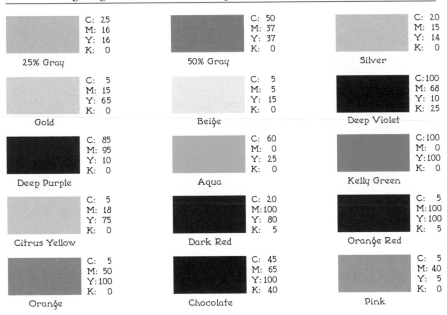

	C	M	Y	K
25% Gray	25	16	16	0
50% Gray	50	37	37	0
Silver	20	15	14	0
Gold	5	15	65	0
Beige	5	5	15	0
Deep Violet	100	68	10	25
Deep Purple	85	95	10	0
Aqua	60	0	25	0
Kelly Green	100	0	100	0
Citrus Yellow	5	18	75	0
Dark Red	20	100	80	5
Orange Red	5	100	100	5
Orange	5	50	100	0
Chocolate	45	65	100	40
Pink	5	40	5	0

A *This chart lists the CMYK values for a series of commonly encountered colors. These values are not absolutes; use them as a benchmark for understanding the relationships between the primary, secondary, and tertiary components.*

H.2   Creating an RGB Monotone

A *Normal contrast.*

B *Purple monotone.*

C *Red monotone.*

D *High contrast.*

E *High contrast: Purple.*

F *High contrast: Red.*

H.3   Creating a CMYK Monotone

A *Original image, desaturated.*

D *A C:100, Y:100 monotone.*

H.5   Recoloring an Element, Retaining Original Tone

A *Original image.*   **B** *Recolored green.*   **C** *Recolored purple.*

H.4   Colorizing an Image, Retaining Deep Tones

A *Colorized using*   **B** *Colorized using*   **C** *Colorized using*
    Overlay mode.   *Soft Light mode.*   *Color mode.*

H.6   Recoloring a White Original

A *Original image.*

B *Recolored image.*

C *Shadows layer set to 35% Opacity.*

D *Shadows layer set to 70% Opacity.*

H.7   Converting a Darker Element to White

A   *The original element.*   **D**   *Recolored to simulate white.*

H.8   Adding Multiple Colors to B&W Artwork

A   *Original line art image.*   **F**   *Final colorized image.*

H.9   Colorizing Line Art: Using Flat vs. Process Black

A *Flat black artwork, knocking out underlying colors.*

B *Flat black artwork, overprinting.*

H.10   Colorizing Line Art: Using an Anti-Aliased Template

E *Colorized line art with hard edges.*

F *Colorized line art with anti-aliased edges.*

I.8   Overprinting a Grayscale Silhouette

A *Original image.*

F *The overprinting silhouette.*

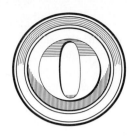

Issues Index

The following table lists the first sentence of over 700 items that appear in the **Mistakes to Avoid** and **Issues to Consider** sections throughout the book. To learn more about a particular issue, use the topic's reference number or page number to flip directly to it.

Items that appear under their topic's **Mistakes to Avoid** section are followed by *"Mistakes."* All other items appear under **Issues to Consider**.

Chapter 1, The Selection Tools

Chapter 2, The Paint Tools

Erasing a layer with locked transparency.

Avoid creating a gradient that is too long, resulting in shade-stepping.
When filling an entire layer with a gradient, create a gradient fill layer.
Resizing the Gradient Editor.

Much more effective fill options exist.

You cannot use one tool to reverse the effect of the other.

Chapter 3, The Vector Tools

Accessing the black arrow tool.

Accessing the white arrow tool.
Accessing the black arrow tool.

Using point text and paragraph text.
Using the Type tool without installing Adobe Type Manager.

Storing a path.
Editing a path.
Transforming a path.

Adding polygonal segments.
Creating open and closed freeform paths.
Creating finely-detailed paths or tracing low-contrast images with the Magnetic Pen tool.
The Magnetic Pen tool only creates closed paths.

Accessing the Add Anchor Point tool.

Accessing the Delete Anchor Point tool.

Accessing the Convert Point tool.

When you define a custom process color, your image must already be in CMYK mode.

Most spot colors do not convert accurately.

Each supported library has a corresponding printed swatchbook.

Chapter 6, The Quick Mask Tools

As long as you're in Quick Mask mode, all colors defined with the Color Picker appear as gray tones.

Toggling back and forth between the Masked Areas and Selected Areas settings.

Painting a Quick Mask with the foreground and background colors.

Toggling between selections and Quick Masks.

Chapter 7, The View Controls

This is the only view that allows you to see any underlying information.

Different images can be set to different views.

The menu bar and all of its commands remain visible.

Photoshop uses a simple trick to display an image this way.

Even though the menu bar is hidden, you can still access a command by selecting its keyboard shortcut.

This is primarily a display mode, especially with all the palettes hidden.

Chapter 8, The File Menu

Failing to accommodate bleeds and trimming. *(Mistakes)*

Entering a resolution too low for the image's intended use. *(Mistakes)*

Creating a new image via copying and pasting.

When blending, start with Transparent Pixels.

Entering the dimensions of an open image.

Determining the default unit of measurement.

Images may not open directly into Photoshop.

Drag-and-drop to open images.

Chapter 9, The Edit Menu

Applying a semi-opaque fill.

Using a blend mode fill to colorize an image.

Use the black, gray, and white options with caution.

You can't stroke type, vector shapes, or layer masks.

Creating a editable, standalone stroke.

Applying a stroke with Preserve Transparency checked.

Stroking the background layer.

Centering a stroke with an odd-numbered width.

Over-manipulating the transformation box. *(Mistakes)*

Applying multiple transformations individually. *(Mistakes)*

When a transformation box is visible on screen, the remaining image-editing commands are shut down.

This command is not available if any of the Pen tools are currently selected.

Transforming a background layer.

Changing transformation options on-the-fly.

This command is not always available.

Entering numerical values.

You don't have to select a path to access this command.

This command is not always available.

Entering numerical values.

Transform vectors or pixels with the same commands.

Cloning while transforming.

Transforming multiple layers.

Applying the same values to layer-based information as well as points and paths.

Don't use the Rotate tool for straightening crooked scans.

Creating irregularly-edged brushes.

Custom brushes are based on active selections between 1 and 999 pixels wide.

Custom brushes are useful to traditional artists who find the elliptical standard brushes too constraining.

Chapter 10, The Image Menu

Chapter 13, The Filter Menu

Chapter 18, The Swatches Palette

There is no command to clear the entire contents of the Swatches palette.

Check the current color mode before loading a swatch.
Be careful when loading a swatch while editing in Indexed Color mode.

Chapter 20, The History Palette

Assuming that history states save with the image. *(Mistakes)*
Attempting to access states that were generated before changing the image's
    dimensions, resolution, or color mode. *(Mistakes)*
Accidentally deleting hidden states. *(Mistakes)*
Incorrectly clicking a snapshot or state. *(Mistakes)*
Higher maximum numbers of history states require more RAM.
Purge history states if you run low on memory.
It's possible to remove the effect of a single command applied to an image by delet-
    ing its history state.
Add the contents of a history state to another image.

Chapter 21, The Actions Palette

The Delete command cannot be reversed by choosing Edit: **Undo**.

You cannot record Edit: **Undo** as part of an action.

Enabling or disabling a Stop dialog box.

Inserted paths are not automatically saved.
An inserted path retains its original position, even if the currenty image is too small.

You don't have to retain the Default Actions set.

Chapter 22, The Layers Palette

Blending modes base their calculations on brightness values, not color mode.

Blending modes work on Grayscale images, too.
Most blending modes have a neutral color.
Utilizing the blending modes' neutral colors.
"Remembering" the keyboard shortcuts for applying blending modes.
Blending modes are not quite the same as brush modes.

Working with hidden layers.

Applying two mask types to the same layer.

Be careful when moving the contents of a selection.

Linking and unlinking layer masks.

Adding layers to an existing group.

Chapter 23, The Channels Palette

Viewing individual channels is a vital part of high-end image editing.

Duplicating a channel.
New channels must be edited before they impact the image.

The effect of this button is affected by channel type and color mode.

A color channel can't be replaced with a mask channel in Grayscale, RGB, CMYK, and Lab Color images.
Rearranging mask channels does not alter the appearance or function of the image or its mask channels.

Bypass the New Channel dialog box.

Be careful when drag-copying a channel between images of different dimensions.
Bypassing the Duplicate Channel dialog box.

Chapter 25, The Character Palette

Ask yourself how much typesetting you really want to perform in Photoshop.
Focusing the range of your edits.
The Character palette only affects live type.

Fonts must be properly installed before you can use them in Photoshop.

Changing the default measurement unit.
Overriding the current measurement unit.
Increasing type size beyond the palette limit.
Changing the image size may change the font size.

Clearing all kerning values.
A single kern unit measures 1/1000 em.

High tracking values are often applied as a typographical effect.
Targeting a single word.

Chapter 26, The Paragraph Palette

Use a bounding text box for more formatting control.
Formatting different paragraphs within the same text layer.
Ask yourself if you really need to format in Photoshop.
Hyphenating manually.

Aligning text in a bounding box.
Aligning point text.

Appendix A, Automation Techniques

Move a copy of an action or command.

Rehearse before recording.
Take your time when recording the steps.

Appendix B, Selection Techniques

Appendix D, File Conversion Techniques

Appendix E, Line Art Editing Techniques

Appendix F, Halftone Editing Techniques

New endpoints are far more predictable when they're applied to an RGB image.

It's easy to pay too much attention to neutral grays.

Always keep an eye on the surrounding image pixels.

As with fleshtones, use this chart as a guide, not gospel.

Learn to make notes as you work.
Printed samples are the best resource.

Appendix H, Colorizing Techniques

Using the Tritone and Quadtone options to colorize an image.

This technique may not produce dead-on accurate colors for print purposes.
An unflattened image provides greater editing flexibility.
Reading the values of a colorized image.
Creating an action for this technique.
Keeping an eye on the blend mode.

Double-check the image before continuing your edits.
When recoloring parts of an image, use paths whenever possible.
Adjusting the new color's tonal depth using Levels.
Adjusting the saturation of the new color.
Sampling colors from another image.
Get more consistent results by converting to Lab Color before desaturating, then
   back again.

You still have to fine-tune the image.

Create a new layer for every colored area.

Don't worry about reducing the resolution.
This technique prepares a line art scan for blending with other images.

Appendix J, Custom Ink Techniques

Index

Symbols

1-bit color
converting to, 314-315
defined, 260

1-bit halftones, creating, 783-785

1-bit mezzotint images, creating, 788-789

1-bit random-screened images, creating, 785-787

3-D Render filter, 497-501

3-D Transform dialog box, 498-501

8 Bits/Channel color mode, 284

8-bit color, defined, 260

16 Bits/Channel color mode, 285

24-bit color, defined, 261

A

Accented Edges dialog box, 462

Accented Edges filter, 462

Action Options command (Actions palette), 623

actions
accessing dialog boxes during, 704
adding paths to, 622-623
batch processing, 180-184
executing, 710-711
file preparation, 709-710
saving settings as droplets, 184-185

copying, 620
creating, 618-619
for RGB monotone creation, 843
creating sets, 619
deleting, 617, 620, 624, 699
dialog boxes in, 618
disabling, 700
disabling commands within, 700
editing commands within, 702
executing, 699
inserting commands into, 701-703
inserting paths into, 706-707
loading, 624, 708
moving, 698-699
pausing, 621-622, 705-706
playing, 620
recording, 617, 620-621, 701
reloadable, 708-709
replacing, 625
replacing commands within, 702
replacing contents of, 702
resetting to defaults, 624
saving, 625, 707-708
selecting, 698
tips for, 711-712
troubleshooting, 707
undoing, 700
uses for, 615-616

Actions palette, 615-616
accessing dialog boxes during actions, 704
Action Options command, 623
assigning keyboard shortcuts, 705
batch processing, 709-711

button controls, 616-618
Button Mode command, 625-626
Clear Actions command, 624
Delete command, 620
deleting all actions, 699
disabling actions, 700
disabling commands within actions, 700
Duplicate command, 620
editing commands within actions, 702
executing actions, 699
executing commands, 699
Insert Menu Item command, 621
Insert Path command, 622-623
Insert Stop command, 621-622
inserting commands into actions, 701-703
inserting paths into actions, 706-707
keyboard shortcuts, 947
Load Actions command, 624
loading actions, 708
moving actions/ commands, 698-699
New Action command, 618-619
New Set command, 619
pausing actions, 705-706
Play command, 620
Playback Options command, 623-624
Record Again command, 621
recording actions, 701

B

X-Z

Solutions from experts you know and trust.

www.informit.com

OPERATING SYSTEMS

WEB DEVELOPMENT

PROGRAMMING

NETWORKING

CERTIFICATION

AND MORE...

**Expert Access.
Free Content.**

New Riders has partnered with **InformIT.com** to bring technical information to your desktop. Drawing on New Riders authors and reviewers to provide additional information on topics you're interested in, **InformIT.com** has free, in-depth information you won't find anywhere else.

- **Master the skills you need, when you need them**

- **Call on resources from some of the best minds in the industry**

- **Get answers when you need them, using InformIT's comprehensive library or live experts online**

- **Go above and beyond what you find in New Riders books, extending your knowledge**

As an **InformIT** partner, **New Riders** has shared the wisdom and knowledge of our authors with you online. Visit **InformIT.com** to see what you're missing.

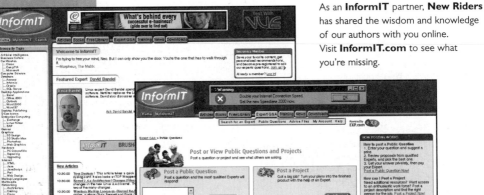

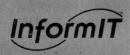

www.informit.com ▪ **www.newriders.com**

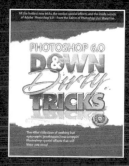

Photo Credits

With a few exceptions from the author's archives, the images that appear throughout this book are from the excellent and extensive John Foxx Images library. For full-size, full-color previews of the entire series, please visit their web site at *www.johnfoxx.com*. If you would like to know more about of a particular image used in the book, contact the author at *donnie@maine.rr.com*.

John Foxx Images, established in 1994, is known for its original, stylish imagery and the professional way the company always incorporates the latest digital techniques into their products. They were recently acquired by ImageState (*www.imagestate.com*). Aiming to be a leader within the picture library industry, selling both rights protected and royalty free photography, ImageState has been built from the acquisition of a number of key industry players: John Foxx Images in the Netherlands, Images Colour Library in the UK, Zephyr Images in San Diego, WestStock in Seattle and Adventure Photo and Film in California.